Characters and Plots in the
Fiction of Graham Greene

ALSO BY ROBERT L. GALE

An Edwin Arlington Robinson Encyclopedia
(McFarland, 2006)

Characters and Plots in the Fiction of Graham Greene

Robert L. Gale

McFarland & Company, Inc., Publishers
Jefferson, North Carolina, and London

All quotations from published materials by Graham Greene are by
the kind permission of the Graham Greene Estate c/o David Higham Associates,
London. Specific information can be found in the Acknowledgments.

LIBRARY OF CONGRESS CATALOGUING-IN-PUBLICATION DATA

Gale, Robert L., 1919–
Characters and plots in the fiction of Graham Greene / Robert L. Gale.
p.   cm.
Includes bibliographical references and index.

ISBN-13: 978-0-7864-2720-8
ISBN-10: 0-7864-2720-5
(softcover : 50# alkaline paper) ∞

1. Greene, Graham, 1904–1991—Characters.
2. Greene, Graham, 1904–1991—Stories, plots, etc.   I. Title.
PR6013.R44Z63335   2006   823'.912—dc22   2006023093

British Library cataloguing data are available

©2006 Robert L. Gale. All rights reserved

*No part of this book may be reproduced or transmitted in any form
or by any means, electronic or mechanical, including photocopying
or recording, or by any information storage and retrieval system,
without permission in writing from the publisher.*

On the cover: Graham Green; landscape ©2006 Photodisc; map ©2006 Pictures Now

Manufactured in the United States of America

*McFarland & Company, Inc., Publishers
Box 611, Jefferson, North Carolina 28640
www.mcfarlandpub.com*

For Maureen and Our Family

Acknowledgments

I quote from the following works by Graham Greene (all published in London except as indicated): *Brighton Rock* (Heinemann, 1938), *A Burnt-Out Case* (Heinemann, 1961), *The Captain and the Enemy* (Reinhardt Books, 1988), *Carving a Statue* (Bodley Head, 1964), *The Comedians* (Bodley Head, 1965, *Complete Short Stories* (New York: Penguin Books, 2005), *The Confidential Agent* (Heinemann, 1939), *Doctor Fischer of Geneva or The Bomb Party* (Bodley Head, 1980), *The End of the Affair* (Heinemann, 1951), *England Made Me* (Heinemann, 1935), *Getting to Know the General: The Story of an Involvement* (Bodley Head, 1984*)*, *A Gun for Sale* (Heinemann, 1936; published as *This Gun for Hire,* New York: Doubleday, 1936), *The Heart of the Matter* (Heinemann, 1948), *The Honorary Consul* (Bodley Head, 1974), *The Human Factor* (Bodley Head, 1978), *It's a Battlefield* (Heinemann, 1934), *The Last Word and Other Stories* (Reinhardt Books, 1990), *Loser Takes All* (Heinemann, 1955), *The Lost Childhood and Other Essays* (Eyre & Spottiswoode, 1951), *The Man Within* (Heinemann, 1929), *The Ministry of Fear* (Heinemann, 1943), *Monsignor Quixote* (Bodley Head, 1982), *The Name of Action* (Heinemann, 1930), *Our Man in Havana* (Heinemann, 1958), *The Power and the Glory* (Heinemann, 1940), *The Quiet American* (Heinemann, 1955), *Rumour at Nightfall* (Heinemann, 1931), *A Sort of Life* (Bodley Head, 1971; New York: Simon & Schuster, 1971), *Stamboul Train* (Heinemann, 1932; published as *Orient Express,* New York: Doubleday, 1933), *The Tenth Man* (Bodley Head and Anthony Blond, 1985; New York: Simon & Schuster, 1985), *The Third Man* (New York: Viking, 1950), *Travels with My Aunt* (Bodley Head, 1970), *Ways of Escape* (Bodley Head, 1980; New York: Simon & Schuster, 1980).

I also quote from *Graham Greene,* revised edition, by A. A. DeVitis, © 1986 Twayne Publishers; reprinted by permission of the Gale Group. I also quote from *Graham Greene: A Study of the Short Fiction,* by Richard Kelly, © 1992 Twayne Publishers; reprinted by permission of the Gale Group.

Although all Greene scholars are grateful to Greene bibliographies published by J. Don Vann (1970), Robert H. Miller (1979), R. A. Wobbe (1979), and A. F. Cassis (1981), work in this area needs to be updated.

I wish to express gratitude to Linda Tashbook, Esq., of the Law School of the University of Pittsburgh, Florence B. Eichin of Viking Press, and Alice Wilson of David Higham Associates, Ltd., for explaining rights to summarize and paraphrase, and to David Higham Associates, Ltd., for permission to quote something under 1,400 words from just under 80 of Greene's fictional pieces long and short.

My special thanks go to Patricia Duff and her corps of interlibrary-loan librarians at Hillman Library, University of Pittsburgh, and to librarians at Pittsburgh's Carnegie Public Library, Oakland Branch, for their quick and amiable help. I am also grateful to Richard Bankert, Jay Dantry, and Donald Wentworth, all of Pittsburgh, for locating books by and articles concerning Greene and making them available to me. I thank the Image Works, Woodstock, New York, for providing the haunting Topham photograph of Greene. And I thank my sister-in-law Christina Merrington-Rust, of Oxford, England, for generously supporting my research activities. Finally, I express my unending love to my wife Maureen, for devotion and encouragement over more than six decades, and my profound affection as well to our family — John, Jim, Christine, Diana, Caroline, Stephanie, Bill, and Lisette — near and scattered.

Table of Contents

Acknowledgments vii

Preface 1

A Chronology 5

The Encyclopedia 9

Bibliography 335

Index 339

Preface

Graham Greene is one of the most important novelists of the twentieth century, indeed, of any century. Although he downgraded himself as a short-story writer, he was also adept in that genre. Many of his novels were phenomenally popular and have remained steadily marketable, while at the same time they challengingly address difficult religious, social, and political issues of abiding importance. At least 18 of his novels and 22 of his short stories have been adapted for movies and television, several more than once.

Greene had a superb intellect, a fine education, insatiable curiosity, and the stamina to travel far and wide from youth to old age. He developed the reputation of being places where international politics and military action were causing or were about to cause controversial change. He was the product of and the spokesman for the so-called "short twentieth century"—roughly from the end of World War One to the collapse of the Soviet Union.

Greene had an allegedly unpleasant childhood with disturbing effects. His father was a rigid headmaster; his mother, bright enough but emotionally austere. His five siblings displayed varied stripes from greatness to shamefulness. Greene says he often experimented with Russian roulette and other suicidal activities. He was psychoanalyzed as a youth but mainly remembered being influenced by his analyst's wife's physique, about which he dreamed. An important part of his creative makeup was his dreams, which he laboriously recorded. He became a Catholic convert in order to marry a woman he loved not wisely but too little. He once publicly defined himself as a Catholic agnostic. In truth he was honestly troubled and questioning, and called himself a novelist who was a Catholic. He became a serial adulterer and a brothel expert, and drank too much and smoked opium whenever he could conveniently do so.

He transmuted a myriad of dangerous influences into living art. He combines dazzling compositional techniques, careful plotting, painterly backdrops, memorable verbal profiles and sketches of characters, their revealing dialogue, religious and socio-political commentary and innuendo, and varied modes and tones from disturbingly quiet to satirical and humorous. He enjoyed being told that he laughed in the shadow of the gallows. Like many compulsive writers—indeed, plenty of workers in most fields—Greene seemed to relish setting a creative challenge for himself and then laboring away, often under stress. He tried to compose 500 words every day, regardless of inner or outer distractions. In emergencies and with stimulants, he could push himself to 2,000 words daily. He tabulated totals.

Greene was a blessedly short-term poet, skillful reporter-editor, indefatigable film and drama critic, movie scenarist, travel-book writer, and essayist and literary critic. This professional activity made his fiction better, often towering and unique. He once said his childhood and adolescent reading of adventure stories inspired his own melodramatic content. Informing it pervasively is the most influential passage of poetry he ever read. It is from "Bishop Blougram's Apology" by Robert Browning, his favorite poet:

Preface

> Our interest's on the dangerous edge of things.
> The honest thief, the tender murderer,
> The superstitious atheist, demirep
> That loves and saves her soul in new French books—
> We watch while these in equilibrium keep
> The giddy line midway: one step aside,
> They're classed and done with. I, then, keep the line
> Before your sages,—just the men to shrink
> From the gross weights, coarse scales and labels broad
> You offer their refinement. Fool or knave?
> Who needs a bishop be a fool or knave
> When there's a thousand diamond weights between?

Greene once asserted that these lines could serve as an epigraph for all of his novels.

I hope this encyclopedia will serve a variety of readers. First, I safely recommend that they read Greene and only thereafter seek further pleasure and perhaps profit by turning to my modest work. It aims to aid novices perhaps confused by their first encounter with Greene, young adults seeking critical perceptions for reinforcement or surprise, and even teachers and scholars studying Greene for sundry purposes. My work is clearly not a substitute for Greene but should serve as a pathway to more enlightenment and fun. Greene is endlessly challenging, and rewards rereading and study. Please believe me: Greene grows upon one with each return to him; I hope this encyclopedia will nourish that growth.

A word about "Greeneland." Greene deplored the frequent use of the term as the locus of his plots and his actors therein. But in addition to being a few bold letters on an imagined cartograph, "Greeneland" is an arresting and useful label. It suggests a murky, muddy, dusty, fetid, steamy, chilly border-shifting place where souls are tortured and find it hard or impossible to rest, where important people work well but often preen, where sinners and criminals gloat and regret and are variously punished, and where lovers glory, sweat, abstain, curse, and pray. My readers will find herein summaries of 26 novels and 56 short-story plots, identifications of 1,352 characters named or given capitalized titles, and biographical data on Greene's family members and some associates. I pay almost no attention here to Greene's nonfictional writing. It has been enough to survey Greeneland fiction and leave adjacent terrains to others.

Please note that in some plot summaries I provide information parenthetically, for clarity, if that information is delayed by Greene—tantalizingly for suspense, or just maybe through carelessness. I have also tried, perhaps not always clearly, to use present and past tenses in order to distinguish Greene's "present" action, interrupted by his occasional sudden "past" flashbacks.

Asterisks (*) in the main text indicate cross-referencing.

In the course of many months devoted to writing this book, I have made tactful inroads on many talented, insightful scholars. Since Greene often lied about his activities, the truth may well never be completely established, and the numerous biographies, long and short, are often at odds with one another. The best of especially canny ones include Norman Sherry's three-volume biography of Greene, which though often unnecessarily subjective is a treasure chest of facts; and Michael Shelden's, whose extensive work is also weighty with data, sometimes disputed and tilted whenever possible toward meanness. The best critics include A. F. Cassis, whose short book is the best possible introduction to green Greene readers; Cedric Watts, for relating biographical data to the fiction; Leopoldo Duran and Mark Bosco, for illuminating Greene's conflicted Catholicism; A. A. DeVitis, Richard Kelly, Neil Sinyard, and Peter Wolfe, for sharp, perceptive judgments; David Parkinson, for skillful work on Greene's film reviews; and Quentin Falk and Gene D. Phillips, for information on film adaptations of Greene's fiction. The reader may easily identify my other favorites when making use of end-of-entry inclusions, the terse form of which I hope won't puzzle anyone for long, once their relation to the bibliography is familiar. I planned not to be explicitly critical of any critic but have slipped on occasion. To one and all of them, I extend my humble thanks. Greeneland has many explorers, and will have more.

A postscript: Like Greene, I was a counter-intelligence officer (though in the American army) during World War II. I too was in London during some of the years when he served there. I too saw some of the V-1s and heard some of the V-2s he saw and heard. My wife Maureen did as well; Maureen was in London from 1939 through 1945.

A Chronology

1896 Marriage of Charles Henry Greene* (1865–1942) and Marion Raymond Greene* (1872–1959), Graham Greene's parents.

1904 Greene born October 2 in Berkhamsted, Hertfordshire, England; siblings were Molly Greene* (1897?–1963), Herbert Greene* (1898–1968), Raymond Greene* (1901–1982), Sir Hugh Greene* (1910–1987), and Elisabeth Greene Dennys* (1914–1999).

1910 Charles Greene becomes headmaster of Berkhamsted School (to 1927).

1912–1922 Greene enrolled in Berkhamsted School (as boarder from 1918).

1921 Treated by psychiatrist Kenneth Richmond.

1922–1925 Attends Balliol College, Oxford; edits *Oxford Outlook*.

1923 Tours Ireland, visits Ruhr.

1925 Graduates at Oxford with 2nd in History; employed gratis by Nottingham *Journal* (to 1926), joins Communist Party very briefly as prank and visits Paris, becomes Roman Catholic, works as sub-editor for London *Times* (to 1929).

1927 Marries Vivienne Dayrell-Browning (*see* Greene, Vivien) October 25, London, with honeymoon near Marseilles, France.

1929 Enjoys Mediterranean cruise; *The Man Within* published.

1930 *The Name of Action*.

1931 *Rumour at Nightfall*.

1932 *Stamboul Train* (U.S. title, *Orient Express*).

1933 Briefly visits Norway and Sweden with Hugh; Lucy Caroline Greene, daughter, born.

1934 Briefly travels in Baltic states; *It's a Battlefield*.

1935 *The Basement Room* (short stories); *England Made Me* (U.S. title, *The Shipwrecked*).

1935 Is film critic for *Spectator* (to 1940).

1936 Travels in Liberia and Sierra Leone; meets Alexander Korda*; Francis Greene, son, born; *A Gun for Sale* (U.S. title, *This Gun for Hire*).

1937 Is co-editor of and film critic for *Night and Day*.

1938 Travels in Tabasco and Chiapas, Mexico, to report on persecution of Catholic Church; sued by Shirley Temple* and required to pay damages; *Brighton Rock*.

1939 Aborts trip in France, having intended to report Spanish Civil War; meets Dorothy Glover*; *The Confidential Agent*.

1940 Works for Ministry of Information, is literary editor of and drama critic for *Spectator* (to 1941); *The Power and the Glory* (U.S. title briefly, *The Labyrinthine Ways*).

1941	Works for British Secret Intelligence Service (SIS, in and out of England, to 1944); in Sierra Leone (1941–1943).
1943	Works under Kim Philby* (SIS) in London; *The Ministry of Fear*.
1944	Works at British propaganda center (to 1946); becomes managing director of Eyre & Spottiswoode, publishers (to 1948).
1945	Writes book reviews for *Evening Standard*.
1946	Visits Spain, collaborates in London with Dorothy Glover on first of several story books for young children, meets Catherine Walston.*
1947	*Nineteen Stories*.
1948	Visits Belgium, Austria, Czechoslovakia, Capri; *The Heart of the Matter*.
1949	Travels in Italy and Africa.
1950	Visits Vienna and Hollywood with Carol Reed*; *The Third Man*.
1951	Travels in Malaya and French Indochina as correspondent; meets Jocelyn Rickards*; *The End of the Affair*.
1952	Travels in Vietnam again (and in 1953, 1955).
1953	Is reporter for *Sunday Times* in Kenya.
1954	*Twenty-One Stories* (mostly repeated from *Nineteen Stories*).
1955	Is reporter for *Sunday Times, Figaro, New Republic,* in Indochina (interviews Ho Chi Minh) and Poland; meets Anita Björk*; *The Quiet American, Loser Takes All*.
1956	Visits Poland and Haiti.
1957	Visits Cuba, China, Soviet Union.
1958	Becomes director of Bodley Head, publishers (to 1968); *Our Man in Havana;* fears vengeance of François Duvalier.*
1959	Takes trip to Belgian Congo, meets Yvonne Cloetta* in Cameroons.
1960	Briefly stays in Tahiti.
1961	Visits Moscow; *A Burnt-out Case*.
1962	Receives honorary doctorate, Cambridge University.
1963	Reports in Haiti and Santo Domingo for *Sunday Telegraph; A Sense of Reality* (short stories); Philby defects to Soviet Union.
1964	Visits Goa; meets Fidel Castro in Cuba.
1966	Appointed Companion of Honor; formally separates from wife, leaves England to establish residence in Antibes, French Riviera; revisits Cuba; *The Comedians*.
1967	Reports in Sierra Leone for *Observer,* reports from Israel during Arab-Israeli Six Day War; *May We Borrow Your Husband? and Other Comedies of the Sexual Life* (short stories); receives honorary doctorate, University of Edinburgh, is made Chevalier de la Légion d'Honneur, France.
1968	Protests Soviet treatment of Czechoslovakia.
1969	Travels in Argentina and Paraguay for *Sunday Telegraph; Travels with My Aunt*.
1971	Visits Argentina and Chile.
1972	*Collected Stories*.
1973	*The Honorary Consul*.

1976	Meets Omar Torrijos Herrera, during first of several visits to Panama; travels in Spain with Leopoldo Duran (again in 1977).
1977	Briefly visits Washington, D.C.
1978	*The Human Factor.*
1979	Operated on for intestinal cancer; receives honorary doctorate, Oxford University.
1980	*Doctor Fischer of Geneva or The Bomb Party.*
1982	Publicly criticizes officials in Nice, France, for corruption; *Monsignor Quixote.*
1985	*The Tenth Man.*
1986	Enrolled in Order of Merit; visits Moscow (again in 1987, 1988).
1988	Receives honorary doctorate, University of Moscow; *The Captain and the Enemy.*
1989	Briefly visits Ireland.
1990	Moves to Corseaux, near Vevey, Switzerland; *The Last Word* (short stories).
1991	Dies in Vevey, April 3, of complications of leukemia.
1997	Graham Greene Birthplace Trust established in Berkhamsted
2004	Greene's centenary celebrated in many places.
2005	"The Nature of Things: Graham Greene on Film," retrospective by UCLA's Film and Television Archive.

THE ENCYCLOPEDIA

ABDUL, GENERAL (*Travels with My Aunt*). Augusta's friend, now 80. He wrote her from Tunis, February 1924, and recently. Taking Henry along, she goes to Istanbul to meet Abdul but learns he has been shot trying to escape. She later learns he's dead.

ABDULLAH (*Travels with My Aunt*). Augusta and Henry have their first lunch in Istanbul at Abdullah's.

ABSALOM (*The Man Within*) *see* **ANDREWS, FRANCIS**

ACKY (*This Gun for Hire*). He is a tall, bald, shifty ex-clergyman, broken-nosed and unfrocked for sexual misconduct. He and his wife Tiny established a bawdy house in Nottwich where Davis takes Anne Crowder. Raven rescues her. Acky has the eyes of a "flawed saint."
In a *Collected Edition* introduction, Greene says he prefers this flawed man of God to more grievously flawed Padre José (*The Power and the Glory*). Michael Shelden believes Acky is partly based on Greene's grandfather Carleton Greene, a Bedfordshire clergyman who at one point felt unworthy to continue in his ministry, demanded to be defrocked, was refused, and enfrocked himself in an open field. Peter Wolfe notes that Greene wrote three essays (1934–1935) on Baron Corvo (the eccentric literary genius Frederick Rolfe [1860–1913], also guilty of misconduct, though within the Catholic church, and defrocked). Greene later confessed a certain affection for Acky, doomed to live in a "world of wounds and guilt." (Sources: Greene, *A Gun for Sale, Collected Edition,* ix; Greene, *Ways of Escape,* 76; Shelden, 106, 219; Wolfe, 73)

ACROSS THE BORDER (1947). An unfinished novel. (Source: Sherry I, 494–96, 499)

"ACROSS THE BRIDGE" (1938). Short story. (Characters: Joseph Calloway, Lucia, Rover.) Beyond a dusty Mexican town along the Rio Grande and the international bridge is a better-lighted American town. The unnamed narrator awaits a driver to take him to Yucatan. He and Lucia observe Joseph Calloway, a precise old British millionaire, hiding to avoid extradition for defrauding Halling Investment Trust shareholders in England. He has Rover, a mongrel he kicks to vent frustration. He doesn't recognize that the two foreigners, just arriving, are detectives seeking him. Like the narrator, he speaks no Spanish. When one detective asks the narrator about Calloway, he denies knowing him. The narrator and Lucia wait in the plaza, expecting, as does a crowd, to see Calloway arrested. But no. What a comedy: Calloway is elevated, untouchable. A detective, not recognizing Calloway, queries him. He agrees — this place is dreadful, real action is "on the other side," one's own country is best. He invites the detective to lunch with him, but his saying he's on duty looking for someone alerts Calloway to danger. The detectives and Calloway journey separately to the state capital, return in a week. The fugitive's wealth again prevented his being identified. Meanwhile, Lucia has crossed the bridge back to America. The narrator feels sympathy for Calloway; he has seen better things beyond the bridge, is now stuck here. The detectives return and see Calloway routinely kick Rover. Although the narrator surprises Calloway by saying everyone speaks English here, he still doesn't talk to others and they regard the millionaire as too important.
The detectives steal Rover. Someone tells

Calloway that Rover was smuggled across the bridge. Calloway gets so jealous of Rover's happiness in America that he crosses also. The narrator, following, sees him and elsewhere the detectives, but lies that Calloway isn't on the American side too. The detectives find Rover, release him from their car, urge him to locate Calloway. Rover does, yappingly. The more sentimental detective drives up, swerves, avoids Rover, crushes Calloway. Rover licks his blood. Calloway drops his hand over Rover's neck. The detective regards the gesture as a caress; the narrator, a blow. Rover bays triumphantly. The scene is comic, pitiable, not tragic. Calling Calloway's dying gesture affectionate demonstrates "our baseless optimism."

The locale of "Across the Bridge" is the Rio Grande crossing between Laredo, Texas, and Nuevo Laredo, Mexico. On one level, it is a parable showing people's frequent alienation from one another by the barrier of unknowingness. The narrator implies that he probably shouldn't even be telling about Calloway, because, although he assumes Calloway's earlier actions were dramatic, he doesn't know "how to treat" them and doesn't want to "invent" incidents he hasn't seen. Richard Kelly explains that the border may be explicated as "the thin geographical and psychological line between sanctuary and danger, boredom and excitement, and life and death."

Quentin Falk, Gene D. Phillips, and Neil Sinyard discuss the 1957 movie adaptation of "Across the Bridge," its action much expanded. Sinyard notes that the film features "a tormented and reviled outsider ... who finally betrays himself through a perverse act of love for his dog," then generalizes that Calloway becomes "that potent Greene archetype — the hunted man at the end of his tether." (Sources: Falk, 127–32, 211; Kelly, 29; Phillips, 38–41; Sinyard, 151)

ADA (*Travels with My Aunt*). She is an ugly woman, 50, for whom Wordsworth was obliged to exchange his date at a porno party near Heathrow.

ADAMS ("The Case for the Defence"). He is Mrs. Parker's murderer or the twin brother of the murderer. Neither can be proved guilty.

ADAMS ("The Case for the Defence"). Either he or his twin brother killed Mrs. Parker.

ADAMS (*It's a Battlefield*). He is a prisoner heard reciting poetry.

ADAMS, MRS. ("The Case for the Defence"). She is the guilty or innocent Adams twin's wife.

ADAMS, MRS. ("The Case for the Defence"). She is the innocent or guilty Adams twin's wife.

ADOLPH (*The Name of Action*). He lives near Kapper, who explains that when Adolph awakens at night, he thinks of something humorous and laughs. He startles Chant by doing so. When Kapper shoots the policeman, Adolph's laugh alarms Chant.

AFTER TWO YEARS (1949). Greene's thin book of love poems inspired by Catherine Walston.* He had 25 copies privately printed. William Cash says that most copies have been lost, one copy valued at about £15,000 is in private hands, and the search for others continues. (Source: Cash, 9, 39)

AGBO (*The Human Factor*). He works for Radio Zaire. Davis tells Castle that British intelligence might recruit Agbo as sub-agent.

AGNES (*Our Man in Havana*). She is a nun in Milly Wormold's school, said to be pretty but sad because of an earlier love affair.

AGNES, MOTHER (*A Burnt-Out Case*). She is the head nun at the leper colony. She cares for Marie Rycker when she arrives, believes her lie that Querry has caused her pregnancy, and demands that Querry stay away.

AITKIN (*This Gun for Hire*). He is a medical student, so serious about his studies that Buddy Fergusson labels him a conscientious objector to having silly fun.

AKIMBU, MARIE (*A Burnt-Out Case*). She is a native living near Dr. Colin, is regarded by Mother Agnes as a hard worker, is criticized by Father Thomas for having a baby a year by different men, but is spoken of tolerantly by the Superior.

By her last name, close to "akimbo," Greene may suggest a figurative pose of non-verbal defiance struck by Marie.

"ALAS, POOR MALING" (1940). Short story. (Characters: Wesby Hythe, Maling, Joshua Simcox, Sir Joshua Simcox.) Maling is the conscientious secretary of the Simcox Newsprint Company. The firm plans a tax-saving merger with the Hythe Newsprint Company. To be legal, it must be completed on September 3, 1940. Sir Joshua Simcox and Wesby Hythe meet, with Maling there to advise. Maling suffers from what his doctors call borborygmi (stomach rumbles). Worse, as he told the unnamed narrator, his stomach audibly replicates recently heard sounds — snatches from a Brahms concerto, Piccadilly street jackhammer, whatever. Earlier that September, air-raid sirens warned Londoners of the German "blitz-and-pieces krieg," but not on the 3rd. During the Simcox-Hythe meeting, Maling's stomach, having picked up an air-raid alarm, sounded off. The two principals, plus Maling, scurried into the basement. The merger was ruined; unfortunately, Maling's tummy never learned to play "All Clear."

The title "Alas, Poor Maling" partly repeats Hamlet's famous "Alas, poor Yorick!" Greene might have used the word "gorge" in mentioning Maling's stomach, since Hamlet's "gorge rises" when Hamlet sees Yorick's skull. The name Maling may derive from *malingre* (French, "sickly"). Richard Kelly believes that "Alas, Poor Maling" is an example of Greene's using humor to "distanc[e] ... himself from the grotesque oddities of the human body." "Alas, Poor Maling," adapted by Greene, was the subject of a 1976 television production. *See Shades of Greene*. (Sources: Falk, 215; Kelly, 32)

ALBERT (*Doctor Fischer of Geneva*). He is Fischer's haughty servant. Albert develops respect for Jones.

ALEC ("May We Borrow Your Husband?"). He is an associate of Stephen and painted Mrs. Clarenty's bedroom mural of a dead faun. She wrote Stephen expressing displeasure with it.

ALEXITCH, CAPTAIN (*Orient Express*). He is Colonel Hartep's obedient subordinate officer at Dr. Richard Czinner's court martial in Subotica.

ALFRED (*The End of the Affair*). He is a waiter at Rules. Bendrix tells Sarah he has eaten there often since their separation. Alfred reveals otherwise to her.

ALI (*The Heart of the Matter*). He is Scobie's black servant, a Temne. He waits on Scobie and his wife, accompanies him to Pende, and runs errands faithfully. When Scobie suspects Ali of conspiring against him with one of Yusef's servants, he says as much to Yusef, who has Ali murdered.

ALICE (*This Gun for Hire*). She is the hunchback servant where Raven lives in London. He buys her a dress knowing she can't wear it. Alice tries to betray him to Mather and Saunders.

ALICE, AUNT ("The Basement Room"). Philip Lane remembers writing a letter to his Aunt Alice to thank her for a teddy bear he was too old to enjoy.

Greene's Aunt Alice was the sister-in-law of his mother, Marion Greene.* Alice ran a school in South Africa, and Marion frequently wrote to her. (Source: Sherry I, 4, 16)

ALICE, AUNT (*Our Man in Havana*). When Wormold writes his sister Mary, he asks her about their Aunt Alice's well-known ear wax.

AMBASSADOR, THE (*The Confidential Agent*). He is the untrustworthy head official in the London embassy of D.'s country.

AMBASSADOR, THE (*Our Man in Havana*). He is the British ambassador — tall, cold, with proper necktie. When informed by Captain Segura about Wormold's being in trouble with the Foreign Office and Segura's forces, the Ambassador summons Wormold and advises him to fly home to England instanter.

AMBASSADOR OF PANAMA, THE (*The Honorary Consul*). Sir Henry Belfrage says this official can legally buy cars and sell them at a profit, whereas British officials can't.

AMBASSADRESS, THE (*Our Man in Havana*). When Wormold reports to the Ambassador, he sees a woman with two children. They immediately disappear. He thinks she is probably the Ambassadress.

AMERICAN AMBASSADOR, THE (*The Honorary Consul*). When this official was at the Jesuit ruins with Fortnum as an English-speaking guide, the revolutionaries kidnap Fortnum, not the Ambassador, by mistake. Sir Henry Belfrage says the Ambassador has New England eyes and wants to be called Wilbur. Belfrage finds Wilbur undynamic.

AMERICAN CONSUL-GENERAL, THE (*Our Man in Havana*). He is the guest of honor at Dr. Braun's European Traders' Association meeting.

AMIS (*Travels with My Aunt*). He is a British agent in *Turkish Delight,* a novel Augusta reads in Istanbul.

AMY ("Jubilee"). She is a London streetwalker turned madam, now comfortably retired though still raucous. She cleaned up the streets during King George V's Silver Jubilee by getting prostitutes to work in her newly established house. She also set up a phony tourist bureau. In the process she made £5,000. Chalfont, an aging gigolo, mistakes her for a former female victim of his. She turns the tables on the ill-garbed fellow, plies him with sherry, and even gives him £5.

Norman Sherry says Amy resurfaces as the more full-blown Ida Arnold in *Brighton Rock.* (Source: Sherry I, 574)

ANA (*The Honorary Consul*). A public-health official's daughter, she is Plarr's pretty secretary. Her father's importance and her starchy piety keep him from seeking sexual activity with her.

ANDERSON ("The Other Side of the Border"). Hands calls on Billings, when Billings is an impoverished photographer in West Africa, reminds Billings of their being at Anderson's Denton store five years earlier, and says Anderson sold out to Bates.

ANDERSSON (*England Made Me*). A factory worker Fred Hall framed to prevent the union from striking.

ANDERSSON (*England Made Me*). He is an abused factory worker's son. When he learns how Erik Krogh's man Fred Hall framed his father, he seeks Krogh for an explanation. Hall slugs him and kicks him out.

ANDRÉ (*The Comedians*). The Pinedas' excellent embassy chef, whose specialty is soufflés. Martha Pineda discharged him so Brown could hire him as his Trianon chef.

ANDREWS (*The Man Within*). He is Francis Andrews's father, owned the *Good Chance,* was a piratical smuggler, was so abusive of his wife that she died, and later was shot and buried at sea. Carlyon, one of his men, inherited everything from him.

Michael Shelden reports that Charles Greene,* Greene's father, so disliked unpleasant parallels to himself and Francis Andrews's father that he vowed not to read any more of Greene's novels. (Source: Shelden, 119–20)

ANDREWS, FRANCIS (*The Man Within*). He is the self-divided hero. Well-educated at Devon, he joins his dead father's smuggler crew, is befriended by Carlyon but demeaned by other crewmembers, informs against them, falls in love with Elizabeth Garnet, testifies at the Assizes in Lewes, and returns to Elizabeth. When she kills herself with his knife, Andrews lets Carlyon escape, claims he killed her himself, and is arrested by the authorities. He seizes his knife and will surely commit suicide with it. Andrews is alternately cowardry and brave, is ridiculed by his inner critic — until the end. Francis calls himself Absalom when Farne asks him his name; he must be thinking about David's loss of his son Absalom (*see* II Samuel:13–19).

Anthony Mockler defines Andrews as "the twisted, tormented, depraved but basically decent Andrews/Graham [Greene]," with Elizabeth being "Elizabeth/Vivienne" (*see* Greene, Vivien, Greene's wife). (Source: Mockler, 49)

ANDREWS, MRS. (*The Man Within*). She was Andrews the smuggler's abused wife and Francis Andrews's loving mother.

ANGELICA (*Our Man in Havana*). She is a member of the secretary pool in the Secret Service office in London, transferred from the accounting office to C.5 at £8 a week, a raise.

ANGELINE, LADY (*Brighton Rock*). She is a character who looks fondly at Sir Mark in a romance Pinkie tells Dallow he read.

ANITA (*The Power of the Glory*). She is a deceased child, five, at whose burial Padre José is afraid to pray.

ANNA (*England Made Me*). She is remembered as a woman whose husband, a night-shift worker for Krogh's, killed her and then himself.

ANNA (*The Human Factor*). She is the stout Russian woman who is Castle's daily servant. She helps him learn some Russian words.

ANNA (*Orient Express*). She is Kolber's maid in Vienna and Josef Grünlich's abused old lover. Josef tells her his name is Anton.

ANNA ("The Root of All Evil") *see* **PUCKLER, HERR**

ANNE (*The Quiet American*). She was one of Fowler's many lovers and the only one, he says, he truly loved. Still, he left her — early enough, his wife says, for Anne to find someone else.

ANNETTE (*England Made Me*). She was the friendly prostitute Anthony Farrant liked. She disappeared. He saves her picture and remembers her.

Greene knew the original Annette, whom he calls "the young tart ... Anthony loved." Greene adds that, like Anthony, he too "walked up those forbidding stairs" to her digs, and he too was saddened when Annette disappeared from his ken. (Sources: Greene, *Ways of Escape*, 39–40; Mockler, 63–68, 93–94; Sherry II, 533–34)

ANTON (*Orient Express*) *see* **GRÜNLICH, JOSEF**

ANTHONY SANT. A novel Greene wrote while he was an Oxford student. Later called *Prologue to Pilgrimage*, it remains unpublished. (Sources: Shelden, 132; Sherry I, 72)

ANTONIO, FATHER (*The Honorary Consul*). Marta tells Rivas that his friend Father Antonio wouldn't marry them.

AN APPOINTMENT WITH THE GENERAL (1982). Novel fragment. (Characters: Jacques Durand, Jean Duval, Marie-Claire Duval, the General, Sergeant Gurdián, Señor Martinez.)

1. A sergeant (Gurdián) admits French correspondent Marie-Claire Duvan to see the General. Señor Martinez, the General's adviser, made the appointment. Since her memory is faulty, it bothers her to be ordered not to use her tape recorder.

2. A month ago Jacques Durand, a respected left-wing weekly editor, invited Marie-Claire to a lunch in Paris, praised her ability to ask hard-hitting political questions, proposed she interview "the General." He knows English; so her not knowing Spanish is irrelevant. Having argued a final time with her husband Jean Duval, Marie-Claire was willing, without being privy to details. Durand cautioned they were suspicious of the General, since he visited Fidel and met Tito in Colombo. She must rush, since Durand said otherwise she might be writing the General's obituary.

3. Struck by the General's doom-filled eyes, Marie-Claire remembers Durand's obituary joke. The General speaks only Spanish here. Gurdián translates. The gist: France should be called liberal, not left-wing; the General follows the people's wishes; American views are considered, not necessarily followed; since Martinez is chauffeuring her but speaks only Spanish, Gurdián will escort her next; Communists are permitted here, but the General resembles a train driver who controls stops and his passengers don't. When the General says he wants Marie-Claire to see his country through her own "beautiful" eyes, she asks whether his power makes women responsive and employs her time-worn gambit. What does the General dream about? His answer? Death. Marie-Claire figures she can use that.

Greene, as he often does, confusingly avoids a straight time line here. First, readers see

Marie-Claire about to start her interview. Second, readers back-track to her gaining the assignment. Third, the appointment takes place. More confusing is this: Part 2 says a month has passed since Marie-Claire lunched with Durand; but Part 3 says Durand talked about a possible obituary two weeks ago. Though sketchy, the story has memorable touches, as when Durand smoothly recommends menu items and when the General answers Marie-Claire's query about dreams with "*La muerte.*"

Richard Kelly explains that the story, originally called "On the Way Back: A Work Not in Progress," was first published in a collection of contemporary fiction entitled *Firebird 1.* It was to have been part of a novel to be called *On the Way Back,* but Greene dropped the idea in favor of his *Getting to Know the General: The Story of an Involvement* (1984), concerning his friendship with General Omar Torrijos Herrera of Panama. In it Greene says Torrijos told him his most recurrent dream concerned death. Yvonne Cloetta* says Greene told her that writing *Getting to Know the General* was a mistake on his part. (Sources: Cloetta, 85; Greene, *Getting to Know the General,* 117; Kelly, 79–80)

ARANJUEZ, SENOR (*The Heart of the Matter*). He is a friend in Lobito (Angola) with whom the Portuguese captain of the *Esperança* stayed for one night.

ARCHBISHOP, THE ("The Blessing"). He is the church official who blesses tanks before they are sent into possible combat.

ARCHBISHOP, THE ("Church Militant"). He is an ever-optimistic church leader in Kenya who drives a Cadillac full of French nuns to the Kikuyu region, and plans to have them settle there despite Mau Mau threats.

ARCHBISHOP, THE (*The Comedians*). He is the exiled Haitian archbishop.

ARCHBISHOP, THE (*The Honorary Consul*). Rivas remembers this old ecclesiast habitually dined well with the General (Stroessner) while Paraguayans suffered in poverty. When the Archbishop heard Rivas was preaching, he ordered him to stop. Blind José said the Archbishop wouldn't deign to visit his dead wife in the *barrio.*

ARCHBISHOP, THE (*Monsignor Quixote*). He is the Catholic superior to whom the bishop of El Toboso writes for advice after Quixote's strange holiday.

ARDEN (*The Honorary Consul*). Fortnum recalls Arden as his schoolmaster in Bueno Aires. Fortnum and his chums called Arden "Smells."

ARNOLD (*Loser Takes All*). He is Dreuther's chief accountant and Bertram's superior. Dreuther promises to promote Bertram and move Arnold to General Enterprises.

ARNOLD, IDA (*Brighton Rock*). She is a fun-loving, justice-seeking London barmaid and raucous drinker, physically and emotionally ample, about 35, living in Russell Square. While in Brighton, she suspects Hale has been murdered. His lucky tip to bet on Black Boy gives her funds to play detective, pursue Pinkie and members of his gang, befriend Rose Wilson, and become the proximate cause of Pinkie's demise. Ida's friends call her Lily. Bookie Jim Tate inaccurately calls her Ida Turner.

Arthur Calder-Marshall calls Ida "[a] cheery sort of Wife of Bath." (In the same essay, Calder-Marshall coined the term "Greeneland" for Greene's fictional terrain.) Norman Sherry notes that Amy in "Jubilee" is a rehearsal for Ida and adds that the busty cinematic model for Ida could be Mae West. ("Amy," "Ida," and "Mae" have three letters each.) Sherry suggests that Ida's loose behavior in pubs resembles that of Dorothy Glover,* one of Greene's mistresses. Anne T. Salvatore faults Ida thus: "[S]he judges Pinkie mercilessly but never internalizes her values as the true ethicist would." When a play based on *Brighton Rock* was being written, Greene, as Sherry reports, wanted the ending to reveal Ida as the true villain, for believing in right and wrong, not in good and evil. (Sources: Calder-Marshall, 373; Salvatore, 33–34; Sherry I, 574, 635; Sherry II, 162, 163, 291)

ARONSTEIN (*England Made Me*). When Erik Krogh reminisces about doing construction work on a Chicago bridge, he recalls his friends Murphy, O'Connor, and Williamson there, and says Aronstein was a friend at another time.

ASHWORTH, MRS. (*Our Man in Havana*). When Wormold goes to the bank for money, the teller keeps him waiting because Mrs. Ashworth phones him and the two chat a while.

ASPLUND (*England Made Me*). He is one of Erik Krogh's less important officials. Krogh feels he needn't consult Asplund, Bergsten, or Stefenson about minor matters, since he has a rubber stamp with their signatures.

ASSISTANT COMMISSIONER, THE (*It's a Battlefield*). He is a faithful Scotland Yard employee. Now 56, he served in the East three years, is concerned with evidence, not justice. He investigates crimes diligently, fusses when asked to prepare reports on the effect hanging the murderer Jim Drover would have on the populace, discusses matters with various people, including his friend Lady Caroline Bury, and has a blank cartridge fired at him by Jim's brother Conrad.

Norman Sherry reports that Greene told him that his uncle Sir William Graham Greene* was a model for the Assistant Commissioner, both being stiff, frustrated, honest bachelors. (Source: Sherry I, 463)

ATTENTION (*A Burnt-Out Case*). He is a leper with bloodshot eyes and sunken chest. He suffers an adverse reaction to dianinodiphenyl (D. D. S.) prescribed by Dr. Colin, who assures the potentially dangerous man, who fears he'll kill his son, that after agonizing through the night he'll become calm.

Norman Sherry says Attention is based on a patient Greene saw at the Congo leprosarium suffering from a dose of D. D. S. (Source: Sherry III, 170)

ATTENTION (*A Burnt-Out Case*). He is the endangered son of a leper whose medicine has made him potentially violent.

A.2. (*The Ministry of Fear*) see **JONES**

AUGUSTUS ("A Little Place off the Edgeware Road"). In the silent movie Craven sees, Augustus betrays Pompilia, who then evidently stabs herself.

"AWFUL WHEN YOU THINK OF IT" (1957). Short story. (Characters: None named.)

The narrator is on the Reading-to-Slough train. A baby winks at him. Has he discovered the narrator's ability to foresee babies' futures in their faces? The mother, smiling, leaves her baby in its basket briefly; the narrator understands he's to watch over him a moment. He asks the baby what he wants at the bar. His white-and-brown burp signals a pint of bitters. His head tilt means a stock-market tip coming. The narrator tells the baby his brokers are Druce, Davis and Burrows. Spittle indicates disapproval. A wail doesn't mean gas but time for more drinks — too early for scotch, therefore gin. To the narrator's voiced optimism concerning tobacco, a wink doesn't indicate disapproval but time for dirty jokes. The narrator starts one. A yawn means the baby's heard it already. He'd respond with his own corker, but laughter strangles his attempt. The mother returns, is sure the narrator is fond of babies, and smiles so lovingly that it's hard not to respond hypocritically. But he says he prefers fishing. The baby's bubbly spurts mean the narrator shouldn't flirt with mum, especially when the narrator sees that he and that kid 25 years later belong to the same dull club and he's calling, right now — doubles for everyone. The narrator hopes he's dead by then.

Richard Kelly locates the theme in the narrator's generalization that it's awful we don't change much; cites William Wordsworth about the child being father of the man; quotes William Butler Yeats's "Among School Children," which warns that a mother would be ill-advised to endure childbirth pains if she could foresee the uncertainties of the adulthood of that lump now resting in her lap; and contends that the baby-grown-up's imagined call for doubles at the club "may suggest the narrator sees his own unhappy twin in the grown child." (Source: Kelly, 54)

AYERS, RUBY M. (*Orient Express*). She is a novelist whose romantic attitude toward chastity Coral Musker thinks about when first considering Carleton Myatt's attentiveness.

AZIKAWE (*The Heart of the Matter*). He is a businessman whose story about a fire in his store Scobie investigates.

BACON (*This Gun for Hire*). He is a plumber the vicar asks to repair a stoppage at St. Luke's.

BAGSTER, FLIGHT-LIEUTENANT FREDDIE (*The Heart of the Matter*). He is a licentious, hard-drinking R. A. F. officer who pursues Helen Rolt, to Scobie's discomfiture.

When Greene was in Freetown on Intelligence duty, he met (January 1942) an unpleasant man he called "Filthy Freddie" in his journal, according to Norman Sherry. (Source: Sherry II, 102, 106)

BAILEY (*The Heart of the Matter*). This corrupt policeman illegally maintained a safe deposit in a city away from Sierra Leone.

BAINES ("The Basement Room"). Baines, a former worker off the African coast, and his wife are the Lanes' servants. Baines, browbeaten by his wife, has a mistress named Emmy living nearby. The Lanes go on vacation and leave the Baineses in charge of their son, Philip. When Mrs. Baines catches the lovers in the best spare bedroom, the Baineses fight and she tumbles over the bannister to her death. Philip witnesses the event and can't hide the fact from the authorities. Caught, Baines wilts.

BAINES ("The Other Side of the Border"). He is the deceased minister in West Africa whom Billings would like to replace.

BAINES (*This Gun for Hire*). Major Calkin praises the police superintendent for catching Baines for street betting.

BAINES, MRS. ("The Basement Room"). She is Baines's viciously domineering wife. The two are servants for the Lanes. Aware of his consorting with Emmy, Mrs. Baines returns early from supposedly visiting her dying mother, catches the two in an upstairs bedroom. The Baineses fight, and Mrs. Baines falls over the bannister to her death.

Thomas A. Wendorf posits that evil is "an operation of radically cruel character and a function of human treachery and betrayal," revealed in "The Basement Room" mainly but not exclusively in Mrs. Baines. (Source: Wendorf, 634)

BAINES, MRS. (*The Human Factor*). She was a friend of Daintry's mother and habitually confided in her, after which Daintry's mother revealed some confidences to Daintry's father.

BAKER (*The Heart of the Matter*). He is a Gambia police official who the Commissioner tells Scobie is coming to replace the Commissioner. When he isn't coming after all, and Scobie will be the new commissioner, the news comes tragically late.

BALLARD (*This Gun for Hire*). Raven recalls Ballard was betrayed by a girlfriend because he went soft on her.

BANKS, COLONEL (*This Gun for Hire*). He is the commanding officer of a training station outside Nottwich. Sir Marcus promises Major Calkin he'll transfer Banks so Calkin can have the position, as colonel, if he will order Raven shot on sight. Calkin hesitates, then declines.

BANNOCK, MRS. (*The Third Man*). She is a member of Crabbin's literary institute. When she mistakes Martins for Benjamin Dexter, she tells him she dislikes his novels because they don't tell good stories. Ironically, she might prefer Martins's cheap Westerns.

BARHAM (*It's a Battlefield*). He is a friend of Conder. A servant in a smoking room tells Conder that Barham hasn't been in this evening.

BARKER (*Brighton Rock*). He is a Brighton bookie.

BARKER (*The Human Factor*). He is a bartender at the Berkhamsted pub where Daintry stops after visiting Castle. Barker's talk is pretty much limited to "Uh."

BARKER (*This Gun for Hire*). Raven remembers Barker as a man betrayed after going soft on a girlfriend.

Since Raven tells Anne Crowder he killed

Battling Kite (mentioned as a victim in *Brighton Rock*), this Barker may be the one mentioned in *Brighton Rock.*

BARKER, DR. (*The Human Factor*). He is Sam Castle's physician, with a flaming strawberry birthmark on his left cheek.

BARLOW (*The Heart of the Matter*). He and his wife are Louise Scobie's friends. When they leave, Louise professes to be friendless.

BARLOW, MAJOR ("The Lieutenant Died Last"). He is the magistrate of the village of Potter. He releases Bill Purves with a caution for poaching after Purves saved Potter from the German invasion.

BARLOW, MRS. (*The Heart of the Matter*). When she and her husband leave, Louise Scobie feels friendless.

BARNES (*The Ministry of Fear*). Major Stone says Barnes was killed, perhaps by Poole or Dr. Forester. Stone may be recalling an old battle experience.

BARON ("The Bear Fell Free"). Baron, a socialist, is Farrell's close friend, can't talk Farrell out of trying to fly across the Atlantic Ocean, and takes a bath in water so hot it kills him.

BARON, PEGGY (*Brighton Rock*). Pinkie frightens Rose by saying Peggy Baron had her face disfigured and lost an eye when she became involved in the mob and vitriol was splashed on her.

BARON SAMEDI (*The Comedians*) *see* **DUVALIER, FRANÇOIS**

BARONIN (*Our Man in Havana*). Hawthorne explains to Wormold how carefully they must do spy work by saying an agent in Denmark in 1940 had to burn incriminating papers but when he flushed them down the toilet, the frozen pipes in the flat below, occupied by Baronin, stopped the flow and ashes floated into her bath water.

"THE BASEMENT ROOM" (1935). Short story. (Characters: Aunt Alice, Baines, Mrs. Baines, Cora Down, Emmy, Lane, Mrs. Lane, Philip Lane, Sir Hurbert Reed, Rose, Lord Sandale, Sir Arthur Stillwater, Mrs. Wince-Dudley.)

1. Lane and his wife, departing for a two-week vacation, leave their son Philip, seven, in their Belgravia mansion with their servants Baines, the butler, and Mrs. Baines, the housekeeper. Philip is ecstatic. Uniquely, he can go past the green baize door and walk downstairs, where the Baineses live. He is greeted by Baines, who offers him cake and swigs ginger-beer. Baines talks about his duty in West Africa, the 40 "niggers" he lovingly controlled, how Philip's father was there, how Baines married and left. Having put dust-sheets over furniture upstairs and gathered Mrs. Lane's makeup items, Mrs. Baines enters, criticizes Philip's eating between meals, rebukes Baines for idle story-telling. He cowers, and Philip feels responsible for him. Philip goes upstairs, doesn't want to handle his toys, returns for lunch, which includes Mrs. Baines's tasty pudding and meringue, asks Baines to take him for a walk. Mrs. Baines says Baines must clean the silver. She and Philip argue; she slaps him, then smiles. Philip retreats to the street.

2. Philip observes a shabby tea shop in Pimlico, sees Baines and a strange girl (later named Emmy). He heard Baines had a niece. She is crying over a cake with pink icing, but Baines importunes her with a jar of powder. Philip wonders who she is. As a joke, he shouts "Baines" the way Mrs. Baines would. Baines starts, recovers, gives Philip some cake, answers, yes, she's his niece, accepts Philip's apology, says he needn't tell Mrs. Baines about this meeting, fears she'll pump him for details. Philip promises silence. Home again, Baines and Philip see Mrs. Baines at the curtained window. In his room, Philip finds his supper laid out. Mrs. Baines slithers in, asks if Philip took any powder pot, notes pink sugar on his shoulder; he blurts out that "they" gave him some cake. He realizes his didn't keep Baines's secret, gripes to himself that adults shouldn't thrust a child into their secrets. Mrs. Baines compounds everything by urging Philip to keep the secret that she knows Baines and the girl were having tea. Mrs. Baines bridles when Philip says why not? the nice girl is Baines's niece. Mrs. Baines bribes him by promising him a Meccano set. He won't

promise, but also won't tell. (The narrator intrudes by saying that Philip 60 years later was an uncreative dilettante, never forgetting Mrs. Baines's viciousness.)

3. Baines joyfully awakens Philip, to announce his wife has been called away because her mother is dying. Philip, disliking Baines's unbecoming childishness, recalls dreaming about witches and a man holding a knife. Baines sends Philip for a copy of the *Mail* and promises celebratory sausages and a long day. The two go to the Park, have a corner-house lunch, visit the Zoo. On the bus home via the Artillery Memorial, Baines boasts of almost shooting a Coastal "black," and answers, yes, he still has his revolver — in case of burglars. Emmy awaits them; the three dine in the basement on sausages, beer, ginger-pop, and burgundy. Sent up for the mail, Philip thinks of French Revolution guillotining. Returning past the baize door, he sees Baines and Emmy kissing. When a letter from Mrs. Baines to Baines confirms her staying away, Philip wonders whether letters, like spoken words, can also lie. Though absent, Mrs. Baines seems present. The adults kiss again before Philip, escort him upstairs, see him safely into bed, and retreat. Their voices, though not distant, fade. Mrs. Baines interrupts Philip's dream of a tricolored man by asking in a whisper where "they" are.

4. Mrs. Baines has searched the empty rooms downstairs. She appeals to Philip, promising that toy, mentioning their secret, asking for his love, threatening him. She combines misery, cruelty, a sour smell. She tiptoes out. Philip feels unwalled between childhood and their adult world; life crashes on him so viciously that his next 60 years were ruined. He sees Mrs. Baines's hand on that spare bedroom door-knob and, feeling loyalty to generous Baines, shouts "Baines." Baines rushes out. While Emmy sits in the best-room doorway, Baines fights Mrs. Baines, whose strength is diminished by her aridity, years, and hopelessness. She goes over the bannister and falls into the hall like a bag of coal destined for the basement. Unseen and seeking to escape everybody, Philip takes the back stairs into the square and its garden. The trees make a forest to hide in from the wolves. Let adults have their world. He seems safe here. But when he sees Baines at their mansion door signal for Emmy to run away, Philip wanders past shops, is lost and afraid, because although Baines was his friend Mrs. Baines had acquired unique power. Can't a policeman come and take him home? He sits and cries. A policeman takes him to the station — to Justice.

5. A constable and others question Philip, who is evasive until a report is telephoned that a Mrs. Baines has been in an accident. Philip feels he must say both Baineses are good to him. The constable takes Philip home. He understands from police gestures that Mrs. Baines is dead. Baines answers the door, stunned into non-deceptiveness at sight of Philip, who would like to help Baines but for his entangling Philip in incomprehensible secrets. Philip shouldn't love; love gets you involved. Glancing at Philip like a begging dog, Baines tells the authorities his wife slipped on the basement stairs. When the police are about to let Baines escort Philip up to bed, the boy — fed up with adult secrecy — blurts that he knows Mrs. Baines lies dead in the hall. The constable, realizing Baines lied and probably tidied up, asks Baines if he were alone. Philip — no more secrets — names Emmy. Baines, ignorantly sympathetic toward a mere child, is quickly asked by the constable who "she" is. The narrator concludes by saying that 60 years later Philip's secretary asked her dying boss the same question.

Greene started writing "The Basement Room" aboard ship while returning from Liberia (1935). Baines's reminiscences about his being a Coaster reflect Greene's experiences there. Baines tells Philip that to Coasters and their native employees food is "chop," gratuities, "dash." Greene uses these words in "A Chance for Mr. Lever" and in *Journey Without Maps: A Travel Book*. The *News Chronicle* paid Greene £50 for "The Basement Room," as a five-day serial. It was the lead story in *The Basement Room* (1935), Greene's first collection of short stories, eight in number.

Neil Sinyard reports that Greene must have been influenced when writing "The Basement Room" by Henry James's *The Turn of the Screw;* both concern "child[ren] stumbling across adult perfidy and passion, with long-term tragic consequences." Michael Shelden theorizes that the witch Philip dreams about and the lurking maneuvers of Mrs. Baines are based on Greene's childhood memories of Marion Greene,* his mother. R. H. Miller compares the five parts of Greene's story to a Renaissance tragedy, with "its construct of rising action, crisis, falling action, and catastrophe, out of which a new awareness ... arises for both protagonist and reader." Gerald E. Silviera regards the story as "a rather explicit Roman Catholic statement on the catastrophe that inevitably follows the rejection of responsibility and the embracing of an egoistic life."

"The Basement Room" has subtleties numerous beyond listing. For example, Baines the adult tells Philip the child on the fatal night that he should get to bed because he's had a long day, whereas Baines is slavering to complete his own long day, by bedding half-child, half-adult Emma; Mrs. Baines's return continues her long day beyond night.

Greene chose the Belgravia neighborhood for its figurative value. Philip descends from beautiful upper quarters into the grave of his innocence. A. A. DeVitis and Richard Kelly focus on the mansion. DeVitis says that it "in Jungian terms symbolizes the integrated personality," adds that the green baize door becomes "a means of distinguishing between the conscious and the subconscious," and concludes that the upper rooms are light (good), while below is dark (evil). Kelly identifies the mansion's many levels: aristocratic upper level, servants' belowground level; conscious level, unconscious level; innocence, experience; known, unknown; even, he adds, "the Jungian archetypes of heaven and hell." In the Greene residence in Berkhamsted, a green baize door separated family rooms and school rooms; and Greene, as well as many critics, have made much of its latent symbolism. In several works, Greene adverts to such a door, often for symbolism. For example, in *The Ministry of Fear* a green baize door in Dr. Forester's sanatorium separates patients' quarters from the evil doctor's sick bay.

This story introduces many of Greene's themes — inexperienced child clashing unwittingly but disastrously with experienced adults, dramatic betrayals, unholy folding of evil into good, paralyzing consequences of innocence lost (often oneirically foregrounded).

"The Basement Room" was the basis of the 1948 movie *The Fallen Idol* (U.S. title, *The Lost Illusion*). Greene wrote the plot-altered script for filmmakers Alexander Korda* and Carol Reed.* In a *Collected Edition* introduction, Greene says Korda tried unsuccessfully to get him to change Baines from butler to chauffeur. William Cash says that Greene's then semi-secret love affair with Catherine Walson* was going so badly that not even "the film rights cheque for £3,000 could raise his wretched and 'dreary' spirits." The British title of the film reflects Greene's habit of suggesting levels of action, while the American title focuses on the child's losing a hero to worship. Gene D. Phillips, discussing differences between story and movie, says the latter concerns "a boy who believes that his friend has committed a murder ... and who lies to the police in an effort to shield his friend"; Philip becomes Felipe, son of a foreign diplomat serving in London; Emmy becomes Julie; the Baineses keep their name, but "Alice" Baines only pretends to leave the house to go visit her "aunt," spies on the lovers from a ledge and is knocked to her death by a swinging window — not murdered, as the boy then wrongly concludes. (Sources: Cash, 101; DeVitis, 173; Greene, *Loser Takes All, Collected Edition,* 126; Kelly, 25; Miller, 151; Phillips, 51–52; Shelden, 108; Sherry I, 571; Sherry II, 239–41; Silviera; Sinyard, 26).

BASIL (*Brighton Rock*). A woman mentions the name Basil in conversation with another woman at Brighton's Cosmopolitan.

BATES (*The Captain and the Enemy*). He is Jim Baxter's school headmaster. Bates writes to Jim's father when Jim doesn't return after his outing with the Captain.

BATES (*The Human Factor*). He is a British defector Castle meets in Moscow. Bellamy, another defector there, tells Castle that Bates married a middle-aged woman from the Union of Writers.

BATES ("The Other Side of the Border"). When Hands visits Billings at his West African photographic shop, he tells Billings that Anderson sold his Denton store to Bates.

BATES (*The Third Man*). He is a British soldier under Colonel Calloway's command. He tells Martins he knows the sewer system as well as he knows London's Tottenham Court Road. While fellow soldiers are pursuing Harry Lime in the sewer, Bates, ordered to protect Martins down there, is shot dead by Harry.

BATES, JOE (*The Confidential Agent*). He is the Benditch coal miners's union leader. Bates, with wild hair and a weak-looking mouth, feels that if Lord Benditch's representative assures him coal won't go to D's war-torn country, he'll authorize the mines to reopen at L's request.

BATES, MRS. UNION-OF-WRITERS (*The Human Factor*). This is how Bellamy identifies to Castle the defector Bates's Russian wife.

BATLOW, MISS (*It's a Battlefield*). She is an elderly filing clerk working in Conrad Drover's office.

BATTERSON (*England Made Me*). On Krogh's orders, Fred Hall fraudulently sells stock to Batterson's company.

BAXTER (*The Captain and the Enemy*). He is Jim Baxter's heartless, tactless, self-absorbed father. Called "the Devil" by many who know him, and by himself, Baxter once worked in Africa. He impregnated Liza and required her to have an abortion. He lost possession of Jim to the Captain in a backgammon game. Black-bearded at his wife's funeral, he is white-haired when Jim sees him later.

BAXTER (*England Made Me*). Minty remembers attending this friend's funeral.

BAXTER, J. (*The Comedians*). He is a pharmaceutical salesman aboard the *Medea*. During the last-night party, he dons a helmet and recites a dramatic monologue inspired by his having been an air-raid warden during the war. It is "The Warden's Patrol," supposedly by Post Warden X. The pursar later tells Brown that Baxter had a heart attack and is buried in Santo Domingo.

BAXTER, JIM (*The Captain and the Enemy*). He is the narrator-protagonist, originally named Victor Baxter. His heartless father, called "the Devil," enrolls Victor in a hated school and loses him, when Victor is 12, in a backgammon game to the Captain, who informally adopts him, renames him Jim, and makes him Liza's surrogate son in London. Jim become a second-rate reporter. His new life begins when Liza dies and he joins the Captain in Panama. They quarrel, after which Jim's careless talk to Cyril Quigly, an agent for the U.S. government, indirectly causes the Captain's death. Jim keeps a running autobiography, leaves it unfinished to seek a different life, and dies in a mysterious accident on his way to the airport. In school, Jim is called Baxter Three by the headmaster, because two other lads named Baxter are also there. In Panama, Jim is sometimes called Smith because the Captain, his alleged father, calls himself Smith.

Greene told Yvonne Cloetta* that Jim at school was based on himself at the Berkhamsted school. (Source: Cloetta, 43)

BAXTER, MRS. (*The Captain and the Enemy*). She was the oppressed wife of Baxter and the mother of Victor Baxter, a.k.a. Jim Baxter. She died a few years before Victor, 12, is won from his father by the Captain in a backgammon game.

BAXTER THREE (*The Captain and the Enemy*) *see* **BAXTER, JIM**

BAXTER, VICTOR (*The Captain and the Enemy*) *see* **BAXTER, JIM**

BEALE (*It's a Battlefield*). He is the Minister, the Home Secretary, often referred to but not appearing in the novel.

BEALE (*The Ministry of Fear*). He is a policeman summoned when Rowe surrenders in Scotland Yard.

BEALE, GEORGE (*Brighton Rock*). He is a Brighton bookie.

"THE BEAR FELL FREE" (1935). Short story. (Characters: Baron, Brigstock, Carter, Tubby Clayton, Conway, Davis, Dolly, Mrs. Farrell, Tony Farrell, Toc H, Jane, John, Mavis, Pamela, Pim.)

Drunk in Earl's Court, London, in June, Tony Farrell, who won substantially in the Irish

Sweepstakes, was dared by the Atlantic Flight Party to fly solo from Croydon to New York. Carter, his buddy from school and army days, and Baron, younger but wiser than the two and a socialist pacifist, warned Tony against the stunt.

Now in the air, Tony ejects his lifebelt, with bravado.

Everyone below is waving, except his frantic mother. At the bar, Baron silently counters Carter's praise of Tony's adventurous spirit by thinking he'd have done something constructive with lottery winnings.

Tony plows through an Irish Channel storm. He can say he lacked a lifebelt, had to turn back for it. As he descends from 1,000 to 900 feet, the teddy bear Jane gave him bumps his back.

John, Jane, and Baron have drinks at the bar. The men have memories of trench warfare, including one about Conway, dead in mud and wire.

Next comes a rainy memorial service, for Tony, dead. Carter and Baron sit together. Tony's mother looks severe and fatigued, her face like that of a distinguished gentleman.

Jane, abed with Tony's replacement, answers Carter's phone call. Yes, she gave Tony a teddy bear; nice it's been found; give it me sometime for a souvenir of our wild love.

In the salty sea's green wash, the bear lifts free, gets coiled in seaweed.

At Tony's memorial, Carter weeps for another war comrade, Davis. Evidently Baron left the bar, took a hot bath at home, and had a fatal heart attack.

Back up with Tony. He reverses his buffeted plane, will admit it was a joke, must fly by compass, descends toward unseen waves going 120 m.p.h.

Carter leaves Baron after the service. Carter proceeds with the teddy bear salvaged from the Irish Sea and boxed, and returns it to Jane; weeps for dead Davis, Jane's bed, dead Tony; imagines Davis, also crying, using his service revolver, his guilt-infused brains staining the wall.

When Tony's plane hits the water, the crumpled wheel and cockpit do their fatal work.

In a final verbal montage, Greene pastes together proof shots of guilt, suicide, money, prayers, memories.

"The Bear Fell Free," which combines stream-of-consciousness bits and flashbacks, is unendurably confusing. It also is foolishly titled. It was published in 285 copies, in 18 unnumbered pages, as a book, of which 250 were numbered and signed by Greene. Why it was ever republished in 150 copies (Folcroft Press, 1970) is another puzzle. Cedric Watts contends that the complex structure of "The Bear Fell Free" owes much to Greene's acceptance of the "theories of precognitive dreams and temporal overlaps" espoused by J. W. Dunne (1875–1949) in *An Experiment with Time* (1927) and *The Serial Universe* (1934). Watts defines "The Bear Fell Free" as Greene's "purgation of experimental ambitions." Greene mentions Dunne and his book in *A World of My Own*. (Sources: Greene, *A World of My Own,* xxi; Watts, 132, 133, 206)

"BEAUTY" (1963). Short story. (Character: Beauty). Amid Antibes's autumnal chills, the narrator hears an old woman in a hideous orange scarf wrapped like an out-of-fashion toque shouting from a balcony. She tells her friends, an English couple, she can't visit them in London because she couldn't torture Beauty, her lovely, passive-looking Pekinese, by quarantining him. She gently lifts Beauty, resembling a cream bun, from her window sill and presses him to her breast. The narrator returns from the Place de Gaulle cinema and sees Beauty, grunting like a disturbed clubman, go to a garbage can and root out the sausage-like, dumped intestines of an animal, drag them to a street corner full of "ordure," squirm his *café-au-lait* fur into it, and mouth his food. But for that toque, the narrator would pity Beauty's owner, as she calls for him post-wee-wee to reappear.

Richard Kelly defines the theme of this farce "the paradoxical relationship between beauty and ugliness, as he [Greene] ... draws together the aesthetic and the excremental views of his subject." Kelly adds that ideal beauty is "enhanced by ... opposites." True, the narrator stresses Beauty's passive "satin eyes," but his calling feces Beauty's "dark shampoo" evokes not the explicator's sense of "paradox" but simply laughter. More evident is Greene's predictable jibe at Americans: Beauty's owner's nationality is not specified; but, calling British MPs "congressmen," she must be American.

"Beauty" is one of the 12 stories in *May We Borrow Your Husband? and Other Comedies of the Sexual Life*; therefore the reader expects at least sexual overtones in it. Though muted, two may be detected—Beauty's owner presses him to her left breast, and the narrator unprovably calls her "sterile." (Source: Kelly, 56)

BEAVIS (*The Ministry of Fear*). He is a Scotland Yard employee who takes down Rowe's statements to Beale and Prentice.

BECKLEY, HENRY (*The Power and the Glory*). He is Director of Private Tutorials. Ltd., a correspondence school Coral Fellows uses for study.

Michael Shelden notes that details of Beckley's school are "intended to be a parody" of Berkhamsted School, of which Greene's father Charles Greene* was headmaster, which Greene attended, and the motto of which—*Virtus Laudata Crescit* (Virtue increases with praise)—also appears on the Berkhamsted coat of arms. (Source: Shelden, 273)

BELFRAGE, SIR HENRY (*The Honorary Consul*). He is the fussy British ambassador in Buenos Aires. When Plarr asks him to help Fortnum, he merely suggests that Plarr start an Anglo-Argentine club and use it to publicize Fortnum's plight in newspapers printed in English.

BELFRAGE, LADY (*The Honorary Consul*). She is the ambassador's wife. She knows Plarr's mother. Plarr gains favor with Belfrage by diverting Lady Belfrage from the tedious attentions of a dull visiting poet.

BELLAIRS, MRS. (*The Ministry of Fear*). She is a flamboyant, gypsy-like fortune-teller who at the fête tells Rowe the weight of the cake. She participates in the spy ring, conducts the phony séance incriminating Rowe, and is raided, arrested, and threatened by Prentice.

Anthony Mockler suggests that Mrs. Bellairs's Campden Hill house might be based on the untidy house of a man named Sir Roger Hollis, 6 Campden Hill Square. Mockler says Roger's brother Christopher Hollis, a Catholic, was at Balliol College when Greene was. (Source: Mockler, 187)

BELLAMY (*The Human Factor*). He is a homosexual British defector, whom Castle meets in Moscow and who welcomes Castle and says he can visit Bellamy's dacha next spring. He tells Castle he was assigned by the British Council in West Berlin and had a German boyfriend in charge of pro-Western agents in East Germany. When his friend got seduced by a woman, Bellamy betrayed his friend's many contacts—but never his whilom friend—to the Soviets and had to escape to Moscow.

Although Anthony Cave Brown doesn't suggest that Bellamy, a homosexual, is based on Guy Burgess,* also a homosexual, he does report that after Burgess defected to Moscow, "he lived with a Soviet lover provided by the KGB, a plumber by trade." (Source: Brown, 517)

BELLEN, LORD ("When Greek Meets Greek"). Lord Bellen employed Lord Driver as a servant, whereupon Driver stole some of his silver spoons.

BELLOWS, DR. (*The Confidential Agent*). He is an elderly, saintly linguist who founded the Entrenationo Language Centre in London in the vain hope that if people speak one language, his Entrenationo, international strife will end. He employs and underpays K., one of D.'s contacts, sneaks around in rubber shoes, and gives Saturday evening soirées.

BELMONT, MONSIEUR HENRI (*Doctor Fischer of Geneva*). He is one of Fischer's toadying Toads. A tax adviser, he is tall, lean, with hollow cheeks and a twitching left eyelid. Belmont shows up at Jones's and Anna-Luise's marriage ceremony, also at the Mass the couple attend on Christmas Eve, and at the bomb party.

W. J. West suggests Thomas Chambers Windsor Roe (b. 1917) as perhaps the basis for much in Fischer's background. However, when West writes of Roe's slick skill in investing other people's money in foreign ventures, setting up tax-shelter companies, and dodging tax laws, Roe seems fully as much Belmont's model. (Source: West, 192–94)

BENDITCH, LORD (*The Confidential Agent*). He controls coal mines in Benditch, a Midlands town. Huge, bullet-headed, big-jawed, with hairy hands, he was a workingman's son, rose to prominence and recognition, is unsympathetic toward his workers, and is Rose Cullen's father. Benditch's commercial associates are Lord Brigstock, Lord Fetting, and Forbes. D. meets and attempts to deal with Benditch.

BENDRIX (*The End of the Affair*). Maurice Bendrix's father. Maurice tells Sylvia Black that he is alive. The reader's absence of knowledge of this man is indicative of Maurice's callousness, caused partly by the fact that when Maurice's mother died his father didn't call him to come home from school.

BENDRIX, MAURICE (*The End of the Affair*). He is the narrator. For 20 years Bendrix has been a competent, doggedly productive novelist of moderate success and moderate confidence. A shortened leg caused a limp and kept him from military service. He seeks Sarah Miles to learn about her husband, Henry Miles, details of whose work he wants to include in his current novel. Bendrix soon lusts for Sarah, and they have a prolonged affair (1939–1944), disturbed by his cynicism and self-hatred, and ended when, thinking him killed by a V1 flying bomb during the war, she promises God she'll stop seeing Bendrix if He revives him — which occurs. Bendrix thinks her quitting him means she has another lover. She has — God. Bendrix tries to wins her back, fails, and comes to realize that her astounding help to others, namely Lance Parkis and Richard Smythe, along with a few so-called "coincidences," may be proof of divine intervention and Sarah's own near-saintliness. When he intrudes on Miss Smythe, Bendrix calls himself Bridges and calls Lance Parkis, who is with him, his son Arthur James Bridges.

W. J. West exaggerates the influence on Greene of the minor novelist John Davys Beresford (1873–1947), who, like Bendrix, had a limp — in Beresford's case, caused by an accident. Evelyn Waugh, liking Greene's use of Bendrix as a main, and unreliable, narrator, says this: "Instead of an omniscient and impersonal recorder we have the chief character giving his distorted version; a character who is himself in course of evolution, whose real story is only beginning at the conclusion of the book, who is himself unaware of the fate we can dimly foresee for him." Gwenn R. Boardman contends Bendrix "wonders whether his hatred [of Sarah] is really as deficient as his love…. Gradually [Boardman adds] he comes to realize that his 'hatred' is really fear — fear of the leap to God." A. A. DeVitis dislikes Bendrix, labeling him "both bitch and fake [in contrast to Sarah], for he is jealous, conniving, sadistic, and foolish." Peter Green labels Bendrix "Greene's atheistical alter ego." (Sources: Boardman, 91; DeVitis, 95; Green, 33; Waugh, 458; West, 134)

BENEVENTO, DR. (*The Honorary Consul*). One of this fellow's professional functions is examining Señora Sanchez's prostitutes every Thursday.

BENEVENTO, SEÑORA (*The Honorary Consul*). She is Dr. Benevento's severe wife. She sports a big cross and watches pseudo-patiently while he enjoys an apératif.

BENNETT (*It's a Battlefield*). He is a gruff Communist who at a big meeting tells Philip Surrogate to keep quiet. Bennett distrusts "intellectual" Reds. Conder the reporter fears Bennett, but Bennett decamps when he thinks Conder is after him.

BENNETT, ARTHUR (*The Confidential Agent*). He may be the alcoholic husband of Mrs. Bennett, Rose Cullen's former nurse. (On the other hand, George Bennett may be her husband. George Jarvis names both names without further clarification when D. asks about Mrs. Bennett.)

BENNETT, GEORGE (*The Confidential Agent*) see **BENNETT, ARTHUR**

BENNETT, MRS. (*The Confidential Agent*). She was Rose Cullen's nurse, comfortably retired in Benditch. When D. asks her about the coal-miners' union there, she clams up even though, earlier, she reminisced fondly to him about Rose.

BERGMAN (*The Honorary Consul*). He is mentioned as an orange-canning factory owner. Plarr has visited it on occasion. Diego Corredo once worked there.

BERGSON ("A Drive in the Country"). He may be the head of the export agency for which the unnamed restless girl's steady father works.

BERGSTEN (*England Made Me*). He is an official in Krogh's company. Krogh doesn't need to consult Bergsten, Asplund, or Stefenson all the time, because he has their signatures on a rubber stamp. Fred Hall is irate when Bergsten boards a chartered airplane at Malmö and Hall has to wait.

BERNAY (*It's a Battlefield*). Bernay, 65, is a church-going, self-important pawnbroker. He burned stock in his shop but decided not to pursue an insurance claim. He now sells items at reduced prices. He sells Conrad Drover a defective revolver and 10 blanks.

BERTHA ("The Over-night Bag"). She is the lesbian lover of Tiny, the obese passenger sitting beside Henry Cooper on their Nice-to-London flight. Bertha's letter to her "darling Tiny" is signed "Your own cuddly Bertha."

BERTRAM (*The End of the Affair*). He is or was Sarah Miles's father. Her mother was his third wife. When the three vacationed in Normandy, his wife suspected it was so he could visit his first wife in Deauville. Bertram disliked Sarah's mother's being a Catholic and deserted both when Sarah was three.

BERTRAM (*Loser Takes All*). He is Dreuther's expert, ill-rewarded accountant, 40. His wife deserted him 15 years ago, and he is engaged to young Cary. Calling him "Bertrand," Dreuther orders him to check errors caused by other accountants. He corrects a serious mistake. When Dreuther hears Bertram plans to marry in London and honeymoon in Bournemouth, Dreuther orders the couple to go to Nice, marry in Monte Carlo, meet him on his yacht there, and honeymoon aboard. They go. He doesn't appear. They wed. Bertram develops a winning roulette system, becomes addicted, and almost loses Cary. Dreuther, appearing nine days late, persuades Bertram that money isn't everything and that romantic poverty appeals to Cary; so he deliberately loses and wins her back. When Bertram takes Bird's Nest for dinner at the Orphée to make Cary jealous, he signs the restaurant guest register as "Robert Devereux."

At the Orphée, Bertram becomes Orpheus-like. The moment he enters the place he sees Cary, surely his Eurydice, love-bitten by Philippe but soon to be returned to reality. Unlike Orpheus, who looks back, Bertram at novel's end lets the sea take the shredded notes of his infernal gambling system "back in our [*Seagull*] wake" and looks only at Cary. (*See also* Hilfe, Willi.)

BERTRAM, AUGUSTA (*Travels with My Aunt*). Henry Pulling calls this spirited lady Aunt Augusta and his mother Angela Pulling's sister. While taking him or ordering him to Brighton, Paris, Istanbul, Boulogne, and Paraguay, Augusta reveals or he learns about her colorful past and present scheming in England, Italy, Havana, and elsewhere, and also about her lovers, including Henry's father Richard Pulling, the Rev. Curran, General Abdul, Achille Dambreuse, Zachary Wordsworth, and maybe Visconti. Wild, hedonistic, romantic, criminal, passionate, sensual Augusta is everything Henry hasn't been. In the course of their hot-cold relationship, he starts changing. Augusta does everything from working in and perhaps running brothels to smugglings, is what she herself would now call a cafeteria Catholic, but remains endearing to all who understand her. But can she do so to all readers?

Should any reader believe Greene when he contended that he started writing *Travels with My Aunt* so indifferently that he "didn't know that Augusta was Henry's mother"? Michael Shelden, Norman Sherry, and William Cash provide details about Dr. Elisabeth Moor, the person on whom Augusta is based. Greene knew "Dottoressa" Moor, an opinionated, amoral Austrian living on Capri. He helped write and wholly edited her autobiography, *An Impossible Woman: The Memories of Dottoressa Moor of Capri* (1975). Greene's friend the novelist Shirley Hazzard (b. 1931), wife of the literary critic Francis Steegmuller (1906–1994), says Greene told her he wrote "his versions of her [Dr. Moor's] presumed" thoughts. Hazzard adds that Dr. Moor was pleased when Greene told her she "look[ed] just like [Nikita] Khrushchev." Hazzard describes Dr. Moor as "[a] squat, categorical figure ... with the rugged, russet complexion of northerners long weathered in the hot south, prominent paleolithic teeth, and memorably pale blue eyes." (Yvonne Cloetta* regards Hazzard's comments on Greene as sometimes "harsh" and inaccurate and adds that Greene regarded Hazzard as a literary snob.) Dr. Moor lived life wildly, had many lovers, including a black man and also Boris Alperovici, the third husband of British comedienne and singer Gracie Fields (1898–1979), on Capri. Hazzard notes that "Graham was fond of Gracie Fields," who "had simplicity, good humour, shrewdness: a human distinction." R. H. Miller generously contrasts Augusta to Ida Arnold (*Brighton Rock*), opining that whereas "Ida exhibits a simple and doctrinaire secular morality, Aunt Augusta takes the world as she finds it, responding to it partly through her own special brand of Catholicism, partly from her experience of living." (Sources: Cash, 169–70; Cloetta, 153; Greene, *Ways of Escape,* 297; Hazzard, 26, 52, 93; Miller, 129; Shelden, 82–83, 460–61; Sherry III, 498–501, 550)

BERTRAM, MRS. (*The End of the Affair*). She is Sarah Miles's mother, from Great Missenden. Her husband married twice earlier. His disliking her being a Catholic inspired her to baptize Sarah secretly when she was two. He deserted both a year later. Sarah's husband Henry Miles's dislike of her mother persuaded her to remain apart from both. Her meeting Bendrix at Sarah's funeral seems fortuitous enough to qualify as miraculous.

In a *Collected Edition* introduction, Greene said he got the idea for Sarah's baptism from the biography of Roger Casement (1864–1916), British consular agent and Irish rebel. Casement, awaiting execution for treason, asked a Catholic chaplain in his prison to baptize him Catholic; the priest inquired and learned Casement had been secretly baptized as a child. (Source: Greene, *The End of the Affair, Collected Edition,* x)

BEYER (*England Made Me*). Minty names him as one of his rival Stockholm journalists.

BILL (*Brighton Rock*). He operates Brighton's Palace of Pleasure shooting booth.

BILL (*Brighton Rock*). He is a waiter at a restaurant where Ida Arnold meets Hale. She asks Bill to "do" Hale a sandwich.

BILL (*The Man Within*). He is an elderly revenuer. While attending the Assizes in Lewes, he slaps Andrews for being a dirty informer. Later, Bill and other authorities enter Elizabeth's cottage in pursuit of Andrews, Carlyon, and the other smugglers.

BILLINGS ("The Other Side of the Border"). He is a friend of Hands. They knew each other in Denton in 1931. In 1936 in West Africa, Hands finds Billings, a pigeon-breasted, dry-skinned impoverished photographer, and persuades him to join his gold-seeking exploration. Billings probably died, or so Morrow hints when he returns to Danvers in Liverpool in 1938. In school, Billings was called Creepy Billings.

BILLY (*Brighton Rock*) see **FRANK, BILLY**

BINNS (*This Gun for Hire*) see **MAYDEW, MISS**

BIRD'S NEST (*Loser Takes All*). She is a middle-aged, broad-shouldered creature with an ugly yellow wig drooping into her earrings, and two gold teeth. She cadges tokens from winning Monte Carlo gamblers. In a failed effort to make his wife Cary jealous, Bertram takes Bird's Nest to a lush restaurant, where, pleading a small appetite, she has lobster and strawberries. To flatter Bertram, she calls him "colonel."

BISHOP, THE (*The Burnt-Out Case*). He is the leading Catholic official of the region. Tall, rakish, nicely bearded, he owns the boat Querry arrives on, is gracious at a party given by Governor and Mme. Guelle, and flirts with Marie Rycker there.

Norman Sherry says Greene, during his stay at Dr. Michel F. Lechat's Congo leprosarium, took a ship belonging to the Bishop to visit other regional missions treating lepers. (Source; Sherry III, 174, 179–84 passim)

BISHOP, THE (*This Gun for Hire*). Acky, defrocked and running a bawdy house with his wife, appeals to the Bishop for reinstatement and hints at the Bishop's former sexual promiscuity.

BISHOP, THE (*Our Man in Havana*). Hasselbacher humorously suggests that Wormold sell a vacuum cleaner to Father Mendez for the Bishop's palace.

BISHOP, THE (*The Quiet American*). He is the Catholic Bishop of Phat Diem and is devoted to Our Lady of Fatima, whose feast day he celebrates. French authorities have disbanded an army he controlled, and now he leads only a brass band. He trades with Communists in his region. When Fowler observes enemy activity near Phat Diem, he argues with the Bishop about Catholic theology. Fowler calls him the Prince Bishop.

Would any war correspondent, during a lull in mortar fire and resting in a cathedral, dispute religion with an expert? Greene here displays his well-known controversial responses to his own adopted religion. According to Norman Sherry, this bishop is patterned on Bishop Monsignor Le Huu Tu, formerly an austere Trappist. (Source: Sherry II, 390)

BISHOP, ARTHUR (*The Heart of the Matter*). He is the hero in a story Scobie invents to entertain Jimmy Fisher, an injured boy taken from the torpedoed passenger vessel also carrying Helen Rolt.

BISHOP, DAVID ("The News in English"). Mary Bishop's husband, he was a mathematics don at Oxford. He and his wife vacationed in Germany. Shortly before the war, he was lecturing in Germany, remained, and is broadcasting pro-German news in English to England as Lord Haw Haw's replacement. Nicknamed Doctor Funkhole by the British, reviled by his super-patriotic mother, but trusted by Mary, David in reality broadcasts valuable military information in a code he and Mary once used and still understand.

BISHOP, MARY ("The News in English"). She is David Bishop's loyal wife. When David is caught during a lecture tour in Germany and broadcasts anti–British propaganda in a Lord Haw Haw fashion, she becomes aware he's using a code she understands and reports the fact to the War Office.

For his own reasons, Greene, after saying Mary prayed, feels obliged to add "she didn't much believe in prayer."

BISHOP, MRS. ("The News in English"). She is David Bishop's mother. She is so patriotic that when her son broadcasts seemingly pro-German propaganda in English to discomfit British listeners she venomously rejects him.

BISHOP OF BATH AND WELLS, THE ("Work Not in Progress"). He is one of the kidnap victims.

BISHOP OF CANTERBURY, THE ("Work Not in Progress"). He is the ecclesiastical leader whom the female fake Archbishop of Canterbury imitates.

BISHOP OF CANTERBURY, THE ("Work Not in Progress"). She is the leader of the thugs, impersonates the real Archbishop of Canterbury, falls in love with the Bishop of Melbourne, and takes ship with him for Australia.

BISHOP OF EL TOBOSO, THE (*Monsignor Quixote*). He is Father Quixote's superior, dislikes Quixote, and cannot stomach his being promoted to monsignor. When reports arrive about Quixote's holiday, the Bishop forbids him from saying Mass.

BISHOP OF MELBOURNE, THE ("Work Not in Progress"). He visits England for the Convocation, penetrates the kidnappers' gang, but falls in love with their leader, the female impersonator of the real Archbishop of Canterbury. They leave together for Australia.

BISHOP OF MOTOPO, THE (*Monsignor Quixote*). He is a traveling bishop, of Italian background. He runs out of petrol near Father Quixote's home. Quixote offers him lunch, of delicious horse meat, and repairs his Mercedes (by filling the tank and greasing his hands). The grateful Bishop has Quixote elevated to monsignor.

BJÖRK, ANITA (b. 1923). Anita Björk, born in Tällberg, Sweden, was a famous actress. She debuted as a teenager (1942), achieved star status in the title role of *Fröken Julie* (*Miss Julie*, 1951, directed by Alf Sjöberg), in *Han glömde henne aldrig* (*Secrets of Women*, 1952, directed by Ingman Bergman), and in *Night People* (1953, American movie shot in Germany). Her husband, the Swedish writer Stig Dagerman, committed suicide (December 1954). She had a son and two daughters. She became a leading performer of the Royal Dramatic Theater in Stockholm and on Swedish television.

Greene met Anita Björk in Stockholm when he was there to consult Ragnar Svanstrom, his Swedish publisher (November 1955). The two became lovers (by December), vacationed in Havana (November 1957), and were together in Stockholm (January 1958). Greene bought Anita a house in the Swedish archipelago (summer 1958). She decided to end the affair (later 1958). While missing her, Greene returned to Catherine Walston,* whom he had characteristically informed about Anita. He also told his estranged wife Vivien Greene* about Anita. It may be cruel, perhaps vengeful, that Greene in his smash play *The Complaisant Lover* (1959 — dedicated to "C[atherine Walston].") has a husband contemplate suicide by carbon monoxide in his garage — the means by which Anita's husband killed himself. Greene and Anita were embarrassed when the play was produced in Sweden (summer 1960). It has been both speculated and doubted that Greene did not receive the Nobel Prize for literature because of the implications of *The Complaisant Lover*. Nonetheless, according to William Cash, Greene and Anita embraced and cried when she visited England (1970s). Michael Meyer, who introduced Greene to Anita, provides details concerning their affair. (Sources: Cash, 93, 105, 250–71 passim; Meyer, 133–36, 173–74, 187–88; Shelden, 418–21; Sherry III, 61, 92–95, 102–08 passim, 216, 720)

BLACK (*The End of the Affair*). He was Sylvia Black's father. During Sarah Miles's cremation at Golders Green, Sylvia tells Bendrix her father was cremated there two years earlier.

BLACK, SYLVIA (*The End of the Affair*). She is the tall, oft-squelched girlfriend of supercilious Peter Waterbury, a minor critic. Bendrix does himself and Sylvia a favor by enticing her to accompany him to Sarah Miles's cremation. The timely appearance there of Mrs. Bertram, Sarah's mother, prevents Bendrix's likely ruinous seduction of Sylvia, who is a thoroughly compassionate young lady.

Paul Hogarth's book illustrating most of Greene's novels includes a grim watercolor of the Golders Green crematorium. (Source: Hogarth, 88)

BLACKBEARD (*The Heart of the Matter*). He is a Bantu pirate in the story Scobie tells to Jimmy Fisher, a survivor of the torpedoed vessel.

BLACK BOY (*Brighton Rock*). Hale tells Ida Arnold to bet on Black Boy, a Brighton horse, to win at 4:00 p.m. Saturday. She bets £25 at 10 to 1, wins, and uses the money to remain in Brighton to hound Pinkie and save Rose.

Norman Sherry says a horse named Blue Boy won a race in June 1936 at Brighton. (Source: Sherry I, 630)

BLACKER ("The Hint of an Explanation"). He was a free-thinking baker in the East Anglian town where David grew up. Blacker tried diabolically to tempt David, when he was an altar boy, to trade him a consecrated wafer for a toy electric train.

Thomas A. Wendorf asserts that "Blacker materializes evil ... but does not undercut an empathic response from storyteller, narrator, or reader." (Source: Wendorf, 627)

BLACKIE ("The Destructors"). Blackie led the Wormsley Common Gang of boys until Trevor, called T., replaces him. Briefly upset, Blackie cooperates with T. and the other boys in destroying Thomas's house.

BLAKE (*The Human Factor*). Davis complains to Castle that Blake was sentenced to 40 years in prison and hence gained freedom from stressful responsibilities. Hargreaves says Blake's case caused the Secret Service to be more careful, even though some agents are still active who worked in the days of Burgess and Maclean.

According to Anthony Cave Brown, George Blake, of Egyptian, Jewish, and Dutch ancestry, was a naturalized Briton, joined the Secret Service (1947), spied on Russians in Berlin, helped American and British agents tap Russian communications to and from Berlin and Moscow, and evidently as a double agent informed the Russians of the fact. Lured back from Beirut, Lebanon, to London (1961), Blake confessed, was arrested, charged, convicted of treason, and sentenced to prison for 42 years — i.e., one year for each of 42 British agents he betrayed to the Soviets' KGB and its executioners. (Source: Brown, 500–01, 595)

BLEEK, ALFRED (*This Gun for Hire*). He is a man Miss Maydew spoke to at an *Aladdin* rehearsal.

BLENDOWE, LORD (*It's a Battlefield*). Just before Conrad Drover enters a gun shop to buy a weapon, the shopkeeper recommends to customer a sporting gun of the type Lord Blendowe used last autumn.

BLENNERHASSET, MAYOR (*Travels with My Aunt*). He is Southwood's mayor and the beautiful, deaf lady's husband.

BLENNERHASSET, MRS. (*Travels with My Aunt*). She was a client in Henry's bank. She was deaf, read lips, and once read his silently mouthed comments praising her outstanding beauty. She returned later, thanked him for his poetic effusion, and added that she was happily married.

"THE BLESSING" (1956). Short story. (Characters: the Archbishop, Caper, Collins, Crowe, Hughes, Martha, Smiley, Tumbril, Weld.)

Smiley, his chief, sends Weld, a reporter, to a port where tanks are to be blessed by the Archbishop before being sent to confront ill-armed enemies. Smiley knows Weld has pacifist sympathies and may hope he'll be professionally embarrassed. First, Weld meets fellow reporters — Hughes (of the AP), Collins (United Press), Tumbril (Reuters) — at a *taverna* for drinks. They dispute the irony of blessing weapons that kill and in a war Weld disapproves of. Collins has brought Martha, a German correspondent's wife, to the Grand Hotel, boycotts the blessing, and asks Weld to phone him if anything untoward occurs. Weld attends. The Archbishop is late but intones blessings. The smelly crowd remains peaceful. Weld talks with a wrinkled oldster who weeps, scorns this "holy war," and explains that if you want to love something but can't manage to do so, bless it, don't hate it. Weld returns to the tavern, phones Collins nothing happened, and drinks further with Hughes and Tumbril. Hughes jokes that Weld, whose persistent coughing indicates he shouldn't smoke, blesses his cigarettes with a hand gesture before lighting up. No, Weld retorts, one doesn't bless what he loves but does bless his hated enemy. He repeats the oldster's statement that blessings don't save lives.

BLIT (*The Human Factor*). He was once Castle's contact in the American Embassy in London. Blit, transferred to Mexico, happens to bump into Castle at the Heathrow airport hotel.

Greene gratuitously suggests the ineptness of American intelligence services by noting that "perhaps" Blit was assigned to Mexico because he couldn't speak Spanish. Blit serves no other purpose in the novel.

BLIXON, MRS. (*Loser Takes All*). Dreuther tells Bertram that Blixon's wife is a nice homemaker, with hands suited to making pastry, but not an exciting woman for Blixon to return to from London on weekends.

BLIXON, SIR WALTER (*Loser Takes All*). He is a small, spotty stockholder in Sitra, a big London company almost completely controlled by Dreuther, of whom he is jealous. Blixon is happily married, is a Hampshire church warden, and is unpopular with Sitra employees, who call him "Blister."

"THE BLUE FILM" (1954). Short story. (Characters: Carter, Mrs. Carter.) Carter is on business in Indochina. His wife is along — beautiful, discontent, frigid. Over coffee at dinner, she says if he were alone he'd find some fancy spots. Bored, she suggests they find an opium den. He says not until they get to Saigon. She vetoes his idea to go see some Japanese stripteasers. Determined to shock her, he finds a guide to take them to some pornographic movies. The first presents an oldster rejuvenated by masseuses. The second features an attractive young couple undressing and copulating. When the male's face turns, Mrs. Carter recognizes her husband. She says she wouldn't have married him had she known of his shameful action. He counters that he loved that girl for about a year 30 years ago, she got a badly needed £50 for the part, he received nothing. Back in the hotel bathroom, he prays his wife will be dead when he emerges. Instead, partly bare, standing like a bird of prey awaiting a fish, Mrs. Carter is turned on. They make love. She even screams, says it's been "years since that happened [to me]." He guiltily feels he's just betrayed his only love.

It is of interest that the reader never knows the first names of these Carters. Norman Sherry reports that Greene told him that a prostitute he was slightly in love with suggested they act in a film together for money; he declined. Grahame Smith avers that "the preposterous coincidence" that the film the Carters chance upon displays Carter decades ago "outdoes even Dickens in sheer unlikeliness." "The Blue Film" was the subject of a 1976 television production. *See Shades of Greene.* (Sources: Falk, 215; Sherry II, 533–34; G. Smith, 196)

BLUE, TONY (*The Confidential Agent*). He was a poor cricket player, whom Captain Currie and two young drunks remember while they are at the Lido with D.

BOLING (*The Heart of the Matter*). He is in charge of sewage, and lives near Harris and Wilson.

BOLTON, LADY (*The End of the Affair*). She was the center of a adultery case investigated by Parkis, who proudly gives Bendrix an ashtray from Brightlingsea's Metropole, involved in the case.

BOMPIERRE, MME. (*The Quiet American*). In the movie Phuong sees at the Catinat theater in Saigon, the widowed Mme Bompierre is Corinne's mother and is being pursued by the postmaster, according to Phuong's excited summary of the movie.

Greene's main purpose here is to indicate Fowler's mistress Phuong's emotional immaturity.

BONE ("Men at Work"). This writer is employed by the Ministry of Information. His pamphlet on the British Empire may have "tactless[ly]" offended other nations, was rewritten, and now Bone objects.

BONNE CHANCE (*The Human Factor*). The name of this horse, and those of Kalamazoo and Widow Twanky, are found in Davis's flat. Taylor, an MI officer, wrongly believes they may be connected with a code.

BOOB, THE ("Jubilee"). Chalfont, a fading gigolo, remembers the Boob and Merdy, probably also gigolos but now vanished.

The name "Boob" is a voiced "Poop." After all, the name Merdy is close to *merde* (vulgar French, "shit").

BORIS (*The Human Factor*). He replaces Ivan as Castle's Soviet contact in England. Boris has a scar, the result of his being wounded as a child when the Nazis conquered Warsaw. Castle and Boris communicate by phone signals and by drops. When Castle contacts him in Watford, Boris is tutoring English. When Castle is sent to Moscow, Boris appears and advises Castle to rely on patience and whisky.

Anthony Cave Brown suggests that Boris, Castle's Soviet control officer in London, is based on Yuri Modin (d. 1995), Philby's Soviet case officer in London (from 1947). Modin's book (1994) on the general subject has a revealing title: *My Five Cambridge Friends: Burgess, Maclean, Philby, Blunt, and Cairncross* (trans. Anthony Roberts). (Source: Brown, 350, 387–88, 583)

BOOJIE (*The Ministry of Fear*) *see* **ROWE, ARTHUR**

BOTTOMLEY, EZRA (*The Human Factor*). He is Castle's mother's friend in Sussex, just returned from missionary work in Rhodesia. He fancies he can talk with Sarah Castle, who finds him dull.

BOWERS (*The Heart of the Matter*). This man was sent home after hitting an assistant of the Governor at a party.

BOWLES (*The Heart of the Matter*). He and his wife are missionaries in Pende.

BOWLES, A. N. (*Loser Takes All*). Bowles is deaf, gray of face, hard, mean, and implacable. He has enough stock in Dreuther's company to help or hurt him in his competition with Sir Walter Blixon. Since Bowles is the other shareholder, the employees dub him "A. N. Other." Bound to a wheelchair, Bowles is pushed by a nurse to tables for gambling, to which he has been addicted for 20 years. He options his shares for money to bet his system is better than Bertram's. Bertram wins but deliberately forfeits the option.

Neil McEwan points out that "enslavement to money looks especially nasty in the capitalist gambler known as A. N. Other, or 'the Other'—Greene's term elsewhere for the devil." This insight is ominously relevant, for, as McEwan also reminds readers, Bertram "discovers a gambling 'system' which has 'the devil in it' and therefore succeeds." (Source: McEwan, 126)

BOWLES, MRS. (*The Heart of the Matter*). She and her husband are Pende missionaries. Scobie finds her abrupt, harsh, and officious.

BOYSTON (*The Heart of the Matter*). Suspected of corrupt activities in Sierra Leone, he was invalided from active service.

BRACER (*The Third Man*). He is a school chum whom Martins and Harry Lime remember. Martins received a Christmas card from Bracer.

BRADDOCK (*The Man Within*). He is the big, scarred, red-faced lawyer who defends six smugglers during their trial at Lewes. He tries to embarrass Thomas Hilliard, the commander of the revenuers who trapped the smuggler crew.

BRADSHAW (*The Honorary Consul*). Plarr tells Rivas his father knew a man named Bradshaw.

BRADSHAW (*The Honorary Consul*). While reading a detective novel, Rivas misinterprets references to *Bradshaw's,* the British railway guide (1841–1961), as references to someone in the novel.

Anthony Cave Brown says that Yuri Modin, Soviet spy in London, helped Donald Maclean,* notorious British double agent, get out of England by making use of *Bradshaw's* (1951). (Source: Brown, 430)

"A BRANCH OF THE SERVICE" (1990). Short story. (Characters: None named.)

1. The narrator had to quit an attractive profession because he lost his appetite for food.

The narrator's father was a great but quarrelsome and job-changing chef. He dragged the boy through England, Switzerland, Germany, Italy, and maybe Russia. So he picked up a smattering of languages, got a job judging the quality of restaurants for the IGGR (the International Guide to Good Restaurants), and was required to eat excessively. Two years passed. He was recruited by "the state" to eavesdrop at restaurant tables and their nest-of-spies lavatories.

2. He judged restaurants for the IGGR, while simultaneously seeking fugitives whose mug shots he was shown. At the Royalty restaurant he sat near a man who used a suspicious foreign accent in welcoming a woman, ate too much with her for the narrator to match comfortably, and disputed with her over pre-dessert cheese. They discussed Flaubert and Madame Bovary. Was she thus naming agents secretly? When she offered the man a cigarette and he took it into the lavatory unsmoked, the narrator followed, seized the suspicious cigarette, and sent it with his report.

3. Over a scrambler his boss told the narrator the suspects' talk about French literature was a cover-up, ordered him to the office, and showed him the interior of the cigarette—wrinkled paper, probably with encoded microdots.

4. Months later the cigarette case led to a suspicious country doctor practicing near a chemical factory where he was a consultant. The narrator was ordered to dine—item for item—beside the doctor at the one-menu Star and Garter near his house. Another agent was posted outside. The doctor looked too honest to be involved with that cigarette affair. Obnoxious onion soup, beef, tart, then cheese gave the narrator diarrhea. Back from the lavatory. The doctor has left. The narrator quizzed the Star and Garter owner about the doctor,

praised the spotless lavatory, presented his IGGR card, and promised a nice writeup. However, outside, the confederate alarmed him by saying the doctor didn't exit out front. They've messed the case.

5. Their boss forgave the narrator because of his cigarette coup. He resigned anyway, saying the doctor was no traitor — a word the boss bridled at. He tried to get the narrator to become a Star and Garter regular, cultivate that doctor, consult him about his diarrhea, send prescriptions the doctor would write to headquarters for analysis. No. The narrator, though appetiteless, is nevertheless happy that the mention he promised for the Star and Garter is in the latest IGGR issue.

Greene has fun here not only by satirizing over-zealous and imperspicacious military-intelligence agents in general but also by having the narrator say his IGGR international food guide caused jealous rivalry between MI6 (international British intelligence) and MI5 (domestic British intelligence).

BRANDON'S ACRE. Title of a novel Greene started, about a spiritualist. Nothing appears to be known about it now. (Source: Sherry I, 424–25, 427)

BRAUN, DR. (*Our Man in Havana*). He is the European Traders' Association president. He invites Wormold, as an important member, to lecture at the association's annual banquet. Braun is Swiss.

BRAUN, HERR ("The Root of All Evil"). He is one of the wine-drinking clubmen. They drink in his cellar.

BREWER (*Our Man in Havana*). He is the London valet of the Chief of the Secret Service. Brewer markets for groceries, and the Chief provides directions, sometimes by phone, for preparing meals.

BREWER, BILL (*Brighton Rock*). He is an elderly Brighton bookie. When he pays Colleoni, not Pinkie, for protection, Pinkie goes to Brewer's home with Dallow, slashes Brewer's face, and takes money owed him.

BREWER, MRS. (*Brighton Rock*). She is Pinkie's disloyal bookie's sick wife.

BREWITT ("The Lieutenant Died Last"). He is the landlord of the Black Boar, Potter's only pub. He and his wife have a 16-year-old son.

BREWITT ("The Lieutenant Died Last"). He is the Brewitts's son, 16. When he tries to escape the German soldiers, three of them shoot him in the legs, "humanely," crippling him permanently.

BREWITT, MRS. ("The Lieutenant Died Last"). She is the Black Boar boss's wife. She doubts her son's statement that the parachutists are German soldiers.

BREWSTER, MRS. (*This Gun for Hire*). She is Anne Crowder's London landlady. They share cold suppers.

BREWSTER, MRS. (*Travels with My Aunt*). She is a member of St. John's Church, whose vicar leaves Henry, Detective-Inspector Woodrow, and Detective-Sergeant Sparrow and talks with her.

BRIDGES (*The End of the Affair*) *see* **BENDRIX, MAURICE**

BRIDGES (*The Ministry of Fear*). He is a courteous employee at the tailor shop where Cost works. He senses Cost's plan to commit suicide but is too late to stop him.

BRIDGES, ARTHUR JAMES (*The End of the Affair*) *see* **PARKIS, LANCE**

BRIGHTON ROCK (1938). Novel. (Characters: Lady Angeline, Ida Arnold, Barker, Peggy Baron, Basil, Beale, Bill, Bill, Black Boy, Bill Brewer, Mrs. Brewer, Pinkie Brown, Carter, Molly Carthew, Charlie, Clarence, Colleoni, Mrs. Colleoni, Annie Collins, T. Collins, Phil Corkery, Crab, Violet Crow, John Cubitt, Mrs. Cubitt, Ted Dallow, Delia, Digby, Doris, Drewitt, Lord Feversham, Billy Frank, Judy Frank, Galloway, General Burgoyne, Gay Parrot, George, Stanley Gibbons, Charles Hale, Harry, Henneky, Innes, Father James, Alfred Jefferson, Joe, John, Johnnie, Kite, Macpherson,

Mais, Maisie, Manders, Sir Mark, Memento Mori, Merry Monarch, Sir Joseph Montagu, Charlie Moyne, Old Crowe, Piker, Pinecoffin, Molly Pink, Sam, Samuel, Snow, Spicer, Sylvie, Jim Tate, Bob Tavell, Tilly, Tom, Willie, Wilson, Mrs. Wilson, Rose Wilson, Zoe.)

(Note: David Leon Higdon collated the first edition [London, Heinemann, 1938], the first American edition [New York, Viking, 1938], and the Uniform Edition [London, Heinemann, 1947], and found 471 substantive variants. The Viking edition is used for this encyclopedia.)

Part One. 1. Brighton on Whitsun. A skinny journalist (Charles Hale) for the *Messenger* distributes "Kolley Kibber" cards, illustrated with his picture. Anyone finding a Kibber and locating Hale wins 10 guineas. The Boy (Pinkie Brown), an evil-looking lad, 17, speaks menacingly to Hale, who also fears (John) Cubitt, who is stalking him. Hale flirts with Molly (Pink), then picks up big-bosomed Ida (Arnold) and, hinting at terror, rushes with her by taxi to the Palace Pier. Ida returns from the Ladies' to continue their hot date. Hale has disappeared.

2. The Boy practices shooting at a Palace of Pleasure booth, asks the time, and waits in a tea room for (Ted) Dallow, Spicer, and Cubitt. Dallow reports that he and Cubitt killed him (Hale, by forcing rock candy down his throat, inducing a heart attack and melting) while Spicer scattered the remaining Kibbers, for an alibi. Pinkie seeks one Kibber dangerously left at Snow's restaurant. Rose (Wilson), a new waitress (age 16), reveals she has that Kibber. Pinkie will lure Rose, for his safety.

3. In London, Ida (a barmaid) meets Clarence, former lover, at a pub. He says someone won the Kibber prize but Hale died (of "natural causes"). She reads newspaper accounts, sees Hale's picture, recalls Hale's leaving a Kibber at a restaurant, attends lonely Hale's cremation, and determines to discover what really killed him. The newspaper says Hale at the Pier met Molly Pink, who works (Ida learns) for London estate-agents Carter & Galloway. Molly tells Ida a kid evidently dunning Hale scared him. Ida goes to her Russell Square flat, and with Old Crowe, a fellow tenant, asks her ouija board about Fred—which Hale lied was his first name. Ida blushes when the board pencils "Phil" (Corkery); the message "FRESUICILLEYE" she translates: Fred, suicide, eye-for-eye vengeance. Despite the troublesome "LL," she gleefully makes plans.

Part Two. 1. Pinkie at the Pier tells Spicer, who mentions their killing Hale, to be cautious. Rose rushes to keep her date with Pinkie, tells him Hale didn't hide the card where she works. Pinkie says nosy girls get mutilated by mobsters, burns a wooden plank with drops from his vitriol bottle, terrifies her, and marches her to Sherry's restaurant. Ordering Rose an ice, he finds the crooner's love song disturbing, calls Rose green, pinches her wrist venomously, and drags her away. Her compact reveals rosary beads. He says he's Catholic too, sings "Agnus dei," and professes belief in Hell and maybe Heaven.

In his bed-sittingroom in the rooming house owned by Billy (Frank?), Pinkie finds Cubitt, Dallow, and Spicer. Since Kite was murdered (in London by Colleoni's gang), Spicer advises caution in collecting "sub" (protection) from Brewer and Tate (bookies). Scared following Hale's death, Cubitt jokes: Rose's evidence could hang them; Pinkie might marry and silence her. Pinkie sneers, takes Dallow along, and visits Brewer's. Pinkie demands £20 as Brewer's sub. Brewer says he paid Colleoni (Pinkie's protection-boss rival), as did Tate. Pinkie carves Brewer's face with a razor. Brewer surrenders the money. Pinkie half-affectionately praises faithful Dallow. They return to Pinkie's room, tell cautious Spicer everything, and learn Rose phoned Pinkie's room to warn of someone's querying her. Pinkie suspects Colleoni's gang and turns in.

2. Dallow brings Pinkie a letter from Colleoni inviting him to his room at the Cosmopolitan. Unimpressed by the luxurious hotel, Pinkie listens to sleek, rich Colleoni, who warns and threatens him, then offers him a job. Coolly sauntering out, Pinkie is detained by a policeman to discuss Brewer's complaint. Pinkie thinks Colleoni ordered Brewer to file charges and admits hitting him, but nothing else. The tired inspector says he doesn't want innocent people hurt in mob rivalries, Colleoni is too strong to be defeated, Pinkie should leave Brighton before next week's races. Pinkie grins, says he's too young to retire, and leaves, planning more killing.

Part Three: 1. Hung-over Ida remains in Brighton. She goes to her bookie, Jim Tate, and bets £25 on Black Boy, on Hale's remembered tip. A phone call from Colleoni interrupts Tate. Outside, Ida asks a bartender who Colleoni is, downs four drinks, and learns Colleoni took over murdered Kite's Brighton protectors and Kite's "kid," age 17, who can't stop Colleoni's monopolizing but razored Brewer. The bartender points out Pinkie on the street. Ida recalls seeing him at the pub behind Hale, walks to Snow's to await her friend Phil Corkery, meets Rose, and asks her about her little fellow (Hale). Rose clams up. Phil enters. Pressed, Rose says Hale ate little and left. Ida tells Phil that Rose fibbed, that Hale wasn't the man who left the Kibber ticket. Though scared, Phil promises to aid Ida. At the police station, with Phil as witness, Ida tells the inspector about "Fred" Hale's actions and Rose's evasiveness, and reads Hale's thorough but unconvincing autopsy report — death by myocarditis. Warning sundry policemen, Ida drags Phil out and starts campaigning at the Pier for truth. Spicer is there.

2. Spicer is uneasy. He saw "It" (Pinkie murdering Hale), and facts may come out. Crab, once Kite's worker, approaches "Spicey," boasts he's Colleoni's employee, and jeers that Pinkie is with the police now. Spicer, scared, goes to Billy's place, and is phoned by Rose, who reports being questioned (by Ida and Corkery). Spicer plans to leave town.

3. Pinkie takes Rose from work by bus into the ugly, cliff-rimmed countryside. She tells him Ida told her to stop thinking Spicer left the Kibber and asks who did. Pinkie quotes the line about "Between the stirrup and the ground," says he won't think about Hell before he dies. He is repulsed by fear of sex with her — he recalls his parents' noisy Saturday-night coition — but is aware she must remain ignorant of his boasted-about actions. He tries his first kiss ever, misses. Back in Brighton, she spots a photographer's window display, points out one of Spicer, which Pinkie tries to buy but is shooed away.

4. Pinkie visits Spicer's room, scares him with talk about Rose, then suggests that he take a holiday. Spicer mentions his ambition to partner with a friend in a Nottingham pub. All the while, Pinkie contemplates eliminating Spicer. Pinkie phones Colleoni, then retires, combining a song about a nightingale and "Agnus dei."

Part Four. 1. Spicer gets Pinkie's old Morris and drives Pinkie to crowded, sunny Brighton, while Pinkie plots his murder. He asks Spicer how one can marry hurriedly. Spicer bets on Memento Mori, which places. Spicer plans to invest in the Nottingham pub. Ida's Black Boy wins. Pinkie, remembering it was "Fred's" favorite horse, learns more about nosy Ida. Pinkie is bidding Spicer goodbye when both are attacked by Colleoni's men. Pinkie, yelling that Spicer was supposedly the target, is kicked and razored across face and knuckles. The police intervene. Weeping, bleeding, too tired to repent, Pinkie hides in a garage, and by moonlight finds Rose at work. She tends to him in Snow's cellar. Hating doing so, he kisses and fondles her, tells her not to tell Ida that Spicer left that Kibber. Snow's manageress chases Pinkie out. He goes to his bedroom, tells Cubitt that Colleoni's men killed Spicer, orders Cubitt to fetch Drewitt, a crooked lawyer. Drewitt arrives, is offered a guinea, and will get Rose and Pinkie married fast. Cubitt, entering, reveals that Spicer is back in his room, alive. Pinkie checks. Loyal Spicer is there, packing.

2. Ida, reinforced by her £200 win, barges into Rose's room over Snow's, pleads with Rose to abandon selfish Pinkie, then yells at her.

3. Pinkie, with Dallow well aware, pushes Spicer down the rotten-banistered stairs to his death. Drewitt quits seeking his guinea beside Pinkie's washstand, is aghast, but is threatened by Pinkie into witnessing Spicer's "fall." Pinkie bribes a waitress to tell where Rose rooms, finds Ida there, is threatened by her with the truth as she leaves, tells Rose they'll wed soon through his lawyer's influence, and kisses her ineptly, reluctantly, remembering his parents' "primeval exercise."

Part Five. 1. Although Spicer's inquest proved innocuous, Pinkie tells Dallow he's worried about untrustworthy Cubitt. Dallow drives the three of them to a roadhouse, where they meet Sylvie, Spicer's drunk ex-girlfriend. Razzed about his sexual abstemiousness, Pinkie swallows his very first drink — Sylvie's dregs — invites her to the car park, but, though she eagerly sprawls in a handy Lancia, wilts and retreats.

2. Kidded on their drive back, Pinki vows

not to marry, plans rationalizing to Rose, but finds her in his room. She shows him newspaper coverage of Spicer's death, says she dreamed Pinkie died, says she's been fired for insulting Ida, and mentions Drewitt. Pinkie will marry underaged Rose, if her father gives permission.

3. Next day Pinkie walks past his childhood Paradise Piece neighborhood, now blighted, to Nelson Place, to Rose's parents' ill-smelling home. He and Mrs. Wilson haggle over Rose's price — £10? £12? £15? — finally 15 guineas. Rose is ecstatic. Pinkie would prefer the annihilation of the world.

4. Ida and Corkery, in the Cosmopolitan, see Colleoni walk by. Ida dispatches Phil for her luggage, books a cushy room, disrobes, and awaits the uneasy fellow's return — for twilight lovemaking.

5. Pinkie boasts to Cubitt and Dallow he'll marry bright Rose and, to their surprise, has a drink. Pinkie silences their jibes. He hints he, not any banister, caused Spicer's death. Cubitt says he'll leave Pinkie's gang. Vowing loyalty, Dallow is sent to Drewitt to arrange the marriage, two days hence.

6. Ida feels considerably unfulfilled by Phil, now asleep, partly clad. Well, hunting for Fred's killer will excite her. She figures on making one of Pinkie's mobsters an informant.

Part Six. 1. Cubitt numbs fear of Pinkie by several whiskies, prowls the Pier, is frightened by the message from a penny fortune-telling machine, and summons courage to go to the Cosmopolitan and ask Colleoni for a job. Colleoni's supercilious man Crab intercepts Cubitt, lets him buy their drinks, then tells him Colleoni couldn't use him and he should escape Pinkie. Cubitt is depressed, angry, and sad, until he sees Ida at a table. She buys him two whiskies (his seventh, eighth), blandishes him, and he blathers about Fred's death, Kite's unplanned murder, broken banisters, Rose's marrying Pinkie, Spicer and the Kibber. He mentions "Brighton rock" (used on Hale). Ida offers him £20 for information, rushes to get Phil to be witness, and returns. Cubitt has left. Ida's gotta save Rose.

2. Saturday. Pinkie, uniquely verbose regarding sex's ugliness, waits at the municipal building with Dallow for Rose, who delayed by unsuccessfully seeking a priest for confession. Before Drewitt, the registrar, and Dallow, Pinkie weds surprised-looking Rose and is hilariously proud of their mortal sins. He stands drinks for the little party at a pub.

When Pinkie demands a room at the Cosmopolitan, he and Rose are rejected. They wander to the Pier, where Rose points out Ida. Rose wants a gramophone record of his voice. No. She surprisingly snarls at him. So he makes a secret recording, in which he curses her and calls her a despicable bitch, and gives it, unplayed, to her. They suck some Brighton rock, attend a romantic movie, go to Billy's empty place and his room, which he rudely calls his. He brutally hugs her, and during and after the slurred-over consummation the door bell rings. Her expressing "love" becomes unfeared Hell to him. Cubitt, at the door, wants Pinkie to take him back, threatens to squeal otherwise, and drunkenly hints at a bribe (Ida's). Unafraid, Pinkie orders him away, returns to Rose, who says she knows about the Kibber.

Pinkie dreams of childhood, Kite, his parents clutched together, drowning. He walks outside, finds in his pocket a loving note from Rose about being with him always regardless, sees a woman praying and therefore saved.

Part Seven. 1. At 7:00 a.m. Rose, alone, finds the kitchen, meets Dallow, sees him boldly kissing Judy, agrees not to tell Billy (her blind husband), and proudly feels accepted by fellow sinners — plus liberated from work. She takes a half-crown from Pinkie's soap dish, goes to Snow's, and tells fellow-waitress Maisie she's married. Though hungry, Rose retreats, sad she's somewhat happy and feeling branded by Pinkie. In Pinkie's room is a smiling woman (Ida), who gently warns Rose this: Rose married a murderer who might kill her; Fred's inquest was erroneous; one witness (Cubitt) won't testify; another (Spicer) was killed; wives needn't but can testify. Rose tries to defend Pinkie but fumbles, is told (dishonestly) she could be jailed. Rose knows Pinkie is evil, whether he's right or wrong. Warned she might have a killer's child, Rose feels glorified.

2. Dallow, seeing Ida leave, tells Pinkie that the visitor (Ida) was Rose's mother. Rose lies to Pinkie in agreement. Pinkie tells Dallow he'll stage Rose's suicide. Dallow fiercely objects. Pinkie approaches Rose, who confesses everything about Ida. Pinkie hints at their double suicide, but only if Ida learns about Spicer, and

says Drewitt was present when Pinkie killed him. Meanwhile, perhaps more "love" and likely security.

3. Pinkie orders Dallow to watch Rose, visits Drewitt, finds him drinking as usual on Sunday, sick, and talkative. So Pinkie promises him £20 tomorrow for a Boulogne vacation.

4. Pinkie resents Rose's tidying their room, reminds her of their mortal sinfulness, and reveals his contingency plan — drive away, in case of more questionings. An infant's squall stirs her to hint at her own possible pregnancy.

5. Next morning Pinkie yells for Dallow and hints at a suicide pact, for Rose only. Dallow says their confederate Johnnie will phone when Drewitt is on the boat for France and unavailable to Ida. A letter from Colleoni offers Pinkie a £200 goodwill buy-out. Pinkie says he's tempted to see new places. Rose enters. Johnnie phones the good news about Drewitt.

6. Sunset in a tea room. Ida and Phil drink and talk: Drewitt gone; Cubitt bribed but also gone. They see Pinkie and Rose with a second couple (Dallow and Judy) there — like fate, says Ida, who cannot be dissuaded from saving dumb Rose.

7. When Dallow tells Pinkie to try country life and stay married 60 years, Pinkie drags Rose away, shoots nervously once in the gallery for an alibi, gets his car, tells Rose in front of the attendant about driving to Peacehaven for drinks, and they're off. Rose acquiesces to double suicide, while he silently expects to survive and go to confession but also resents his ugly life. Half-despairing, she wants to share his damnation. They stop, dash through rain into a hotel, where Pinkie orders drinks, tells Rose to write a suicide note, and loads his revolver in the lavatory.

8. Dallow wonders where Pinkie and Rose went, accepts Judy's kiss, sees Ida, and asks her what's up. She mentions Fred's murder and knowing Johnnie, and lies that the police have Drewitt. Overhearing, Judy approaches. Ida offers Dallow £20 for information, but he leaves for the Gents', looks for Pinkie, hears about his planted alibi, fears for Rose, and learns from the car-park attendant about Pinkie and Peacehaven. Ida, hearing, persuades Dallow to rent a car and seek Pinkie with her.

9. Two sporty drinkers give Rose the once-over and leave. Rose tells Pinkie she wrote the farewell note he wants, feels an urge to escape, but drives on with him. Doubts buffeting him, he stops by the sea-battered cliff. His will impels her to take Dallow's gun from Pinkie, wondering if he would shoot himself first if she delayed, thinking of Christmas images. He says he'll walk off, listen for her shot, then shoot himself. She is unconvinced by prayer phrases and feels that a bold evil act is honest. Someone shouts Pinkie's name. Rose discards the gun. Dallow, that woman (Ida), and a policeman rush up. Dallow yells that Drewitt is arrested. Pinkie goes after Dallow with his vitriol bottle. A policeman smashes it into Pinkie's face, which steams. Pinkie hurls himself over the cliff.

10. Over drinks in London, Ida explains to Clarence: Drewitt was in France; Cubitt wouldn't confess, drunk or sober; Pinkie died, not Rose, now back with her parents. Ida returns to her flat, finds a letter from Tom, figures now that "sui" in "SUICILLEYE" means Pinkie's agonized scream, and tells Old Crowe to ask the ouija board if she should rejoin Tom.

11. Rose at the confessional tells a priest she wants damnation, not absolution. He replies thus: God's mercy is appallingly strange; Pinkie's love, if present, showed goodness; we must hope; return for absolution; if you have a baby, make him saintly, pray for his father. Rose feels comforted, will resume work at Snow's, approaches Billy's place, but will face horror. (Pinkie figured she would never hear his gramophone recording, but she survives — and will.)

The intriguing title of the novel relates to stick candy called Brighton Rock, which, no matter where it is snapped apart, reads "Brighton Rock."

Norman Sherry reports that *Brighton Rock* sold poorly at first and earned Greene only £256 the first nine months. Later, it sold well and intrigued countless critics. A. A. DeVitis's analysis is centered thus: "In terms of ... allegory, the chief polarities of good and evil are established by Rose and Pinkie; the middle ground is represented by Ida Arnold." According to Lawrence Grobel, Truman Capote said that *Brighton Rock* is "just an incredibly beautiful, *perfect* novel. It has the greatest last four paragraphs of any modern novel I can think of."

Stylistically *Brighton Rock* is fascinating —

with true and false foreshadowing, irony, tonal horror, gangster dialogue, imagery, echoes of other writers, and use of Brighton place names. Jean-Yves Monnier regards to know and knowing as "almost a leitmotif" performing "a major structural function" in *Brighton Rock*. Thug-slang includes milky, bogies, buers, carving, geezers, grassing, lamping, polonies, totsies, and touts. The 300-plus metaphors and similes are often startling, as when celibate Pinkie is aware of sexual action the way a gunnery student understands movements diagrammed on a chalk board; or when poor Rose compares fat Ida's stare to an idiot's at the window of a bombed house. *Brighton Rock* echoes aspects of T. S. Eliot's *The Waste Land*. Both mention gramophones, Lil, a sea change, a weekend at the Cosmopolitan (the Metropole is named in later editions), a key in a door, burning. Sherry provides a map of Brighton, with a running commentary on many locations. Peter Mudford notes that "[t]he influence of faith upon action, without effect in *Brighton Rock,* is seen as the determining force in *The Power and the Glory.*" Sherry discusses a dramatic version based on the novel. It was to be produced in fall 1939, but World War II delayed it until February 1943. Greene despised almost everything about it.

A movie version called both *Brighton Rock* and *Young Scarface* (1947) starred Richard Attenborough as Pinkie. It also disappointed Greene. The novel is cinematic, its 29 numbered sections juxtaposing action/inaction, noise/quiet, opulence/drabness, carnival/slum, daylight/darkness. (Sources: DeVitis, 71; Falk, 209; Grobel, 139; Higdon, 177; Monnier, 31; Mudford, 28; Phillips, 159–66; Sherry I, 629–34; Sherry II, 15, 163–64)

BRIGITTA (*The Power and the Glory*). She is the daughter of the whisky priest and Maria. When the three met after six years, he finds Brigitta impudent, disrespectful, and perhaps corrupt and without saving grace.

Calder-Marshall opines that Brigitta's "precocious sexuality ... is untrue of an Indian village child." (Source: Calder-Marshall, 374)

BRIGITTA (*The Power and the Glory*). The whisky priest was so drunk that he conferred this name to an infant intended to be Pedro.

BRIGSTOCK ("The Bear Fell Free"). Baron sees Brigstock's hat on the hat stand at Earl's Court.

BRIGSTOCK (*The Confidential Agent*). He is the sharpest business partner of Lord Benditch, Lord Fetting, Forbes, and Goldstein. Brigstock tells D. they want payment in gold.

BRIGSTOCK (*The Heart of the Matter*). This naval officer is a heavy drinker at the Sierra Leone club.

BRITISH AMBASSADOR, THE (*The Honorary Consul*). Crichton tells Plarr that Sir Henry Belfrage, his superior, received instructions from London, as did this British Ambassador in Asunción, to cooperate with the American Ambassador concerning the Fortnum-kidnapping incident.

BRITISH AMBASSADOR, THE (*Travels with My Aunt*). He, the Dutch Ambassador, and the Nicaraguan Ambassador attend Visconti's party in Asunción.

BRITISH MINISTER, THE (*The Quiet American*). Fowler recalls how tedious it is for him to explain the situation in Vietnam to visitors, including the British Minister.

BRITON, JULES (*It's a Battlefield*). He is a Catholic and a café waiter. His mother gave birth to him in England, browbeat him, and died. His French father, Heysan-Bretau, abandoned wife and son, recently died in France, and bequeathed Jules 10,500 francs. This enables Jules to rent a car, take Kay Rimmer into the country, make love a few times with her, and think of proposing marriage to her. His deciding to remain circumspect doesn't bother Kay.

BROMLEY, MRS. (*The Heart of the Matter*). Louise Scobie keeps a photograph of Teddy Bromley, his wife, and Louise. They are in a Yorkshire scene.

BROMLEY, TEDDY (*The Heart of the Matter*). He, his wife, and Louise Scobie are in a photograph Louise treasures.

"BROTHER" (1936). Short story. (Characters: None named.) The elderly proprietor of a Paris café watches as several Communists proceed from a town called Combat to Menilmontant toward his establishment. After sunset, firing was audible. The proprietor is glad he sent his wife out of danger. A girl and a man with an injured leg lag behind the others in the group, then enter, demand cognac, but don't pay. The girl helps the hurt man drink. A billiard player in a back room feels unthreatened. He callously explains he's poor. The proprietor remembers a police barricade at the Place de la République but closes his shutters anyway. Four men, obviously "Reds," enter, demand cognac, say they needn't pay because comrades share and share alike. Emboldened by awareness of machine-gun fire, the proprietor criticizes the Communists for free-love notions, points to the injured man and the girl, but is told that the two are brother and sister, that they are Germans, that the man was hurt in a concentration camp. The proprietor, feeling pity for the two and envy for the group's "camaraderie," fetches some Napoleon brandy from the billiard room for everyone. He's just observed the Gardes Mobiles placing a machine gun on the Faubourge opposite his café. The girl is asleep now, and her brother has pained, despairing eyes. The proprietor recalls German words from old—*Kamerad* and *mein bruder*. Gunfire rakes the front room. Shattered glass falls. Policemen enter. The four Reds are gone. An officer orders drinks for himself and his men, dramatically pays the nine francs fifty the proprietor mechanically requests, and promises the government will reimburse him for property damage. He goes to the other room, finds the girl and her brother shot dead, the latter staring at him. When he mumbles the words "mein Bruder," the officer voices his disbelief and rattles his coins.

Richard Kelly reminds readers that Greene was so bored as a student in Oxford that he "visited the Communist headquarters in Paris in 1926." Kelly adds that although nothing politically consequential followed, Greene drew on "[t]his flirtatious experience with communism" when he wrote "Brother." A. A. DeVitis concludes rather too liberally that in it Greene "make[s] the point that all men are brothers, while observing that Communists at least are equal to one another whereas those who live under more traditional political systems are arbitrarily subject to class restrictions." (Sources: DeVitis, 170–71; Kelly, 21)

"BROTHER AND SISTER" see *ENGLAND MADE ME*

BROTHERS (*The Ministry of Fear*). He is a policeman under Prentice. After years of following Prentice, Brothers might ultimately resemble him in expertise.

BROWN (*The Captain and the Enemy*) see **CAPTAIN, THE**

BROWN (*The Comedians*). He is the hero-narrator, almost 60, and owner-manager of the Trianon hotel in Port-au-Prince. Born in Monte Carlo, Brown was educated by the Jesuits, was abandoned by his mother, became a waiter in London, sold fake paintings throughout England, and reported to his dying mother in Haiti. Calling herself the Comtesse de Lascot-Villiers (perhaps truly), she wills her Trianon to Brown, who improves it until Duvalier's Tontons Macoute scare tourists away. Brown's mistress is Martha Pineda, an ambassador's wife. Sexually too active, but always with pain and regret, and without religious or political beliefs, Brown aids friends in Haiti, notably William Abel Smith and his wife Mrs. Smith, Jones, Dr. Magiot, Joseph, and Henri Philipot, against repressive Haitians officials represented by Captain Concasseur and his men. Doing so costs Brown his Trianon. When Martha accompanies her husband to Peru, Brown, having escaped to Santo Domingo, begins to work for Fernandez, an undertaker. Brown regards his former Catholic faith replete with "doctrines and myths of childhood," calls himself no hero, talks indiscreetly and takes chances for others, all the while feeling he is a comedian assigned a part in a farce.

In a *Collected Edition* introduction, Greene says he gave Brown, Jones, and Smith the common names he did to avoid lawsuits. Before or after significant action, Brown often records his dreams. Leopoldo Duran, Greene's friend, says that "I call them dreams of grace, for poor Brown is saved through these dreams." (Sources: Duran, 209; Greene, *Stamboul Train, Collected Edition,* xiii)

BROWN (*The Comedians*). This is possibly the name of the narrator Brown's father, whom Brown's mother calls a swine and says he's probably dead.

BROWN (*The Heart of the Matter*). This is a code name one of Yusef's servants uses to be admitted to Wilson's office.

BROWN ("Work Not in Progress"). The Archbishop of Melbourne once thought about loving a girl to be named Brown.

BROWN, DR. ("Proof Positive"). He is the "pet sceptic" of the Psychical Society before which Weaver lectures. He notices that Weaver is very ill, urges Crashaw to make him quit speaking, when he collapses rushes to his side, and pronounces him dead for a week at least.

BROWN, PINKIE (*Brighton Rock*). He is the skinny, spiritually poisoned boss, 17, of a Brighton bookie gang. He lives in Paradise Place, also called Paradise Piece. His childhood experiences with careless parents, sadistic schoolmates, and unsatisfying Catholicism make him a unique combination of ageless-eyed evil and abstemiousness. He loathes the idea of drinking, smoking, or fornicating. His weapons are demonic rhetoric, razor, gun, and bottled vitriol. Pinkie causes the murder of Hale, a reporter influential in the murder of Kite, Pinkie's adored boss. The loyalty of his closest associates, including Bill Brewer, John Cubitt, Dallow, and Spicer, is then tested. Ida Arnold's nemesis-like search for clues about Hale's death causes Pinkie to persuade his girlfriend Rose Wilson, whose testimony could ruin him, to marry him and join him in a suicide pact, which he wouldn't honor. Since Pinkie is underaged, their wedding, arranged by Drewitt, his corrupt lawyer, is illegal. Pinkie hates to be called the Boy.

Norman Sherry says the name Pinkie may derive from a 1936 Brighton gang leader named Spinks, whose nickname was Spinky. Grahame Smith compares little Pinkie and "Macbeth in his 'borrowed robes,'" both being studies "of the incremental nature of evil," and both having killed too much ever to turn back. Sherry relates Pinkie's background, his response to sexuality, and his irreligious beliefs to Greene's childhood, his thoughts about suicide, his responses to Catholic doctrine and rites, his attitudes toward good-evil, right-wrong, and death, his sociological concerns, and his reading. A. A. DeVitis suggests that "Pinkie is in many ways like Milton's Satan — his mind is its own place and can make a hell of heaven, a heaven of hell." Trevor L. Williams adds to the insight concerning Milton's Satan by contending that "Greene creates a Satan in Pinkie whom he tries to condemn through repellent descriptions, but while Milton's Satan becomes sympathetic *despite* the poet's best efforts to turn the party line against him, Greene actively intervenes on Satan's behalf by suggesting constantly that Pinkie's dedication to evil is superior to Ida's obsession with right and wrong." Gene D. Phillips, a Jesuit priest, posits that many critics' contention that "Pinkie is certainly damned [is] a trifle too facile." Among better arguments, he quotes Pinkie's notorious "Between the stirrup and the ground" line, which is played on six times in the novel. (The original of Pinkie's slightly garbled quotation is from "Epitaph for a Man Killed by Falling from his Horse," by William Camden [1551–1623]: "Betwixt the stirrup and the ground, / Mercy I asked, mercy I found.") Pinkie's spiritual destination puzzles critics. K. C. Joseph Kurismmootil has it both ways, saying, first, that although "Pinkie confesses his fear of death by drowning," he "is cleansed by it [the sea] and, now redeemed, he is snatched up by a life that goes on and on, into eternity," but, second, that he is "the hell-bound Boy of *Brighton Rock*." Heinz Antor so stresses Greene's belief in "the preponderance of divine grace over evil and sin" that he cautions readers "against making too facile an indictment of the wrongdoer," namely Pinkie. (Sources: Antor, 99,100; Kurismmootil, 56, 134; Phillips, 156; Sherry I, 635, 637–49; G. Smith, 64; Williams, 69)

BROWN, ROGER (*The Captain and the Enemy*) see **CAPTAIN, THE**

BROWNE (*The Captain and the Enemy*). Jim Baxter addresses a telegram to Browne, a nonexistent "friend," to please the Captain by pretending to ask Browne to report on Liza's condition. Jim knows she's dead.

BROWNE (*The Human Factor*). He is a man with a bowler. Percival and Hargreaves see him in Pall Mall. Percival, who dislikes Browne, says he is an economic advisor of the Prime Minister.

BRÛLE, PÈRE (*The Heart of the Matter*). Scobie fondly remembers this Catholic priest, who after 20 years of service in Africa without leave died of blackwater.

BRUTUS (*The Comedians*). He is the owner of a Petit Guave bakery.

BUFFY (*The Human Factor*). He, Dicky, Dodo, and Harry are boisterous guests at Hargreaves's weekend shoot. Buffy, who talks with Daintry, explains that he wears a wedding ring but isn't married and that an untrustworthy dating service used a computer and sent him a mismatched date. Buffy sees Daintry in London, and invites him to his exclusive White's club on St. James's Street for some drinks.

Paul Hogarth includes a fine watercolor of "White's Club, Pall Mall, London" among his illustrations of Greene's novels. (Source: Hogarth, 145)

BULLEN (*It's a Battlefield*). He is one of the Assistant Commissioner's assistants.

BULLEN, MISS (*Loser Takes All*). She is Dreuther's secretary in London. Dreuther orders her to arrange for Bertram and Cary to have rooms in the Hotel de Paris in Monte Carlo, and even where and when to get married.

BULLER (*The Honorary Consul*). He is the manager of the Bank of London and South America. He attends Sir Henry Belfrage's cocktail party.

BULLER (*The Human Factor*). He is Castle's boxer, notable for being too affectionate for watchdog duties. Castle dislikes Buller, but Sam Castle adores him. As part of his escape, Castle must shoot Buller.

Greene drops uproariously funny lines relating to Buller as casually as Buller deposits lines of spittle on guests' clothing. Greene even makes Buller's "*crotte*" (poop) dryly comic.

BULLER, CAPTAIN (*The Heart of the Matter*). He is a character in the story Scobie tells to Jimmy Fisher, an injured survivor of the torpedoed vessel.

BURGESS, (GUY) (*The Human Factor*). In conversation with Hargeaves and Percival, Daintry mentions Burgess and Maclean as Secret Service men from years back. Later Percival calls Burgess "an advanced alcoholic."

Guy Francis de Moncey (Moncy, Morney) Burgess (1911–1963) was recruited by the Soviets while he was a Cambridge University student and was making it obvious to one and all that he and some of his friends, including Donald Maclean,* deplored capitalist democracy. Burgess worked for England's Secret Intelligence Service and helped recruit Kim Philby* (1939), was in the Foreign Office news service (1944), defected (1951), and surfaced in Moscow (1956), by which time it was known that he had been a double agent for years. Greene was a good friend of Burgess, well known in British social circles as brilliant, unstable, alcoholic, boorish, and with homosexual tendencies. *See also* Bellamy.

A BURNT-OUT CASE (1961). Novel. (Characters: Mother Agnes, Marie Akimbu, Attention, Attention, the Bishop, Cassin, Mme. Cassin, Sister Clare, Dr. Colin, Mrs. Colin, the Commissioner, the Commissioner of Police, Deo Gratias, Emanuel, the General, the Greek, the Director of Public Works, Grison, Mrs. Grison, Governor Guelle, Mme. Guelle, Henri, Father Henri, Hoghe, Father Jean, Father Joseph, the King, the Manager of Otraco, Maxime, Marie Morel, Henry Okaka, Thomas Olo, Parkinson, Montagu Parkinson, Father Paul, Perrin, Mrs. Perrin, Brother Philippe, Querry, André Rycker, Marie Rycker, Simon, the Superior, Sister Thérèse, Father Thomas, Toute à toi.)

Part One: Chapter 1: 1. The Bishop's boat goes sluggishly up-river, amid heat, humidity, and insects. The captain is a priest; the crew, black. The white passenger (Querry) smokes, plays dice with the captain, and drinks whisky. Otraco (Office de l'Exploitation de Transports Coloniaux) controls commerce (in the Belgian Congo).

2. They reach their destination, an African mission (containing a leproserie, a school, a hospital, and living quarters, and with a native village nearby). Earlier, the captain taught Greek in the school there. The laughter of the priests playing cards irritates Querry. Isolated, they seem innocently immature. He explores the moonlit village, returns to his assigned room, is asked by the Superior if he wants anything. Suffering from nothing, he wants nothing.

Chapter 2: 1. Dr. Colin, at the leproserie 15 years, discharges Deo Gratias, a deformed ex-leper, as cured, tends other patients, and meets the boat. Its one passenger, Querry, greets Colin by name, and says his "boat goes no farther."

2. Colin is perusing his new leprosy atlas, brought by the boat, when the Superior enters. They talk: (André) Rycker, who wasted six years in seminary study, has just upset the Superior by visiting and talking about his spiritual problems, didn't mention his wife, wondered about Querry; Colin assigned Deo Gratias, "a burnt-out case" because leprosy has eaten all it can, as Querry's servant "boy," when Querry, having just seen some lepers and being unafraid of them, asked for him; there are leprophils, usually female; the Superior probes few people's motives.

Part Two: Chapter 1: 1. Querry starts a routine life. He sees Father Paul and Brother Philippe, managing electricity for the mission and the lepers' village, Father Jean, handling the nuns' prayers, and Father Thomas, supervising the schools. Querry, burnt-out and seeking isolation, attends no Mass, tells Colin he is neither writer nor criminal, volunteers to help with his 800 patients, agrees to drive a truck to Luc, the provincial capital, to buy food and ask about ordered electrical equipment.

2. With Deo Gratias along, Querry drives through forests and rain, dreams the first night of a former girlfriend, who slaps him and whom he tells he's leprous.

3. At Luc, Querry gets the run-around until Rycker officiously intervenes, calls Querry by name, says he's read of his fame, and says he must stay with him until the rain ends.

Chapter 2. Rycker drives Querry, with Deo Gratias following, past the palm-oil factory he manages and to his house, gives Querry whisky drinks, and introduces his wife Marie. He tells Querry, who says was married, that he married Marie, who is child-like and usefully young, two years ago. Rycker orders Marie to fetch that copy of *Time,* issued 10 years ago, featuring a cover essay on Querry. After dinner, Marie excuses herself. Rycker says she's probably recording Querry's visit in her simple diary. Rycker presses glum Quarry about his profession, praised in *Time,* and about his Catholic faith; says he reads about love — Agape, not Eros — demeans Marie for inadequate convent education and sexual reluctance, criticizes the leproserie priests for their mundane concerns, boasts of his brilliance in seminary moral-theology courses, asks about Querry's prayers. Querry says Rycker has everything figured out and asks permission to go to bed.

Chapter 3: 1. Colin's equipment arrives by boat. Since native rumors, often justified, concerning European miracles, jealousy, and ferocity, might prejudice observers of the items, Colin hides everything until the new hospital is built. Rycker, violating his promise not to reveal Querry's profession as a world-famous Catholic architect, told the Superior, who told Colin. Querry says rich parishioners spoiled his artistically modern churches by redecorating, he is now tired of architecture, women, and prayer, and he thought he'd come here, mutilated, to die. Colin compares Querry's injuries to hopelessly advanced leprosy — the disease in such cases must "must burn itself out." Querry follows Colin to the hospital, sees lepers' disfigurements, notices Catholic and African religious items, listens to one sufferer who says he'll die tomorrow. Colin examines patients requiring care in that new hospital.

2. In his journal, Querry mentions his pitiless attitude toward humans. In a letter to Colin he expresses the death of his desire and of his vocation, says he built for self, not God's glory nor buyer's joy. Colin asks "Who cares?" about Querry's explanations. Querry dreams he finds a priest, says he himself is a priest despite his civilian clothes, must confess, must hold Mass, but women interfere and a second priest takes their wine. Querry cries, awakens yelping. "Who cares?" bobs in his mind. In the morning he seeks a desk and a drawing board.

Chapter 4: 1. For two months Deo Gratias, often stumbling, serves Querry, then disappears.

When a leper finds Deo Gratias's staff at the bush's mysterious edge, Querry goes at night in search — wondering why. At last he find his boy, in a marsh, his ankle broken, muttering "Pendélé."

2. Querry tells Colin he saw to Deo Gratias's rescue at dawn. Deo Gratias hinted that Pendélé was his boyhood village, replete with dancing, singing, waterfall, simplicity. Colin equates Pendélé with the lepers' final disease, namely hope. Querry jokes that, if missing, he could be found in Pendélé.

Part Three: Chapter 1: 1. Two weeks later Rycker takes Marie to a party given by Governor Guelle and his wife. Mme. Guelle asks Marie about Querry, has read the *Time* essay praising his creativity while ignoring his unsavory actions, would like to meet him, and listens as Rycker says Querry — a veritable Catholic Schweitzer — protected a runaway, rained-on leper in the bush by lying on his body, and persuaded him to return to the leproserie. Mme. Guelle is about to wonder whether Querry is a homosexual when Guelle hints at Querry's saintliness. Rycker says world-famous Querry is designing not a simple hospital of the sort the Director of Public Works would oversee but a modern African church. The Bishop enters. Rycker starts praising Querry to him, but the Bishop wonders if Querry plays bridge and then flirts with Marie, who says Querry is someone for her learned husband to talk to.

2. Rycker, driving home drunk, reminds Marie she mustn't play bridge, interrupts her thoughts of her parents and the convent in Belgium, criticizes himself aloud, and thinks to himself about their unsatisfactory wedding night. She says aloud she might be too young for him. He wants intercourse this night. She says it's unwise given their regimen of rhythmic birth control. Nevertheless, he orders her in baby talk, and, stripped for action, awakes her reluctant compliance under his mosquito net, convinced that Christian marital acts symbolize Christ's marriage to His Church.

Chapter 2. Two weeks later Marie drives to the leproserie with drums of oil for the Bishop. He is busy hoping Rycker might buy some bidets for lepers' footbaths. Because her husband demanded it, she badgers him to give an invitation to Querry, who, when informed, tells the Bishop that he has just received a forwarded letter from his ex-mistress, abandoned three months ago but signing herself "toute á toi," that he dislikes Rycker, that he half-fears Marie, but that he'll see her. Overhearing, Marie drives away. The two men debate love, Marie's plight and her goodness, Pendélé as a lost childhood paradise, man's immaturity, remorse, and Querry's nothingness now. Querry tells the Bishop to keep Rycker away from him and summons Deo Gratias, who, when asked, says he was happy when little.

Part Four: Chapter 1: 1. Querry and Colin sit across the road listening to the Superior's sermon to some lepers and nuns, about so-called Klistians' sins, their creator Yezu's love and mercy, non-believer Colin's Klistian-like goodness, the value of prayer. Colin wishes Christianity could make cortisone cheaper, then disputes with Querry about love and mercy. Querry praises Colin for being good without belief. Colin says it's easy because he likes without victim-making love-making. Querry unconvincingly pronounces himself cured.

2. At Sunday dinner of cheese soufflé, prepared by the nuns, Father Paul, the Superior, Father Thomas, Father Jean, and Brother Philippe discuss care of eggs, prioritizing electricity use, school curriculum, Rycker's intrusiveness. The Superior draws Father Thomas aside, admonishes him for criticizing Marie Akimbu, a promiscuous native teaching catechism under the nuns, says they must use what's at hand, wonders whether Father Thomas should transfer out of Africa. He replies by asking the Superior why oppose Querry, who is famous, helpful, and heroic in saving Deo Gratias. The Superior cautions Father Thomas not to regard Querry as saintly.

3. Father Thomas, in his room, homesick for Liège, fearing the dark, hears Querry near and invites him in. He confesses to weak eyesight, wanted martyrdom in China, was rejected, volunteered to come here, implies teaching reading here is trivial, fears losing his faith here, welcomes talking to humble Querry, who replies he has no doubts, no faith. Father Thomas hopes Querry has "the grace of aridity," is experiencing St. John's *noche oscura*. Querry, gently irritated, rejects Father Thomas's offer to ponder faith together, pray, be telepathic.

Chapter 2: 1. The Bishop's boat delivers supplies from Luc. Aboard is a fat passenger, (Montagu) Parkinson (a journalist for the London *Post*), feverish but recovering. Colin speaks in French encouragingly to him; Querry translates into English, is critical of Parkinson's self-centeredness. He has a camera and a typewriter, tells Querry to take his picture as he is carried ashore by six men. Father Thomas offers to let Parkinson bunk in his room.

Chapter 3: 1. Colin remembers an old Greek shopkeeper in Luc who after witnessing his clerk making love with the Greek's young wife drove his car over the clerk, crushing his legs and pelvis, told the police not to worry about what he had done but "what I am going to do," and promptly committed suicide. The quoted phrase holds meaning for optimistic Colin, who treats a leper adversely reacting to medicine called Dianinodiphenyl sulfone, then talks with Father Thomas and Parkinson, who has come to learn about Querry. Father Thomas admits he told Parkinson what Rycker reported about Querry's saving Deo Gratias and building a new hospital. Parkinson disgusts Colin by ranting that his truth-distorting, internationally syndicated journalism creates history, publicity creates propaganda, and both generate money for Colin's patients. Querry enters, and Parkinson grabs him.

2. Parkinson interviews Querry. Querry reveals this: Parkinson and he are both burnt-out cases; like lepers, when their disease runs its course and eats all it can, they can be cured; Querry got burned out by his wealth, vanity, professional success in architecture, pretended Catholicism, and misuse of women; Parkinson's lust for journalistic popularity and for food burned out his writing skills and caused ruinous obesity. Objecting to Rycker's gossip, Querry tells Parkinson he'd like to seduce Rycker's wife for revenge. He corrects misinformation Parkinson also got from his *Post* files concerning his love affairs with Marie Morel and Mrs. Grisson, then ends the interview. Parkinson recites religious questions he could ask, vows to extol Querry so much that after his death pilgrims will visit a statue of him by the River Congo. Alone, Querry vows to do no further harm with happiness of the sort a leper feels when cured and able to touch another safely. He whispers an apology — sincere? — to the young lover whose girlfriend, Marie Morel, he seduced.

Part Five: Chapter 1. Parkinson leaves. A magazine arrives, featuring an ugly British colonial cathedral. Police come by, seeking a fraudulent Salvation Army leader. Father Thomas visits a bush seminary seeking a new teacher. An illegitimate baby, born with polio, is baptized. Colin tells Querry he suspects him of kindness; reveals he was "chosen" by accident to treat lepers; talks about leprologists' suicides, suffering vs. discomfort; shows Querry blind lepers; says patients declared non-lepers often dislike being discharged; hopes evolution can produce better humans; believes "the Christian myth" may be evolution's only valuable contribution; says love is planted in us, like hate; praises Pascal's gamble; confesses his only love, his wife, is buried in the leproserie.

Chapter 2. Querry's planned hospital is progressing. Father Joseph hopes an occupational-therapy structure is next. Querry, planning to remain, hopes he can be buried beside Mme. Colin as Colin will be later. Father Thomas returns early. The Superior announces his summons to Luc; Father Thomas will be in charge. This upsets everyone except mock-modest Father Thomas. After farewell toasts, the Superior leaves, advising Father Thomas to curb his enthusiasm. Father Joseph tells Querry that Father Thomas was chosen to supervise because he knows accounting. During a siesta, Querry dreams of accompanying the Superior voyaging with a corpse to bury in Pendélé. Father Thomas awakens Querry: Mme. Rycker told Rycker something about Querry that made Rycker think more highly of Querry. Father Thomas reads Querry the newspaper essay by Parkinson; a copy came on the boat with the Superior. Parkinson mentioned interviewing André Rycker about illustrious Querry, whom he found, after much exploring, as a repentant lover who has embraced God and become a selfless saint helping lepers. Querry, angered, says his ultimate refuge is jeopardized and he must straighten out that liar, Rycker.

Part Six: Chapter 1: 1. Three days later Marie Rycker is reading *The Imitation of Christ* listlessly while Rycker naps feverishly. She reminisces, hears a noise outside, is told by Rycker to check. She finds Querry, who has driven toward Luc, to do errands for Colin, and has stopped here to order Rycker to quit lying about him, which spoils his reclusiveness. She says Rycker wants to latch onto Querry childishly, loves God not her, must learn she's possibly pregnant, and Querry mustn't add to his annoyance. When she says Rycker wants no child, Querry, touched by her helplessness, offers to speak gently to Rycker, and drive her to Luc for pregnancy testing. He tells Rycker this: Parkinson's embarrassing writings must cease; Querry had talent, not genius; seeking reclusiveness here, he found useful work; he is atheistic; Rycker pretends to love God because he loves nothing else, not even his wife. Rycker answers every comment with hypocritical casuistry, calls Querry saintly. Baffled, Querry leaves — without telling Rycker he's taking Marie to Luc.

Marie doesn't say goodbye to Rycker. She accompanies Querry, who regrets not explaining this action to Rycker and drives into darkness toward Luc. Querry tells Marie he flew by chance to Africa rather than Tokyo, with credit card, using surname only. She says she wishes she'd never met Rycker, says she lacks friends in Luc, asks Querry for a loan to fly straight to Europe, is refused, and sleeps — like a pitiful child.

2. In Luc, Querry engages two rooms in a hotel. He mistakes Marie's laughter over a book for crying; so he knocks, enters, and offers her whisky. Getting steadily drunk himself, he recites a fairy tale about a boy who matures, marries, is unhappy, and becomes the worshipped King's jeweler, highly successful not only as lover — especially of another Marie, a suicide — but also as creative artist, but realizes the King exists only in his mind and his prideful work must cease. Despite Querry's disclaimers, Marie recognizes the jeweler is an architect and his jewels are buildings.

Chapter 2: 1. In the morning, Querry handles Colin's errands, goes to the Bishop's boat. The new captain seems unaware of Querry's notoriety. At the hotel bar he encounters Parkinson, who has a room near Querry's and Marie's, which he jokes about. He boasts of the popularity of his Querry essay, a translation of which is in the scandal-mongering *Paris-Dimanche*. Marie strolls in, cockily accepts a whisky. They leave Parkinson. At lunch Marie tells Querry the doctor suspects her of being pregnant. Parkinson intrudes, asks to photograph Querry, is refused. Marie, at Querry's suggestion, tries unsuccessfully to phone her husband, then says she'll go to the cathedral and pray for happiness.

2. Parkinson accosts him, says Rycker is in the hotel seeking Marie, says his next essay on Querry can either continue to make him saint or wreck him. Rycker rushes in, questions Querry about his actions yesterday, then says he read in Marie's diary just now that she spent the night with Querry, who says he doesn't seduce children although Rycker deserving cuckolding, and scoffs at threats of law suits. Querry pays his bill, finds Deo Gratias in the truck, mentions Pendélé, drives past the cathedral, finds Marie. When he mentions her diary entry, she mostly giggles, then agrees she should tell Rycker about her pregnancy. He looks about the cathedral, dimly nostalgic. She ponders prayer and belief. He expresses almost total disbelief regarding God, love, vocation.

Chapter 3: 1. Querry is back at the leper colony. The erection of the roof-tree for the finished hospital is celebrated by a feast, including too-sweet champagne for the white men, many toasts, beer for the workers, and stale *petits fours* for the nuns. Dissidents from the Lower Congo appear, and sing irreverent and critical songs. All the priests except Father Thomas have fun. Sudden lightning and thunder. Querry sees Deo Gratias in the darkness outside, joins him, and although Querry assures him he intends to remain here, Deo Gratias repeatedly says he'll depart with Querry.

2. At the leproserie the sisters phone Father Thomas to report Querry drove Mrs. Rycker to Luc. Querry re-enters, wet from rain, and answers their startled questions nonchalantly. Father Thomas reports Mme. Rycker has just arrived, after a three-day drive alone, and has told the sisters she is pregnant by Querry, who calls it nonsense. Father Thomas rebukes Querry for scandalously betraying their hospitality.

3. Querry accompanies Father Thomas to the nuns' house. Marie says the baby is Querry's. He says it's nonsense. Lying histrionically, she reminds everyone she and Querry were together alone once, says she loves him, is his "toute à toi." Alone with Querry, Marie says when she reluctantly, dangerously slept with Rycker she imagined he was Querry; so she's

only half-lying. She adds that after Rycker read her diary in Luc, he ranted until in fatigue she said she had slept with Querry. Rycker hit her. Parkinson was there, intervened, and heard later the pregnancy test was positive. She half-apologetically rationalizes for burning her bridges and his unique home here. Leaving, he tells Mother Agnes that Mme. Rycker confessed her lie, will deny it, is dangerously innocent; he is rancorously told to get out. He goes to Colin, says Marie will lie to escape Rycker and Africa, but gets invited to stay with Colin and build mobile units. Querry says he suffers anew, surprisingly, and must depart but not for Pendélé.

4. The priests discuss matters. Only Father Thomas criticizes Querry and fears newspaper accounts and Rycker's possible legal action. They agree Mrs. Rycker must leave. Some hope everything will blow over. Parkinson suddenly appears, says he came with Rycker, who is seeking Querry. Rycker bursts in, maunders about his agony, trusting Querry, not wanting Querry's bastard, then exits to find Querry's buddy Colin. Some of the priests liken the situation to a Palais Royal farce. Brother Philippe, wondering if Rycker has a gun, exits.

5. Colin and Querry are talking about mobile units, Colin's wife's fatal sleeping sickness, Querry's half-faith, success ruined by praise, when someone shouts Querry's name. He steps into the dark. Brother Philippe says Rycker may be armed. Rycker appears. They trade comments about Marie's lie and her baby. Querry seems to laugh. Rycker shoots him. Querry fails to explain he laughed at himself because of some absurdity.

6. They bury Querry near Mme. Colin, with space between reserved for Colin. The Superior, having returned, discusses Querry with Colin, who says Querry lost faith in God, love, and architecture, was crippled by fame, was tough, finally may have been cured and wanted to live since he learned to serve others. The Superior predicts Rycker, now praying in prison, will be acquitted of his *crime passionel*. Colin begins to see his 60 patients, including a newly infected little boy.

Norman Sherry reports that in September 1958, shortly before *Our Man in Havana* was published, Greene wrote a friend in Belgium to learn who might arrange for him to live for some weeks in an African leper hospital, of a Schweitzer sort and managed by a religious order. (The name of Albert Schweitzer [1875–1965] appears eight times in *A Burnt-Out Case*.) Greene's friend recommended Dr. Michel F. Lechat, a young Belgian leprologist working in the Congo. Lechat replied to Greene's request. The result was that Greene flew to Leopoldville (February 1, 1959) and then flew to Coquilhatville, where Lechat met him and took him ten miles farther to his leprosarium in Yondo, under the auspices of the Missionaries of the Sacred Heart. (Since Leopoldville is called Leo and Coquilhatville is called Coq, it seems likely that Greene's Luc is short for Luozi, southwest of Coq.) Lechat showed Greene around his establishment and encouraged him to visit leprosy sites nearby (until February 26). Greene left the Congo via Brazzaville, French Equatorial Africa (early March) and so to Paris. He recorded his observations in "Congo Journal" (January 31–March 8, 1959), in *In Search of a Character: Two African Journals* (1961), often transferred almost verbatim to *A Burnt-Out Case*. According to Sherry, Greene wrote *A Burnt-Out Case* in steady morning stints in Jamaica (November 1959), Tahiti (January 1960), and London and Brighton (March 1960). Michael Meyer traveled with Greene (1959–1960) and adds this detail: Greene wrote one-quarter of *A Burnt-Out Case* during that one month in Tahiti. The novel was published January 1961.

Robert Pendleton says *A Burnt-Out Case* "is written quite explicitly against *Heart of Darkness*, as the number of parodic inversions of [Joseph] Conrad's novel demonstrates." For example, Pendleton notes that Querry's final words, totally unlike Kurtz's — "the Horror!" — comprise "a cryptic hint of an existential leap of faith." A. A. DeVitis regards Querry as "too old a hand [with women] to be caught by such a feminine wile" as Mrs. Rycker's getting him to the Luc hotel overnight with her. Neil Sinyard says that events toward the end "build to a climax where tragedy teeters on farce" and reenforces this interpretation by citing numerous theatrical images. Greene's parable about the King and the jeweler, which is an autobiographical allegory about Greene the worn-out, self-absorbed, sexually athletic writer, is simultaneously fun, transparent, and prolix. Paul O'Prey admires Greene's sketching of "[t]he leper colony ... briefly but vividly and convincingly, without sensationalism or sentimentalism." David Parkinson details Greene's superciliously expressed relief that *A Burnt-Out Case* was never filmed, despite Otto Preminger's having bought two unexercised options on it. (Sources: DeVitis, 119; O'Prey, 97; Miller, 91; Parkinson, 707; Pendleton, 112, 113; Sherry III, 165–75, 224, 228–32, 237–41, 820; Sinyard, 71)

BURTON, ARTHUR ("The Moment of Truth"). He has been a waiter, wifeless and childless, at Chez Auguste in London for 20 years. He discovers he needs surgery for cancer. Though stoical, he feels it would help to converse sympathetically about the approach of that crime called death — with a stranger, not a friend or fellow worker. He seeks out Dolly Hogminster, whom he has waited on, as he has with her husband, to do so, and hints about his condition — to no avail. She leaves him a note tipping him and thanking him for recommending certain shops for bargains.

BURY (*The Human Factor*). He is Castle's mother's lawyer. She offers to have him advise Sarah Castle, her daughter-in-law.

BURY, LADY CAROLINE (*It's a Battlefield*). She is an eccentric, strangely dressed, wealthy old widow living in a Bloomsbury mansion. She knew Henry James, Thomas Hardy, and Oscar Wilde. On her walls hang paintings by the late Margaret Surrogate. Lady Caroline still wields political influence. Devoted to various liberal and charitable causes, she tells Philip Surrogate and the Assistant Commissioner she wants justice for Jim Drover, sentenced to be hanged for murdering a policeman.

The model for Lady Caroline is Lady Ottoline Morrell (1973–1938), liberal English socialite. Norman Sherry says she was tall and ugly, cosmetized and dressed garishly; was a patroness of talented writers; and threw glittering soirées, attended by the likes of Henry James, Katherine Mansfield, and John Middleton Murry. Greene first glimpsed her when he was a student at Oxford but first socialized with her in 1930 after she invited Greene and his wife Vivien Greene* to tea, wrote her in 1931 when his career wasn't doing well, and was encouraged by her. (Source: Sherry I, 142, 464–46)

BURY, LORD JUSTIN (*It's a Battlefield*). He is mentioned as Lady Caroline Bury's late husband. While in Spain during the hot summer of 1921, he died of a cold.

BUTLER, INSPECTOR (*The Human Factor*). He is the Sussex police officer who calls at Castle's mother's home to question Sarah Castle. He has heard from Berkhamsted police that her dog Buller was shot. Sarah thinks Butler's mild blue eyes indicate childishness until she looks at them more carefully.

BUTLER, MRS. (*The Man Within*). She is Elizabeth Garnet's bosomy servant. She testifies as to the alleged immorality of Elizabeth and Andrews. She says Elizabeth said Andrews was her brother.

BUTTERWORTH (*The Heart of the Matter*). He was a Bamba official who, becoming ill, was replaced by Dicky Pemberton.

C (*The Human Factor*). Maurice Castle remembers this Chief of British Intelligence as Sir John Hargreaves's predecessor. C, who had a black glass eye, told Castle to escape BOSS agents because he was being pursued for having fallen in love with a black girl. Hargreaves is also called C.

The Chief in *Our Man in Havana* has a glass eye, but it is blue not black. Anthony Mockler chillingly discusses two of Britain's real Cs. (Source: Mockler, 175–76, 190, 193)

CALKIN, MAJOR JOSEPH (*This Gun for Hire*). He is Nottwich's chief constable. He served in the World War I. He is now fat, a bit alcoholic, and over the hill. His wife browbeats him. He disobeys Sir Marcus's order to kill Raven, even when offered a bribe and then threatened.

CALKIN, MRS. (*This Gun for Hire*). She is the constable's hen-pecking wife. At a party they give, she caters to Sir Marcus and Mrs. Piker, the mayor's wife.

CALLITROPE (*This Gun for Hire*). He is a financial supporter of Nottwich stage shows. Dreid owes Callitrope's uncle.

CALLOT, ANNETTE-MARIE (*Travels with My Aunt*). According to Augusta Bertram, she was a friend who was murdered and dismembered on the Paris-Calais train by the Monster of the Chemins de Fer.

CALLOW (*The Honorary Consul*). Sir Henry Belfrage tells Plarr that an embarrassing episode of flying the Union Jack upside down occurred during "Callow's time."

CALLOWAY (*England Made Me*). He is a servant under Sir Ronald at the British Legation in Stockholm. He tries unsuccessfully to stop Ferdinand Minty's interloping.

CALLOWAY (*The Heart of the Matter*). He is a mail censor.

CALLOWAY, COLONEL (*The Third Man*). He is a Scotland Yard man and an officer ranked colonel while assigned to the British section of Vienna. He investigates the "death" of Harry Lime, who he knows is involved in black-market trade in illegal and diluted penicillin. Calloway works reluctantly, then cooperatively, with Lime's friend Rollo Martins, first to prove Lime is alive, then to stop him. Calloway contrasts his dogged professionalism and Martins's sometimes more effective amateur sleuthing. When drunk, and for a time thereafter, Martins calls him Callaghan.

CALLOWAY, JOSEPH ("Across the Bridge"). He is an aging British millionaire swindler, on the run in Mexico. When two detectives seize his dog Rover and take him across the bridge into the United States, Calloway follows. They spot him. One detective chases Calloway and Rover in his car, avoids the dog, and kills the man.

CALLUM, ARTHUR ("Murder for the Wrong Reason") *see* **MASON, DETECTIVE-INSPECTOR**

CALVER, JAMES (*The Power and the Glory*). He is a Yankee criminal, who robbed a Houston bank of $10,000 and killed two government agents. His particulars are circulated in Mexico, to which he escaped. He may have killed Coral Fellows. The police wound him badly, but he escapes. The police entice the mestizo to lure the whisky priest to Calver, to hear his dying confession. Calver won't confess and tells the priest to use his knife to try to escape.

Michael Shelden suggests that Calver's name suggests Calvary but foolishly concludes that the result "make[s] the whisky priest look like a ludicrous imitation of Christ." (Fortunately, Shelden says nothing about James Calver's initials.) Anthony Mockler oddly feels that Calver's "tardy entrance" late in the novel is "perhaps the only real false note in the book." Surely he is a magnet attracting the priest ineluctably. (Sources: Mockler, 155; Shelden, 269)

CAMILLA (*Travels with My Aunt*). She is the pretty daughter of the Chief of Police at Asunción. Henry dances awkwardly with her at Augusta's dinner party.

CAMPBELL (*Orient Express*). He is a *News* reporter who Mabel Warren recalls tried unsuccessfully to interview Dr. Richard Czinner five years ago.

CANBY ("A Day Saved"). This is one of the names by which Robinson refers to the man he is pursuing. Robinson also calls him Douglas, Fotheringay, Jones, and Wales.

CANTERBURY, THE ARCHBISHOP OF ("The Improbable Tale of the Archbishop of Canterbury"). When Satan visits Britain and causes trouble, the Archbishop of Canterbury shoots him.

CAPER ("The Blessing"). He is Collins's boss, evidently an Associated Press editor.

CAPRIOLE, FATHER THOMAS (*The Comedians*). He is a Jesuit priest in England. When Brown left school in Monte Carlo, he promised the priests he would go see Father Capriole but evidently didn't.

CAPTAIN, THE (*The Captain and the Enemy*). This enigmatic adventurer says he was a prisoner of war in Germany during World War I and learned Spanish after escaping into Spain, and evidently did learn to fly toward war's end. Bored, he became a criminal. In his 40s he adopts Victor Baxter, renames him Jim Baxter, gives him to Liza in London as her surrogate son, and periodically visits them. He provides for Jim and Liza, loving the latter in his own way. He tutors Jim in Spanish and geography. He is ambitious to be a latter-day buccaneer in the admired mode of Sir Francis Drake and Sir Henry Morgan. He goes to Panama in hopes of loading gold on mules. He gets involved with Cyril Quigly, an American agent opposed to Colonel Martínez of the Panama National Guard, tries to aid anti-Somoza insurgents, and is killed. Liza tells Jim that Roger is the real name of the Captain, whose birth name was Brown — or so he told Jim. At different times he calls himself Carver, Colonel Claridge, Smith, and Captain J. Victor.

THE CAPTAIN AND THE ENEMY (1988). Novel. (Characters: Bates, Baxter, Jim Baxter, Mrs. Baxter, Browne, the Captain, Clara, Harding, Liza, Lunardi, Mrs. Lowndes, Colonel Martínez, Muriel, Pablo, Quigly, Twining.)

Part I: 1 (1). The narrator, Victor Baxter, 12, is at an unpleasant boarding school, hectored by fellow students, when, a tall, lean, dark stranger calling himself the Captain looms before him. The Captain says he won Victor at backgammon last night from his father, named Baxter but also called the Devil. The severe headmaster lets the Captain take Victor into town until 6:00 p.m. The Captain ducks into the Swiss Cottage, a pub, for gin and tonics. Baxter, outside, dreams of sailing a raft on the nearby canal to Valparaiso. The Captain leaves his worn bag (containing two bricks) at the Swan counter, and engages rooms. They enjoy lunch, and he signs the bill "J. Victor (Capt.)." He gives Victor his choice — afternoon movie called *The Daughter of Tarzan* and his return to school, or escape to London. Soon they are in a railway compartment heading for Euston station.

(2). They proceed by taxi to a rundown neighborhood, then walk back a quarter-mile. The Captain asks Victor about his mother. He hardly knew her; she died years earlier. They get to a mostly empty Victorian house in Alma Terrace (Camden Town, London). The Captain rings the only untaped bell (one long, two short rings). Liza responds. The Captain tells Victor to call her mother or Mum, treat her gently, and decide to remain or not, as he chooses. Victor says he doesn't want to return to school.

2 (1). Liza, young and pale, welcomes Victor, whom they call Jim. She is apprehensive concerning any kidnapping; but the Captain says he won the lad at backgammon, and his father and his aunt (Muriel) won't care. Jim calls her mother but can't manage the kiss the Captain suggested. The Captain dismisses Liza's queries about money, doesn't anticipate jail time, and recalls army experience in Germany 20 years before. Living in the basement, Liza is caretaker of this house, to discourage squatters until it can be demolished. They give Jim his choice of rooms, then a chamberpot, washing utensils, and blankets. He imagines traveling to Africa, as the Devil did. The Captain brings in "pyjamas" for Jim, who dislikes their orange color and sleeps on his sofa in his pants.

(2). In the morning, Jim goes downstairs and Liza soft-boils an egg for him. He asks questions until she says it's all right with her but don't question the Captain, who returns from outside — to see that all's well. Jim senses shyness and fear in both adults.

(3). Time passes. Liza mostly stays inside, apart from buying newspapers, perhaps to read whether a schoolboy was missing. Jim does much of the shopping. Captain suddenly appears on the street, gives Jim money to buy two éclairs, tells him to tell Liza he'll be away for some months but on his honor will return, tells him to give her his love, hands him an envelope for her, says she kinda likes him. He reveals that Liza once knew that devil Jim's father. When Jim gets home, Liza says she hopes Jim likes the Captain.

(4). When the Captain reappears, he takes Jim to see the movie *King Kong*, which puzzles the boy. The teary-eyed Captain explains King Kong and the girl loved each other despite her meaningless kicks at "[t]he poor chap." Jim hopes that love doesn't stop him from liking the Captain. Before vanishing, he gives Jim a newspaper; Liza is to read the second page but not worry a bit.

3. When Liza delays reading page two, Jim finds evidence thereon that a military man asked of a night jeweler in Wimbledon where

Baxter Street was, after which a gang entered the open door and robbed the jeweler thoroughly. Next morning Liza says the Captain hopes Jim will look after her when he's gone. She says he first saw her in the hospital, ill, when he accompanied Jim's father there.

4. Jim's father suddenly appears—Jim shouts "The Devil." He demands to see Liza. Their rancorous talk over tea reveals this: The Captain, whom the Devil calls Roger and a phony, wrote from Bruges saying where Liza and the boy are; the boy was won over a chess game, not backgammon; the Devil caused her to bear "a dead child"; the boy is a replacement; the boy's mother's vile sister may hire a detective to seek him; the Devil won't tell.

5 (1). Weeks later the Captain reappears, with beard, big stick, and car. He tells Liza she probably should have let the Devil provide help, and suggests that instead of Jim's attending school he should read the Bible, have the Captain tutor him occasionally about geography, learn German and Spanish by gramophone records with some help from the Captain. Jim could walk toward a school, sneak home again, and be tutored with an atlas by the Captain. His German, through being a prisoner of war, was better than his Spanish, since he briefly escaped through Spain and was helped at a monastery. He lauds Sir Francis Drake and Henry Morgan for being pirates and stealing millions, whereas thieves grab trash. But for needing to be near Liza, the Captain would go where Panamian gold is. He prefers Kipling's rugged verse to Jim's recitation about namby-pamby Horatius and a bridge. When he recounts his war experiences, details get altered.

(2). The Captain returns, shaves off his beard, leaves, and Liza feels desperate. To obey the Captain, Jim and Liza study the Bible, which often silences her, especially words such as "virgin" and "whoredom."

(3). The Captain returns. Then at the door are Jim's father and also his mother's sister from Richmond. Jim hates her. After an acidulous discussion, it is decided Jim must attend a local school.

(4). About two years later, the Captain is away, Liza is shopping, and Jim answers the door to a policeman. Jim's answers to various questions about his father, his aunt, and Liza puzzle the courteous fellow. When Liza bursts in, she proves uncooperative. Jim, writing all this later, says years passed before he again saw the Captain, who visited Liza sometimes. Jim now wonders about love. Did Jim love generous Liza? Did he ever learn about love except through books? Sometimes, reappearing, the Captain would ask, disinterestedly, about his journalistic career, but would mainly pressure him not to leave Liza, whose relationship to Jim became more "aunthood" than motherhood. Jim, having left, feels that the Captain likely sends Liza money and that the two are growing old together without his being there. His memoirs end here, temporarily.

Part II: 7 (1). Years pass. The Captain is away terribly long. Police come and go. Jim moves to a Soho bed-sitting room and becomes an apprentice reporter, suddenly hired because — inspired by the Captain's crooked examples — he submitted a scoop to an eager editor about a weird non-existent accident. From Spain, the Captain sends Liza a letter enclosing a Swiss-bank check for £3,000. With a share, Jim moves to a two-room flat. Liza is hit by a car. Jim visits her in the hospital; she tells him to take her long-treasured packet of the Captain's letters and destroy them. He promises but instead retrieves them from her basement quarters, together with Jim's own memoirs. He reads, for the first time, the letter accompanying that Swiss check: The Captain is off to gold-rich republics near Panama, hopes one day she and Jim can join him. She never heard from him again. Jim, having been in and out of affairs, still wonders if she and the Captain were lovers—indeed, what love is. An earlier letter from the Captain records his dream that Liza would be in a strange hospital after a car accident. Another letter came from Colombia. Another wrote of his drinking only moderately because he had to be sharp for his work. Jim wonders what work?

(2). Ambitious to be a writer, Jim wonders also what Liza might have written to the Captain. Hoping for information, he writes the Devil to meet him. Then he finds a new letter to Liza, saying the Captain is enclosing £1,500 to bearer, for her to use to fly to him in Panama City. He meets the Devil, looking older, for lunch, shows him the letter and the check, and the Devil figures Jim will cash it for himself. The Devil says Aunt Muriel phoned that Liza was in the hospital; then Muriel, the "bitch," died. He tells Jim the Captain saved him from a teen-age robber in the London Underground. The Devil put the Captain up for a week. The Captain met Liza, four months pregnant by the Devil, and fell for her. The Devil made her have an abortion — botched, with no chance for more children. She left with the Captain. The Devil and Jim agree that the letter hints that the Captain is after big money. The Devil won't go see Liza.

(3). Jim cashes the check, gives the Devil £50 he fibs the Captain owed him, half-enjoys a lush Soho dinner, doesn't write the Captain. Another letter to Liza tells her to wait since money is temporarily short. Jim reads this letter three times, compares it to the draft of a love letter he wrote to a girlfriend, and thinks that both men are liars but that either the Captain's lies are worse, by making Liza his loyal emotional prisoner, or that Jim, never truly loving, envies the Captain. Liza dies. Jim handles arrangements and wires the Captain as from Liza that Jim is leaving for Panama. Jim quits hack reporting, wants to write for serious publication — perhaps these memoirs, which he corrects and will continue.

Part III: 8 (1). Jim flies London-to-Amsterdam, skips New York because the Captain has avoided the U.S., then Caracas-to-Curaçao, updating his "history" en route. The Captain, though liar and crook according to the Devil, was always dependable; Jim hopes, though, for gold from him, not fatherly affection. Quigly, a tall, skinny man, meets Jim at the Panama airport, tells him his father, "Mr. Smith," is away, installs him in a two-person Continental Hotel room, and provides him with Pablo, an armed bodyguard sent by Colonel Martínez. Pablo, whom Jim likes and trusts more than Quigly, shows him Panama City — 123 international banks, luxurious American Zone, and slums. A week passes. Quigly treats Jim to a Peruvian dinner. With Pisco Sours, they get informative: Quigly was born in England (Brighton), lived there 16 years, works here for an American newspaper as a financial consultant, and is usefully knowledgeable about troubles in Nicaragua, Guatemala, El Salvador, elsewhere; Jim hopes to work with Smith, whom he calls his adopted father; Smith has been in and out of trouble, with Americans and others; Quigly could hire Jim as a stringer to provide useful information.

(2). Two nights later Pablo says Colonel Martínez has released him and Señor Smith is back. The Captain appears, clean-shaven, gray, and more wrinkled. He and Jim share whiskies in their room. The Captain cautions that Quigly is acquaintance not friend, asks about Liza, and Jim says only that a car accident hospitalized her. More lies deepen the hole. They reminisce on their double lives. The Captain reveals that he has a dangerous job, that Jim can help by checking on copy-hungry Quigly.

(3). Next morning the Captain is gone. Jim sees an unfinished letter to Liza. Outside, Quigly offers Jim money for help with a story indirectly about Smith. No.

(4). While reviewing what he has written, Jim remembers feeling no sadness when Liza died but wishes he hadn't destroyed her last letter, unmailed, to the Captain. Sending it would have prevented his lying to the Captain that she was hurt not dead.

(5). Jim, lonely, misses even Quigly. The Captain returns, shows Jim some ruins, says he prefers Sir Francis Drake, who robbed but rarely killed, to city-ruining Morgan. The Captain says he could ruin a carefully built city by bombing it from his plane, which he then regrets telling Jim he owns — as a hobby. He admits he's working now with three others and participated in that harmless jewel theft (only £3,000 in value) mentioned in the *Telegraph*. He augments his warning about Quigly, untrustworthy and involved in a swapping game with him.

(6). The Captain leaves a note for Jim — off again on a short flight — and $100. Preferring work to gifts, Jim turns sullen, exits, blows too many dollars at breakfast, and encounters Quigly. He says he would pay Jim $600 a month for scraps of news, true or not; in Panama, yarns could concern finance, politics, even war; he wonders where the Captain keeps his plane. Quigly interests Jim, who, after all, also got his start writing by falsifying a story.

(7). Jim finds the Captain, back again and shaving. He says this: Beards could be no disguise here; everything is politics here; he could be killed, not jailed; he doesn't fear death, which is inevitable; he wants to leave Liza secure; he plans a huge caper involving mules (his often-used code for gold) and hopes he can trust Jim, who agrees he's the Captain's friend.

(8). The Captain drives Jim in his old Renault through the American Zone to a hidden airstrip. He points to his plane proudly, confusing Jim by referring to it and Liza as "her" and expressing worry over both. He says he took flying lessons to get out of the infantry. He takes Jim for a spin over the Atlantic, the Pacific, ships awaiting Canal passage, and down again. The Captain gets Jim to think of a London friend and telegraph him to inquire about Liza, and stands over him at the hotel desk while he sends a message to an imaginary friend. Jim hints that Liza might be getting worse. The Captain demands that Jim fly back to her. Refusing, Jim says Quigly offered him work. Captain turns threatening. Jim snarls: Liza is dead.

(9). Jim escapes down the stairs. He rationalizes that the Captain's generosity was only for Liza, that both he and Jim lie only to gain individual independence. In desperation, Jim phones Quigly. They meet where Quigly bought him sours. He tells Quigly he quarreled with the Captain, that is, Smith, and needs work. Quigly by means of whisky gets Jim to talk freely — about his real father, Liza, Smith's disappearances and name changes, police visits, the plane. Quigly connects that plane to Colombia, drugs, and something more dangerous than drugs, and boasts that finance — his expertise — connects with politics, crime, in fact everything. He mentions Colonel Martínez, of the National Guard and surely Smith's protector; says anti–American Panamians oppose Nicaragua's (Anastasio) Somoza (Debayle [1925–1980]) and El Salvador's death squads, hints Smith is supplying guerrillas by plane, says he could've worked with Smith, asks where he hides his plane. Jim, drunk, wants a room. Quigly says he could help Smith; Jim, drunk, vaguely describes where the airstrip is, thinking Quigly wants intelligence not information.

(10). Next morning Quigly phones Jim, says Smith is gone, has a letter from England which Jim can get from the porter. Jim pockets it. The two search the Captain's room. Jim takes another letter, from the Captain's jacket. Quigly says Smith's flying route is over Costa Rica to drop arms to the (anti–Somoza) Sandinistas at Estelí (Nicaragua). This is exciting to Jim, who is persuaded by Quigly that they should stop the Captain, with whom Jim is still angry. They drive off in Quigly's Mercedes, but the Captain's plane is gone. Quigly sends a telegram. Jim uses the old room in the Continental, ignores a message at the desk from the Captain to phone Colonel Martínez, and instead reads the first letter. It is from the Captain, with a check for getaway money: Jim, you should've continued lying; I supported you only for Liza, whose child the Devil made her lose; avoid Quigly, whose damnable employers I told nothing; I first stole for risky fun, then to support Liza; I don't know that she really cared for me; now she's dead I'm free; I thank God if He exists; I can do one thing for my friends; you stay out of my life. Jim reads the second letter, from Liza to her Captain: I am dying and want you to know I've loved you from first sight, you kindest of men. Jim feels jealous, inferior, isolated. He plans to keep the letter, to comfort the Captain should he return. He dreams of trying to penetrate an obscure, ever-retreating wood. Quigly phones: Pablo, at the door, will take you to Martínez, to whom reveal nothing.

(11). Pablo escorts Jim to Martínez's office. Martínez fusses with papers, calls Jim Mr. Smith until Jim says his name is Baxter, asks where Baxter's missing father and his plane are, says his plane took the wrong direction, and says Quigly is a "gringo" informant but no friend. Jim reveals nothing but that Quigly offered him work, which Martínez advises him to refuse until he can give Jim word concerning his father.

(12). Jim returns to his room. He wonders who Somoza was, who the Sandinistas were — names he heard earlier. Quigly appears, tells him Smith crashed his explosive-laden plane into a Managua bunker where President Somoza was, to please his friends but, missing Somoza, pleased Quigly's side. Quigly could have used Smith more; now offers to aid Jim and, like Martínez, use him; is asked to leave; drops $1,000 for him. Pablo phones that Martínez wants Jim, despite Jim's retort that Quigly gave him the news.

(13). While waiting, Jim updates his memoirs. The Captain cared for Liza, not him, is safely dead. Should Jim follow that last dream, which also included mules, unladen with the gold the Captain sought? Jim gives up his ambition to write. Did King Kong love the girl he held despite her kicking him? What is love?

(14). After seeing Martínez, Jim returns to his room, finds in the waste basket a torn-up letter that the Captain probably intended for him, partly assembles it and reads it. The Captain complains he gave to others who needed him, was in need himself, lacked King Kong's strength. Jim counts his money, can cash his unused air ticket, adds in writing his intention to follow his own mules and find his own future, and puts his presumably never-publishable memoirs in the waste basket.

Part IV: 9 (1). Martínez puzzles over Jim's "novel" and tells Quigly he got it first. He wonders if Quigly warned Somoza about Smith's route. Quigly answers how could he? Martínez asks if King Kong is something in code. Quigly thinks he was a gorilla. Martínez wants nothing to go wrong before President Carter and General Torrijos sign the Canal Treaty in a few weeks. Quigly counters that Jim is probably flying home to London and doubts Martínez's contention that Quigly warned Somoza and Smith was shot down. Martínez warns Quigly to get to the safe American Zone.

(2). Martínez works with a translator on the last of Jim's writings. Pablo reports Jim has booked a flight to Valparaiso. Martínez is puzzled: Smith and Jim weren't involved in Chile. Yet Americans cooperate with (Augusto) Pinochet (Ugarte, b. 1915). King Kong distresses Martínez, who thinks his General might recommend Jim's book as publishable about "gringo espionage." By phone Martínez learns Jim has just died in an accident en route to the airport.

The Captain and the Enemy was a long time aborning. Norman Sherry reports that by telegram to Antibes and signed Señor V, General Omar Torrijos Herrera (1929–1981) invited Greene, all expenses paid, to visit him (1976). Greene later figured that perhaps Fidel Castro, knowing of the anti–American political bias of Torrijos, suggested that Torrijos might use Greene somehow during Panama-U.S. discussions concerning the Panama Canal and the American Zone. Torrijos and Greene got along splendidly. Torrijos was a friend of the Sandinistas, who were battling Nicaraguan dictator Anastasio Somoza Debayle (1925–1980), and Greene could and did provide journalistic support for both Torrijos and the Sandinistas. At Torrijos's invitation, Greene was also present in Washington, D.C. at the signing of the two Canal Treaties by Torrijos and President Jimmy Carter (September 7, 1977; *see Travels with My Aunt*). Torrijos died in an airplane crash (1981). Greene attended his funeral in Panama. (Sherry summarizes shadowy evidence permitting the allegation that the CIA and General Manuel Antonio Noriega [b. 1939, ex–Panamian dictator and currently U.S. prisoner for drug trafficking] sabotaged Torrijos's airplane.) Greene abandoned a idea for a novel about Torrijos, to be titled *On the Way Back*. Instead, he did three things. He published *An Appointment with the General* (1982, originally called "On the Way Back: A Work Not in Progress"). He reminisced, often sentimentally, about his friendship with Torrijos in *Getting to Know the General: The Story of an Involvement* (1984). And he wrote *The Captain and the Enemy* (1988). Readers uneasy about America's releasing control to Panama of both the Canal Zone and the Canal may find their concerns reenforced by David Pryce-Jones, who in his review of *Getting to Know the General* says that in writing it Greene "place[d], without qualification, his talent and reputation at the service of a campaign against the United States and its purposes in the contested arena of Central America. Using the privileges and freedom of residing in Antibes, Greene is praising and promoting those who would destroy such privileges and freedoms elsewhere." Pryce-Jones does call Torrijos "an eccentric but on the whole benevolent autocrat."

Robert Pendleton suggests that Greene was influenced by Joseph Conrad in structuring this final novel. Pendleton believes that it resembles *Under Western Skies* slightly; that Jim, like Marlow, tries to understand himself by understanding "his mysterious counterpart the Captain"; but that the effort is unsatisfactory. Judith Adamson regards Greene's novel as "held together by Greene's habit of playing with names, turning the plot with irony, and cutting through time with letters, journals and dreams."

The Captain and the Enemy may be downgraded for many reasons. Jim excessively dwells on his unpleasant schooldays. Seeing *King Kong,* together with the Captain's response to it, makes too great an impression on Jim. Jim couldn't learn much Spanish during the Captain's infrequent visits to the basement digs that the pre-adolescent Jim shares with Liza. Jim is preternaturally speedy updating his memoirs while awaiting more trouble to crash about him. Doesn't Liza have any independent ambition? Robert Hoskins curiously contends that when Martínez asks "Who is King Kong?" the question may really be "Who is the Captain?" and ultimately "a question about writing itself."

The Captain and the Enemy seems to remain, mostly, an inchoate document attesting to Greene's inability to stomach American political efforts in Central America in the 1970s. (Sources: Adamson, 180; Falcoff; Hoskins, 300; Kelly, 79–80; Pendleton, 156; Pryce-Jones, 35; Sherry III, 562–88 passim)

CAREY, FATHER ("The Hint of an Explanation"). David remembers Father Carey as the priest in the Catholic church in the East Anglian town where David grew up.

CAREY, J. G. (*The Third Man*). When Martins stops at Frankfurt en route to Vienna, a reporter mistakes him for Benjamin Dexter, the novelist, then says his assignment is to interview J. G. Carey, whom he also can't identify.

CARL (*Orient Express*). He was a waiter at the Moscowa in Belgrade, remembered by Mabel Warren but now, she knows, replaced by a Frenchman.

CARLOTA (*The Honorary Consul*). She is Castillo's daughter in a novel by Saavedra.

CARLYON (*The Man Within*). He was the elder Andrews's smuggling partner aboard the *Good Chance,* inherited his wealth and vessel, and persuaded Andrews's son Francis to join his crew. Young Andrews reveres Carlyon despite being abused by the crew. Carlyon escapes when revenue officers led by Hilliard try to arrest him and his crew. Although Andrews informs against Carlyon, he evades capture, encounters Andrews at Elizabeth's cottage, forgives him, and escapes.

CAROSSE (*The Tenth Man*). He is an experienced actor, middleaged, portly, cocky, and possessed of a genius's imagination. At a Paris urinal, he mistakes Chavel for someone named Pidot and pays Chavel to deliver a message to Carosse's wife. The Mayor of Bourge tells Carosse about Chavel. Carosse goes to Thérèse Mangeot's inherited house, pretends he's Chavel; briefly out-prevaricates the real Chavel; when identified as Carosse the actor, who murdered Toupard, shoots Chavel and disappears.

CAROSSE, MADAME (*The Tenth Man*). She is the unwanted wife of Carosse, the actor. He calls her a bitch to Chavel, when he thinks Chavel is Pidot and when he wants Chavel to deliver a dishonest message to her that he must hide briefly in Switzerland.

CARPENTER, EDWARD (*Travels with My Aunt*). Aunt Augusta tells Henry she attended a literary figure's funeral, also attended by Edward Carpenter ([1844–1929], Brighton-born socialist writer), Dr. Havelock Ellis, [James] Ramsay MacDonald, E[dith]. Nesbit, [George] Bernard Shaw and his wife, and H. G. Wells.

CARPENTER, MISS (*The Confidential Agent*). She is Dr. Bellows's Entrenationo Language Centre secretary. D. distresses her at the Saturday soirée.

CARSON (*The Human Factor*). He was a Soviet agent in South Africa. Castle knew and admired him. Carson helped Sarah Castle escape via Swaziland and Mozambique. Muller tells Castle that Carson was apprehended and died of pneumonia in prison. Castle believes Carson was murdered by South African security officers. Castle becomes favorably disposed toward Communism because of Carson's humanity.

CARTER ("The Bear Fell Free"). Carter, a former officer during World War I, is Tony Farrell's faithless friend. After Tony's death, Carter telephones Tony's girlfriend Jane. She says she gave Tony the teddy bear. Carter returns the teddy bear to Jane, feels guilty, and muses about Tony's friends.

According to Cedric Watts, Greene named Tony Farrell's "duplicitous friend" Carter to get back at Lionel A. Carter,* his "tormentor" at Berkhamsted School. Greene himself discusses this sadistic Carter briefly. (Sources: Greene, *A Sort of Life,* 82–84; Watts, 32)

CARTER ("The Blue Film"). This businessman takes his bored wife to a hut near Saigon showing pornographic movies. In one, filmed 30 years earlier, he appears with his only love, a girl, 21. Mrs. Carter disapproves but is sexually excited by the film. After the Carters make love for a big change, Carter feels he has betrayed his only beloved.

CARTER (*Brighton Rock*). He is a member of the London real-estate agency Carter & Galloway, which employs Molly Pink.

CARTER (*The End of the Affair*). Some people leaving Sarah Miles's cremation say the Carters have invited them for the week-end. Their chat suggests that after a death life goes on smoothly.

CARTER (*The Third Man*). He is Calloway's junior officer. Carter apologizes to Calloway for losing track of Harbin, is forgiven, and redeems himself by suggesting that the coffin supposedly containing Harry Lime's body be dug up. Harbin's corpse is found inside.

CARTER (*This Gun for Hire*). Raven remembers him as a man hurt by going soft on a girlfriend.

CARTER, JULIA ("Mortmain"). She is Philip Carter's fair-haired wife. Instead of despising his former mistress, Josephine Heckstall-Jones, for vindictively leaving in his home items including letters evidencing their supposed affection, Julia praises Josephine for her friendliness and criticizes Philip for his distress.

CARTER, LIONEL A. (1904–1971). He was a fellow student when Greene attended the school in Berkhamsted. He made Greene's life miserable, memories of which affected Greene throughout his life. Gwenn R. Boardman pointed out early that "Carter ... is a recurrent figure, the bully of 'The Revenge'— one of Greene's personal school memories." Cedric Watts reminds readers that Greene's "childhood foe, Carter, is vicariously defeated in the form of fictional namesakes." Greene says he often had trouble when he gave characters names beginning with C. (Sources: Boardman, 125; Greene, *Ways of Escape,* 22–23; Watts, 153, 204)

CARTER, MRS. ("The Blue Film"). She is Philips Carter's still-beautiful but now bored wife. When Philip takes her to see some pornographic films, one happens to feature him with a long-ago girlfriend. Julia disapproves but is so turned on by the movie that she beds Philip to her satisfaction—first time in years.

CARTER, MRS. (*The Heart of the Matter*). She is a mail censor. This tough woman survived the deaths of her husband and three children. Though kind to Helen Rolt, Ms. Carter writes Louise Scobie, vacationing in South Africa, that her husband is having an affair with Helen.

CARTER, PHILIP ("Mortmain"). He is a fiction writer who had a stormy relationship with Josephine Heckstall-Jones for 10 years, then married Julia. Their marriage is imperiled when Josephine leaves letters in Philip's home, now Julia's also, purporting to be affectionate but in reality to demonstrate continued possessiveness.

A. A. DeVitis notes that "[t]he fact that Greene uses the name Carter disparagingly in other works suggests that the man [Philip Carter] gets what he deserves." (*See* Carter, Lionel A.) (Source: DeVitis, 178)

CARTER, WILLIAM (*Our Man in Havana*). He poses as a vacuum-cleaner salesman from Nottwich, England, and meets Wormold on the airplane back from Jamaica to Havana. In reality Carter is an enemy spy. Carter attends the European Traders' Association and attempts to poison Wormold, shoots Hasselbacher to death in the Wonder Bar, and agrees to sample Havana's night-life with Wormold. Wormold shoots at Carter, misses, is shot at, then kills Carter.

Greene suggests Carter's unattractiveness by making him a tweedy, pipe-smoking, stammering snob, and by having him criticize Oxford and Cambridge for backwardness "in technology." Grahame Smith notes that "the apparently reassuring Carter ... comes from Nottwich, that Nottingham of *A Gun for Sale,* while his surname is that of Greene's boyish tormentor from his schooldays" (*see* Carter, Lionel A.). (Source: G. Smith, 140)

CARTHEW, MOLLY (*Brighton Rock*). She was a pretty girl who, Rose believes, deserves eternal damnation because she committed the unforgivable sin of despair and then killed herself.

CARVER (*The Captain and the Enemy*) *see* **CAPTAIN, THE**

CARY (*Loser Takes All*). She is Bertram's peppy fiancée, 20. They plan to marry in London and honeymoon in Bournemouth. But Dreuther, Bertram's boss, demands that they wed in Monte Carlo and honeymoon on his yacht offshore. They proceed to Monte Carlo. Dreuther doesn't show up. They wed. Bertram gambles so well and so exclusively that their marriage is jeopardized. She flirts ineffectively with Philippe Chantier. Dreuther arrives, advises Bertram; he gambles to lose, is reunited with Cary.

Greene particularizes Cary first by saying that her parents were killed during the Blitz, then by praising her "flashes of disquieting wisdom," and finally by having her memorably name Bertram's first wife "Dirty."

"THE CASE FOR THE DEFENCE" (1939). Short story. (Characters: Adams, Adams, Mrs. Adams, Mrs. Adams, Henry MacDougall, Mrs. Parker, Mrs. Salmon, Wheeler.) The unnamed court reporter-narrator calls Adams's trial for hammering Mrs. Parker dead the strangest he ever attended. She lived on Northwood Street. So does Mrs. Salmon, who saw Adams emerge from Mrs. Parker's house at 2 a.m. on that moonlit February 14th night and drop the hammer from his gloved hand. Minutes later, Henry MacDougall almost ran Adams over on Northwood. Wheeler, a next-door neighbor, heard a thud, looked out, and spotted Adams. Adams testifies he was home with his wife at that hour. When the defense counsel presses Mrs. Salmon, she insists she can identify Adams. He is ugly, stout, with "pekingese" eyes, thick of body, with muscular thighs. At counsel's request, Adams's twin brother, at the back of the court room, stands up. He is identical, even dressed the same, and says he too was home with his wife. Mrs. Salmon cannot be certain. The accused goes free. Outside is a crowd, through which the twins brashly rush. One is hit by a bus and dies, his skull smashed. The surviving twin weeps. The narrator asks himself but can't say whether the accident represents "Divine vengeance," then wonders whether Mrs. Salmon's sleep will be troubled.

Greene foreshadows the one twin's death by having one or the other of them almost run down earlier by MacDougall. Is it divinely poetic justice, or devilish misjustice, that the unlucky twin's cause of death somewhat resembles Mrs. Parker's?

"The Case for the Defence" was the subject of a 1976 television production. *See Shades of Greene.* (Source: Falk, 215)

CASSIDY (*It's a Battlefield*). This Irish poet is a talkative guest at a big luncheon held by Lady Caroline Bury and attended by Philip Surrogate.

CASSIN (*A Burnt-Out Case*). He is the Director of Public Works in the Upper Congo.

CASSIN, MME. (*A Burnt-Out Case*). She is the Public Works director's fat wife and attends Governor Guelle's party.

CASTILLO (*The Honorary Consul*). He is Carlota's fisherman father in a novel by Saavedra.

CASTLE (*The Heart of the Matter*). He is evidently a government official. Scobie says he talks too much.

CASTLE (*The Human Factor*). Maurice Castle remembers that a Castle was an artisan at the Berkhamsted castle.

CASTLE (*The Human Factor*). Castle, Maurice Castle's father, was an old-fashioned general practitioner in Sussex and a Liberal Party advocate. Upon retiring, he bought an Edwardian house near a golf course but soon died of a stroke. Castle remembers his father told him about the reality of fairies to encourage him to believe that life is worthwhile.

Norman Sherry suggests that the relationship of the elder Castle and his wife is based on that of Greene's own parents, Charles Greene* and Marion Greene.* (Source: Sherry II, 150)

CASTLE, MARY (*The Human Factor*). She was Maurice Castle's first wife, killed in London by a buzz bomb during the Blitz. Castle feels guilty because he was then safely stationed in Lisbon. Castle also has feelings of inadequacy because he has been a sterile husband.

CASTLE, MAURICE (*The Human Factor*). He is the protagonist, 62, employed by the British Secret Intelligence Service 30 years. Before the war, he worked in a bank. When SIS assigned him to Pretoria, South Africa, he loved and married Sarah MaNkosi, a black, and adopted her black son, Sam. Carson, a Communist, helped them all remain together. Partly through gratitude to Carson, Castle became a double agent in London, now handling African information in MI6, working with Daintry, Davis, Hargreaves, and Percival, and sending coded data to Boris, his Soviet controller. When Soviet agents need to make physical contact with Castle, they approach him and ask him if he is William Hatchard, as a mutually identifying code. His leaks are attributed to Davis, who is murdered. Castle's sending Boris information, of no direct use to the Soviets, about the Uncle Remus project blows his cover, and he escapes to Moscow, alone.

Castle comments that it is amusing that his fake passport, provided by a Soviet agent near the Heathrow Airport, names him as Partridge, a bird hunted during "[t]he shooting season." All Castle wanted was to remain Sarah's devoted (though sterile) husband and Sam's careful father, be loyal to peace, and write a book deploring apartheid.

Michael Shelden feels that Maurice's last name relates to the Berkhamsted castle. Shelden explains that "[t]he fragmented walls [of the castle] seem to be an omen for Castle, the sign of the bleak future awaiting him when he will have to flee Berkhamsted for Moscow." Tim Armstrong finds the name Castle apt since Castle is "obsessed with the security of his family." In giving Castle his first name, Greene undoubtedly also thought of Maurice Oldfield (1915–1981), the experienced British Military Intelligence officer in Egypt (1944), later in and out of London's headquarters (1944–1981), including Singapore (1950–1958) and Ireland (1979–1980). Oldfield knew and was ineffectively suspicious of Kim Philby.* Also when Greene named the happily married Maurice and Sarah Castle as he did, he was thinking about Maurice Bendrix and Sarah Miles, energetic lovers from *The End of the Affair*.

A. F. Cassis tersely concludes that Castle prefers "the ideal of ... individualism and humanism to patriotism." Probing the Castles's marriage, Mark Bosco begins by saying that "[i]t is new to Greene's characters that Castle and Sarah are *happily* married and very much in love. This representation of married love differs sharply from Greene's earlier Catholic cycle," signaling his "new conception of marriage" and an awareness "of the developing Catholic discourses" about marriage. Bosco continues: "This once normative pattern of the Catholic literary revival was challenged by post-Vatican II theological discourse," all of which may be related to "Greene's late novels [which] offer glimpses of married love as the new *Imago Dei*." With the Castles mainly in mind, Bosco says that when "God seems absent, married love becomes God's trace, the gleam of hope in an otherwise dark world, the text's tenuous signifier." Nonetheless, many readers must wonder about the Castles: Maurice, though sterile, is still only 62, and after sexually avoiding the much-younger Sarah for months, has intercourse with her only once in the course of the novel. (Sources: Armstrong, 591; Bosco, 123; Brown, 388, 581; Cassis, 22; Shelden, 480)

CASTLE, MRS. (*The Heart of the Matter*). She is a government worker's wife. She tells Louise Scobie that Scobie won't be promoted to commissioner. She also praises Louise for writing so well she could become a professional.

CASTLE, MRS. (*The Human Factor*). She is Maurice Castle's widowed mother, 85, living in East Sussex and dutifully visited once a month by Maurice. She was given a medal for service as a head warden during the Blitz, and is such a patriotic Conservative that she tells Sarah Castle, her daughter-in-law, that she would inform on Maurice if she knew he was a "traitor." She has a Burmese cat named Tinker Bell, which Maurice's boxer Buller would eat if given a chance.

Norman Sherry contends that Mrs. Castle resembles Greene's mother Marion Greene.* If so, the family portrait is not flattering. Leopoldo Duran says he and Greene "agreed that the one evil person in the book is Mrs. Castle." (Sources: Duran, 234; Sherry III, 608–09)

CASTLE, ROGER (*The Human Factor*). He is mentioned as Maurice Castle's snobbish cousin. He works in the Treasury. Daintry knew him at Oxford.

CASTLE, SAM (*The Human Factor*). He is Sarah Castle's black son by a black African father. Davis amiably calls him "the little bastard" in conversation with Maurice Castle, who adopted and loves him. Sam goes with Sarah to her mother-in-law Mrs. Castle's home in East Sussex, where he is likely to be miserable.

CASTLE, SARAH (*The Human Factor*). She is the former Sarah MaNkosi, a Bantu African. Educated in a Methodist school and at the African University in the Transvaal, Sarah was Maurice Castle's MI6 agent in Pretoria. They violated South African apartheid laws by marrying, and escaped, with her natural black son Sam, to Mozambique and England. Sarah, a non-believer, and Sam are lonely but try to adjust. When Castle escapes to Moscow, she and Sam begin to live with his widowed mother, cannot both follow, and she refuses to leave without Sam. An ignorant British golfer in Sussex sees her on his course and calls her Topsy.

CATARINA (*The Power and the Glory*). This is the name called out by her demented father when the whisky priest is jailed with him.

CATERINA (*The Honorary Consul*). She is the wife of a prison warder, ranked sergeant, in a novel by Saavedra.

CATHERINE, MÈRE (*The Comedians*). She is a popular Port-au-Prince brothel manageress, with a face similar to a pleasant nanny's in a Deep-South movie.

Norman Sherry relates this sympathetically treated madam to the madam in *A House of Reputation*, a play Greene wrote (c. 1957), couldn't get produced, and once denied in writing he ever wrote. Sherry adds that Greene based Mère Catherine's establishment on a Port-au-Prince brothel run by a madam named Georgette. According to Michael Shelden, when Anita Björk* ended her affair with Greene (1958) and Catherine Walston* was unavailable, he began his consorting with Yvonne Cloetta* (1959) and thought it would be a good joke to name the madam of Haiti's best brothel Mère Catherine. (Sources: Shelden, 446–47; Sherry III, 301–10, 348, 351–52)

CATO (*The Comedians*). He is the owner of a Petit Guave garage.

CAVE, DR. ("Under the Garden"). He is Wilditch's London physician. He points out from evidence in x-rays taken of Wilditch's lungs that further examination is necessary and recommends Sir Nigel Sampson as a specialist.

CAVEDA, RAMON (*Rumour at Nightfall*). He remains loyal to Carlos the Pretender, becomes a guerrilla leader, believes in liberty, free thought, and democracy, and plans to attack San Juan, a provincial Spanish town. To spite her mother, Eulelia Monti sleeps one night with Caveda. Chase intercepts mail from Caveda, hoping it will aid in Caveda's capture. Crane, Chase's friend, sees the elusively ghostlike Caveda but only from the rear.

Brian Diemert magnifies the importance of *Rumour at Nightfall* by discussing it with reference to classical mystery novels: "Caveda is the signifying value that determines all else in the novel"; Chase, "unlike the sleuth of detective fiction, ... is not attuned to the possibility of there being more than one reading of things"; consequently Chase "sees Caveda as the author of a univocal text and is indifferent to the indications in Caveda's story that he comes across." (Source: Diemert, 99, 100)

CERRA, FATHER MIGUEL (*The Power and the Glory*). This Jesuit priest is the author of a sentimental book about the martyrdom of a lad named Juan. A pious mother reads portions of it to her two daughters and her son Luis.

"CHAGRIN IN THREE PARTS" (1966). Short story. (Characters: Jacques Dejoie, Madame Emmy Dejoie, Félix, Pauline, Madame Volet, Paul Volet.)

1. Antibes, in rainy February. The narrator, an English writer now unmarried, enters Félix's restaurant, where he dines almost nightly, although big, aggressive Madame Emmy Dejoie, inside, glares at him. Madame Volet, amazingly pretty, comes in. The two women chatter, thinking the narrator, an *anglais* or *américain,* won't understand. Anyway, he's reading a Trollope novel featuring Mr. Crawley. The narrator learns Emmy's husband Jacques Dejoie, tall but unimpressive, died; Madame Volet's husband Paul Volet, a large but routinized lover, left her for a bitch with dyed hair. Emmy plies Madame Volet with wine before dinner and during Félix's carved fish with the *bouillabaisse.*

2. Madame Volet gripes that Paul talked politics perpetually. Emmy responds. Emmy adored husband Jacques; post-coitus, he emitted cock crows; after his death, she found true and more gymnastic love with Pauline, who died five years ago; now Emmy knows her "capacity"; Emmy confesses she might have relished Jacques's "little object" as a smoked eel. Madame Volet giggles

3. After trying Trollope further, the narrator surveys sleepy Madame Volet, whom Emmy promises not only sleep tonight but love lessons soon. The women leave. The narrator thinks Paul was a fool and feels chagrin himself for lost opportunities.

Informed readers realize that the Rev. Josiah Crawley's courtship, as presented in the Victorian novelist Anthony Trollope's *The Last Chronicle of Barset* (1867), provides a decorous contrast to Emmy's siege of Madame Volet. "Chagrin in Three Parts" was the subject of a 1976 television production. *See Shades of Greene.* (Source: Falk, 215)

CHALFONT ("Jubilee"). He is a gigolo, 50 but looking younger, still trim. In slightly frayed array, he enters a pub and tries to pick up Amy, an expensively dressed woman who turns out to be a retired madam. Amy gets revenge on numerous "uncongenial partners" by buying Chalfont drinks, giving him money, and making him realize his current seediness.

"A CHANCE FOR MR. LEVER" (1936). Short story. (Characters: Davidson, M. Golz, Lever, Emily Lever, Lucas.)

Mr. Lever has sold British heavy machinery for 30 years in Europe and the United States but hasn't done well recently. Five weeks ago he left London for Africa. Lucas, a businessman, persuaded him to invest his savings in Lucas's heavy machines, consult in Brussels with M. Golz, Lucas's partner, and locate a man named Davidson. Davidson has been digging for gold in Liberia in a rift running from Nigeria to Sierra Leone and will happily sign a contract to buy Lucas's digging machines. Lever will make a handsome commission.

Now in Africa, Lever encounters difficulties. His cook and his tired carriers want more money, get sick, require his treating them with his salts, aspirin, and iodine, and occasionally lose their way through horrifying forests. Chiefs at successive villages offer Lever unattractive palm wine, and sell him rice and palm oil for his group. Diseased natives dance oddly, have scraggly livestock, fumble through dust and dung. Heat from vertical sun rays is terrifying. At night, rats, cockroaches, jiggers, and mosquitoes are constantly frightful. Lever begins an initially cheerful letter to his wife Emily, ill back home — don't skimp on milk and stout. Everything grows worse. Rumors of the whereabouts of Davidson, that mysterious white man, are misleading. In panic one night, Lever, having secreted his clothes to prevent their being gnawed by rats and insects, steps barefoot into the dust to pray; a jigger attacks a toe. His diminished crew finds a native's bloated corpse shoved into one of Davidson's gold holes. Lever finds Davidson's tent near a place called Greh. Davidson lies unconscious, horribly yellow, his chest covered with black vomit. Next morning, Lever, fatally disoriented, types a letter as from Davidson to Lucas contracting for machinery, carefully forges Davidson's signature, figuring a follow-up agent from Lucas will report Davidson's death by yellow fever and complete the transaction. Lever flails at one of Davidson's mosquitoes but slaps only his bitten ankle, has two carriers cram Davidson into a handy hole, destroys his letter to Emily since he will quickly be home himself, and dreams of vacations on the Continent for the two of them.

The omniscient narrator concludes otherwise.

Readers, unlike Lever, know this: While carrying sloppy forgeries for three euphoric days toward civilization, he also carried fatal yellow fever in his system; there's no loving divinity in the impenetrable forest that soon caught him, where nature constantly presents evidence of shriveling, decay, and death; let those in safety, however, believe otherwise.

Robert Pendleton says "there is a vein of absurdity, almost farce, about the disintegration and corruption of the white anti-hero [Lever] in Africa that recalls [Joseph] Conrad's short story 'An Outpost of Progress.'" Many logistical, sanitary, and gory details presented in "A Chance for Mr. Lever" have their origins, Norman Sherry reports, in Greene's own intrepid, dangerous travel in Liberia (January-March 1935), narrated not only in Greene's *Journey Without Maps: A Travel Book* (1936) but also in *Land Benighted* (1978; republished as *Too Late to Turn Back,* 1981) by Greene's cousin Barbara Greene (later Countess Strachwitz), his trek companion when she was a tender 23. "A Chance for Mr. Lever" was the subject of a 1976 television production. *See Shades of Greene.* (Sources: Falk, 215; Mockler, 132; Pendleton, 105; Sherry I, 522–61 passim, 566)

CHANT, OLIVER (*The Name of Action*). He is a rich young London idealist. A desire for adventure impels him to Trier, where he finances a revolution against its dictator, Paul Demassener, and falls in love with Demassener's wife, Anne-Marie. Chant helps smuggle arms from Coblenz to Trier, sleeps with Anne-Marie one night, and regards this act as love whereas she says he has merely satisfied her lust temporarily. While drunk, Chant reveals to Kapper, a leading conspirator, that Anne-Marie told him her husband is impotent. Kapper's distribution of a broadside trumpeting this fact contributes to Demassener's being wounded and deposed. Chant feels sympathetic toward Demassener and accompanies him on a train to Luxemburg. An immature lover, Chant combines lack of religious faith and a half-hearted desire to die with Anne-Marie.

CHANTIER, PHILIPPE (*Loser Takes All*). He is a handsome, hungry young gambler whose losses and appearance attract Cary. When Cary and her brand-new husband Bertram argue because of his sudden gambling addiction, worsened by winning, she flirts with Philippe — harmlessly, even though he spins an appealingly romantic story of his past. Bertram gives him more money to lose.

CHAPLAIN (*It's a Battlefield*). He is the chaplain at Leeds prison. The Assistant Commissioner meets him there while visiting Jim Drover. Later, the Chaplain visits the commissioner to explain he's retiring, exhausted by having to break sad news to relatives of inmates, softly and indirectly.

CHARGE, MAJOR (*Travels with My Aunt*). He is Henry's pro-Empire neighbor. He agrees to water Henry's dahlias but does a poor job. He asks Henry to feed and water his fish.

Greene particularizes Charge by saying that his laugh resembles a merciless nose-blowing.

CHARLIE (*Brighton Rock*). While returning to Brighton after his unsatisfactory meeting with Sylvia, Pinkie passes Charlie's Pull-in café.

CHARLIE (*This Gun for Hire*). This fat man runs a London dive which Mather and Saunders raid in an unsuccessful search for Raven.

CHARLOT, JEAN-LOUIS (*The Tenth Man*) *see* **CHAVEL, JEAN-LOUIS**

CHARTERIS, CELIA (*Loser Takes All*). She is a person Dreuther describes to Bertram as agreeable. He says she'll be boarding his yacht at Portofino. Celia doesn't figure in the story beyond the hint that Dreuther wouldn't mind if Bertram forgot his wife and dallied with Celia.

CHARTERS (*The Comedians*). Jones recalls that Charters, his friend in Imphal, could smell water. This inspires Jones to fib he can too.

CHASE, FRANCIS (*Rumour at Nightfall*). He is a British correspondent, 38, in Spain two years, and chasing the guerrilla leader Ramon Caveda for six months hoping for a scoop. His friend for 10 years is Michael Crane. Chase is rational, extroverted, and so secular that he regards Catholic Spain as rotten. Crane's and

Crane's rivalry over Eulelia Monti, along with their opposite frames of mind, leads to Chase's tragic betrayal of Crane.

Taking Chase and Crane ultra-seriously, Robert Hoskins opines that "[t]he dual protagonists ... are clearly two halves of a single personality," and "Crane is figuratively the imprisoned 'man within' Chase who must die to be released." (But then what happens to that "single personality"?) Michael Shelden suggests that the names Chase and Crane "together ... sound like those of a bad comedy team." Peter Wolfe incorporates the two names in a discussion of characters in Greene's fiction whose names begin with the letter C, including numerous Carters and Caveda too. (Sources: Hoskins, 5; Shelden, 157; Wolfe, 159–60)

CHAVEL (*The Tenth Man*). He was Jean-Louis Chavel's distinguished lawyer-grandfather. The family had lawyers back into the 17th century. Chavel's lost house, now 223 years old, has portraits of many of them.

CHAVEL (*The Tenth Man*). He was Jean-Louis Chavel's distinguished lawyer-father.

CHAVEL, JEAN-LOUIS (*The Tenth Man*). He is the protagonist, a middle-aged Parisian lawyer who, imprisoned by the Germans as one of 30 hostages, avoids random execution by deeding his fortune, including his country mansion in Brinac, to Janvier (Michel Mangeot), who replaces him as victim. Calling himself Jean-Louis Charlot at war's end and feeling wretched, Chavel can't find work, returns to Brinac, and tells Michel's sister Thérèse Mangeot he knew Michel in prison. Carosse appears, pretending to be Chavel. The two men could exploit Thérèse together; but Chavel unmasks oily Carosse, a murderer, and protects Thérèse at great cost.

Anthony Mockler stretches in thinking Greene may have given Chavel the first name Louis because the first name of the hero of *Le nœud de vipéres: roman* (1932; trans., *The Vipers' Tangle,* 1933) by his esteemed friend François Mauriac (1885-1970) is Louis and he is a lawyer. (Does Chavel choose the name Charlot because he plans to be a charlatan?) A. A. DeVitis believes he is named so as to "suggest ... not only by his name but also in his appearance and demeanor Charlie Chaplin's Little Tramp." (Evidently DeVitis regards Jean-Louis's last name to be Charlot-Chavel. Good, but his "appearance and demeanor" are anything but Chaplinesque.)

Norman Sherry details Greene's relationship with Chaplin (1889-1977). Greene knew and admired Chaplin's films, praised him in a controversial open letter (September 27, 1952) in times of McCarthy-era unrest, and sought to have his Bodley Head publishers bid for Chaplin's autobiography (1957). Greene met Chaplin in Vevey, Switzerland, dickered further, and volunteered to edit his autobiography (1960); spent two weeks going over it and making suggestions to tighten it, which Chaplin ignored (1960); and when it appeared (*My Autobiography,* 1964) was falsely accused of having ghostwritten it. Greene and Chaplin, among other celebrities, consulted with Thomas Roe, a Swiss-based lawyer, con man, and eventually convicted criminal, to be tutored in the niceties of income-tax avoidance (1964–1965). Gene D. Phillips expatiates on Greene's 1952 open letter. Yvonne Cloetta* touches on Greene's friendship with Chaplin. (Source: Cloetta, 48–49, 152–53; DeVitis, 146; Greene, *The Graham Greene Film Reader,* 436–37; Mockler, 206; Phillips, 134; Sherry II, 444–46; Sherry III, 115–18, 127, 408–11)

CHAVEL, MADAME (*The Tenth Man*). She is Jean-Louis Chavel's grandmother. Jean-Louis remembers she chose the wallpaper in his old bedroom. When 14, he drew a face on it.

CHAVEL, MADAME (*The Tenth Man*). She was Jean-Louis Chavel's mother. He remembers she used to watch from an unseen spot for visitors she didn't wish to admit.

"CHEAP IN AUGUST" (1964) Short story. (Characters: Henry Hickslaughter, Joe Hickslaughter, Margaret, Charlie Watson, Mary Watson.)

1. Mary Watson, British and 39, vacations cheaply in Jamaica, in August. Charlie Watson, her husband, a professor of English literature in a Connecticut university, is in London researching James Thomson, the pre-Romantic poet. Inexperienced 12 years ago in London, she met Charlie — an adventure for her. Their

10-year marriage has become routine. She reads Charlie's daily letters, arriving in bundles, and less conscientiously replies, sometimes by postcard. She fibs she's with Margaret, a nonexistent friend. Mary would like a fling before turning 40, surrendering to old age, and dying. The Americans she sees, especially hippo-fat ones, aren't appealing to party with. She rebuffs them by accentuating her accent. Three weeks of rum punches and the humid-evening calypsos prove boring.

2. Half-missing Charlie, Mary swims in the hotel pool. An elephantine old American, Henry Hickslaughter, with white hair, splashes over, introduces himself, and learns she's English, married to an American temporarily in England. Later, nursing a warm martini, she is approached but declines Hickslaughter's offer for drinks with him, goes off to lunch, ignoring his childish blurt about wanting company. He follows, planks himself down, and when she gripes that the black waiter served tomatoes with her trout, corrects her pronunciation of "tomatoes." Accepting her unwanted tomatoes, he answers her questions. He doesn't like St. Louis, his home town, got retired, vacations here in August because it's cheap. He says their rooms are on the same floor. Declining dessert, she heads for a nap, walks past his room, sees the maid cleaning it, lacks iced water in her room, and enters his to ask the maid for some. No maid. She sees an incomplete letter, reads it, and learns Hickslaughter is demanding that his brother Joe repay a loan — or else — since he himself had to borrow in Curaçao. Appearing, Hickslaughter suggests a drink after her nap. Feeling guilty about snooping, she agrees, naps, contrasts her Charlie's demure letters with Hickslaughter's menacing one, phones him, and agrees to avoid the expensive bar by sharing his bourbon in his room. An adventure. Entering, she observes drink set-ups, senses his solitude, confesses reading his letter. He says he saw it was moved, doesn't care, would do the same in her room hoping to find a love letter the likes of which he never wrote and is overage to, now. His bourbon-loosened tongue and her curiosity create revelations. To her answer that her husband studies 18th-century poetry, Hickslaughter expresses surprise they wrote poetry then, confesses liking only Longfellow at school long ago, quotes something about bearded pirates. Feeling uniquely curious about another human being, since Charlie sparked only quick-dying sexual curiosity, Mary asks about Joe, learns he managed money better than Henry Hickslaughter, gradually feels in control of their talk, has more bourbon. Somewhat fuddled, she quotes Longfellow about "the thoughts of youth," gets Hickslaughter to discuss Joe, who he says calls Hickslaughter a pirate but who'll pay up. He's too conservative to accept her offer to treat him to dinner. They stagger, though, to the dining room and overhear a pair of homosexuals discussing Tennessee Williams. Mary suddenly feels scared of Hickslaughter, despite their age differences and his not getting fresh. They chat about more bourbon, how it aids sleep, his inability to sleep. They avoid the homosexuals and head for the lift. His key won't unlock his door, which, already unlocked, she opens. He says he needs a bourbon after seeing those "nancies," but she thanks him for the "lovely evening," and leaves for her room.

4. Mary dips into Thomson's *Seasons*, contrasts predictable, patronizing Charlie and old Hickslaughter, safe as a rusty shipwreck on a rock, probably now trying to drink himself unconscious. Deciding to offer him her sleeping pills, she gets into her dressing gown, knocks at and enters his room, and finds him in ugly pajamas — crying. He says he thought she was the maid, whom he summoned, hoping to get her compliantly drunk. He says he fears darkness and loneliness, pays for companionship in Curaçao, is over 70, has occasionally looked for sudden death. She gets him to sleep, lies beside him, hears him mutter, and later they make love, quietly, quickly. She cries, unseriously, at the brevity of this encounter. Slipping, is he carrying her anonymous infant away to Curaçao? They agree it was unplanned but understood. What was? While packing to return home, she concludes they assuredly know Jamaica was cheap that August.

"Cheap in August" A. A. DeVitis calls "in some ways Chekhovian" but doesn't particularize. Richard Kelly calls it "tender and compassionate." Perhaps, but conservative readers might object. Mary Watson may be moved by generous feelings toward rollypoly old Hickslaughter. But if she wanted sexual adventure, why not flirt with a stalwart Jamaican or two?

Perhaps a waiter's brother? If she wanted to alleviate boredom more decorously, how about a tour with or without dull fellow vacationers to a botanical garden, old church, museum, university library, rum factory? Native rum might be better than a hick's bourbon, certainly superior to a warm martini. Couldn't she have ordered a martini with ice, shaken, or even stirred? Compassionate toward Hickslaughter? Back home in dull New England again, how will she process guilt feelings near Charlie? How compassionatize his concavity? Demand manhattans first, over striped "pyjamas"? "Cheap in August" was the subject of a 1976 television production. *See Shades of Greene.* (Sources: DeVitis, 178; Falk, 215; Kelly, 59)

CHESTER ("The Man Who Stole the Eiffel Tower"). He is an American tourist who, with his unnamed girlfriend, goes by taxi, twice, in an effort to see the Eiffel Tower. When it's gone, they don't understand (nor does the Parisian taxi driver). Nor when it's back, do they understand either.

CHICK, MISS (*It's a Battlefield*). She is the bar maid in the building where Conder lives.

CHIEF (*It's a Battlefield*). He is the head reporter in the newspaper office where Conder also works.

CHIEF, THE (*Our Man in Havana*). He is the head man in London's Secret Service. He wears a black monocle, which hides a baby-blue glass eye. He is the boss of Angelica, Hawthorne, Beatrice Severn, etc. He admires Wormold because he seems traditional and overlooks his inadequate recruits and reports. To cover his own deficiencies, the Chief ultimately rewards Wormold. The Chief in *The Human Factor,* called C (*which see*), has a black glass eye.

Norman Sherry says that the Chief is based on Sir Stuart Menzies, the head of the British Secret Intelligence Service for which Greene worked (1943–1944). (Source: Sherry II, 171–72)

CHIEF CLERK, THE (*The Honorary Consul*). While Crichton is talking with Plarr at the British Embassy in Buenos Aires, he complains that the Chief Clerk just issued a new directive concerning entertainment expenses.

CHIEF ENGINEER, THE (*Our Man in Havana*). He is an officer serving on the *Juan Belmonte.* On his trip to Cienfuegos, Wormold spots him drinking and fictionalizes him into one of his agents.

CHIEF OF POLICE, THE (*The Honorary Consul*). Colonel Perez tells Plarr that this official in Asunción just told him Plarr's father Henry Plarr was killed trying to escape.

CHIEF OF POLICE, THE ("The Lottery Ticket"). He is a corrupt official in the Mexican town where Thriplow is vacationing. He uses Thriplow's donated lottery winnings to capture and execute a political opponent of his friend the Governor.

CHIEF OF POLICE, THE (*Our Man in Havana*). While playing draughts with Wormold, Captain Segura boasts he knows about the spies in Havana, will go to the Chief of Police, and they will tighten the net.

CHIEF OF POLICE, THE (*The Power and the Glory*). He is the fat jefe who confers with the lieutenant about catching the whisky priest. He has a toothache, which the dentist Tench drills on at the moment of the priest's execution. The late Lopez's daughter lives with this jefe.

CHIEF OF POLICE, THE (*The Power and the Glory*). He figures in the story read by the pious mother to her children.

CHIEF OF POLICE, THE (*The Power and the Glory*). He is the crooked jefe in the capital city. He helps himself to the whisky priest's contraband brandy.

CHIEF OF POLICE, THE (*Travels with My Aunt*). He is an important officer in Rome. Henry informs Visconti that the chief called Visconti a viper.

CHIEF OF POLICE, THE (*Travels with My Aunt*). He is an important Asunción officer. O'Toole tells Henry he knows this man.

CHIEF WARDEN, THE (*The End of the Affair*). He is a Bigwell-on-Sea official. When Henry Miles visits him to inspect air-raid facilities, Sarah goes along and, eager to forget Bendrix by becoming sluttish, exchanges kisses with the Chief—unproductively.

CHILTON (*The Human Factor*). He is the MI6 agent with the most seniority. He has a dog-bark laugh and specializes in Ethiopia.

CHINE (*It's a Battlefield*). He is an employee at the insurance company where Conrad Drover works. Their director tells Conrad he's appointing Conrad to Chine's position.

CHINKY (*This Gun for Hire*). This is the Pekinese dog brought by Mrs. Piker to the party given by Major Calkin's wife, who worries because fellow-guest Sir Marcus hates dogs.

It would now be considered politically incorrect to name a Pekinese "Chinky." Peter Wolfe makes much of Sir Marcus's dislike of dogs, when he says that the old armament maker "naturally opposes peace and love." Wolfe continues by asserting that Greene often "used dogs to signal the budding-forth of these divine values." (Source: Wolfe, 65)

CHOLMONDELEY (*This Gun for Hire*) see **DAVIS**

CHOU (*The Quiet American*). He lives in Cholon, the Chinese suburb in Saigon. He is Dominguez's contact to Heng in Quai Mytho.

Greene's hilarious description of this feeble old Chinese man, totally addicted to opium and surrounded by a congeries of family—old, young, and crawling—pets, and junk, provides welcome if situationally inappropriate comic relief.

CHUBBY (*The Confidential Agent*). He has a room at the Lido. Pig, another person there, looks through D.'s window thinking the room is Chubby's.

The young men having fun at the Lido may be pursuing sex, since the well-traveled Greene dubs one of them Chubby ("chubby" being an American vulgarism for penis).

"CHURCH MILITANT" (1956). Short story. (Characters: the Archbishop, Father Donnell, General Kimathi, Patsy One-Eye, Father Schmidt.)

Northeast Kenya. Just after the Mau Mau, who are Kikuyu tribesmen, have been forced back by British troops (1953?). In his jeep, Father Donnell is driving the narrator-journalist, when they encounter the Archbishop, driving his new Cadillac, with women passengers in gray clothes marked by gray crosses. The Archbishop arranges to meet the two men at the Niguru mission later. Donnell and the narrator visit some brave nuns, now settlers at Niguru, near the Kikuyu reserve. Awakening Father Schmidt, old and gullible, Donnell fibs that Mau Mau have attacked his settlement, poisoned his well, driven his cows off, and killed his chickens. He requests supplies, especially wine. Catching on, Schmidt deplores Donnell's persistent childishness. Donnell says the Archbishop wants his new nuns—Little Sisters of Charles Foucauld—to settle, build huts, and farm like natives. The over-confident Archbishop enters and is indifferent to Schmidt's comments that murders were recently uncovered at Moragumbi. No matter, the Archbishop explains; the nuns have their vocation. While he is wrangling with Donnell, the narrator and Schmidt load Donnell's jeep with empty wine bottles. Their rattling might unsettle the Archbishop when the two vehicles leave. The narrator observes, however, that neither Donnell, lost in thought, nor the Archbishop, driving directly behind, seems to notice. Darkness falls.

Greene's reports about his visit to Kenya are reprinted in *Ways of Escape*. Norman Sherry reports on Greene and Kenya in general, and Greene in the Mau Mau region in particular (August–October 1953). Greene toured the Kikuyu Reserve, conferred with a Father McGill at a mission, saw loyal and disloyal Kikuyu natives, was driven in a jeep by a British officer who was named Candler and was later ambushed and beheaded by Mau Mau. Greene wrote about these experiences and also about Dedan Kimathi, Mau Mau leader, who is mentioned in "Church Militant," which, considering Greene's Kenya travels, is a singularly unrevealing story. Richard Kelly writes that it is "not ... especially funny or memorable" and, further, that the "invisible pious women and the authoritarian archbishop are stock characters who never come alive." A. A. Devitis contends that the story presents "two believably drawn priests." (Sources: DeVitis, 176; Greene, *Ways of Escape*, 192–216 passim; Kelly, 47; Sherry II, 461–69)

CIFUENTES, ENGINEER (*Our Man in Havana*). Called Dr., he is a member of the Country Club and a friend of the Minister of the Interior. Wormold obtains Cifuentes's name from the Club membership list, makes him into one of Wormold's non-existent agents, and accords him technical expertise. Cifuentes, 65, is tall and squinty. At one point, he is shot at and wets his pants. One of Sanchez's mistresses knows Cifuentes.

CLARA (*The Captain and the Enemy*). She is a girl Jim Baxter once felt he loved. When he finds the draft of a love letter he wrote her, he concludes he merely wanted her for sex.

CLARA (*The Confidential Agent*). She is a prostitute, with coarse but friendly features. Else Crole knows Clara and offers to hire her as a servant-companion. After Else's death, however, Clara criticizes her to Mr. Marie Mendrill.

CLARE, SISTER (*A Burnt-Out Case*). She is a nurse at the leproserie. When Dr. Colin is phoned, he thinks she's about to report a death.

CLARENCE (*Brighton Rock*). He is a Londoner. He seduced Ida Arnold by pretending he was going to die soon. When they meet again, she calls him a ghost but discusses Hale's murder with him. Some weeks later, Ida talks with Clarence about Pinkie's death.

CLARENTY, MRS. ("May We Borrow Your Husband?"). She is Stephen's and Alec's client. She complains to Stephen that she dislikes Alec's painting of a dead faun for her bedroom. In the end, Stephen will leave Tony and do work for Mrs. Clarenty.

CLARIDGE, COLONEL (*The Captain and the Enemy*) see **CAPTAIN, THE**

CLAY, FATHER (*The Heart of the Matter*). Formerly a Liverpool priest with experience counseling prisoners, he is now the Bamba mission priest. Scobie confers with him after Pemberton's suicide.

CLAYTON, TUBBY ("The Bear Fell Free"). He is a buddy Carter muses about.

CLIVE (*The Heart of the Matter*). He is a Department of Agriculture employee living near Harris and Wilson.

CLOETTA, YVONNE (1923–2001). She was Greene's last mistress. Yvonne shared a home with her husband, Jacques Cloetta, and their daughters, Brigitte and Martine, at Juan les Pins, near Antibes. (Martine later married and was mistreated by Daniel Guy, a southern French criminal.) Greene happened to stop at Douala, in the French Cameroons, French West Africa, on his way out of the Congo leper colony (March 1959), which figures in *The Burnt-Out Case*. Yvonne was there with Jacques, an employee of the United Africa Company, Ltd., an Anglo-Dutch import-export firm active in Douala and nearby Dahomey. She regularly lived 10 months a year with their daughters in politically safer France. She agreed to show Greene Douala's night life, and they danced at a club until 4:00 a.m. Next day she visited his hotel room, talked philosophically, learned he was single, and considered seeing him in Antibes. They dined in Nice (August 1959) and spoke of their love. She was aware, sometimes uneasily, of his previous sexual liaisons. In Paris, he shocked her by taking her to a bordello he had frequented (1959). She was with him in the Barbados and in England (1963). Greene liked Antibes, where he and Yvonne often met (from 1964). Although she wanted Jacques to know (in 1964) that she was Greene's lover, he wasn't told until later. Greene and Yvonne frequently went to Capri, from which Greene once wrote Catherine Walston* (August 1967) about Yvonne's gardening and their swimming there. When Greene moved permanently to Antibes (1966), their relationship became enduring. They visited Israel (1981), the Soviet Union (1986), and elsewhere. In *Getting to Know the General*, Greene calls Yvonne "my greatest friend." He often labeled her his "HHK" (happy, healthy kitten).

William Cash reports that Yvonne, whom he interviewed, was disgusted with Norman

Sherry, when in the second volume of his biography of Greene he theorized that Sarah Miles, heroine of *The End of the Affair,* was identical to Catherine Walston. Cash seeks to clarify the record: "Far from being Greene's petite, poodle-like Cote d'Azure 'companion,' as she has been portrayed, Yvonne has an immediately apparent, feisty, no-nonsense, sexual authority — bordering on the bossy — that Greene clearly seemed to like." Yvonne translated some of his works and edited some, including *A World of My Own.* She stayed with him, his last year and a half, in Vevey, Switzerland, and was with him moments before he died. Leopoldo Duran presents details concerning Yvonne's son-in-law Daniel Guy. Yvonne Cloetta knew Greene more thoroughly than any other woman ever did. (Sources: Cash, 23, 154, 162–64; Cloetta, 6–10, 20–23, 25, 32, 39, 5l, 106, 107, 174–83 passim, 190–91; Duran, 247–59 passim, 288–89; Greene, *Getting to Know the General,* 155; Shelden 446–455 passim; Sherry III, 224, 404, 435, 464)

CLOUGH, COLIN (*The Human Factor*). He works for advertiser Edward Joiner. Clough's promotes Jameson's Baby Powder, which is overshadowed by Johnson's in the market. Daintry attends Clough's wedding to Elizabeth Daintry, his daughter. Daintry gets Clough's name wrong and calls him "Clutters."

CLOUGH, MRS. (*The Human Factor*) *see* **DAINTRY, ELIZABETH**

COHEN (*This Gun for Hire*). He may be a backer of Nottwich theatricals. He is uncertain whether Davis quarreled with Cohen or with Cohen's nephew.

COHEN, ALF (" A Drive in the Country"). Mike recognizes Alf Cohen's tune on his car radio while he is driving the uneasy girl home.

THE COLD FAULT *see **THE HUMAN FACTOR***

COLIN ("Dear Dr. Falkenheim"). He is a pleasant British couple's son. While they were vacationing in Canada, Colin, six, saw a man playing Father Christmas scatter presents from a helicopter, land, emerge, and get beheaded by the rear propeller. Far from believing Father Christmas was dead, Colin associated him with Christ, dead yet alive and so, like Christ, Father Christmas lives. Having such faith occasions Colin, now l2, to come home regularly from school beaten up by schoolmates who dislike his position.

COLIN, DR. (*A Burnt-Out Case*). He is an unselfish physician who has worked at the leproserie for 15 years. He has lost his religious faith, but his devotion to others is saintly. He was happily married to a woman who died at the colony of sleeping sickness. Unlike Querry, Colin was evidently never a womanizer and as a widower is uninterested in female relationships. He is ambitious to improve medical facilities at the colony. He is an understanding friend of Querry, who admires him so much that he wants to be buried where Colin's wife is buried and where Colin intends to be. At one point, Colin says his mother is vacationing in the Swiss Alps.

It seems macabre of Greene to accord Colin an anatomical name. Greene describes one leper's scrotal elephantiasis but stops at that juncture.

Colin is patterned after Dr. Michel F. Lechat (b. 1927), respected Belgian epidemiologist specializing in leprosy. While a medical student, he explored the Congo by bicycle (1951), returned with his wife Edith (1953) and became medical director of a leprosarium in Iyonda (also spelled Yonda), in the Congo's equatorial forest. After serving there for six years (until 1960), he enrolled at Johns Hopkins University and obtained his doctorate in Public Health (1983), became president of the School of Public Health, University of Louvain, and launched a brilliant career. Of his more than 330 publications, some 200 concern leprosy (*see International Journal of Leprosy* 70 [March 2002]: 49–50).

Norman Sherry wrote Dr. Lechat for information concerning Greene during the weeks he spent at Lechat's Yonda leprosarium. In one letter, he wondered whether Lechat was a regular Catholic, a troubled Catholic, or an atheist. Lechat replied testily that he might be regarded as all three. Paul O'Prey observes that Dr. Colin "[d]espite his atheism ... is 'religious' in his concern for man and in his metaphysical ponderings on man's origins and spiritual state." Paul

Hogarth's watercolor depicting "The Léproserie at IYonde" is especially stark, with diseased eyes in the brooding sky above it. (Sources: Hogarth, 113; O'Prey, 98; Sherry III, 175)

COLIN, MME. (*A Burnt-Out Case*). She was Dr. Colin's wife. She died after contracting sleeping sickness.

Greene suspensefully delays telling about this selfless woman, who, the reader may think, was perhaps a leper.

COLLEONI (*Brighton Rock*). He is Pinkie's overpowering rival in Brighton's protection racket, ever since Colleoni's men killed Kite, Pinkie's boss. Colleoni lives in a Cosmopolitan hotel suite, insulated tycoon-like from danger, is smug and catered to, offers Pinkie a job but when refused orders his men to attack Pinkie and his friend Spicer, and rejects Pinkie's friend Cubitt's plea for a job.

In a *Collected Edition* introduction, Greene says Colleoni is based on a retired Brighton gang leader. Michael Shelden feels that Greene may have had movie-mogul Alexander Korda* in mind when he made Colleoni a kind of interloping Jew. Malcolm J. Turnbull, in a study of Jewish characters in English detective fiction, curiously contends that "Colleoni plays Mephistopheles to ... Pinkie, and ultimately leads him on to catastrophe;" a Jewish devil leading a Faustian Pinkie? Greene ironically names Colleoni after Bartolomeo Colleoni (1400–1475), the Venetian general, a brilliant tactician and disciplinarian. Colleoni tells Pinkie that Napoleon III (1808–1873) and his wife Eugénie (Marie de Montijo de Guzmán [1826–1920]) slept in the room he now occupies at the Cosmopolitan. The reference to Napoleon is lost on Pinkie but not on Robert Hoskins, who expatiates on "Pinkie as Napoleonic Strategist." Norman Sherry reports that the slashing and kicking of Pinkie and Spicer at Colleoni's behest replicates details of a 1936 Brighton bookmakers' feud. David Leon Higdon notes that Colleoni's being Jewish is muted in later editions of the novel. W. J. West goes too far in whitewashing Colleoni by calling Colleoni "almost an avuncular figure." (Sources: Greene, *Brighton Rock, Collected Edition*, xi; Higdon, 181–82; Hoskins, 80–87; Shelden, 213; Sherry I, 634–35; Turnbull, 102; West, 79)

COLLEONI, MRS. (*Brighton Rock*). She is the protection boss's wife. She evidently likes flowers and fruits.

COLLEY ("The Other Side of the Border"). He was a down-and-out, alcoholic clerk, in Brazil at 17, then in Africa. He obtains a job through Danvers in Liverpool. Colley joins Hands's expedition to prospect for West African gold (1936) and, according to hints from Morrow to Danvers (1938), probably died there.

COLLIER (*The Ministry of Fear*). He attends Mrs. Bellairs's séance, patronized as former waiter, tramp, stoker, but also admired as a poet now of rough but acceptably spiritual poetry.

COLLIER (*This Gun for Hire*). He is the Nottwich producer of stage shows, including *Aladdin* at the Royal Theatre. Small, fierce-eyed, with straw-colored hair, he attained his position maybe through pull, maybe through merit.

COLLIER, JOE (*The Man Within*). Fat and huge, he is one of Carlyon's smugglers. When several crew members were arrested, Collier escaped. Collier accompanies Carlyon to Elizabeth's cottage, tortures her, and escapes after she kills herself.

COLLINS ("The Blessing"). He is a United Press reporter. Although dispatched to cover the Archbishop's blessing of the tanks, he stays with Martha in the Grand Hotel and asks Weld phone him if anything unusual occurs at the ceremony. When Weld reports nothing untoward happened, Collins hangs up.

COLLINS (*England Made Me*). Minty reminds Farrant that Collins taught history at Harrow. Farrant pretends he went there.

COLLINS (*The Heart of the Matter*). He and his wife are Louise Scobie's friends now living in South Africa.

COLLINS (*It's a Battlefield*). He is a policeman at the scene of Mrs. Janet Crowle's murder. Superintendent Crosse orders Collins to remain and tidy the place with Jenks.

COLLINS ("Murder for the Wrong Reason"). When Detective-Inspector Mason telephones Scotland Yard, he learns that Collins is on night duty and orders Groves sent to him instead.

COLLINS, ANNIE (*Brighton Rock*). She was a girl Brown remembers from school days. At 13, she was promiscuous and had a baby. Annie remembered her difficulties then; so when she got pregnant again at 15, she committed suicide by putting her head on railroad tracks and waiting for a delayed train.

COLLINS, BEATRICE (*The End of the Affair*). Bendrix finds a program in one of Sarah Miles's books. It says Beatrice recited lines from William Wordsworth at a July 23, 1926, school event.

COLLINS, LADY (*It's a Battlefield*). The Home Secretary's male secretary thinks of Lady Collins, and her Montagu Square abode, when the Leeds prison warder says Jim Drover and his wife Milly were quiet when she visited Jim. Since Lady Collins's husband is imprisoned now, the secretary is likely her lover.

COLLINS, LORD (*It's a Battlefield*). He is serving a five-year prison sentence, evidently for a Stock Exchange crime.

COLLINS, MRS. (*The Heart of the Matter*). She and her husband, now living in South Africa, are Louise Scobie's friends. Louise visits them.

COLLINS, NELLIE ("Murder for the Wrong Reason"). Detective-Inspector Mason recalls her singing at the Old Bedford.

COLLINS, T. (*Brighton Rock*). This is a phony name on one of several empty filing boxes purportedly containing records of the unsuccessful lawyer Drewitt's cases.

COLLINSON, HUBERT ("Murder for the Wrong Reason"). Having blackmailed Detective-Inspector Mason, perhaps because of their mutual interest in Rachel Mann, Collinson got murdered.

COLONEL, THE ("The News in English"). He is a War Office official. Mary Bishop reports details of a code developed by Mary and her husband David. The Colonel uses it when David, broadcasting anti–British propaganda from Germany, simultaneously relays German military information valuable to Britain.

Greene conveys his distaste for out-of-danger wartime officials by saying the Colonel's attractive tweeds make him look as though he just popped into town for a day or so to handle the war.

COLONEL, HERR ("Dream of a Strange Land"). He is the military officer who gets Herr Professor to let him illegally convert his country house into a casino to entertain Herr General. Herr Colonel boasts he's so healthy he shouldn't wear out.

COLONIAL SECRETARY, THE (*The Heart of the Matter*). In the police station, Scobie catches a glimpse of the secretary's wife in a photograph of a bathing party.

COLONIAL TREASURER, THE (*The Heart of the Matter*). Scobie sees the treasurer's wife in a beach-party photograph.

THE COMEDIANS (1966). Novel. (Characters: André, the Archbishop, J. Baxter, Brown, Brown, Brutus, Father Thomas Capriole, Mère Catherine, Cato, Charters, Captain Concasseur, the Dean of Studies, Dechaux, Mme. Dechaux, Alexandre Dubois, Clement Dupont, Hercule Dupont, Dr. François Duvalier, Emil, Fernandez, the General, the General, Geoff, Colonel Gracia, Hamit, Wilbur K. Hochstrudel, H. J. Jones, Joseph, the Comte de Lascot-Villiers, the Comtesse de Lascot-Villiers, Louise, Luigi, Dr. Magiot, Man Friday, Marcel, Mère Merlan, Chick Nelson, Henry S. Ochs, the Papal Nuncio, Petit Pierre, Philipot, Dr. Philipot, Henri Philipot, Mrs. Philipot, Angel Pineda, Luis Pineda, Martha Pineda, the Rector, the Secretary for Public Works, the Secretary for Social Welfare, the Secretary for the Interior, the Secretary for Tourism, the Secretary of Education, the Secretary of State, Mrs. Smith, William Abel Smith, Tin Tin, Schuyler Wilson.)

Part One: Chapter 1: 1. Brown, the narrator, is a British passenger aboard the *Medea*, a passenger-cargo ship from Philadelphia in August, toward Haiti. Others include William Abel Smith, an unsuccessful American vegetarian-ticket candidate for president (1948), and his wife; "Major" Jones, British, with a (phony) letter to a Haitian official; and a British pharmaceutical salesman (Baxter). The Smiths have brought canned food.

2. A neat black named Fernandez, also aboard, heads for Santo Domingo. Brown is returning to a hotel he owns outside Port-au-Prince. And to Martha. The pursar invites the passengers for drinks. They mention Haiti's Tontons Macoute and their rebellious opponents. The Smiths aren't scared. Jones says with a small squad he could bring peace. Brown suggests that Jones and the Smiths stay in his mostly vacant hotel.

3. Brown dozes on deck. Smith comes by, tells Brown he and his wife supported the black Freedom-Rider movement in Tennessee. Brown warns him to proceed to Santo Domingo because the Tontons Macoute, though black, murder blacks. Smith explains their mission — promulgate vegetarianism, eliminate bodily acidity, especially in the war-mongering rich, thus create universal peace. Smith's idealism shames Brown's cynicism. The Dutch captain asks Brown to report anything untoward about Jones, about whom his home office queried him by cable. Brown says he'll observe but not spy on Jones.

4. Over drinks, Jones tells Brown that people are either toffs — well-paid, intelligent, established, responsible — or tarts — witty, flighty, opportunistic, fun-loving. At gin rummy, Jones wins $6 and explains his clever card psychology. He tells war stories, and both Smiths say Smith got votes from conscientious objectors and Anti-Blood Sports League members. Baxter, former air-raid warden, asks whether Smith would fight to protect his wife. Maybe, though sadly.

5. Brown finds the pursar inflating condoms into balloons for the ship's final-night party. They discuss President François Duvalier, Haiti's tyrant. The pursar asks why Brown returned to his endangered hotel. No answer.

6. During dinner, marked by swaying balloons and embarrassment at the Smiths's eating their own supplies of odd foods, the captain is called away. The pursar produces company liquor. The Smiths abstain. Entertainment starts in the salon: kitchen orchestra, chef's song, nervous Baxter's "Warden's Patrol" poem. Fernandez weeps, is comforted by both Smiths, and exits. Others sing "Auld Lang Syne."

7. In his room Brown destroys letters regarding his hotel that government agents shouldn't see. Jones raps, enters, asks if Brown knows any "big boys" in Port-au-Prince. Brown explains where some of Papa Doc's untrusted army officers are, warns Jones about presenting letters of introduction in shaky Haiti. Jones answers enigmatically, recommends "Shut-eye" as the solution for all problems.

Chapter Two. Brown clears Port-au-Prince customs, encounters Petit Pierre, a courageous half-blood journalist, accompanies him by taxi toward the Trianon, Brown's unsold hotel at nearby Pétionville. Brown sees Martha (Pineda), his mistress, in the diplomat-corps car of her husband (Luis Pineda). She drives Brown to the dark Trianon, formerly jumping with tourists and workers. After their three-months' abstinence, they make love. Joseph, Brown's sole employee remaining (limping since the Tontons Macoute broke his hip), reports: Dr. Philipot, Haitian Secretary for Social Welfare, hid here from authorities; Philipot heard Martha's car, feared the Toutons Macoute were coming, slit his throat, lies dead in the hotel's empty swimming pool. Brown orders Joseph to usher the Smiths, arriving, into the John Barrymore Suite, drive Martha home, fetch Dr. Magiot. The Smiths have a letter of introduction to Philipot. Martha and Mrs. Smith notice Philipot's body. Brown says he's a sleeping beggar.

Chapter Three: 1. The narrator's background: Born 1906, Monte Carlo; British parents — the Comtesse de Lascot-Villiers (last revealed name of mother), who abandoned him (after 1918 Armistice); father unnamed (Brown?) — educated at Jesuit College of the Visitation; playing Frère Laurent in French adaptation of *Romeo and Juliet* stirred sexual desires; using fake credentials, won £300 gambling, slept with lady winner; was expelled from college.

2. Brown became a London waiter, did wartime Foreign Office service sending propaganda to Vichy-controlled territory, bought fake paintings from an art student and toured

England selling them, answered his long-silent sick mother's appeal from Haiti to visit, sold out, flew to Kingston and Port-au-Prince.

3. At the Trianon, where his mother was dying, Brown met Petit Pierre, Joseph, and Dr. Magiot. Dying in cheerful resignation, she explained that after quasi-legal maneuvering with the Trianon's owner Dechaux, who put the place in her name, she owned the Trianon outright, because he though younger died. Brown would inherit two-thirds, the rest mostly going to Marcel, her Haitian lover, rooming next-door. Brown determined to make Trianon first-rate. He saw Marcel, when summoned, enter sexually insatiable mamma's room. She died that night. Her will gave Brown 66 shares, Marcel 33, and one each to Magiot and her lawyer, Alexandre Dubois. Although Magiot advised Brown to liquidate and leave, and predicted political problems if an unnamed doctor (Duvalier) came to power, Brown bought out Marcel with a bundle of hundred-dollar bills and remained. At the casino he saw Marcel lose his hundreds. Brown won and first glimpsed Martha Pineda, German, young, dark, nervous, an ambassador's wife, who also won. She said she knew about him, admired his mother, asked for a rendezvous. Next night she secreted him in an embassy car. Under Columbus's statue, near the port, he felt impotent because, as he blurted, later last night he found Marcel, a suicide by hanging in his mother's bedroom. Potency returned to Brown. They became clandestine lovers for a year. His hotel prospered. Brown met, disliked, and feared Martha's fat son Angel Pineda, five. The lovers rented a room over the store of Hamit, a Syrian. They argued about Angel, whom she would lose if she divorced. Martha pleased Brown by getting an embassy chef fired so Brown could hire him; the Trianon cuisine became famous — until political unrest scared tourists away. Brown escaped by air to New Orleans. After four weeks in New York comfort, he returned to Haiti.

Chapter Four: 1. Now. Dr. Magiot removes possible clues from Philipot's body in the pool. He and Brown carry it to Magiot's car. Evading a Toutons Macoute patrol, they deposit Philipot, an unsuspicious suicide, behind a bougainvillea in a seedy neighborhood.

2. At breakfast the Smiths say they saw Joseph clean the pool and intend presenting their plan for a vegetarian cooking center to Philipot. Or his successor, Brown suggests, changes being frequent. Petit Pierre enters with his morning newspaper column, reporting the arrivals of Smith, narrowly defeated by Truman (1948), and the Trianon owner, but not of Jones, who, Petit Pierre tells Brown, has been arrested. Against Petit Pierre's advice, Brown complains to the British chargé, a sickly fellow who says he'll protest, but cautiously, since America is supplying arms to Haitian rebels via Santo Domingo. After Smith finishes swimming in the pool, Brown reports about Jones. Smith promises help, fearlessly.

3. Brown takes Smith to an exhibition building where are located the office of the Secretary of State and offices of foreign ambassadors not yet recalled. Brown glimpses Martha's husband Luis Pineda. Brown demands to see the Secretary, whom he tells Smith to bribe with $200 — in case Jones has hurt any policemen in a scuffle.

4. Next afternoon Brown and Smith wait before the hidden eyes of a Tontons Macoute sergeant, then see Jones, whose face reveals a beating. Brown writes a letter to a Tontons Macoute officer, gets Smith to bribe the sergeant $20 to deliver it.

Chapter Five: 1. Next day Joseph reports that Philipot's body was found, caused ambassadorial unrest, was taken to a funeral parlor. Smith, whose pollyanna essay about Jones's treatment, which Brown critiques helpfully, insists on joining Philipot's cemetery-bound cortège. Clement and Hercule Dupont, twin funeral directors, drive Philipot's coffin in their hearse near the Trianon, accompanied by magnificently stony Mme. Philipot and her little boy, who wants ice cream. Brown, the Smiths, and Joseph observe. Tontons Macoute arrive, stop everything, and one (Captain Concasseur) shoves Mrs. Smith when she protests. Smith can do nothing. Brown stares recklessly. Concasseur breaks the hearse glass and extracts Philipot's coffin. Joseph whispers that Duvalier may convert Philipot's corpse into an office ghost-buster. The Duponts and the Philipots have Trianon ice cream. Smith feeds his wife something vegetarian and tells Brown he'll destroy his article and lecture on Haiti when home again in Wisconsin.

2. Brown attends an evening embassy function. He chats with Luis Pineda. Hamit approaches, then dead Philipot's nephew Henri Philipot, then Martha. Young Philipot talks about wanting a Bren gun to assassinate Papa Doc, his Tontons Macoute head (Colonel Gracia), and his palace-guard colonel. Brown recommends Jones, who he says was battered by the police and professes combat experience. Luis says let's all be comedians, not real-life sufferers. Martha says she smells of mumps-sick Angel's vomit, is no comedian. Angel wants Brown to visit him. Martha takes Brown upstairs. Angel plays a puzzle, cheats to win, and tells Brown the two can keep secrets. Brown tries to lure Martha into a nearby bedroom. She says no, embraces him, suddenly surrenders; reminded of dead Philipot's posture, he can't achieve; she promises a later rendezvous. Downstairs, Brown bids Luis good-night.

3. Frustrated and blaming Martha, Brown drives to Mère Catherine's brothel. A Tontons Macoute is asleep outside. Brown enters, is told his favorite prostitute, Tin Tin, is occupied. Concasseur, also there, says he's brought an important white customer to Tin Tin. Over rum, Concasseur and Brown needle each other — about Haitian capitalism, anti–Communist Haitian peasants, American protection in case of trouble. Brown suddenly recalls Petit Pierre's telling him Concasseur filched American equipment to build a chic ice rink that failed. Brown reminds Concasseur of it and is scared when Concasseur fingers his revolver. Suddenly Tin Tin and Jones emerge. Jones is confident again, says trouble's over, transport's arranged. Departing, Brown warns him against Concasseur. Tin Tin, outside, tells Brown that Jones made her laugh.

Part Two: Chapter 1: 1. On their way to the new Secretary for Social Welfare, Brown gets Smith away from beggars at the post office. The new official equivocates regarding Philipot, maleficent and body missing, and the Dupont twins' arrest. Smith explains his plan for his non-profit vegetarian center — with restaurant, library, auditorium, theater, etc., and 20 or more workers. Brown finds Smith's unrooted dreaminess astonishing. The welfare secretary phrases his on-sight pay-off discreetly and suggests Smith write home for cash. Smith is encouraged.

2. Martha drives to the Trianon to tryst with Brown. With the Smiths unexpectedly staying up, the lovers try beside the dark pool. Reluctant again, Brown confesses Philipot killed himself there. With unique joy, they talk about her Nazi German father, hanged by the Americans; Brown's and Luis's Jesuit education and politics.

3. Next day the welfare secretary takes Smith, Brown, and a Tontons Macoute to the dusty plain where Duvalierville is planned. He presents little but a cockpit, askew housing, broken machinery, and puffery. A legless man shows a statuette. Smith purchases it. The soldier fingers his gun belt. Smith's disillusioned request to be driven back depresses the secretary.

4. At the Trinon, Smith confers with his wife while the British chargé awaits Brown. Soon to be transferred, the chargé says Jones has persuaded authorities he wants to do business with Duvalier, has a Tontons Macoute driver, and is rooming at the Villa Créole, where Concasseur stays. Brown and the chargé fear for Jones. Young Philipot, suddenly appearing, tells Brown he consulted Jones about getting Bren guns and some training, to attack Duvalier's forces. When Jones was evasive, Philipot let the Villa Créole guard see him, to make the Tontons Macoute distrust Jones. Smith says they'll stay longer.

5. Saturday. Philipot declines Brown's dinner invitation. Magiot comes, so Brown can introduce the Smiths. They discuss American election methods, vegetarianism, crimes around Duvalierville; Magiot expatiates on Catholicism, Voodoism, Communism, Cuba, rebellion, American power, martyrdom.

Chapter Two: 1. Past midnight. Brown promised to drive Joseph up a mountain past Kenscoff to an hours-long Voodoo ceremony, financed by a rich man. The event includes rums, fire in brazier on earthen floor, priest, Latin prayers, sacrificial cock, invocation of Voodoo gods, including warriors' god. Joseph brandishes a machete, drinks, and seemingly endangers Philipot, who is there and whose arm has been purified by scorching fire. Brown returns to the Trianon.

2. Pre-dawn. Concasseur leads a squad to ransack the Trianon, seeking Joseph. It seems some rebels attacked a police station, killed one

policeman, took weapons from the rest, and scared them away. When Brown unsatisfactorily answers Concasseur's queries about Joseph's whereabouts, Philipot's actions, and "Colonel" Jones's plans, a Tontons Macoute slugs Brown, another kicks him, and he wets himself. Suddenly Mrs. Smith, in hair-curlers, bellows in self-taught French that Concasseur is *dégoutant,* demands to see *votre warrant,* and after more mangled French forces the enemy out, laughing in embarrassment.

3. Afternoon. Luis is in South America for a week. Martha sleeps with Brown in his bedroom. They feel peaceful, away from horrors outside. The Smiths notice Brown escorting Martha to her car. Returning, Brown is told by Mrs. Smith, unexpectedly charitable, that she would have liked to know Martha better, and is tearfully told by Smith that he realizes the Home Secretary and his cronies were intent on shaking him down and not planning any vegetarian center.

Chapter Three: 1. Next evening. On the way to the plane flying the Smiths to Santo Domingo, Brown lets them stop downtown, scatter money, but see the slightly crippled take it from the severely crippled, and policemen converge. That night Brown visits Jones at the Villa Créole. Elated at gin-rummy victory over a treasury worker, Jones offers Brown a martini, romances about his military episodes, says he saw and could help Philipot, and offers Brown a share in a $250,000 scam to trick Concasseur. Diabolically tempted, Brown listens as Jones says Brown could shed his endangered hotel, take his share, build elsewhere in the Caribbean or Bora-Bora, while Jones dreams of creating a ritzy golf course, with clubhouse, bar, girls. He knows just where.

2. Brown drives to the casino, sees an Italian electrician win a little, bets, and sees the pursar of the *Medea,* docked again. The pursar says Baxter died of a heart attack, was buried by Fernandez, who is a Santo Domingo undertaker. Brown drives the pursar to the *Medea,* declines to have a drink aboard, and mentions Jones's offer, which he will refuse. Rain.

Part Three: Chapter 1: 1. In his room, Brown dreams of being refused communion. Jones awakens him, says Concasseur went to Miami, discovered Jones's dishonest scam, and is back gunning for him. Brown drives Jones to the *Medea.* They awaken the captain. As a gold-toothed policeman approaches, the captain saves Jones's life by hiding him in his cabin lavatory and telling the policeman no passenger named Jones is aboard his ship and that *"vous êtes en Hollande."* The policeman leaves. The pursar dresses Jones as a woman from the ship's theatrical-box costumes. Brown drives Jones to Luis's ambassadorial residence, mistakenly thinking Luis is still away. Fearing Brown plans to grab his wife, Luis is relieved to offer Jones refugee status. Enter Martha, laughing.

2. Brown drives to his empty Trianon, has a lonely drink, misses Joseph's limping step, and broods self-pityingly on his countrylessness, and being in terror-stricken Haiti by chance.

Chapter Two: 1. For parts of 10 days at the Trianon, Brown and Martha make love, discuss religion, and quarrel, because she and Angel both like Jones. Three weeks later they quarrel anew, because Jones likes the Pineda dog Don Juan, and they fuss about Jones, who has charmed Martha and whose danger from Duvalier scares her. Brown is jealous of Jones. Martha retorts that Brown assigns false dramatic roles to everyone and hints that this makes him as murderous as her Nazi father.

2. Magiot drives up, awakens Brown, and wants companionship, saying most Haitian physicians have purchased exit permits and escaped. He expatiates on corrupt American political bulwarking of Duvalier against Communists like himself, as it did with (the late) Trujillo (earlier in Santo Domingo [Rafael Leonidas Trujillo Molina [1891–1961]). Magiot says Hamit is missing and the rebels, like Philipot and Joseph, are uselessly brave as guerrillas without experienced leadership. Magiot happily recalls Brown's courageous, fun-loving mother. Brown says all he wants is to run his Trianon profitably and maybe have a girlfriend. Magiot reports that Philipot wants to establish a training base for his 40 or more rebels, near the Dominican border. Countering Brown's criticism of Jones, Magiot wonders if Jones could provide leadership. Petit Pierre approaches. Magiot vanishes. Petit Pierre says Concasseur was shamed in Miami about Jones, therefore wants to kill him. Petit Pierre adds that Pineda, in whose embassy Jones has sanctuary, may be replaced.

3. Brown visits the Pinedas. Jones is there. Brown tells Luis that Hamit may need diplomatic assistance. When Pineda professes inability to oppose Concasseur, Jones, needled by Brown, boasts he can rescue Hamit, says Philipot asked for assistance, and foolishly agrees to have Brown help him leave sanctuary for guerrilla work. Returning to Magiot, Brown formulates plans to spirit Jones to Philipot.

4. Brown gets police permission to drive to Les Cayes. That afternoon Martha visits him, and they make love. They discuss his foolhardy plan to take Jones to Les Cayes, his pretended suspicion she sleeps with likeable Jones, and the unlikelihood of their own future together. Heavy rain. Brown says he hates Concasseur, the Tontons Macoute, Papa Doc, and thinks Jones possibly can fight. Martha will help Jones escape the embassy.

5. Brown receives a letter from Smith, in Santo Domingo. The Smiths met Fernandez, whose sick mother Mrs. Smith improved by vegetarianism. The Smiths hope to start a center there. Brown learns that Hamit has been murdered, Mère Catherine's girls are scared, Mme. Philipot and her child are in the Venezuelan embassy. Magiot invites Brown to dinner. They formulate plans for Brown to get Jones to a cemetery rendezvous with Philipot and others. Brown will proceed to Les Cayes. Magiot will treat Angel for mumps, as an alibi.

Chapter Three: 1. Next day Martha writes Brown: Jones is sick. On Sunday two days later, Concasseur sees Brown, reminds him his pass to Les Cayes permits one night there. They fence verbally, mainly about Jones. Brown looks at the few Haitian paintings still hanging at the Trianon, then visits the empty Barrymore suite, his mother's altered room, Marcel's too.

2. Brown visits Martha. Luis is absent. They quibble about Jones, who is dressed for escape and whom Brown suspects of sleeping with her. Her affirmative he only half believes.

3. Brown drives Jones south in heavy rain, past unmanned police posts, through Petit Goave. They swig Brown's whisky and climb into the hills. Queried, Jones says Martha was a remarkable "lay," then naps. They break an axle and a headlight on a boulder. They walk to the rendezvous point — a hut in the cemetery near Aquin — to await Philipot. Brown can take a daytime bus from Aquin to Les Cayes. Jones? He's on his own. They bivouac in the cemetery. Jones confesses he lied about almost everything, from military service to Martha. They share a sandwich and nap. Before dawn, Brown walks forth but is captured by Concasseur, lies to protect Jones, who, however, appears and is grabbed. Suddenly materializing, Philipot shoots Concasseur, while Joseph kills the driver and begins extracting his gold teeth. Jones vomits, secretly.

Chapter Four: 1. Brown, safe in Santo Domingo for a month now, gets a car through Fernandez and via Smith's introduction drives to see Schuyler Wilson, a fat American working at a bauxite mine. Wilson needs a catering manager. Brown, applying, isn't hired once he praises Haitian insurgents.

2. Brown, back at a hotel near Santo Domingo the town and awaiting Smith, recalls his last few weeks. He saw Jones with Philipot, went next day with Joseph to the frontier, spent 11 days with him, parted from him and got to Santo Domingo and a hotel. Smith happened by in Fernandez's car, pressed $1,000 on him, told him Fernandez needed an assistant undertaker, said Martha and Angel were in town and Luis was assigned to Lima.

Behold Brown driving by jeep to seek work at a Monti Cristo fruit company. Past Juan and Eilias Pinas, he is halted at a frontier military post and told by a friendly lieutenant that soon after he crossed from Haiti 20 guerrillas also crossed. Brown pauses, muses on his Jesuit-trained conscience eased by his feeling rootless, sees insurgent stragglers, including Philipot, with a broken arm, a walking-wounded guerrilla named Emil, and dead, stretcher-borne Joseph. Philipot extols brave Jones, also dead. Brown drives Philipot and Emil to San Juan.

4. Mass is held for Joseph, the three dead insurgents, and presumably non-Catholic Jones, attended by Brown, Martha, weeping Angel, the Smiths, and Fernandez. Martha addresses Brown: Tontons Macoute, calling Magiot a Castro agent, killed him; she leaves for Lima tomorrow; will you write? Certainly. He has dinner with the Smiths and Fernandez. A letter comes mysteriously from Magiot, expressing love for Brown's mother, reviling the Establishment for atrocities to Jews, Catholics, and Communists, praising fighters for the *mystique*

not the *politique* of their beliefs (such as Catholicism and Communism) and for preferring blood on hands rather than Pilate's water. Brown becomes Fernandez's junior partner dealing with bereaved French- and English-speaking families of "the dignified and disciplined" dead.

Norman Sherry summarizes Greene's trips to Haiti. When Greene first visited Haiti (1954), tourism was flourishing and he met Aubelin Jolicoeur, a journalist who arranged for him to witness a voodoo ceremony, who introduced him to Georgette John-Charles, the model for Mère Catherine, and who himself was the model for Petit Pierre. Greene returned to Haiti (June 1956), staying at the Oloffson Hotel, on which he patterned Brown's Trianon. During his third visit (August 1963), he returned to the Oloffson. While visiting near Haiti a final time (1964), he observed Dominican-border activities. According to Sherry, Greene wrote *The Comedians* off and on (mostly December 1964–June 1965). Cedric Watts reports a quick 60,000-copy success. Marie-Françoise Allain records that Greene told her he began *The Comedians* "with the intention ... to fight the horror of Papa Doc's dictatorship." Daphna Erdinast-Vulcan explicates the title *The Comedians:* "Brown believes that he disparages the characters in his story, himself included, when he calls them 'comédiens.'" Erdinast-Vulcan adds that Brown derogates the two types of comedians—ones who disguise themselves by role-playing, and those involved in comedies—by affirming Brown's twin awarenesses that life is a comedy, which itself is "an inferior art form," and that individual lives are directed by some sort of practical-joking authority. Incidentally, the words "comedian[s], " "comedy," and varieties thereof appear 21 times in the novel. A. F. Cassis bluntly calls *The Comedians* "black comedy at its best."

R. H. Miller notes that, "[t]rue to the realism of Greene's political narratives, ... Brown provides just the right perspective on the political situation in Haiti. An outsider and a European, he gives readers 'Western eyes,' through which, like him, they can be horrified at what transpires in this novel, from the death of Dr. Philipot at its opening to the death of Jones at its close." Gene D. Phillips suggests that *The Comedians* is unified by "the underlying theme of commitment" and by "Brown's reactions" as he witnesses several characters' "various" responses to challenges. Incidentally, a smaller unifying thread also helps to knit the novel: Brown mentions reading Henry James's short story "A Great Good Place," which concerns a frenzied person's dream escape to a quiet haven (where his servant is named Brown). The words of James's title are played with four times later in *The Comedians,* finally when Jones says the rocky plain where he is going to die is "a good place." Neil McEwan makes two generalized statements, hardly credible but provocative: "Most of the plot concerns Jones's attempt to pose as an arms dealer and defraud Papa Doc"; and "[a]lthough the Smiths' story is a subplot, they are the heart of the novel." Dorothea L. L. Barrett finds enough evidence in *The Comedians* and other Greene novels to conclude that "the affinities and antitheses of Communism and Catholicism constitute a central issue in modern political history and intellectual life."

Before *The Comedians* was published, MGM bought film rights and hired Greene to adapt it for the screen (1967). Phillips reports that Greene told him he was tempted to decline the offer, since he had to cut the flashbacks and also avoid narrating his plot from Brown's unique point of view. Phillips explains how Greene altered the end action: Brown and Jones await Philipot in cemetery; Jones confesses fibbing about military adventures and receives mock absolution; Concasseur appears, kills Jones, is killed by Philipot; Brown replaces Jones, finds guerrillas, harangues them as ragged bastards in English only Philipot understands, will lead them although he is uncommitted to their cause and combat inexperience. Quentin Falk says "the film had everything an MGM big budget could offer—star cast (including [Richard] Burton at $750,000 and [Elizabeth] Taylor at $500,000), exotic settings and lavish production values." Falk praises several members of the cast: Burton, for "the right sort of world-weariness and cynicism as Brown"; Alec Guinness, "just right" as Jones; Peter Ustinov, "low-key as the cuckolded ambassador"; Lilian Gish and Paul Ford, "the rapidly disillusioned Smiths descend[ing] with dignity"; and James Earl Jones, "excellent" as Magiot. Still, Falk concludes that the result is "perhaps the most disappointing of all

Greeneland excursions on film," partly because "Taylor was a mistake." Greene never wrote a film script based another of his novels. Yvonne Cloetta* presents evidence that the Haitians were grateful to Greene for writing *The Comedians*. David Parkinson tells why Greene never adapted another of his novels for the big screen. (Sources: Allain, 78; Barrett, 119–20; Cassis, 24; Cloetta, 102–03; Erdinast-Vulcan, 74; Falk, 155, 161; McEwan, 91, 93; Miller, 117–18; Parkinson, xxxvi-xxxvii; Phillips, 172, 175, 182; Sherry III, 337–43 passim; Watts, 75–76)

COMFORT (*Travels with My Aunt*). Augusta tells Henry she once knew a girl named Comfort. Comfort fell in love with a coward named Courage, married a man named Payne, and killed herself in a comfort station.

COMMANDANT, THE (*Rumour at Nightfall*) see **DIAZ, GENERAL**

COMMANDER-IN-CHIEF, THE (*The Quiet American*). Fowler complains that after casualties are removed, he and other reporters will be flown safely to Hanoi to hear a speech by the Commander-in-Chief. The officer also sends a two-star general to Phat Diem to represent the French government at peasant-quieting religious festivals.

COMMISSIONER, THE (*A Burnt-Out Case*). Rycker reminds his wife Marie that Mme. Guelle, Governor Guelle's wife, was displeased at an earlier function when Marie committed a breach of etiquette in front of the Commissioner's wife.

COMMISSIONER, THE ("Dream of a Strange Land"). According to Herr Colonel, the Commissioner once said that the only wars Herr Colonel's country ever fought were fought by his men.

When Herr Colonel, smarting at the jibe, wonders to Herr Professor how crime can relate to war, Greene is obviously complaining about the unsavory interrelationships of crime, war, and politics.

COMMISSIONER, THE (*The Heart of the Matter*). He is Scobie's superior in the police office. He tells Scobie he won't be promoted to commissioner when he, age 53, resigns. He sends Scobie to Bamba to look into Pemberton's suicide. Although the commissioner trusts Scobie, he grills him when Tallit is suspected of diamond smuggling. Finally, he tells Scobie he will be promoted to commissioner, but by then Scobie is fatally entangled in problems.

COMMISSIONER OF POLICE, THE (*A Burnt-Out Case*). In Colin's parable, this official sees the Greek discourage his clerk's licentiousness by deliberately running over him.

CON (*Orient Express*). She is a cousin of Mabel Warren. Mabel writes her a letter because, she writes, she has nothing better to do on the train.

CONCASSEUR, CAPTAIN (*The Comedians*). He is a Tontons Macoute officer. He tortures Jones, steals Dr. Philipot's hearsed coffin, shoves Mrs. Smith, orders Brown slugged and otherwise threatens him, and follows him to the rendezvous with the insurgents, only to be shot by Dr. Philipot's nephew Henri Philipot.

The word *concasseur* in French means "steamroller." Norman Sherry says Captain Concasseur is based on Major Franck Romain, a trusted killer employed by François Duvalier. (Source: Sherry III, 321)

CONDER (*It's a Battlefield*). He is a persistent crime reporter, short, bald, aging, and liberal. He collects foreign coins and currency. He fibs that he's married, with six children, whereas he rents a bed-sittingroom in a building where Jules Briton is a waiter. Conder seeks information about the Streatham Common murder; attends a Communist meeting with Jules, where he sees and fears Bennett, a Communist there; pumps Milly for information about her husband Jim Drover; and tries unsuccessfully to interview Rose, the murdered policeman Arthur Coney's widow.

R. H. Miller notes that Greene's depiction of Conder makes use of his own "experiences working for the *Nottingham Journal* and the *Times*." (Source: Miller, 23)

CONEY, ARTHUR (*It's a Battlefield*). He was a policemen participating in crowd control during the Communist riot at Hyde Park.

When he threatened Milly Drover with a truncheon, her husband Jim Drover stabbed him fatally.

CONEY, ROSE (*It's a Battlefield*). She is Arthur Coney's abused wife, 10 years her husband's elder. When Milly Drover, Arthur's wife's killer, asks her to sign a reprieve petition, Rose is so timid and befuddled that she does so.

THE CONFIDENTIAL AGENT (1939). Novel. (Characters: the Ambassador, Joe Bates, Dr. Bellows, Lord Benditch, Arthur Bennett, George Bennett, Mrs. Bennett, Tony Blue, Brigstock, Miss Carpenter, Chubby, Clara, Conway, Crikey, Else Crole, Monty Crookham, Rose Cullen, Captain Currie, D., Mrs. D., Fennick, Lord Fetting, First Secretary, Forbes, Fortesque, Frankie, Emily Glover, Goldstein, Sir Terence Hillman, Hogpit, George Jarvis, Joe, Joey, K., L., Dr. Li, the Liberal, Mrs. Marie Mendrill, Lady Mersham, the Minister of the Interior, Mr. Muckerji, Nell, Peters, Pig, Row, Sally, the Second Secretary, Spot, Mrs. Terry, Conway Tearle, Tony, Peter Triffen, the Undersecretary for Overseas Trade, Winifred, Z.)

Part I: The Hunted: One. Dover, late-autumn evening. D., 45, a confidential agent for the common people in his country's civil war, docks, sees L., an aristocratic agent for the other side, and chances to meet Rose Cullen, just after his passport, with out-of-date photo, was checked and she was fined by customs for bringing in brandy. Rose, 20, is the spoiled daughter of coal-baron Lord Benditch, whom D. is to consult secretly about buying coal for his compatriots. Rose gives D. a lift to London in a hired Packard. It develops a flat tire. They stop at a roadhouse for repairs and dinner. L. appears. In the lavatory, D. is about to be attacked by L's thuggish chauffeur that D. caught looking for his credentials (hidden in his sock) when Captain Currie, the roadhouse owner, enters. Rose doesn't believe D.'s partial explanation about himself. He declines a £2,000 bribe from L. Seeing Rose drinking with others, D. leaves her a message, takes her Packard, and leaves.

Forty miles from London, a Daimler blocks D. Currie drives up. With Rose drunk in the back seat, L. watches his chauffeur slug D. Failing to find his credentials, they seize the Packard, leave D's wallet and toilet case, and let him hitchhike to London.

Two. London, 6:00 a.m. D. reports to a shabby Bloomsbury hotel, is taken to room 35 by Else (Crole), the sweet, skinny servant, 14, of the mean manageress (Mrs. Marie Mendrill). A message orders D. to the Entrenationo Language Centre. He naps, asks Else to lock his room, reports to Dr. Bellows, idealistic founder of the Centre, and meets K., his shabby, ill-paid contact (from D.'s country), who loudly tutors him on Entrenationo, whom D. briefs about last night's actions, including L.'s offered bribe, and who softly tells D. that Bellows holds Saturday office soirées and reminds D. he must leave England Monday. D. returns to his room. Else, devoted to D. because he speaks considerately to her, reveals that Mrs. Mendrill searched his room and gave Else a week's notice for objecting. Else says she could be a maid for her prostitute friend Clara. Rose, who got D's hotel name from his dropped diary, phones him to meet at Russell Square Station at 7:00 and dine with her. Promising to help Else more than Clara could, D. gives the child his credentials to hide in her stocking, and rests.

D. walks to meet Rose, is lured into a mews by a begging decoy, is shot at but missed, then finds Rose. She says she told Currie about their date and gives D. his diary, which Currie had, but disbelieves much that D. tells her—until she finds the bullet that missed him. They have brandy and sandwiches in a pub. D. asks Rose to employ Else somehow, discourses on his duty to aid his amoral country's downtrodden, and says he lectured on medieval French and discovered the Berne MS of *Song of Roland,* better than either the Oxford and the Venice versions because it establishes Oliver as more heroic than glory-seeking Roland. Rose, hardly following, says her father resembles Roland. D. calls L. a traitor like the epic's Ganelon. Rose takes D. to a movie they abandon before the predictable ending. D. thinks K. is following them. She drops D. at his hotel by taxi, feels immature love toward him, dislikes his commitment to duty, won't hire Else, wants to go to his room with him. No. He kisses her, departs, and is told by Else that Mrs. Mendrill is in her den with a man (K.). Mrs. Mendrill produces a letter saying their superiors order D. to surrender his credentials. No. She hits him. Else pseudo-naively enters and gets D. to his room. He promises freedom for her tomorrow.

Three. Morning. Else tells D. about Mr. Muckerji, an Indian lodger who questions people and writes down their answers (for a mass-observation agency). D. tells Mrs. Mendrill he'll pay for Else's week's wages and take her away tonight. D. waves at the smiling girl. After Muckerji quizzes him trivially, D. heads for Lord Benditch's address. Approaching Knightsbridge, D. sees Currie, who walks him to Benditch's Chatham Terrace mansion, points out L.'s chauffeur, suggests D. go shake hands with him. No. Currie leaves.

A servant takes D's coat and presents him to big, hairy-handed Benditch, whose advisors are Forbes, Lord Fetting, and Brigstock, all of whom Rose told D. about. While Fetting sleeps, Brigstock dickers coal-sales terms. Benditch asks for D.'s credentials as his country's agent. Missing. D. says Rose can vouch for him. The coal dealers delay. L. waits outside, gloats as D. is dismissed, but seems worried. Benditch summons L. Rose enters, surprised to see D., who says the servant filched his papers. Rose orders Forbes to come out, tells him to help D. Forbes, long wanting to marry her and eager to open idle coal mines he controls, agrees. The three drive to D.'s country's embassy, where D. says the honest Second Secretary under the untrustworthy Ambassador may help. But the First Secretary tells Forbes the Second Secretary has moved away, disbelieves Forbes's comments about D., and says D.'s passport isn't D.'s. Rose, convinced of D.'s sincerity, identifies a certain book by D. in the embassy. The First Secretary, now armed, says rebels executed that author. The phone rings, and the First Secretary holds D. for questioning about a certain girl's death.

Four. Detectives arrive, say Miss Crole was murdered. She was Else. D. blames himself. Neither Rose nor Forbes can help. The detectives reveal this; Muckerji saw Else take down one of her stockings in D.'s presence; her diary says a man will take her away forever. Suicide pact. D. answers their questions, blames Mrs. Mendrill and K., quietly vows vengeance, is led out. He slugs the First Secretary, takes his gun, threatens everyone, tells Rose he gave an inscribed copy of his Berne MS study to the British Museum, hides in an empty basement flat nearby and occupied according to the address marker by (Emily) Glover, shaves his moustache to alter his appearance, and vows to become the hunter.

Part II: The Hunter: One. After a cornershop breakfast, D. goes to his hotel, shouts he is Muckerji, is admitted by Mrs. Mendrill's voice, spies on the room where dead Else lies; hears Rose's friend Clara lie to Mrs. Mendrill, then hides and hears Mrs. Mendrill talking with K., who is painting over evidence where Else struggled while Mrs. Mendrill pushed her out her window. D. also hears Mrs. Mendrill talking with Muckerji, who says a witness saw her and Else there. Mrs. Mendrill sees D. in a mirror and lets him follow K. out. On to Bellows's soirée. While watching K., D. phones Benditch's home, obtains Rose's number, phones her, gives her his Glover address, tells her he must kill Else's killer, and learns Forbes has contracted to sell L. coal. D. forces K. into the street, follows him by taxi, and when he causes a commotion tells a policeman near Marble Arch that K. is drunk and has the policeman get K. into his taxi, over objections from a witness named Hogpit.

Two. D. takes K. into Emily Glover's empty flat, grills him, learns L. bribed Mrs. Mendrill and K., and backs him into the bathroom. While K. jabbers about Entrenationo, how he thought D. sold out, and having six months to live, D. fires one of the gun's last two bullets but misses. Rose, suddenly at the door, says L.'s coal from Benditch et al. will be shipped via neutral Holland (really on to L.'s country). D. suggests appealing to the miners, though idle a year, not to send coal to L.'s soldiers. They check K. Dead of a heart attack.

Three. D. and Rose, loving him now, kiss. He feels love for her but no desire, instead gratitude for her patience and trustworthiness. Miss Glover's neighbor Fortescue rings, is admitted. Rose explains they're partying in Emily's absence. She deflects his concern about K., placed on the divan, "ill." Fortescue leaves.

Part III: The Last Shot: One. Sunday, pre-dawn. D., up alone from Euston Station by train, is at Willing in the Midlands, waiting for a connection to Benditch, a town beside Benditch's mines. D. talks with a lame old porter, then proceeds with the porter's friend George

Jarvis to Benditch. Jarvis tells D. where Mrs. Bennett lives. Mrs. Bennett, once Rose's nurse, reminisces about her and reluctantly gives him the address of Joe Bates, the union leader. But Bates is at the Red Lion inn, with L. and Benditch's agent. The people cheer at news from Bates that the mines will reopen for coal for Holland. L., whom D. resists killing with his gun, tells D. that Miss Glover and Fortescue found K., possibly murdered, perhaps can identify D., whom he loudly calls a criminal. Shouting "Comrades," D. tells the crowd that the coal is going to his country's anti-labor regime, which their union pledged not to supply. D. evades the fat constable, escapes over a wall, and is hidden in a shed by "the Gang," including three underaged anarchists, who watched D. at the Red Lion. D. surrenders his gun, to use to shoot the lock off a shed, where they will get dynamite to blow up the mines.

Two. At 7:00 p.m., by prearrangement with "the Gang," D. emerges, tired, hungry, and apprehensive, to meet Crikey, a Gang member, at the Chapel wall, past which a choir's hymns roll. Crikey is to take him by bus to safety in nearby Woolhampton. But a sudden explosion exposes D., and the police capture and jail him. Fed in welcome comfort, he learns he's to be escorted to London.

Part IV: The End: One. D. is a prisoner in London. But neither Fortescue nor Hogpit can identify him; and Forbes has hired Sir Terence Hillman to represent him, with help from a brisk solicitor, who tells D. that his passport has been validated, and Mrs. Mendrill confessed to killing Else and is adjudged insane. Hillman gets a remand, with D. out on bail, of £2,000. Forbes, who provided it, drives D., after a quick stop at Forbes's mistress Sally's abode, to the Lido, a Southcrawl hotel Forbes owns. En route, Forbes says this: Forbes kept Rose from the court; Rose will marry him; a motorboat will take D. to a tramp steamer heading for D.'s country with food; the Benditch explosion caused Benditch and associates to cancel L.'s coal contract for fear of governmental action. In the hotel recreation room, Currie appears and announces D. is wanted for murder, as the hotel's newspapers indicate.

Two. Currie and some drunks hold D. for the police, summoned by phone. Two heavies appear, bundle D. in a car, drive him to a motorboat, which whisks him to the steamer in offshore darkness. Surprisingly, Rose, who says Forbes rejected her, is already aboard. She agrees D. may be dead soon but they have, ah, the meantime.

(Cedric Watts reminds scholars less thorough than he that the original British edition of *The Confidential Agent* concludes with a three-line paragraph, all of which Greene deleted from later editions, and which ends with D. feeling that "trust seemed to be returning to the violent and suspicious world.")

Stimulated by benzedrine daily, Greene wrote *The Confidential Agent* in the mornings of six weeks (April-May 1939), for the express purpose of potboiling a thriller for family cash. Even so, as David Lodge points out, "Greene ... avoided the cruder kind of political simplifications that characterize much of the writing of the thirties ... D. is by no means convinced of his side's ideology" as a pop-thriller's hero should be. From the start Greene was displeased with *The Confidential Agent* and even used the pseudonym Henry Gough in the manuscript. In afternoons of the same period of time, Greene continued writing *The Power and the Glory*. He felt sure that the public would buy thousands of copies of his fast-paced thriller, its action occurring in three frenzied days, while his masterpiece about the whisky priest would make its way more slowly. Michael Shelden reports that the reverse was the case: *The Confidential Agent* gradually sold only 5,000 copies in England, and *The Power and the Glory* by 1941 sold 30,000 copies.

Although Greene barely hints at the fact, the civil war in Europe in the late 1930s in *The Confidential Agent* is the Spanish Civil War (1936–1939). More clearly, D. is fighting for the Republicans, who lost, while L. is fighting for the Nationalists under Francisco Franco (1892–1975), who won. Greene typically excoriates both bellicose sides for viciousness, although his sympathies are with D., who succeeds (or at least doesn't fail) in his mission to England but is probably doomed to an early death back home. Peter Wolfe presents an overarching interpretation of "the D.-L. pairing": "D., representing the underdogs in a civil war, stands for death and ... L. serves the forces of life." Wolfe, however, continues: "[T]he difference between them is not so clear-cut as the life-death dualism first suggests. D. keeps alive under his burden of decay and destruction, and L., dyspeptic and effete, does not stand for vigorous, abounding life."

Warner Brothers purchased film rights to *The Confidential Agent* before it was published (England, September 1939; the United States, October 1939). The novel was timely, because World War II started in Europe in September 1939. The movie (1945) presents rival Spanish Civil War agents in October 1937 and stars Charles Boyer (D., called Denard), Lauren Bacall (Rose Cullen), Katina Paxinou (Mrs. Mendrill, called Mrs. Melandez), and Peter Lorre (K., called Contreras). Gene D. Phillips regards the film as "too sophisticated for the general public and not sophisticated enough for the critical minority." He laments the fact that the movie couldn't be shot on location in London, because of the war, and was mostly filmed in a Hollywood studio. He does, however, praise the lines in the script, which "often have the ring of Greene's original dialogue." David Parkinson reports that Greene planned a movie with Alexander Korda* about a Spanish government agent coming to London during the Civil War and being followed, but that Korda's associates thought the project was too dangerous at the time. (Sources: Greene, *Ways of Escape*, 90–94; Lodge, 17; Parkinson, 701; Phillips, 34, 35; Shelden, 279–80, 284; Sherry II, 13–16; Watts, 46; Wolfe, 89)

CONNELL (*England Made Me*). Minty recalls his schoolmate Connell's death after a one-week bout with scarlet fever and his attending the funeral.

CONNETT, MISS MAY (*This Gun for Hire*). She is Davis's secretary and has an office adjoining his at Midland Steel. She evidently has been intimate with him, because she calls him Willy but stops when she sees him with another person.

CONNOLLY (*The Human Factor*). Castle knew a priest who worked so admirably in the Soweto slums that Castle "half believed" in the priest's God, just as he half-believed in Communism because of Carson's unselfishness.

CONNOLLY (*The Quiet American*). He is Bill Granger's assistant, who at a critical juncture is off in Singapore chasing women. Granger has to stay in Saigon to cover for Connolly or he'll get fired.

CONSTANCE (*This Gun for Hire*). She must be a servant at St. Luke's in Nottwich. The vicar and his wife call for her.

CONSUL, THE (*The Honorary Consul*). Fortnum tells Plarr this Sante Fe official was hospitable and helpful when he and Clara got married.

CONWAY ("The Bear Fell Free"). Carter recalls seeing Conway killed in the trenches during World War I.

CONWAY (*The Confidential Agent*). He is a sweets-loving boy, about seven. His mother encounters D. at the Russell Square underground station and wrongly thinks his apprehension is due to fear of elevators. She tells Conway to let D. hold his sticky hand.

CONWAY (*The Ministry of Fear*). He is Dr. Forester's patient whose murder Forester's labeled suicide.

COOLER, COLONEL (*The Third Man*). He is a crooked American officer, with tired, kind eyes. He is involved in Vienna's black market, first with tires, then in the penicillin scheme masterminded by Harry Lime, whose supposed death he says he witnessed. Cooler gives money to Martins from Harry, is in league with Kurtz, but is let go by Colonel Calloway.

COOPER (*Our Man in Havana*). Wormold tells Hasselbach their mutual friend Cooper has gone home and therefore won't be a guest at Milly Wormold's birthday party.

COOPER ("The Over-night Bag"). He is the dead, week-end baby boy, according to Henry Cooper, whose wife's it is, not his. The child may be fictional.

COOPER, HENRY ("The Over-night Bag"). During his Nice-to-London flight, he tells fellow passenger Tiny that his over-night bag contains a dead baby. He doesn't tell his mother, with whom he lives and who welcomes him home.

Greene obviously has fun giving this unassuming little Henry the same name as that of Henry Cooper (b. 1934), the English heavyweight boxer, and the only man to win three Lonsdale belts, which he did in 1961, 1965, and 1970—1965 being the year Greene published "The Over-night Bag."

COOPER, MAJOR (*The Heart of the Matter*). He is the dentist for the British in Sierra Leone. He sponsors Wilson to become an honorary member of his club.

COOPER, MRS. ("The Over-night Bag"). She is Henry Cooper's mother. The two live together in London. She welcomes him home, questions him about his trip, but isn't told about any dead baby in his over-night bag. While he unpacks, she bakes a shepherd's pie.

A. A. DeVitis says that "events [in the story] are given meaning by the Hieronymus Bosch reproduction" Cooper likes but avoids saying why Cooper's mother doesn't like it. She should, especially when, as DeVitis opines, the toe in the marmalade, mentioned by her son, "adds a further nuance to the morbid obsession that Cooper and his mother share." If both are morbidly obsessed, both should relish Bosch. (Source: DeVitis, 178)

COOPER, MRS. ("The Over-night Bag"). She is Henry Cooper's wife and the mother of the dead baby in his over-night bag; he is not the father. Or both may be creatures of Henry's imagination.

CORAL (*This Gun for Hire*). She is a nubile brunette dancer who appears when Collier orders a rehearsal. Davis looks her over but invites Ruby to lunch.

CORINNE (*The Quiet American*). In the movie Phuong attends at the Catinat theater in Saigon, Corinne is Mme Bompierre's daughter.

CORKERY, PHIL (*Brighton Rock*). He is a former, seemingly unsatisfactory lover of Ida Arnold, who blushes when his first name is spelled by Old Crowe's ouija board. When Ida and Phil meet again in Brighton, she encourages him, even shares a room with him in the Cosmopolitan, but only, or mainly, to force him to help her pursue clues to convict Pinkie.

CORNFORTH, WILLIAM P. (*The Heart of the Matter*). In Wilson's office is a calendar with Cornforth's name, along with his message about honesty and enterprise.

The message is appropriate only in part, whether or not Wilson pays attention to it, because while he professes to be an accountant when he's actually a spy he does tell Scobie's wife Louise he loves her.

CORREDO, DIEGO (*The Honorary Consul*). He is a member of Rivas's gang, who kidnapped Fortnum. Diego, 35, unmarried and asthmatic, and Pablo are fellow Argentinians. Diego worked for Bergman at one time. Diego drives Plarr to Rivas's hut, later deserts, and is shot by the police while he is trying to escape.

COSSA (*Travels with My Aunt*). When Detective-Sergeant Sparrow asks Henry if Augusta ever mentioned Cossa, and also Passerati, Stradano, and Tiberio Titi, Henry says no.

COST (*The Ministry of Fear*). He is a member of the spy ring and has three identities. As Ford, Cost is a tailor at the Pauling and Crosthwaite shop. As Cost, he is a businessman at Mrs. Bellairs's séance and helps fake his own murder to throw Rowe underground. As Travers, Cost awaits supposed books to be delivered by Rowe to a hotel. When Prentice, Rowe, and Davis, the hotel clerk, confront Ford at his shop, he phones Anna Hilfe, expresses his hopelessness, and plunges shears into his throat.

COURAGE (*Travels with My Aunt*). Augusta tells Henry she once knew a man named Courage, who was afraid of mice. A girl named Comfort loved him, married Payne, and committed suicide.

CRAB (*Brighton Rock*). He is a cocky mobster, forced out of town by Kite's gang but back when Colleoni hires him.

In the first edition of *Brighton Rock*, Greene describes Crab as formerly Jewish until a hairdresser and a surgeon changed him. In later versions, Crab is depicted as an ape until altered. Michael Shelden points to this quiet emendation, and others like it, as evidence of Greene's early anti–Semitism and his later fear of being called anti–Semitic. (Source: Shelden, 151–52)

CRABBE (*It's a Battlefield*). He is a poet and is a guest at Lady Caroline Bury's luncheon. Crabbe is passé and suspicious of other guests.

CRABBIN (*The Third Man*). He is the fat young man, fussy, serious, and knowledgeable, who is part of a literary institute in Vienna. When Crabbin mistakes Martins, who writes under the pen name Buck Dexter, for Benjamin Dexter, a significant British writer, he stakes Martins to a week's hotel stay plus meals if he will lecture on the modern novel. The lecture makes for needed but too-protracted comic relief.

CRADBROOKE, LADY (*The Ministry of Fear*). She is a dowager whose name is used on thank-you letters sent by the Free Mothers in gratitude for flour and tea.

CRANBEIM, MRS. (*This Gun for Hire*). She is or was a close friend of Sir Marcus and is privy to secret British government information about the legality of shipping nickel to neutral countries in wartime.

CRANE (*The Name of Action*). He is an American engineer selling illegal weaponry in Coblenz. An amoral businessman, he sold arms to Demassener, Trier's dictator, and now sells revolvers, machine guns, and ammunition to Chant, who is eager to overthrow Demassener.

Greene depicts this American as fat, with tiny eyes and baggy trousers, lustfully outlining Demassener's wife Anne-Marie's curvaceous body with air-groping hands, using bad German to tell anecdotes about Prohibition in the United States, and eager to sell anything to anyone with money. Greene was critical of *The Name of Action* and felt that Crane was the "one redeeming character" in it and deserved a part in *The Quiet American* later — because he was yet another reprehensible American, doubtless. W. J. West notes that Crane "bears more than a passing resemblance to Harry Lime of *The Third Man*," then comments more importantly that Greene "admired American writers such as [John] Dos Passos and Edmund Wilson [and perhaps Stephen Crane?], but here is the first appearance of his hatred of another side of American life." (Sources: Greene, *Ways of Escape,* 21; West, 29)

CRANE, MICHAEL (*Rumour at Nightfall*). He is a British ex-journalist, 33, in Spain for rest and contemplation. Down from Madrid to San Juan, he meets up with active-correspondent Francis Chase, his friend for 10 years. Crane is romantic, spiritually open, and introverted; these traits clash with Chase. Crane's seeing elusive Caveda, the guerrilla sought by Chase, throws the two friends closer. Their both being attracted to Eulelia Monti, however, makes them rivals, especially since Crane is positively influenced by her religious faith, which Chase deplores. Crane marries Eulelia and is betrayed by Chase.

Robert Hoskins oddly regards Crane and Chase as "two halves of a single personality" and yet Chase as Crane's "alter-ego." (Source: Hoskins, 4, 14)

CRANE, MRS. (*Rumour at Nightfall*). She was Michael Crane's mother. He disliked her for being vulgar and grasping, and opposed to travel. An inheritance from her enabled him to visit France, then Spain. His friend Francis Chase, who knew Mrs. Crane, remembers her as interesting and reliable.

CRASHAW, COLONEL ("Proof Positive"). As president of the Psychical Society, he arranges for Major Weaver to lecture to a group of old ladies and fellow retired officers. Despite growing audience disapproval, Crashaw notes some "shrewdness" in Weaver's rambling about the power of the spirit over the flesh and lets him continue.

CRAVEN ("A Little Place off the Edgeware Road"). He is a sick, self-loathing man, close to insanity. He dreams of buried bodies, hopes they won't experience physical resurrection, and prays for his own permanent bodily decomposition. When he attends a silent movie in a theater near Edgeware Road, a man sits beside him, mutters about a murder scene, splatters him with blood, and leaves. Craven telephones the police about the murderer, only to learn that the gory man is the murder victim.

Craven's name suggests a person too cowardly to face reality.

CRAYSHAW (*The Heart of the Matter*). Scobie remembers Crayshaw as a person caught with illegal diamonds, either stolen or smuggled.

CRICHTON (*The Honorary Consul*). He is the British Embassy press attaché. The incoming telephone calls about Fortnum distress him. Crichton attends Plarr's funeral and alerts Fortnum to his being both retired and honored.

CRIKEY (*The Confidential Agent*). The anarchistic Benditch gang tells D. to wait for Crikey, a fellow member and a bus driver, to give him a lift to nearby Woolhampton. D. is apprehended before Crikey can help.

CRIPPEN (*It's a Battlefield*). He is a meticulously clean prisoner the Assistant Commissioner remembers from when they were both in the East.

CROLE, ELSE (*The Confidential Agent*). She is the small, bony, scared maid, 14, under Mrs. Marie Mendrill's thumb at the hotel D. reports to. D. is kind to Else, and she hides his credentials in her stocking. Mrs. Mendrill discharges her for being ultra-loyal to D., who, when he hears she may go and work for a prostitute named Clara, promises to help her. But Mrs. Mendrill kills her and tries to put the blame on D.

When Greene wrote *The Confidential Agent* in the late 1930s, he undoubtedly knew his brother Hugh Greene,* then a correspondent in dangerous Nazi Germany, had his ever-roving eye on actress Tatjana Sais there. But did Greene know that the real name of Hugh's target was Else Neumann, and that she was married? Did he name Else Crole as he did and then kill her off, as a warning to Hugh? Brian Diemert notes how sad it is that Else "sees her relationship with D. in terms of her experience with these texts," i.e., the cheap, trashy, sentimental stories which she reads and which condition her limited response to real-life situations. (Source: Diemert, 149)

CROMBIE, DOCTOR ("Doctor Crombie"). He was the Bankstead school physician. His theory, repeatedly presented in hygiene classes, that sexual activity, including masturbation and even marital love-making, is the leading cause of cancer forced him to resign when kids apprised their parents. Thereafter, he lived on a private income, wrote learned articles rejected by medical journals, and died of pneumonia. The narrator, a Bankstead day-student, was relieved when his father told him that playing by himself with toy trains was safe. Later, the narrator, 60 and married four times, facetiously validates Doctor Crombie's theory by blaming his lung cancer on something more fun than being an inveterate smoker.

CROMPTON, FATHER (*The End of the Affair*). He is a competent priest, compassionate, he says, after 25 years in the confessional. He has a powerful upper body but short legs. Sarah Miles consults with him, without immediately evident satisfaction. He holds his own, logically and politely, when Bendrix tries to undercut his faith.

The family name of Catherine Walston* was Crompton. David Crompton was the full name of both Catherine's father and her brother. One of Catherine's sisters, Belinda Crompton Strait, was so upset by Greene's using the name Crompton that she wrote Catherine in an unsuccessful request to have Greene change it. William Cash reports that the elder David Crompton's older brother and his six children were lost at sea when the *Lusitania,* the Cunard liner, was sunk by a German submarine (1915). A. A. DeVitis, comparing Father Crompton to Father Clay and Father Rank (both in *The Heart of the Matter*), pronounces Father Crompton "a more forceful character." (Sources: Cash, 75; DeVitis, 98; Shelden, 358; Sherry, II, 223, 258, 336, 379)

CROOKHAM, MONTY (*The Confidential Agent*). He is a person whom Captain Currie, when he is about to greet Rose Cullen at the roadhouse near Dover, slips away to go after.

CROOKS (*The Ministry of Fear*). Rowe remembers him as one of several friends who abandoned him after he was tried for killing his wife.

CROSS, ELISABETH ("When Greek Meets Greek"). She is Nicholas Fennick's niece. When the two start a phony school in Oxford called St. Ambrose's College, she meets a student named Frederick Driver. The two outwit both her uncle and his father, Lord Driver, and plan to marry and take over St. Ambrose's.

CROSS, SUPERINTENDENT (*It's a Battlefield*). He works in Scotland Yard, phones the Assistant Commissioner that Mrs. Janet Crowle's murderer has been located, and reluctantly lets him accompany the Flying Squad that apprehends him.

CROSTHWAITE (*This Gun for Hire*). This name is mentioned as involved in the grocery business in Nottwich.

CROWDER (*Travels with My Aunt*). He is a Chicago meat packer who Colonel Hakim tells Augusta was asked by General Abdul for money to promote a scheme in Istanbul. Hakim adds that the CIA surveilled Crowder and a German named Weissmann, also approached by Abdul, and that all three are arrested and talking.

CROWDER, ANNE (*This Gun for Hire*). She is a feisty chorus actress, living in London but having performed in provincial theaters for five years. She has been engaged to James Mather six months, gets a job dancing in *Aladdin* in Nottwich, goes there on the same train with Davis and Raven, and is almost killed by Davis in Acky's and Tiny's bawdy house. Raven saves her. They escape the authorities by hiding in a shed. Thinking Raven can stop a threatened war, Anne promises not to betray him. But when he tells her he murdered the Czech minister and his secretary, she tells the police he's gunning for Sir Marcus. Her conscience bothers her for only a few hours, because an upcoming reward will enable her to marry Mather. (In *A Gun for Sale,* the British title of *This Gun for Hire,* Anne Crowder is called Anne Weaver.)

CROWE ("The Blessing"). He is mentioned as the chief sub-editor handling foreign news at the paper for which Smiley and Weld work.

CROWE (*Brighton Rock*) see **OLD CROWE**

CROWLE, MRS. JANET (*It's a Battlefield*). She was murdered and her dismembered body was found in a trunk in Paddington Station. A man named Ruttledge was arrested but soon released. Scotland Yard personnel track down the real killer.

Michael Shelden points out parallels between Mrs. Crowle's murder and a 1920s murder case in which the victim's body was found in a trunk at the Charing Cross station, and which was solved and the killer tried and executed. (Source: Shelden, 245)

CROWN PRINCE, THE (*England Made Me*). This member of the Swedish royal family is at the opera with his Princess when Krogh and Farrant are present. The Prince is described as having a square, intelligent face.

Gustav VI (1882–1973) began his rule after the death of his father Gustav V (1858–1950). The first wife of Gustav VI was Margaret Victoria Wettin (1882-1920); his second, Lady Louise Alexandrine Mountbatten (1889–1965).

CRUICKSHANK (*The Human Factor*). He is a British defector, who Ivon tells Castle is living comfortably in Moscow.

CUBITT, JOHN (*Brighton Rock*). He is a graying member of Pinkie's Brighton mob. Cubitt's having served time in prison back in 1923 makes him wary. When Pinkie kills Spicer, another mob member, Cubitt deserts Pinkie, tries to find employment in Colleoni's strong gang, is rejected, drinks excessively, and when drunk is lured by Ida Arnold to reveal details of Pinkie's murder of Hale.

CUBITT, MRS. (*Brighton Rock*). John Cubitt's mother, deceased 20 years. Cubitt recalls getting in touch with her once in a Brighton séance, at which time her voice sounded familiarly boozy.

CUDLOW ("The Other Side of the Border"). He was a friend of Hands and Billings. When Hands drops in on Billings in West Africa in 1936, Billings tells him that Cudlow died of yellow fever a year ago.

CULLEN, ROSE (*The Confidential Agent*). She is Lord Benditch's liberal daughter, indulged, alcoholic, and rebellious. D. meets her by chance at Dover when she is stopped at customs. They drive to a roadhouse, near which she sees D. attacked. The two meet in London. She begins to believe in his mission, helps him, begins to be in love with him, persuades Forbes, in love with her, to arrange for D.'s escape out of Southcrawl. When D. boards the tramp steamer, Rose is already there.

Peter Wolfe says that D. "needs Rose ... to escape the police and to restore his humanity," then outrageously wonders whether Greene is punning to the effect that "D. comes to see life through Rose Cullen glasses?" (Source: Wolfe, 88)

CUNDIFER, LADY (*This Gun for Hire*). She buys a hat at a low price at the jumble sale at St. Luke's.

CURLEW, MELANY (*Travels with My Aunt*). She was the wife of Richard Pulling's partner William Curlew, according to Augusta. Augusta tells Henry that Melany was so sexually demanding that poor William indirectly informed her that he was an adulterer. Melany virtuously forgave him and continued to press him.

CURLEW, WILLIAM CROWDER (*Travels with My Aunt*). According to Augusta, this man was so tired of his wife Melany's sexual demands that he and his partner, Henry Pulling's father Richard, wrote her anonymously that William had been unfaithful. Melany generously forgave him and continued with her fatiguing demands.

Curlew the man seems appropriately named, for curlew the bird is noted for having slender parts and possessed of the instinct to migrate.

CURRAN, THE REV. (*Travels with My Aunt*). He was one of Augusta's lovers. An animal trainer, he needed a career change when an elephant mashed one of his toes. He and Augusta started a Brighton dog church. They married dogs, baptized dogs, gave the road-killed absolution, but never countenanced canine divorce. Unable to stop his religious practice, Brighton police exiled him for flirting. Augusta explains "the Rev." merely meant "Revered," and says Curran must be 90 now.

CURRIE, CAPTAIN (*The Confidential Agent*). He owns the roadhouse north of Dover where D. and Rose Cullen stop. Stiff, jolly, and loquacious, Currie appears in the action at times unlucky for D. His attempt to have D. arrested at the Lido fails. Lido girls call him Curly.

CURTIS, TOM (*The Ministry of Fear*). Rowe remembers him as one of several friends who drifted away after his trial for murdering his wife. Rowe guesses Curtis would have joined the military once war was declared.

CYNTHIA (*The Human Factor*). She is a peppy secretary in MI6 and answerable to Castle and also Davis, who is in love with her. Since she is the daughter of a major general, she evidently aims higher. But Davis's murder causes her considerable sadness.

CZINNER, DR. RICHARD (*Orient Express*). He was formerly a Catholic and now, 56, a Communist allegedly atheistic. He testified against Colonel Hartep in Belgrade (August 1927), escaped arrest, fled to England, became a schoolmaster (calling himself Richard John) at Great Birchington-on-Sea. Five years later, he is now returning to Belgrade on a forged passport to head a Communist revolt, but is captured at Subotica, and becomes the victim of a perfunctory court martial held there by Hartep. Josef Grünlich helps him escape, but he is mortally wounded, and tended by Coral Musker until he dies.

Christopher Hitchens sees Czinner as a Christ-like figure returning to his homeland and offering himself as a sacrificial figure. Hitchens interprets Czinner's capture and death as coalescing into "a subliminal Passion Play." The name "Czinner" could be a pun on "sinner," according to Brian Diemert, who defines Czinner as a "communist revolutionary" both inarticulate and offended by third-class passengers' smell. (Sources: Diemert, 48; Hitchens, xiv)

D. (*The Confidential Agent*). D. is the confidential agent, 45, from a country torn by civil war. A former university lecturer on medieval French, he is a specialist in *Song of Roland* and studied at the British Museum almost 18 years ago. War-scarred, he sides with the common people and against aristocrats represented by L., another agent. Each wants to buy coal from Lord Benditch. Neither succeeds. D. is a pessimistic pacifist, saddened by his wife's death during the war three years earlier. The murder of Else Crole, who tried to befriend D., turns him violent and makes him eager to kill K., his turncoat London contact. The devotion of Rose Cullen, Benditch's daughter, half-persuades him to believe in love again. Forbes, Benditch's partner and hopelessly in love with Rose, books D. as Davis in the Lido, a Southcrawl resort he owns, to help D. escape.

In a *Collected Edition* introduction, Greene says he named D. and L. as he did to avoid localizing their conflict. Peter Wolfe says D. is "[a]n intellectual by profession and a skeptic by temperament," and doubts his ability to succeed in his mission, whereas a "summary of his adventures reveal[s] him as perhaps the outstanding male character in the Greene canon," because in the process of "win[ning] the day" he retains "his sense of humor and self-irony" and employs "quick thinking and decisiveness." (Sources: Greene, *The Confidential Agent, Collected Edition*, viii; Wolfe, 86, 87)

D., MRS. (*The Confidential Agent*). She was D.'s wife. The two courted in London. After 15 years of marriage, she was executed during the civil war in their country. Three years later, D. undertakes his confidential mission to England.

DAINTRY (*The Human Factor*). He was Colonel John Daintry's clergyman father, who served as a chaplain in the British navy during the Battle of Jutland (May 31, 1916).

The only pun in *The Human Factor* is devoted to this man, who Greene says was "washed up after the Battle of Jutland" into an "obscure rectory in Suffolk." Norman Sherry contends that Daintry's parents are largely based on Greene's parents, Charles Greeene* and Marion Greene.* (Source: Sherry III, 608)

DAINTRY, COLONEL JOHN (*The Human Factor*). He is the security officer brought into MI6 as a "new broom" to see whether Castle, Davis, or Watson is the source of security leaks. Daintry shoots well and drives his Jaguar over a hundred. He was married to Sylvia Daintry 15 years, grew estranged, and hasn't seen her for five years — until he attends Sylvia's daughter Elizabeth's wedding to Colin Clough. Daintry gets to know Hargreaves and Percival, wrongly suspects Davis, and is outraged when Percival murders Davis. Daintry didn't forcefully pursue definite evidence against Castle and vows, instead, to resign.

Yvonne Cloetta* says Greene told her that although none of his characters deeply resembles him, Daintry comes closer than others. Greene told Leopoldo Duran he felt Daintry was "one of the most successful characters" in *The Human Factor*. Michael Shelden reports that Daintry's name, St. James's Street residence in London, and efforts to find secret-service moles (in 1978) all parallel aspects of Colonel Claude Dansey (d. 1947), deputy director of the Secret Intelligence Service (in the 1940s). Norman Sherry makes much of the fact that Daintry's flat is modeled on Greene's, at 5 St. James Street, but doesn't mention Colonel Dansey's having lived there. (Sources: Cloetta, 49; Shelden, 35–36, 326–27; Sherry III, 605–06)

DAINTRY, ELIZABETH (*The Human Factor*). She is the beautiful daughter of Colonel Daintry and his estranged wife Sylvia. Daintry and Castle attend Elizabeth's registry-office wedding to Colin Clough. Elizabeth is more loyal to her flashy mother than to her lonely father.

DAINTRY, MRS. (*The Human Factor*). She was Colonel Daintry's gossipy mother. She relays confidential comments by friends to her clergyman husband as second-hand confessions.

DAINTRY, SYLVIA (*The Human Factor*). She is Colonel Daintry's estranged wife. Accompanied from Brighton by Edward Joiner, she attends her daughter Elizabeth's wedding. Well-wishers go to Sylvia's flat, where she has countless china owls.

DALLOW, TED (*Brighton Rock*). He is a member of Pinkie's gang. Heavy, easygoing, and loyal to Pinkie, he enjoys a sexual relationship with Billy Frank's wife Judy which Pinkie finds ugly. Pinkie's plan to marry and kill Rose

Wilson causes Dallow to betray him to Ida Arnold. Dallow's friends call him Dally.

DAMBREUSE, ACHILLE (*Travels with My Aunt*). He is one of Augusta's especially prevaricating lovers, though certifiably robust. The two enjoyed rendezvousing on an unvaried evening schedule in the Albany part of the St. James and Albany Hotel in Paris, until she, Louise Dupont (his afternoon mistress), Achille's wife, and some of his children chanced to meet. Augusta told Henry she admired the stamina of this semi-retired metallurgist, who was over 50, who said he was from Toulouse, but who was from Paris. She was sad that his unnecessary embarrassment ended their relationship. Later, they met on a boat near Panama, after which he sent her a pleasant postcard tactfully signed "A. D." She tells Henry that Achille must now be almost 90.

What was Achille's goddess-held Achilles heel? It was exposed when Achille's macho reared its head: Achille's wife wanted tea at the Ritz; therefore, he said no and chose instead the garden between Augusta's Albany and Louise's St. James, where Augusta and Louise happened to be — motivated, Augusta felt, by "a Higher Power."

DAMBREUSE, MADAME (*Travels with My Aunt*). She is or was Achille Dambreuse's plump wife. Achille told Augusta he lived in Toulouse with his wife and six children. In reality, he, his wife, and four children lived in Paris.

DANVERS, JIMMY ("The Other Side of the Border"). He is a corrupt Liverpool businessman who organizes syndicates and sends gold-seeking expeditions to West Africa. As the New Syndicate general manager, he obtains investors for Hands's disastrous expedition 1936–1938, and, despite Morrow's dire warnings about Hands, prepares another expedition and expresses unshaken faith in Hands.

DAVENANT (*This Gun for Hire*). He is a backer of shows in Nottwich. He has known Callitrope. Davis bought out Davenant. Collier is terrified when he repeatedly confuses the names Davis and Davenant when speaking to Davis.

DAVID ("The Hint of an Explanation"). He is the fellow train passenger, not initially identified as a priest, who tells the narrator about Blacker, a free-thinker. When David was an altar boy in an East Anglian town, Blacker tried to get him to swap a consecrated wafer for a toy electric train. Though tempted and frightened, David resists. Partly because this experience was a "hint" from God, David became a happy priest. David says his anti–Catholic schoolmates nicknamed him Popey Martin. Therefore, David's last name may be Martin.

DAVID (*The Ministry of Fear*). When Rowe phones a wrong number, someone hysterically calls him Ernest and tells him David must have told him that Minny, a pet cat, was killed in last night's air raid.

DAVIDGE (*England Made Me*). He, his wife, and their daughter Lucia, all of Coventry, are vacationing in Stockholm. They meet Farrant at Gothenburg, on the way. Davidge likes to read the Scottish author John Lockhart (1794–1854).

DAVIDGE, LUCIA (*England Made Me*). Farrant consorts with Lucia while she and her parents are voyaging to and are in Stockholm briefly. They fall into sleazy love. Farrant, who calls her Loo, promises to rendezvous back in Coventry, her home city.

Tony attends the Wagnerian opera *Tristan und Isolde* with the Crown Prince and finds the love-potion part of the plot silly. He complains about "a poisoned draught, irreparable love, death that ends everything," Yet his recalling how Loo "drank the schnaps ... in Gothenburg" permits the conclusion that schnaps became a tawdry "love" potion contributing indirectly to Tony's death — at the hands of the minion (Hall) of King Mark (Match-King Krogh). Norman Sherry shows that Loo is partly based on one of two unnamed young English girls Greene and his brother Hugh Greene* flirted with in Stockholm (August 1932). Robert Hoskins suggests that the names of Lucia Davidge and her brother Roderick Davidge may derive from siblings Lucia and Roderick in Sir Walter Scott's *The Bride of Lammermoor,* old Mr. Davidge's favorite novel. (Sources: Hoskins, 50; Sherry I, 488)

DAVIDGE, MRS. (*England Made Me*). She and her husband are vacationing with their daughter Lucia in Stockholm. Farrant shows them around.

DAVIDGE, RODERICK (*England Made Me*). He is mentioned as the Davidges's son and Lucia Davidge's brother.

DAVIDSON ("A Chance for Mr. Lever"). He is a prospector for gold in Liberia. Lever, who wants to sell him digging equipment, finds him. But Davidson is unconscious, is oozing black vomit, and soon dies of yellow fever, which Lever fatally contracts.

DAVIS ("The Bear Fell Free"). Davis, when Carter telephones Jane, Tony Farrell's girlfriend, about Tony's death, is evidently busy with her in her bed. Feeling guilty, Davis commits suicide.

DAVIS (*The Confidential Agent*) see **D**

DAVIS (*It's a Battlefield*). He is Surrogate's sleep-out servant, who is obsequious but silently calls him a bastard for womanizing.

DAVIS (*The Ministry of Fear*). He is a patient whom Forester sent to his so-called sick bay for weeping excessively.

DAVIS (*The Ministry of Fear*). He is the hotel clerk where Rowe delivered the suitcase supposedly filled with books. Davis identifies Rowe to Prentice, who takes both men to the shop where Cost works, as Ford. They identify Cost, who then kills himself.

DAVIS (*Our Man in Havana*). William Carter tells Wormold that Davis was his college roommate in Nottwich and went into Gripfix sales in the Caribbean area.

DAVIS (*This Gun for Hire*). He works for Sir Marcus, the Nottwich steel magnate, Davis is fat, indulges himself on sweets, and likes to seduce girls, to whom he calls himself Willie. Marcus orders Davis to hire Raven to assassinate the Czech pacifist. Calling himself Cholmondeley, Davis pays Raven in stolen money, numbers of which are known to the police. Anne Crowder and Davis take the same London-to-Nottwich train. Raven pursues Davis, who suspects Anne and tries to kill her at the bawdy house run by Acky and Tiny. Raven saves her, follows Davis to Marcus's offices, and kills Marcus and Davis.

Peter Wolfe notes that Davis's often-mentioned emerald ring, "with its cold glitter and resemblance to a snake's eye, symbolizes treachery." (Source: Wolfe, 66–67)

DAVIS, ARTHUR (*The Human Factor*). He is Castle's assistant security officer, knowledgeable in physics and mathematics. Davis was educated at Droitwich Royal Grammar School and Reading University, drinks too much, and is still a bachelor. Happy-go-lucky, somewhat careless at work, and in love with Cynthia, his and Castle's secretary, Davis pines for an assignment to Lourenço Marques, and even romance there with Cynthia. Daintry relays tentative suspicions to Percival that Davis is the source of security leaks, whereupon Percival kills him with traceless poison in Davis's whisky.

W. J. West suggests that Greene lampooned his friend Malcolm Muggeridge* (1903–1990), British author, journalist, and Christian apologist, in aspects of his portrayal of Davis. Both served in military intelligence, both liked Raymond's Revuebar, and Davis wanted to serve in Mozambique, where Muggeridge served during part of World War II. Other points of comparison, however, seem strained or missing. Michael Shelden too confidently contends that "Greene ... knew of no attempts to silence an officer [in the secret service] by killing him. The episode was invented not only for dramatic purposes, but also as a way of embarrassing the service." (It is difficult to prove negative assertions.)

Anthony Mockler discusses Muggeridge's military assignment in Lourenço Marques and also Muggeridge's hatred of Soviet Russia. (Sources: Mockler, 185, 196; Shelden, 481; West, 235–37, 241)

DAVIS, BATTY (*The Heart of the Matter*). This lieutenant insanely rages in the made-up sea story Henry Scobie tells Jimmy Fisher, when the boy is recovering after being rescued from the torpedoed vessel.

DAVIS, FATHER (*The Heart of the Matter*). He is a priest in Durban, South Africa. While vacationing there, Louise Scobie met him. Home again, she snidely tells her husband Henry that Father Davis is more intellectual than Father Rank, their priest in Sierra Leone.

DAVIS, WILLIAM (*The Human Factor*). He was Arthur Davis's father. He attended the Droitwich Royal Grammar School, won in English composition (1910) a prize of a selection of Robert Browning's poems, and passed it to Arthur for achieving a "First in Physics" (1937).

DAYRELLE-BROWNING, VIVIENNE *see* **GREENE, VIVIEN**

"A DAY SAVED" (1935). Short story. (Characters: Canby, Douglas, Fotheringay, Jones, Robinson, Wales.)

Robinson, the narrator, shadows a person he doesn't know. This ordinary-looking person has umbrella, bowler, and gloves. He conceals something Robinson is willing to kill him to get. Robinson wonders if his name is Canby, Douglas, Jones, Wales, or maybe Fotheringay. Under a railway bridge, the man meets someone, perhaps a friend, and reveals he's going from Dover to Ostend. The friend tells him he can save a day by flying instead of going mostly by train. Robinson wonders — save a day for what? Accompanying him, he observes the man's uneasiness during the flight. At customs, Robinson translates for the grateful man — obviously "stupid and good-natured." The two drink together for a while, then take a night train, punctuated by meaningless talk. They get to the man's destination, a house full of his friends. Though invited in, Robinson declines. Remaining outside, he observes the foolish fellow being welcomed by a woman, a girl, and three men. Robinson thinks he saw the man say he saved a day. Robinson, calling himself Fotheringay, Wales, and Canby, as well as Robinson, hopes the fellow has to replicate his own experience of doubting himself, following someone, and thus also expending 86,400 seconds fruitlessly.

A. A. DeVitis calls "A Day Saved" "a haunting tale of obsession, schizophrenia, and paranoia, [which] employs, ambiguously, a doppelganger motif." Other readers might call it pretty silly. (Source: DeVitis, 171)

DEAN OF STUDENTS, THE (*The Comedians*). This official at the Jesuit College of the Visitation in Monte Carlo dismissed Brown after his exploit at the casino, which the dean half-admired.

DEAN OF WARBURY ("Under the Garden"). He was an official at Warbury, the school Wilditch attended as a child. When Wilditch's mother criticized the school, the Dean replied defensively but accurately by letter, saying the school complied with her demand that the boy not be given further religious instruction but adding that it helped students develop their imagination.

DEANE, RICHARD (*Doctor Fischer of Geneva*). He is one of Fischer's Toads. He was a popular British movie actor, and is now old-and-young looking, with an alcoholic smile. Fischer goads him for his alleged sex appeal and lack of acting skills. He drives a Mercedes, attends Fischer's parties, and gets drunk at the bomb party.

"DEAR DR. FALKENHEIM" (1963). Short story. (Characters: Colin, Dr. Doppeldorf, Jeff Drew, Dr. Falkenheim, Father O'Connor.)

The narrator has read an insightful book by Dr. Doppeldorf recommended to him by Dr. Falkenheim, a psychiatrist to whom the narrator writes a letter. He is worried about a traumatic event that occurred to his son Colin. When the boy was six, the narrator and his wife left England and spent some months in a western Canadian city near the Rockies. When Christmas approached, they wanted to disabuse Colin of belief, if he still believed, in Father Christmas. The narrator equates the idea of several Father Christmases and the concept of the Trinity that kids are also supposed to accept. But when one store competed with its rival, by hiring a helicopter to fly a Father Christmas to its parking lot on Christmas Eve, they took Colin for a last episode involving the mythical figure. Father Christmas dropped presents, landed, stepped out jollily, and was decapitated by the rear propeller. Colin's mother tried to explain that a poverty-stricken codger named Jeff Drew was hired to play the role; the papers crudely headlined the death of

Father Christmas; but nothing has shaken the boy's belief. Six years later, Colin still comes home beaten up by his wise schoolmates, because, "like an early Christian," he insists Father Christmas exists, is dead, and therefore is "indestructible."

Richard Kelly relates undercurrents of "Dear Dr. Falkenheim" to Greene's memory of his own "recording and disclosing the details of his psychic traumas to the psychoanalyst Kenneth Richmond," some details having to do with "naive beliefs in heroes, love, and loyalty" echoed by confused little Colin. Michael Shelden and Norman Sherry detail Greene's relationship (1921–1925), with Richmond, a self-trained, Jungian psychoanalyst and spiritualist, and with his wife Zoe Richmond. Neither Shelden nor Sherry connects the Richmonds with "Dear Dr. Falkenheim," although it seems obvious that, when Colin's father writes Dr. Falkenheim about Colin, Greene is twitting Richmond. (Sources: Greene, *A Sort of Life*, 98–104; Kelly, 51; Shelden, 65–67, 104–05; Sherry I, 92–107 passim, 214–15)

DEAR SANITY see ***THE MAN WITHIN***

DECHAUX (*The Comedians*). He designated Brown's mother, who was Dechaux's secretary, owner of the Trianon, for tax purposes, but then died driving his Mercedes too fast for Haitian roads.

DECHAUX, MME. (*The Comedians*). Dechaux's wife. Brown's mother says Dechaux detested her so much that he would have been delighted had he known Brown's mother got the Trianon instead of his large, fat, black, uneducated wife's getting it.

DEDHAM, SIR SILAS ("Under the Garden"). In the story Wilditch wrote at school, this man is a City resident holding the mortgage to Tom's mother's house.

DEDICATIONS. To his parents Charles Greene* and Marion Greene,* Greene dedicated *Rumour at Nightfall;* to his wife Vivien Greene,* *England Made Me, The Man Within, The Name of Action, Stamboul Train;* to Vivien and their children, *The Heart of the Matter;* to his daughter Caroline, *Doctor Fischer of Geneva or The Bomb Party;* to his sister Elisabeth Dennys,* *The Human Factor;* to Dorothy Craigie (Dorothy Glover*), *The Confidential Agent;* to Catherine Walston,* *The End of the Affair;* to Yvonne Cloetta,* *The Captain and the Enemy, Travels with My Aunt;* to A. S. Frere, a director at Heinemann, publishers, *The Comedians, Loser Takes All;* to Dr. Michel Lechat, *A Burnt-Out Case;* to Carol Reed,* *The Third Man;* to Father Leopoldo Duran (and Aurelio Verde, Octavio Victoria, Miguel Fernandez, Tom Burns), *Monsignor Quixote;* to Dave, Anne, Nils, Ingeborg, *It's a Battlefield;* to "Gervase," *The Power and the Glory;* to Victoria Ocampo, *The Honorary Consul;* to René Bernal and Phuong (friends in Saigon), *The Quiet American.*

DE GAULLE, TANTE YVONNE ("Two Gentle People"). She is the wife of General Charles De Gaulle (1890–1970). Marie-Claire Duval tells Greaves she once saw Tante Yvonne shopping for cheese.

DEJOIE, MADAME EMMY ("Chagrin in Three Parts"). She is an aggressive widow, married to the late Jacques Dejoie, then the lesbian lover of Pauline, deceased, and currently making a lesbian-activities target of Madame Volet, whose husband has just left her.

DEJOIE, JACQUES ("Chagrin in Three Parts"). He was Emmy Dejoie's late husband. He was able to satisfy Emmy sexually during their early married years but not later, because — as Emmy tells Madame Volet — he didn't have *fantasies.*

Richard Kelly contends that in having Emmy tell Madame Volet that Jacques's death was caused by infected bowels, Greene reveals his "delight in juxtaposing excremental and romantic images." (Source: Kelly, 67)

DELAINE, THE HON. CAROL (*Orient Express*). She is the daughter of Lord Gathaway. An actress, she will play Emmy Tod, the chargirl in the movie adaptation of *The Great Gay Round,* Quin C. Savory's novel.

DE LASZLO (*England Made Me*). He is an artist whose portrait of Sir Ronald illustrates *Viol and Vine,* Sir Ronald's book of poetry.

DE LETTRE, GENERAL (*The Quiet American*). (Full name: Jean Joseph-Marie de Lettre de Tassigny [1889-1952]). He is the French general said by Fowler to be mortally ill in Paris. Soon after Fowler is supposed to write about the political and military consequences of De Lettre's departure from Vietnam, his death is announced.

De Lettre was the commander of all French forces in Vietnam until he was recalled to France, where he died of cancer. His death (January 11, 1952) dates the action of *The Quiet American* (September 1951 to February 1952).

DELIA (*Brighton Rock*). She is Molly Pink's young friend, who squeals frequently. Hale tries to pick up both girls in Brighton, in an unsuccessful attempt to shield himself from Pinkie.

DELIA (*England Made Me*). Aunt Ella mentions in a letter to her nephew Ferdinand Minty his cousin Delia and the affair of Delia's twins.

DEMASSENER, ANNE-MARIE (*The Name of Action*). She is the wife of Trier's dictator, Paul Demassener. Her father was French. She has dark hair, slanting eyes with gold and green and gray specks, a beautiful face, and an alluring figure. She has been married five years to an impotent husband. Chant appears and attracts her lust. She tells him about Demassener's affliction, which Chant reveals to Kapper, a revolutionary, who uses it to depose Demassener. Anne-Marie won't leave with Chant or accompany Demassener, when, wounded, he is taken by train to Luxemburg.

This beautiful, sensual woman is one of Greene's most unbelievable characters. Loyally married for five years to an impotent, aging, stooping stick of a man, she waits and waits— to go to bed with Oliver Chant? Surely Captain Kraft, the erectly standing ex-duelist, was handier earlier.

DEMASSENER, PAUL (*The Name of Action*). He is Trier's dictator, tall, slightly stooped, with cloudy blue eyes. Married to Anne-Marie Demassener for five sexless years, impotent Demassener has profound affection for her. He captured the city three years earlier. He closed cabarets and brothels, outlawed music, and imposed puritanical morality. When Kapper, a would-be rebel, taunts him with a poster depicting him as impotent and his wife as sluttish, Demassener aims a revolver at Kapper but is gravely wounded by another rebel. Chant, who loves but loses Anne-Marie, admires Demassener and helps him into exile.

Michael Shelden analyzes Demassener's puritanical character, notes that he disdainfully "dismisses the loss of civil liberties as a small price to pay for purity," but strangely adds that "perhaps Greene was thinking of his father when he created the character of Demassener." (Source: Shelden, 142)

DEMPSTER (*The Heart of the Matter*). The Elder Dempster Company has premises in Freetown. H. R. Harris is assigned a work room there.

There was a company in Freetown of that name when Greene was there (1942–1943). (Source: Sherry II, 100)

DENNYS, ELISABETH GREENE (1914– 1999). Greene's sister. She was her mother's favorite daughter and Greene's adored sister. She was train-bearer at his wedding to Vivienne Dayrell-Browning (1927; *see* Greene, Vivien). During World War II, Elisabeth worked as a secretary to the regional head of the Secret Intelligence Service (MI6) in the Middle Eastern Theatre and helped Greene's assignments to MI6 and West Africa (1941). She married Rodney Dennys, an intelligence officer in Cairo and Turkey during the war; they lived in Istanbul later. Their three children are Nicholas Dennys (now in England), Louise Dennys (in Canada), and Amanda Dennys Saunders (in England). Later in Greene's life, Elisabeth sometimes acted as his secretary. While writing *J'Accuse* (1982), he sent her dictabelts about governmental corruption in Nice. When Greene was about to travel again with Leopoldo Duran in Spain (1977), Elisabeth found them a beautiful portable communion set. Elisabeth suffered a debilitating stroke (1989), after which her daughter Amanda Dennys Saunders became Greene's occasional secretary and was at his death bed (1991). Yvonne Cloetta* reports that Louise Greene Dennys, Elizabeth's other daughter, edited Greene's *Monsignor Quixote* and *Ways of Escape,* and was executive publisher of Alfred A. Knopf and executive vice president of

Random House, Canada. (Sources: Cash, 35; Cloetta, 89; Mockler, 175, 177; Sherry I, 48, 354; Sherry II, 83–84, 384; Sherry III, xxviii, 53, 631, 645, 699, 782–84)

DENTISTA ("The Lottery Ticket"). When the bank manager wants to confer with the Governor in the Mexican state about Thriplow's lottery winnings, he finds the Governor being treated by the Dentista.

DEO GRATIAS (*A Burnt-Out Case*). He is a leper, with fingers and toes destroyed. Though cured, because leprosy has burned out all it can, Deo Gratias wants to remain. Dr. Colin has him be Querry's servant "boy." When Deo Gratis escapes into the bush, Querry persuades him to return. When Deo Gratias describes Pendélé, his home village, as a kind of paradise, Querry says he'd like to go there with him.

Greene seems bitterly ironical when he names this mutilated creature "Thanks Be to God"; however, both name and character are based on a leper Greene met at the Congo leproserie in Yonda he visited (February 1958). Leopoldo Duran says he "came across the name Deo Gratias" in St. Augustine. A. A. DeVitis observes that Querry "and Deo Gratias come to parallel one another: Querry's spiritual mutilation matches Deo Gratias's physical handicap." (Sources: DeVitis, 118; Duran, 236; Sherry III, 167)

DERMODY, MRS. (*The Ministry of Fear*). She works with the Free Mothers. When Rowe goes there, she gives him Mrs. Bellairs's address.

DERRY (*The Heart of the Matter*). The Commissioner tells Scobie that Derry has reported thefts in the diamond mines.

DESPREZ (*The Quiet American*). She is a public-relations officer's wife in Saigon. She is one of Bill Granger's guests at the Vieux Moulin, along with Captain Duparc, on the night Pyle is killed. Fowler sees the group.

"THE DESTRUCTORS" (1954). Short story. (Characters: Blackie, Joe, Mike, Summers, Thomas, Trevor.)

1. Trevor, called T., is the most recent recruit of the Wormsley Common Gang of boys. During the August Bank Holiday, they meet each morning to plan mischievous actions, which include stealing rides on buses. Their leader is Blackie, until T. takes over by ingeniously suggesting they organize to destroy the nearby mansion owned by Mr. Thomas. He is a kind, retired builder-decorator. His is the only building in the neighborhood not flattened during "the old blitz." Propped by wooden struts, it sticks up "like a jagged tooth." The lot of a house once next door is now a car-park. Thomas's bathroom plumbing was disrupted; so Old Misery, as the boys call him, now has a backyard privy with a star-shaped aperture and resembling a graveyard tomb. T. tells the gang that his father, once an architect but now a clerk, told him the mansion was built by Christopher Wren 200 years ago. Mr. Thomas, who courteously let T. in and showed him the 200-year-old "corkscrew" staircase, said he'd be away this Sunday. T. orders his followers to bring multiple tools.

2. Sunday. Mike, a nine-year-old gang member, avoiding church because his parents have overslept, reports. Blackie brings a hammer and a stolen sledge. T. organizes his minions to hollow out the place, leave only the outer walls, clip the wiring, unhinge the doors, smash, break, and tear up the bathroom, kitchen, and bedroom. T. philosophizes that "destruction ... is a form of creation." They lunch on sandwiches brought along. By 6:00 p.m., Thomas would be able to sleep only on "a bed of broken plaster." T. and Blackie remain. T. found a cache of £70 in notes, tells Blackie they're not thieves, and carefully burns them. Blackie says T. must hate Thomas. No, he avers; it wouldn't be fun with hate involved.

3. Monday. Mike and another boy must go with their families to Southend. T. orders the others to remove floors, windows, and stairs, and saw the joints. That evening T. opens a remaining pipe to flood everything. Mike rushes up with news that Thomas, spotted at Southend, became cold and is heading home early. Challenged by his gang and almost superseded by Blackie, T. improvises, greets Thomas sweetly, says a boy got caught in his "lav" and must be rescued. Muttering that his horoscope warned him about a crash, Thomas finds himself pushed into his "loo" and locked there by T., who advises him to be quiet. Thomas sits,

ponders wisely, hears hammering, suspects burglars, and emits an "experimental yell." No rescuer from the car-park hears.

4. All the boys except Mike, abed at home, chisel out the mortar between damp sections and bricks. Through the loo aperture, Thomas is passed a blanket, buns, and sausage-rolls, for night-time comfort and sustenance. At 7:00 a.m. a lorry driver backs from the car-park to Thomas's wall, shored by a wooden strut. Turning towards the street, he hears an avalanche of bricks; he brakes, climbs out, and surveys an altered landscape: no house, hill of rubble, bricks on lorry, shout from loo, rope from lorry to strut. He releases Thomas, who wonders where his house is. The driver responds with a laugh, and apologetically adds that his guffaw wasn't personal but that the episode is funny.

Greene, his wife Vivien Greene,* and their daughter Caroline moved into a beautiful house at 14 North Side, Clapham Common, London (1935). It was destroyed by German incendiary bombs during World War II (October 1940). Peter Green says that "[t]he hatred of his [Greene's] marriage ... lay behind ... 'The Destructors,' which described the vandalism of a house based ... on the last London home the Greenes shared." John Ower calls the story a "minor masterpiece ... of modern fiction," explaining that "Greene's ... vision" therein "embraces psychology, sociology, history and theology." A. A. DeVitis asserts that readers of the story "become ... aware that the energy expended in the act of total destruction [of Thomas's mansion] is in fact liberating." DeVitis adds that its having been spared during the Blitz "becomes an unacceptable absurdity to the boys," and that they must therefore "deal it the same kind of rude justice" accorded all other residences in its block. However, Neil McEwan says the truck driver's climactic laughter exemplifies a "sense of humour [that] includes a graduated awareness of what is not amusing"; Paul O'Prey calls the destruction of the house "senseless"; Cedric Watts labels the entire story "cynical." It was the subject of a television production in 1976, the 1978 showing of which, according to Norman Sherry, raised a public outcry. (*See also* Shades of Greene.) Yvonne Cloetta* claims she and Greene helped Hugh Greene,* Greene's brother and a director of the BBC, film the story.

(Source: DeVitis, 171; Cloetta, 53; Falk, 215; P. Green, 33; McEwan, 52; O'Prey, 58; Ower; Sherry II, 66; Watts, 24)

DEVEREUX, ROBERT (*Loser Takes All*) *see* **BERTRAM**

DEVIL, THE (*The Captain and the Enemy*) *see* **BAXTER**

DEWES, FATHER ("Special Duties"). This Catholic priest lives in a room near Mrs. Ferraro, who is supposedly sickly. He is available by bell call if she feels she's dying.

DEXTER, BENJAMIN (*The Third Man*). He is a distinguished British novelist, just under 50. Crabbin invites Martins, whose pen name is Buck Dexter, to lecture to his literary group because he thinks Martins is Benjamin Dexter. Calloway, having read Benjamin Dexter, likens him to Henry James in both complexity and subtlety, but says he displays a greater degree of femininity not only in style and but also in personal behavior.

Greene had the British novelist E. M. Forster (1879–1970) in mind when sketching Benjamin Dexter. Greene has Calloway criticize Dexter's "wide ... feminine streak" and his "interest in embroidery and ... tatting." Forster was a homosexual whose name is associated with the literary "Knitting Circle." Greene has Miss Wilbraham, a member of Crabbin's group, buttonhole Martins, who she thinks is Benjamin Dexter, and tell him she doesn't approve of his works because they don't good stories. Neil Sinyard reminds readers in detail that "it was with Forster that Greene had his first quarrel with Modernism, notably to do with Forster's passage about 'The Story' in *Aspects of the Novel* (1927). 'Yes — oh dear yes — the novel tells a story,' Forster famously intoned. 'That is the fundamental aspect without which it could not exist. That is the highest factor common to all novels, and I wish that it was not so, that it could be something different — melody, or perception of the truth, not this low atavistic form.'" Sinyard continues, "But Greene resented this. 'I'm a story-teller,' he insisted." (Sinyard's discussion of the Forster-Greene disagreement does not mention *The Third Man*.) (Sources: Phillips, 64; Sinyard, 114; Wolfe, 132)

DEXTER, BUCK (*The Third Man*) *see* **MARTINS, ROLLO**

DIAZ, GENERAL (*Rumour at Nightfall*). He is the Commandant at San Juan. Aged, thin, haughty, and suffering from bleeding coughs, he rebukes Colonel Riego for associating with Francis Chase, whom he also chastises.

DIBBA, PHILIP (*The Human Factor*). He was an MI6 agent in Kinshasa. He had to accept forced retirement from the position of Kinshasa's Director of the Post Office when he was caught misprinting postage stamps and privately collecting them.

DICK (*Orient Express*). Coral Musker remembers him as one of her minimally successful theatrical friends. Others are Flo, Ivy, and Phil.

DICK ("Work Not in Progress"). The fake Archbishop of Canterbury wonders if her former boyfriend Dick will be any impediment.

DICKY (*The Human Factor*). He, Buffy, Dodo, and Harry are boisterous guests at Hargreaves's shoot. Dicky later sees Daintry with Buffy at White's, the latter's club. Buffy excuses drunk Dicky's rudely questioning Daintry on the grounds that Dicky was an MI5 interrogator during the war.

DIEGO (*Monsignor Quixote*). He was a fellow student during Enrique Zancas's student days in Salamanca. Diego knew Marquez, the rich stockbroker.

DIEGO, SEÑOR (*Monsignor Quixote*). He is a gracious old farmer and vintner. He won't sell wine to wealthy Mexicans, because they buy favors from the priests in nearby Learig. But he welcomes Father Quixote and Zancas, treats them to wine, and gives them cases for themselves and the Osera Trappists.

Leopoldo Duran says that the famous wine grower "Señor Antonio [Nogueiras] de las Regardas is Señor Diego in *Monsignor Quixote*." (Source: Duran, 156)

DIGBY (*Brighton Rock*). Crab, working in the Cosmopolitan for Colleoni, learned manners by watching the way a man named Digby looked carefully at a woman.

DIGBY, RICHARD (*The Ministry of Fear*) *see* **ROWE, ARTHUR**

DIRECTOR OF AGRICULTURE (*The Heart of the Matter*). He is a Sierra Leone official. He gave the Indian fortune teller £1 for reading his palm, and also a letter of recommendation. Wilson, who hears this, pays him 10 shilling for a reading.

DIRECTOR OF EDUCATION, THE (*The Heart of the Matter*). A beach-party photograph in the police station near Scobie's office includes this director holding a dead fish.

DIRECTOR OF POSTS AND TELEGRAPHS, THE (*Our Man in Havana*). To create a life for his imaginary Teresa in his spy reports, Wormold says she is this official's mistress.

DIRECTOR OF PUBLIC WORKS, THE (*A Burnt-Out Case*). At Governor Guelle's party, he and the Manager of Otraco wonder who Querry, newly arrived, might be.

DIRTY (*Loser Takes All*). This is the name Cary assigns to Bertram's first wife when she talks about her. For humor, Greene has Bertram, the narrator, gratuitously add that Dirty was a fat, sexy brunette with pekingese eyes.

"A DISCOVERY IN THE WOODS" (1963). Short story. (Characters: Fox, Liz, Moon, Number One, Number Three, Number Two, Pete, Tort.)

1. In Bottom, a village in the hills five miles from the sea, children play two age-old games—"Old Noh" and "Ware That Cloud." Pete, perhaps nine, is the son of a demented fisherman, who fears to go to sea during cloudy days, and his misshapen little stammering wife. Pete wants to leads timid, bandy-legged Liz, seven, and three boys he calls Number One, Number Two, and Number Three, to seek blackberries in the woods dangerously beyond Bottom's boundary. They must vow not to tell their parents. Only Number One won't promise; so he is pinioned, jabbed with a spittle-dampened wooden cross, and towed along by a string. The children march to the edge of

their territory, see a ravine, and imagine "luscious untouched fruit" beyond.

2. Number One says that fruit belongs to Two Rivers, the next village. It might be uninhabited, Pete counters. Liz says giants might be over there but, when asked, makes a pannier to hold berries. Her buttocks show. Even though Number One promises to make trouble, Pete orders Numbers One, Two, and Three to advance as a rear guard. He and Liz descend to the ravine and beyond.

3. The two climb through undergrowth, hear the three coming along behind, hope for blackberries but also perhaps a treasure, then smell something hot and metallic, and suddenly see the ocean.

4. Among rocks, Pete and Liz see a strange, long structure, like a house but curved, partly overgrown, and split in two. It has enormous chimneys and floors, and could have accommodated thousands of people. Pete whistles for the others to advance.

5. He swings down through tree branches, drops onto a shell-like surface, slides to where he sees the red rock that broke the structure. A leaping squirrel leads him to a hall, with treelike wooden pillars along a floor, moss-covered humps, a multi-colored slab, drinking vessels, skull-like round things. Whistling for the others, Pete thinks this big house resembles a huge fish tossed like a strong wave onto rocks to die. Number One is released. They gather "forfeits" and put them in Liz's skirt. They survey the hills beyond the windows of the house. Pete remembers the Noh legend, about a boat with beasts. Number Three twangs a musical instrument.

6. The children explore rooms filled with mysterious, discolored fixtures. They find a partly sunken, tiled square with dead leaves and splashes of bird droppings. Another hall contains bones of children in seemingly defiant postures. The live children assemble in fading sunlight. Number One calls the place only a big house, but Pete says it's a big boat—Noh's. Pete and Number Three conjecture that the "Cloud" might have frightened Noh, but where are the corpses? Well, when the waters receded, the animals escaped in pairs, except water rats. Pete tells doubtful Number Three he saw stony snakes in one room. Up high above the top floor is a house with "a meaningless design"—FRANCE. Pete plans to trace that pattern on the dust, for his father to explain, perhaps. All five children climb the steps, covered with yellow dust, and into the house. They see "the man," a long straight skeleton with the skull relaxed on a shoulder bone. Pete calls it Noh; Liz, a giant. Number Three, pacing, measures its six feet. It has crumbling blue material over the loins. The four boys walk away, crunching scattered forfeits. No treasure here. Pete looks for Liz, sees her with her naked bottom squatting on the skeleton's thigh bones, rocking, weeping, keening, praising the giant's six feet of straight bones and gleaming teeth. Pete suddenly calls Liza pretty, tries hard to stand straight, feels a "first ... sensation of love" for that rocking creature with the twisted legs. The two see their three friends scrambling away like crabs. Liz keens once more "for a whole world lost."

"A Discovery in the Woods" is Greene's only science-fiction piece. The futuristic story features tiny humans deformed by an atomic explosion, living in ignorance, and conflating a redaction of the Biblical Noah's ark, from which the colony survived to devolve, and a mythologized racial memory of that nuclear mushroom in the sky.

Cedric Watts lists several similar 1950s "post-nuclear-holocaust works," which include William Golding's *Lord of the Flies* (1953). Watts adds that Greene here "exploits the techniques of delayed decoding and covert plotting." Watts explains that Greene narrates an effect while holding back an explanation (delayed decoding) and presents elements of action so incoherently (covert plotting) that a re-reading is required to make sense of it all. It may be added that Greene employs a good deal of disarming fairy-tale diction in this horror story. (Source: Watts, 70, 71)

THE DIVIDED HEART see **THE MAN WITHIN**

DOBEL, HERR ("The Root of All Evil"). He is one of the wine-drinking clubmen.

"DR. CROMBIE" see **"DOCTOR CROMBIE"**

"DOCTOR CROMBIE" (1965). Short

story. (Characters: Doctor Crombie, Colonel Parker, Horace Turner, Miss Warrender, Wright, Fred Wright.)

Something "unfortunate" has just reminded the narrator of Doctor Crombie, the Bankstead school physician when the narrator was a day-student.

Doctor Crombie advised boys age 13, that playing with oneself causes cancer. The day-students commuted back home to London and told their parents. The narrator's father (who had long heard masturbation progressively caused loss of energy, nervous weakness, melancholy, and insanity) told him playing by oneself with toy trains was safe. The narrator felt reassured. After leaving school but before entering the university, the narrator met with Doctor Crombie for a picnic by Bankstead Castle. He told the narrator the school had demanded his resignation, wouldn't say why. The narrator learned that Bankstead day-student Fred Wright had visited a prostitute off Leicester Square during a half-day excursion, experienced some testicular pains, suspected venereal disease, and consulted Doctor Crombie. He told Fred that not merely masturbation but also frequent sexual intercourse caused cancer. Fred relayed this news home. Many parents conferred, then talked with their boys. Unknown to Fred, his peppy father had cancer. Doctor Crombie lost his job. The narrator, in love and interested, consulted Doctor Crombie and was told all this: Making love, in or out of marriage, causes cancer; immoral youngsters lay the foundation for cancer later; saints could die of cancer sans sex; married couples have little sex, and the more the worse; nearly 100 percent of cancer victims have had sex; Doctor Crombie lived alone, and untempted; if any species deviates wrongly and accidentally, natural evolution will cause its extinction; man may suffer the fate of the dinosaurs.

Today the narrator, married four times and over 60, has been told he has lung cancer. Caused by smoking? Oh, he believes with Doctor Crombie, who died of pneumonia a while back, that more pleasant excesses have been the cause.

Comments by Greene, Norman Sherry, and Richard Kelly provides proof that Greene was thinking of his father Charles Greene,* headmaster of Berkhamstead School, when he presented Doctor Crombie and his warnings to students, and the obviously hyperbolized consequences thereof. (Sources: Greene, *A Sort of Life,* 80–81; Kelly, 62; Sherry I, 43–46 passim)

DOCTOR FISCHER OF GENEVA OR THE BOMB PARTY (1980). Novel. (Characters: Albert, Monsieur Henri Belmont, Richard Deane, Monsieur Excoffier, Madame Faverjon, Anna Fischer, Doctor Fischer, Monsieur Groseli, Alfred Jones, Anna-Luise Jones, Lady Jones, Mary Jones, Sir Frederick Jones, Kips, General Krueger, Madame Krueger, Montgomery, Mrs. Montgomery, Secretary of Embassy, Steiner.)

1. Alfred Jones, the protagonist-narrator, was the son of Sir Frederick Jones and Lady Mary Jones. Diplomatic work took the family abroad, enabling Jones to learn French, Turkish, and Spanish. A German air raid (London, December 1940) killed the parents and destroyed the left hand of Jones, a fireman. He wears a gloved prosthesis. With a small pension, he became a translator-correspondent for a chocolate factory in Vevey, Switzerland. When Anna-Luise Fischer of Geneva was visiting in Vevey, she and Jones by chance had lunch at the same place, chatted, fell in love, and married — despite his being in his 50s and her being under 21. She has a small income from her deceased mother's invested capital. Anna-Luise hates her father Doctor Fischer of Geneva for mistreating her mother. Fischer, wealthy inventor of Dentophil, a perfumed toothpaste, is the object of Jones's detestation, because of Fischer's pride, contemptuousness, and cruelty. Guests of Fischer's notorious parties, whom Anna-Luise called Toads (meaning toadies), include Richard Deane, movie actor; General Krueger, retired Swiss army officer; Kips, international lawyer; Monsieur Belmont, tax adviser; and Mrs. Montgomery, American widow. Jones regards his love for and marriage to Anna-Luise as a miracle, and remembers their first meeting more clearly than events on the day she died.

2. Anna-Luise and Jones, widowed 20 years, since his wife and daughter died in childbirth, meet at Lausanne to see movies, sleep together one Sunday, and casually consider marriage. Soon she leaves her father's home and moves in with him.

3. Jones drives his Fiat to Versoix to see Fischer, is ushered by a surly servant (Albert) to a

waiting room in his gigantic lakeside estate, and meets Mrs. Montgomery, an American widow and Fischer's shopper-hostess. She asks if he knows Richard Deane, Krueger, who selects party wines, Kips, or Monsieur (Henri) Belmont, tax man. No. Kips, Fischer's bent-over lawyer, is admitted. Jones is told to return Thursday at 5:00.

4. Anna-Luise wants Jones to avoid her father, who she says is hellish and God-like, smiles dangerously, mocks but mustn't be mocked, and is ashamed Dentophil provided his fortune. Regardless, Jones meets Fischer, who proves indifferent to his daughter's marrying, is relieved to learn Jones's hand wasn't lost because of heredity deformity, and, noticing his Welsh name, asks about porridge.

5. Weeks later Jones and Anna-Luise marry in the mayor's office. She spots a Toad there — Belmont, who bears an invitation to Jones alone to a Fischer party. He wants to go. Anna-Luis doesn't want him to, says Fischer will be like Satan tempting Christ. He says he's no Christ but won't go. She persuades him to go.

6. After meeting a Spanish confectioner in Geneva on business, Jones is seen by Mrs. Montgomery, who asks what expensive gift he'd like Fischer to give him — gold cigar cutter? platinum watch? He hits a nerve by saying guests probably sell their gifts back to the stores selling them.

7. Anna-Luise tells Jones her mother, who liked music while Fischer didn't, heard classical music records with a clerk. Fischer found out, bribed the clerk's employer, Kips, to fire the clerk, hired Kips as his therefore enriched and silent lawyer, and punished Anna-Luise's mother sexually thereafter — until she willed herself to die.

8. Jones worries as the dinner date approaches. Anna-Luise tells him to arrive, resist being humiliated, leave. She suggests her getting off the pill after the ski seasons ends. Ill omens crowd Jones while dressing for the party.

9. Albert reluctantly admits Jones. To the five hostile toadying guests Fischer introduces Jones as his son-in-law, says he has a deformed hand and translates letters concerning chocolate — proving he had investigated Jones. Fischer insults Deane for not speaking French and being an ineffective, alcoholic actor. Mrs. Montgomery praises Fischer as a prize-giving host and says she selected tonight's prizes. For what? Jones asks Fischer, who says if prizes rewarded intelligence Kruger wouldn't win, then criticizes Mrs. Montgomery's blue hair. She demurs — until he says contradicting him will mean no prize, and even deaths, as in the past. Remaining out of curiosity, Jones concludes the conversation isn't based on rowdy good humor but on "hollowness and ... hypocrisy" and all-around hatred. Fischer demands a toast to Madame Faverjon, who, Fischer says, was the greediest of his guests and died two years earlier. Fischer eats caviar while his guests must eat cold, unsweetened porridge if they want their presents. While they eat, Fischer says Deane prematurely ejaculates. Fischer says a one-handed man must have trouble making love. Fischer explains that his presents-for-food experiment is designed to see if the greed of the rich has limits, that though rich he may find his own greed has limits, and that God, in whom he doesn't believe, isn't limitlessly greedy for our love but for our humiliation. Jones says perhaps God gave him Anna-Luise's love; Fischer suspects it's less lasting than Mrs. Montgomery's gold necklace, and if we are in God's image He must be disappointed.

10. Home again, Jones tells Anna-Luise about the porridge-gorged guests' presents — jewelry, watches — and promises not to attend another party. Snow falls in November. But death will annul that promise.

11. During December weekends, Jones takes Anna-Luise to ski while he reads. She hopes he lives very long and they can die together. He dreams he saw Fischer weeping at a grave. On Saturday they shop at a Vevey music store for a Mozart cassette, are waited on by someone named Steiner. He was Kips's employee and Fischer's deceased wife's fellow music lover until Fischer had him fired. Seeing the mother's face in the daughter's, Steiner faints and is hospitalized. Jones visits him. Steiner, whose name Anna-Luise never knew, tells Jones he loved her mother but she never loved him, he attended her burial, and — unknown by Fischer — saw Fischer weep. When Jones relays this to Anna-Luise, she doubts her father's tears.

12. During the Christmas season, Kips goes to Jones's office, gets him to translate a letter in Turkish evidently involving an American arms

purchase from the Skoda company in Prague, Czechoslovakia, for a Turkish company to ship perhaps to Palestine or Iran. Jones declines a gift in payment, agrees to keep the matter confidential, but tells Anna-Luise. She says her father wants to get his hooks into Jones. Though non-Catholic, Jones and Anna-Luise attend Christmas eve Mass, where they see every Toad except Kips. They wonder: Do Toads have souls? Jones thinks souls evolve in humans and believes Anna-Luise has one; Kips and Krueger, maybe; Belmont, Deane, and Mrs. Montgomery, no; Fischer has one, probably damned.

13. One Saturday after Christmas Jones drives Anna-Luise, in a nice sweater he gave her for Christmas, to ski again. He persuades her to go on a slope with others, where it's safer. He bribes a surly waiter for a window table, to watch for Anna-Luise. He reads from *The Knapsack*, a poetry anthology selected by Herbert Read. News of an accident interrupts him. Anna-Luise swerved to avoid an inexperienced, fallen skier, hit a tree, injured her head, bloodied her sweater. Leaving his Fiat, Jones rides in the ambulance to the hospital. He phones Fischer's house, but Albert tells him Fischer is busy and Jones should write him. After an agonizing time, an emergency physician informs Jones that Anna was anethetized for surgery but died.

14. Jones writes Fischer about Anna-Luise's death. Fischer doesn't appear at her burial at Saint Martin's cemetery, in Gibraltan-controlled Anglican ground. Jones returns to their flat, prepares a suicidal drink of whisky and 20 aspirin tablets. Mrs. Montgomery interrupts by phone to say Fischer wants to discuss a trust. Jones tells her he'll consider visiting, gulps the whisky, figures Fischer wants Anna-Luise's trust money from her mother, and sleeps.

15. After an 18-hour slumber, Jones determines to humiliate Fischer, borrows a car, drives to Versoix, and is admitted by Albert. Fischer, smiling with "ineffable superiority," tells Jones this: Fischer didn't attend Anna-Luise's funeral because she resembled her mother, Jones thinks he despises Fischer but really just hates him; to despise a person, one must experience deep disappointment which most people can't do; forgiveness is only Christian; if he believed in God he'd attack Him for making him capable of disappointment. Jones calls Fischer insane. Fischer says Jones isn't intelligent enough for that opinion, rambles about each Toad's greed, mentions Kips, then the trust. Anna-Louise's mother's will says if daughter died childless mother's capital goes to father. Since this proves she forgives him, he won't accept it. After rebuking him about Steiner, still alive, Jones is told the capital is his, replies that Anna-Luise's income was all saved for the child they hoped to have. Fischer challenges him to attend his final party, with ultra-gourmet food and huge checks as presents tempting the guests' ultimate greed. He holds up a golden Christmas cracker as though he were a priest with the Host.

Home again, Jones dreams of Fischer as a clown juggling eggs exploding when they drop. Next day, too cowardly for suicide, Jones works at the office, goes to an unexciting soft-porn movie. Next day he mails his acceptance of Fischer's party and plans to kill himself later by carbon monoxide in his garage.

16. Jones drives to Fischer's estate, is ushered by Albert to the snowy lakeside lawn, with a servant-tended log fire, brilliant lights, and a bran tub, which, Mrs. Montgomery explains, is full of crackers to be drawn out blindly after dinner. Caviar, wines, vodka, roast beef, cheese. Resisting bloody meat, Jones seeks oblivion with wine-bibbing. Fischer explains that guests may safely forfeit prizes if any wish and that each of five of the six identical cracker cylinders in the tub contains a blank check for 2,000,000 francs, each to be named as the recipient wishes. Fischer says Kips might seek research to cure his spinal curvature, Mrs. Montgomery might buy a lover, Deane might finance a movie, Belmont might try a tax-avoidable investment. Krueger says accepting a check is like accepting caviar. Fischer says that he's researching greed vs. fear since the sixth cylinder contains a bomb killing only the cracker-tape puller, that his party resembles Russian roulette, and that anyone wishing may leave now. Kip does. His lost share, Fischer says, will be split among survivors. Krueger and Belmont boast of previous risky gambles. Mrs. Montgomery calculates extra winnings, grabs a cylinder. It pops it harmlessly. Belmont pulls. Pop. Fischer suggests Jones try next since the odds are worsening. Jones replies he'll watch the entire infernal

greed experiment. Deane, drunk and reciting lines of a war movie starring, takes a cylinder. No bang. Krueger delays. Jones takes a cylinder, doesn't pull. Krueger, confessing his non-combat service, wants to sneak out. Fischer orders him to obey party rules. Krueger takes a cylinder, doesn't pull, steps away from Jones, who bites his tape and pulls with his good hand. His hope to join Anna-Luise in death fails. Fischer taunts cowardly Krueger. Krueger weeps in fear; so Jones pulls out another cylinder. Pop. Fischer calls him greedy only for death. Jones returns Kips's check to Fischer, with his own check buys Krueger's unpulled cylinder, escapes down the lawn near the lake and Anna-Luise's spiritual presence, pulls the tape. Tiny pop. Is Fischer laughing because he stole Jones's death? Steiner suddenly sloshes up, tells Jones he's sorry about Anna-Luise's death and has come to spit in Fischer's "God Almighty" face. Fischer tardily recognizes Steiner, who accuses him of causing Fischer's wife's death. Fischer wishes he'd had Kips double Steiner's salary to make him and Fischer's wife succumb to greed too, confesses his failure to buy Jones, then walks toward the lake. Steiner says hate can't last and now he only pities Fischer. The two hear Fischer shoot himself to death. Steiner won't let Jones take the revolver. Fischer resembles a dead dog, fearful no longer.

17. Jones finds his office work dulls his courage, while despair is deeper than irrelevant death. Reminders of Anna-Luise — two photos, one handwritten note, her chair, boiling an egg — seem to this half-believer like words heard at their midnight Mass — "you shall do [these things] ... in memory of me." He occasionally has coffee with Steiner and was once shouted at as "Mr. Smith" by Mrs. Montgomery near a jewelry shop.

Doctor Fischer of Geneva or The Bomb Party may be one of Greene's easiest novels to read but one of the most difficult to understand. Norman Sherry avoids it entirely. Michael Shelden devotes an irrelevant paragraph to it. It is tempting to dismiss it, the way Cedric Watts does, for being "slight and trivial." Source-hunting critics find much in it to occupy them. R. H. Miller suggests that Fischer's "prototype ... is Erik Krogh," since both "made their fortunes from products that meet a particular need" and both are "sociopath[s]." (Erik Krogh, in *England Made Me,* was based on Ivar Kreuger [1880–1932], the Swedish industrialist-swindler.) Haim Gordon, who writes much about Erik Krough [*sic*], suggests that activities within Roche, a Swiss-based pharmaceutical company, and particularly by its criminal employee Stanley Adams, "could easily have served as the model for *Dr. Fischer of Geneva or The Bomb Party,*" since Roche and Adams were both convicted of economic espionage and betraying trade secrets. W. J. West offers Thomas Chambers Windsor Roe (b. 1917) as a partial inspiration for Greene in adumbrating Fischer's nature. Roe was a shady, Brighton-born international lawyer with headquarters in Lausanne. He established a falsely advertised and quickly failing company called Royal Victoria Sausages, Ltd. (1961–1964, with a factory near Horsham, Sussex), tax-efficient Swiss companies, and lucrative tax-dodging off-shore shelters for some of Greene's foreign royalties (and those of Charlie Chaplin, Noël Coward, American actor George Sanders, etc.). Roe was arrested in Switzerland for criminal conspiracy (1965), convicted, and sentenced to six years in prison. Richard VanDerBeets, Sanders's biographer, summarizes Roe's crimes and mentions Greene. Greene gives Sir Herbert Read (1893–1968) a plug by having Jones read from *The Knapsack,* an anthology Read compiled; however, it doesn't include Ezra Pound's "The Seafarer," which Jones miraculously finds in it. (In both *The Lost Childhood and Other Essays* and *Ways of Escape,* Greene accords Read extraordinary praise.)

Georg M. A. Gaston regards *Doctor Fischer of Geneva* as akin to "allegory, fable, fairy tale, and detective story." He adds that it can be approached as a "study of ... evil; a dialectic ... between hating and despising; a commentary on ... greed; a ... love story; ... an ironic presentation ... of a novelist's self-created world and mind [and] Greene's most pessimistic word on his life-long pursuit of salvation." Mark Bosco approves of Gaston's approach but says that the novel must also be regarded as "a carnivalesque play on the major themes of Greene's religious imagination." Bosco adds that "Catholic ritual, tropes, and images are turned upside down or are transgressed ... to display the macabre effects of jealousy and greed on love," and thoroughly explicates.

Quentin Falk discusses the made-for-television movie based on and entitled *Dr. Fischer of Geneva* (1984, BBC/Consolidated), starring James Mason (as Fischer), Alan Bates (Jones), and Greta Scacchi (Anna-Luise). Cedric Watts describes it as "effective," "thanks largely to the sardonic acting of James Mason." (Sources: Bosco, 131; Falk, 198, 218; Gaston, 131; Gordon, 57; Greene, *Lost Childhood,* 137–42; Greene, *Ways of Escape,* 41–46; Miller, 145; Shelden, 454; VanDerBeets, 168–73; Watts, 81; West, 180–201 passim)

DODO (*The Human Factor*). He, Buffy, Dicky, and Harry are boisterous guests at Hargreaves's shoot.

DOLLY ("The Bear Fell Free"). She is evidently Farrell's pet. He paid Carter £3 per week to care for her.

DOMINGUEZ (*The Quiet American*). He is Fowler's loyal, conscientious, intelligent Indian assistant, from Bombay and then Goa. Fowler thinks he may be Catholic. Unwilling to kill any living creature, he is distressed when Fowler bats at a mosquito.

DOMINGUEZ, RAUL (*Our Man in Havana*). He is a Cuban pilot. Wormold makes up the name Raul Dominguez in his spy reports and says his creation is really a pilot to be recruited for aerial photography work. Enemy agents get wind of the report and cause the real Dominguez to die in a car accident.

DOMINGUEZ, RAUL (*Our Man in Havana*). He is a fictitious creation of Wormold in his list of imaginary recruits. Wormold reports that he is a pilot and should be hired to take aerial photographs of enemy constructions in the Oriente mountains, near Santiago. A real pilot of the same name is murdered by the opposition.

DONGEN (*England Made Me*). His is a name Hall mentions during his telephone conversation from Amsterdam with Krogh.

DON JUAN (*The Comedians*). Luis Pineda's yapping little dog. While residing with the Pinedas in sanctuary at their embassy, Jones calls the dog Midge.

DONNELL, FATHER ("Church Militant"). He is a missionary priest in Kenya. He warns the Archbishop that settling French nuns in the Kikuyu region is ill-advised — to no avail. Donnell's playfulness is evident in jokes he tries on Father Schmidt and the Archbishop.

DOPPELDORF, DR. ("Dear Dr. Falkenheim"). He is the author of a book Dr. Falkenheim recommended to the narrator, who read it with alleged pleasure.

DORA (*This Gun for Hire*). A sales girl says that certain silk knickers for sale at the jumble at St. Luke's would be tasty on Dora.

DORIS (*Brighton Rock*). She is Snow's senior waitress and habitually sneers at other waitresses' work.

DOUGLAS ("A Day Saved"). One of the names by which Robinson refers to the man he is pursuing. Robinson also calls him Canby, Fotheringay, Jones, and Wales.

DOUGLAS, JAMES (*Orient Express*). He is a reader who, Mabel Warren says, might like to read works by Quin C. Savory.

DOWN, CORA ("The Basement Room"). She is a person whose fourth marriage Baines reads about in the *Mail*.

DOWSON (*England Made Me*). He is the person to whom Sir Ronald dedicated *Viol and Vine,* his book of poetry.

"DREAM OF A STRANGE LAND" (1963). Short story. (Characters: Herr Colonel, the Commissioner, Herr General, Herr Director of the National Bank, Herr Professor.)

1. Herr Professor, 67, has been retired from the hospital for two years, lives in a house a few minutes from the capital, surrounded by firs and rocks. He treats only a few favored patients. His office features a bronze paperweight showing an eagle pulling on Prometheus's liver. One winter day a poor patient, with leprosy, appeals to Herr Professor to minister to him secretly, so that he won't be discovered, be released from his bank cashier's job, and live on a tiny pension. He foolishly offers to keep everything secret

and even suggests a bribe. Ejecting the fellow, Herr Professor leaves his office, enters his capacious dining room., finds a green apple on his sideboard, and crunches into it with his fine front teeth.

2. That same morning healthy Herr Colonel drives up in his Mercedes-Benz, not for medical advice but to report that Herr General, who on multiple leaves has enjoyed gambling at Monte Carlo for 50 years, and is to be surprised for his 70th birthday by a special party. Herr Colonel persuades, nay, orders, Herr Professor to let a squad of his men handle logistics and convert Herr Professor's house into a gaming establishment, discreetly away from authorities' "absurd laws" enforced by the jealous Commissioner. Herr Colonel has formulated plans to redo the dining room by installing chandeliers, roulette tables and chairs for 100 players, an orchestra to waft music from the summerhouse outside, and to convert the sideboard into a bar. Herr Professor smirks to cover his timidity and says nothing when Herr Colonel interprets this violation of the law as in a good cause.

3. An army of workers arrives, with all necessary equipment, three black-suited croupiers, musicians in winter coats, and Herr Colonel in his regimental evening suit. Herr Professor took his bronze Prometheus to his bedroom and was reading Schopenhauer, until Herr Colonel orders him to be host when Herr General arrives.

4. The rejected leper sloshes in galoshes toward the house, to appeal again before facing hospitalization or maybe drowning himself in the nearby lake. He sees a uniformed old man driven by in a Mercedes. The would-be patient plans to tell Herr Professor that it's better to obey the spirit of the law than the letter, that he'll handle "filthy" bank notes with gloves to protect clients. Puzzled by dazzling house lights, he spies two officers stagger outside, drunk and "betrayed," they complain, by roulette numbers. One pulls his revolver, considers suicide, but carelessly drops the weapon. They see the patient, think he's the gardener, decide on more champagne, and wobble inside. The patient, peering through a widow, concludes this is the wrong house — instead of crammed office, chandeliers, gamblers, shouting croupiers, even diaphanously clad ladies, tuneful music. Not merely wrong place, whole "wrong country." He can't find his way home again. He sees Herr Professor, who sees only a pressed face in outline, but he can see Herr Professor "clearly," looking like a guest at "the wrong party." The patient gives a you're-lost-too gesture, unseen because of outside darkness. The patient realizes the two can't meet, in this house, into which both have wandered by accident. Nothing here, for help. He hears a make-your-bets cry.

5. Herr Colonel drags Herr Professor to gamble alongside busy Herr General, who says he's had little good fortune yet. He advises Herr Professor to hedge by also betting zero. He does, and doesn't lose. They hear an explosive sound. Champagne corks, no doubt. But Herr General, remembering incidents in the Monte Carlo of old, grins and says he hoped for a gunshot.

Marie-Françoise-Allain reports details Greene shared with her about a dream that triggered this story: Location, Sweden; leper shoots self through forehead; Greene believed he himself was partly the leper, partly the professor. Greene writes about the dream in *A World of My Own*. Brian Thomas observes that the betrayer (Herr Professor) and the victim (the leper) both become strangers, each "the mirror image or double of the other," and both ultimately lost. Musically knowledgeable literary critics might make much of the selections Herr Colonel's musicians play, which include something from Franz Lehar (1870–1948), melodies from *La Belle Hélène* and *La Vie Parisienne* by Jacques Offenbach (1819–1880), and waltz strains out of Johann Strauss (1804-1849) or more likely Johann Strauss Jr. (1825-1899). "Dream of a Strange Land" was the subject of a 1976 television production. *See Shades of Greene*. (Sources: Allain, 28–29; Falk, 215; Greene, *A World of My Own*, xx-xxi; Thomas, 105)

DREID (*This Gun for Hire*). In talk about financing *Aladdin* in Nottwich, Dreid's owing money to Callitrope's uncle is mentioned.

DREUTHER, HERBERT (*Loser Takes All*). He is the powerful, white-haired boss of Sitra, a big company with headquarters in London. His competitive associate is Sir Walter Blixon. A. N. Bowles holds enough shares to tip the balance either way should he choose to sell. Dreuther has been married four times, finds "good" women dull, has a yacht called the *Seagull* along the Mediterranean coasts, and speaks flawless French. His employees call him the Gom (Grand Old Man). He orders Bertram, one of his accountants, to marry not in London but in Monte Carlo, then honeymoon on the *Seagull*. They wed, but Dreuther arrives almost disastrously nine days late. He advises Bertram that his bride Cary may prefer romantic poverty to a life of sterile wealth that Bertram could provide by virtue of his sudden gambling success.

Norman Sherry quotes the description of Dreuther at the Monte Carlo bar, where Bertram finds him having a Pernod, chatting with the bartender in French, with yachting cap, growth of white whiskers, sweat shirt, and baggy old pants; then Sherry calls the paragraph a "sketch" of Alexander Korda,* the film mogul aboard whose yacht the *Elsewhere* Greene once sailed for a month (beginning September 27, 1951). Sherry adds that on the *Elsewhere* Greene rubbed elbows with Laurence Olivier, Vivien Leigh, and Margot Fonteyn, among other beautiful people. Paralleling this, Greene has Dreuther inviting writers, actresses, hypnotist, rosarian, research physician, etc., aboard his *Seagull* for a month at a time.

Herbert Dreuther is complex, as Greene wants readers to understand, since he has Dreuther quote Charles Baudelaire and understand Jean Racine. Also, Dreuther's advice to Bertram, which is both astringent and self-revelatory, rewards consideration. Greene says Dreuther "is undeniably Alexander Korda, and the story ... is soaked in memories of Alex, a man whom I loved." Earlier, in a *Collected Edition* introduction, Greene avers, not honestly, that Dreuther is his only fictional character based on a real person. (Sources: Greene, *Loser Takes All*, *Collected Edition*, 124–25; Greene, *Ways of Escape*, 224; Sherry II, 381, 383–84)

DREW, JEFF ("Dear Dr. Falkenheim"). He was an indigent old man hired by Browne's department store in Canada to play Father Christmas. He dropped presents from a helicopter and landed in the store parking lot. When he got out, he was beheaded by the rear propeller.

DREW, LORD BREWITT ("The Lieutenant Died Last"). He owns private grounds in Potter. His absence makes it easier for Bill Purves to practice his lifelong habit of poaching for rabbits and birds in the lord's preserves.

DREWITT (*Brighton Rock*). A graduate of Lancaster College, Drewitt is a corrupt lawyer in Brighton, married 25 years, living in a shaky, sooty house near the railroad line, and suffering from chronic indigestion. When Pinkie engaged him, Drewitt lost his job representing the Bakely Trust. He labels empty file boxes with fictitious clients' names, for show. Drewitt is in Pinkie's room when Spicer is killed just outside. Bribed, Drewitt arranges Pinkie's marriage to Rose. Pinkie distances Drewitt from inquisitive authorities by sending him to Boulogne. Ida Arnold's lie to Dallow that Drewitt is in police custody precipitates final action against Pinkie. Drewitt's numerous literary quotations to Pinkie includes Christopher Marlowe's ominous one from *Tragedy of Dr. Faustus*: "Why, this is Hell, nor are we out of it." Leopoldo Duran says Greene "didn't much like Marlowe's *Faustus*." In a *Collected Edition* introduction, Greene says when Prewitt (as Drewitt is called in some editions) envies typists carrying cases, the idea reflects writing by Beatrix Potter (1866–1943), whose works Greene relished. (Source: Greene, *Brighton Rock*, *Collected Edition*, xiii)

"A DRIVE IN THE COUNTRY" (1937). Short story. (Characters: Bergson, Alf Cohen, Fred, Joe, Mike, Harry Roy, Peter Weatherall.) An unnamed girl is tired of her life, secure but boringly routine, with her staid parents and sister. Her stodgy father, head clerk at Bergson's Export Agency, has steadily improved their house in Golding's Park, and it will be paid for in 15 more years. Her boyfriend, Fred, 30, is unemployed in these hard times, is unstable, drinks a bit, and is regarded as "crazy" by his father. One night the girl, after hearing through the thin wall her parents' tender and comforting lovemaking, exits to meet Fred, who takes her for a drive into the country. She is willing to go away with him. He suggests a roadhouse where his friend Mick may be, have a few drinks, and then perhaps sleep in the car, which he admits he didn't borrow but stole. They agree to drive past the place, off the road, and into a field. They kiss. He has a drink from his bottle. She notices a revolver in his pocket. They walk away from the car. It begins to rain. He complains that, being "of the ruling class" and hence an uninsured worker, he can neither rely on the dole nor find work nowadays. He wants to shoot her, then himself. She protests. She wants not only irresponsible excitement but also loving security. He goes among the trees and kills himself. She returns to the car, turns off the switchboard light, avoids taking anything, finds the roadhouse, hears Mike say he is a "Bolshie," and catches a ride from Mike to her home. Mike wants to come in with her, but she says no. He drives off. She re-enters her home, tells her awakened and concerned father that she was checking the door bolt. She concludes that weak, crippled people aren't tragic but merely somewhat repulsive, remembers that her father recently checked their roof for leaks, and tenderly notes that the door bolt, though flimsy, was precisely there — installed by "a Man," namely, that Bergson's head clerk.

Richard Kelly reports that Greene, who says he attempted suicide several times, first "embodied this dramatic and personal subject" in "A Drive in the Country," which in Kelly's opinion is "flawed" because Fred is vaguely characterized and the girl is "poorly motivated." A. A. DeVitis finds that the background of the story "suggest[s] the economically deprived period of the thirties." Gangeshwar Rai contends that the story existentially "embodies the theme of anxiety and hopelessness man is suffering from in the modern busy urban life and points out that both possession and deprivation have dehumanizing effect on man." "A Drive in the Country" was the subject of a 1976 television production. *See Shades of Greene.* (Sources: DeVitis, 170; Falk, 215; Kelly, 27; Rai, 109)

DRIVER ("The Lieutenant Died Last"). He is Potter's constable. The German soldiers herd Driver and the other villagers into the Black Boar.

DRIVER, FREDERICK ("When Greek Meets Greek"). He is Lord Driver's son. Released from prison, Fred, as he called, enrolls in Nicholas Fennick's phony St. Ambrose's College, in Oxford, meets Fennick's niece Elisabeth Cross, and plans with her to outwit both his father and her uncle, marry, and take over St. Ambrose's.

DRIVER, LORD ("When Greek Meets Greek"). He is a pretend aristocrat. He enrolls his son Frederick in Nicholas Fennick's phony St. Ambrose's College, in Oxford, without paying. Eventually, Fred and Elizabeth Cross, Fennick's niece, meet. They outwit both of the oldsters, and plan to marry and take over St. Ambrose's.

DROVER, CONRAD (*It's a Battlefield*). He is Jim Drover's brainier but mixed-up brother. He clerks for £6 a week in the Regal Assurance Company, is passively in love with Jim's wife Milly. When Jim is imprisoned for murder and awaits hanging or a reprieve and an 18-year sentence, Conrad timidly sleeps a couple of times with Milly. Taunted for cowardice by Milly, Conrad buys a revolver, stalks the Assistant Commissioner, fires what proves to be a blank cartridge at him, and is immediately crushed by a car skidding on the rainy street. He is hospitalized, operated on, but dies.

Conrad's parents named him after a merchant seaman who lodged with them. This is a tip of the hat to Joseph Conrad, whose works Greene admired. Another Greene touch occurs when Conrad's parents told him there was no point in naming him Herbert, after his uncle. One of Greene's brothers was Herbert Greene.* Michael Shelden and Norman Sherry note that Greene's description of Conrad's horrible pains after being hit by the car were made more vivid by Greene's experiencing pain himself but, more significantly, his taking note of the effects of pain witnessed by others, when he was hospitalized for appendicitis (October 1926). Greene's paragraphs detailing Conrad's agony seem unduly protracted. (Sources: Shelden, 134–35; Sherry I, 324)

DROVER, JIM (*It's a Battlefield*). He was a bus driver, 38, earning £3 a week, and has inchoate Communist leanings. During a Red-led strike, he observed his wife, to whom he was married five years, being threatened by a club-wielding policeman named Arthur Coney, stabbed him fatally, and is now in prison awaiting sentencing. After Conrad, his brother, is killed by a car, Jim is reprieved but must serve 18 years in prison.

DROVER, MILLY (*It's a Battlefield*). She is Jim Drover's frail, so-so pretty, clumsy wife, 27 after five years of marriage. She misses her husband in prison for murder, visited him there, and doesn't know how she can stand either his execution or his being sentenced to 18 years in prison. She sleeps a couple of times with Jim's brother Conrad Drover, who has long loved her from a distance. Milly can't even crochet straight.

DRUCE (*The Man Within*). He is one of Carlyon's crew of smugglers. He is caught at the beach by the revenuer Hilliard and his men. Andrews identifies Druce at the Assizes in Lewes.

DRUCE, CAPTAIN (*The Heart of the Matter*). He is a police officer who searches various ships, including the *Esperança,* with Scobie accompanying him.

DUBOIS, ALEXANDRE (*The Comedians*). He was the lawyer retained by Brown's mother. She willed him one share of her Trianon hotel.

DUBOIS, M. DESPREZ (*The Quiet American*). He is or was a friend of Captain Trouin's father in Vietnam. Trouin tells Fowler that the first time he dropped napalm on a village he imagined he might be killing old Dubois.

DUCKER (*The Heart of the Matter*). Ducker and Tierney are praised in the *Downhamian* news bulletin, read by Harris, for being good soccer forwards.

DUKE (*The Quiet American*). He is Pyle's black dog. His paw prints on wet cement provide Vigot the clue that Pyle visited Fowler shortly before Pyle's death.

DUNCAN, MISS (*The End of the Affair*). She was a musician performing during a function (July 23, 1926) at a school Sarah Miles attended as a child — this according to a program that fell out of a book of hers that Bendrix was looking at after Sarah's death.

DUNLOP ("A Visit to Morin"). He is the narrator, an unmarried non-believer. When he was in Collingworth school, Dunlop read works by Pierre Morin, a Catholic novelist. After service in the war, Dunlop becomes a wine merchant, visits Morin in a village near Colmar, Germany, and discusses religion, faith, and belief with him.

Norman Sherry incorrectly suggests there is something of the persistent reporter, à la Montagu Parkinson of *A Burnt-Out Case,* in Dunlop's questioning and listening to Moran. Dunlop is not a reporter, and Morin knows it. Sherry says Dunlop interviews Morin, but he doesn't. In fact, Dunlop rebukes Morin for thinking he was a child when he was first influenced by Morin's writings, and would have returned to town at once if he had his car. (Source: Sherry III, 249, 250, 689)

DUNN, SIDNEY ("SID") (*Orient Express*). He is a Constantinople theater manager. Coral Musker signs in London to be a chorus dancer for Dunn's Babies. Carleton Myatt and Janet Pardoe see the show, but Coral isn't part of it.

DUNSTAN (*The End of the Affair*). He is Henry Miles's chief. At one point, Sarah Miles flirts with him, in an unproductive effort to try to forget Bendrix.

DUNWOODY (*The Ministry of Fear*). Prentice carelessly names Dunwoody to Rowe. Prentice adds that Dunwoody is watched as a traitorous courier of Home Security papers but is protected by his powerful father's political clout.

DUNWOODY, LADY (*The Ministry of Fear*). She phones Willi Hilfe at the Free Mothers' office. Later she is involved in his failed attempt to leave via Paddington station for transportation to Ireland.

DUNWOODY, LORD (*The Ministry of Fear*). Prentice reveals to Rowe that Lord Dunwoody has clout enough to protect his son, who may be a traitor.

DUPARC, CAPTAIN (*The Quiet American*). He is a member of the Press Liaison Service in Saigon. He is one of Granger's guests at the Vieux Moulin, along with Madame Deprez, at the time Pyle is killed.

DUPONT ("A Visit to Morin"). Morin mentions to Dunlop the name of Monsieur Dupont. He is perhaps an imaginary debating opponent of Morin and Dunlop.

DUPONT, CLEMENT (*The Comedians*). He and Hercule Dupont, his twin brother, are middle-aged owners of a Port-au-Prince funeral parlor. They manage Dr. Philipot's funeral, only to have their hearse broken into by Captain Concasseur and Philipot's coffin stolen.

DUPONT, HERCULE (*The Comedians*). He and his twin Clement Dupont are funeral directors. Captain Concasseur interrupts Dr. Philipot's funeral cortège.

DUPONT, LOUISE (*Travels with My Aunt*). She is or was one of Achille Dambreuse's mistresses, the other being Augusta. Achille established Louise (for afternoons) in the St. James part of the St. James and Albany Hotel in Paris, and Augusta (for evenings) in the Albany part of the St. James and Albany. His ménage à beaucoup ended when he, his wife, two of their four children, Louise, and Augusta all chanced to meet at tea-time.

DUPONT, MADAME (*Loser Takes All*). Bertram invents this woman. When Cary tells Bertram she's going to dinner with Philippe Chantier, Bertram counters by lying that he is dining with Madame Dupont, who, he adds, is young, beautiful, intelligent, rich, and recently widowed.

DUPONT, MLLE. (*The Heart of the Matter*). Helen Rolt remembers her as her bad-tempered French teacher at her school in Seaport, England.

DURAN, MIGUEL (*The Honorary Consul*). He accompanies Señora Vallejo, perhaps as her latest lover, to Plarr's funeral. Her husband couldn't attend.

DURAND (*The Heart of the Matter*). Scobie remembers Durand, a police chief in French Guinea. When Scobie tells the French naval officer at Pende that he went shooting with Durand, a pleasant Norman, he is curtly informed that Durand is now a prisoner in Dakar.

The implication is that Scobie's French friend probably didn't cooperate with the Vichy French.

DURAND, JACQUES ("An Appointment with the General"). He is the suave, handsome editor who hires Marie-Claire to interview the General.

DUROBIER ("A Visit to Morin"). He is a character in Pierre Morin's novel *Le Diable au Ciel*. Durobier's literal acceptance of orthodox Catholic dogma is wrongly thought to reflect Morin's beliefs.

DUTCH AMBASSADOR, THE (*Travels with My Aunt*). He, the British Ambassador, and the Nicaraguan Ambassador attend Visconti's party in Asunción.

DUVAL ("Two Gentle People"). He is Marie-Claire Duval's homosexual husband. Duval's lovers include François (painter), Toni (ballet dancer), and — new to Marie-Claire — a fellow named Pierre.

DUVAL, JEAN ("An Appointment with the General"). He is Marie-Claire Duval's husband, charming but impossible. Their "final" argument helps motivate her to take the assignment to interview the General.

DUVAL, MARIE-CLAIRE ("An Appointment with the General"). She is Jean Duval's childless, unhappy wife, who decides to get a divorce. She is an expert journalist, whom Durand hires to interview the General.

DUVAL, MARIE-CLAIRE ("Two Gentle People"). She is the middle-aged, childless, passively unhappy wife of a homosexual. She is pretty, with long, unsexy legs. By chance, Marie-Claire meets Henry C. Greaves, also unhappily married. They enjoy a harmless dinner together, then, too late to change fate, part.

DUVALIER, DR. FRANÇOIS (*The Comedians*). He is the hated, feared dictator of Haiti — president, ex-communicated Catholic, and resident of his palace afraid to step outside. His portrait resembles that of Baron Samedi, with graveyard black tail-suit and myopic, expressionless eyes behind thick-lensed spectacles. Duvalier remains unseen in the novel. Sufficient to suggest his control are appearances and actions of his stooge cabinet officials and his Tontons Macoute, with their sunglasses, black clothing, and weapons.

François Duvalier (1907–1971) was born in Port-au-Prince, Haiti, graduated from the University of Haiti School of Medicine (1934), was on its staff (1934–1943), was active in the U.S.-sponsored anti-yaws campaign, was director-general of the National Public Health Service (1946), and served as Minister of Public Health and Minister of Labor. Duvalier unsuccessfully opposed the coup of President Paul Eugène Magloire (1950), fled to the interior, practiced medicine, and benefited from the general public amnesty (1956). With army support, Duvalier was elected president (1957) for a six-year term but after a fake re-election (1961) declared himself president for life. During his regime, unprecedented in duration, Duvalier terrorized all and summarily executed many of his political opponents. He regimented and intimidated his subjects through his private army of death squads, known as Tontons Macoute. "Tontons Macoute," meaning "Uncle Grab Bag" in Creole, derives from a Haitian fairy tale in which the bogeyman grabs children, puts them in his sack, and kidnaps them. Under Duvalier the Haitian economy worsened and illiteracy never fell below 90 percent. He practiced Voodoo, partly to make the people believe he possessed supernatural powers over them. By some Haitians he was called Baron Samedi, a character in Voodoo mythology known to haunt cemeteries, wear a top hat and tails, and smoke a cigar. Duvalier's wife was Simone Ovide Duvalier; their son, Jean-Claude Duvalier. Before his death, Duvalier made arrangements for Jean-Claude to succeed him (1971). Duvalier was known as Papa Doc; his wife, Mama Doc; their son, Baby Doc.

Norman Sherry reports this about Duvalier and his opinion of Greene: Duvalier accused Greene of racism in a fancy pamphlet; Duvalier ordered Lucien Montas, his Cultural Affairs head and a journalist for *Le Nouvelliste,* to write what became *Graham Greene Démasqué: Finally Exposed.* Marie-Françoise Allain reprints Montas's introduction, in which Greene is called a drug addict and a torturer, while his novel *The Comedians* "n'est pas bien écrit ... le livre n'a aucune valeur." In an interview (1979), Greene told Sherry he feared Papa Doc might send goons to murder him. (Sources: Allain, 74–75; Sherry III, 372–73, 850)

ECKMAN (*Orient Express*). He worked in Constantinople in Carleton Myatt's company. Since he is a Jew turned Christian, Myatt neither likes nor trusts him. Eckman did badly, sold to Leo Stein, and disappeared.

Norman Sherry suggests that Greene's friend André Raffalovitch, a cultivated Jew who converted to Catholicism, was a model for Eckman. (Source: Sherry I, 426)

ECKMAN, EMMA (*Orient Express*). She is Eckman's wife, a Christian. She sews for Constantinople's Anglican Mission. When Myatt and Stein interview her, she appears mousy and says her husband may not wish to return to her.

EDITH (*Our Man in Havana*). When Wormold goes to his bank to withdraw some money, the teller delays when a friend named Henry phones him and the two discuss a friend named Edith. The teller says Edith looked "swell" yesterday.

EDITH (*Travels with My Aunt*). She is a British tourist in Paris whose loud voice at Maxim's is embarrassingly "ventriloquial."

EDWARD, UNCLE (*Our Man in Havana*). He is or was Wormold's uncle. Wormold asks in a letter to his sister Mary if he's still alive.

EDWARDS (*Orient Express*). He is a London *Clarion* journalist. From Vienna, Mabel Warren phones Edwards and expertly dictates her stories about Dr. Richard Czinner and Quin C. Savory.

EGERTON, COLONEL MARK (*This Gun for Hire*). In his letter to the Bishop, Acky blames Egerton for instigating an inquiry full of bribed and perjured testimony. It got Acky defrocked.

EGERTON, MRS. (*This Gun for Hire*). She is the wife of Colonel Mark Egerton, who started the inquiry against Acky. In his letter to the Bishop, Acky calls her a deceitful, scandal-mongering bitch.

EKMAN (*England Made Me*). He and his wife live on the fourth floor of the building in which Minty lives. Ekman is a dustman.

EKMAN, FRU (*England Made Me*). She is Minty's jolly neighbor.

ELIJAH ("The Trial of Pan"). God has a brief vision of this "minister," described as foul of breath and cruel.

ELIZABETH (*The Man Within*) see **GARNET, ELIZABETH**

ELLA, AUNT (*England Made Me*). She is Minty's aunt. She writes him after a silence of almost 20 years.

ELLIS, DR. HAVELOCK CARPENTER, EDWARD (*Travels with My Aunt*). Aunt Augusta tells Henry she once attended an important literary figure's funeral, also attended by Edward Carpenter, Dr. Havelock Ellis ([1859–1939] English scientist and author), [James] Ramsay MacDonald, E[dith]. Nesbit, [George] Bernard Shaw and his wife, and H. G. Wells.

ELSIE (*England Made Me*). This is a girl, perhaps from Brighton, whose name Hall mutters while napping on his Amsterdam-to-Copenhagen flight.

ELSIE (*Orient Express*). In a letter, Mabel Warren asks Con to give her love to Elsie.

EMANUEL (*A Burnt-Out Case*). This is the name given at baptism to a baby fathered by a leper and given birth by a wife, crippled with polio. Her husband, when cured of leprosy, left her. The priests ask no questions.

EMIL (*The Comedians*). He is a straggler from Henri Philipot's army of insurgents. Brown drives Emil, wounded in the foot, to Domingo.

EMILIO (*Rumour at Nightfall*). He delivers the Aljerema-San Juan mail, is also a San Juan brothel-keeping street pimp. He worked three years as a waiter in London; so his English is good. Emilio is killed by Caveda's men for blathering to Chase.

EMMA ("The Basement Room"). She is Baines's mistress and lives near where the Baineses are the Lane family's servants. When Philip first sees Emma, he notes she seems pinched, skinny, and not someone he can concoct a story about. Baines introduces Philip to Emma as his niece. Mrs. Baines leaves supposedly to visit her dying mother, returns secretly, and finds the lovers in an upstairs bedroom. Philip witnesses the Baineses' fight, Mrs. Baines's accidental death, and Baines's sneaking Emma from the mansion before summoning the authorities. When questioned, Philip reveals the truth and blurts Emma's name.

R. H. Miller sees Emma as a precursor of Rose in *Brighton Rock*—both, though ready for love and joy, are pathetically "frail and identity-less." (Source: Miller, 152)

EMMA (*This Gun for Hire*). She is the German-speaking secretary of the Czech that Raven assassinates. Since she is present, he kills her also. Visions haunt him of his shooting her through both eyes.

THE END OF THE AFFAIR (1951). Novel. (Characters: Alfred, Bendrix, Maurice Bendrix, Bertram, Mrs. Bertram, Black, Sylvia Black, Lady Bolton, Carter, the Chief Warden, Beatrice Collins, Father Crompton, Miss Duncan, Dunstan, Jones, Sir William Mallock, Maud, Miles, Henry Miles, Sarah Miles, Alfred Parkis, Lance Parkis, Mrs. Parkis, Mary Pippitt, Prentice, Russell, Savage, Miss Smythe, Richard Smythe, Peter Waterbury, Wilson, X, Y).

Book One: 1. Maurice Bendrix, novelist, is the narrator. He could start this story anywhere. Like other stories, it has neither beginning nor ending. He starts thus: Bendrix sees Henry Miles one rainy night (January 1946). They live opposite each other at (Clapham) Common (Bendrix at 14 Cedar Road; Miles, at 17). They haven't seen each other since June 1944. Bendrix slept with Henry's wife Sarah Miles, now hates her. The two men drink at a pub, go to the Mileses' home. Henry suspects Sarah of infidelity, may hire detective Savage to investigate, but is reluctant. Bendrix offers to talk with Savage. Returning from a rainy walk, Sarah is startled to see Bendrix. Both men worry about her health.

2. Bendrix engages Savage's agency at three guineas per day plus expenses to check on Sarah.

3. Bendrix recalls seeking Henry (summer 1939). Henry worked at the Ministry of Pensions, and Bendrix needed material for a novel about a senior civil servant. Invited by Henry to a party, he first met beautiful, friendly Sarah.

4. Bendrix's landlady tells him Mrs. Miles called. He calls back, but the number has been changed. Sarah phones again. He fibs he was about to phone. She wants to have lunch. He feels hopeful — for one final bed time.

5. They rendezvous. He suggests Rules for lunch, where they formerly went and where he lies he's often gone since. She wants him to be friendly with Henry, who is lonely and aloof. They part on the street. She coughs violently.

6. Bendrix's lame leg kept him in civilian life during the war. He served in Civil Defense. His and Sarah's love delighted him. He wrote on schedule, but not when love became a love affair and he snarlingly knew it would end. The Rules lunch stymied his creativity. Alfred Parkis, Savage's self-deprecating man assigned to follow Sarah, reports to Bendrix: Sarah lunched with some strange man and then sadly visited a Catholic church. Bendrix admits he lunched with Sarah.

7. Bendrix, half-jealous of Henry, who doesn't possess Sarah physically but sees her at home, recalls dining with her, discussing Henry's work habits, kissing her, seeing a movie based on one of his novels, their eating onions because Henry disliked onions, and making love in the Bristol hotel — destroyed Bendrix adds, during the Blitz. He casually took her home to Henry, who offered him a drink and whom Bendrix oddly liked more than he liked Sarah.

Book Two: 1. Bendrix muses on his arrogance, lack of trust, self-doubt, while making love to Sarah and afterwards. Once on the floor downstairs while Henry was abed with a cold. Henry meandered down for a hot-water bottle minutes later. Sarah felt no remorse, lived for the moment, indifferent to eternity, then. She told Bendrix she and Henry had been celibate a decade; Bendrix was unique among her lovers; none would replace him. This proved true.

2. Seven years later, Parkis writes Bendrix. Through contact with Sarah's maid (Maud) at 17 Cedar Road, Parkis obtained a letter she started to Bendrix (he thinks, however, to another lover) and discarded. She also walked to 16 Cedar Road nearby. Bendrix ponders his jealousy, his badgering Sarah so as to end their affair, her uncritically calm responses.

Back in May 1940, with Henry working late in Home Security, Bendrix, intending to hurt Sarah, took a teen-age streetwalker to a pub for pre-sex drinks but paid and dumped her there. Sarah's calmly phoning next morning caused him to wonder whether, if there's a God, His enemy the devil's function is to kill love.

3. In his next report, Parkis says Sarah approached 16 Cedar Road, where the maid met Parkis's son (Lance), stationed there to help. In a newspaper at his authors' club, Bendrix sees a picture of Henry, honored for Ministry services, and with Sarah. Bendrix decides to see Sarah again and therefore invites Henry for a knowingly untasty lunch at the club. Henry tells Bendrix he didn't hire Savage the detective after all. Bendrix said he did, gives Henry the second report, watches him, outraged, burn it in the club's lounge fireplace, and leave. It's been only weeks (since January 1946), and Henry seems dignified.

4. Bendrix follows Henry. They sit in the rain. Henry, crying, guesses Bendrix and his wife were lovers, wonders why Sarah didn't leave him. Bendrix venomously replies: Henry was both her meal ticket and easy to fool, as other men had done before; it's fun to discuss it, now that it's all over; you, passionless, pimped for her; she's got a Cedar Road lover; I ultimately bored her; our professional labors don't matter. Henry is tactful. Bendrix remembers Sarah's farewell.

5. June 1944. Sarah comes to Bendrix's place. She says that their love isn't ended simply by their no longer meeting, that we love God without seeing him. They make love during a V1 buzz-bomb attack. He wouldn't mind dying during this climax. V1s come nearer. He checks the basement; if the landlady isn't there, they'll be more secure there. An explosion hurls him into brief unconsciousness. He recovers slightly, walks up through debris, and sees

Sarah, astonished he's alive, says she saw his covered body, thought he was dead, prayed — for a miracle — says she'll return to Henry, adds that love never dies.

6. January 1946 again. After Sarah sees Bendrix and Henry when she returns from that rainy walk, Bendrix is hopeful but learns that she's gone to the country. No letters. No answer to his. Weeks pass. He thinks of suicide. Did she hope that bomb killed him? He calls her lover "X." After six months, hate stops, happiness returns, and Parkis reports. The other man at 16 Cedar is Richard Smythe, living with his unmarried sister. Bendrix plans to take Lance Parkis with him to Smythe's place, pretend the boy is ill, and thus meet X.

7. Miss Smythe admits Bendrix. Lance plays his part cleverly, as Arthur James Bridges, son of Bendrix, who is Bridges. Richard Smythe enters, handsome but for a disfiguring strawberry birthmark on his left cheek. Bendrix wonders how he could be Sarah's lover. Smythe reveals he is an atheistic "rationalist" eager to disabuse everyone, including Arthur pronto, of widespread religious lies. Bendrix counters that he too believes in nothing, though with touches of hope. Smythe shows puzzling embarrassment when Bendrix says he should meet Sarah Miles. Bendrix rules out Smythe as Sarah's lover.

8. Parkis reports he attended a cocktail party at Henry's and Sarah's home and filched her journal, which he gives Bendrix. Driven by envy, hatred, and suspicion, and expecting revelations of Sarah's new love, Bendrix finds the credible answer in her own words. He reads the last pages first, then the rest.

Book Three: 1. ... Only You remain; accord needful him my own peace.

February 12, 1946: I dreamed of love with Maurice, was denied; God, delay giving me Your anguish.

Bendrix then reads entries in chronological order.

2. June 12, 1944: I ponder love surviving physical love. Maurice queries me. I can't manufacture belief in omnipresent, all-loving God. Maurice and I are happy when we love but cause each other sorrow.

June 17, 1944: On the Common I saw a handsome man with a bad birthmark arguing against foolish belief in God. Maurice and I love and bicker. I am in the country with Henry, whose happiness I hope for. London again. More air raids. I can't both despair and believe in "dear" God. Why "dear"? After we made love, Maurice checked downstairs, and a bomb blasted us. I went down, saw him evidently dead, prayed to God that he should have been alive and happy without me, that I could return to Henry, that if God restored him I promised I'd give him up. When he walked back up, hurt but alive, I wished he were dead.

July 9, 1944: I dropped Henry by taxi at work, proceeded past Maurice's boarded windows, got home, found a letter from him, destroyed it unread.

3. July 10, 1944: In the Common the birthmark-stained neighbor, Richard Smythe, was inveighing against God, Gospel dating, and Christ, while his gray-haired sister distributed invitations. At dinner while Henry rambled about widows' pensions with Sir William Mallock, an insurance expert, I resisted interrupting to describe my nakedness with Maurice when that V1 fell.

July 15, 21, 22, 1944: I tried to forget Maurice by flirting with Dunstan, Henry's chief. No luck.

July 23–30, 1944: When a group visited a shelter at Bigwell-on-Sea, the Chief Warden and I kissed, fruitlessly. I asked God whether I should break my promise about Maurice, or keep it and become self-destructively sluttish. I dialed Maurice's number, but a girl said she'd borrowed the flat while he was away. I asked God, not quite believed in, to show me, a bitchy phony, what to love and I'd rob Him of my love.

4. September 12, 1944: Henry told me he's been promoted. So? When asleep, he smiled primly. I forget why I married him. Now I'm all virtuous, love nothing, not even You.

5. May 8, 1945: V.E. Day. I dislike peace. Henry said he might get shifted to another office, said peace meant quiet. I have nothing but quiet.

September 10, 1945: I chanced upon Smythe's card, consulted him, hoping he could destroy my belief so I could renege on my vow to You. I told him all about Maurice, Henry, my prayerful promise. He replied that most prayers aren't answered, we created God, therefore we love him, distorting his image in the process. I secretly wished, self-sacrificially, to touch, perhaps thus heal, Smythe's ugly birthmark. He advised my creating partial happiness by choosing either Henry or Maurice. I fed unwanted Richard's illusion by thanking him for the help and promising to return weekly; I prayed doing so would help him.

October 2, 1945: A rain drove me into a church, happening to be a Catholic one. I disliked its ugly statues. Richard had said we invent doctrines to satisfy desires. Why want the resurrection of our bodies? Mine, no. But, suddenly, Maurice's? Yes. If my body were vapor, could it love his resurrected body? I'd prefer my resurrected body instead of vapor. But Richard's resurrection fairy-tale is right. Henry called transubstantiation during Mass superstition. Christ suffering crucifixion was no nailed vapor. I can't hate vapor. What would hating God signify? Did God's body exist? I left the church hating Henry's talk about glandular deficiency as faith's source and crossing myself with so-called holy water.

6. January 10, 1946: I remembered piercing my nails into my hands when I prayed to You to let Maurice live; You were moving in my pain. Wanting to learn love of You, I reluctantly returned home shivering in the rain, and saw Henry there with Maurice, thus given back a second time.

7. January 18, 1946: I phoned Maurice and had lunch with him at Rules. Was this breaking my promise? If he argued, he would hate himself, and that always hurt me. Leaving, I wanted him to kiss me, but my violent coughing prevented it. I entered a church, told God I was tired.

8. February 3, 1946: I followed Maurice toward his pub unseen. Richard's opinions made me believe their reverse, recognize a true not legendary Christ. Outside, I saw Maurice again. Should I sit by him, have a drink, leave Henry, live with Maurice, type his ill-paying novels to save us money? If God turned Maurice around to see me, I'd greet him; He didn't. I went home, planned to phone Maurice, leave Henry, who wouldn't mind, planned to quit worrying about God, packed, wrote a letter saying dear Henry I'm going off with still-beloved Maurice. Henry popped in, started weeping, said Bendrix treated him to lunch. Henry said he loves me. I wanted him to become angry so I could leave him and go to Maurice. Henry's promising to try to be a better husband made me remain, destroy the letter. I lost Maurice again. God didn't do this; I did, and promised Henry to stay. I can't talk to anybody; I ask God to let me talk. I bought a crucifix, prayed to the crucified God; let me think of others, of Henry's tears, Richard Smythe's disfigurement, give me pain to love, then be healed.

February 4, 1946: Henry childishly escorted me places.

February 5, 1946: Henry's planning a vacation in France or Germany for us turned me selfish again. God, I'm still a bitchy phony; do away with me.

February 6, 1946: When Richard proposed marriage, I joked I was already married, then said he and Maurice had taught me to believe in God, plus. Richard said I'm beautiful therefore couldn't love anyone with an ugly birthmark, which he hates God for giving him. Seemingly at God's direction, I kissed his metal-tasting strawberried mark. We parted, he wrongly feeling I pitied him; I envy his God-mirroring pain.

February 10, 1946: Finally, I needlessly wrote God. You were with us always; when our little lovings were spent, You were there. Of You, ever good, I asked for pain but You gave peace. Let him have mine.

February 12, 1946: I was lovingly peaceful. But then I dreamed of ascending stairs to meet Maurice, whose love I sought; a stranger's voice warned me; I descended into waist-high waters. God, I want Maurice now and Your pain a bit later.

Book Four: 1. Bendrix, having read Sarah's diary, mainly feels sexual desire again, figuring physical love will cancel her stupid vow. He phones her. She says she's ill, in bed. Good, he sneers; he'll be right over. She hurriedly dresses, walks into the sleety night. He follows, loses her, and finds her in that same church. He is certain he, a man, can defeat Christ on that cross. She coughs, sees him, asks why he doesn't leave her alone. He says Parkis gave him her diary. Coughing again, she leans on him. He touches her fondly, says he'll wait until she's healthier, then they'll go to his Dorset cousin's empty cottage, worry about lawyers later; he'll write a commissioned biography of General (Charles George) Gordon, finish his novel, and money won't be a problem. But Sarah has fallen asleep. He childishly whispers love words in her ear. She awakens, says she's tired, will say goodbye here, promises to phone him — with fingers crossed, he notes — asks him to have mercy and leave, asks God to bless him. He thinks a God might well bless her.

2. Eight days pass. Bendrix takes notes on Gordon in the British Museum Reading Room, chances upon Parkis there, and back home he gets a phone call. Henry tells him Sarah has died and invites him for a drink.

Book Five: 1. Bendrix and Henry drink Sarah's whisky and talk. Henry says she asked for Father, wonders if she turned Catholic, says she'll be cremated. Bendrix, sneering at her intrusive God, challenges You to resurrect her after burning, feels her dying diminishes himself. Henry takes sleeping bills and gets Bendrix to remain overnight. Wanting to remember yet forget Sarah, he dreams of shopping with her, unsuccessfully but unworriedly.

Morning. Henry sleeps. The undertaker comes; then Smythe, who tells Bendrix that Sarah was becoming a Catholic, should be given a Catholic funeral not cremated. When Smythe goes upstairs and takes a lock of Sarah's hair, Bendrix calls her body refuse now and available for silly relic-taking. Smythe says she wrote asking him to pray for her. Confused, Bendrix returns home, incompletely repaired. A letter is there from Sarah: I am sick. I won't leave with you. I told a priest I wanted to be a Catholic, asked if he could marry us? No. I slammed out but then saw a crucifix. Maybe I'm a phony, but I've caught total belief like a disease, like love; I pray for death. Bendrix concludes he can't write a novel about Sarah, because life is unending.

2. Before Sarah's cremation at Golders Green, Bendrix grants Peter Waterbury, a patronizing critic, an interview. Waterbury's girlfriend, Sylvia Black, senses Bendrix's disgust with Waterbury and offers to accompany him part-way to the funeral.

3. Henry the day before phoned Bendrix to return. Father Crompton, the priest Sarah had consulted, was there. He said Sarah desired to become a Catholic and wouldn't like cremation. But Bendrix rudely disputes with him, saying plans shouldn't be altered.

4. Sylvia stays with Bendrix. They arrive at the crematorium late. Henry leaves, crying. Smythe leaves, silently. Parkis is there and, when asked, says his son Lance is very ill. Bendrix blandishes Sylvia into a dinner, to be followed — he feels sure — by inexpert or expert sex, as he decides. Feeling love/hate toward Sarah, he implores her to keep him from hurting Sylvia, next. Sarah's mother, Mrs. Bertram suddenly appears, asks if he is Mr. Bendrix, says Sarah called him her best friend. He courteously dismisses Sylvia, takes Mrs. Bertram to dinner, plies her with wine. Mrs. Bertram, a lapsed Catholic, was deserted and remarried, tells him she had Sarah secretly baptized Catholic in France when she was two, wishes Catholicism had taken hold of Sarah, like a vaccination. Alone again, Bendrix tells God that, though magic, He hadn't taken Sarah but Bendrix had, though now You have won. Bendrix dreams of shooting at unbreakable glass bottles.

5. Henry calls on Bendrix, asks about his work, invites him to reside with him, paying part of the rates, asks whether he believes in personal survival. No; further, like characters in fiction, the notion is undisprovable; but God is a lie. Henry confesses his long-lived sexual inability; says, unlike the widowed hero in Bendrix's novel *The Ambitious Host,* he feels his wife's presence in their house and, being dead, she can't be elsewhere; says Parkis, whom Bendrix identifies for him shamefacedly, visited him, reported his boy Lance's illness, wanted something of Sarah's, and was given a fairy-tale book she kept from her childhood.

6. Bendrix moves over to Henry's, brings a prostitute in, discovers he's permanently impotent, dreams joyfully of Sarah, evocatively reads some of Sarah's marked-up childhood books. In one he finds a 1926 school program involving music and poetry; in another, Sarah's marginal note about God. Ah, even then, he muses.

7. Henry attends a Mass for Sarah, invites Father Crompton to dinner. Bendrix, included, badgers him with critical remarks, gently answered. Parkis sends the fairy-tale book back by messenger, with a letter to Bendrix. In it he wrote that Lance, afflicted with appendicitis, ran a dangerous fever and needed surgery. Lance rambled about Mrs. Miles, whom he spoke with once on the street, and said he dreamed she gave him a present, which was this

book. Bendrix notes on its fly-leaf Sarah's childish hand expressing the wish that a sick person might read it. Father Crompton, shown this early message, counters Bendrix's doubts by quoting St. Augustine about time's non-durational present. Bendrix raves that Sarah was a lewd liar and he wants no pity, is countered by Father Crompton's praise of saints' versatility, reviles Catholicism, is told he hates well, goes upstairs, begins to fear these coincidences represent divine intervention, starts hating himself and his conduct, thinks nothing is worth loving/hating except You. He tells Sarah he's afraid. He ponders saints' sinning.

8. Bendrix sees Smythe on the Common. He says he's given up public speaking and private tutoring, doesn't know what to believe, and reluctantly reveals his birthmark — almost gone. He says electrical touches in a nursing home cured it. Bendrix compares saints to certain characters in his fiction hindering his creative progress. Henry tells him that Sarah's mother visited him at work and told him about Sarah's being baptized. Henry thinks it odd she was unconsciously Catholic and turned to Catholicism years later. Bendrix calls it coincidental. Smythe phones Bendrix, confesses his facial cure was not by electricity but ... Bendrix hangs up, lies to Henry about Smythe's message, but begins to fear coincident-like miracles — Mrs. Bertram? Lance's dream? Smythe? A dangerous tide is sweeping him. But he must save Henry from curiosity seekers. Bendrix resists destroying Sarah's journal, tells God he hates Him as though He exists, then tells Sarah she wins, he believes she has survived and God exists, but will retain hate to disturb God. He exits with Henry for a drink, sees his own damaged house where God gave him back his injured life, and asks God to leave him alone now.

Norman Sherry reports this: Greene began writing *The End of the Affair* while living on Capri (1948), continued writing it during an especially love-filled time there with Catherine Walston* (May 1950), and finished it aboard the *Elsewhere,* the private yacht of movie-mogul Alexander Korda,* then off San Remo (August 1950); Greene called *The End of the Affair* "his 'I' book — maybe because it is such a close transcript of his triangular relationship with Catherine and Harry [Walston, her husband]"; and further, its working title was *The Point of Departure.* In a *Collected Edition* introduction, Greene says use by Charles Dickens of first-person-singular narrators inspired him to try the method in *The End of the Affair.* He adds that he constructed the novel with ingenuity to avoid using tedious straight chronological narration and further was comforted by praise of the novel from William Faukner. *The End of the Affair* was published in London September 3, 1951.

As for source material influencing Greene's thoughts while writing this novel, A. A. DeVitis cites the study of St. Catharine of Genoa by Friedrich von Hügel (1852–1925), St. John of the Cross, "Ash Wednesday" by T. S. Eliot, and *The Good Soldier* by Ford Madox Ford (1873–1939). Philip Stratford says that, given "saint"-like Sarah's "miracles" and Bendrix's "reluctantly accept[ing]" God, *The End of the Affair* "came closer than any of Greene's [other] novels to an out-and-out demonstration of faith."

William Cash devotes an entire book to explain that Greene's "secret passion" for Catherine Walston, his most momentous fellow adulterer, inspired *The End of the Affair.* Cash also relates how Greene brought to bear on the novel elements from his vast knowledge of literature, especially by authors unhappy in marriage and often faithless. In "Shocker," the anonymous *Time* reviewer of *The End of the Affair* writes the following: "In this story, Greene apparently intended to show two things: 1) that saints are real human beings, who 'happen' nowadays just as they always will; 2) that no love affair, however sordid, can escape the terrible, endless implications of love." In his review, Greene's novelist-friend Evelyn Waugh (1903–1966) asserts (totally incorrectly) that this is the first of "Mr. Greene's works [in which] there is humor." Leopoldo Duran spends a whole chapter on Greene's sense of humor. David Lodge calls *The End of the Affair* not only "an enormously complicated ... detective story, in which a divine culprit is pursued by a godless detective," but also "the story of an 'eternal triangle' in a highly significant sense: Bendrix's rival for Sarah's love is not another man, not Henry, but God." DeVitis, highly praising *The End of the Affair,* lists its brilliantly managed stylistic and structural features: "[T]he emotionally involved and therefore unreliable narrator, stream-of-consciousness, the flashback or time shift, the diary, the letter, the inner reverie, the use of dream for symbolical as well as foreshadowing purposes, and the spiritual debate." Ronald G. Walker reports that of 20 novels by Greene that he studied, *The End of the Affair* has the most narrative divisions, 60, averaging only 990 words each. Its time-line is surely the most difficult of Greene's fictions to keep straight.

Given the latitude of contemporary standards, it may be difficult nowadays to realize that when *The End of the Affair* was published, there was talk of its being prosecuted or banned. Acceptable novels weren't supposed to mention, as Greene's account of Bendrix and Sarah together does, pubic hair, penetration, and orgasm. John Atkins posits that "[i]f we are to fix a time for Greene's emergence into sexual maturity in his fiction it must be 1951 with the publication of *The End of the Affair*. The snigger is completely gone, mere prurience is set aside, and he faces the sexual relationship uncompromisingly, even if bitterly. Sensibly, he judges sex by its results as well as by its pretences. The lover's instinct he encounters head-on."

The End of the Affair was made into a movie (1955), starring Deborah Kerr (as Sarah), Van Johnson (Bendrix), and John Mills (Parkis). Gene D. Phillips comments that the action in it is in chronological order, to Greene's displeasure, that the "miracles" (the disappearance of Smythe's birthmark, Parkis's son's recovery) are omitted, that Mills is splendid while Van Johnson was miscast. Regarding Van Johnson, Quentin Falk reports Greene's agreement, also that in the British version of the movie the lambasting of Father Crompton by Bendrix was deleted. Anne Piroëlle praises the performances by Deborah Kerr and John Mills, says Van Johnson's lacks "subtlety and depth," and adds that Greene's desire to play "all the scenes in flashback" was overridden by the producers, who thought flashbacks "would ... proving confusing to audiences." Cedric Watts dismisses the movie as "an indifferent version."

Neil Jordan (b. 1950), the Irish novelist, short-story writer, and movie writer-director-producer, was already famous before gaining added lustre by writing and directing *The Crying Game* (1992). Later he wrote an adaptation of *The End of the Affair* and directed it brilliantly (1999). It starred Ralph Fiennes, Julianne Moore, and Stephen Rea. (Sources: Atkins, 52; Cash; Duran, 75–84; Falk, 109, 114, 155–56; DeVitis, 93–95, 95, 99; Greene, *The End of the Affair, Collected Edition,* vii-xi passim; Phillips, 129, 131, 132; Piroëlle, 83; 129–32; Sherry II, 333, 334, 379; "Shocker," 99; Stratford, 307; Walker, 231; Watts, 62)

"THE END OF THE PARTY" (1929). Short story. (Characters: Colin Henne-Falcon, Mrs. Henne-Falcon, Joyce, Morton, Francis Morton, Mrs. Morton, Peter Morton, Mabel Warren.)

Peter Morton, nine, awakens his twin brother Francis, on the rainy morning of January 5. Colin Henne-Falcon, a neighborhood friend, is 10 today. His mother is giving him another birthday party. The twins are invited again. Peter was born minutes earlier than Francis, that extra time in the light making him more self-reliant. Francis says he just dreamed he was dead and also dreamed about a big bird. He doesn't want to go to the party, where Mabel Warren and Joyce will be guests again and, older than the twins, chronically domineering. When they played hide-and-seek in darkness at last year's party, Mabel frightened him by suddenly touching him. Francis pretends he has a cold, takes a Biblical oath he won't go, hopes God will intervene. Peter tells his mother Francis is ill. But their nurse advocates cool air for Francis, and their mother imperceptively says one need fear neither death nor darkness. Off they go. Once there, Francis tries to avoid playing hide-and-seek. But when Peter, attempting to help, says Francis fears the dark, Francis boldly says he'll play. The bright chandelier is extinguished. Darkness descends like a hooded-winged bat. The boys scatter to hide. The girls will do the seeking. Peter intuitively guesses Francis is hiding between a certain bookcase and settee, finds him, puts a comforting hand on him, and promises to stay close. When lights bloom again, Francis is dead, beyond terror and darkness, and Peter wonders why he can feel in himself Francis's scared pulse beating on.

Norman Sherry, Neil Sinyard, and Richard Kelly note parallels between Greene and Francis Morton. Both feared bats, darkness, parents' misunderstanding, strangers' footsteps. Kelly finds irony in Peter's waking Francis in the morning from a dream of death, only to touch him into death that evening. A. A. DeVitis says Peter "inherits his dead brother's fear." Roland A. Pierloot theorizes that the Morton twins, who "represent opposite complementary poles," foreshadow the Farrant twins in *England Made Me* "in a nuclear form." (Sources: DeVitis, 60; Kelly, 17, 18; Sherry I, 15; Sinyard, 89)

ENGLAND MADE ME (1935). Novel. (Characters: Andersson, Andersson, Anna, Annette, Aronstein, Asplund, Batterson, Baxter, Bergsten, Beyer, Calloway, Collins, Connell, the Crown Prince, Davidge, Lucia Davidge, Mrs. Davidge, Roderick Davidge, De Laszlo, Delia, Dongen, Dowson, Ekman, Fru Ekman, Aunt Ella, Elsie, Farrant, Anthony Farrant, Kate Farrant, Foreign Secretary, Fuzzy Wuzzy, the General Manager, Gouldsmith, Gower, Grey Lady, Captain Gullie, Fred Hall, Professor Hammarsten, Hammond, Henriques, Jack, James, Erik Krogh, Lagerson, Uncle Laurie, Laurin, Loewenstein, GL, Mabel, the Manager, Marina, Maud, Ferdinand Minty, Mrs. Minty, Miss Mollison, Murphy, Nils, O'Connor, Partridge, Patterson, Pihlström, the Princess, Herr Redaktur, Sir Ronald, Scott, Sparrow, RS, Stefenson, Stodger, Tester, Puffin Travers, Whitaker, Major Wilbur, Williamson, Mrs. Wisecock.)

Part I. 1. London, autumn. Kate Farrant drinks gin in a pub, awaiting her brother Anthony ("Tony") Farrant. They are twins, 33. Born a half-hour earlier, Kate domineers while Tony charms. She works for Erik Krogh in Sweden. He will hire Tony. Tony, a charmingly irresponsible sponger, unemployed again, arrives and lets Kate take him by taxi for his passport to his digs, redolent of girlfriends. The twins remember when he played hookey and she forced him to return to school.

2. By boat to Gothenburg to report to Krogh, Tony rationalizingly reminisces about school, Kate, the cut under his eye caused by his carelessly skinning a rabbit, the scar he lies is a war wound, his unearned Harrow necktie, prostitutes, cadged money, crooked deals from Aden to Bangkok, getting caught pretending to be an army captain, and rich Krogh.

3. At Gothenburg Tony meets and fibbingly charms Lucia Davidge and her parents, vacationing from Coventry and heading for Stockholm by an English pleasure-cruiser. Tony and Kate drink schnapps — she too many. Tony shoots expertly at a booth and wins a blue vase for Kate, a toy tiger for himself. When Kate takes his arm, she loosens his grip on the vase. It drops and breaks. They separately muse about, and together talk about, his shady deals, his missing 21st-birthday signet ring ("popped?," i.e. sold), their father's death. Kate, remembering her careful professional climb, disapproves of but needs to aid Tony, who ripostes her complaints with panache.

Part II. 1. Krogh surveys his five-floor, steel-and-glass Krogh building, ponders the modern statue in the court, asks about Miss Farrant's arrival, and taxis to the British Legation, whose minister is Sir Ronald (from Harrow). Krogh's peasant father shot ducks for their food on Vätten; Krogh worked in American and French factories, speaks English and German in addition to Swedish, is now Europe's richest man and lends money to the French government, needs but ignores police protection because authorities would check his past and learn about his American monopoly.

2. At the legation, Krogh's observations of Chippendale, tea cups, and a hawk-like woman talking about poetry mix with memories of Chicago and that money-making, frictionless cutting machine in Barcelona. He takes two phone calls in Sir Ronald's office. Fred Hall, involved in the cutter, reports from Amsterdam about falling stock; Krogh orders a buy, to shore it. The second call requires instant action. After giving Sir Ronald a stock tip, Krogh returns to his office, checks quotations, and rushes to mollify Andersson, a Socialist causing labor unrest at his Nyköping factory (south of Stockholm).

3. Kate and Tony await Krogh in Krogh's apartment, in a tall building. Tony brashly fingers the man's suits and ties, suggests rewardrobing the tasteless fellow. Tony fears Kate's intimacy with Krogh is blotting their childhood memories. The two spar verbally, then turn calm. Krogh appears, fatigued. Tony senses easy victory over the gauche man, however rich. Kate introduces Tony. Krogh promises to interview him tomorrow, awkwardly lets him go, tells Kate that Laurin, a timid Krogh director, is ill.

Outside, two reporters, Ferdinand Minty, a

Harrow man 20 years in Stockholm, and Nils, a young Swede, accost Tony. Krogh brushed them off earlier. Minty offers to bribe Tony for information on Krogh. Cocky Tony gets to his hotel, unpacks, broods, displays some pin-ups, and reminisces.

4. Kate lies awake beside Krogh, asleep, his cold hand on her. When she told him about Tony's marksmanship at Gothenburg, he promised to hire him. Kate reminisces — training to be a nurse, learning shorthand, working well at Leather Lane, her father's moral maxims, his death, first sleeping with Krogh, rising stocks. Krogh's (i.e., the company) is safe.

Part III. 1. Minty feels lucky today, Tuesday, September 23 (1930?), picks up two general-delivery letters. The first remits his customary £15 family monthly allowance. The second, from Aunt Ella, breaks long silence and mentions his mother's failing memory, Uncle Laurie's death, Ella's seeing a Harrow lad at the Fakenhurst station. Minty sees a film star's limousine, a thrown bouquet, and Nils's grabbing its attached card. Minty gets it, reports to his editor, who rebukes him for missing an interview with Krogh but who happily hears Minty can pump Miss Farrant's gossipy brother.

2. Tony, the rain drenching his only suit, pauses for beer. Minty happens by. They talk about Harrow and about Krogh. Tony rushes to Krogh's. Bubbling, Kate says he's hired and she's delighted he's here with her — for now. Krogh, seeming shy, makes Tony his U.S.-style bodyguard. Tony criticizes the courtyard statue as highbrow and asks for wardrobe money.

3. Minty goes to Captain Gullie, Sir Ronald's military attaché, teases him by saying Tony calls himself a Scotsman, urges Sir Ronald to hold a Harrow dinner, and says Tony may be a fake and Krogh's company may tumble. He goes out, phones Tony at Krogh's, strikes a deal to buy inside information. Though Anglo-Catholic, Minty attends a Lutheran church service.

4. Tony accompanies Krogh, tired and bored, to the opera (*Tristan und Isolde*), phones Lucia Davidge during intermission, offers to give her his toy tiger, learns she'll meet him for breakfast tomorrow. Krogh sneaks out, is photographed once, and he and Tony avoid the crowds by taxiing to Tivoli. Tony gets rid of Pihlström and Professor Hammarsten, two journalists, and wins prizes for Krogh at a shooting booth. While Tony picks a girl and dances, Krogh remembers his shyness, working in Chicago, the cutter, present fiscal dangers. Hammarsten finds Krogh, would interview him but for Tony's arrival — with a girl from Lund. Hammarsten yammers about his translation of *Pericles* and about a play he has written. The girl reads Krogh's palm, has some beer, leaves. Suddenly Krogh promises 25,000 crowns for Hammarsten to produce his play.

5. Minty climbs to his fourth-floor flat, notes that his landlady let his tortured spider under glass escape, catches it, gets into a cold bed, and prays for success with Tony.

Part IV. 1. Tony meets Lucia — "Loo" — at the North Bridge. They embrace awkwardly while taxiing to Drottningholm for breakfast, try to find a love nest at the palace, but return to the city and arouse Minty. After clumsy efforts at offering more breakfast, Minty, who hates girls, learns from Tony about Krogh's encouragement of Hammarsten's play, and leaves his visitors to report the scoop. Tony, who grows indifferent, and Loo, who boasts of two former sexual encounters, make odd love.

2. When Hall phones from Amsterdam, Krogh persuades him to continue buying, to keep their stock steady, says America can be handled, tells himself to continue forgetting the past, asks Kate where likable Tony is.

3. In her office, Kate worries about Krogh's manipulated books and short-term loans. Tony enters. She envies his sexual alliance with Loo, seeing herself completed in him. She contrasts their passé human nationalism with Krogh's cold internationalism, fears Tony's old pleurisy weakened his chest, learns he's squiring the Davidges around, watches him depart.

Feeling linked between Tony and Krogh, Kate visits Krogh in his office and expresses worry about the short-term loans. He says they must keep them secret now and must spend lavishly for publicity, and suddenly proposes marriage. For his legal safety? No, for a future in England. She requests his promise of a settlement on herself and Tony. He agrees.

Returning to her office, Kate finds Tony reading confidential materials and guessing correctly that Krogh is "bolstering" Amsterdam by loans, brashly suggests blackmailing him and escaping to England together. Saying no, she agrees she loves Tony not Krogh. Tony plans a party at Saltsjöbaden, where he knows Laurin is recuperating.

Part V. 1. Andersson works at the Nyköping factory, hears a news item (about his father), leaves, ruminates on his father's tedious socialistic advice, and takes a train to Stockholm to see Krogh. When the porter won't open the gate and compares Krogh's wealth to Andersson's grubbiness, the lad suddenly thinks of his fellow workers' tragic unhappiness. Told that Krogh is at Saltsjöbaden, 20 kilometres distant, Andersson determines to get there.

2. Tony drives one of Krogh's fast cars with Kate and Krogh through the night toward Saltsjöbaden. At some stops, Krogh drinks excessively. At another stop, Krogh enjoys inspecting night work on a bridge.

3. Summoned by Krogh, faithful Hall, having steadied stock quotations, boards planes for Amsterdam-Copenhagen-Malmö-Stockholm flights. During the first leg, he reads, naps, recalls his Brighton bookie days, caresses his brass knuckles, envies director Laurin. At Malmö, Bergsten, a Grogh's director, boards a chartered air taxi and Hall, furious, must await a later one.

4. At the Saltsjöbaden party, Krogh drinks, Tony and Kate dance to voluptuous music, Hammarsten brings possible actors and actresses for his play, and when Tony and a blonde actress go outside they see young Andersson. The actress translates Andersson's gripe that his father was fired. Tony goes inside and reports Andersson's presence to Krogh, who tells Tony he framed old Andersson thus stopping a union strike and orders Tony to throw young Andersson out. Feeling kinship with the fellow's plight, Tony refuses. Kate begs Krogh to take her home. Hall suddenly enters. Hearing Andersson isn't wanted, Hall goes outside, bloodies him with his brass knuckles and kicks him in the stomach. Meanwhile, would-be thespians are shouting parts and the orchestra plays on.

Part VI. 1. Tony, remembering former disengagements, says a quick goodbye to Loo. The Davidges' cruiser is leaving. Tony promises to meet Loo in Coventry in a week. She tells him exactly where, half-doubting him. Sir Ronald gets into his first-class cruiser compartment, to return for a week back home.

Tony has coffee with Minty. Fellow losers, they discuss surgeries they suffered. Minty thinks of visiting his English aunt. Tony prefers recklessness to joy, plans to get money from Kate and try Coventry, gives Minty a valuable scoop — Kate will marry Krogh — goes to Krogh's, and carelessly tells a publicist there to criticize Krogh. Tony enters Kate's tidy office, his conceited failure opposing her humble success. He says he needs a loan to get to Coventry and Loo, laments Andersson's injury; won't play dirty for Krogh, avoids Kate's penknife jab, recalls their childish telepathic tricks. His yen for Loo overcomes his love for Kate. Wanting him to stay, Kate, resists giving him money. He says he told Minty about Krogh's marrying her. Labeling him naive, she surrenders some cash, asks him for dinner tonight.

2. Hall sees a newspaper headline about Krogh's approaching marriage to Kate, enters Krogh's, warns Krogh that Tony leaked about the wedding, could reveal their illegal loans in England, and should be stopped. Krogh says they'll keep Tony here by continuing his pay. Entering, Kate says Tony is going to England. Hall offers to frame Tony, à la Andersson. No, says Kate. Suggesting a poker game with Tony, Hall gets Kate to invite him to dine with Tony and her.

3. Behold vicious Hall, happy Tony, Krogh, Gullie, and Kate at poker. She folds, memorizes the dramatic scene within and beyond the windows. She would almost ask God to make beloved Tony stay with her. Tony's straight flush beats Hall, whose money Tony boasts will pay for a shoot in Scotland. Calling the game finished, Kate is scared by Hall's malice. Tony, offering to walk away with Hall, breezily bids Kate goodbye with a promise to write, as she begs him to stay to reminisce a little. She jealously curses Loo, whom, he counters, he loves. Gullie entertains Krogh and Kate with card tricks. Krogh finds some ties Tony bought and left for him. Krogh doesn't want them. Kate fondles them. Hall reappears, says he left Tony, needs a drink to cut the fog. Kate phones Tony's hotel, is told he's not there, leaves a message for him to call.

Part VII. Present at the cremation are Bergsten, Gullie, Hall, Hammarsten, Kate, Krogh, Laurin, and Minty. Minty wishes the body had been left in the water. He remembers three friends who also died. He proudly comments that the dead man's recent girlfriend is in England, unaware. Hammarsten tells Minty that his news item about a certain marriage almost cost Minty his job, comments on Krogh's new American stock issue. Minty and Gullie discuss the Harrow dinner, wonder how the man who drowned could have simply walked into the water. Minty says he saw Hall leave the scene, asks Hall for a statement, gets snarled at. Krogh, the brain, and Hall, the hand, drive away, together yet lonely. Kate tells Minty the wedding's off, Krogh and Hall have argued, Hall is culpable, Laurin will manage in New York, all here are non-socialistic thieves together, she has a job in Copenhagen. Minty thinks of his withered spider.

According to Norman Sherry, discarded titles for *England Made Me* were *Brother and Sister* and *The Shipwrecked*. Sherry adds that the title chosen is ironic and has to do with "the forming of a certain type of character [namely Tony] ... by the English public school." (If so, bad cess to Harrow and God help England.)

England Made Me, never popular, suffered weak early sales — only 4,500 copies in England and 930 in the United States — according to Michael Shelden and Sherry.

Cedric Watts calls *England Made Me* "hollow and unconvincing" with an "awkwardly contrived" plot and characters as "artificial constructs." Nonetheless, some minor figures are viable, especially over-powdered Loo, busy Gullie, bespectacled Hammarsten, pretentious Sir Ronald, thuggish Hall. Better are Greene's broad- and fine-brush treatment of scenery — urban, from the air, and during Tony's wild night drive. Greene made excellent use of sights seen during a visit with his brother Hugh Greene* to Sweden (August 1934). Michael Meyer, Greene's friend and an expert on Scandinavian sights and literatures, praises Greene for having "caught uncannily" the "atmosphere" of Stockholm. Not one to waste any experience, Greene patterned Tony's cremation on that of the mother of his wife Vivien Greene* (May 1933).

England Made Me was adapted into a movie (1972) starring Michael York (as Anthony Farrant) and Peter Finch (Erik Krogh). Locale and action are moved to a Germany corrupted by nascent Nazism for its historical appeal; Krogh becomes an unprincipled German industrialist-financier; and the Farrants are not twins but siblings. Quentin Falk discusses these changes. (Source: Falk, 170–77; Meyer, 134; Phillips, 184–85, 194; Shelden, 228; Sherry, I, 476–77, 484, 491, 503, 578; Sinyard, 155; Watts, 31, 217)

ENRIQUE (*Rumour at Nightfall*). He is one of Caveda's men. Because Enrique saw Chase report to General Diaz, Enrique and five of his men take Chase to the inn where Miguel, their leader, is. Described as handsome, fleshly, stupid, and resembling an opera tenor, Enrique carelessly looks out the window and gets himself shot dead.

ENRIQUE, FATHER (*Monsignor Quixote*). He is a Trappist at Osera whom Father Leopoldo wants to open the monastery gates when he hears gunfire.

ENTERTAINMENTS. Greene provided a distinction between his thriller novels and his more serious novels. He subtitled each of the following "an entertainment": *Stamboul Train* (1932), *A Gun for Sale* (1936), *The Confidential Agent* (1939), *The Ministry of Fear* (1943), *The Third Man* (1950), *The Fallen Idol* (1950 reprint of "The Basement Room"), *Loser Takes All* (1955), and *Our Man in Havana* (1958). From the start, the distinction was essentially meaningless. Almost every "entertainment" has content as serious as most of the other novels.

THE EPISODE. An unpublished novel Greene wrote in part while working for ten days at the British American Tobacco in London (1925). Greene sent a chapter to Vivienne Dayrell-Browning, his fiancée (later his wife; see Greene, Vivien). In it he presents a lover's proposal to and rejection by his girlfriend. Vivienne objected to being fictionalized; Greene pretended to her it was all fiction, then confessed the truth. Later Greene said *The Episode* was about "a young man caught up idealistically in a disappointing revolution." (Sources: Greene, *A Sort of Life*, 202; Shelden, 122, 132–33; Sherry I, 203, 269–70)

ERNEST (*The Ministry of Fear*). Rowe gets a wrong number when telephoning, is mistaken for Ernest by a hysterical person who tells him David must've told him that Minny, a pet cat, was killed in an air raid last night.

ERNEST ("Under the Garden"). He is or was the gardener at Winton Hall when Henry Wilditch, Wilditch's uncle, owned it and lived there. As a child, Wilditch regarded Ernest in his 20s as old. When Wilditch returns home, Ernest, though retired, still helps around the place and is really old. They reminisce about the garden and its environs.

As Michael Shelden notes, Ernest is based on Ernest Northrop, the gardener of Sir William Graham Greene,* Greene's uncle and at one time owner-resident of Harston House, Cambridgeshire. (Source: Shelden, 49–52)

ERTZÜGER, FRAU (*The Name of Action*). Kapper tells his wife Bertha she'll find the murdered policeman's blood stains past Frau Ertzüger's house and must cover them with dripping strips of raw liver to fool the street cleaners.

ESCOBAR, GUSTAVO (*The Honorary Consul*). He is Margarita Escobar's unfaithful husband, moustached, ruddy, deaf, and having a nose rearing like a *conquistador*'s horse. On the Chaco side of the Paraná river Escobar owns an *estancia,* with an airstrip useful when he smuggles whisky and cigarettes. He attends Plarr's funeral, despite perhaps knowing his wife was one of Plarr's ex-mistresses.

Greene later explained that in limning Escobar he "borrowed features" from the friend of a friend he had consulted in Buenos Aires in an unsuccessful effort to locate a public brothel. (Source: Greene, *Ways of Escape,* 302)

ESCOBAR, MARGARITA (*The Honorary Consul*). She is Gustavo Escobar's unfaithful wife. She was Plarr's mistress, whom he remembers as speaking French when being coarse in bed. Later Margarita was Colonel Perez's mistress, then Gaspar Vallejo's. She and her husband attend Plarr's funeral.

ETHEL (*Our Man in Havana*). She is the secretary of Miss Jenkinson, who is the security-pool supervisor in London's Intelligence headquarters.

EVANS (*The Heart of the Matter*). He is a police officer under Captain Druce's command during inspections of neutral ships off Sierra Leone.

EXCOFFIER, MONSIEUR (*Doctor Fischer of Geneva*). He is the nervously hovering official civil witness at Jones's and Anna-Luise's marriage.

FALKENHEIM, DR. ("Dear Dr. Falkenheim"). He is presumably a psychoanalyst to whom the narrator writes the letter constituting the short story. The narrator needed professional advice, explains how his and his pleasant wife's son Colin, when six, saw Father Christmas beheaded by helicopter propeller, refused to accept his physical death, but insisted, even when 12, that Father Christmas was dead like Christ and therefore is indestructible.

"FALLS THE SHADOW" see *THE NAME OF ACTION*

FANATIC ARABIA. Unfinished novel. (Source: Sherry I, 9, 584)

FANSHAWE (*It's a Battlefield*). He is a clerk at the gunshop which Conrad Drover enters. Drover thinks of buying a weapon but doesn't.

The name Fanshawe is so unusual that Greene may well have derived it from *Fanshawe, a Tale* by Nathaniel Hawthorne.

FARNE (*The Man Within*). He is the small, trim, efficient barrister working under Sir Henry Merriman. To prepare his case against the smugglers at the Assizes in Lewes, Farne tricks Andrews into talking too much. Farne still fails. The smugglers, acquitted of murder, are soon indicted for smuggling.

FARRANT (*England Made Me*). He was the father, deceased, of twins Kate and Anthony. They have numerous memories of him, often unpleasant.

FARRANT, ANTHONY (*England Made Me*). He is the slightly younger twin of Kate Farrant. They have an enigmatic relationship, are telepathically linked, and partly enjoy reminiscing. When Tony, as a child, was skinning a rabbit he accidentally cut himself under his left eye. Later he pretends the scar was the result of a war wound. (Michael Shelden's contention that Tony deliberately cut himself seems nonsensical.)

Tony is experienced in numerous shady deals, largely in the East. Now 33, Tony leaves London to accompany Kate via Gothenburg to Stockholm, where she works. At Gothenburg he meets Lucia Davidge, about to go to Stockholm for a holiday. In Stockholm, Tony is hired as bodyguard to Erik Krogh, a millionaire whose mistress Kate is. Tony sleeps briefly with Lucia in the bedroom of Minty, a reporter to whom he is willing to sell damaging business secrets. Tony pleases Krogh but soon outlives his usefulness. Krogh remains more tolerant than Hall, his tough associate, who murders Tony.

Richard Kelly, Norman Sherry, and Cedric Watts echo Greene's revelation that the model for Anthony Farrant was his oldest brother, Herbert Greene,* the family black sheep who was involved in espionage, held a variety of brief jobs, and was an alcoholic. If so, he must have been a superb talker; Tony's quick comebacks comprise a rhetorician's upmanship handbook. (Sources: Greene, *Ways of Escape,* 39; Kelly, 88; Shelden, 60; Sherry I, 493; Sherry III, 22; Watts 207)

FARRANT, KATE (*England Made Me*). She is Anthony Farrant's twin brother. Born a few minutes first, Kate is dominant and steady; Tony, mercurial and often dependent on her. She worked her way up in the commercial world to become the secretary and mistress of Erik Krogh, Stockholm business titan. At 33, Kate gets Tony to accompany her from London to Stockholm, where Krogh makes Tony his bodyguard. Kate responds to Tony as best she can when he is depressed and truthful, and when he is joyful and false. After his death, she plans to leave Stockholm for a job in Copenhagen. At one point, Kate tells Tony she is sterile.

Greene felt that he drew Kate "better than any other [woman]," except perhaps Sarah Miles in *The End of the Affair.* Were the Farrant twins incestuous? Critics differ. Greene says that apart from threats to capitalism, "the subject" of *England Made Me* is simply "a brother and sister in the confusion of incestuous love," with "self-protective instinct" keeping each from "self-discovery." (Source: Greene, *Ways of Escape,* 40, 41)

FARRELL, MRS. ("The Bear Fell Free"). She is Tony Farrell's widowed mother, unhappily watches him fly off from Croydon, and laments his death.

FARRELL, TONY ("The Bear Fell Free"). Farrell is a veteran of World War I, has a number of friends as well as a faithless girlfriend named Jane, wins money in the lottery, drinks excessively, accepts a dare to fly from London's Croydon airfield to New York, and crashes in the Irish Sea.

Ironically, the lottery was the Irish Sweepstakes and winner Tony's final resting place is the Irish Sea. Tony Farrell may be a sketch for the more portrait-like Anthony Farrant in *England Made Me.*

Michael Shelden suggests that the name Farrell may have come from *Foe-Farrell* (1918), a novel by Sir Arthur Quiller-Couch (1863–1944) that Greene often read as a youth. Cedric Watts sees something autobiographical in Farrell, partly because like Farrell Greene made a daring trip (to Liberia, 1935), more credibly because like Farrell he took a teddy bear along as a mascot when he traveled. Richard Kelly finds Farrell akin to Greene's brother Herbert Greene* in irresponsibility and recklessness. (Sources: Kelly, 88; Shelden, 71; Watts, 32, 132)

FAVERJON, MADAME (*Doctor Fischer of Geneva*). She was an especially greedy Toad at Fischer's earlier parties. Two years earlier, she was distressed at the Quail Party, because she loved birds. She committed suicide, perhaps because of self-loathing. At the first party Jones attends, Fischer proposes a toast in her memory.

FAVORITES, GREENE'S OWN. In a *Collected Edition* introduction, Greene named as his best stories "A Chance for Mr. Lever," "Cheap in August," "The Destructors," and "Under the Garden." To Leopoldo Duran, he named "The Basement Room," "Doctor Crombie," "The Destructors," "Dream of a Strange

Land," "The Hint of an Explanation," "Two Gentle People," "Under the Garden," and "A Visit to Morin." As for novels, to several friends at different times he expressed special satisfaction with *Brighton Rock, The Honorary Consul, The Human Factor, Monsignor Quixote, Power and the Glory,* and *Travels with My Aunt.* To a four-novel edition of his favorites he added *The Quiet American* to *The Honorary Consul, The Power and the Glory,* and *Travels with My Aunt.*

(Sources: Brydon, 84; Duran, 49; Greene, *Collected Stories, Collected Edition,* viii; Sinyard, 58)

FELIPE, FATHER (*Monsignor Quixote*). He is an elderly Trappist at Osera, now functioning as guest master.

FÉLIX ("Chagrin in Three Parts"). He is in charge of Félix au Port, an Antibes restaurant where the narrator observes Madame Emmy Dejoie and Madame Volet. Félix serves the women.

Once Greene had established his permanent residence in Antibes, he frequented this fine establishment.

FELLOWES (*The Heart of the Matter*). He is a sanitary inspector. While Scobie was on leave, Fellowes and his wife were assigned Scobie's bungalow. Scobie finds Fellowes unpleasant. Fellowes attended school in Lansing, England.

FELLOWES, MRS. (*The Heart of the Matter*). She gives a big dinner party featuring Argentine beef brought by Wilson. Scobie and Helen Rolt are among the guests.

FELLOWS, CAPTAIN CHARLES (*The Power and the Glory*). He is a banana plantation manager, with a big, empty face. He saw action in France during World War I. His happiness at work is indicated by tuneless singing. He is Trixy's solicitous husband and Coral's father. After Coral's death, Trixy wants to leave Mexico. So they do.

FELLOWS, CORAL (*The Power and the Glory*). She is the daughter, about 13, of Charles and Trixy Fellows. She helps out at the banana plantation. When the murderer James Calver sends the whisky priest a message written on one of Coral's lessons, the implication is that he murdered her.

In *The Lawless Road: A Mexican Journey* Greene writes about Fru R., who home-schooled her daughter from mail-order textbooks, as Coral's mother tries to do. (Source: Greene, *The Lawless Roads,* 150–59)

FELLOWS, TRIXY (*The Power and the Glory*). She is Charles Fellows's wife and Coral's mother. Trix, as Charles calls her, is a hypochondriac. She tries to home-school Coral by using materials from the London correspondence courses directed by Henry Beckley. After their daughter dies, Trix persuades Charles to take her back to England.

FENNICK (*The Confidential Agent*). He is the police counsel during D.'s court hearing. Fennick has a birdlike appearance. The magistrate prefers the arguments of Sir Terence Hillman, the opposition counsel.

FENNICK, NICHOLAS ("When Greek Meets Greek"). He is a white-haired old cheat. He worked as a servant for Lord Charles Manville, then for Lord Bellen, then went to prison. Fennick and his niece Elisabeth Cross establish a phony school called St. Ambrose's College, in Oxford. They award a degree and diploma to Lord Driver's son Frederick Driver, who Fennick mistakenly believes is a fine military-family scion. Elizabeth and Frederick plan to marry, with the financial blessings of their hoodwinked elders, and then take over St. Ambrose's.

FERDINAND OF CASTILE (*Our Man in Havana*). He is the father of Milly's chestnut horse Seraphina.

FERGUSSON, BUDDY (*This Gun for Hire*). He is a Nottwich medical-school student. He tries to compensate for intellectual mediocrity and an inevitable peacetime provincial professional future by macho bluster. During the student frolic, he tries to lord it over competent fellow students but is humiliated when Raven forces him at gunpoint to undress in a garage and give Raven his clothes. Fergusson later has an obscure medical career.

Michael Shelden says that Greene's description of the student rag is modeled partly on an event in the life of his father Charles Greene.* He was headmaster at Berkhamsted School when Armistice was declared. He refused to give the students the day off to celebrate. Led by rowdies from a nearby training camp, schoolboys probably resembling Buddy joined in the fun. Peter Wolfe suggests that since Furgusson is undistinguished in peacetime he imagines himself to be a trench-warfare daredevil." (Sources: Shelden, 25–26; Wolfe, 26)

FERNANDEZ (*The Comedians*). He is a black passenger on the *Medea*, often answers questions by saying yes or no inappropriately, proceeds to Santo Domingo, and resumes his work directing a funeral parlor. He worries, even weeps, about his mother's health, which Mrs. Smith offers to improve. Fernandez hires Brown to be a junior partner.

FERNANDEZ (*Travels with My Aunt*). Augusta tells Henry she met Fernandez in Rome. He owned a cattle farm in Camaguey, Cuba, invited Augusta for a month's holiday, and they sampled Havana's bawdy Shanghai Theatre.

FERRARO, MRS. ("Special Duties"). She is William Ferraro's wife. For ten years she has imagined herself to be near death and has therefore installed a Catholic priest in a nearby room in the Ferraro mansion. The latest such priest is Father Dewes.

FERRARO, WILLIAM ("Special Duties"). He is a successful London businessman. The firm Ferraro & Smith was founded by his grandfather, who exiled with Giuseppe Mazzini (1805–1872). Three years ago, Ferraro, apprehensive after a pneumonia attack, hired Miss Saunders to accumulate indulgences for him. When he checks on her, supposedly at prayer for him, he finds the church she named non-existent and herself not pious but with a boyfriend. He must get a better personal secretary.

FERREIRA, P. (*The Heart of the Matter*). Wilson decodes a message concerning this man as a passenger on a ship from Lobito (Angola) possibly involved in smuggling diamonds.

FERRY, MME. (*The Comedians*). She is Dr. Magiot's servant.

FETTING, LORD (*The Confidential Agent*). He is Benditch's fatigued partner. While D. is presenting his case to buy coal, Fetting mostly sleeps, then rouses only to decline signing any contract.

FEVERSHAM, LORD (*Brighton Rock*). Crab, working for Colleoni at the Cosmopolitan, has learned manners by watching Lord Feversham speak to porters. (Feversham is called Heversham in some editions.)

FIRST SECRETARY, THE (*The Confidential Agent*). He is a London official in the embassy of D.'s country. He is probably crooked, doesn't help D., and says he's armed. D. punches his Adam's apple, grabs his gun, and escapes.

FIRST SECRETARY, THE (*The Honorary Consul*). He is a British Embassy official in Buenos Aires. His having the flu caused Crichton to be sent to attend Plarr's funeral.

FIRST SECRETARY, THE (*The Quiet American*). He is a Saigon official who threatens to stop imports to Pyle when plastics, rather than medical supplies, are discovered.

FISCHER, ANNA (*Doctor Fischer of Geneva*). She was Doctor Fischer's unhappy wife and Anna-Luise's loving mother. Anna taught her daughter to ski. Anna loved music; so her husband caused her music-loving friend Steiner to lose his job and for added revenge turned their marital relations into a kind of torture. Anna-Luise believes her mother willed herself to death.

FISCHER, DOCTOR (*Doctor Fischer of Geneva*). He is probably in his 50s, has fading red hair and moustache, heavy eyelids, and pouches under his eyes. He invented a perfumed toothpaste called Dentophil, which turned him into a vicious, contemptuous millionaire. No one knows what he's a doctor of. He has a gorgeous estate at Versoix, outside Geneva. He indirectly caused his wife Anna's death, which intensified his misanthropy. He is icy toward their daughter Anna-Luise. His pleasure in life is throwing parties for five already wealthy guests toadying to him and letting themselves be ridiculed, demeaning themselves, for lavish gifts. The Toadies, as Anna-Luise calls them, are Monsieur Belmont, Richard Deane, Kips, General Krueger, and Mrs. Montgomery. Jones attends two of Fischer's parties, the first out of curiosity, the second to discomfit him.

Haim Gordon carelessly generalizes thus: "When he succeeds in totally unmasking the cowardly avarice of his guests, [and] when, at the bomb party, Dr. Fischer succeeds in exhibiting their baseness for what it is, nothing is left for Dr. Fischer except despair and suicide." Fischer has not unmasked all of his guests: Jones remains undefeated by Fischer, whose motivations remain too complex to be fully understood. (Source: Gordon, 30)

FISHER (*The Honorary Consul*). He is the Secretary of the Anglo-Argentinian Society. He attends a cocktail party given by Sir Henry Belfrage.

FISHER, JIMMY (*The Heart of the Matter*). He survived the torpedo attack on the ship carrying Helen Rolt, among others. While recuperating at Pende, he is treated to a seagoing-pirate story invented by Scobie and told to him.

FISHGUARD (*The Ministry of Fear*). He and Still have admitted themselves to Dr. Forester's sanatorium, argue at tennis and chess, but reconcile through fear of being committed to Forester's sick bay.

5 (*The Human Factor*) see **PHILIPS**

FLAGEOLLET (*Travels with My Aunt*). This is the name of a family whose remains are buried in one tomb in the Boulogne cemetery.

FLIC, M. (*The Quiet American*). In their humorous conversation about detective work, Fowler says Vigot, the French detective, whom he names M. Flic here, might question Gustave about bashing an old lady's skull much as a priest might query someone in the confessional.

FLIGHT see **THE MAN WITHIN**

FLO (*Orient Express*). Coral Musker remembers her as one of her somewhat successful theatrical friends. Others are Dick, Ivy, and Phil.

FORAGE (*The Honorary Consul*). He is an old gentleman who frequents the Hurlingham Club in Buenos Aires. He attends a cocktail party given by Sir Henry Belfrage.

FORBES (*The Confidential Agent*). He is a rich businessman in and out of London. He is one of Lord Benditch's partners, along with Brigstock, Lord Fetting, and Goldsmith. Forbes wants to marry Rose Cullen even though he has been keeping a mistress named Sally. Later he rejects Rose. He helps D., first by providing his bail (£2,000, to be forfeited), then by arranging his escape to sea via Southcrawl, where he owns the Lido. Rose calls him Furt — short for Furtstein, his original family name.

Greene stresses both Forbes's Jewish background and his desire to conceal it. Greene says the shape of Forbes's skull reveals his past. Forbes turns out to be D.'s most selfless ally and should never be called an old Furt. Michael Shelden gathers, quotes, and paraphrases every possible hint at anti–Semitism in Greene's fleshing out Forbes and concludes Greene was more biased than he was. In the process of finding parallels between Forbes and Alexander Korda,* the filmmaker of Hungarian-Jewish background, Shelden notes that the Entrenationo word for "heart" in Dr. Bellows's school is "korda." When asked about his alleged anti–Semitism, Greene, according to Shirley Hazzard, said he reread "the book in question, *The Confidential Agent,* to see if the accusation held water. 'And ... [he admitted], there is anti–Semitism in it. I don't believe [he rationalized] I was anti–Semitic.... But the thing was in the air.'" (Sources: Hazzard, 77; Shelden, 148–50, 212–13, 281)

FORBES (*The Heart of the Matter*). He and Newall, both elderly, survived the torpedo attack on the ship carrying Helen Rolt, among others.

FORD (*The Ministry of Fear*) see **COST**

FORDHAVEN (*This Gun for Hire*). He is Miss Maydew's father. He doesn't figure in the action.

FOREIGN MINISTER, THE (*The Honorary Consul*). He is a British Embassy official in Buenos Aires who tells Sir Henry Belfrage that Fortnum's being kidnapped is "a purely Paraguayan affair."

FOREIGN SECRETARY (*England Made Me*). He speaks formally to Kate Farrant when she, Anthony Farrant, and Krogh are having a pleasant evening at Liseberg.

FORESTER, DR. (*The Ministry of Fear*). He is an old physician, kindly-looking but part of the spy ring. Rowe meets him through Mrs. Bellairs, is imprisoned in Forester's private sanatorium as Richard Digby, spies on his inhumane treatment of fellow inmates, escapes, and returns with Prentice too late to prevent Johns, Forester's assistant, from shooting him.

Interesting to Greene critics is "the green baize door" separating Forester's obedient patients and his sick bay for the recalcitrant. (*See* "The Basement Room.") (Source: O'Prey, 51–52)

FORTESCUE (*The Confidential Agent*). He is a protruberant-eyed neighbor and friend of Emily Glover, who is absent when Fortescue intrudes on D. and Rose Cullen, in Miss Glover's flat, immediately after K. has died there of a heart attack. Asked to identify D. by the police, Fortescue tries but cannot. He and Emily are fellow Oxford Groupers.

FORTNUM (*The Honorary Consul*). He was Charley Fortnum's alcoholic father. He liked horses, tried unsuccessfully to get Charley to ride horses and to conquer fear, and died in Argentina. Charley treasures his father's pictures of sporting events.

FORTNUM (*The Human Factor*). Fortnum & Mason's is an elegant Piccadilly department store where Castle tells Daintry he can buy Maltesers chocolate candy to take to the Hargreaveses' party. Daintry later goes to Fortnum's to buy food.

FORTNUM, CHARLEY (*The Honorary Consul*). He is the functionally useless Honorary Consul in the Argentine city where Plarr lives. Fortnum's middle name begins with "Q," but he won't tell anyone what that name is. Born and educated as a Catholic in Buenos Aires, Fortnum is disliked his father and was married to Evelyn (September l939). Fortnum, now over 60 and an alcoholic, owns acreage outside the city, grows maté, and drives a Land Rover he calls Fortnum's Pride. He says he has a split personality and since school days calls his bad side "Mason." (Fortnum and Mason's was a Piccadilly department store.) Forbes met and respected Clara at Señora Sanchez's brothel, and married her. By mistake, he was kidnapped by Rivas's gang, behaves bravely in captivity, talks at length with his captors and also Pharr, and is rescued. Fortnum and Clara will undoubtedly raise her child, sired by Pharr.

Yvonne Cloetta* says Greene told her it was going to be tedious for him to have to live three years with Charley Fortnum, whom, she added, she came to like. Norman Sherry quotes one of Greene's diaries (March 28, 1970), in which he mentions that a guerrilla group in Corrientes province, Argentina, kidnapped the Paraguayan Consul, probably by mistake, and released him, and further that President Alfredo Stroessner* remained indifferent during the incident. Mark Bosco, calling Fortnum an "undefeated failure," traces his "beginning as a comic caricature and developing into a fully realized character," and in the process learning about fatherhood and forgiveness. (Sources: Bosco, 112; Cloetta, 71; Sherry III, 531)

FORTNUM, CLARA (*The Honorary Consul*). She is Charley Fortnum's wife, 18, partly of Tucumán descent. They encountered each other in Señora Sanchez's brothel. Plarr purchases her sexual favors with a pair of gaudy sunglasses. Clara's response to both Charley and Plarr, preferring the latter, is to try to please. She gets pregnant by Plarr, after whose death she awaits Charley's response, timidly realizing that his tender love trumps Plarr's roughness.

The relationship of Clara and Plarr is complex beyond analysis. Plarr himself dies with an unasked question from Clara unanswered in his mind. Some of Greene's ugliest sex images are inspired by Plarr's attitude toward Clara.

FORTNUM, EVELYN (*The Honorary Consul*). She was Charley Fortnum's first wife (married September 1939). He tells Pharr he was married 25 years ago and Evelyn was an intellectual who therefore didn't understand human nature, was a Christian Scientist, and died of cancer in Idaho.

FOTHERINGAY ("A Day Saved"). One of the names by which Robinson refers to the man he is pursuing. Robinson also calls him Canby, Douglas, Jones, and Wales.

FOWLER, HELEN (*The Quiet American*). She is Thomas Fowler's estranged wife. Roman Catholic living in London, she denies her philandering husband a divorce so he can marry Phuong, writes him a bitter letter, but writes again saying she's starting divorce proceedings.

Norman Sherry draws parallels between the reluctance of Helen Fowler, being a staunch Catholic, to grant Fowler a divorce, and the probable arguments of Vivien Greene,* Greene's Catholic wife, from whom he wished to separate in the early 1950s (and wrote her thus) because he loved Catherine Walston.* (Source: Sherry II, 405–09)

FOWLER, THOMAS (*The Quiet American*). Fowler, the narrator, is a war correspondent, with experience in pre-Hitler Germany, London during the Blitz, and India and Burma. He is in his 40s, cynical and agnostic if not atheistic. Assigned to Vietnam during the French Indochina war, this experienced, pleasure-loving and -resisting, opium-smoking, death-wishful womanizer long separated from his wife Helen Fowler, remains politically neutral, deploring French and American bureaucracy and actions alike. He has enjoyed a two-year sexual relationship with young Phuong and intensely dislikes Pyle, the quiet American, when Pyle falls for Phuong. The two men are nearly killed outside Phat Diem. Fowler is so disgusted when Pyle masterminds a Saigon street bombing to support General Thé that he helps plan Pyle's death. In the end, Helen will divorce Fowler, enabling him to continue sleeping with Phuong. Pyle would like to address Fowler as Tom, but Fowler tells him to call him Thomas.

Personally involved in his complex depiction of Fowler, Greene lets Fowler vent his own anti–American asseverations (sometimes sadly true but not always), and many of Fowler's sexual, drug, and religious activities and opinions parallel Greene's. Fowler's weapons, to defeat unselfish, sentimental, quiet people are cynicism and blatant hedonism. In *Ways of Escape,* Greene writes in self-aggrandizing detail about his own use of opium, because "it played an important part in the life of Fowler." Yet Greene and Norman Sherry both dispute the obvious conclusion that Fowler is Greene's partial self-portrait. Sherry presents Greene's denial: Fowler is an atheist, Greene, not; Fowler lost a girlfriend to an American, Greene never did. Sherry inaccurately adds *The Quiet American* is both anti–American and anti–British, the latter because Fowler betrays his friend Pyle, whereas, Sherry blatantly asserts, no Britisher, in Greene's view, would. (Did Sherry forget Greene's friend Kim Philby,* among other betrayers of mutual friends?) Uwe Böker traces Fowler's four-stage progress — self-distancing, sympathizing, participating, reasoning — toward knowledge that his motives are ambiguous. (Sources: Böker, 141–45; Greene, 173, 173–85; Sherry II, 474–75)

FOX ("A Discovery in the Woods"). This is the name of one of the two sets of parents in Bottom who had more than one child. The other family is named Tort.

FRANCISCO, FATHER (*Monsignor Quixote*). He is a Trappist at Osera who manages the gift shop. He gives Pilbeam the number of a doctor in Orense to phone for assistance when Father Quixote is injured.

FRANÇOIS (*The Quiet American*). In the movie Phuong goes to at the Catinat theater in Saigon, Mme Bompierre's daughter Corinne is with François in his room when the postmaster, looking for Mme Bompierre, climbs into Corinne's window.

FRANÇOIS ("Two Gentle People"). He is a painter and is one of Marie-Claire Duval's husband's homosexual partners.

FRANK, BILLY (*Brighton Rock*). He is Judy's blind husband. He rents rooms to Pinkie, Cubitt, Dallow, and Spicer in his rooming house. Billy presses clothes and doesn't know Judy fools around with Dallow.

David Leon Higdon asks, "Is Pinkie Brown's oft-mentioned but never-present landlord

Frank or Billy?" It seems possible, though uncertain, that his name in Billy Frank. (Source: Higdon, 169)

FRANK, JUDY (*Brighton Rock*). She is blind Billy Frank's wife. She has unseen trysts with Dallow. She delivers Colleoni's scented note to Pinkie and enjoys an off-color ribbing of Pinkie about sex.

FRANKIE (*The Confidential Agent*). Fortescue tells Rose Cullen, in Emily Glover's flat, that he and Emily knew Frankie as a reliable guest or member of their Oxford Groupers.

FRASER (*The Heart of the Matter*). He is a young officer whose criticism of Louise Scobie's love of poetry maddens her husband Henry.

FRAU GENERAL (*Travels with My Aunt*). She was a German general's wife in Rome. She approached Visconti, who was disguised as a priest, to confess three adulterous affairs. He rushed her, both escaped the American advance in her husband's staff car, and headed for Florence.

FRED (*The Captain and the Enemy*) see **QUIGLY, CYRIL**

FRED ("A Drive in the Country"). He is the unemployed, half-crazy loser who drives his uneasy girlfriend in a stolen car into the country to execute a suicide pact. Although she demurs, he shoots himself to death anyway.

FREDERICK, SIR ("The Other Side of the Border"). When Morrow reports to Danvers in his Liverpool office, Danvers's secretary tells him Sir Frederick is outside, waiting to be admitted. He is probably an investor in Danvers's gold-prospecting schemes.

FRENCH AMBASSADOR, THE ("An Old Man's Memory"). He is an official in England and is with the President of France at Dover for the opening of the Channel Tunnel. The French train arrives in England, but the English train is destroyed in the tunnel.

FRITZ (*The Name of Action*). He is one of Kapper's thugs. Big, heavy, and sleepy, Fritz guards Lintz's door to prevent Chant from precipitously entering an inner room. Fritz stands near Karl.

FRITZ (*The Name of Action*). He is the bargekeeper's dog. Fritz dragged the murdered policeman's body from the Moselle to the barge.

FROST (*This Gun for Hire*). He is the policeman whom Mather directs to drive him and Saunders to various dives, beginning with Charlie's, in fruitlessly seeking Raven.

FUERABBIA (*The Honorary Consul*). He is be to an assailant in Saavedra's projected idealistic political novel, entitled *The Intruder* but destined to be unfinished, Saavedra laments, because he's too old.

FULLOVE (*The Ministry of Fear*). He is a seedy-looking old man feeding birds. He gets Rowe to deliver a heavy suitcase purportedly full of books to Travers at the Regal Court hotel. Its explosion is supposed to kill Rowe and Anna Hilfe.

FUNKHOLE, DOCTOR ("The News in English") see **BISHOP, DAVID**

FURTSTEIN (*The Confidential Agent*) see **FORBES**

FUZZY WUZZY (*England Made Me*). Farrant allegedly remembers Fuzzy Wuzzy, the headmaster's wife at his school. When Krogh thinks of jobs for Farrant and asks if he can act, Farrant says Fuzzy Wuzzy rewarded his histrionic prowess with some chocolates.

Farrant plays roles, all right, but never in a Stockholm theater.

GABRIEL ("The Trial of Pan"). He is Lady Hope-Smithies's defense counsel, ineffective against Michael.

GALLOWAY (*Brighton Rock*). He is a member of Carter & Galloway, a firm that employs Molly Pink in London.

GALVÃO, FATHER (*The Honorary Consul*). He is a Portuguese Jesuit priest serving in Buenos Aires. Said to be friendly to women, he is Señora Plarr's special friend. They attend her son's funeral.

GARNET (*The Man Within*). This is the surname, given by neighbors, of Elizabeth's mother. If the name is correct, she is Elizabeth Garnet. Jennings roomed and boarded with the two, and purchased their cottage to provide money for Elizabeth. Soon thereafter, the mother died.

GARNET, ELIZABETH (*The Man Within*). She is the radiant, innocent, loving daughter of a woman whose surname was supposedly Garnet. After her mother's death, Jennings continued to live in the Garnet cottage with her daughter, was alternately loving and abusive, and was killed by smugglers shortly before Andrews appears. Elizabeth and Andrews fall in love. She encourages him to go to Lewes to testify against smugglers he worked with. Upon his return, two smugglers, Carlyon and Joe Collier, attack the cottage while Andrews is at the well. Joe tortures Elizabeth, who stabs herself to death with Andrews's knife. Andrews learns the truth, tells the authorities he killed her, and prepares to commit suicide with his knife.

Michael Shelden suggests that Elizabeth is Greene's "idealised portrait of his Vivienne [Dayrell-Browning]," later his wife (*see* Greene, Vivien). Anthony Mockler conflates the two as "Elizabeth/Vivienne aged nineteen." (Sources: Mockler, 49; Shelden, 116)

GATHAWAY, LORD (*Orient Express*). He is the father of The Hon. Carol Delaine, the actress who is to play Emmy Tod, the chargirl, in the movie version of *The Great Gay Round,* Savory's novel.

GALVÁN, DOCTOR (*Monsignor Quixote*). He is an El Toboso physician. He has known Father Quixote for 30 years. When Quixote is found near León by Galván and Father Herrera, Galván gives him a sedative by injection and they get him back to El Toboso.

Leopoldo Duran and Robert Hoskins note that when Greene visited Madrid (July l980) he met Mayor Enrique Tierno Galván, on whom he patterned what Hoskins calls "Father Quixote's kindly doctor." (Sources: Duran, 16; Hoskins, 258)

GAY PARROT (*Brighton Rock*). This is a horse a grocer asks Cubitt about in a coming race.

GENERAL, HERR ("Dream of a Strange Land"). He is a military officer. To celebrate his 70th birthday, his friend Herr Colonel gets Herr Professor to stage a surprise by letting Herr Colonel and his men convert Herr Professor's country estate into a casino. For 50 years, during regular leaves, Herr General has relished gambling at Monte Carlo.

GENERAL, THE ("An Appointment with the General"). He is the Latin-American leader Marie-Claire Duval flies from Paris to interview. She finds him exuding power, sensuality, and doom. When she asks him what he dreams about, his answer is "death." Although neither he nor his country is named, the General is Omar Torrijos Herrera (1929–1981) of Panama.

GENERAL, THE (*A Burnt-Out Case*). He is the ecclesiastical head of the order, based in Europe (probably Brussels), of the priests and brothers serving at the leproserie. They fear the General will hear through their Bishop about the Ryckers-Querry scandal.

GENERAL, THE (*The Captain and the Enemy*). He is the never-seen commander from whom Colonel Martínez, of the Panama National Guard, takes orders.

The General is Omar Torrijos Herrera (1929–1981), dictator of Panama (1968–1978). He was educated in military classes in El Salvador, the United States, and Venezuela. He was commissioned second lieutenant in Panama's National Guard (1952), advanced to lieutenant colonel (1966), then colonel (1968). He and Colonel Boris Martínez led a coup that overthrew President Arnulfo Arias (1968). Torrijos exiled Martínez and promoted himself to brigadier general (1969). He initiated economic and social reforms. An elected assembly gave Torrijos complete civil, political, and military control (1972–1978). He visited Fidel Castro in Cuba at Castro's invitation and, once home again, suppressed agitation by labor unions and liberal students. In efforts to gain control of the Panama Canal, he threatened to blow it up if negotiations went badly. He signed two Canal

Treaties with President Jimmy Carter (September 7, 1977), giving Panama control of the Canal Zone (1977) and the Canal (2000). Torrijos decided not to seek elective office again (1978) but retained unique power as head of the National Guard (from 1978). He died in an airplane crash (1981). In *A World of My Own,* Greene says he once dreamed of a CIA plot to kill Torrijos but was unable to warn him. Greene wrote *Getting to Know the General: The Story of an Involvement* (1984) about his friendship with "Omar." In it, Greene avers he shouldn't respond skeptically to rumors that Torrijos was assassinated by the CIA. (Sources: Falcoff; Greene, *Getting to Know the General,* 193, 223–24; Greene, *A World of My Own,* 30–31; Pryce-Jones)

GENERAL, THE (*The Comedians*). Captain Concasseur hints to Brown that the Haitian president has written to the General in France about their common culture. The general is presumably Charles de Gaulle (1890–1970).

GENERAL, THE (*The Comedians*). He is the president of the unnamed South American country Luis Pineda represents in the Haitian embassy. He is said to be fairly benevolent.

GENERAL, THE (*The Honorary Consul*). The President (of Argentina) cannot disturb the General to intervene in the Fortnum affair, because he is happily fishing in the south of Argentina. (The General is President Alfredo Stroessner.*)

GENERAL, THE ("The Last Word"). He is the military leader presiding over a futuristic world order, sans religion, war, freedom. He has kept Pope John, an amnesiac, in ignorant seclusion for about 20 years until, finally being the last Christian, Pope John can be executed. At the precise moment of shooting him, the General wonders if what the Pope believes is true.

Richard Kelly calls the General an unconvincing "hybrid character," being a combination of the priest-killing Lieutenant in *The Power and the Glory* and Enrique Zancas, the Communist ex-mayor in *Monsignor Quixote.* (Source: Kelly, 85)

GENERAL, THE (*Travels with My Aunt*). O'Toole tells Henry that he and the General are cooperative friends and that Paraguay needs a strong leader. Henry says he's heard this strongman is a dictator. (He is Alfredo Stroessner.*)

GENERAL BURGOYNE (*Brighton Rock*). This is a horse seen to be restless before the race begins that Black Boy wins.

GENERAL DIRECTOR OF THE NATIONAL BANK, THE ("Dream of a Strange Land"). Herr Colonel would have held Herr General's surprise birthday party, illegal though it would have been, at this man's house except that it's quarantined with scarlatina. Herr Colonel commandeers Herr Professor's house instead.

GENERAL MANAGER, THE (*England Made Me*). He owned a Fiat, according to an unlikely story Farrant tells Kate.

GEOFF (*The Comedians*). He is a character in a pornographic American novel entitled *No Time Like the Present* that Jones was reading shortly before Brown visits him.

GEORGE (*The Honorary Consul*). When Plarr is having tea with his mother, he hears someone twittering in French that George is "coupable."

GEORGE (*The Man Within*). He is a servant at the Lewes inn where Farne meets Andrews.

GIBBONS, STANLEY (*Brighton Rock*). Ida Arnold sees this man, or a person at an establishment named Stanley Gibbons, near Charing Cross, examining a postage stamp.

GL (*England Made Me*). These are reference initials used by Scott and James, solicitors in England, in the letter they sent Minty accompanying his September allowance. Minty notes that "GL" are new initials to him.

GLOVER, DOROTHY (1901–1971). She was one of Greene's mistresses, born in London, of Irish and Scottish extraction. Living in Bloomsbury, Dorothy was a theater-costume designer. To write without the distraction of his wife Vivien Greene* and their two children, Greene rented a studio in the London home of

Dorothy, unmarried, and her mother (spring 1939). When World War II started (September 1939), Greene dispatched his family to his mother Marion Greene* in Crowborough and later to Oxford, but remained in London himself. When Greene met her, Dorothy may have been the ex-wife of an American soldier met during World War I. During World War II, she was a warden of air-raid shelters and a fire watcher. Despite Greene's deceptive tactics, Vivien knew about Greene's affair with Dorothy but hoped it would blow over. Vivien told William Cash that Greene and his brother Hugh Greene* probably "shared" Dorothy, who they nicknamed "Dolly Tear Sheet." When Greene returned from Sierra Leone (1943), he picked up with Dorothy again. Using the pen name David Craigie, Dorothy wrote a children's book entitled *The Voyage of the Luna* (1948). As Dorothy Craigie and collaborating with Greene, she wrote and illustrated *The Little Train* (1946), *The Little Fire Engine* (1950), *The Little Horse Bus* (1952), and *The Little Steamroller* (1953). She also wrote *Dark Atlantis* (1952).

Greene celebrated VE Day (May 8, 1945) with Dorothy, not Vivien, who knew then her life with Greene was finished. Greene soon preferred a new mistress, Catherine Walston* (starting 1946), to either Vivien or Dorothy, and persuaded Dorothy to take a three-months' vacation in Africa (1947) so he could be with Catherine unencumbered. Greene took Dorothy on trips, to Paris and then Africa (1948), where he presented her a letter explaining his love for another (Catherine). He took Dorothy on a vacation to Italy, writing Catherine, however, that it might be hell for him (May 21, 1949). His awareness of betraying Vivien and Dorothy tormented him for years (and he fictionalized his pangs in *The Heart of the Matter* and *The End of the Affair*). Dorothy took instructions to become a Catholic (1951) and, oddly, immediately made friends with fellow Catholic-convert Catherine. Curiously amiable, Dorothy and Greene edited *Victorian Detective Fiction* (1966), a catalogue of a collection of mystery novels they had assembled over the years, with Hugh's help; Greene and bibliophile John Carter provided introductions. Greene flew from Antibes to Dorothy's funeral (1971), after which her aged mother, with whom she had resided, had to be comfortably moved by a welfare agency to what was called a safe house. Anthony Mockler provides details concerning Greene's and Dorothy's coauthored works. Cash reports that Yvonne Cloetta* said Greene was more regretful and sorrowful for his treatment of Dorothy than of any other woman and saw him weep when he learned of her death. Yvonne adds that Greene once helped Dorothy buy a house for herself and her mother and assigned a small pension on her. (Sources: Cash, 65, 271; Cloetta, 65; Mockler, 200; Shelden, 275; Sherry II, 19–25 passim, 62, 215, 266, 280–89 passim, 318, 532n14)

GLOVER, EMILY (*The Confidential Agent*). She owns a Chester Gardens flat. While she's away, D. hides in it and forces K. into it. When he shoots at but misses K., K. has a fatal heart attack. Rose Cullen and then Fortesque, Emily's neighbor, come there too. Emily is pious.

Michael Shelden notes that Emily Glover's last name is that of Dorothy Glover,* one of Greene's mistresses. Shelden adds that D.'s leaving K.'s corpse on fictional Miss Glover's "floor" (actually her divan) for her to discover might have given Dorothy Glover a kick when she read *The Confidential Agent*. (Would it?) (Source: Shelden, 279)

GOD ("The Trial of Pan"). He presides in the court, allows Pan to plead his case by music rather than words, and is distressed as a consequence.

GOERING, FIELD-MARSHAL [HERMAN WILHELM] (*Travels with My Aunt*). Visconti tells O'Toole an Italian prince gave him a picture to present in 1945 to Field-Marshal Goering, one of Visconti's patrons. O'Toole says it was a stolen Leonardo da Vinci drawing.

Goering (1893–1946) was one of several German military leaders under Adolf Hitler sentenced to death at Nuremberg for Nazi war crimes. He committed suicide.

GOLDSTEIN (*The Confidential Agent*). He is or was one Lord Benditch's partners, along with Brigstock, Lord Fetting, and Forbes. Goldstein is absent when D. confers with the others at Benditch's home.

GOLDTHORB (*The Confidential Agent*). At Dr. Bellows's soirée, D. mentions Goldthorb as a writer of detective stories and asks K. if he has read any of them.

GOLZ, M. ("A Chance for Mr. Lever"). He is a Brussels associate of Lucas, the London heavy-machinery manufacturer. On his way from London to Liberia to sell equipment to Davidson, Lever gets advice from Golz.

GOM, THE (*Loser Takes All*) see **DREUTHER, HERBERT**

GONZALEZ, FATHER (*Monsignor Quixote*). He was a Valladolid priest. When he died, a local undertaker prepared him for burial, stole the brass handles of his coffin, and leads Father Quixote to a lavatory to confess the sin to him there.

GOTTMANN, WOLFGANG (*The Third Man*). He is a Viennese civil servant whose bust Martins sees in the Central Cemetery on his way to Harry Lime's burial.

GOULDSMITH (*England Made Me*). This is a name in the cryptic telegram Farrant sent his twin sister Kate when their father died.

GOVERNOR, THE (*The Heart of the Matter*). He is the leading official, 60, for the British presence in Sierra Leone.

GOVERNOR, THE (*The Honorary Consul*). He is the leading official of the province where Plarr lives. The two occasionally fly in the Governor's airplane. The Governor invited Fortnum to a dinner honoring the American Ambassador because Fortnum speaks English. This caused fatal woes, because Rivas and his men, aiming to kidnap the Ambassador, grabbed Fortnum by mistake.

GOVERNOR, THE (*The Human Factor*). When the Governor of the Gold Coast was Hargreaves's superior, Hargreaves unknowingly ate human flesh, being courteous to his host — or so Hargreaves told the Governor.

GOVERNOR, THE (*It's a Battlefield*). He is the top official at Leeds prison, where Jim Drover is incarcerated. The Governor is attending a concert there when the Assistant Commissioner visits Drove.

GOVERNOR, THE ("The Lottery Ticket"). He is the leading official in the Mexican state where Thriplow is vacationing. When the bank manager seeks the Governor for advice on using the lottery winnings Thriplow wishes to donate, he evidently agrees that the manager should give them to the Chief of Police. This little, plump, middle aged, boyish-looking Governor is corrupt, and the Chief uses the money to have the Governor's rival for reelection murdered.

GOVERNOR, THE (*The Power and the Glory*). He is the ruthless governor of the state where the whisky priest often hides. The Governor's message to the Chief of Police in the capital city, as relayed to the lieutenant, encourages him to shoot hostages to persuade the priest to surrender. The Governor's cousin sells contraband wine and brandy to the priest, then drinks much of the wine himself.

GOVERNOR OF THE CHACO, THE (*The Honorary Consul*). This official was unwilling to spend money dredging the Chaco side of the Paraná river; so plans to deepen port waters to accommodate bigger ferries were abandoned.

GOWER (*England Made Me*). This is the name of a character in Professor Hammarsten's play. When an actor seems suitable for the part, his friends call him Gower.

GRACIA, COLONEL (*The Comedians*). He is the head of the Tontons Macoute and is nicknamed Fat Gracia.

Robert I. Rotberg says that the leader of the palace guard protecting François Duvalier was Colonel Gracia Jacques. (Source: Rotberg, 226–27, 356)

GRAND DUKE, THE ("The Root of All Evil"). Rumors indicate that during an uprising in a town near B — an attempt was made to assassinate this man.

GRANGER (*The Quiet American*). He is Bill

Granger's son, eight. He is reported as having polio but later is said to be better.

GRANGER, BILL (*The Quiet American*). He is an American war reporter. He is noisy, alcoholic, and obscene, and frequently files dishonest reports — traits Fowler regards as typically American. Granger criticizes Fowler's accent and says he's from Pittsburgh, proud of it. When Fowler learns Granger's son has polio, he is sympathetic and wishes he could cover for Granger so he could fly home immediately.

Granger is based on Larry Allen (b. 1908), a correspondent who won a Pulitzer Prize (1942) for his work during World War II and whom Greene met in Saigon (1951), when Allen's best days were regarded as behind him. (Source: Sherry II, 398–402 passim)

GRANGER, MRS. (*The Quiet American*). She is war-correspondent Bill Granger's wife. From home, she cables him about their son's polio and later about his being out of danger.

GRANNY BROWN (*Our Man in Havana*). The Chief of the Intelligence headquarters in London uses Granny Brown's Ipswich Roast recipe when preparing a dinner for the Permanent Under-Secretary.

GRAVES (*The Ministry of Fear*). He is a fat little policeman who questions Rowe at Scotland Yard. His dealing in routine crimes causes him to dislike Prentice's intricate cases.

GRAVES (*This Gun for Hire*). He is the prospective purchaser of a house in the Nottwich development. He meets with Green, the salesman. Anne Crowder upsets their deal by giving Green two of Raven's stolen £5 notes as down payment for the place.

Peter Wolfe opines that Graves, described in the same sentence as looking both young and old, wearing a black suit, and emanating the notion of losing sleep because he has babies, thus "carries the extremes of birth and death within himself." (Source: Wolfe, 77)

GRAVES, H. ("Men at Work"). He is a member of the Book Committee in the Ministry of Information. He suggests that Richard Skates, with nothing to report, should list a report on progress on his agenda.

GREAT DANE, THE (*This Gun for Hire*). Raven names him, among other thugs, hurt by girlfriends.

GREAVES ("Two Gentle People"). He was Henry C. Greaves's grandfather, a British consul in Nice.

GREAVES ("Two Gentle People"). He was Henry C. Greaves's father and, according to Henry, sought adventure in America.

GREAVES, HENRY C. ("Two Gentle People"). He is shrewish Patience's middle-aged husband. They are childless. Discontent with America, Henry, tall, thin, and decorously moustached, expatriated himself and Patience to Antibes. By chance, he meets Marie-Claire Duval, also unhappily married. The two have a harmlessly pleasant dinner, but it is too late in their ruined lives to do anything more intimate.

GREAVES, PATIENCE ("Two Gentle People"). She is Henry C. Greaves's nagging wife. She reluctantly accompanied him from the United States to France. Her lack of a positive approach to life is indicated by her disliking the taste of Coca Cola as manufactured in France. When Henry returns from a harmless dinner with Marie-Claire Duval, met by chance, she accuses him of consorting with a woman she can smell on him.

This ironically misnamed harridan is weakly characterized. As Richard Kelly notes, she is "a stereotype of the vulgar American, ... addicted to Cola-Cola, cigarettes, and sex." However, if addicted to the last on Kelly's list, she shouldn't have insultingly offput poor Henry by (incorrectly) suggesting he is too worn out by this evening's *fille* to accommodate her addiction. (Source: Kelly, 69)

GREEK, THE (*A Burnt-Out Case*). In Colin's parable, he was a Luc shopkeeper. In his late 70s, he married an illiterate young American, whom he saw bedded down with his African clerk. The Greek bought a car, ran it over the clerk, and permanently damaged his pelvis, among other things. The police asked the Greek why. He replied that his past action wasn't important but "what I am going to do" was, then shot himself to death. Colin uses as personal advice the Greek's statement concerning the importance of future action.

Norman Sherry says that this story is based on a story Greene heard during his visit to the Congo. (Source: Sherry III, 167)

GREEN (*This Gun for Hire*). He is the housing-estate agent who is trying to sell a home in a development section to Graves but takes Anne Crowder's offer instead. Later summoned by Mather to describe Anne, Green, though breezy in plus fours, is of no help, which is ironic, because Anne is Mather's fiancée.

Over-ingeniously equating Graham Greene and this Green, Michael Shelden opines that the scene in which Green starts talking to Graves and thus saves Anne, upstairs and about to be shot by Raven, "is Greene's coy little reminder that every action is in his hands. Characters live or go to their graves on his whim." Peter Wolfe, also ingenious, sees the conjunction of Green and Graves as "mirroring ... the fusion of birth and death in Raven." (Sources: Shelden, 218; Wolfe, 77)

GREENE, CHARLES (1865–1942). Charles Henry Greene was Greene's father. Charles's grandfather Benjamin Greene was a Bury St. Edmunds brewer and owned sugar plantations in St. Kitts. Charles's father William Greene, at 15, was sent to manage the sugar plantations, returned to England, married a master mariner's daughter, was a farmer and solicitor, returned to St. Kitts (1881), and died there. (William was joined at St. Kitts by a brother who died, age 19, of yellow fever, having, it was said, sired 13 children.) Charles was educated at Bedford School and Wadham College, Oxford. He wanted to be a barrister but began teaching at Berkhamsted School (from 1889), where he became second master (1896) and headmaster (1909). He married Marion Raymond (1896), a first cousin once removed, and was a devoted, pampered husband. Their six children were Molly Greene,* Herbert Greene,* Raymond Greene,* Graham Greene, Sir Hugh Greene,* and Elisabeth Greene Dennys.* Charles Greene was remembered by students as a Christian, Liberal Victorian, and strict disciplinarian fearful of juvenile sexuality, especially masturbation and homosexuality. He occasionally enjoyed winter vacations abroad and alone, for example, to Egypt (1904–1905). During World War I he combined patriotism, anti-imperialism, and anti–Marxism, agonized over the military fates of Berkhamsted graduates in France, and was disturbed by having to increase school enrollments and hire female teachers.

Greene was psychologically damaged by his father's being both an eccentric school headmaster and an ineffectively nurturing father. There was a green baize door past his father's study, beyond which was the Berkhamsted School. That door figures in several of Greene's fictional pieces. Roland A. Pierloot theorizes that from his early to his late fiction Greene used his father as a "paternal imago," beginning with old Andrews in *The Man Within* to the Captain in *The Captain and the Enemy*. Common plot ingredients are son losing mother early, split-personality father, son struggling to avoid resembling father, hence betraying him. When Greene was psychoanalyzed by Kenneth Richmond (1921), his father was compassionate but bewildered, and never understood the traumatic consequences of his son's having been bullied at school. When Greene became a Catholic (1926), his father never said a contrary word to him about it. Charles Greene retired from Berkhamsted because of worsening diabetes (1927), moved with his wife to Crowborough, Sussex (1927), and enjoyed better relations with his son. Suffering more severely, Charles Greene continued to be injected with insulin by his wife, who also read detective stories to him, and their son's books, bowdlerized where necessary to prevent upsets. Greene was in Sierra Leone when his father died (1942) and had a Mass said for him then. (Sources: Greene, *A Sort of Life;* Pierloot, 193; Sherry I, 3–46 passim, 53–64, 88–103 passim, 345–46, 498–99; Sherry II, 27–28, 150, 151)

GREENE, ELISABETH (1914–1999). Greene's sister. *See* Dennys, Elisabeth Greene.

GREENE, HERBERT (1898–1968). Greene's brother. An indifferent student, he never sought advanced schooling, worked in Santos, Brazil, in the coffee firm of his uncle Edward Greene, got a girl pregnant, and went to Argentina. He obtained family funds and started a tobacco farm in Rhodesia. Everywhere Herbert Greene went, he was flashy, irresponsible, and dishonest, traits all aggravated by gambling and alcohol addictions. He conned Imperial Japanese Navy agents in London into paying him for information, most of which he found in journals available to the public (1934). According to his book *Secret Agent in Spain* (1938), he made two trips to Spain and did spy work — trivial, in all likelihood — for agents of General Francisco Franco. Greene defines his brother's book as "of dubious authenticity." Michael Shelden says it "does not inspire confidence in his sanity" and indicates why by tersely summarizing its ridiculous plot. Anthony Mockler calls it "the most incredible mish-mash" with, however, "little details" convincing him that Herbert was a courier in Spain. He often returned to England to sponge on family members, including his elderly parents. Greene grew so disgusted with this black sheep that more than once he expressed his wish in writing that Herbert would commit suicide. (Sources: Greene, *A Sort of Life*, 149; Mockler, 130; Sherry I, 171, 496–500, 613–15; Sherry III, 22, 784; Shelden, 26, 27–28)

GREENE, HUGH (1910–1987). Sir Hugh Carleton Greene, Greene's favorite brother, was handsome and tall, at 6 feet 6 inches. After attending Berhamsted School, where their father Charles Greene* was headmaster, Hugh spent time in Germany and studied at Merton College, Oxford (until 1933), where he was the first president of the Oxford Film Society. He and Greene vacationed together in Burgundy (1931) and Sweden (1932). Hugh was a stringer in Munich for the London *Daily Herald* and the *New Statesman,* then worked for the *Daily Telegraph* in Berlin, where Greene visited Hugh (1934). When Hugh was in Berlin writing for the London *Daily Telegraph* and possibly spying on the Nazis, Greene tried unsuccessfully to pull strings enabling Hugh to accompany him to Mexico (1936). Hugh observed with foreboding the advent of National Socialism in Germany, wrote frankly about his dismay, and was expelled (May 1939), only a few months before World War II began (September).

Hugh was assigned to Warsaw until driven out by the Germans (1939), reported from other European cities including Brussels and Paris, then escaped to London (June 1940). He worked for the British Broadcasting Company's German service (from October 1940). He flew to Sweden to investigate the effectiveness of German jamming of BBC broadcasts (1942). From London (1942), Hugh sent word to Greene, then in Sierra Leone, that a secretary named Doris Temple was being dispatched to Freetown and would be a good drink-and-sleep companion for him; Greene evidently found her useful only as a source of valuable gossip. After the war, Hugh helped control broadcasting in Berlin's British zone (1946–1948). While working for the BBC's eastern European service (1948–1950), he went on loan to head the British Emergency Information Services in psychological warfare against Communist insurgents in Malaya. While there, he enabled Greene to pay him a dangerous visit (November 1950–January 1951). Greene was thus able to write "Malaya, the Forgotten War" (*Life,* July 30, 1951). Greene's affair with Catherine Walston,* whom Hugh disliked and saw as menacing Greene's marriage, caused a cooling of the brothers' friendship (into the 1950s). In London again (1952), Hugh held important posts with the BBC, was director-general of the BBC (1960–1968), supervised expanding BBC's television news programs, and became a member of its Board of Governors (1968–1971). Perhaps the BBC's racier dramatic presentations were influenced by the popularity of Greene's forward-looking fiction. On retiring, Hugh was appointed chairman of the brewing establishment Greene, King and Sons, and also became chairman and honorary head of The Bodley Head Press. He and Greene co-edited *The Spy's Bedside Book: An Anthology* (1957) and *Victorian Villainies* (1984). Hugh also wrote *The Third Floor Front: A View of Broadcasting in the Sixties* (1969).

Hugh Greene married (1934) Helga Mary Guinness (b. 1915), had two sons with her, one named Graham Carleton Greene (b. 1936) in the novelist's honor, before Hugh and Helga were divorced (1948); married (1951) an American named Elaine Gilbert Shaplen (b. 1920) and had two sons with her before the marriage ended (1969); married (1970) his long-time mistress Else Hofler Neumann ([1909–1981], German actress known as "Tatjana Sais," ex-wife of Günter Neumann, writer and theater director); and married (1984) a script supervisor named Sarah Mary Manning Grahame (b. 1940). Sir Hugh Greene, knighted in 1964, died of prostate cancer and heart complications. Michael Tracey provides details concerning Hugh Greene, his friendship with Graham Greene, and his many sexual and marital activities. Both brothers were immensely talented and astonishingly promiscuous.

William Cash says that Greene's wife Vivien Greene* believed Greene and Hugh shared Dorothy Glover* and called her "Doll Tear Sheet." (Sources: Cash, 65; Shelden, 20, 189, 312, 390; Sherry I, 396, 486–87, 586, 656–57; Sherry II, 10, 12, 128–29, 225, 239–58 passim; Sherry III, 781; Tracey; Watts, 207)

GREENE, MARION (1872–1959). Greene's mother. Born Marion Raymond, she was the daughter of the Reverend Carleton Greene, vicar of Great Barford. She was a first cousin of Robert Louis Stevenson. Six feet tall, thin, shy, keenly intelligent, and socially reliable, she married her cousin Charles Greene* (1896), and became the loving, reserved, aloof mother of Molly, Herbert, Raymond, Graham, Hugh, and Elisabeth. She supervised Greene's pre- and early-teenage reading admiringly, followed his professional and personal career with joy tempered by misgivings, all the while doting on Charles, to whom she read aloud and whose diabetes she controlled by personally injecting him with insulin. In his play *The Potting Shed* (1958), Greene allegedly based the character Mrs. Callifer on his mother. His remoteness from his mother is indicated when in *A Sort of Life* he images his mother's pre-death coma as a crusader lying on a tomb. He probably didn't actually see her then, and he certainly didn't cancel his scheduled business trip from France to New York to attend her funeral. He did request masses for her. Greene records a dream he had in which he was obliged to handle his mother's corpse and that it resembled his deceased sister Molly Greene,* who spoke frighteningly about being cold. (Sources: Greene, *A World of My Own*, 115; Sherry I, 16–18, 35–37, 46–49; Sherry II, 27–28, 150, 152; Sherry III, 28, 212–13)

GREENE, MOLLY (1897?–1963). Greene's sister and oldest sibling. Few details have been published about her. Greene says he once dreamed about his deceased mother's resembling Molly, who spoke about feeling cold. According to Norman Sherry, Molly died of cancer. (Sources: Greene, *A World of My Own*, 115; Sherry III, 784)

GREENE, RAYMOND (1901–1982). Greene's brother. He was better in school studies and sports than Greene was. When Greene displayed suicidal tendencies (1920), Raymond suggested that Kenneth Richmond should psychoanalyze him. Raymond was best man at Greene's wedding to Vivienne Dayrell-Browning (1927; *see* Greene, Vivien). Raymond became a successful surgeon, with a practice in Oxford and later in Harley Street, London. Also an avid mountaineer, he conquered Kamet, a Himalayan peak (1931), and even tried Everest (1933). (Source: Sherry I, 92, 397)

GREENE, SIR WILLIAM GRAHAM (1857–1950). Greene's uncle, he was an officer in the Admiralty, helped establish the Intelligence Service, and lived in Cambridgeshire. Greene said that Sir William was a source of his character the Assistant Commissioner in *It's a Battlefield*. (Sources: Sherry I, 463; Watts, 207)

GREENE, VIVIEN (1905–2003). Greene's wife. She was born Vivienne Dayrell-Browning. Her mother, Marion (also called Muriel) Green-Armytage Dayrell-Browning, courageously left her unfaithful husband Sidney Dayrell-Browning (1915), forced Vivien to reject him, broke a hip or leg in a fall, and died (1933). Vivien wrote and published some juvenile poetry entitled *The Little Wings* (1918). She was working for Basil Blackwell in his Oxford publishing firm when she read something by Greene, then a student, about worshipping the Virgin Mary (1925). A Catholic convert (when 17), Vivien wrote Greene to say the Virgin is to be venerated, not worshipped. He replied, invited her for tea, fell in love foolishly fast, and soon proposed. She declined — mainly because of his alleged atheism — but agreed to a secret engagement. Greene suggested a celibate marriage (1925). After Greene became a Catholic (1926), they were married at Saint Mary's, Hamstead, London (October 25, 1927). They had two children, Lucy Caroline Greene (1933, later called Caroline) and Francis Greene (1936). Greene was an indifferent father and a notoriously unfaithful husband. A year after Caroline's birth, he started his trek through Liberia. He took Vivien to the United States on business (1938), proceeded as planned to Mexico and left her in New Orleans to get home alone by Dutch cargo boat. Greene's affairs with Dorothy Glover,* Caroline Walston,* Anita Björk,* and Yvonne Cloetta* put strains on Vivien.

Early in her marriage, Vivien suspected Greene's relationship with Dorothy, which began (spring 1939) shortly before World War II erupted (September). Greene moved his family for their safety and his convenience to Crowborough and then Oxford during most of the war. Vivien celebrated VE Day (May 8, 1945) in Oxford; Greene, in London with Dorothy, though then less in love with her too. In New York on business (October 1947), Greene took Vivien along, neglected her, and unsuccessfully sought Catherine, who was busy with another lover. Remnants of Greene's relationship with Vivien were ruined when an undelivered love letter he wrote Catherine was returned to sender and Vivien read it and told Greene so (November 1947). He considered a deed of separation, a judicial separation, and even an annulment (1948). He was with Vivien and their children one final time (1958). Supported financially by Greene, Vivien lived on in London, was devoted to her children, wrote *English Dolls' House in the Eighteenth and Nineteenth Centuries* (1955), and became known at the world's leading expert on dolls. Vivian suffered a broken hip (about 1989). She offered to go see Greene (1990) when he was dying in Switzerland, did view him in his coffin in Vevey (April 4, 1991), and attended his funeral there (April 9, 1991). Present also were Greene's and Vivien's daughter Caroline Bourget's son Andrew Bourget, Greene's brother Hugh Greene[*]'s son Graham Carleton Greene, Greene's last mistress Yvonne Cloetta,* Greene's friend the leprosy-specialist Dr. Michael Lechat (*see The Burnt-Out Case*), and Greene's father-confessor Leopoldo Duran, who exuberantly conducted the ceremony.

William Cash provides a vivid image of long-suffering Vivien, who was nearly blind but very alert when he interviewed her (2000) three years before she died, age 98. He also quotes what evidently is the only extant letter (April 14, 1948) from Vivien to Greene, in which she rebukes him for his much-bruited affair with that American blonde culture-vulture Catherine Walston.* (Sources: Cash, 43–71 passim, 121–30, 258–60; Duran, 344; Shelden, 110–14, 135–36, 255–56, 318, 346–47; 486; Sherry I, 179–230 passim, 256, 347–55, 473–74, 504, 529, 662–65; Sherry II, 20, 206–07, 275–85 passim; Sherry III, 790, 795–96)

GRETA (*It's a Battlefield*). She is one of the 150 girls employed in the Battersea match factory.

GREY LADY (*England Made Me*). This is the name of a horse Hall writes his mother to bet on.

GRIGGS (*The Ministry of Fear*). Among Rowe's confused memories of childhood is his recollection that Griggs, a clumsy dentist, first acquainted him with pain as a child of seven.

GRISON (*A Burnt-Out Case*). He is or was a senior worker in the Post Office. Querry slept with and abandoned Grison's wife, and was challenged by Grison to a phony duel. Querry says Grison didn't mind the affair until Querry left and Mme. Grison embarrassed Grison in public.

GRISON, MME. (*A Burnt-Out Case*). She was one of Querry's many lovers back home. Only when Querry dumped her did her husband object.

GROENER (*This Gun for Hire*). He is the old German owner of the café in the Soho building in which Raven rooms.

GROENER, FRAU (*The Heart of the Matter*). She is the daughter of the Portuguese captain of the *Esperança*. Scobie catches the captain trying to smuggle a letter to his daughter, married to a German in Leipzig. The captain tearfully explains her mother is dead, he sends her money, and she hates his mistress in Lisbon.

GROENER, FRAU (*This Gun for Hire*). She is the wife of the Soho café owner. Raven forces

Alice to pretend to be phoning her so he can learn details of actions by the police attempting to capture him.

GROSELI, MONSIEUR (*Doctor Fischer of Geneva*). He was a guest at two of Doctor Fischer's parties before dying of cancer.

GROVES ("Murder for the Wrong Reason"). He is an evidently able Scotland Yard detective whom Detective-Inspector Mason summons to come to the residence of Collinson, murder victim. While Groves is getting there, Mason solves the crime.

GRUBER (*The Honorary Consul*). He is a German immigrant. His parents, too old to leave Germany to escape Adolf Hitler (l936), concealed their rings in a cake for him to take with him while escaping. He made his way to Argentina. Now an optician and a photographer, Gruber is Plarr's friend and sold him a pair of sunglasses, which he wooed Clara Fortnum with. Gruber attends Plarr's funeral.

GRUNER, FRAU (*The Name of Action*). She is tall, bony, gray, and old. She pleads with Demassener for permission to give her executed son's body a Mass of Christian burial. He allows her to have a priest attend the burial within prison grounds.

GRÜNLICH, JOSEF (*Orient Express*). He is a fat career criminal in Vienna, nominally Catholic. He pretends to be Anna's lover in order to enter her bedroom, go to her employer Kolber's room nearby, and rifle his safe. When Kolber unexpectedly appears, Grünlich shoots him to death and escapes by the Orient Express. He is arrested in Subotica on an arms violation but escapes again and surfaces in Constantinople. Anna believes his name is Anton.

Michael Shelden strangely contends that Grünlich is so successful that some readers might half-admire him, even that perhaps "Greene identified with him" and therefore gave him a name which means "greenish" in German. (Source: Shelden, 155)

GUELLE, GOVERNOR (*A Burnt-Out Case*). He is the tiny, short-sighted governor of the Congo province, and resides in Luc, the capital. He once decorated Rycker, who meets Querry at the governor's home. Guelle squelches his wife's query whether Querry may be queer.

GUELLE, MME. (*A Burnt-Out Case*). She is Governor Guelle's wife. Rycker demeans his wife Marie by telling her to ask Mme. Guelle for Perrier not *orange pressée*, which Marie would prefer. Mme. Guelle wonders whether Querry is a homosexual.

GULLIE, CAPTAIN (*England Made Me*). He is the military attaché at the British Legation in Stockholm. Farrant meets Gullie there. Minty tells the porter he must see Gullie, who discusses Harrow with him. Gullie plays poker at Krogh's apartment the night of Farrant's murder.

Without elaborating, Anthony Mockler suggests "Major Giffey, Head of Station, SIS, Tallinn [Estonia]" as a model for Gullie. (Source: Mockler, 94)

A GUN FOR SALE (1936). Novel. *See This Gun for Hire.*

GURNIÁN, SERGEANT ("An Appointment with the General"). He is a military man serving the General. He speaks excellent English, translates when Marie-Claire Duval interviews the General, and is going to chauffeur her around so she can see the unnamed Latin-American country for herself.

GUSTAVE (*The Quiet American*). While they are having a humorous conversation about detective work, Fowler calls Vigot, the French detective, and says Gustave might be persuaded to explain how he hit an old lady in the head much the way a sinner might be urged by a priest to speak in the confessional.

H, TOC ("The Bear Fell Free"). He is a buddy Carter muses about.

HACKENFURTH, FRAU ("The Root of All Evil"). She dresses suspiciously to Puckler. Thinking she might be a man dressed as a woman, he pulls off her wig to determine her gender. She kept knowledge of her wig a secret even from her husband.

HAKE (*The Man Within*). He is a big, bearded smuggler in Carlyon's crew. When the revenuers under Hilliard attempt to arrest the 10 smugglers, four escape, but not Hake. During the smugglers' trial at Lewes, Hake threatens Andrews, defends his behavior eloquently, and says Tims killed Rexall.

HAKIM, COLONEL (*Travels with My Aunt*). He is a police officer in Istanbul. Asthmatic and partly deaf, he courteously questions Augusta in her hotel room about General Abdul and his criminal associates, including Visconti.

HAKIM, COLONEL (*Travels with My Aunt*). He is a character in *Turkish Delight*, a novel Augusta happens to be reading when the real Colonel Hakim arrives to question her.

HALE, CHARLES (*Brighton Rock*). He is a newspaper reporter who gave information about Kite to Colleoni. This resulted in Kite's being killed by Colleoni's men in London. Pinkie, Kite's assistant, wants revenge on Hale, seen in Brighton. Hale places Kolley Kibber tickets in obscure spots for a contest. Aware of being followed, Hale picks up Ida Arnold but leaves her at the Palace Pier. Hale's murder by members of Pinkie's gang is diagnosed as death by heart failure. Ida wins money by acting on Hale's tip to bid on Black Boy in the races, and uses the money and her own doggedness to exact vengeance on Pinkie. Hale tells people in Brighton his first name is Fred.

Paul Hogarth includes a watercolor of Brighton's Palace Pier among his illustrations of Greene's fiction. Norman Sherry suggests that details of Hale's murder are based on a real-life grabbing and fatal beating of Ernest Friend Smith, 67, in Brighton (April 1928). Michael Shelden discusses two 1934 murders in Brighton: Tony Mancini, a petty thief, was acquitted of murdering his girlfriend but later freely confessed; a murdered woman's body parts were found in Brighton and in London, and neither she nor her murderer was ever identified. (Sources: Hogarth, 49; Shelden, 244–45, 508; Sherry I, 634)

HALIFAX (*The Heart of the Matter*). He is a bubbly Public Works Department officer. When his wife Mary and Scobie's wife Louise board ship for South Africa, Halifax warns them about "bow-bow" (bowel) troubles at sea. He'll probably seek sexual gratification while Mary is away.

HALIFAX, MARY (*The Heart of the Matter*). She is a Public Works officer's untidy, vapid wife. She repeatedly reads the same novel, unaware of doing so. She and Louise Scobie voyage to South Africa together.

HALL, FRED (*England Made Me*). He is a tough former Brighton bookie. Long Krogh's loyal employee, Hall phones Krogh stock quotations from Amsterdam, helps frame Andersson to prevent a strike at Krogh's Nyköping factory, flies to Stockholm, pummels Andersson's son, and plays poker with Farrant and others at Krogh's apartment. Hall leaves with Farrant and causes him to be drowned. (Early in the novel, he is referred to as Jim Hall.)

Erik Krogh is based on the Swedish industrialist Ivar Kreuger (1880–1932), whose rise to international notoriety as a swindler started when he partnered with Paul Toll. Greene may have had Paul Toll's crisp name in mind when he named Fred Hall.

HALL, JIM (*England Made Me*) *see* **HALL, FRED**

HALLIDAY (*The Human Factor*). He is the learned operator of an Old Compton Road bookshop. At 17 he joined the British army hoping to go to France. Instead he served during the post–World War I Archangel campaign and spent four years in a Russian prison. He studied Communist literature and became a romantic Marxist. Castle thinks he can pass coded literary messages, using novels he buys there, via Halliday's son, who has a pornographic shop across the street. But old Halliday is the Soviet contact. When his son is arrested, Halliday helps effect Castle's escape to Moscow.

HALLIDAY (*The Human Factor*). He is the book-dealer's son and runs a nearby pornographic shop selling books and films. When the police arrest him for selling a pornographic film to a 14-year-old, his father disabuses Castle, who thinks he is passing coded messages through the younger Halliday to Boris, Castle's

Soviet contact. Old Halliday, the real conduit, is aware his son will ingratiate himself with the authorities by blowing Castle's cover.

HALLOWS (*This Gun for Hire*). He is the courteous Metropole hotel porter, thrice-wounded First World War veteran. He gives Anne Crowder information about Davis, takes Ruby to lunch after Davis stands her up, and naively praises Sir Marcus because he gives Christmas turkeys to his workers.

HAMIT (*The Comedians*). He is a Syrian merchant. He rents a bedroom for Brown and Martha Pineda to use, receives mail for Henri Philipot concerning the revolutionary movement, is tortured but doesn't reveal information implicating Dr. Magiot, and is murdered.

Ian Thomson and Norman Sherry identify a Syrian named Issa el Saiëth (Saieth) whom Greene met (August 1963). Thomson reports this: Issa, as he was called, was born in Haiti of Palestinians from Bethlehem. At five, he was sent to New York City, learned to play baseball, became a band leader, and played clarinet and saxophone at the Society Club in New York. He returned to Haiti, opened the first department store in Port-au-Prince, dabbled in real estate, established an art gallery behind the Oloffson Hotel, and lived in the gallery. He met Greene, sold him a valuable painting by Haitian artist Philippe Auguste for $50, drove him to a brothel "for research," and observed that Greene was very religious and had a huge crucifix beside his bed in his Oloffson room (#11) to ward off trouble. Issa told Thomson that when Greene learned Issa had been arrested by François Duvalier, Greene killed him off (i.e., Hamit) in *The Comedians*. Sherry adds this: Issa was a secret partner of Al Seitz, who owned the Oloffson, on which Brown's Trianon is based, that Issa's brief arrest was on suspicion of betraying Duvalier, that he was found not guilty and released. (Sources: Sherry III, 341, 363–64; Thomson, 230–31)

HAMMARSTEN, PROFESSOR (*England Made Me*). He is a Stockholm language teacher, newspaper stringer, hence one of Minty's rivals. For years Hammarsten has been translating Shakespeare's *Pericles*. Krogh, on a generous whim and for publicity, offers to underwrite a production of a play by Hammarsten. Hammarsten brings would-be actors and actresses to Krogh's party at Saltsjöbaden, where they drink too much. Hammarsten calls Farrant "Fecund" and "Ferrett."

HAMMOND (*England Made Me*). Kate Farrant studied bookkeeping and short-hand at Hammond's school in Leather Lane, in England. She recalls this "rat-faced" man gave her a prize for her short-hand speed and Krogh met her there.

HANDS ("The Other Side of the Border"). He is a retired Denton bank manager, almost 70. A noble-looking Liberal but with a breaking-up face, this widower is suspicious of his pro-Fascist son's schemes, yet hopeful he'll succeed in finding gold in West Africa.

Greene takes a gratuitous poke at Liberals by saying that old Hands felt that people could govern themselves if allowed, that money doesn't corrupt, and that statesmen love their native lands. Norman Sherry regards Greene's sketch of old Hands as a portrait of his own father, Charles Greene.* (Source: Sherry II, 149)

HANDS ("The Other Side of the Border"). He is a flashy, prevaricating, self-deceived phony from Denton, outside London. He seeks gold in West Africa. Financed by Danvers of Liverpool, he marries Ethel, the niece of Millet, Denton's photographer, and explores the West African interior with Ethel, Billings, Colley, and Morrow (1936–1938), with unspecified disastrous results. He returns to Danvers to try again.

Greene explains in a prefatory note he stopped working on "The Other Side of the Border" as a novel partly because he had previously treated Hands in portraying Anthony Farrant in *England Made Me*. Richard Kelly adds that Hands is based on Greene's brother Herbert Greene,* whom Kelly defines as also a conniving adventurer in Rhodesia and Brazil among other places, a self-fantasizer justifying repeated failures, and the son, like Hands, of a naively liberal man (i.e., Charles Greene*). (Source: Kelly, 90, 91)

HANDS, ETHEL ("The Other Side of the Border"). She is the niece of Millet, the Denton photographer. Ethel is captivated when she eavesdrops on Hands's fibbing boasts to Millet. Hands marries her and takes her with him to West Africa (1936). At once, Ethie doesn't feel well. Nothing more is said about her.

HANDS, MRS. ("The Other Side of the Border"). She is the deceased wife of old Hands. Her photograph depicts her as a long-haired, spaniel-eyed woman, "devoted but not to Mr. Hands."

Greene tantalizingly says Hands knew the object of his late wife's devotion but adds nothing more. Did she love God, her son, another man?

HANNIBAL (*Travels with My Aunt*). This was the name of the elephant that trod on the Rev. Curran's toe, ending his circus career as an animal trainer.

HANS (*Our Man in Havana*). He is the younger of the two K.L.M. pilots whom, along with Miss Pfunk, their stewardess, Wormold and others see resisting alcoholic beverages at the Tropicana. They aren't supposed to drink before flying back home via Montreal to Amsterdam.

HANSEL (*The Third Man*). He is a little boy who tells his Papa he heard Ilse Koch crying and a big foreigner talking to her at the time of Koch's death. Martins worries when Hansel looks at him and calls him a foreigner.

Hansel's murderous foreigner was probably Cooler, not the shorter Harry Lime.

HARBIN (*The Third Man*). He was a criminal associate of Lime and his group. Word spread that Calloway caused him to become a double agent and inform against Lime; so Lime, Cooler, and Kurst killed him and had him buried in Lime's coffin.

HARDING (*The Captain and the Enemy*). He is the housemaster of the school from which the Captain rescues Victor Baxter, whom he renames Jim. Harding doles out allowances to pupils on Sundays so they can't spend everything immediately.

HARDING, YORK (*The Quiet American*). He is a professor whom Pyle knows and idolizes, and whose political philosophy inspires him. Harding briefly visited the Far East, including Korea and Vietnam, two years earlier. His several books, notably *The Advance of Red China*, contain warnings and advocate establishing a defensive Third Force against Communism and colonialism alike. Pyle's belief that General Thé might be a third-force advocate leads to Pyle's undoing. Hence, Fowler is accurate in saying Harding indirectly killed Pyle.

HARGREAVES, LADY MARY (*The Human Factor*). She is Sir John Hargreaves's American-born wife. A pleasant hostess, she limps, one leg weakened by rheumatism. She and her husband decided not to have children. She wanted to preserve her figure and her freedom.

HARGREAVES, SIR JOHN (*The Human Factor*). He is C, the Chief of England's Secret Intelligence Service. Blue-eyed, serene, with a limp, Sir John served as District Commissioner on the former Gold Coast and reminisces about his old Africa, where he had a black mistress before he got married. He and his wife decided not to have children. He felt children would cause anxious times in Africa. The report of security leaks where Castle is employed causes Sir John to authorize Daintry and Percival to investigate and act. Percival's murdering Davis on inadequate evidence ruffles Sir John but doesn't much disturb his London club life, weekends at his country estate, and his novel reading.

Norman Sherry says that "[t]he Hargreaves's home life is derived from the weekend parties that Catherine [Walston*] and Harry Walston organised." Anthony Cave Brown hints that Hargreaves may be based on Sir Stewart Graham Menzies (1890–1968), the long-time Chief of the British Secret Service (1939–1952). (Sources: Brown, 583; Sherry III, 609)

HARRIS, H. R. (*The Heart of the Matter*). He is a cable censor in Sierra Leone. He was a student at Downham school (1917–1921). He shares living quarters with Wilson, first at the Bedford Hotel and later in a hut. While in the hotel, the two competitively hunt cockroaches. When reading the *Downhamian*, his old school magazine, Harris comes across "The Tick of the Clock," a fantasy. In reality, this item is the first one ever written by Greene. It appeared unsigned in his *Berkhamstedian* school magazine (1921; reprinted in London *Star,* January 18, 1921, paying the author three guineas). Grahame Smith regards Harris as "a splendid comic character." (Sources: Sherry I, 80–81, 103–04; Sherry II, 112; G. Smith, 98)

HARRIS, HENRY (*This Gun for Hire*). He is the vicar at St. Luke's. He ineffectively supervises the jumble sale.

HARRIS, MRS. ("May We Borrow Your Husband?"). She is William Harris's first wife. He recalls that she liked Arpège perfume, which he sniffs as it wafts off Poopy Travis.

HARRIS, MRS. (*This Gun for Hire*). She is the dry but peppy wife of the vicar at St. Luke's. She urges Harris to watch over the jumble sale more carefully, since committee members are grabbing bargains before the sale officially commences.

HARRIS, WILLIAM ("May We Borrow Your Husband?"). He is a successful novelist, twice married and at least 50. While on a working vacation in a hotel in Antibes and writing a biography of the Earl of Rochester (1647–1680), he enjoys observing the activities of newly-weds Poopy and Peter Travis, and of homosexual interior decorators Stephen and Tony. Harris wishes he had nerve enough to warn Poopy, of whom he grows fond, that Stephen and Tony may borrow her husband to seduce him, which they do. But he figures that Poopy is too innocent and self-critical to understand.

In his 30s Greene wrote *Lord Rochester's Monkey,* a biography of John Wilmot, Earl of Rochester, but it was too racy to be published until decades later (1974). Greene has Harris theorize that the queer-sided ménage he observes could end as a tragedy if Poopy catches on and a comedy if she doesn't. He hopes for a tragedy, but it winds up a "comedy," a word often used here—and elsewhere—in Greene. In fact, Gwenn R. Boardman in a comprehensive chapter entitled "Exploring 'Under the Garden': We Are All Comedians," mentions the "farcical adventures" in "May We Borrow Your Husband?" (Source: Boardman, 159)

HARRY (*Brighton Rock*). He is a casual London drinking friend of Ida Arnold's.

HARRY (*The Human Factor*). He, Buffy, Dicky, and Dodo, are boisterous guests at Hargreaves's shoot.

HARRY ("Work Not in Progress"). The woman posing as Archbishop of Canterbury hopes her having Harry as a previous boyfriend won't interfere with her loving the Bishop of Melbourne.

HARRY, COCKNEY (*The Man Within*). He is a crafty member of Carlyon's crew of smugglers. When Hilliard and his fellow revenuers try to arrest them on the beach, Cockney Harry and three others escape. Harry boldly sits in the gallery at the Assizes in Lewes during the trial of the six who were captured. Andrews, who also escaped, testifies but doesn't finger Harry. In gratitude, Harry warns Andrews that the smugglers on the loose plan to get revenge on him.

HARTEP, COLONEL (*Orient Express*). He attended the 1927 trial of General Kamnetz in Belgrade for rape. Czinner testified against Kamnetz and was sought by Hartep for doing so. Five years later Hartep finds Czinner in Subotica, tries him by court martial, and has him executed.

Greene found little that was promising in *Orient Express* "except in the character of Colonel Hartep" but later told Leopoldo Duran he felt better about the novel. (Sources: Duran, 241; Greene, *Ways of Escape,* 33)

HASSELBACHER, DR. (*Our Man in Havana*). He is an expert code-cracker and does research in the blue coloration of cheese to avoid confronting reality. He is Wormold's best friend and drinking buddy. Hasselbacher tells Wormold he was a German cavalry officer 45 years ago and displays two photographs—one taken in 1913, the other after World War I began. Wormold ignores Hasselbacher's advice to avoid siding with either Democracy or Communism. While trashing Hasselbacher's residence, Captain Segura exposes Wormold's code system and endangers his fictionalized agents. Hasselbacher warns Wormold about enemy plans to kill him. Carter kills Hasselbacher. Wormold kills Carter. All over nothing. Hence, Hasselbacher's espousal of neutrality was wise.

Greene and Michael Shelden identify the partial model of Hasselbach. He was Baron Ekkehard von Schack (sometimes misspelled Schacht), an impoverished German veteran of World War I living on Capri. In the 1950s Schack was granted a small pension, could then repay friends' hospitality, drank too much, went swimming, and had a fatal heart attack. Greene knew about Schack's military photograph, his helmet, his gloves, and his celebrating the Kaiser's birthday every year. Greene attended Schack's funeral. As Schack did, Hasselbacher celebrates the Kaiser's birthday by donning his German army uniform, helmet, and breastplate. Hasselbacher tells Wormold that the Kaiser spoke to him once and called him Captain Müller. Much remains untold about enigmatic Dr. Hasselbacher, incompletely adumbrated on purpose. (Sources: Greene, *Ways of Escape*, 258–59; Shelden, 82–83, 500)

HASSELBACHER, EMMA (*Our Man in Havana*). When Wormold is questioned by the Santiago police and they find an unsent post card addressed to Dr. Hasselbacher in his wallet, he fibs about loving a Dr. Emma Hasselbacher and leaving Havana because her husband is suspicious.

HATCHARD, WILLIAM (*The Human Factor*) *see* **CASTLE, MAURICE**

HATTY (*Travels with My Aunt*). Hatty was a fellow worker with the Rev. Curran and Augusta in their Brighton dog church. After Curran decamped, Augusta also left but Hatty remained. Augusta, 40 years later, looks her up and finds she is a fortune teller. Hatty accurately reads Henry's fortune in tea leaves.

HAWTHORNE, HENRY R. (*Our Man in Havana*). He is British Secret Service agent 59200 out of London. He recruits Wormold in Havana, believes his outrageous fibs about agents he is hiring and supervising, and goes to London to praise "our man in Havana" to their Chief. He looks at Wormold's sketch of a military installation but doesn't quite recognize it as based on vacuum-cleaner parts. During Wormold's conference with London authorities, Hawthorne is understandably offish with him.

W. J. West says that Greene's number as a secret-service agent in Sierra Leone during the war was 59200. (Source: West, 169)

THE HEART OF THE MATTER (1948). Novel. (Characters: Ali, Azikawe, Senor Aranjuez, Flight-Lieutenant Freddie Bagster, Bailey, Baker, Tom Barlow, Mrs. Tom Barlow, Arthur Bishop, Blackbeard, Boling, Bowles, Mrs. Bowles, Boyston, Brigstock, Mrs. Bromley, Teddy Bromley, Brown, Père Brûle, Captain Buller, Butterworth, Calloway, Mrs. Carter, Castle, Mrs. Castle, Father Clay, Clive, Collins, Mrs. Collins, the Colonial Secretary, the Colonial Treasurer, the Commissioner, Major Cooper, William P. Cornforth, Crayshaw, Batty Davis, Father Davis, Dempster, Derry, the Director of Agriculture, the Director of Education, Captain Druce, Ducker, Mlle. Dupont, Durand, Evans, Fellowes, Mrs. Fellowes, P. Ferreira, Jimmy Fisher, Forbes, Fraser, the Governor, Frau Groener, Halifax, Mary Halifax, H. R. Harris, Helen, Jagger, F. J. K., Corporal Laminah, Lane, Loder, Makin, Miss Malcott, Ethel Maybury, Newall, Mrs. Onoko, D. C. Parkes, Pemberton, Dicky Pemberton, Perrot, Mrs. Perrot, Father Rank, Rees, Reith, Robinson, Molly Robinson, Helen Rolt, John Rolt, Snakey, Catherine Scobie, Henry Scobie, Louise Scobie, Dr. Jessie Sykes, Tallit, Thimblerigg, Tierney, Tod, Dr. Travis, Vande, Miss Wilberforce, Edward Wilson, Colonel Wright, Yusef.)

Book One: 1. I. (Freetown, Sierra Leone, early 1940's.) E. Wilson, new accountant for the United African Company, sits on the Bedford Hotel balcony when H. R. Harris, a cable censor, enters. They drink and chat. Harris criticizes black workers, identifies Major Henry Scobie, assistant police commissioner walking below, and criticizes Scobie's artsy wife.

II. In his station, Scobie thinks about his 15 years here and about Louise, his faded wife. The Commissioner tells Scobie he's retiring, says it's unfair but Scobie won't become commissioner, names Baker as the new commissioner. Scobie hears the complaint of black Miss Wilberforce, whose sexiness he scans indifferently. Her landlady mistreated her. Scobie no longer takes sides concerning native squabbles.

III. Scobie goes to his residence, finds Louise sweaty under a mosquito net. She tells him Mrs. Castle gossiped that Scobie won't be promoted. She can't persuade him to transfer or retire, twits him about missing Mass. Mention is made of their deceased daughter Catherine, the Vichy French beyond the border (in French Guinea), Syrians, and diamond smuggling nearby. Ali, Scobie's faithful black "boy," will serve food.

IV. Scobie drives Louise to the Cape Station Club. They encounter sundry members and wives. Fellowes, sanitary inspector, complains that Major Cooper, dentist, is sponsoring Wilson as an honorary member. Scobie is relieved when Louise meets shy Wilson. The two discuss literature. She invites Wilson to dinner soon. Scobie hopes she won't be patronizing, as usual.

V. Leaving Louise to be driven home by Mrs. Halifax, Scobie drives on his rounds. He sees Yusef, corrupt Syrian storekeeper, having car trouble, drives him home. The two discuss Yusef's rival, Tallit (Christian Syrian), and ongoing diamond smuggling.

VI. Scobie continues his rounds, walks on the wharf with a black policeman, drives past the brothel, checks on newly jailed felons, is happy that Louise will relax after talking about books at the club.

VII. Scobie cuts his hand on a splinter. Ali bandages it in Scobie's bathroom. Wilson has been reading poetry with Louise. Scobie drives Wilson to the Bedford.

VIII. Louise feels disliked by everyone, except Wilson now, wants a vacation in South Africa. Scobie promises to find funds to send her there.

2. I. Robinson, local bank manager, declines to loan Scobie the requisite £250.

II. To enforce wartime naval laws, Scobie, Captain Druce, Evans, and other policemen search for smuggled diamonds on the *Esperança*, neutral Portuguese ship, before allowing it through the blockade. They know they won't find any diamonds in lard cans or bags of rice. The fat captain is affable with wine and jokes. Scobie, alerted by a Portuguese steward, searches the captain's bathroom and finds an illegal letter from the captain to his daughter in Leipzig. Scobie confiscates the letter, despite the weeping, bribe-offering captain's plea about being widowed, having a Lisbon mistress jealous of his daughter, and being Catholic like Scobie.

III. In his office, Scobie illegally opens the captain's letter, which discusses his sins and love for his daughter . Scobie burns the letter out of sentimentality. Fraser, a junior officer, happens to see him doing so, mentions Druce's suspicion of the captain, Unfounded, says Scobie. Scobie goes home, knowing Louise will ask about his day, only to grouse about hers.

IV. Over several gins, Scobie and Louise talk. The bank refused. He'll get the vacation money somehow. She is miserable, lonely, wants him to be peaceful. He wishes he'd taken the Portuguese's bribe, and fibs he loves her.

Part Two: 1. I. Wilson and Harris share a Bedford apartment. Wilson prepares to dine at Tallit's house. Harris persuades Wilson to let an Indian, just outside, tell his fortune: Ah, he will succeed in love and work, enjoys poetry, will capture a man. Harris tells Wilson to pursue unworthy Scobie's wife Louise.

II. Tallit provides dinner for Wilson and Father Rank, local Catholic priest, who laughs heartily, kids Tallit for competition with Yusef, talks about illegal diamonds, liquor, hoarded cotton, and tells Tallit that if he saw Scobie drive Yusef home all was innocent. Wilson listens carefully.

III. When Wilson gets home, he and Harris have a contest squashing cockroaches, especially numerous in Harris's slovenly room; they argue about scores but in the morning apologize amiably. Scobie sees Wilson at the station, and invites him to walk with Louise and stay for dinner. The Commissioner tells Scobie that Wilson just requested a wharf ticket.

2. I. Louise Scobie leads Wilson, already enamored, to a beautiful sunset spot near an abandoned station, reveals this: Scobie, whose nickname "Ticki" he dislikes, is sending her to South Africa, doesn't love her, is happier alone because she hates him. Wilson half-accidentally kisses her. Father Rank happens to see them and shouts about rain. Wilson tells Louise he loves her. Calling him too young, she laughs at him.

II. Louise and Wilson, drenched, return to her house. Scobie says there's trouble concerning Dicky Pemberton, the Gambia district commissioner; the Commissioner ordered Scobie to drive overnight to check; Wilson must please stay a while for drinks with Louise. Scobie leaves. Obeying Louise, Wilson checks her bedroom for rats; he smells her face powder.

Part Three: 1. I. Scobie, with faithful Ali, gets to Gamba. Scobie interviews Father Clay, who says Pemberton, a gambler and drinker, hanged himself, but the priest hopes it was murder — to prevent Pemberton's losing God's mercy. He adds Yusef supplied Pemberton's liquor. Scobie finds that Pemberton, inefficient with reports, left a note to his widowered father, hanged himself from a brass nail. Scobie tells Father Clay that God must forgive such an unformed fellow's act. Scobie takes quinine to ward off fever, and sleeps. When he awakens, Yussef is there. He says Pemberton bought items at his regional store and signed IOUs, which Yusef ostentatiously burns in front of Scobie, who talks feverishly with him about not wanting a bribe. Yusef hints that a man has come from England to check into diamond smuggling, expresses gratitude for Scobie's friendship, and offers him a 4 percent loan. Scobie dreams about Louise locking him out and also about resisting suicide.

II. Scobie recovers from fever, rests, returns home. Louise says Wilson has been kind. Scobie notices she's writing Mrs. Halifax a letter, learns she is going to South Africa and a berth is open for Louise. Scobie tells Louise he'll borrow the money, and she can go. She seems only moderately pleased.

III. The liner arrives Saturday. Scobie and Louise go to Sunday Mass. Servants help her pack. She warns him that Wilson is a phony. Halifax cheerily bids his wife goodbye. Scobie does the same and returns alone to what he hopes will be comfortable changelessness.

IV. Back home, silence. Rat in bathroom. Vulture on roof. Yusef, from whom Scobie borrowed money for Louise's trip, drives up. He reminds uneasy Scobie that the British seek unsuccessfully to stop little industrial diamonds from getting via cross-border Vichy French agents in Africa, and also from Sierra Leone, through Portugal to Nazi Germany. He tells Scobie that Tallit's cousin will try to smuggle a big diamond in a parrot's crop aboard the next Portuguese ship.

Book Two: 1. I. Behold Scobie at Pende(mbu), south of Freetown, on May 5, to interview survivors of a torpedoed liner after 40 days at sea. Also there are Druce, a doctor, Perrot (the Pende district commissioner), Mrs. Perrot, and Wilson. Wilson updates the Perrots: Tallit's cousin's parrot's crop concealed a diamond, but authorities couldn't prove the parrot was Tallit's cousin's. After drinks, Scobie retires, makes cryptic notes in his diary, and falls asleep praying.

II. Next morning survivors get ashore, some walking, several on stretchers. The French officer responsible for their rescue talks with Scobie, who looks at a child close to death and at a young woman, only 19 — just wed, husband lost at sea, and clutching a stamp album.

III. Scobie visits the rest house where Mrs. Bowles, a missionary, cares for the weakest survivors. He sits beside the child, asks God to take his peace and give it to her, comfortingly whispers, yes, he is her father. She soon dies.

IV. Scobie gives his place in the van to Miss Malcott, a survivor heading for Lagos, Portugal, to teach. Mrs. Bowles asks him to read to Jimmy Fisher, an injured young survivor. Scobie picks the biography of a bishop among the Bantus, pretends to read it, but instead tells a made-up story of pirates. Helen Rolt, the nineteen-year-old, regaining consciousness, listens.

V. Wilson confronts Scobie with news of corruption in his company's local store, says military items have come from Yusef, hints Scobie and Yusef are too close. Scobie rebukes him for naiveté. Wilson says Scobie sent Louise away because of him, adds he kissed her. Scobie's serene response angers Wilson, who upbraids him for somehow getting money for her vacation, snarls that Scobie is after Mrs. Rolt, then weeps — with hatred.

2. I. Six weeks later. During an alert, Scobie sees a light in a hut near his house, knocks to tell the occupant to close the blackout curtain. Helen Rolt, there, invites him in for gin. She tells him much about herself. He listens gravely. They become friends, separated by two spouses, one dead, one alive. Scobie returns in the rain, happy briefly, alone surely.

II. After hearing cases involving necessary native lies, Scobie writes Louise — truthfully, therefore without affection. Scobie is hauled before the Colonial Secretary, the Commissioner, and Colonel Wright from Cape Town to investigate, and grilled about Tallit's parrot. He answers thus: Yusef has given him nothing but information; Yusef is unreliable, as is Tallit; Parliament prefers Moslems to Catholics. The authorities appear aware Yusef's money financed Louise's trip.

III. Exiting, Scobie sees Harris and learns from him that the two of them and Wilson all attended the Downham school in England, further, that Harris and Wilson are moving from the hotel into a hut near Scobie.

IV. Scobie enters Yussef's home and awakens him in the ugly room where they consummated their loan. Yusef admits he planted diamonds in his enemy's cousin's parrot's crop. Scobie says Yusef wants Tallit out of business, chills their friendship, promises to pay monthly interest on the loan, and disbelieves Yusef's joking threat to tell the Commissioner that Scobie took money to arrest Tallit but then says he wouldn't do so.

V. Scobie goes to confession, tells Father Rank he has doubts, feels empty, is given an unneeded absolution, kneels, prays for Louise's happiness, feels God is too approachable.

3. I. Scobie visits Helen, to give her some stamps. They talk about her husband and her one-month's marriage, about death, about the two cables Louise sent when their daughter died in England, about Helen's lack of faith in God. Helen's ugly appearance makes him feel responsible—unlike what one need feel about the dead. They agree they feel safe together. Flight-Lieutenant Freddie Bagster, whom Helen met by the beach, shouts at her door for admittance (as he will often do). Staying quiet until he leaves, Scobie and Helen kiss.

II. Scobie sleeps with Helen, leaves before first light, ponders on lies he must now tell through responsibility for both Helen and Louise.

Part Two: 1. I. Harris and Wilson occupy a hut near Helen's. When Harris is reading a periodical from the Downham school, he encounters a love poem addressed to L.S. and signed E.W., and concludes Wilson is after Louise.

II. Harris sleeps. Wilson regrets sending his poem to Downham, goes outside late, spots Scobie near a hut, and recognizes as a lie Scobie's excuse he couldn't sleep.

III. Wilson interviews a black lad who works for Yusef, orders him to spy on Scobie's activities, threatens jail if he lies. Then Wilson checks a coded message about diamonds coming up from Lobito (Angola).

IV. In his recently purchased old car, Wilson drives through the rain to a brothel, reluctantly pays, and engages a girl, who, first, serves palm wine.

Part Three: 1. I. After a month of sneaky lovemaking in her hut, Helen and Scobie argue. She says his being a Catholic doesn't permit their marriage but enables him to confess adultery and be forgiven. He offers to put her on an outward-bound vessel. She tells him to go to hell. He leaves, pities her, writes a letter dated September 5, signed but without naming her, and thus putting his security in her hands, saying he loves her more than he loves God perhaps, and shoves the letter under her door.

II. Father Rank visits Scobie, has some beer, and says he feels useless and is called only to help the dying. Scobie can't tell Father Rank he loves two women and won't look after his own soul.

III. Scobie notices Wilson searched his office. Scobie goes to the Commissioner's bungalow for dinner and drinks, asks why he's the last to know Wilson is a spying intelligence agent, learns Wilson spies on every Britisher hereabouts and trusts Tallit, tells the Commissioner about borrowing £200 from Yusef, is told diamonds are being stolen at the mines.

Reluctantly, Scobie visits apologetic Helen, learns she never picked up his note, seems unworried by that fact, promises to care for her needs as long as he lives. At home he finds a telegram from Louise announcing her return (after seven months). He feels desperate for being so needed always. He prays only for death. How about taking too many aspirin? God breaks laws. Christ, being God hence unmurderable, surely hanged himself. Scobie records recent action in his diary, dated Wednesday, September 6.

2. I. Scobie, Helen, Wilson, Dr. Jessie Sykes, and others have dinner, featuring Argentine beef obtained by Wilson, at Mr. and Mrs. Fellowes's. Pemberton's suicide is discussed. Rejecting Wilson's suggestion of suicide by sleeping-draught overdose, Dr. Sykes would prefer faking angina and having a colleague prescribe hoardable pills for it. They discuss

Catholicism and suicide. Helen, annoyed, goes outside with Scobie, who tells her Louise is returning. Wilson interrupts them and drives Helen to her hut. When Scobie gets home, he finds a letter from Helen there and Yusef asleep there. Helen writes: Scobie needn't honor any promise; she loves him; she'll leave or be his "hore," as he chooses. Yusef implores Scobie to deliver a packet secretly to the *Esperança* captain, soon to dock. No. So Yusef reveals this: Helen's native boy, employed by Yusef, filched Scobie's letter intended for Helen and read it to Yusef; Yusef will give it to Louise, unless ... Scobie feels he can never return to the land of truth.

II. When Druce leaves the *Esperança*, Scobie hands the captain, who is grateful that Scobie never reported his earlier crime, Yusef's packet with instructions to give it to the Lisbon pilot.

Book Three: Part One: 1. I. Scobie meets Louise at her boat. Home anew, she starts arranging for better relations. Scobie calls on Helen. When he tells her Louise wants him to go to confession and then Mass, Helen rebukes him — naively, he feels — for spiritual niceties, and suggests he remain in mortal sin. She fears he'll abandon her. No, he replies.

II. Next morning Scobie silently pities Louise for danger at sea, childbirth, death of child. When she starts the two of them for Mass, he feigns heart pains, sips some brandy, and hence can't receive when she does. This is but a temporary escape.

2. I. Wilson brings his poem, addressed to L.S., to Louise. She laughs at its romantic exaggeration of love. Angry, he wonders if Louise returned to her husband out of love or jealousy. Questioned, he reveals Scobie's affair with Helen. Louise hits him, causing a nosebleed. Lying down, Wilson adds that Yusef is too close with Scobie, who suddenly enters and innocently helps Wilson away.

II. Scobie brushes off Louise's mentioning Wilson's crush on her, is forced by Louise to promise to go to communion tomorrow, and while rushing to the confessional is in confusion. Abandon Louise? Abandon Helen to horny Bagster? Put his own soul first? Abandon God and be punished so others may be happy? To Father Rank he confesses adultery, is told he must promise not to be with that other woman alone again, says he can't promise that, is told he can receive absolution only upon contrition, repentance, and that promise. Scobie retreats, in despair. That night he dreams his dead body stinks. In the morning Louise reminds him of communion today. He goes, consumed with contrary thoughts of self, others, pity, responsibility. Offering his damnation to God, Scobie takes the wafer.

3. I. Scobie reads about angina in a medical book in the bank-manager Robinson's office. The Commissioner tells Scobie that he'll become the new commissioner after all, also that Robinson is terminally ill. Scobie sees Ali talking with a strange lad, begins to suspect Ali, and feels guilty for doing so. He takes new furniture to Helen, tells her of his promotion. When she selfishly upbraids him, he persuasively says he's damned and believes in Hell, loves and would spare both mistress and wife (they need him more than God does), mentions chest pains. They drive together until dusk. Ali, acting suspiciously, sees them.

II. In total loneliness, Scobie writes in his diary. A strange black lad enters with a diamond wrapped in a paper (Scobie's letter to Helen) from Yusef, and leaves. The gift means the diamonds Scobie gave the sea captain got through to Lisbon. Ali enters with the other boy. Scobie returns the diamond, orders him to warn Yusef, hears Ali and the boy whispering outside, doubts Ali's loyalty. Louise calls down to remind him of communion tomorrow (November 1). He seems to be striking God, feels damned.

4. I. Next day, on his way to Yusef, Scobie encounters Wilson, who tells him he loves Louise better than Scobie can. They speak frankly. Wilson, misunderstanding, leaves. To Yusef, Scobie admits he worries about Louise, Helen, and now Ali, fears consequences of worrying, is persuaded to have Ali report to Yusef for advice. Yusef leaves for a long while, then returns and they talk. Someone screams. Scobie goes to the wharf and finds Ali, his throat slashed.

Part Two: 1. I. Scobie finds Helen. She knows about Ali, and says, though loving Scobie deeply, she must depart. He thinks his death would ease everything for her. She elaborates on her leaving. He prays to die. They cannot part. He says he must think.

II. After dinner, Louise, happy about Scobie's promotion and indifferent concerning Ali's murder, suggests throwing a Christmas Eve party and then attending Mass. He equivocates, lets her retire, and records in his diary his pains and fear of angina.

2. I. Scobie is examined by Dr. Travis, describes his pains, wonders about angina, and is given evipan, plans his diary entries, goes into the church, envies the saved, and promises God that He will be rid of him soon. But his monologue is answered: I love you, have wept for you, go to the confessional, or reject me now but return later. Scobie feels unable to accept this message, feels too responsible, leaves, clutching his pills.

3. I. Scobie loads his diary November 3–11 with deceptive comments on work and retiring, and adds comments on evipan in earlier entries. On the 12th, while Louise is at the beach, he goes to Helen's hut. Empty. Is she with Bagster? At dinner with Louise, he mentions his illness, his medicine, and his retirement. She'd like a house in Kent, reads some poetry to him about salvation he can't accept, pops off to bed ahead of him. Alone, he takes 12 pills and whisky, sits rigidly, hears pain, stands, tries to pray, tells God he loves ... but falls.

Part Three: 1. I. Three days after Scobie was buried, Wilson calls on Louise, proposes, is fended off for now, is told Scobie's diary indicates he saw Helen the day he died. He asks how long Louise knew about Helen. She replies thus: Mrs. Carter wrote her; Scobie thought he was so clever; he probably confessed, took communion, and continued sinning. Wilson says Scobie was bribed by Yusef, is allowed to see Scobie's diary, and points out the added-in references to evipan. Louise doubts he committed suicide, because after all he was a good Catholic.

II. Having drunk plenty on the beach, Helen and Bagster convene in her hut. He proposes some lovemaking. Her passively supine acquiescence is off putting. They'll probably meet tomorrow. Alone, she prays raggedly, feels an adjacent pillow hoping another's presence is still there.

III. Louise shows Scobie's diary to Father Rank. They conclude from it that Scobie committed suicide. The priest says Scobie needs more comfort now than she does, feels sorry Helen got commingled with all of them, says the Church can't fathom the human heart, expresses hope for Scobie, believes he loved God. But when Helen says he didn't love anyone else, Father Rank says she's probably right.

Norman Sherry theorizes that Greene may have first thought of writing a novel in which the protagonist kills himself after Greene had a dream when he was 25 and was interested in Vivienne Dayrell-Browning, his future wife (*see* Greene, Vivien). In the dream he so hated her for spurning him that he planned to shoot himself to make her feel miserable. Much action and scenery in *The Heart of the Matter* was based on Greene's wartime duty in Freetown, Sierra Leone, and his later visits to other African regions (1941–1946). In "Convoy to West Africa," which is part of *In Search of a Character: Two African Journals* (1961), Greene writes about voyaging from Liverpool to Freetown (December 9, 1941–January 3, 1942), to assume duties there.

Dating the action of *The Heart of the Matter* is difficult. Scobie says many generals have been ignored for promotion since l940. He arrives at Pende May 8, according to his diary. Wilson hires a native boy to spy on Scobie June 27, then opens his safe with numbers enabling the reader to conclude he was born in 1910 and is now 32. So the year of this action is probably 1942. Scobie writes Louise September 5. He tells Father Rank that Louise has been gone seven months, which would make the action of the novel commence early in February 1942. But Scobie dates an entry in his diary Wednesday, September 6, which fell in 1944. (Either Scobie or, more likely, Greene was careless.) Scobie adds to his diary October 31 and November 1–11, and dies the following night.

Critics wonder whether Scobie's soul is saved. Several have upbraided Greene for not telling us. Neil McEwan, for example, says "Greene surrenders his decision to God but Scobie's soul is subject only to the novel's laws; the last judgment on him should be there. Novels ought not to raise a central question and leave it unanswered." Greene, however, won't play God. If readers can answer Greene's closing riddle, aren't they playing God?

Sherry reports that with the publication of *The Heart of the Matter* Greene found himself "the most famous and most pursued writer in

England." The novel raises many controversial issues, especially for Catholic readers. This fact was reflected in many opinionated reviews and a few outright bans against the novel. All of which resulted, as Michael Shelden reports, in soaring sales — 300,000 copies in England in three years, not to mention record sales elsewhere — and its being chosen as a main selection by the Book-of-the-Month Club in the United States. Some of Greene's earlier novels were reissued, and his world-wide popularity, and notoriety, were assured. Prophetically, Greene generalizes toward the end of *The Heart of the Matter* that beauty resembles success, because neither can be loved very long.

Cedric Watts says "[t]he 'heart of the matter,' it seems, is pity." R. H. Miller explains better: "The 'heart of the matter' is fundamentally the totality of vision that rests with an omniscient God that can account for the problem of evil, natural and moral, and how one is to reconcile it to one's belief in that loving God." Miller compares the structure of the novel to that of a typical Elizabethan tragedy, with exposition, triggering events, mounting action, climactic situation, and acts descending to ruination; complicating this structure is the twining through it of two plots, one ending in Ali's murder (public plot line), the other in Scobie's suicide (private plot line). Lynne Cheney contends that "[b]y referring to the structure of *The Heart of the Matter* as a series of strands binding Scobie ever more tightly, we indicate that our particular angle of vision on the book causes us to perceive its happenings as related parts rather than as [separate] events."

Quentin Falk reports that Greene wrote a stage adaptation of *The Heart of the Matter,* which Richard Rodgers and Oscar Hammerstein bought and presented in Boston (1950); but it soon failed and never moved to New York. The novel was adapted as a movie (1953), for the rights to which Shelden notes that Alexander Korda* paid Greene £4,000. It starred Trevor Howard (as Henry Scobie), Peter Finch (Father Rank), and Maria Schell (Helen Rolt). Since Schell (1926–2005) was an Austrian beauty, her accent required that in the movie plot she is an Austrian wife of an Englishman. The final action is altered in the movie: Scobie, about to shoot himself, hears a street fight, rushes to break it up, is mortally injured, asks his servant to tell Mrs. Scobie that "God made it all right, for her." This mitigates distress suffered by Catholic film-goers anticipating the protagonist's suicide. For another reason, the movie was banned in Hong Kong, Singapore, and Malaya, according to Falk: British colonial audiences oughtn't see British police commissioner Scobie unfavorably depicted. Greene told Pierre Joannon (1981) that *The Heart of the Matter,* along with three of his other novels, had been banned in Ireland at one time. In truth, it was banned in Hong Kong, Singapore, and Malaya, but was permitted in Ireland after substantial cutting — according to David Parkinson. (Sources: Cheney, 119; Greene, *The Graham Greene Film Reader,* 720; Joannon, 163; Falk, 105, 108, 210; McEwan, 68; Miller, 70–71; Parkinson, 720; Phillips, 120, 122; Shelden, 214, 356; Sherry II, 292, 293–94; Watts, 58)

HECKSTALL-JONES, JOSEPHINE ("Mortmain"). She was Philip Carter's tempestuous, dark-haired mistress for 10 disquieting years. She once scorched Philip with a cigarette butt. When he marries Julia, Josephine attends the wedding exhibiting tears. She writes Philip a letter during his honeymoon with Julia in Greece, the malevolent purpose of which Julia naively misunderstands. Josephine leaves notes in the home which she shared with Philip and where he and Julia now live. Continuing to misunderstand, Julia upbraids Philip for being unsympathetic toward Josephine.

HEI, MISS (*The Quiet American*). She is Phuong's older sister. Their parents are dead. Having worked in Singapore, Miss Hei knows English and through Pyle's efforts obtains work in his boss Joe's office. She wants Phuong to marry well, and therefore dislikes Fowler and prefers Pyle for her.

HELEN (*The Heart of the Matter*). Helen Rolt tells Scobie that the games mistress at her Seaport school was named Helen, as she herself is.

HENG (*The Quiet American*). He is Chou's knowledgeable Communist associate. Heng tells Fowler about Pyle's plan to deliver plastic explosives to General Thé. After they are used in the Place Garnier massacre and Pyle turns callous, Heng smoothly persuades Fowler to participate, indirectly but surely, in Pyle's murder, details of which Heng manages.

HENNE-FALCON, COLIN ("The End of the Party"). Colin is a boy whose mother celebrates his 10th birthday with a party.

HENNE-FALCON, MRS. ("The End of the Party"). She is a big-bosomed hostess giving her son Colin a birthday party.

Her name, combining fluttery smother-loving and scary swooping, is underlined by her regarding her juvenile guests as "a flock of chickens."

HENRI (*A Burnt-Out Case*). He is Dr. Colin's efficient young African dispenser at the leproserie.

HENRI, FATHER (*A Burnt-Out Case*). He was a visiting priest who damaged a chair by trying to balance on the back of it, as in a circus act. The priests push it against a wall so it's still serviceable. When Parkinson sits in it, it tumbles.

Norman Sherry reports that Dr Michel F. Lechat, Greene's real-life model for Dr. Colin, wrote Sherry that Greene was a Father Henri's close friend when Greene was visiting Lechat's Congo leprosarium. Greene did some river traveling with Father Henri then. (Source: Sherry III, 173, 177, 180)

HENRIQUES (*England Made Me*). He was a person at Harrow, along with Patterson, before Farrant's alleged time there. So says Minty, when he and Farrant are discussing the school. Minty knows Farrant never attended Harrow.

HENRY (*Our Man in Havana*). He is an American businessman in Havana. Wormold's getting a withdrawal of cash at his bank is delayed when the teller takes a phone call from Henry and the two discuss their friends Edith and Mrs. Slater. Wormold feel insignificant when he hears the teller tell Henry he can have a four-year loan of $200,000 at 5 percent.

HERBERT (*It's a Battlefield*). He was Conrad Drover's uncle. Conrad's parents named Conrad after a merchant seaman who lived with them. They said it was pointless to name him after Uncle Herbert, who was broke.

"HERETICS IN LOVE" see *THE NAME OF ACTION*

HERRERA, FATHER (*Monsignor Quixote*). He is a priest who earned a doctorate in moral theology at Salamanca, then was the secretary of the Bishop of El Toboso three years. When the Bishop learns Father Quixote is going on holiday, he sends stiff, austere Herrera to replace him temporarily. Herrera, whom Zancas calls a "black Fascist," does all he can to bother Father Quixote.

Jae-Suck Choi observes that "[f]rom the first meeting, Monsignor Quixote disagrees with Father Herrera on two issues — moral theology and God's mercy. The Monsignor talks about God's mercy, but Father Herrera puts emphasis on God's judgement." (Source: Choi, 193)

HEVERSHAM (*Brighton Rock*) see **FEVERSHAM**

HEYSAN-BRETAU (*It's a Battlefield*). He was Jules Briton's father. He abandoned Jules and Jules's mother, returned to France, might have become mayor of Petit Tourville but died, leaving Jules 10,500 francs. Jules is delighted.

HICKSLAUGHTER, HENRY ("Cheap in August"). He is an obese, shady American, over 70, up from Curaçao to Jamaica, where August rates are cheap. He aggressively beseeches Mary Watson for friendship, doesn't mind her reading a threatening letter he is writing to his brother Joe Hickslaughter, and hints at his own piratical past. Mary finds him needing affection because of loneliness and fear of dying slowly somewhere. She lies down beside his bulky body, boozy and asleep, and soon they make brief, quick, unregretted love.

Greene demonstrates his chronic prejudice against Americans, fat or otherwise, by graphically depict this one, whom he also names strangely. Does Henry slaughter hicks or bray with a hick's laughter? Also, Greene spells Hickslaughter's informal affirmatives as "Ye-eh."

HICKSLAUGHTER, JOE ("Cheap in August"). He is the brother of Henry Hickslaughter, who writes a menacing letter to Joe. Henry asks Joe to give his love to their sister.

HIGGINBOTHAM (*This Gun for Hire*). He is the Westminster bank clerk in Nottwich who tells the police his daughter Rose found Buddy Fergusson in their garage.

HIGGINBOTHAM, ROSE (*This Gun for Hire*). According to her father, she found Fergusson stripped, bound, and gagged in the Higginbothams' garage.

HIGGINS (*The Honorary Consul*). Sir Henry Belfrage commends Plarr for being true British, unlike the Higginses and the O'Briens hereabouts. Is Greene indicating his anti–Irish bias or this British functionary's snobbery?

HIGH COMMISSIONER, THE (*The Quiet American*). Fowler mentions seeing this official's Saigon house, with French Foreign Legion guards in front of it, as he walks home to Phuong after Pyle's death.

HILFE, ANNA (*The Ministry of Fear*). She is Willi Hilfe's brother. Both are refugees from Vienna. They use the Free Mothers' office as a cover. Anna is aware of Willi's spying activities, hates his genius for creating fear, but loves him like a twin. She aids Rowe when Willi wants to hurt him, falls in love with Rowe, breaks Willi's wrist to prevent his using a gun, and tells Rowe of Willi's escape plans. Anna hopes Rowe will remain Richard Digby, caught in amnesia, because his past is troublesome. Rowe regains his memory but pretends he hasn't, to love a blander Anna, who, however, knows the truth but pretends otherwise.

W. J. West contends that Anna is patterned on Greene's cousin Barbara Greene, who married Count Rudolf Strachwitz, a German aristocrat, and lived with him in Germany during the war. (Source: West, 99–100)

HILFE, WILLI (*The Ministry of Fear*). He is Anna Hilfe's twin-like brother, both refugees from Vienna. Willi needs the film that Rowe, an amnesiac, unknowingly possesses. Willi helps stage Cost's pretended murder at Mrs. Bellairs's séance, urges Rowe to hide from its consequences, and when his and Cost's plans to murder both Rowe and Anna fail cooperates with Dr. Forester to get Rowe into Forester's sanatorium. Willi tries to escape to Ireland with Lady Dunwoody's help; but Anna tells Rowe, who confronts him at Paddington station. Willi gives up the second copy of the damaging film, vengefully reveals Rowe's distressing past to him, and commits suicide.

Brian Diemert notes Hilfe's "name ironically means 'help' in German." Elliott Malamet explicates Willi's reading in *Sonnete an Orpheus* (1923) by the Austrian poet Rainer Maria Rilke (1875–1926). He says that the four Rilke lines quoted in the novel concern Orpheus as "a symbol of continual transformation or metamorphosis" and "accentuate the Orphic elements of loss and transformation" in Greene's novel; however, another part of the Orphic myth — poetry conquering death — doesn't work for Rowe, who realizes juvenile literature doesn't prefigure happy endings in adulthood. (Sources: Diemert, 153; Malamet, 49)

HILL, D. ("Men at Work"). He is a member of the Book Committee in the Ministry of Information. He proved of positive value by writing a negative defense of the existence of the Ministry.

HILLIARD, THOMAS (*The Man Within*). For four years he has been in command of revenuers and gaugers trying to interdict smugglers. When he gets Andrews's anonymous letter tipping him off, he and his men trap 10 smugglers on the beach, are shot at, and capture six. Rexall, one of Hilliard's men, is killed during the action. During the trial of the arrested smugglers, their defense attorney, Braddock, tries to embarrass Hilliard.

HILLMAN, SIR TERENCE (*The Confidential Agent*). He is a parrot-nosed barrister of considerable clout. Forbes engages him to represent D. in court. He argues that, to gain time, the police are improperly holding D. on minor charges. D. is released on bail provided by Forbes, who then helps him escape.

HILTON, MR. (*Our Man in Havana*). One night Wormold and Beatrice see "H.H." impressed in the sky and designed to advertise Mr. Hilton.

Mr. Hilton is Conrad Hilton (1887–1979), the American businessman who founded one of the world's largest hotel organizations. During the Cold War, Hilton built luxurious, American-style hotels abroad to present America's face to Communism. He announced plans for the Hilton Havana (1950), to have 850 rooms, 450-car garage, swimming pool, and rooftop space. Completed (1958), it was popular with tourists both American and non-American, entertainers, gamblers, and gangsters. As Claudia Lightfoot adds, "the Havana Hilton in Vedado on Calles and L was completed more or less just in time to be taken over by Fidel Castro who renamed it the Habana Libre and set up his first headquarters there in 1959."

The Habana Libre was then called the Habana Libre-Guitart (1993–1995), the new name deriving from that of a Spanish investment group. The hotel was refurbished, and the work force was reduced from 1,200 to 400. It was again called the Habana Libre (from 1996). Meanwhile, the Meliá-Cohiba hotel, a 22-story structure and allegedly a copy of a hotel in Japan, was built nearby, financed by a Spanish-Cuban group (1995). It took over most of the foreign-tourist trade from the aging Habana Hilton. Many Cubans regard the Meliá-Cohiba as "Spain's second conquest" of their island. (Sources: Lightfoot, 126; Scarpaci, Segre, Coyula, 121, 240, 301)

"THE HINT OF AN EXPLANATION"

(1948). Short story. (Characters: Blacker, Father Carey, David, Aunt Lucy.)

The unnamed narrator is on the train with David, whose talk reveals that he is Catholic. Bundled against the December cold, they converse amiably, even while differing. David, seemingly happy, listens courteously to the narrator's espousal of agnosticism, complaints about free will, and occasional corruption even of children. David's measured reply: Our questions get no answers, only "hints" making sense to the individual recipient but tending to frustrate that "thing behind the human actors"— call it Satan. David asks permission to relate his own childhood.

David was an altar boy in an East Anglian town with a minority of mistreated Catholics. His father was a bank manager. An ugly, free-thinking baker named Blacker sought to corrupt David. He enticed David, 10, by inviting him into the bakery to play with his toy electric train. One day he offered David a wafer he had baked, challenged him to tell its difference from Catholic wafers, was told it wasn't consecrated, and asked David to filch him one from Mass for him to taste. For the first time, the topic of transubstantiation confronted David. Blacker offered the train for a wafer — consecrated, mind you. He threatened to cut David with a razor if he didn't comply. Sunday at communion, David held his host under his tongue, took it to the sacristy, wrapped it, by then pulpy, in a piece of newspaper. Family visitors occupied David's family into the evening. He put the matted paper beside his bed, sensing it had infinite value. He couldn't sleep for worry. Blacker, frustrated at David's delay, whistled at his window, reached up, hungrily, half mad. David told where the wafer was but denied it to him, ignored the promise of the train, outfaced threats of the razor. He felt that when Blacker called the wafer only a piece of bread it had to mean more to him than that. The boy "picked it — Him — up," and swallowed Host, paper, and all. When David told Blacker, the man wept.

On the train now, David offers the inquisitive narrator his adult conclusion: Blacker seems to have been "that Thing weeping for its inevitable defeat." Their train jolts and stops. When the narrator says he would have given Blacker what he sought and wonders what Blacker would have done with it, David says he might first have put it under a microscope but then have tried other actions. The narrator asks about "the hint," to which David says it was all a beginning. The puzzled narrator is suddenly enlightened: David moves to reach the baggage rack, his coat parts to reveal his priestly collar, and he says, yes, he owes much to Blacker and is happy.

There is something charming in David's resisting as a child a unique kind of temptation, trading for a toy train, and then surrendering as an adult to another unique kind of temptation, confiding to a stranger on a real train. A. R. Coulthard circuitously suggests that David's feeling that his youthful act of resisting evil Blacker contained God's powerful hint, and led him to become a priest, colored his memory of the event, and made him demean Blacker and remember him as almost indescribably ugly and with reason to dislike Catholics; but Blacker's wanting a wafer, far from being a satanic ploy, "was really his clumsy attempt to reach out for God." Coulthard also contends that David's "sense of superiority over Blacker pervades the story." Perhaps more acceptably, Paul O'Prey reasons that Blacker wanted to "'seduce'" young David by means of the toy train so as to lay hands on "a consecrated host" and with it "prove to himself that there is no such thing as transubstantiation." (Sources: Coulthard, 122, 124; O'Prey, 62)

HOBBS (*Orient Express*). Opie mentions Hobbs and Sutliffe as cricket players.

HOCHSTRUDEL, WILBUR K. (*The Comedians*). His name is mentioned as someone expected by a guest at the Ambassador Hotel, just past Santo Domingo.

HOGHE (*A Burnt-Out Case*). This is the name, Querry believes, of the architecture student whose girlfriend, Marie Morel, he seduced briefly.

HOGMINSTER ("The Moment of Truth"). He is an American tourist, about 60, in London with his wife Dolly. When Arthur Burton, their Chez Auguste waiter, mentions he must go to the hospital for a check-up, Hogminster says he believes in check-ups. Dolly chimes in that he has had four, maybe six.

Greene's anti–American bias shines through the name Hogminster, which Greene needn't call "curious" but does.

HOGMINSTER, DOLLY ("The Moment of Truth"). She is an American tourist, in her late 40s, in London with her husband. Both are mainly interested in dining and shopping. Arthur Burton, their Chez Auguste waiter, is dying of cancer, angles for words of sympathy from Dolly, but gets none.

HOGPIT (*The Confidential Agent*). This vociferous Londoner tries to stop a policeman from arresting K. for public drunkenness. D. gets K. into his taxi, which ironically contributes to a chain of events resulting in K.'s death. Hogpit could incriminate D. in that death but is unable to identify D. in a police lineup.

Greene often gives characters strange names. Hogpit is clearly a loser; yet Greene does make him clever enough to respond when people laugh at his name by retorting it's no more humorous than the name Swinburne. Greene carelessly names three characters Joe in *The Confidential Agent*.

HOME SECRETARY, THE (*It's a Battlefield*). He is the official whose decision is to order Jim Drover's execution or his being reprieved and ordered to serve an 18-year prison sentence. The decision will have to do with politics, not justice.

THE HONORARY CONSUL (1973). Novel. (Characters: the Ambassador of Panama, Ana, Father Antonio, the Archbishop, Arden, Sir Henry Belfrage, Lady Belfrage, Dr. Benevento, Señorsa Benevento, Bergman, Bradshaw, Bradshaw, the British Ambassador, Buller, Callow, Carlota, Castillo, Caterina, the Chief Clerk, the Chief of Police, the Consul, Diego Corredo, Crichton, Miguel Duran, Gustavo Escobar, Margarita Escobar, the First Secretary, Fisher, the Foreign Minister, Forage, Fortnum, Charley Fortnum, Clara Fortnum, Evelyn Fortnum, Fuerabbia, Father Galvão, George, the Governor, the Governor, the Governor of the Chaco, Gruber, Higgins, Doctor Humphries, Captain Izquierdo, Juan, the Junior Minister, Lopez, Señora Lopez, Mallea, María, María, Marta, Martin, Miguel, the Minister of the Interior, Montez, Julio Moreno, Señora Moreno, O'Brien, Pablo, Pedro, Pedro, Father Pedro, Colonel Perez, Dr. Eduardo Plarr, Henry Plarr, Señora Plarr, the President, Pride, the Representative of the British Council, Aquino Ribera, Rivas, Léon Rivas, Señora Rivas, (Ken) Russell, Dr. Jorge Julio Saavedra, Sabato, Señora Sanchez, General Stroessner, Teresa, El Tigre, Gaspar Vallejo, Señora Vallejo, Señora Vega, Captain Velardo, Wilbur.)

Part One: 1. Dr. Eduardo Plarr, Argentine physician, practices in a small town (Corrientes, Argentina) on the Paraná river, 800 kilometers north of Buenos Aires. When Eduardo was 14, Henry Plarr, his English father, went missing in Paraguay. Eduardo left Buenos Aires to escape his self-absorbed Paraguayan mother. At sunset by the (hot November) port, Plarr indifferently reads *The Taciturn Heart*, a macho novel by Dr. Jorge Julio Saavedra, his patient and friend. He meets his friend Doctor Humphries, an old British teacher. They discuss alcoholic Charley Fortnum, the Honorary British Consul, and his pregnant wife Clara. Humphries asks who the father is; Plarr, her lover, opposes any need for truth. The Honorary Consul imports a Cadillac every two years, sells them to generals in the capital. The Governor had Fortnum show the visiting American Ambassador, along with other non-Spanish-speaking dignitaries, some Jesuit ruins.

2. Plarr naps in his riverside apartment. He and León Rivas, a schoolmate turned priest turned revolutionary, once joined the Juventud Febrerista guerrillas. Recently Plarr gave Rivas's band details about the American Ambassador. Awakened by phone, Plarr learns they have just mistakenly kidnapped Fortnum, not the Ambassador. They've drugged Fortnum, hope for ransom money, but now he's sick. Plarr must treat him. Brought in by the guerrillas, Plarr identifies their victim. Valueless Fortnum. Aquino, a gunman, says their leader El Tigre won't like this development. Fortnum is in a two-room mud hut near the *barrio,* resting in a coffin. He recognizes Plarr and mumbles about losing his wife's sunglasses. Plarr recommends releasing Fortnum. Rivas intends either ransom or murder for him.

Part Two (flashback): 1. Some weeks after arriving from Buenos Aires, Plarr first encountered Fortnum, in a club drunk. Humphries and Plarr got him to Humphries's hotel room. Fortnum wanted to visit Señora Sanchez's brothel to help his girlfriend María. Plarr drove him instead to the Consolate, where he was the Honorary Consul, listened to his chatter, got nicknamed Ted, declined a drink, and left.

Soon Plarr needed some documents witnessed, returned to the Consolate to have it done, chatted with forgetful Fortnum, diagnosed him as dreadfully alcoholic, prescribed some medicine, suggested his cutting down on what Fortnum called regular "measures" of drink, and departed to see more-deserving patients.

2. Almost two years later, Plarr visited Señora Sanchez's brothel with Saavedra, who visited Teresa weekly here — strictly for physical discipline and research about poverty. Saavedra babbled about his symbolic characters and how abstract, not real, politics are timeless in fiction. Plarr wondered if his realist-politician father was imprisoned or dead in Paraguay, compared brothel customers to clinical patients, and asked about Fortnum's María — dead, he's told. Teresa led Saavedra inside. Waiting outside, Plarr glimpsed a prostitute with a facial birthmark, like a Hindu's spot. More than a year later he visited the place and selected Teresa.

3. Time passed. Plarr grew fond of the small city, occasionally entertained Humphries, dined with Fortnum, visited Teresa. He flew east with the new Governor to see his maté plantation, visited Bergman's orange-canning factory, was driven once by Fortnum around his maté acreage (camp), and during one of his frequent flights to Buenos Aires to see his mother met Sir Henry Belfrage, the new British Ambassador, at a cocktail party. He asked Plarr about Consul Fortnum and revealed this: Fortnum was bothersome, useless; Humphries troublesomely wrote Sir Henry of Fortnum's remarriage; Plarr would please Sir Henry by hushing Humphries.

Back home, Plarr was called to Fortnum's camp, where Clara, that new wife, partly Tucumàn Indian and under 20 — Fortnum reported — was ill. Fortnum drove "Fortnum's Pride" — his Land Rover. While examining Clara, Plarr noted that tell-tale Hindu-like birthmark, hinted about Señora Sanchez's establishment, diagnosed her illness as intestinal inflammation. When Plarr added he knew only Teresa, he and Clara are mutually understanding. Over whisky, Plarr revealed awareness of the past of Clara, whom Fortnum insisted he adored and whose freedom Señora Sanchez sold him. The two men discussed love — Fortnum romantically, Plarr cynically. Fortnum said he hoped for 10 years, then Clara would inherit his valuable camp. Driving home, Plarr obsessed on Clara's past, present, and ill-curved body.

A few weeks later Plarr visited his friend Gruber, who escaped from Nazi Germany (1936) and became a photographer-optician here. Over beer, Plarr gossiped about Fortnum, who said Fortnum's wife died and he really married Clara. Gruber said two civilians asked about Plarr recently; one calling the other "Father." Suddenly Clara entered the shop, driven there by her husband's worker. Plarr, obsessing again, bought her some begemmed sunglasses.

They sat by the river, talked frankly about Señora Sanchez, marriage, Clara's not being pregnant. With indifferent obedience, Clara accompanied Plarr to his flat, slept with him, spoke obscenities. He felt freed, void. She declined payment. She said Charley liked her to be tender. Plarr wanted her to be herself next time. Planning how to meet again, she left to find her driver.

Part Three: 1. Now see Dr. Plarr, escorted home by Diego (Corredo) after seeing kidnapped Fortnum. At dawn he drives to Fortnum's camp and finds Colonel Perez, the clever police chief. Perez tells passive, now-pregnant Clara that Charley's empty car (new Cadillac) was near the river; tells Plarr he suspects kidnappers; catches Plarr lying about phoning Fortnum's office; disagrees that an honorary consul isn't a kidnappers' target; suggests the American Ambassador could have been Paraguayan criminals' object; says Plarr, who once mentioned his father was jailed or dead in Paraguay, might be indirectly involved; opines Plarr could betray a friend like Fortnum. After Perez departs, Plarr beds with Clara, less roughly. Fortnum's maid serves lunch. They discuss Charley's Cadillac, his borrowing her sunglasses, why he married Clara, whether he's dead. The radio reports the kidnappers' demand: British Consul to be released by midnight Sunday for 10 named political prisoners in Paraguay (including Plarr's father). Clara tells Plarr she doesn't want Charley either back or dead. Again, they make "love," a counterfeit word, he gloomily feels. She tardily says two journalists came while he slept, interviewed and photographed her, learned from Perez the newsworthy item that she's pregnant. She tells Plarr she pretended ecstasy just now in bed with him, thinking to please his *machismo*.

2. Driving home, Plarr recalls how his friends Léon Rivas and Aquino (Ribera) appeared at his office, told him they planned to kidnap the American Ambassador when he would come north in November, and wanted details about their target's movements. Aquino showed Plarr his right hand, with three fingers cut off by Paraguayan police to make him talk — which he did. He said it was awkward to write now, even short poems. He escaped by bribing a policeman, who was killed accidentally in the venture.

3. Fortnum awakens in the hut. Daylight. Splitting headache. No Clara. No Ted. A man called Léon passes an armed Indian guard (Miguel) and brings coffee, doubts Fortnum's talk about seeing any Dr. Plarr, and explains they wanted to grab the American Ambassador but retaining Fortnum will cause negotiations enabling a few men to avoid torture and be released. Léon fries Fortnum some eggs, lets him sleep, has his wife Marta brings him whisky. Léon and Fortnum disagree about Fortnum's ever being freed. They discuss their common religion. Fortnum cunningly asks to confess to Léon, once a priest, before they kill him; Léon voices shame for reading the Gospels to poverty-stricken Paraguayans. Fortnum, drunk, jokes about his coming death. Léon tries to reassure him.

Twilight. Fortnum lures courteous Aquino in for whisky. They discuss Aquino's poems, pain, Fortnum's desire to see his child, his death. Fortnum gets Aquino to provide writing materials, starts a lugubrious letter to Clara, drunkenly has an idea, talks Aquino into arming himself with Miguel's gun and escorting him to the privy. In darkness he flees, is shot at, and falls.

Part Four: 1. (Thursday) Sir Henry Belfrage fusses over his improperly fried eggs, chats with his wife, and worries about the political consequences of Fortnum's being kidnapped. Plarr, having flown to Buenos Aires, is announced, which spoils Belfrage's siesta. Plarr tells him Fortnum is insignificant. Belfrage replies that the Americans don't pay off terrorists, the Americans won't ruffle (Alfredo) Stroessner (Paraguayan president) by asking him to aid, and London also regards Fortnum as unimportant. Plarr mentions his father's possibly being alive in a Paraguayan jail, offers to intercede with the kidnappers. Cogitating, Belfrage suggests that Plarr form an English Club back home, telegraph something about Fortnum's patriotism, and stir international journalistic commentary.

Tea time at the Calle Florida. Plarr meets his mother, dressed in mourning for her lost husband — if alive, 71 today, she reports — and gorging on éclairs. This sponge — Plarr sends her money — makes him doubt she ever loved and thus accounts for his diagnostician-like passionlessness. He remains courteous to his critical, selfish mother, who hasn't heard about any kidnapping.

On the return flight, Plarr's hope for quiet is spoiled. A former mistress, Margarita Escobar, and her husband Gustavo Escobar, are aboard. The three flirt conversationally about sex. Margarita hopes Plarr isn't involved with Clara, whose employer Señora Sanchez both men know. Also aboard is Colonel Perez, who tells Plarr that there are no developments concerning Fortnum, that his Governor advised delays and ordered him to Buenos Aireas to consult the Minister of the Interior, who, however, favors troop action. Plarr says he saw Belfrage, who's disinterested. Perez adds that today a hijacker's grenade destroyed a BOAC airplane and 167 died in the crash, that Fortnum is comparatively insignificant, and that a bomb in a church was found, unexploded—a miracle, Catholic natives believe.

2. That evening Plarr invites Humphries and Saavedra to a hotel terrace for salmon and wine. Plarr establishes the phony Anglo-Argentine Club with them. He drafts a cable from their "Club" about the missing honorary consul to send London *Times*. Saavedra, dilating the while on his *macho* writings, won't sign it—too crudely styled—but courageously offers to replace Fortnum as hostage. Plarr, impressed, sends his message to London and *El Litoral*, the local newspaper.

Plarr drives Saavedra to his dingy digs, downs some Johnny Walker, feels respect for the shoddy novelist, who perhaps deserves a footnote in Argentine literary history. Saavedra says he visits some of Señora Sanchez's girls; few, including Clara, of whom he speaks perceptively, are suitable models for his fictive characters. He believes Plarr's father is listed among hostages to be exchanged.

Home again, Plarr commingles thoughts of his father and of Fortnum. Tempted to phone Clara, he is surprised. She's right here on his bed. She drove Fortnum's Pride in from the camp, wrecked and abandoned it, hitched a ride, had a cut knee bandaged by Señora Sanchez, and evasively walked here. Clara says Charley's sex acts have been boringly gentle, unlike Plarr's. She wonders if she loves Plarr. He has always hated the word "love" because of his pseudo-sentimental mother. He preferred his father's restraint. He can't figure out love.

Perez rings, is admitted, has a drink, tells Plarr he knows about his messages to London and *El Litoral*, says he wants the Communist blackmailers to fail but Fortnum to live. Queried, Plarr fibs he's alone. Léon phones, is ingeniously put off. Perez says Clara wrecked Fortnum's Pride, was followed, is on the loose. Saying affairs require lies, Plarr admits she's here. Perez warns Plarr to avoid the kidnappers, says a Paraguayan official just told him that Plarr's father was killed trying with a man named Aquino Ribera to escape, then departs. Léon phones again. They need him. Asked, Léon confesses Plarr's father is dead, but he feared that telling Plarr would drive him away. Plarr tells Clara his father is dead, says he must aid Fortnum — still living, he implies — pats her tummy tenderly, wonders what she just asked him that he didn't answer and now can't recall.

Part Five: 1. Plarr is taken to Fortnum, shot in the Achilles tendon. Léon won't let Plarr leave. They rest. Léon tells how Plarr's father, weak after 15 years in a police station 100 kilometers southeast of Asunción, couldn't run fast during the escape and was shot. Plarr and Fortnum talk — about Fortnum's limited life, his noisy Christian Scientist first wife's pitying him and ignoring her cancer, his love for quiet Clara. Again Plarr wonders what Clara asked him.

Morning. Marta brings local papers, which mention Saavedra's offer. Aquino queries Saavedra's exchange value. Afternoon. Radio reports never mention Saavedra. A cataract-blind old villager named José follows a path, addresses Pablo, approaches the gang, says his wife just died, wants Father (Léon Rivas) to anoint her, and needs that coffin his friend Juan said Pablo bought. Fortnum shouts "Ted"—a *gringo* voice, says José, but soon is hypnotized by sounds from the radio, a magic box to him. Pablo vetoes Aquino's idea of killing blind, talkative José. Marta wishes her husband, whom she calls Father, had guided José home but then turns subservient.

Time passes. The men wish they could move to a new hideout. Pablo says José has been talking about their radio. Aquino mentions killing Fortnum.

Evening. Marta brings the Buenos Aires *Nación*, which mentions Saavedra's offer. Silence and rain fall. Surly, all sit in darkness.

Fortnum is given more whisky. Plarr shares it, but not Aquino, caught earlier by Léon. Fortnum lauds Clara's innocence so much that Plarr finds it hard not to blurt who got her pregnant.

2. Friday morning. A helicopter circles the *barrio,* blowing leaves onto the hut. Should they shoot Fortnum? Phone to extend the deadline a week? They're glad their car's hidden. Marta and Plarr dispute with Rivas over his status as uncooperative priest. Even Aquino chides Rivas.

Fortnum asks Rivas to let Plarr give Clara a letter he's been laboring over. Rivas continues it by taking dictation — full of loving, modest words, plus advice on rearing their "little bastard." Entering, Plarr silently listens.

Feeling reproached by Fortnum's message to Clara, Plarr exits. Aquino, armed, stops Plarr, says he doesn't write poetry now. Rivas sends Marta and another (Diego) to buy provisions. Plarr defeats impetuous Aquino at chess. Aquino asks Plarr if Clara's baby is his. A gunshot outside. Rivas says it was nothing. Aquino and Plarr discuss God.

Returning, Marta says Diego remained to get gas for their car. Though worried, Rivas reads a detective story, with a predictable plot — unlike life, he comments. Plarr fears the worst, recalls Clara refused an abortion, wonders about their child's tangled future, with one cane-cutting Tucumán grandfather, one liberal English grandfather shot in Paraguay. Aquino tunes the radio to night-time news. Nothing about them.

3. Midday Saturday. The radio reports that England plans no action about Fortnum, since he was never a member of its diplomatic corps. Aquino favors killing him. Plarr pretends to believe there's hope.

Plarr lets sullen Aquino win at chess; sees Fortnum asleep smiling, wonders if he's dreaming of Clara or of measured booze; wonders if Clara will have a son resembling Plarr; fancies Fortnum with the lad, reared Catholic. Plarr and Rivas talk, partly about their fathers. Plarr admits his relationship with Fortnum's Clara. Plarr silently feels he and Rivas are hopeless. Rivas dilates on Christ the man, the Holocaust, God the pitiable. The radio reports that Diego Corredo was shot dead evading the police and seeking the Paraná's Chaco shore.

Marta cooks up more old stew. Aquino demands Fortnum's death, to avenge Diego. Fortnum worries about Clara and the child.

Rivas commends macho Aquino for never countenancing failure, says killing hostages is effective, recalls sinful types at confession, reluctantly agrees when Marta begs him to say mass tomorrow — Sunday. Obscurely motivated, Plarr calls such talk "mumbojumbo," disbelieves in any God letting deformed children be born. Aquino chimes in: God is evil capitalism. Rivas believes that God is responsible for evil as well as for saints, that what Plarr calls horror is God's night side, that God like mankind is evolving. Plarr queries any evolution producing Hitler and Stalin in one generation. Rivas says evolution will eventuate in Christ-like goodness everywhere. Marta voices fear. Plarr admits to a germ of faith. Rivas says Plarr is jealous of Fortnum, now calling for his Ted, because Fortnum loves Clara. Marta washes Rivas's shirt for tomorrow's mass.

Darkness, lightning, rain. On the radio, Perez announces the hut has been surrounded; by eight o'clock tomorrow morning Fortnum must emerge first; the others must follow in surrender; all will remain in Argentina. Aquino suggests killing Fortnum and sneaking out one by one, opens the door, and calls to Miguel, on guard outside. Floodlights flash on, off, on again. Miguel is shot. Pablo suggests surrendering, for the sake of Marta, who still wants mass. Aquino suggests voting on killing Fortnum and running. Plarr, regularly jibing, hopes for an appropriate ending — i.e., comic, not tragic. Plarr checks on Fortnum, who heard Rivas say Plarr was jealous, slugs at him, knocks the bottle down. Questioned, Plarr explains details of his indifferent sessions with Clara. Fortnum expresses relief at finding the bottle unbroken, starts gulping. Rationalizing that God is a joker, Plarr feels exhausted.

4. Early morning. Marta prepares candles and bread for Mass, awakens Father Rivas. Aquino won't attend. Pablo asks to confess.

Griping at Plarr, Fortnum destroys his letter to Clara and a photo of her standing beside Fortnum's Pride. He and Plarr admit to possibly having faith, but Fortnum calls whisky his sacrament.

Plarr watches Rivas read the Latin Gospel. Aquino seems puzzled. Rivas consecrates the bread. Plarr remembers the exact words. Perez shouts they have one hour to release Fortnum. Pablo asks for a vote. Aquino, armed, wants Fortnum's death. Rivas wants God's mercy.

Going to Fortnum in the other room, Rivas says his orders are to kill him. Almost weeping, Rivas asks Fortnum to make his confession however brief, wishes he himself could confess to a priest. When asked to confess sorrow for having insufficient hope, he does, is given absolution. They share whisky. Fortnum says it's too bad no priest can absolve Rivas.

Perez announces the 15-minute mark. When asked, Aquino comments about Plarr's father. He was affectionate, courteous, tortured simply by being 15 years in police station (CIA wouldn't tolerate amputating his fingers), white haired, stooped, rheumatic, limping, sadly bored, praying for a final pain. Aquino says he's afraid, not bored. Plarr muses. Ten minutes left. Aquino asks Rivas to let him shoot Fortnum now. Plarr offers to go speak to Perez. Pablo wants to release Fortnum. Aquino remains trigger-happy. Marta fears death for all. Rivas agrees to let Plarr go ask Perez for an extension. Plarr tells Aquino he's jealous of Fortnum, who thus wins. Five minutes. Again, Plarr can't remember Clara's question to him.

Plarr exits into violent sunlight, sees dead Miguel, walks forward, is shot painlessly in the leg from behind, falls, rests peacefully. Plarr hears the close voice of Rivas saying he simply had to help but has been shot in the stomach. Plarr says Father and absolves him in Latin. Three armed paras (CIA-trained paratroopers) advance.

5. At Plarr's funeral are his affected mother, her priest Father Galvão, Perez, unhappy Fortnum, bored Clara, Gaspar and Margarita Escobar, insincere Señora Vallejo and Miguel Duran (her current lover?), pompous Saavedra, Crichton (from the British embassy), offish Humphries, and Gruber. Over the Union Jack-draped coffin, Saavedra preaches the official version: Fanatic Father Rivas killed Plarr; Plarr and Saavedra planned an Anglo-Argentinian culture club; etc. Leaving, Fortnum, whose ankle is mending, recalls being driven from the revolutionaries back to Clara, who gave his damaged Pride to the police and revealed nothing to him about Plarr. Crichton asks permission to visit Fortnum at his camp.

Back home. Fortnum rests; hates Clara's mechanical kiss but concludes she's faultless, considering her background, and couldn't even love Plarr; resents having seen Rivas shoveled into unconsecrated ground; sleeps.

Crichton arrives, accepts some whisky, but doesn't drink any. Fortnum counters Perez's dishonest report that Rivas shot Plarr and was shot by the paras. Fortnum says this: When the paras shot Plarr once, Rivas left his gun, told Aquino he wouldn't shoot Fortnum but must aid Plarr; the paras shot Rivas, then Plarr twice more, in the head; Aquino shot at Fortnum, missed, was shot by the paras. It seems Marta and Pablo are alive. Crichton tells Fortnum he must retire but says the Ambassador is recommending him for an order-of-merit honor. Fortnum is incredulous.

Fortnum dreams Plarr is on a road with him, laughing. Awakening, he sees his workers' pre-dawn lanterns and finds Clara. She says she dreamed of strangling the baby. He says people get "caught up" into affairs by mistake. Crying, she says she never loved unloving Plarr. He says they'll name the baby Eduardo, if male, since in a manner he loved Plarr. Her lie about not loving Plarr is necessary. Fortnum is happy that part of much-loved Plarr will survive.

Norman Sherry reports that Greene worked on *The Honorary Consul* intermittently for three years (beginning late 1970). It was published to critical acclaim in England and the United States, in the latter by Simon & Schuster (September 1973), since Greene was disaffected with Viking after a dispute over the title of *Travels with My Aunt* (1969). Nor was Greene displeased with this change, since Simon & Schuster paid $150,000 in advance for *The Honorary Consul* and promised $30,000 more for his autobiography. Moreover, *The Honorary Consul* was a Book-of-the-Month Club selection (1973).

The descriptive vividness in *The Honorary Consul* is partly owing to Greene's revisiting Buenos Aires, Chile, and thereabouts (September 1971, September 1972). Paul O'Prey regards *The Honorary Consul* as "Greene's most subtle, complex and accomplished novel," with its characters having unique "depth and range." In *Ways of Escape* Greene says he preferred it to his others. According to Marie-Françoise Allain, he said it was his "favorite book," and "the one that brother[ed him] ... the least."

Leopoldo Duran says Greene liked it best because the characters develop and because "Fortnum matures as a father" and even regards traitorous Plarr as a kind of son. Yvonne Cloetta* says that Greene told her that it was his novel he liked best (to 1976) but later preferred *Monsignor Quixote*.

After probing *The Honorary Consul* skillfully, Mark Bosco generously concludes that "[t]he end of the novel emphasizes two places in which the religious and the political imagination intersect: hope and love," that "hope can ground political belief ... when ... experienced in ... commitment to others," that "love has a stake ... in creating communities of commitment ... [and] in the evolutionary union of humanity with God," and that "love ... in the novel ... keeps human action focused on correct practice." Brian Thomas discusses the relationship of *The Honorary Consul* to legends and myths concerning Christianity, fathers and sons (including Oepidus), usurpation, King Arthur, the nocturnal vigil, and so on. Cedric Watts feels that *The Honorary Consel* "would have been improved by editorial pruning. The ratio of ethical debate to action, particularly in the last third of the novel, is too high; suspense wilts as discussion extends."

Greene makes a fugue out of this novel by developing most of the characters contrapuntally: Clara is a deceptive/considerate whore/wife; Fortnum is/isn't what he seems; Perez follows/breaks laws; Plarr is detached/attached; Rivas is a multiply divided priest/criminal, calling his seminary honeymoon site/prison, even defining God as diurnal/nocturnal, good/evil.

Watts reports that *The Honorary Consul* was made into a 1983 movie (American title, *Beyond the Limit*), starring Michael Caine (as Fortnum) and Richard Gere (Plarr). Anne Piroëlle explains how the movie necessarily compresses the novel, says Caine and Gere were both miscast, praises Perez's credible maturing, but concludes that it caters to immature audiences.

In *Getting to Know the General* (1984), Greene tells how he successfully arranged ransom to free two English bankers kidnapped in El Salvador by guerrillas (1979). If so, then truth is stranger at least than Greene's fiction. (Sources: Allain, 129; Bosco, 117; Cloetta, 76; Duran, 239; Greene, *Getting to Know the General*, 155–58; Greene, *Ways of Escape*, 308; O'Prey, 128; Piroëlle, 80–82; Sherry III, 544–53 passim, 612; Thomas, 176–89; Watts, 77, 217)

HOGARTH, PAUL (1917–2001). Artist, illustrator, and author (Arthur) Paul Hogarth was born in Kendal, Westmorland, England, and studied at Manchester's School of Art and London's St. Martin's School of Art. He established offices in Majorca and later in Chipping Campden, Gloucestershire (where Greene and his wife Vivien Greene* once lived). He traveled very extensively, often publishing and illustrating "walking tours." Of his several books, *The Artist as Reporter* (1967, rev. ed. 1986) was the most influential. In addition to magazine work, he illustrated upwards of 30 books. Hogarth will be best remembered for following and sometimes accompanying famous writers, illustrating their travel writings, and on occasion including his own journal notes. These writers include Brendan Behan, Sir John Betjeman, Lawrence Durrell, Robert Graves, Doris Lessing, Malcolm Muggeridge, Stephen Spender, and Greene.

To track Greene's locales, Hogarth traveled some 50,000 miles (June 1985 – May 1986), visiting 50 cities, towns, and villages in more than 30 countries on four continents. The result is his book *Graham Greene Country* (1986), which contains watercolor illustrations based on 23 Greene novels plus "May We Borrow Your Husband?," together with quotations from Greene's fiction relating to the pictures and pertinent commentaries by Hogarth. An illuminating way to read or reread Greene's fiction is with Hogarth's splendid book as accompaniment. (Source: Hogarth)

HOPE-SMITHIES, LADY ("The Trial of Pan"). She was convicted in one of the trials preceding Pan's trial. Her crimes were generosity, hitting the Anglican curate, and losing at bridge.

HOPE-SMITHIES, LORD ("The Trial of Pan"). He was Lady Hope-Smithies's husband. He wrongly paid when she lost at bridge.

HOPKINSON ("Special Duties"). He is Ferraro's timid confidential secretary. He supplies Ferraro with Miss Saunders's home address.

HOPKINSON, MRS. (*This Gun for Hire*). Her name is mentioned in conversation at the jumble sale at St. Luke's.

HOWELL ("Under the Garden"). This is the name of a farmer who owns or owned a field near Winton Hall.

HUGHES ("The Blessing"). He is an Associated Press reporter sent to cover the Archbishop's blessing of the tanks. Unhappy at the assignment, he drinks with the other reporters, gripes that tanks kill what opposes them, but tells Weld his report will be neutral.

HUGHES (*Travels with My Aunt*). Miss Barbara Keene writes Henry Pulling from South Africa that Hughes, a neighboring widower in his late 50s, has proposed marriage to her. Asking Henry's advice, Barbara obviously hopes he will answer with his own proposal.

HUGHES, JOHN ("Mortmain"). He is Philip Carter's oldest friend. Josephine Heckstall-Jones includes Hughes's name in a list she types and leaves in the overseas telephone directory, supposedly to be helpful to Philip.

HUGHES, MISS (*Travels with My Aunt*). She is the widower Hughes's teenage daughter. Miss Barbara Keene writes Henry that she likes Miss Hughes moderately.

THE HUMAN FACTOR (1978). Novel. (Characters: Agbo, Anna, Mrs. Baines, Barker, Dr. Barker, Bates, Mrs. Union-of-Writers Bates, [George] Blake, Blit, Bonne Chance, Boris, Ezra Bottomley, Browne, Buffy, Buller, [Guy Francis de Moncey] Burgess, Inspector Butler, Burry, C, Carson, Castle, Dr. Castle, Mary Castle, Maurice Castle, Mrs. Castle, Roger Castle, Sam Castle, Sarah Castle, Chilton, Colin Clough, Connolly, Cynthia, Daintry, Colonel John Daintry, Elizabeth Daintry, Mrs. Daintry, Sylvia Daintry, Arthur Davis, William Davis, Philip Dibba, Dicky, Dodo, Fortnum, the Governor, Halliday, Halliday, Lady Mary Hargreaves, Sir John Hargreaves, Harry, Ivan, Jameson, Joe, John Thomas, Edward Joiner, Kalamazoo, Laker, Lord, Lulu, [Donald Duart] Maclean, Meredith, Mimi, Cornelius Muller, Naomi, Mark Ngambo, Patricia, Penelope, Dr. Emmanuel Percival, [Kim] Philby, Philips, Piper, Porton, Portland, Pullen, Raymond, Rita Rolls, Rougemont, Rougemont, Taylor, Tinker Bell, Brigadier Tomlinson, Captain Van Donck, Vassall, Watson, Mrs. Whitehouse, Widow Twanky, Wilkins, Willie.)

Part One: Chapter 1. Maurice Castle, 62, lives in Berkhamsted and likes to appear a conformist. He has worked for the British Secret Service 30 years. His flashy assistant, Arthur Davis — both are in MI6 — returns from lunch. Castle can then go. But Davis says Brigadier Tomlinson, an MI6 superior, wants to see him. Castle is introduced to Colonel (John) Daintry, whom Tomlinson calls "our new broom" and who as a security official examines Castle's harmless briefcase, just to check, because of recently suspected document leaks. Davis was seen removing a classified document to read over lunch.

Chapter II. Castle takes the Euston-to-Berkhamsted train, then bicycles home to his lovable, loving black South African wife Sarah and her illegitimate little boy, Sam Castle, adopted by Castle. Castle has double whiskies. They discuss Sam's measles-induced fever. Buller, their spittle-dribbling boxer, slumps in. The phone rings; no one is on the other end.

Chapter III: 1. Lady (Mary) Hargreaves greets Daintry, and then noisy Buffy, Dicky, Dodo, and Harry, their bird-shooting guests. Portly Dr. (Emmanuel) Percival, another guest, offering Daintry a martini, reminds him they once met. Daintry says C (Sir John Hargreaves, chief of Military Intelligence) has arranged a conference. At lunch, Daintry envies beer-guzzling Percival his obvious conviviality and Sir John his rich American wife.

2. The raucous guests leave. Hargreaves has a whisky-laced confab with Daintry and Percival. A Soviet defector has reported a leak, concerning the Chinese. The source is narrowed to one of three in Section 6: Castle, whose dull background Daintry summarizes; Davis, young, free-spending; and Watson, Castle's chief, head of MI6. Hargreaves wants no scandal. Daintry wants no cover-up. They decide Daintry must probe deeply and Percival must arrange the likeliest suspect's undetectable murder.

3. At midnight Percival taps and enters Daintry's room. Daintry analyzes a varicolored geometric painting by Ben Nicholson (1894–1962) on his room wall, and suggestively tells Daintry to be cool about Hargreaves's strategem, regard himself as confined in the painting's yellow square, do his job within it, and not worry about action in separate nearby blue and red squares.

Part Two: Chapter I: 1. In London early, Castle orders two copies (one for a friend) of Tolstoy's *War and Peace,* Aylmer Maude's translation, at a Soho bookshop owned and operated by Halliday. Halliday laments that his son runs a pornographic bookshop across the street.

2. At work, Castle and Davis review coded material from Zaire, some given them by Cynthia, a pert secretary. Davis unrequitedly loves her. He wishes their work were more glamorous, like James Bond's. Castle, 62, feels stuck here, says he'd prefer to write apartheid books. Davis is ordered by Dr. Percival for a medical check-up—something connected with insurance. Davis longs for an exciting assignment to Lourenço Marques (Mozambique). Castle wishes for a modest, secure retirement—with his wife and "the little bastard," as Davis affectionately calls Sam. Castle says seven years ago he, Sarah, and Sam escaped Pretoria, a step ahead of apartheid-enforcement agents of BOSS (the Bureau of State Security) to Lourenço Marques (and then England), and offers to ask Watson to consider transferring Davis to L.M. Watson phones Castle: Hargreaves wants to see both of them.

3. After introducing Castle to Hargreaves, Watson is requested to leave. Hargreaves praises Castle for fine Pretoria reports, commends him for rescuing Sarah before BOSS agents caused embarrassment, and orders him to share intelligence secrets with Cornelius Muller, even though Muller, a BOSS agent here briefly from South Africa, tried to blackmail Castle in Pretoria after he violated race laws with Sarah. Hargreaves acquaints Castle with the secret American Uncle Remus project, involving joint efforts by the United States, South Africa, and England to counter possible Russian and Cuban penetration of African gold, diamond, and uranium sources. Castle must share secrets with Muller but soft-pedal China data. He must also keep Uncle Remus from Watson and Davis. Castle tells Hargreaves that Davis wants a transfer to Mozambique.

Chapter II. Sunday in October. Castle though a non-believer pops into the Berkhamsted church, then takes Sam, recovering from the measles, for a walk with Buller. He tells the bright boy about a dragon he imagined nearby that helped him when he was afraid at school. That night he informs Sarah he's been asked to invite their nemesis Muller, now in London, to dinner. Feeling secure, she doesn't mind.

Chapter III: 1. Davis persuades Castle to dine in town, attend a striptease with him and Percival, and sleep over at Davis's flat. Castle is to phone Sarah of these plans.

2. The three visit Raymond's Revuebar. Percival watches his first striptease. He mentions that Daintry disapproves of him because he prefers fishing to bird shooting. When Davis eyes stripper Rita Rolls, Percival cautions him about his high blood pressure. Davis and Castle leave Percival at his flat. In Davis's unkempt rooms, at 2:00 a.m., they have whisky and discuss Percival. Castle wonders what motivated Percival to spend the evening with them. Davis says that earlier that evening Percival hinted at British research in bacteriological warfare at a center called Porton. Sarah phones, says she's afraid because their home phone rang twice with no one speaking on the line. Castle disabuses her worry, tells Davis that his instinct tells him Davis's phoned is tapped and—with loud music from the gramophone drowning more talk—says maybe Davis's room is bugged and Percival planted false talk about germ warfare for Davis—or even Castle—to be caught repeating.

Chapter IV: 1. Castle agrees to let Davis slip out from 11:00 a.m. to 1:00 p.m., pretend to have a dentist's appointment, and meet Cynthia at the zoo on her day off. Davis carelessly takes more confidential material out, to read. Watson phones for Davis. Castle lies to cover up Davis's absence and is ordered to report immediately, in Davis's place, to Hargreaves.

2. Their conference concerns fence-mending between MI5 and MI6, concerning safe Tanzania and Zanzibar, unsafe because it has Chinese training camps. Pullen, an MI5 man, clarifies zones of responsibility. When Hargreaves wonders where Davis is, Castle says with a dentist. Percival says Davis's teeth looked fine

under examination and demands the dentist's name.

Part Three. Chapter I: 1. After Percival treats Hargreaves to lunch at his Reform Club, they walk into Pall Mall, chilly in October, to talk clear of any bugging. Percival says that after conferring with Daintry he is convinced Davis is the leak. Percival adds the following: Davis is schizoid, if assigned to Lourenço Marques could escape; Watson is cleared; Castle has a splendid family and personal background; Davis lied about the dentist and, followed by Daintry's man, met Cynthia, and lied about putting a report in his safe, took instead to lunch and perhaps elsewhere; Percival planted a phony report about Porton research. Percival suggests poisoning Davis with aflatoxin, produced in mouldy peanuts. It causes unsuspicious liver necrosis and kidney engorgement. Percival adds this will be doing Davis a favor; he already drinks too much and could have a more painful death. Demurring weakly, Hargreaves would prefer hard evidence first.

2. Daintry leaves his St. James flat to meet his daughter, beautiful but distant Elizabeth, for dinner at Stone's. She is more loyal to her mother than to him. Elizabeth tells Daintry she's marrying Colin, an advertising man, on Saturday the 21st. Daintry silently fumes: Percival plans to kill poor Davis on no hard evidence of wrongdoing.

Chapter II: 1. Davis drives his Jaguar to Berkhamsted to join Castle, Sarah, Sam, and Buller for an October Sunday picnic. Sam adores Davis, remembers they played hide-and-seek once. While they play it again for Sam, Davis expresses fear he's being followed. Castle says that since they're both innocent there's no danger. When found by Sam, Davis jokingly confesses he's a double agent with a 007-like poison pen.

2. At his bookshop Halliday talks with Castle, laments atrocities that occurred during the Vietnamese War, and agrees to mail him two copies of Anthony Trollope's novel *The Way We Are Now*. Castle finds a public phone, dials, says wrong number, and hangs up.

3. Sarah catches Castle with *War and Peace*. He says he's trying planning to write an essay on it.

Chapter III: 1. Castle is at home drinking whisky and awaiting the arrival of Muller, whom Hargreaves ordered Castle to entertain and introduce to Sarah. Castle remembers being interrogated in Pretoria by smoothly intelligent Muller when he had been three years in South Africa and was illegally loving Sarah — his black Bantu agent. Captain Van Donck, brutal but simple, was threateningly present. Muller called Castle imprudent, stupid, and ignorant, and recommended dumping Sarah rather than getting tried, sacked, and sent home. Castle recalls that his Communist friend Carson in South Africa warned him to fear intelligent enemies more than merely brutal ones. Muller arrives by chauffeur, accepts drinks and dinner, not turning a hair when introduced to Sarah, whom he didn't know Castle married after she escaped through Swaziland to safety. Sam asks if Muller is a spy like Davis. Muller boasts his ancestors arrived in South Africa in 1700, included an "ostrich millionaire" wrecked by the 1914 war, reports Castle's naive friend Carson died in prison, says they'll talk about Uncle Remus soon, and, after Buller licks his trousers affectionately, departs.

2. Castle and Sarah discuss Carson, who saved Sarah from prison, where Sam would have been born, by getting her to Lourenço Marques seven years ago. She says they are all grateful but Castle shouldn't let gratitude carry him too far.

Chapter IV: 1. Once a month Castle goes by train with Sarah, Sam, and Buller to visit his mother in East Sussex. This time, while Sarah, Sam, and Buller are in the garden, old Mrs. Castle, 85 and starchy, expresses fear that if she, her son, and his wife all died at once, Sam would be grabbed by South Africans seeking the boy's sizable inheritance.

2. Home again. The phone rings on and off thrice. Castle won't answer. Sarah says she knows he's worried but fears he'll never be "free" to explain.

Chapter V: 1. En route to London, Castle reads in *War and Peace,* gets off at Watford, phones his office he's checking here with Buller's veterinarian, and proceeds to a certain house. Boris, who tutors here, greets him. Castle's wrong-number phone calls alerted him to meet Boris, who has replaced Ivan as Castle's Soviet-agent contact. Boris tells Castle that information from him about Muller and about Porton may be British traps, but that details about Uncle Remus, confirmed by Soviet contacts in Washington, are doubtless authentic. Castle says he hates what Muller tried to do to Sarah and Sam, hate like love causes mistakes, he wants out. Boris says Castle is required for two more years and reassures him the Soviets have Castle's escape prepared — in case — and for Sarah's and Sam's also.

2. Hargreaves hosts Percival at his Travellers Club. Hargreaves wishes he were back in the old Africa instead of heading to Washington for 10 days. He grouses that Uncle Remus has "incompatible allies," adds that Muller is off to West Germany, and hints that Percival and Daintry will snare Davis.

Chapter VI: 1. When Castle arrives late to work, Cynthia tells him Davis is ill and Percival is advising Davis. Castle checks with Daintry and finds him disputing with Percival, who seems knowledgeable and exits. Asked by Daintry, Castle says he thoroughly trusts Davis. Daintry shows Castle his soon-to-wed daughter's photograph and expresses feelings of loneliness.

2. Castle gets Cynthia to visit Davis in his slovenly digs. While she helpfully makes his bed, Davis laments his condition to Castle, who warns him to drink less, says don't worry about Daintry's obligatory security checks, and tells him he recommended Davis for Lourenço Marques.

Chapter VI: 1. Daintry takes Castle, for moral support, to his daughter's registry-office wedding to Colin Clough. They follow well-wishers to Daintry's long-estranged wife Sylvia's Kensington flat. A crowd. Champagne-cork explosions. Sylvia's collection of china owls. They meet Edward Joiner, Sylvia's companion, with her from Brighton for the ceremony. Sylvia phones Castle here, having obtained the number via the registry: Davis is dead. Castle tells Daintry, who smothers remarks about Percival, accidentally breaks Sylvia's special gray owl, and incurs her venomous wrath.

2. Castle and Daintry rush to Davis's flat. Percival, already there, brought Piper and Taylor, Special Branch detectives. They snoop about. Percival seems talkatively embarrassed to Castle. Daintry is glumly suspicious. Taylor wonders about certain names scribbled by Davis. Castle explains they're horses Davis bet on. Piper and Percival note suspicious lines from Robert Browning marked with a "c," until Castle deciphers "c": Cynthia, Davis's beloved.

Chapter VIII: 1. With Davis's death, Castle figures he won't be needed in the African section further. He'll use *War and Peace* once more, then burn it, both happy he aided the Soviets and thus repaid for Carson's sacrificial help, and also sorry he can't assist with Uncle Remus and thus get revenge on Muller. He has too much whisky, tells Sarah about Davis, and resists her plea to escape to color-blind France. They both fear Davis was criminally careless.

2. Castle and Buller walk to a preplanned message drop. Castle recalls a similar hole-in-wood location where he as a child left a love message for an unattractive girl, thus balancing redressing ugliness with kindness. He sees a fat man get out of a car. Home again, he tells Sarah they should be inarticulately happy. His message to Boris was goodbye.

Part Four: Chapter I: 1. With Davis gone, Castle's handling information from Zaire lessens. His dreams concern South African apartheid lavatories, never Davis. Castle tells Sarah about Rougemont, a Free State farmer, through whom he met Carson. Rougemont said Castle could never understand apartheid. Castle wishes he could share more secrets with Sarah.

2. Thursday. Muller, back from Bonn, works with Castle and seems sincere. But they needle each other — about Carson's allegedly dying of pneumonia, about Uncle Remus's projected use of tactical atomic weapons with German acquiescence, about apartheid even in heaven, about Davis's funeral today, which Castle deliberately avoids. Muller gives Castle notes about his Bonn meetings, to be read and destroyed. Muller leaves. Castle pockets the notes.

Chapter II: 1. At Davis's funeral, Hargreaves, back from Washington, thinks of food; Percival silently questions the Vicar's texts; Cynthia weeps; Daintry is sullen; Watson, worried. Davis's dentist-cousin from his hometown of Droitwich and Davis's Department of Environment fellow-lodgers also attend.

2. During their Travellers Club lunch, Hargreaves half laments possibly innocent Davis's death. Percival calls the present-day Cold War a game, longs for peace and better medical facilities, says Davis leaked Percival's "fantasy"

Porton information, admits aflatoxin Percival added to Davis's whisky hurt his liver. Mixed with their talk are comments about their lunch wines.

3. Walking toward his flat, Daintry is persuaded by Buffy to have a drink at his club. Inside are Dicky and others. He has three martinis, blabbers about funerals and weddings, meanders home, nibbles sardines, silently rebukes conspiratorial Percival and Hargreaves, dismisses the evidence against Davis as slight, feels guilty, evokes his dead parents for advice, phones his daughter, gets his answering son-in-law's last name wrong, and hangs up.

4. Castle reads verses to Sam from one of Sam's favorite books [Robert Louis Stevenson's *A Child's Garden of Verses*]. In his study, Castle copies Muller's notes for Boris, including the phrase "A Final Solution," supposedly from Bonn meetings.

5. Sarah has a nightmare, tells Castle it concerned their being separated at an apartheid railroad station, and wonders about their future safety. He can't give a simple answer.

Part Five: Chapter I: 1. Rainy Friday in November. Castle delivers the copy of Muller's report via old Halliday to young Halliday for Boris, chats with old Halliday, takes a train to Watford, finds Boris's house. Empty. Castle enters a new Roman Catholic church, half-envies a woman battling loneliness by confession. He might have to confess — in court. He enters the confessional to unburden himself safely, but is queried and then rejected. He knows his story is too long.

2. Home alarmingly late, Castle suddenly tells Sarah this: Davis, thought to be a security leak, was murdered; Castle became a double agent to repay Carson for saving Sarah; he's been in constant danger; he may now be the suspect; he sent a supposedly final message to his Soviet contact but then sent another because of information from Muller. Sarah scorns his excuse about helping black Africans, asks what to do. He says she should go with Sam to his mother's, he's been promised an escape alone, she and Sam can follow. Meanwhile, no communication. Denying he should be called a traitor, she says he, she, and Sam are their own private unbetrayed country. They make love for the first time in months.

Chapter II. Friday. Hargreaves is reading *The Way We Live Now*, regretting his calling Davis a traitor but telling himself Percival did the killing, when Muller phones him about Castle and gets invited to potluck dinner. Lady Hargreaves can't make small talk and soon leaves Hargreaves and Muller to whisky and business. Muller wonders if Davis or Castle leaked, says he gave Castle some Bonn material incorrectly drafted, and gets chauffeured back to London. Hargreaves plans to confer with Percival.

Chapter III: 1. Saturday. Castle hears the morning radio report of young Halliday's arrest for selling a youngster pornographic material. Castle knows he'll trade his copy of Muller's report for leniency. Castle awakens Sarah, tells her to go with Sam immediately to Castle's mother. He'll phone Monday. The two taxi away. He signals an emergency Soviet-spy line. No answer. His phone rings. He won't answer.

2. Hargreaves meets Percival in the Reform Club by arrangement and says Muller is alarmed. Hargreaves couldn't get Castle by phone, will dispatch Daintry to check, suspects Davis was innocent. Percival says Davis was ineffective, hence no loss.

3. Castle anxiously stays home. His mother phones, and he unsettles her with lies. Seeking whisky and pocketing a revolver, he, as well as Buller, spots a stranger's legs outside a basement window. The door bell rings. Castle admits Daintry. Over drinks, Castle mentions Davis, imprudently involves himself by saying he knows Davis was innocent, covers by saying Watson or a pool secretary could have leaked, and says his wife quarreled and is away. Castle is tempted to confess to Daintry, who suddenly seems human but whose watch may contain a recording device. Daintry drives off in the rain.

4. Daintry stops at a Berkhamsted pub, phones Percival, blurts that he killed the wrong man, that he saw Castle and Castle said Davis was innocent. Percival says that all exits are closed to Castle but that Hargreaves wants hard evidence against Castle. Daintry, lonely now, resolves to resign.

5. Old Halliday visits Castle in his lonely home and tells him he retained the Muller copy intended for his son, thus revealing he and not his in-custody son has been the book-code Soviet conduit all along. Halliday offers Castle £25 for his attractive library and help in escaping England. Halliday tells Castle to shoot affectionate Buller, which he does.

6. While proudly driving Castle through the rain to temporary safety, Halliday explains he was a prisoner of war near Archangel (from 1914), read Communist essays, was converted, and became a London mole. Castle says he'll never be a Communist, hints at Stalin's atrocities, is answered by "Hamburg, Dresden, Hiroshima," and gets cheerfully dumped at a Heathrow airport hotel — headed for Moscow.

7. Castle enters the hotel, bumps into Blit, a former contact in the American Embassy later assigned to Mexico, then goes to his room. A bearded agent enters with a fake passport for "Partridge," alters Castle's appearance to resemble its photograph, gives him a ticket to Paris and a blind man's cane to appear to need assistance in boarding, and tells him to fly without baggage and await instructions in Paris.

Part Six. Chapter I: 1. Saturday. Sarah is at her mother-in-law Mrs. Castle's home. The old woman is officiously worried. Sunday, no news. Monday. Sarah walks into town, rashly phones Castle's office, isn't told anything, hangs up, and returns to Mrs. Castle, who says some man is here to talk with her. Inspector Butler tells Sarah the Berkhamsted police learned where she was, reported Buller was shot, and suspect robbery. She tells Butler she and Castle quarreled and she doesn't know where he is. Butler leaves.

2. Days pass. Sarah enrolls Sam in the local school. She senses loneliness of such permanence that she welcomes a phone call from Percival. He persuades her to come to London for lunch. She feels she'll soon be with Castle.

3. Sarah and Percival have a fancy lunch. He contends Castle has absconded traitorously, and separately from her for safety, and is in Moscow. When she says she'll follow him there, Percival replies threateningly: Carson, a Communist, aided Castle and Sarah; Muller has Sam's black father in jail and he could claim paternity; Sam could be denied a passport. Sarah walks out.

Chapter II: 1. Castle, met by Ivan in Prague and debriefed near Irkutsk, is given a dingy, two-room apartment in snowy Moscow, and some rubles. The phone doesn't work. Fat Anna, his "daily," teaches him some Russian, walks him around, cooks a little. He buys and reads old British novels, including *Robinson Crusoe*. Two weeks pass. He snarls at Ivan, who cautions patience.

2. Ivan takes Castle to a library. A benign-looking "comrade" explains, with Ivan translating: Castle will become known as a defector via an internationally bruited press conference, and is to help select the most suitable African novelists to be invited to a Writer's Union meeting here. First, Castle insists on a phone line to Sarah and then her arrival with Sam here. Gloom descends; Ivan is soon gone.

3. Bellamy, a homosexual and a defector from the British Council stationed in Germany, visits Castle and is friendly and helpful, though prissy.

4. One night Castle finishes *Robinson Crusoe*. The phone startlingly rings. No voice. In the morning he gestures to Anna toward the phone and at a photo of Sarah. Anna will help.

5. Boris visits Castle, bringing duty-free scotch. While they drink, Boris explains everything: Castle sent reports from London to a supposed British agent in Moscow; said agent was a Soviet plant; thus authenticated to the British, he passed disinformation to British agents in London; they believed it; Uncle Remus jeopardized Castle's usefulness; his transmitting Muller's notes ended it; the Soviets got him to Moscow; Sam's not being on Sarah's passport means only Sarah can try to escape; if she tries, the British could arrest her for complicity with dead Carson; Boris, unlike Ivan, is Castle's friend here; Boris advises patience and more whisky.

Chapter III: 1. Castle's mother, seeing her son at a televised news conference, disputes with Sarah. The old woman says her son is a traitor and she would have exposed him had she known. The young woman says her husband helped her people in Africa and once said she and Sam were his country. The old woman says if Sarah tries to escape she will make Sam, who is a British subject, "a Ward in Chancery." Puzzled, Sarah recalls she was told by a mysterious phone call she could be helped to Moscow now and perhaps Sam could also be — "in time." She refused.

2. Sarah knows no one except her mother-in-law, that woman's friend Ezra Bottomley, back from a religious mission in Rhodesia, and Sam. One day Castle phones, asks about everyone, agrees she couldn't leave Sam, agrees they must be patient. The Moscow line goes dead.

Greene told Ronald Bryden that when he

started writing *The Human Factor* (in 1967) he called it *A Sense of Security*. Mark Bosco says its first-draft title was *The Cold Fault*. Tim Armstrong calls it Greene's "most disillusioned Cold War novel." After Greene's friend and former MI6 supervisor Kim Philby* published *My Silent War* (1968), Greene abandoned *The Human Factor* for obvious reasons but later decided to continue (1975). In *Ways of Escape,* Greene explains both his delay in writing it and his dissatisfaction with it when finished. He sent a copy to Philby in Moscow. According to Norman Sherry, Philby's response combined professional criticism and personal friendship. Bryan Forbes writes about Greene and Philby thus: "I don't believe his [Greene's] defiant friendship and defence of Philby was another of his calculated tilts at an Establishment he had little time for; I think his affection for Philby was genuine on a human level and that it was no coincidence that his last novel on divided loyalties was called *The Human Factor*." Yvonne Cloetta* writes too profusely about Greene's relationship with Philby.

In the aftermath of American post–Vietnam angst, *The Human Factor* not surprisingly made the *New York Times* best-seller list six straight months; in fact, according to John Bear it was Greene's only novel to achieve #1 status on that list. Not all Americans, however, admire *The Human Factor*. Donald Greene, for example, notes that in it "[w]e find sympathy for Kim Philby, condemnation of American 'imperialism,' and the like." The critic continues: "Castle ... seems to owe more than a little to Philby. He is a 'mole,' regularly transmitting secret information to his Russian paymasters. The villains are the heads of MI5, who callously murder the wrong suspect, using that old standby of whodunits, an undetectable poison. Castle, like Philby, is conveyed by his employers to safe exile in Moscow. The reader seems expected to feel sorry for him."

Bosco, intrigued by the title of *The Human Factor,* says "[t]he search for a stable 'factor' — the human factor ... — is uneasily negotiated in a universe denied and deprived of Greene's usual recourse to explicit Catholic images and beliefs." Grahame Smith contends that if *The Human Factor* were Greene's last novel, it could be seen as a "rich resumé ... of his literary career," since, as Smith demonstrates, it has details "link[ing]" it to elements in *A Burnt-Out Case, The End of the Affair, The Comedians,* and *The Honorary Consul.* Robert Pendleton summarizes various comparisons of *The Human Factor* and Joseph Conrad's *The Secret Agent,* and then "place[s] *The Human Factor* in the full context of Greene's developing relationship with Conrad," including similar narrative form, spies' reluctance to act followed by isolation, British governmental ineptness, and their heroes' lack of circumspection. Roger Sharrock contends that with *The Human Factor* "Greene clearly invites comparison with practitioners of the secret service romance like Len Deighton and John Le Carré. The comparison [Sharrock adds] is very much to his advantage." A. A. DeVitis argues that "the chessboard imagery" in *The Human Factor,* first "suggest[s] the nature of espionage" but gradually turns "structural, and the theme of flight and pursuit ... dominates the action."

Greene provides two inconsistent hints for dating the action in *The Human Factor*. The Clough-Daintry wedding day was Saturday, October 21; therefore the action must occur in 1972 or 1978. Davis won a "First in Physics" in 1953 at age 16; since he is now just over 40, the action should occur in 1978. However, the novel was published in March 1978, half a year before Castle's troubles start.

When Castle recalls having been kind enough as a child to leave a note for an ugly girl, Greene is rehashing part of his short story "The Innocent." Paul O'Prey finds two weaknesses in *The Human Factor:* Castle's being disguised as a blind man walking through Heathrow would have called for considerable "acting skills from a man in an extreme state of nervous tension"; and "Percival's one-man decision to eliminate Davis on the flimsiest of circumstantial evidence" is "unconvincing."

A motif pulsating through this novel about persons good and bad, in agony or callous, is loneliness. Castle loves, is Trappist-like, loses; his first wife died alone; his second wife, out of Africa, is exiled to Suffolk; Sam is black amid white pupils, loses Buller; Castle's mother's rigid righteousness alienates; Hargreaves reads cozily, while his childless wife has tea, often alone; Daintry's ex-wife and daughter despise him, and he despises murderous colleagues; old Halliday is a book-isolated mole.

Quentin Falk discusses the movie version of *The Human Factor* (1979). Otto Preminger (1906–1986), its director, had financial problems almost from the outset, and most of the cast was miscast. Its stars include Richard Attenborough (as Daintry), John Gielgud (Brigadier Tomlinson), Derek Jacobi (Davis), Robert Morley (Percival), and Nicol Williamson (Castle, age 37). Falk regards the result as "a failure of such staggering dimensions — artistically, technically and logistically — that it seems to transcend the bounds of mere criticism." *Philby, Burgess and Maclean* (1977) was a television film starring Anthony Bate (as Philby), Derek Jacobi (Burgess), and Michael Culver (Maclean). (Sources: Armstrong, 591; Bear, 127; Bosco, 119, 181n40; Bryden, 89; Cloetta, 114–44; DeVitis, 138; Falk, 178, 179–86 passim, 216; Forbes, 215; Greene, *Ways of Escape,* 306–09; D. Greene 20, 183–84n27; O'Prey, 137; Pendleton, 135–38; Sharrock, 147; Sherry III, 601–02; G. Smith, 186, 187)

HUMPELNICKER (*Our Man in Havana*). Wormold hears tourists at the Nacional Hotel discussing how a stray bullet recently killed another tourist and smashed his Leica camera, and how a surviving tourist plans to take a fragment of the lens to his friend Humpelnicker as a souvenir.

HUMPHRIES, DOCTOR (*The Honorary Consul*). He is an old, white-haired, thin, nicely dressed, seedy pedagogue, in town 20 years. Living in the Hotel Bolívar, Humphries defeats his friend Plarr at chess, and dislikes Fortnum. Humphries writes critically about Fortnum to Sir Henry Belfrage, who calls Humphries "Jeffries" in conversation with Plarr.

HYTHE, WESBY ("Alas, Poor Maling"). He wants his Hythe Newsprint Company to merge with Sir Joshua Simcox's Simcox Newsprint Company. But Maling's stomach rumbles the sound of an air-raid alarm and ruins the deal.

"THE IMPROBABLE TALE OF THE ARCHBISHOP OF CANTERBURY" (1924). Short story. (Characters: the Archbishop of Canterbury, Satan.) Satan, a lunatic, visits Britain, causes wars, hopes for multiple killings, but is shot by the Archbishop of Canterbury, who then fears God will judge him adversely. Telling the archbishop not to worry since he'll find no God, Satan says he's God, performed some nice miracles, but then rashly made himself man. In blood-drenched laughter, he dies. (Source: Sherry I, 126–27).

INDIAN QUEEN (*Travels with My Aunt*). This was a race horse whose yearling's speed, according to Augusta, reminded Jo Pulling of the swift passage of time.

INNES (*Brighton Rock*). This is the name of a non-existent client of the unsuccessful lawyer Drewitt, who has empty filing boxes with such names on them.

"THE INNOCENT" (1937). Short story. (Character: Lola.) One autumn day, the narrator invites his casual girlfriend Lola to go to Bishop's Hendron, where he was born and lived 12 years, for dinner, drinks, and bed together. Although much is the same about the village, the inn seems differently placed and the cinema, café, and garage are new. A group of children leaving from a dancing lesson remind him he took lessons in that house up that hill. He wishes Lola weren't with him. So, after drinks and before dinner, he gets her permission to leave, briefly. He walks toward that house, hears the piano inside, and remembers how with unique intensity he felt love for a girl who also took dancing lessons. She was almost eight; he, a year younger. They danced in class but never became friendly outside. He drew a picture for her, shoved the paper into a hole in the wooden gate, and told her; she never looked for it. Now, 30 years later, when he buys females for brief affection, he finds that paper. The sketch was one of a man and a woman — innocent then, but obscene to him now. Abed later, he feels that his Lola, having earned "a fiver" and asleep, is part of his present scene.

Features that Greene provides of Bishop's Hendron — sand, canal, bridge, alms-houses, school, church, paving stones, High Street, Town Hall — mirror those of Berkhamsted, the town of his own first years. "The Innocent" moralizes that an experienced adult can find smut in a child's innocent expression. Greene's movie-director friend Bryan Forbes (b. 1926) writes that "I spotted that he [Greene] had used

The Innocent again in *The Human Factor* and asked him whether he was conscious of this. He replied that the repetition was intentional." (Source: Forbes, 216)

INSPECTOR, THE (*It's a Battlefield*). He is the superior of the Assistant Commissioner, who at one point says he must telephone the Inspector.

"THE INVISIBLE JAPANESE GENTLEMEN" (1965). Short story. (Character: Dwight.)

Bentley's restaurant, London. The narrator, an experienced, middle-aged writer, observes and hears a girl, no more than 20, "pretty and *petite*," confidently telling her fiancé that Mr. Dwight, her publisher, has given her a £500 advance on her first novel. She wanted to call it *The Ever-Rolling Stream* but made him happy by letting him call it *The Chelsea Set*. The narrator also observes eight courteous Japanese gentlemen, speaking, bowing, and dining on fish. He would like to warn the girl that future years could be filled with work, defeat, and challenges to endurance. She tells her fiancé, who works for his unliked wine-merchant uncle, they can marry next week, he can probably get a job with her publisher, and they can go to St. Tropez, which she hasn't visited but which will be the scene of *The Azure Blue,* her next novel. She rebukes him when he criticizes the redundant title, says Dwight has praised her powers of observation, says she needn't cast her second novel in now-"done" London, snatches the bill, and calls the dinner "my celebration." Meanwhile, two of the Japanese gentlemen talk and bow simultaneously. The narrator hopes the girl's first novel fails, she becomes a photographers' model, and her fiancé sells wine successfully. When her fiancé casually asks her what the crowd of Japanese are doing here, she says "What Japanese?" and adds that he's so "evasive" he really mustn't want to marry her.

To carp, the title "The Invisible Japanese Gentlemen" is only half accurate. The girl's absence of observational powers is manifest (and should doom *The Azure Blue* to failure), but the narrator's powers are formidable. He not only notes the essentials about the very visible eight Japanese, all of whom voice "their incomprehensible tongue" and one of whom wears glasses, but also modifies his opinions concerning the affianced couple in the course of their revealing talk. The narrator's unspoken advice to the cocky girl is advice Greene might in 1965 have said he'd have been happier if he had heard and acted upon back in his own twenties. Richard Kelly praises the efficiency of the first four sentences of this story: They introduce characters, set scene, give details concerning Japanese diners, locate seats, and present the budding novelist's attractiveness and self-absorption. "The Invisible Japanese Gentlemen" was the subject of a 1976 television production. *See Shades of Greene*. (Sources: Falk, 215; Kelly, 65)

ISAACS (*The Ministry of Fear*). Rowe adds numbers, over and over, to the partial phone number Cost phoned just before his suicide and dials combinations to learn whom Cost called. To one person who answers, he asks for Isaacs but is told he is speaking to Wilson.

ISAACS (*Orient Express*). He is, or was once, a friend of Carleton Myatt, or perhaps was his chauffeur. Myatt recalls that the two chased girls together.

ISAIAH ("The Trial of Pan"). God has a brief vision of this "minister," described as ceaselessly crying for repentance.

"I SPY" (1930). Short story. (Characters: Charlie Stowe, Mr. Stowe, Mrs. Stowe.) As soon as Charlie Stowe, 12, hears his mother snoring one night, he feels free to sneak downstairs to his absent father's ground-floor tobacconist shop. Charlie's pals have rebuked him for never smoking. He plans to try tonight. The darkness is pierced by searchlights combing the sky for enemy Zeppelins. Before Charlie can light up, he is surprised to hear his father enter, braced by two policemen. They let Mr. Stowe take away a few cigarettes, laugh when he says he'll put off talking to his wife until tomorrow, and march him out again. Charlie returns to his bed, sad that he can't tell his distant, wraith-like father he loves him—which he doesn't. He's going to be alone with his too-demonstratively loving mother.

Richard Kelly admires the way Greene deftly

touches on the boy's sudden maturing, and uses a third-person narrator to limit the reader's knowledge of background details. (Source: Kelly, 19–20)

IT'S A BATTLEFIELD (1934). Novel. (Characters: Adams, Assistant Commissioner, Barham, Miss Batlow, Beale, Bennett, Bernay, Jules Briton, Bullen, Lady Caroline Bury, Lord Justin Bury, Sean Cassidy, Chaplain, Miss Chick, Chief, Chine, Collins, Lady Collins, Lord Collins, Conder, Arthur Coney, Rose Coney, Crabbe, Crippen, Crosse, Mrs. Janet Crowle, Davis, Conrad Drove, Jim Drover, Milly Drover, Fanshawe, Governor, Greta, Herbert, Heysan-Bretau, Home Secretary, Inspector, Jenks, Fred Jones, "Gee-Gee" Jones, Marlene, Flossy Matthews, Michael, Norma, Patmore, Pierpoint, Kay Rimmer, Rowlett, Ruttledge, Mrs. Amy Simpson, Margaret Surrogate, Philip Surrogate, Symond, Lord Taveril, Winston.)

1. London, autumn. The Assistant Commissioner in Scotland Yard is efficient but timid, despite three years' service in the East in dangerous jungles. He meets the Home Secretary's young assistant secretary for dinner, after which they drive in the secretary's car through depressed areas of London past Battersea to Leeds prison. The secretary wants to see, not talk to, Jim Drover, a bus driver who during a Communist street demonstration near Hyde Park thought a policeman, named Coney, was threatening Drover's wife Milly and therefore stabbed him fatally. The secretary wants the Assistant Commissioner to write about political consequences if Drover is hanged. The chief warder shows the secretary the prison Blocks (A., B., C.), describes the 400 inmates' activities, and shows the visitors Drover — motionless, with childish eyes, stubborn, obtuse. When the warder says Milly visited quietly, the secretary thinks of Lady Collins, while the Commissioner thinks of hell's circles.

2. Conder, dogged crime reporter, finishes some writing in the office: Ruttledge, Streatham Common murder suspect, is to be released. Conder, living in a bed-sittingroom and collecting coins and currency as a hobby, fictionalizes to everyone he's going home to his wife and six children.

Kay Rimmer, Norma, Greta, and Marlene are working mechanically at machines in the Battersea match factory. They are among 150 female employees. The manager explains to a visitor about three "Blocks" (A, B, C.) of work, of different skill levels. Yes, there are accidents, through carelessness or stupidity. After the overtime bell rings, the girls scatter to sundry destinations. Kay sees Jim Drover's brother Conrad, a brainy insurance company's chief clerk, waiting for her. He wants her to circulate petitions favoring Jim, whose wife Milly is Kay's sister.

Surrogate, Fabian-turned-Communist writer, tenderly handles several books from his library bookcase, only to find a mouse back there nibbling his cobnuts. He offers the tiny creature some cheese, orders a taxi, and tells his dayservant Davis to set a mouse-trap.

Lonely Jules Briton, café waiter whose French mother bore him in England, domineered him, and died, brings Conder a smuggled rouble. Learning Jules knows Kay, Milly's sister, Conder hopes to interview Milly, discusses a clemency petition for Jim, and off they go to a Communist meeting. Jules says he and Conder pretend to be Reds, but once in the meeting Kay's tears make him want to act. Surrogate drones that Drover's death would weaken capitalistic oppression. A man named Bennett squelches Surrogate and doubts the present intellectuals' honesty. Jules wishes Kay would become his girlfriend, temporarily. The meeting ends. Jules introduces Conder to Kay, who rebuffs him and he leaves. Kay sees Surrogate and says Drover is her brother-in-law. Surrogate says the Party can't help Jim but he'll speak to Lady Caroline Bury, and invites Kay home.

At a pub near his digs, Conder rendezvouses with Patmore of Scotland Yard, who promises an exclusive on the Streatham Common murder in exchange for Communist plans concerning Drover. Learning Drover is to be sacrificed, Patmore leaves. Conder sees Bennett outside. Eavesdropping? Scared, Conder walks through dark slums and phones his office about having a lead on the murder.

Surrogate takes smiling Kay by taxi to his "man's den" of a flat. She finds everything sumptuous. A portrait of Surrogate's indifferent wife Margaret, deceased, hangs near his circular pink bed. Kay thinks about that bed, happily.

Conrad Drover muses: Jim, his strong, beloved, long-jealous brother, needs Conrad's brains now; Conrad loved but lost Milly to Jim. After work, Conrad visits Milly. They rent rooms in the same building. They kiss. She reminisces about Coney the policeman. He tried to batter her and cried when Jim stabbed him. Conrad cooks bacon for Milly, offers to sleep in the kitchen to protect her, speaks encouragingly, senses their own insignificance, then suggests Milly asks Mrs. Coney to sign Jim's reprieve petition. Milly reluctantly agrees. She chides him for loving her, for being too nervous even to hold a gun, and contrasts herself with her man-crazy sister Kay, also rooming in the house.

Alone, Milly broods about Jim, half-welcome death, poor neighbors; she wanders through the partly unoccupied house, encounters Kay's perfume, then Kay, who says at the meeting everyone signed Jim's petition and mentions influential Surrogate, who simply talked without intimacy and sent her home by taxi. Maybe tomorrow.

The Assistant Commissioner goes to his rooms, hoping for a later dinner prepared by Mrs. Simpson, his fussy day-servant. But Superintendent Crosse phones: Mrs. Janet Crowle's murderer is cornered. The Assistant Commissioner rushes to Scotland Yard, and he and Crosse speed to where the murderer rooms. The Assistant Commissioner watches at the fire escape as they arrest the man while he's preaching into his mirror about Christ's forgiveness.

3. At 8:30 a.m. Davis awakens Surrogate, but he resumes sleep until 11:00. The match-factory girls take a five-minute morning break for tea and biscuits. Conder sends up some truth-bending copy, aware the paper disseminating it will be pulp soon — his body too, soon enough.

Surrogate tells his dead wife's portrait he didn't "bed" that girl last night, dresses, and calls on Lady Caroline Bury in her Bloomsbury mansion. This wise, liberal, weird literary-salon hostess promises to get the Assistant Commissioner to help Drover. Her luncheon guests include novelist Crabbe, Irish-poet Sean Cassidy, and others. Surrogate, glad to escape, goes to Oxford Circus to meet Kay. Not there.

Milly phones Conrad at work, but he can't accompany her; so she calls alone on old-looking Mrs. Coney, who invites her in for tea and cake, relieved she isn't another reporter. Milly senses the two could come to an understanding of justice but for the expensive, vengeful legal system. Mrs. Coney signs Jim's petition only when another of those intrusive reporters comes and Milly promises to get him away. He is Conder. She identifies herself, wants him to write something to get her husband justice, can't fathom his cynicism, accepts his lies about his six-kid family, hears him promise help, and waits with him in a traffic jam while Queen Mary is chauffeured up Regent Street.

On Saturday, Conrad at work senses the younger clerks' hostile eyes, is constantly afraid the company director's nephew will replace him, is tentatively happy when the director surprisingly praises his discipline, promotes him. He lunches at his usual tea-room, buys quickly wilting flowers for Milly, thinks of her comment about guns in his hands, shops for a gun but buys none, and visits Milly in her rooms. She boasts of getting Mrs. Coney's signature and having three drinks with a reporter named Conder. Milly and Conrad argue about doomed Jim, consider the future, discuss love and his shopping for a gun, and laugh. Darkness falls. Conrad reviews his bookkeeping notes, stares with nonsensual hunger at Milly while she crochets, badly. Preparing a two-chair bed, Conrad confesses he felt love for her even at her wedding. Milly says goodnight and leaves. Kay enters, sleek with man smell, taunts him, goes upstairs to Milly. While Conrad spies, Kay boasts about Surrogate's bed prowess, his talk about his dead artist wife, the mouse he threw a shoe at. Kay exits to her room. Milly whispers for Conrad, knows his talk is lies. He thinks she'll feel less shame if he seeks intimacy first-off. Only lust could assuage guilt, briefly. Afterwards, lust became love through his experiencing hate, pain, guilt, and her crying.

Lady Caroline phones the Assistant Commissioner to invite him for dinner, Monday. They knew each other 10 years ago. Though buried in dispatches about Drover, he agrees. He muses — his job is to uphold a system.

4. Sunday. Surrogate, lolling abed, thinks of Kay and her condemned brother-in-law, addresses his wife Margaret's portrait, rationalizes his egocentrism, then promises Margaret

he'll give up Kay. Davis, silently critical, prepares Surrogate's breakfast.

5. Conder, though well paid, saves money for coins and vacations (like that one near the Schaffhausen falls, where he betrayed a girl) by having a cheap breakfast in the café below his room, waited on by his friend Jules. Conder says maybe he shouldn't aid Milly, because he fears Bennett is stalking him. Jules says he'll help Milly. Conder boards a bus, reads a paper, goes to Bennett's address to apologize, but is told by a toughie that Bennett was followed (by Conder) and "skedaddled."

Jules, a Catholic, attends Mass offered in French, feels he should aid Milly's husband, would ask the priest to sign the petition but for his being surrounded by Knights of Columbus, and returns home to open a letter from France. From his long-absent father in Petit Tourville? No, it reports both a bequest of 10,500 francs from his father, now dead, and his cautionary warning to be prudent. Ah, £150 for him. He seeks Kay, finds her at Leicester Square waiting for a no-show, shares his news, almost proposes immediate marriage but caution restrains him, and drives her outside London in a rented car: Refreshments at Huntonbridge, on to Berkhamsted, tea at a cottage place, spirited love-making in the Park. Kay is happy, thoughtful/thoughtless, worries about getting careless in the grass, and feels cold; more love-making; she mentions marriage; cautious, he prefers her free-love chatter. They drive to Ivinghoe, barely avoid a night crash, get to a cottage room, make love again — too fast. They dispute about eating something, the permanence of marriage to a Catholic, how long £150 would last. She fears commitment; he, loneliness. In the dining room, he ignites Drover's petition to light the hearth gas.

Conrad goes to Bernay, a pawnbroker suspected of arson until he dropped his insurance claim. Bound for Sunday church service, Bernay cows Conrad ostentatiously but then sells him a rusty gun and 10 rounds for £4.10, leaving him only pennies. Ever since sleeping with a murderer's wife, Conrad feels as strong as a murderer, happens near Trafalgar Square to see the Assistant Commissioner clutching some reports, wants to ask him to spare Jim, holds out a hand, and says "Sir." Recoiling, the Assistant Commissioner spurns the beggar, thinks his job is catching people not serving justice, but turns back for the fellow. Gone. The Assistant Commissioner thinks first of jungle fever in the past, and then retirement, of jungle death then or in London soon. Feeling followed, he enters a corner house, orders whisky, and studies contradictory Drover reports. Oh, let the Minister decide. The Assistant Commissioner gets to his flat, opens the building door, turns back, sees that beggar retreating.

Still walking, Conrad feels like a wasted, hate-filled coward. Are his thoughts aloud? He no longer loves Milly. Churches let out. He walks into the afternoon, sits on a park bench, watches idle and varied crowds. Nobody regards him. Lucky Jim, escaping all this. Returning to Milly resembles a dog's returning to its vomit. Her unmalicious sneers were better than unloving lust. Darkness and rain. People stare at him. He thinks of the grim office tomorrow, of easeful suicide. A Battersea bus gets Conrad to Milly, awaiting him. Both are stupid, he thinks.

5. Monday evening. Mrs. Simpson warns the Assistant Commissioner she saw someone loitering nearby, then fussily helps him leave for dinner with Lady Caroline. He avoids taking a taxi, since taxis skid in this rain, and, though aware of being followed, walks to Caroline's fancy place. The weirdly garbed woman misses her dead, rubicund husband Justin, tells the Assistant Commissioner she's tired of being charitable and of discovering the talented early, but wants to prevent Drover's execution and requests confidential details. He says she must consult Minister Beale, says Surrogate has gone Communist. "It's fashionable," Caroline counters. He frowns at a Margaret Surrogate painting on Caroline's wall. "Too phallic?" she counters. She wonders about a hanged or reprieved Drover's wife's sex life. Hostess and guest dine. She says she needs painful surgery, wonders where to bequeath her £200,000 estate, gripes at inequitable wage scales, questions him as to faith, which she has. Mumbling something, he rises in nausea, silently wishes he could forever watch the world evolve from nationalistic chaos to economic order — but to be enjoyed by whom? The Assistant Commissioner can't help Drover and apologetically leaves. On her outside steps, he sees his stalker with a revolver and ecstatically knows all about remaining calm.

Conrad steadies his weapon, aims at everything he hates, imagines telling Milly the "fairy tale" that he did it well and was as unfrightened as Jim; but a car skidding in the rain fractures his spine. Someone says the bullets were blanks. Horrendous pain is like a frantic bird's wings beating in his brain. In the hospital, Milly, summoned because he left a note to her in his pocket, gently asks why, wants to tell him about Jim, but a nurse gets her away. Conrad screams through his broken jaw.

Back at his flat, the Assistant Commissioner encounters the prison chaplain, who says that, fed up with capricious injustice, he is resigning. The Assistant Commissioner, concerned about the blanks fired at him, is shocked when the chaplain says Drover has been reprieved, adds that his wife can't be faithful during his 18-year prison sentence and that Drover's brother will look after her. On the heels of the chaplain's departure, the Assistant Commissioner is informed by phone that Conrad's surgery was successful but he died of shock. The Assistant Commissioner concludes that Scotland Yard is more essential to his well-being than the reverse, envies Lady Caroline's faith, and meticulously pens a report on the Streatham Common murder.

Greene wrote *It's a Battlefield* in a hit-or-miss fashion. While despising best-sellers, he hoped to make it a best-selling thriller like *Stamboul Train*. It was not. Michael Shelden reports that early sales were about 7,500 copies in England and 2,000 in the United States. In the political background of *It's a Battlefield* looms the General Strike in England (May 3–12, 1926). A. F. Cassis says the novel presents "a luckless tragic world reminiscent of [Thomas] Hardy's universe." A significant literary inspiration for the novel was Joseph Conrad's *The Secret Agent*. As Lynne Cheney and Norman Sherry observe, both novels are cast in London, and along the spectrum of characters in each novel are lady patroness, assistant police commissioner, cabinet minister cum secretary, and "lower" working-class members. While Conrad's novel features a bomb plot by anarchists, Greene's germinal action is the killing of a policeman by a dumb Communist. Cheney continues: "In looking at these two novels to see what their structures emphasize, one notes that the most obvious structural fact about both is that they are arrangements of the effects of an event, and in both cases the causes of the actions presented, unlike the actions themselves, happen." It may be added that the killer's brother's first name is Conrad. In school, Greene's fictional Conrad, who dislikes the name, felt that boys with more common names "locked together and shared secrets."

London embraces everyone and most events in *It's a Battlefield*. Greene presents its action by manipulating rapidly changing points of view — once in mid-sentence and signaled only by a dash. Unity is enhanced by war imagery and other figures often more startling; by mini-motif verbal echoes such as "blocks," "wasted food," "go to hell," "lust and love," "pushed aside," "beret," "shaking [i.e., trembling] hand," "matches"; and by predictable disappointments wounding Greene's squadron of lonely, mis-connecting, afraid, disappointed, unjustly treated, boxed in, unsuccessful fighters. In a *Collected Edition* introduction, Greene calls its last 60 pages uniquely successful. The novel was never made into a movie, although, as Gene D. Phillips remarks, many of its scenes are "constructed as if for a film." (Sources: Cassis, 19; Cheney, 123–24; Greene, *It's a Battlefield, Collected Edition,* x; Phillips, 15; Shelden, 228; Sherry I, 457)

IVAN (*The Human Factor*). He is Castle's Soviet controller, who replaced Boris for a while. Castle prefers Boris, because Ivan tried to blackmail Castle. After Castle resurfaces in Moscow, Ivan, venomously jealous of nice treatment of defectors, becomes his escort to a library where he is to work. When Castle tries to make demands, he never sees Ivan again.

IVY (*Orient Express*). Coral Musker remembers her as one of her occasionally successful theatrical friends. Others are Dick, Flo, and Phil.

IZQUIERDO (*Travels with My Aunt*) see **VISCONTI**

IZQUIERDO, CAPTAIN (*The Honorary Consul*). Fortnum promised to tell Plarr about this fellow but never does.

J., F. G. (*The Ministry of Fear*). F. G. J. was Jones's father. His wife and Jones's mother celebrated their silver wedding anniversary on

3.8.15, as indicated when she as N.L.J. gave F.G.J. a watch so engraved. The elder Jones died (1919).

Does the date 3.8.15 have any significance in Greene's life?

J., N. L. (*The Ministry of Fear*). N. L. J. was Jones's mother. She had the watch she gave her husband engraved with details of their silver wedding and had it further engraved and gave it to their son in memory of the father's death (1919).

JACK (*England Made Me*). In a letter written to his mother, Hall mentions seeing Jack in Amsterdam.

JACK (*The Ministry of Fear*). Mrs. Bellairs tells this boy's fortune at the fête Rowe attends.

JAGGER (*The Heart of the Matter*). Harris tells Wilson he roomed in Jagger's house at the Downham school, which both young men attended.

JAIME (*Rumour at Nightfall*). He is Eulelia Monti's hairdresser. Caveda tells Eulelia to have Jaime get a message to him.

JAMES (*England Made Me*). Scott and James are British solicitors. They send Minty his £15 monthly allowances. Minty is pleased when his September 20 remittance arrives.

JAMES, FATHER (*Brighton Rock*). He is the Catholic priest to whom Rose tries but fails to confess before her marriage to Pinkie.

JAMESON (*The Human Factor*). Clough works for Jameson's Baby Powder Company, a rival of Johnson's.

JANE ("The Bear Fell Free"). She is Tony Farrell's girlfriend. She throws a teddy bear into the cockpit of Tony's airplane before he tries to fly across the Atlantic Ocean. When Carter telephones Jane about Tony's death, she is in bed with Davis. Carter returns the salvaged teddy bear to her.

JANVIER (*The Tenth Man*) *see* **MANGEOT, MICHEL**

JARVIS, GEORGE (*The Confidential Agent*). He is a laconic old resident of Willing, in the Midlands. Some say he's married; others, not. He goes by train with D. to Benditch. Along the 14-mile run, he rattles off place names. His favorite response to queries is "Ah." He may be going to visit a woman friend. (Could she be Mrs. Bennett?) The Gang's badly managed explosion at the mines allegedly shocked him.

JAVITT ("Under the Garden"). He is the tall, one-legged, bearded man whom Wilditch finds under the garden in his dream and fantasy. Ageless, with weakening eyesight, Javitt lives with Maria, not to be regarded as his wife but rather a person so intertwined on occasion with him that a daughter sprouted, named Miss Ramsgate. Half-afraid of and half-admiring Javitt, Wilditch absorbs much wisdom from him, about time — non-existent, brief, astronomically long — about sexual "spilling," about disloyalty and double-agency as requirements for humanity to survive and evolve, and about the necessity to travel to find beauty, its relationship with ugliness, and love. Javitt explains their real names aren't Javitt and Maria. When Wilditch ties up Javitt to escape him, Javitt admires this evidence of Wilditch's disloyalty.

Paul O'Prey theorizes thus: Wilditch says not only that he learned more from Javitt than from all of his schoolteachers but also that Javitt never lived; therefore, "in other words, [Wilditch learned] from his own imagination." (Source: O'Prey, 65)

JEAN, FATHER (*A Burnt-Out Case*). He is a priest at the leproserie. He is tall, pale, concave in shape, bearded, with a Flemish appetite. He supervises the nuns when they pray. He was a fine student of moral theology but hides the fact by professing great interest in movies.

JEFFERSON, ALFRED (*Brighton Rock*). He is a chief clerk from Clapham, who, the newspapers report, found Hale's body.

JEFFRIES (*The Honorary Consul*) *see* **HUMPHRIES, DR.**

JENKINSON, MISS (*Our Man in Havana*). She is the secretary-pool boss in London's Intelligence headquarters. Every "inhabitant" of the building except Miss Jenkinson goes by a Christian name. She assigns Beatrice Severn, who speaks French, to be Wormold's assistant in Havana, explaining that both French and Spanish are Latin languages.

JENKS (*It's a Battlefield*). He is a policeman on duty when Superintendent Crosse and others apprehend Mrs. Janet Crowle's murderer. Her body was found in a trunk in Paddington Station. Crosse orders Jenks to stay and clean up with Collins.

JENNINGS (*The Man Within*). He was a Customs employee. Later the eccentric old man roomed and boarded in the cottage of Mrs. Garnet and her daughter Elizabeth. He bought their cottage so Elizabeth could survive financially after her mother's death. Jennings both loved and abused Elizabeth. He was killed by smugglers before Andrews arrives at the cottage.

JEROME ("A Shocking Accident"). He is a school student, nine, when headmaster Wordsworth tells him his father was killed when a pig fell off a broken balcony in Naples and landed on him. Jerome shocks Wordsworth by asking what happened to the pig. Relaying the event to a school friend, he gets nicknamed Pig. When his aunt tells his fiancée Sally about her brother's death, Jerome is overjoyed that she too asks him what happened to the pig.

JERVIS (*Orient Express*). He figures inexplicably in Carleton Myatt's business-based dream, in which Eckman is criticized.

JIM (*Orient Express*). His name is mentioned in conversation about beer in the restaurant car of the train.

JIM (*This Gun for Hire*). While confiding in Anne Crowder, Raven tells her Jim was a friend of his at the orphanage.

JIM BRADDON AND THE WAR CRIMINAL. An unfulfilled film project by Greene while he briefly lived in Hollywood (mid–1940s). (Source: Parkinson, 700, 704)

JIMINEZ, SEÑORA (*The Power and the Glory*). She believes that after the whisky priest's execution, one can purchase a piece of handkerchief soaked in his blood, as a relic. Or so Luis's pious mother said.

JOE (*Brighton Rock*). He is a flashy-toothed black to whom Ida Arnold speaks outside a London pub. She asks sympathetically about his hay fever.

JOE (*The Confidential Agent*). He is one of two fake policemen Forbes engaged to prevent authorities from capturing D. at the Lido. The two hussle D. onto a motorboat.

JOE ("The Destructors"). He is a fat member of the Wormsley Common Gang of boys.

JOE ("A Drive in the Country"). He is a fellow a skinny girl tells Mike she prefers to Mike.

JOE (*The Human Factor*). He is the bartender at White's, where Buffy takes Daintry for drinks.

JOE (*Our Man in Havana*). He is a black man who limps, counts his steps as he walks, and sells pornographic cards.

Greene, with pre-1960s insensitivity, lets a couple of his characters call Joe "a nigger."

JOE (*The Quiet American*). He is the American Economic Attaché in Saigon and hence is Pyle's superior. Joe is 50, with nut-brown eyes, and something of a buffoon. His decency is indicated when Granger brings a drunk Frenchman he calls Mick to a bar and then leaves him, and Joe takes him to his own residence to rest up.

Greene enjoys demeaning yet another American official in Vietnam by saying Joe spent three years in Paris but can't speak French.

JOE (*This Gun for Hire*). He owns a gambling dive where Saunders tells Mather they might find Raven. No luck.

JOE ("Under the Garden"). This was Wilditch's dog when both were young. In theorizing about the need to change names, Javitt says that if Wilditch had a dog named Jupiter he wouldn't believe that was its real name.

JOEY (*The Confidential Agent*). He is a member of the youthful anarchistic gang in Benditch. They try to dynamite the coal mines.

JOHN ("The Bear Fell Free"). Baron sees John immediately after Tony Farrell begins his fatal flight.

JOHN (*Brighton Rock*). This is the name signed on the slip Cubitt buys at the fortune-telling machine. He is drunk enough to believe the message is ominous.

JOHN (*Orient Express*). In a letter to Con, Mabel Warren mentions her Uncle John's recent death.

JOHN, POPE ("The Last Word"). He is a proscribed Christian in the futuristic new-world order. Suffering from amnesia following General Megrim's attempt to assassinate him, he has been kept in virtual isolation for about 20 years. When he is the last Christian alive, he is subject to execution by the General. Pope John fervently believes death will be followed by the light, not darkness.

JOHN, RICHARD (*Orient Express*) see **CZINNER, DR. RICHARD**

JOHNNIE (*Brighton Rock*). He is a member of Pinkie's gang. Pinkie orders Dallow to tell Johnnie to make sure Drewitt gets aboard the ship bound for Boulogne. Johnnie phones yes. Ida Arnold says Johnnie was mistreated by his mother.

JOHNS (*The Ministry of Fear*). He is a bespectacled young attendant working for Dr. Forester in his sanatorium. Forester assigns Johns to care for Rowe, admitted as Richard Digby with amnesia. Digby alerts Johns to Forester's misconduct. Johns continues to admire Forester for his alleged idealism, until he discovers that he and Poole murdered Major Stone, another inmate. Johns then shoots them both, saying doing so protected Forester from any whimsical jury's actions.

JOHN THOMAS (*The Human Factor*). Davis refers to his easily aroused penis as John Thomas — an oblique allusion to Mellors's identical cocknonym in *Lady Chatterley's Lover* by D. H. Lawrence (1885–1930). Greene records his dream that Lawrence amiably praised his writings. Leopoldo Duran says Greene didn't consider Lawrence a good novelist. (Sources: Greene, *A World of My Own,* 11; Duran, 45)

JOINER, EDWARD (*The Human Factor*). He is Sylvia Daintry's companion. He drives her from Brighton to her daughter Elizabeth's London wedding. Joiner tells Castle he virtually is Jameson's Baby Powder, for which company Elizabeth's brand-new husband Colin Clough works. Jameson's big competitor is Johnson's.

JONES ("A Day Saved"). One of the names Robinson uses to refers to the man he is pursuing. Robinson also calls him Canby, Douglas, Fotheringay, and Wales.

JONES (*The End of the Affair*). When Bendrix takes an unnamed Sackville Street prostitute to a pub, she tells him she has a canary she named Jones after the John who gave it to her.

JONES (*The Ministry of Fear*). He assists Rennit at the Orthotex detective agency. Rennit calls Jones A.2 and assigns him to Rowe's case. Willi Hilfe learns about this from Rowe and has Jones murdered, with his remains buried in the pond island at Dr. Forester's sanatorium. .

JONES, ALFRED (*Doctor Fischer of Geneva*). He is the narrator-protagonist, perhaps 55. His father Sir Frederick Jones was a minor diplomat. Through traveling with his parents, Alfred learned French, Turkey, and Spanish. He was a fire warden in London during World War II. His parents were killed in the Blitz, and he lost his left hand (December 1940). His first marriage ended when his wife Mary died in childbirth, as did the female child — this about 20 years before the present action. Jones is a translator-correspondent for a Swiss chocolate factory in Geneva. He marries loathsome Doctor Fischer's delightful daughter Anna-Luise, attends one of Fischer's infamous parties, suffers Anna-Luise's death, and attends Fischer's final bomb party with discomfited suicidal intentions.

Paul Hogarth suggests that the chocolate factory Jones works for is modeled on the Nestlé factory in Vevey and includes a watercolor of the Nestlé building. Mark Bosco believes Jones's "memory of Anna-Luise and the relics of their life together become for Jones the closest claim to a kind of religious faith, captured in Catholic imagery and liturgical language." Discussing allegory as a structural device in Greene, Peter Erlebach finds "the Everyman type of person" in Alfred Jones because of his common last name. (Sources: Bosco, 138; Erlebach, 28; Hogarth, 149)

JONES, ANNA-LUISE (*Doctor Fischer of Geneva*). She is villainous Doctor Fischer's bright, pretty daughter. She hates him, mainly for what he did to her mother. Before she turns 21, Anna-Luise and Alfred Jones, 30-plus years her senior, chance to meet and fall in love. They marry. She warns Jones about Fischer. She loves to ski, a sport her mother introduced her to when she was about four. Skiing causes Anna-Luise's death, following which are Jones's suicidal loneliness and despair.

Mark Bosco finds in Greene's use of Anna-Luise's "human-divine image" aspects of religious allegory. Bosco explains: Anna-Luise through resembling her mother is the opposite of Fischer, who therefore rejects her; sight of her face renders Steiner ecstatically, if perilously, happy; and remembrance of her image arms Jones "as he goes to one last battle at Fischer's party." (Source: Bosco, 136)

JONES, FRED (*It's a Battlefield*). The shopkeeper at the gun store Conrad Drover is about to enter gossips to someone Fred Jones is away shooting with Lord Taveril.

JONES, "GEE-GEE" (*It's a Battlefield*). The shopkeeper at the gun store where Conrad Drover is about to enter tells someone "Gee-Gee" Jones didn't rent a moor this year.

JONES, H. J. (*The Comedians*). This British con-artist was born in Assam. His father was a tea planter, according to his mother. Calling himself Major Jones, he is a passenger on the *Medea,* where he meets Brown, William Abel Smith, and Mrs. Smith, among others. He pretends to be an experienced British soldier, even though he had flat feet and his only duty was to entertain troops near Burma as part of the Entertainments National Service Association. Jones hopes to lure the Haitian government into a fraudulent arms deal. Learning this, Captain Concasseur beats him up. Brown spirits Jones out of sanctuary in the embassy administered by Luis Pineda, whose wife Martha, Brown's mistress, becomes Jones's friend. Jones makes contact with insurgents under Henri Philipot. Jones finally admits to Brown he never was a soldier; nevertheless he dies in combat fighting Haitian forces. Several people pay Jones a great compliment when they say he makes them laugh.

Norman Sherry identifies three possible models for Jones: Colonel Hubert Julian, a prevaricating arms dealer; Father Thomas Gilby, a close, unprincipled friend of Greene and Catherine Walston;* and a journalist who impersonated Greene and whom Sherry labels "Greene II." V. S. Pritchett says "Jones is a *comic* comedian ... committed to making something out of the anarchy that the deeply comic are drawn into." (Sources: Pritchett, 85; Sherry III, 341–43, 366–67, 372, 398–99)

JONES, LADY (*Doctor Fischer of Geneva*). She was Sir Frederick Jones's wife and Alfred Jones's mother. She and her husband were killed in London during the Blitz (December 1940).

JONES, MARY (*Doctor Fischer of Geneva*). She was Alfred Jones's first wife. Twenty years earlier she died in London giving birth to their daughter, who also died.

JONES, SIR FREDERICK (*Doctor Fischer of Geneva*). He was Alfred Jones's father, a minor diplomat, with assignments in France, Turkey, and Paraguay. He and his wife were killed in the London Blitz (December 1940).

JOSÉ (*The Honorary Consul*). He is a blind old *barrio* man. He wanders into the hut where Rivas and his men hold Fortnum. He needs a coffin for his wife, who just died. He marvels when he hears Rivas's radio.

JOSÉ, FATHER (*Monsignor Quixote*). He is the priest-grandson of Señor Diego, the vintner outside Learig. Diego would have preferred it if his grandson hadn't become a priest but had married, managed the family vineyard, and had a son to do so later.

JOSÉ, PADRE (*The Power and the Glory*). He is a failed priest, 62. After 40 years, he saved his life by succumbing to anti-Catholic government pressure and getting safely married. He is ridiculed by his fat wife and mocked by street urchins, refuses to pray at Anita's burial, and won't hear the whisky priest's confession even though the lieutenant promises him immunity if he does so.

In a *Collected Edition* introduction, Greene says he prefers Acky, a flawed man of God, to Padre José. (Source: Greene, *A Gun for Sale, Collected Edition*, ix)

JOSEPH (*The Comedians*). He is Brown's faithful employee at the Trianon. He was crippled by the Tontons Macoute and has a permanent limp. He notifies Brown of Dr. Philipot's suicide. Joseph leads Brown to a Voodoo ceremony in which Henri Philipot undergoes a ritual to become an insurgent. Joseph joins young Philipot and is killed in combat. Brown attends his funeral Mass in Santo Domingo.

JOSEPH, FATHER (*A Burnt-Out Case*). He is a priest with such long service in Africa that his speech has African inflections. He supervises native construction workers and works beside them happily.

JOSSY (*This Gun for Hire*). He is one of several thugs known by Raven to have regretted being soft on girls.

JOURNALIST ("Work Not in Progress"). He notes that the 12 kidnappers, posing as Anglican bishops, have wrongly counted the Bishop of Bath and Wells as two.

JOYCE ("The End of the Party"). She is a guest, 11, at Colin Henne-Falcon's 10th birthday party. Her parents permit her more freedom than Francis Morton's mother allows him.

JOYCE (*Orient Express*). He is a faithful agent in Constantinople for Myatt, Myatt and Page. Carleton Myatt plans to put him in charge, replacing Eckman. When Myatt gets to Constantinople, Joyce aids him.

JUAN (*The Honorary Consul*). Juan is the local coffin maker. Blind José tells Pablo that Juan told him Pablo bought a coffin from him. José needs it for his wife.

JUAN (*The Power and the Glory*). He is the pious hero in the smuggled religious book read by the pious mother to her two daughters and her son Luis. The account of Juan's execution, sanitized and sentimentalized, is unlike that of the whisky priest.

JUAN (*Rumour at Nightfall*). He is the skinny husband of the manageress of the San Juan inn where Chase and Crane stay. Juan associates with Emilio.

"JUBILEE" (1936). Short story. (Characters: Amy, the Boob, Chalfont, Merdy.)

Chalfont, a gigolo, though 50 looks younger. He is tall, still somewhat erect, with a military moustache. He seldom leaves his tiny bed-sitting room off Shepherd's Market during the Jubilee. In frayed clothes, he doesn't want to encounter any former female acquaintances. His pals Merdy and the Boob might remind him playfully of his pickup game. Still, needing money, he drifts into a pub for some heartening sherry. A nicely dressed woman there seems familiar. She winks. He sidles over and asks if she remembers him. She offers him a second sherry and says the name Amy will do for her. She encourages his dishonest reminiscing. When he wonders if they might repair to her "little nest," she says she's retired, then reveals she was once a prostitute near Bond Street and temporarily mistakes him for an ex-client. She boasts that she sanitized some of London's streets for the Jubilee by gathering girls from her business area, establishing a profitable "House" with them, and opening a phony tourist bureau. In the process she made £5,000 and set up a place in Brighton. She stands another sherry for deflated Chalfont, who's sad she's brimming with "bright plebeian spontaneity" while his neuritis would prevent any dance with her now. She completes his ruin by pressing £5 on him and saying customers in her past paid her a "quid" and also did nothing thereafter.

To his feeble protest she offers to take him to her home, where "you [can] do your stuff." On the street, Amy turns joyful and, for revenge, slaps Chalfont on the back to inspire some Jubilee enthusiasm in the manifestly old fellow.

Norman Sherry discusses circumstances surrounding the Silver Jubilee of King George V (1865–1936, reigned 1911–1936). Greene implicitly invites readers to spread their London maps and trace Chalfont's way along Berkeley Street, Bond Street, Curzon Street, Jermyn Street, Limehouse, Mayfair, Paddington, Piccadilly, Shepherd's Market, and Wardour Street — all named in "Jubilee." (Source: Sherry I, 572–74)

JUDY (*Brighton Rock*) *see* **FRANK, BILLY,** and *also* **FRANK, JUDY**

JUICY JULIET (*This Gun for Hire*). According to Buddy Fergusson, a pseudo-macho fibber, she is a Metropole hotel barmaid he was intimate with.

JULES (*The Tenth Man*). He is the headwaiter at Chavel's favorite Parisian café. When Chavel orders an apéritif, Jules serves a moneyed American soldier first. Recognizing Chavel, Jules offers him food, drink, and a room, and half-boasts he served Frenchmen ahead of high-ranking Germans during the now-ended occupation.

JULIAN (*Travels with My Aunt*). He is Lucinda O'Toole's hippie-artist boyfriend. Lucinda tells Henry that Julian studied at Oxford, almost got trapped by Trotskyists, and would like to paint soup cans after the school of Andy Warhol (1928?–1987). Lucinda is distressed that while with Julian she "forgot the pill" and may be pregnant (not so). He hitchhikes to Istanbul while she takes the Orient Express there.

JUNIOR MINISTER, THE (*The Honorary Consul*). He is an London official who demeans Fortnum's kidnapping in a BBC broadcast. In the process, he misnames Saavedra, calling him Savindra.

K. (*The Confidential Agent*). He is a shabby, ink-stained, bespectacled tutor, 55, at Dr. Bellows's Entrenationo Language Centre. K. is D.'s contact. K. thinks D. has turned unpatriotic and informs on D. to L., who promises him a university appointment back home. K. is complicit in Mrs. Marie Mendrill's murder of Else Crole. D. forces K. into Emily Glover's empty flat, shoots at him but misses. K. dies of a heart attack. When Fortescue blunders in and sees dead K., Rose Cullen says he's ill and calls him Jack Owtram, for no discernible reason.

K., F. J. (*The Heart of the Matter*). In an *Downhamian* periodical, Harris reads that Lane praises F.J.K. for his persuasive performance as Bunthorne in *Patience* (by Gilbert and Sullivan).

K., J. (*This Gun for Hire*). These are the initials on the hairbrush of the Czech minister Raven assassinated. His name remains unrevealed.

KALAMAZOO (*The Human Factor*). Taylor, an intelligence officer, finds the name of this horse, and those of Bonne Chance and Widow Twanky, in Davis's flat and wrongly believes they may be connected with a code.

KALEBDJIAN (*Orient Express*). He is the efficient, obsequious Armenian reception clerk at the hotel in Constantinople where Myatt regularly stays. He makes useful guidebook-like suggestions to two gushy American girls asking about tour sites. He welcomes Myatt, as well as his companions Janet Pardoe and Quin C. Savory.

Greene felt that Kalebdjian and Leo Stein were "presented with excellent brevity." (Source: Greene, *Ways of Escape*, 33)

KALNITZ, MAYOR ("The Root of All Evil"). The wine-drinking clubmen discuss his death, which occurred in 1887 or 1888.

KAMNETZ, GENERAL (*Orient Express*). He was tried for child-rape in Belgrade (1927), Czinner bravely testified against him, but Colonel Hartep's connivance got him off.

KAPPER, BERTHA (*The Name of Action*). She is Joseph Kapper's wife. She is untidy, pale, skinny, and with poor teeth. She reluctantly obeys his order to go sabotage the murdered policeman's blood stain with dripping raw liver.

KAPPER, JOSEPH (*The Name of Action*). This poet and revolutionary plots to depose Demassener, dictator of Trier. Kapper fancies his scurrilous verse is mightier than arms purchased by Chant. But the two, plus Kapper's thugs, work together. Kapper heads a deputation of rebels into the palace. They confront Demassener, wound him, and let Chant take him into exile. Before meeting Kapper, Chant romanticizes him because he is a poet, even fancying he probably resembles Christopher Marlowe. Not so.

Greene over-emphasizes Kapper's Jewishness, criticizes only Kapper among the revolutionaries, often refers to him as "the Jew," and describes him, when standing before a statue of the Madonna, as viewing "the mother of his eternal enemy," and later as regarding gold "with the reverence of Aaron." David Leon Higdon shows how in 1970 Greene revised *Brighton Rock* (published 1938) to reduce passages that could be regarded as anti–Semitic. (Did Greene suppress republication of *The Name of Action* partly because of anti–Semitic tinges in it?) (Source: Higdon, 182)

KARL (*The Name of Action*). He is one of Kapper's thugs. Large, heavy, and sleepy, he stands beside Fritz, to guard Sebastian Lintz's door and thus keep Chant from entering an inner room.

KASTNER, HERR ("The Root of All Evil"). He is one of the wine-drinking clubmen.

KATE, GREAT-AUNT (*Our Man in Havana*). When discussing possible combinations for his safe with Beatrice Severn, Wormold suggests the telephone number of his great-aunt Kate, who lived in Oxford until her death 15 years ago.

KEENE, DORIS (*Travels with My Aunt*). When Augusta tells Henry she is thinking about a love affair, the inexperienced fellow is reminded only of Doris Keene photographs he saw in *Romance*.

KEENE, MISS BARBARA (*Travels with My Aunt*). She is Sir Alfred Keene's daughter, just under 40. When Sir Alfred died, Barbara invited Henry to dinner. He was tempted to propose but didn't. She goes to live with cousins in Koffiefontein, South Africa, writes to him that a neighbor named Hughes proposed to her, and undoubtedly hopes Henry will counter with a proposal. Nothing happens.

KEENE, SIR ALFRED (*Travels with My Aunt*). He was a valued client of Henry when Henry was a bank manager. Sir Alfred forced Henry's superiors to make him a real manager, not acting manager. Sir Alfred sought but ignored Henry's advice on investments.

KEYSER (*The Ministry of Fear*). Rowe tells Rennit, the detective, that Keyser recommended Rennit to him. There probably is no Keyser.

KING, THE (*A Burnt-Out Case*). In the fairy tale Querry tells Marie Rycker, the King is the being that the jeweler tries to please. The King may be equated with God, a being Querry contends we individuals create.

KING, R. ("Men at Work"). He attends a meeting of the Book Committee in the Ministry of Information. A former advertising man, he got into trouble writing about the meat ration and therefore was promoted to be in charge of the Books Division of the Ministry. He also includes among "right authors" one he names Priestley. (J. B. Priestley* perhaps?)

KIPS (*Doctor Fischer of Geneva*). He is an attorney with a spinal malady that bends himself into the shape of a "7." Kips attends Fischer's gift-laced parties, thus making him a Toad. He employed Steiner, who caused Fischer marital embarrassment. Therefore Fischer financed the publication of *Adventures of Mr. Kips,* a cartoon book spoofing poor Kips. Fischer then bought Kips's silence by hiring him at a big fee. Kips attends the bomb party but won't participate in the Russian roulette-like event.

KITE (*Brighton Rock*). He was the leader of a Brighton protection gang, befriended Pinkie, and became a father figure to him. Kite was surrounded by thugs from his rival Colleoni's men at London's St. Pancras railway station and fatally slashed with razors. Pinkie assumed command of the gang. Hale, the reporter, was somehow involved with Colleoni, which causes

Pinkie to obtain revenge by ordering Hale's murder.

Cubitt tells Ida Arnold that Colleoni's men meant only to wound Kite. But Raven in *A Gun for Sale* tells Anne Crowder that he and some others purposely killed Kite, here called Battling Kite, because he was a member of a rival racing gang. Raven says Kite was betrayed by "a skirt."

KITE, BATTLING (*This Gun for Hire*) *see* KITE

KNOCK-ME-DOWN (*Travels with My Aunt*). Lucinda O'Toole tells Henry she knew of a fellow who was baptized Knock-Me-Down.

KOCH (*The Third Man*). He is Harry Lime's neighbor in their building. Koch, the mortuary head clerk, tells Martins he saw the accident that killed Harry and shows Martins Harry's flat. Ilse, Koch's wife, cleaned it thoroughly. When Harry and his fellow criminals regard Koch as too talkative, he is murdered, probably by Cooler.

KOCH, ILSE (*The Third Man*). She is Koch's wife, then widow. She is mountainous but domineered by Koch, after whose murder she is evidently terrorized into silence.

KOLBER (*Orient Express*). He is the assistant station-master at the Subotica railroad station. He is Anna's employer. When Kolber discovers Grünlich trying to rob his room safe, he confronts Grünlich with a revolver, but Grünlich distracts him and shoots him to death.

KOLLEY KIBBER (*Brighton Rock*). This is the pseudonym Charles Hale uses on the cards he hides here and there in Brighton as clues to the newspaper prize.

Kolley Kibber is a variation of the name of British poet Colley Cibber (1671–1757). Norman Sherry relates the Kolley Kibber contest to an identical contest conducted in Brighton (August 1936) by a *News Chronicle* reporter calling himself Lobby Lud. (Source: Sherry I, 630–31)

KORDA, ALEXANDER (1893–1956). He was a movie director, producer, and executive. Born to Jewish parents, as Sándor Laszlo Kellner, in Hungary, he was a Budapest journalist, entered the Hungarian film industry, changed his name (1909), and became a director (1914). He was married (1919–1930) to Maria Farkas, a temperamental actress calling herself Maria de Corda. After World War I, Korda's leftist tendencies caused him to flee to Austria, then Germany, then Hollywood, where over-extending caused difficulties (by 1930). Korda went to London, made high-quality movies, but again over-extended (by 1939). His second wife (1939–1945) was the beautiful actress Merle Oberon (1911–1979). Korda went partners with MGM, was the first moviemaker to be knighted (1942), borrowed £3 million from the British government (1948), and was involved in ventures losing most of it (by 1954). Korda directed at least 25 movies (1914–1919), 24 or more (1920–1932), then, mostly in England, more than a hundred more.

David Parkinson, Michael Shelden, and Norman Sherry detail Greene's relationship with Korda. For the *Spectator* and the *Fortnightly,* Greene adversely reviewed several of Korda's films (late 1930s) and in the process deplored the Jewish influence in the British film industry (late 1930s). Then Greene and Korda met (November 1936) and became friends. Korda was involved in spy intrigues during World War II, as was Greene. Korda paid Greene handsomely for movie rights to his fiction: £2,000 for *The Power and the Glory* (1940, resold to John Ford), £3,000 for working on *The Fallen Idol* (1948, based on "The Basement Room"), £4,000 for *The Heart of the Matter,* £9,000 for *The Third Man.* Greene was the occasional guest, among other luminaries, for trips to Mediterranean ports and islands aboard the *Elsewhere,* Korda's yacht (1950, 1951). Greene came to love Korda, and after his death he wrote movingly about their friendship. (Sources: Greene, *Ways of Escape,* 50–51, 224–28; Parkinson, xxx–xxxi, xxxv, 701, 703–04; Shelden, 34–36, 212–14, 281; Sherry I, 590–603 passim; Sherry II, 239–43 passim, 334–35, 376–84 passim)

KRAFT, CAPTAIN (*The Name of Action*). He is the small, rigid chief of police, obedient to Demassener, dictator of Trier, until Kraft observes discontented citizens massing in front of the palace. Kraft's face is pitted with tiny dueling scars.

KROGH (*The Tenth Man*). He is an Alsatian hostage held by the Germans. When told 10 hostages are to be shot in the morning, he naively asks if they have to volunteer. The 30 slips for drawing are put in his shoe, the biggest in their cell.

KROGH, ERIK (*England Made Me*). He is a self-made millionaire of Swedish peasant stock. He did construction work in the United States, developed a frictionless cutting machine in Barcelona, and established his headquarters in Stockholm and a factory nearby. Krogh met Kate Farrant when she was studying bookkeeping and short-hand in London, hired her as his secretary, and made her his mistress. Trouble for Krogh begins when he hires her twin brother Anthony as his bodyguard. After Krogh orders his henchman Hall to squelch labor unrest among his employees and Anthony won't go along with strongarm tactics, Hall misunderstands Krogh's discontent and murders Tony. This ends Krogh's relationship with Kate.

Erik Krogh is based on Ivar Kreuger (1880–1932), Swedish industrialist, financier, and swindler. He migrated to the United States (c. 1893), where he made millions as a building-construction engineer. He and Paul Toll established Kreuger & Toll (1908), struck it rich in the match industry, and organized the Swedish Match Co. (1917), soon an international monopoly. Kreuger obtained unfair competitive advantages by lending funds to foreign governments in exchange for concessions. Consequences of the Big Crash of 1929 devastated his empire, and he committed suicide in Paris.

While introducing Krogh, Greene gratuitously mentions Krogh would instantly kill himself if things became desperate. Greene comments that Krogh is in *England Made Me* to advance the plot but never becomes a living character. This is unfortunate, since Greene read and reviewed (1933) *The Financier: The Life of Ivar Kreuger* (1933) by Michael George De Solovetytchik (1902–1982), which describes Kreuger's personality quirks Greene might have used to vivify his Krogh. (Sources: Greene, *Ways of Escape,* 39; Watts, 31)

KRUEGER, GENERAL (*Doctor Fischer of Geneva*). He is properly ranked divisionnaire, i.e., a high-ranking officer in the Swiss army, but is courteously called a general. He has never seen combat but postures, showing ramrod erectness, conqueror's nose, fierce moustache. A Toad, Krueger sometimes selects wines for Doctor Fischer's parties. Fischer reminds Krueger that he married money, wasn't content when his wife died and left him wealthy, but remained greedy. Krueger displays both cowardice and humility by refusing to take a crack at Fischer's bomb party and then weeping.

Haim Gordon inaccurately generalizes when he says that "the greedy Toads who participate in Dr. Fischer's bomb party ... act with false courage when they pull the string [tape] that they believe will either blow them up or present them with a check." Mrs. Montgomery, Deane, and death-seeking Jones all show courage viz-a-viz odds morphing from good to so-so to worse. Even Krueger, a guest who participates in the bomb party though not the tape-pulling, shows genuine courage, not "false," when he admits he was never in combat. (Source: Gordon, 70)

KRUEGER, MADAME (*Doctor Fischer of Geneva*). She was General Krueger's wealthy wife, who died.

KRUGER (*Orient Express*). Mabel Warren remembers Kruger's Belgrade beer garden. So does Czinner, who also notes that the region has been turned into apartments.

KURTZ (*The Name of Action*). He is a small, misshapen revolutionary banished from Trier by Demassener. Exiled in London, Kurtz eagerly continues the republican revolt. When he meets Chant at Mrs. Meadmore's London house, Kurtz persuades him to go to Trier and try to finance Demassener's downfall.

KURTZ (*The Third Man*). He is an Austrian living in Vienna's Russian zone. He occasionally disguises himself by wearing a toupée. Kurtz phones Martins to tell him he witnessed Martins's friend Harry Lime's being struck and killed by the car. His story puzzles Martins. After Martins sees Harry, he seeks Kurtz in the Russian zone and orders him to tell Harry to meet him at the Prater wheel.

KUSACK (*This Gun for Hire*). He is Mather's superior at Scotland Yard. Mather is polite to and works harder than Kusack.

L. (*The Confidential Agent*). He is a confidential agent, opposed to D. in their country's civil war. Both L. and D. are in London to purchase coal from Benditch. D. regards L. as an effete aristocrat, the result of half a millenium of inbreeding. L. orders his chauffeur to slug D., closes the deal for coal after D. fails with Benditch and his partners, promises K. a professorship back home in the university where he is allegedly the chancellor, and probably is in league with Captain Currie to have D. seized at the Lido, where Forbes's men effect D.'s escape.

THE LABYRINTHINE WAYS see ***THE POWER AND THE GLORY***

LAGERSON (*England Made Me*). He works as a publicity writer for Krogh. Farrant callously talks Lagerson into becoming discontent and possibly subversive.

LAKER (*The Human Factor*). This ginger-haired ex-guardsman covers Arab republics in North Africa for MI6 and regards himself as one of the few military men among London's MI6 and MI5 agents.

LAMINAH, CORPORAL (*The Heart of the Matter*). He is a native policeman who, according to Miss Wilberforce, is her landlady's brother. He later appears when Scobie finds Ali's body.

Greene first visited Freetown, Sierra Leone, with his cousin Barbara Greene (from January 1935), on their way to Liberia. A lad who was one of several black servants hired to help the Greenes was named Laminah. When Greene was ordered to Sierra Leone by British Intelligence (1941), he looked up Laminah, then an adult, and found that the war had enabled him to prosper. (Source: Sherry I, 518)

LANCE (*This Gun for Hire*). He is the leader of the scout troops at St. Luke's. The vicar asks Lance to bring some lads to flatter Miss Maydew by asking her to sign their autograph books.

LANE ("The Basement Room"). He had an evidently important position with the British government in an African coastal country and evidently knows important governmental officials in London. Lane, now married, and his wife live in a Belgravia mansion with their son Philip, seven. The Baineses are their servants. The Lanes go on holiday and leave the Baineses in charge of Philip.

LANE (*The Heart of the Matter*). Harris reads in an *Downhamian* periodical that Lane praises F.J.K. for a skillful performance in *Patience* (by Gilbert and Sullivan).

LANE, MRS. ("The Basement Room"). She and her husband go on holiday and leave the Baineses, their servants, in charge of their son Philip.

LANE, PHILIP ("The Basement Room"). He is the bright, imaginative son of the Lanes, seven, and subject to unpleasant dreams. The Lanes live in a Belgravia mansion. Philip's parents go on a two-week holiday, leaving him to be cared for by their bickering servants, the Baineses, who live in the basement. For the first time, Philip can descend past the green baize door into the Baineses' quarters. At a nearby restaurant, Phil, as Baines calls him, happens to see Baines with his mistress, Emma. Baines beseeches Philip to keep mum. Mrs. Baines learns about Baines's so-called niece, and menacingly cajoles Master Philip to keep her knowledge of the affair their secret. These grown-up machinations combine with Philip's not only seeing Baines and Emma kissing, but also seeing Mrs. Baines's later fighting her husband and falling to her death, to propel Philip Lane into an escapist, useless, dilettantish adulthood, ending in his death 60 years later.

LASCOT-VILLIERS, THE COMTE DE (*The Comedians*). He may or may not exist. If real, he may be dead. He may have been Brown's mother's husband.

LASCOT-VILLIERS, THE COMTESSE YVETTE DE (*The Comedians*). She was Brown's mother and later employed this name. There may also have been a real Comte de Lascot-Villiers. An earlier husband or lover was presumably a man named Brown, hence young

Brown's father. She gave birth to Brown at Monte Carlo. She enrolled him in a Jesuit school there. She called herself Maggie Brown when she was working as a saleswoman for a dressmaker (1934). She abandoned Brown, evidently went to France, and was a member of the French resistance movement during World War II. She worked as the secretary of Dechaux, the owner of the Trianon, a Port-au-Prince hotel. For tax purposes, Dechaux put her name on the deed but then died in a car crash. She wrote Brown to come visit her, which he did in time to see her a final days, be impressed by her ultra-sensual love of life, meet her young black lover Marcel, and inherit the Trianon.

"THE LAST WORD" (1988). Short story. (Characters: the General, Pope John, General Megrim.)

1. The old man, in a small apartment with a monthly pension, has non-speaking neighbors, remembers only a flash, then darkness. He talks to a figure with a broken-off arm, on a crucifix. He will be taken to the airport on December 25, which is not Christmas Day. That holiday has been abolished. His book is confiscated by a stranger who says he's loyal to the General.

2. An officer at the airport lets him retain the book. The old man flies four hours on the General's well-appointed United World airline airplane, reads in the book he has virtually memorized, declines caviar and vodka. Its clinking glass jars a memory—of bowing strangers, a crack, darkness.

3. An officer whisks him by car to a hotel room and says the General will see him tomorrow. He asks if the general is General Megrim. No; he died almost 20 years ago. The officer tells the concierge the old man is the Pope. The concierge asks what the Pope is.

4. The old man unpacks the crucifix, sleeps on a "succulent mattress," awakens, and remembers dreaming of speaking uncomprehendingly to a contemptuous woman in an ever-shrinking barn and of saying "Pax" and "Love." A servant orders him to dress in garments provided—white surplice and cape, lent by the World Museum of Myths—reminds him he was once a priest, says he won't need the cross after seeing the General. The old man cuts himself shaving.

5. Taken to a large square, the old man is told that as a former head of state he is being honored. A gun salute reminds him of the cracking sound preceding his long darkness.

6. The General reveals this: General Megrim was wrong to try assassinating the old man, whose Church caused many wars; wars have ended; those soldiers, eventually unnecessary, preserve world peace; the old man is the last living Christian; he is Pope John; he and the General are similarly ambitious; the Pope was shot at for conducting an illegal Mass; the General's predecessors didn't want to martyr him; religions simply withered, Catholicism being last and having been first to follow that Jewish carpenter; 20 years of solitude have passed for Pope John, who now has zero followers; Christianity and Communism are both dead. The old man says he has had a friend, with a broken arm, to talk to. Calling such nonsense mythic, the General exposes a weapon. Pope John expresses joy to be sent not into death's darkness but into "the light." The General pours two glasses of wine. Pope John raises his, says "Corpus domini nostri," is shot dead. The General frighteningly wonders if what the Pope believed could be valid.

Greene told Leopoldo Duran that "The Last Word" had a historical basis. A story once circulated in the Vatican about Pope Pius XII's fear that while German troops were occupying Rome Adolph Hitler would have him arrested and taken to Germany. Greene's rendition has an evocative title. It makes one think of Christ's Last Supper, of the fictional Pope John's last words here, and, not least, of his having the last word over the General, who is spiritually challenged, at last, by the last of the last words—"nostri." (Source: Duran, 242)

THE LAST WORD AND OTHER STORIES (1990). Collection of 12 short stories, 11 of which were previously published. The title is poignant, since this book was the last by Greene to appear before his death.

LAURIE (*England Made Me*). He was Minty's uncle. Minty's Aunt Ella writes him about Laurie's death.

LAURIN (*England Made Me*). He is a director in Krogh's company. Laurin, cowardly, weak, and untrustworthy, is ill at Saltsjöbaden.

LAWRENCE ("Men at Work"). R. King, chairman of the Books Divisions in the Ministry of Information, reports that Lawrence, a novelist, wrote *Parson's Pleasure,* which King calls naughty. Therefore King is deemed competent to advise the Book Committee, in the Ministry, about India. (Is Greene thinking of naughty D. H. Lawrence here?)

LEADBETTER, HENRY (*Our Man in Havana*) see **WORMOLD, JAMES**

LEADBITTER, GENERAL ("Proof Positive"). He is a member of the Psychical Society before which Major Weaver lectures. Weaver's overpoweringly lily-scented pocket handkerchief causes Leadbitter to want to smoke for relief, but Weaver tells him not to.

LEHR (*The Power and the Glory*). He is a German-American who left Germany to avoid military conscription. He and his unmarried sister have a farm home in a relatively safe Mexican state. Although he is a Lutheran and disapproves of inessential Catholic luxuries, Lehr welcomes the whisky priest and allows him to say Mass to Mexicans and Indians in his barn. Lehr's mention of "that scoundrel [Herbert] Hoover" and "Hiram Long," probably meaning Huey Long (1893–1935), helps to date the action of the novel.

In *The Lawless Roads: A Mexican Journey,* Greene writes about a Mer W, Herr R. and Fru R, who befriended him when he was riding sick on a mule, much the way the Lehrs were hospitable to the priest. (Source: Greene, *The Lawless Roads,* 150–62)

LEHR, MISS (*The Power and the Glory*). Formerly a hotel manager, probably in Pittsburgh, she has lived comfortably with her brother after he was widowered. She is kind to the whisky priest.

LEHR, MRS. (*The Power and the Glory*). She was the wife of the German-American living in Mexico. Lehr unemotionally tells the whisky priest that she is buried in his paddock.

LENÔTRE (*The Tenth Man*). This old clerk is one of the 30 prisoners held as hostages by the Germans. He is the eighth man to draw a slip. When he draws one marked to indicate he is to be shot, he starts writing a letter to his daughter.

LEOPOLDO, FATHER (*Monsignor Quixote*). He is the ecclesiastical head of the Spanish Trappist monastery at Osera, near Orense. When Father Quixote is hurt in the car accident outside his church, Father Leopoldo forbids the Guardia from taking him away, tends to him graciously, and gives sanctuary to Zancas. Father Leopoldo follows the thoughts of Descartes that it is hard to distinguish fact from fiction, debates with Professor Pilbeam on the subject, and proves his preference by giving credence to Quixote's claim that Don Quixote was his ancestor. Leopoldo is a bad cook.

Greene named this superb priest Leopoldo out of respect for his closest priest-friend, Father Leopoldo Duran, who devotes a chapter in his book about Greene to the Cistercian Abbey of Osera and Greene's enthralled response to it during several stays there. The imposing monastery is featured in Paul Hogarth's book illustrating Greene's novels. (Sources: Duran, 318–26; Hogarth, 163)

LEVER ("A Chance for Mr. Lever"). He lives in Eastbourne, England, and is an experienced salesman of heavy machinery. He invests his moderate savings in Lucas's business in London, goes to Liberia to find Davidson, a gold digger, and get him to buy digging machinery. After an ill-fated trek with native helpers, Lever finds Davidson dying and soon dead of yellow fever. Lever, who has written his wife Emily back home, forges papers indicating Davidson's agreement to purchase, tears up his letter thinking he will beat it home, but after three delirious days trying to return to civilization, dies.

The name "Lever" is both appropriate, since Lever sells machinery, and ironic, since in Africa the poor fellow ultimately lacks leverage.

LEVER, EMILY ("A Chance for Mr. Lever"). She is Lever's sick wife in Eastbourne, London. He writes solicitously to her from Liberia, where he is trying to sell digging equipment. In his fatal fever-induced delirium, he imagines success and their vacationing in Switzerland and on the Riviera.

LEWIS, F. ("Men at Work"). He is a member of the Book Committee in the Ministry of Information. During World War I he fought at Gallipoli. When the committee meets, he dozes. Miss Manners mentions B.L. and F.L.; so B.L. could be Lewis.

LI, DR. (*The Confidential Agent*). He is a professor from Siam's Chulalankarana University. He is a conscientious student of Entrenationo at Dr. Bellows's Entrenationo Language Centre in London.

LIBERAL, THE (*The Confidential Agent*). He is a liberal cabinet member in D.'s country. D. suspects him of informing on D. to L., D.'s rival agent, since only five cabinet members were privy to D.'s coal-buying mission.

LIEUTENANT, THE (*The Power and the Glory*). He is the complexly ruthless, unemotional police officer whose deprived childhood causes him to hate wealth, social injustice, and Catholicism. He pursues and captures the whisky priest, jails him, but offers him illegal brandy and the illegal services of Padre José, who declines. Next morning, the lieutenant has the whisky priest shot and calmly delivers the coup de grace.

George M. A. Gaston regards the lieutenant as "a secular counterpart of the priest" and also "a mystic," but one who encounters only vacancy, since he regards the priest's loyalty to the Church as meaningless albeit admirable. Gaston continues: The lieutenant devotes his life to what he regards as social, political, atheistic justice; but since "his idealistic hope depends ultimately on imperfect men, it is ... doomed." Michael Shelden notes that "[i]n the end he [the lieutenant] is neither good enough to spare the priest, nor evil enough to enjoy his death." Michael W. Higgins comments that "at the novel's end the lieutenant, like Golgotha's centurion, is not quite the same, for he has been shaken by what he has witnessed and his righteous certitude, shattered." To illustrate Greene's frequent use of parallelism, Peter Erlebach notes "the antithesis of [whisky] priest and lieutenant" and continues by saying "[t]he lieutenant has all the features of a conscientious priest with the exception of the love of man." (Sources: Erlebach, 25; Gaston, 33, 33–34; Higgins, 14; Shelden, 267–68)

"THE LIEUTENANT DIED LAST" (1940). (Full title: "The Lieutenant Died Last: An Unrecorded Victory in 1940.") Short story. (Characters: Major Barlow, Brewitt, Brewitt, Mrs. Brewitt, Lord Drew, Driver, Mrs. Margesson, Bill Purves, the Vicar.)

Potter is a village in England's Metroland, isolated but important to commerce and communication north of London. Spring afternoon (1940). Some German parachutists land, cut telephone and telegraph wires, and herd the locals into Brewitt's pub, the Black Boar. When Brewitt's son, 16, tries to escape, three Germans wound and capture him. Bill Purves, a poacher whose activities are interrupted, watches the Germans from gorse near Lord Drew's grounds, sees several soldiers near railroad lines near a gravel pit, chuckles in anticipation of fun, shoots two with his old Mauser rifle, a relic from his 1914–1918 service. Fired on, he moves, counts four Germans with rifles, two more unarmed up the line with an explosives box plus a guard, and a lieutenant with his revolver. Purves circles through a trench, and shoots but only wounds another soldier. The lieutenant barks an order. Two men respond. Purves kills them. The lieutenant moves to safely. The guard wounds Purves in the shoulder. The explosives men grab their rifles. A goods engine puffs by, eclipsing Purves, who finds concealment behind a gravel truck, sees in waning light the men opening their box, fires, and it explodes. A massacre. The mangled lieutenant shouts to be killed. Without rifle bullets left, Purves accommodates the German with his own revolver. In the lieutenant's wallet Purves finds the photo of a baby on a hearthrug. While the villagers mop up, Purves enters the Black Boar, accepts the surrender of the wounded Germans, and is let off with a caution for evidence of his poaching—two rabbits in his pockets. Purves, though still poaching, became a temporary celebrity, telling his story for tips. But he kept that baby picture all to himself. Seeing it made him feel bad, without knowing why.

Greene praises the German soldiers for "humanely" shooting young Brewitt non-fatally but says Purves, the old British combat veteran, is incapable of understanding why looking at the picture of the dead German's baby makes him uneasy. In Greene's opinion, were Nazi soldiers regularly more warm-hearted than callous old Brits?

In *A World of My Own,* Greene mentions several dreams he had that are germaine to "The Lieutenant Died Last." Gene D. Phillips and Quentin Falk report that the story was the basis of a British movie entitled *Went the Day Well?* (1942; American title, *Forty-Eight Hours*). Phillips adds that the title of the movie derives from the epigraph that opens it:

> Went the day well?
> We died and never knew.
> But well or ill,
> Freedom, we died for you.

The movie was produced by Alberto Cavalcanti, a Brazilian friend of Greene, who says in *The Last Word* that he "regret[ted] never having seen it," owing to his being on a wartime assignment "out of England [in West Africa] ... when it was shown." Although Anthony Mockler calls "The Lieutenant Died Last" "one of Greene's most moving short stories," his plot summary contains four major errors. Mockler does discuss *Went the Day Well?* expertly, concluding that it "is still stirring to this very day." (Sources: Falk, 26, 207–08; Greene, *The Last Word,* vii; Greene, *A World of My Own,* 39–42; Mockler, 169–70, 202; Parkinson, xxxv, 692; Phillips, 21)

LIME, HARRY (*The Third Man*). Stocky, broad-shouldered, hunched, and paunchy, he is a heartless criminal in Vienna allegedly for the purpose of helping an international-refugee program. He invites Rollo Martins, his idolizer from their schooldays together, to Vienna to write about refugees. Harry's current crime involves stealing penicillin, diluting it, and selling it on the black market. Its use causes sickness, insanity, and death, especially among children. When things got hot, Harry faked his death by car accident, aided by Kurtz and Cooler. Martins discovers Harry is alive, meets with him, is cavalierly handled, and is even told he can have Harry's ex-mistress Anna Schmidt. Aware of Harry's depravity, Martins cooperates with Colonel Calloway, participates in tracking Harry in Vienna's sewer system, and kills him.

In his book illustrating Greene's fiction, Paul Hogarth includes a watercolor of Vienna's Central Cemetery, where Lime was "buried." In naming Lime, Greene says he "wanted ... a name natural and yet disagreeable, and to me 'Lime' represented the quick-lime in which murderers are said to be buried." The word surely first brings to mind the wince of bitter fruit. Martins at the bar would do more than wince if he saw a hairy lime in his drink. Orson Welles immortalized Harry Lime in the movie *The Third Man* (1949). (Sources: Greene, *Ways of Escape,* 244; Hogarth, 81)

"LIMITED EDITION" (1948). Short story. (Characters: None named.)

Michael Shelden discusses "Limited Edition," an unpublished pornographic short story by Greene about a man who sits next to a pretty woman in a movie theater and later in a railroad car, caresses her, licks his finger, excites her, and thus initiates their friendship. (Source: Shelden, 364–65)

LINTZ, SEBASTIAN (*The Name of Action*). He is a sparsely bearded, bespectacled shoemaker whose shop is across the street from the Jesuit Seminary in Trier. Kurtz gives Chant old Lintz's address, enabling him to meet Lintz and be introduced to Kapper and Torner, would-be revolutionaries.

LITTLE DWARF DOODOO (*Our Man in Havana*). He or she is a character in Milly Wormold's cereal-box advertisement. The tiny creature scares a rat by pretending to be a cat.

"A LITTLE PLACE OFF THE EDGEWARE ROAD" (1939). Short story. (Characters: Augustus, Craven, Lucius, Pompilia.)

One rainy summer day Craven walks along the Park, past the Marble Arch, onto Edgeware Road. He has dreamed thrice about a honeycombed cemetery of undecayed bodies "ready to rise again"—warts, erupting boils, and all. Craven is so poor he can buy lust but not love, and has a body so unhealthy that he prays against its resurrection. He enters a dingy theater on Culpar Road showing a silent movie to a sparse audience. Subtitles concern Augustus betraying Pompilia, Roman centurion named Lucius, his death-defying girlfriend. A little man with a wet beard brushes past Craven and sits beside him. The man's bubbling speech concerning coincidence, blood, murder, and

£50 seems so incomprehensible that Craven feels comparatively sane after all. The man puts a sticky hand on Craven's hands, blurts "Bayswater Tragedy," "Cullen Mews," answers Craven furtively, exits. The film breaks. Lights come on. Craven checks his smeared hands, recalls reading about a Cullen Mews murder, alerts the police by telephone, and learns that, yes, there was a murder there, the killer is in custody, but the victim — his neck cut with a bread knife — has disappeared. Craven wonders why such things happen to him, tells himself it was all a dream, then checks his blood-besprinkled face in the phone-booth mirror. Even as he screams that he won't go mad but is sane, a crowd gathers and a policeman arrives.

Richard Kelly says this story presents Greene's "ultimate ... nightmare, the immortalization of the human body with all of its disgusting defects." "A Little Place off the Edgeware Road" was the subject of a 1976 television production. *See Shades of Greene.* (Sources: Falk, 215; Kelly, 31)

LIZ ("A Discovery in the Woods"). She is Pete's timid friend, seven. Liz accompanies Pete and three other boys exploring the woods beyond Bottom. She makes a pannier of her skirt to hold blackberries they pick. When they find a tall, straight skeleton in the ruined boat, she sits in its lap and laments her dwarfism.

Greene concentrates excessively on details of Liz's anatomy. A. A. DeVitis contends that Liz represents "intuition and the promise of beauty"; Pete, "the future." (Source: DeVitis, 177)

LIZA (*The Captain and the Enemy*). She is the Captain's girlfriend. Liza lives in a flat in Camden Town, London. The two have a liking-loving relationship. Its dynamics puzzle and challenge Jim Baxter. When the Captain gives Jim to Liza as a surrogate son, she is about 24. The Captain provides for Liza and Jim, and she nurtures Jim until he tires of the relationship, leaves, and becomes a journalist. She is hit by a car and is hospitalized. Jim visits her. When she dies, Jim takes money the Captain sent for her to join him in Panama and goes there himself. She leaves the Captain a letter expressing her love.

LODER (*The Heart of the Matter*). He is the dour Scottish chief engineer of the vessel the German submarine torpedoed. Loder carefully reports their lagging behind the fleet with engine trouble, attack details, events during nearly two months since the sinking, and the casualties. Then Loder collapses.

Greene memorably depicts this minor character as self-sacrificial, honest, thorough, and with a well-rendered accent. By contrast, the French officer, also on the scene, is curt, cold, and Vichy.

LOEWENSTEIN (*England Made Me*). While falling asleep at one point, Kate Farrant names Whitaker and Loewenstein as made by God when He made the lamb. Kate may thus be regarding the two as investors, gentle or rapacious, in Krogh's shaky stock. However, "löwe" is "Lion" in German.

LOLA ("The Innocent"). She is the narrator's casual overnight date.

LOPEZ (*The Honorary Consul*). He is a banker whose wife is Plarr's last mistress.

LOPEZ (*Our Man in Havana*). He has been Wormold's sullen assistant in the vacuum-cleaner store for 10 years. He mispronounces the name Wormold in several different ways. Wormold makes him one of his fictitious agents.

LOPEZ (*The Power and the Glory*). He was a ticket agent whom the whisky priest sought help from to escape aboard the *General Obregon*. However, Tench tells him Lopez was executed weeks ago.

LOPEZ, SEÑORA (*The Honorary Consul*). She is a banker's wife and Plarr's last mistress.

LORD (*The Human Factor*). When Daintry sees beer at Hargreaves's lunch table after the bird shoot, he recalls with distaste that Lord was "boyish" for serving ginger beer.

"THE LORD KNOWS" (1925). Short story. (Characters: None named.)

A cynic and a drunk try to disillusion an innocent young man by suggesting that his fiancée isn't a virgin. The drunk illustrates his point by seducing a delicate spider to come into his hand by putting whisky on a finger. (Source: Kelly, 14–15)

LOSER TAKES ALL (1955). Novel. (Characters: Arnold, Bertram, Bird's Nest, Sir Walter Blixon, A. N. Bowles, Miss Bullen, Cary, Philippe Chantier, Celia Charteris, Dirty, Herbert Dreuther, Madame Dupont, Aunt Marion, Naismith, Ramage, M. Tissand, Truefitt, the Vicar.)

Part One: 1. The narrator, Bertram, 40, and Cary, his fiancée (20), are talking (in the Monte Carlo hotel lounge). She sees an equestrian statue, rubs the horse's knee for luck, and tells Bertram he's about to marry a superstitious woman. He hopes they have luck at the tables.

2. In their talk that evening, Bertram reminds Cary of various things. He was married 15 years before. When his wife ran away, he took a friend named Ramage to dinner and champagne, then slept well, relieved. Two weeks ago, Bertram's luck changed. Working for five dull years as an assistant accountant in London (for a firm called Sitra), he planned a simple wedding and a Bournemouth honeymoon. But his rich old boss, Herbert Dreuther, to whom he had never spoken, summoned him to his lofty office.

3. Dreuther entertains ritzy guests on his yacht (the *Seagull*), is opposed inside the firm by jealous Sir Walter Blixon, knighted, it was said, only after Dreuther refused the honor himself.

4. Bertram entered, timidly. Present were Dreuther; feisty Blixon; Blixon's friend Naismith; Arnold, chief accountant, who was Bertram's supervisor; and Miss Bullen, Dreuther's secretary. An accounting error caused consternation. Blixon and Naismith huffily left for lunch. Bertram, known for passionate mathematical brilliance, solved the matter by rightly blaming an out-of-date computer for confusing "2" and "7." Elated, Dreuther quizzed Bertram, learned of his wedding plans, ordered him instead to get to Nice with his fiancée, board Dreuther's yacht with him there, and wed in Monte Carlo. Miss Bullen would handle details and even schedule their civil wedding — 30th, 4:00 p.m.

5. Bertram told Cary about the change of plans. Initially objecting, she brightened when they saw an ugly wedding bunch emerge from a hideous London church. Two weeks later, the two are in the Monte Carlo, awaiting Dreuther, not yet here.

6. Bertram recalls their arrival. Miss Bullen booked them into two rooms, a sitting room between, all with balconies. He and Cary hadn't ever slept together. She gave mixed signals: I'm tired. Why two rooms? I could sleep in sitting room. See double beds. They watched gamblers in the Casino's small-stakes *cuisine,* determined not to buck the bank by silly systems. When Cary sympathized with a gambler, handsome but wan and hungry, Bertram seemed jealous. They argued, stormed into separate rooms, but soon conversed from separate balconies. After more mixed signals, they wound up in no bed or beds but innocently asleep on the sitting-room balcony floor.

7. After breakfast they taxi to a government building, check their marriage date and time, observe ultra-serious gamblers at the Casino, and try their luck. Cary bets on a number indicating her age and loses. Bertram bets on it, twice backs, and wins, jokes about buying one of the many systems advertised to guarantee winning, and looks vainly for Dreuther's *Seagull*. Low on money, they change to one room. They see a deaf old gambler (A. N. Bowles), wheeled by a nurse. Cary looks superstitiously for signs signaling their fate. They return to the government building and are duly married.

8. No word from Dreuther. Bertram and Cary lose 2,000 francs at the Casino. Next morning, still no *Seagull*. They see Bowles again. He owns enough shares in Sitra which if sold to Blixon would damage Dreuther. Bowles is wheeled to the gambling tables. Bertram recalls Pascal's sensible wager favoring the existence of God, figures he might gamble on a system of his devising, which, like God, just might exist. They see a woman they call Bird's Nest because of her hair-do. She touches up big winners for 200-franc chips, bets half, saves half, and usually concludes the evening ahead. Cary can't get Bertram to borrow from Bowles — too sharp and stingy, says Bertram, who thinks he can win by reducing losses and increasing gains. Cary tries Bird's Nest's strategy, unavailingly. The hungry young man gives her 100 francs, all he can spare. She wins 500. Bertram is jealous again.

9. Three days. Cheap meals. Only 5,000 francs left. Having developed his system, Bertram takes 1,000, bets, loses, then sees his numbers rising. It's a matter of having sufficient capital. A porter asks him to report to the manager, who speaks so tortuously that Bertram blurts that he and Cary are broke. To which the hotelier says they like their client Dreuther so much that here's a 250,000-franc loan.

Bertram and Cary drive a rented car to Peille, a mountain village, enjoy a meal, but argue when he insists on showing how his gambling system works back at the Casino's *Salle Privée*. He loses all but 1,000. She leaves. Later he follows, crying. She hugs him, says she doesn't care. But, he gloats, he won five million francs.

Part Two: 1. Chauffeured car, makeover for Cary, vintage wine, beach bungalow, winnings to nine million. Bertam wants Cary not to sit at his elbow but go shop. She sarcastically hopes he'll retire from this "work" so they can be together more. Fifteen million. Bertram spoils the cocktail hour by griping about his Martini, then spoils the dinner by trying to order for Cary. She wants roll and coffee, volubly longs for when they were poor, generous, and happy, watches him at his *estragon* and caviar, pleads a headache. They were going to the ballet; he goes, alone. Though tempted to surrender to Cary's request to fly away, he returns to the Casino, surprises his audience by losing in accord with his system. To bedroom. No Cary. At 2:30 a.m. she returns, says she and that hungry gambler, Philippe Chantier by name, went walking and talking. She gives details of Philippe's background, says she's dining with him tomorrow. So Bertram lies he's to dine with a "Madame Dupont" he saw winning at baccarat.

2. Back at the tables. Thinking a certain beauty is Bertram's new love, Cary is off with Philippe again. Controlling £15,000, Bertram loses more, on purpose. Bowles, also losing badly, asks Bertram to lend him five million francs. Refusing, Bertram brilliantly offers to buy Bowles's shares in Sitra for fifteen million francs, handy in his hotel safe box. The two boast of their infallible gambling systems, challenge each other regarding loans, share sales, options. Bowles finally bets anticipated winnings against an option, signed and witnessed, on his shares.

3. Bertram savors thoughts of pitting Dreuther and Blixon against one another. He would tell Cary, but she's off with Philippe. Having no Madame Dupont, Bertram settles on Bird's Nest as a willing dinner guest. She suggests the Orphée, a hideous place where Cary and Philippe by chance are also dining. Bertram listens as Cary, seeing him, complains to Philippe about her husband. Bertram, pretending she's a stranger, loudly criticizes her for it. After paying for the dinner with Philippe, Cary leaves with him. Bird's Nest praises Bertram for chivalrously rebuking that young woman, pleads a tiny appetite, has only *langouste thermidor*. The two leave. Bertram finds Cary in bed studying French. Soon after saying Philippe proposed, Cary cries. Bertram gloats about his power to help or hurt Dreuther. But she prefers a poor husband to a rich gambler, predicts a callous, moneyed future for him, defends forgetful Dreuther, retires solo.

4. Alone mid-afternoon, Bertram gambles disheartedly, wins, arranges to pay Bowles for his lost options, and suddenly sees the *Seagull* in the harbor, and Dreuther, bewhiskered and with yachting cap, at the hotel bar. Nine days late. Dreuther doesn't remember Bertram until reminded of everything, blames his delay on engine trouble, offers to pay Bertram's expenses, and invites him to sail away tonight. In his room, Bertram finds a farewell letter from Cary to "Darling" saying they don't fit any more. He leaves his packed bags at the desk and formulates plans.

5. Bertram boards Dreuther's yacht. They drink and talk frankly. Bertram confides in Dreuther almost completely. Limitlessly ambitious, Dreuther mentions his four wives, says he doesn't like unsanitary cash but relishes things and power it buys, gently advises Bertram even though his advice may sound cynical, says Philippe's poverty appeals to Cary, and offers a plan.

Part Three: 1. Bertram returns to the Casino, changes his money to tokens, finds Cary and Philippe in a café, and bribes Philippe with some tokens to gamble further. Philippe departs. Cary cries, knowing Philippe is consumed by gambling. Bertram asks her to visit Dreuther's yacht for one celibate night and disembark at Genoa tomorrow, promises to discard his system and not gamble again, sees Bowles gambling, sees Philippe winning, and donates his last tokens.

2. Dreuther is a perfect yacht host for Bertram and also Cary, who retires early. Amid more drinking, Dreuther tells Bertram he'll promote him to chief accountant. Bertram approaches Cary's cabin. Unlocked. He tells her Dreuther told him how to act to get her back but says he hasn't told Dreuther what he did. He retrieved the money he left for Bowles, thus forfeiting the option, and gave all to Philippe, now probably broke. They are poor again but happy. He tears up his system notes and tosses them overboard.

Both in a *Collected Edition* introduction and in *Ways of Escape,* Greene says he wanted to destroy his reputation as always serious by attempting "an amusing, agreeably sentimental *novella.*" *Loser Takes All* is that, and often hilarious too, Bertram the narrator being such a goof. A. A. DeVitis notes that *Loser Takes All* "is important ... because it demonstrates that Greene can be lighthearted if he likes and can develop a theme that is primarily comic if he wants." Neil McEwan more seriously contends that Greene not only presents A. N. Bowles as an object of satire because he associates "gambling and capitalism," but also presents Dreuther as, though charming because of his "generosity and worldliness," still "dangerous to poorer people." William Cash rings a nice change on the title *Loser Takes All* by giving the title "Loser Takes Nothing" to his chapter on the worsening (1950–1951) of Greene's affair with Catherine Walston.* Paul Hogarth's watercolor of Monte Carlo's famous Casino is a beautiful part of his book illustrating Greene's most vivid fictive locales.

Loser Takes All was made into a movie (1956, adapted by Greene; American title, *Strike It Rich*), starring Robert Morley (as Dreuther) and Glynis Johns (Cary), and miscasting Rossano Brazzi (Bertram, but called Bertrand). Gene D. Phillips demonstrates that the inferior movie was uselessly beefed up into a "wide-screen ... 'travelogue'" by having the newlyweds enjoy a day in the French countryside. Neil Sinyard says Greene wanted Trevor Howard for Bertram and Orson Welles for Dreuther. Quentin Falk fully explains why Greene, and the reviewers, disliked the movie. James Scott, film director, did a remake of *Loser Takes All* (1989). (Sources: Cash, 205–31; DeVitis, 46; Falk, 5, 107, 120–24 passim; Greene, *Loser Takes All, Collected Edition,* 123; Greene, *Ways of Escape,* 224; Hogarth, 99; McEwan, 126; Phillips, 92; Sinyard, 150, 151, 158).

"THE LOTTERY TICKET" (1947). Short story. (Characters: The Chief of Police, the Governor, Henry Thriplow.)

Henry Thriplow, a well-to-do, timid London bachelor, about 40, regularly vacations where they aren't other tourists. Now in Vera Cruz, he buys a lottery ticket, boards a barge for a 40-hour sea trip to a backward Mexican state, and settles in a hotel. On the third day, a lottery-ticket chart reveals his number won 50,000 pesos (roughly £2,500). Ashamed of gaining amid such poverty, he goes to the bank and volunteers to be a local benefactor here. Endow a library, hospital, alms house? The manager takes him to the Governor and explains matters in rapid Spanish. Outside again, Thriplow, British liberal as he is, thinks some nearby soldiers could use better schooling. He asks the manager about an ill-clad girl leaving the Workers' and Peasants' Syndicate. "Religious," is the answer. They find the English-speaking Chief of Police playing billiards. He blandly persuades naive Thriplow that his gift will be used for non-political progress to oppose German-, Italian-, and Japanese-fomented rebellion and stem a reactionary movement seeking to reinstall the inquisitorial Church. Thriplow objects that he wants no political distress. The Chief offers "Señor Tipno" a marble seat in the plaza with his name inscribed as progress's friend — perhaps near the Presidencia. Thriplow responds modestly.

That evening Thriplow talks with his cautious hotel proprietor. Language limitations create difficulties. The gist: Governor's opponent in election made advances until unpaid policemen, indifferent to opponent's accusatory placards, received money to remove placards; opponent now being pursued. When Thriplow counters that Mexico is a democracy, the proprietor provides ironic hints in Spanish and French about the opponent's defamatory treachery and tells him where the opponent lives. Rushing there, Thriplow learns from the opponent's convent-bred daughter, who was the girl from the

Syndicate, that her father has been shot by liquored-up soldiers, and now he "knows ... all there is to know." Easing Thriplow's tortured conscience, she says he doesn't understand and asks for and receives money to get an out-of-state priest to bury her father. Thriplow leaves, experiences manifold hate — of lottery ticket, bank manager, Governor, Chief, dead opponent, new ideas. As Thriplow weeps for "the whole condition of human life," a passer-by mistakes him for a poor Mexican.

"The Lottery Ticket," written in 1938, remained unpublished for nine years. Greene delayed because his travelogue *The Lawless Roads: A Mexican Journey* (1939, U. S. title, *Another Mexico*) and especially because *The Power and the Glory* (1940) treated more fully and better what Richard Kelly describes as "seedy ... Mexican towns, ... vultures waiting for another death, ... roaches, ... dentist, the fat chief of police preaching social progress, and the themes of fatalism and betrayal." Greene also delayed publication of "The Lottery Ticket" because it is ineffective. Readers surely wonder why a rich, liberal Londoner would be so naive as, first, to go to and be bored in a backwater Mexican town and, second, to be hoodwinked by Spanish-spouting con artists. Greene has a narrator tell the story, so both he and Greene can get in some comments on fate. Twice the narrator suggests that fate, when it operates, seems to do so with malicious humor, as, for instance, with poor Thriplow. (Source: Kelly, 73)

LOUCHARD, PIERRE (*The Tenth Man*). Carosse mentions him as a character in a play, a seducer somehow loved by his victims. Carosse boasts of playing the role well, thus hinting to Chavel that he can sweep Thérèse Mangeot off her feet.

LOUISE (*The Comedians*). She is Captain Concasseur's favorite *putain* in Mère Catherine's brothel. He says he will "treat" Brown to her. Brown declines.

LOU-LOU ("May We Borrow Your Husband?"). She owns and operates a restaurant near the Antibes cathedral. Harris takes Poopy to lunch there.

LOULOU (*The Name of Action*). Chant dreamily recalls Remnant once asked him if he ever heard the delightful story about Loulou and Michael.

LOWNDES, B. ("Men at Work"). He is a member of the Book Committee in the Ministry of Information. Lowndes endorses R. King's suggestion to have the novelist Lawrence attend the next committee meeting, since he may know something about India.

Miss Manners mentions B.L. and F.L.; so F.L. may be Lowndes.

LOWNDES, MRS. (*The Captain and the Enemy*). She is a neighbor Liza criticizes for being a busybody. Liza thinks Mrs. Lowndes told the authorities Jim Baxter should attend school, not stay home.

LUCAS ("A Chance for Mr. Lever"). He heads a London firm manufacturing heavy machinery. He persuades Lever, an out-of-luck salesman, to risk his savings and go to Liberia to sell digging equipment to Davidson, a gold prospector there.

LUCIA ("Across the Bridge"). She is a bright American with whom the narrator discusses Calloway in the Mexican town across the bridge.

LUCIUS ("A Little Place off the Edgeware Road"). He is a Roman centurion in the silent movie Craven sees. Lucius has a brave girlfriend in a nightgown.

LUCY ("The Hint of an Explanation"). She is Father David's aunt. He remembers that her visiting his home with other relatives after Mass prevented any daylight meeting with Blacker.

LUCY (*The Man Within*). For three years, she has been Merriman's curvaceous mistress in Lewes. She has little trouble seducing Andrews at the White Hart inn. Afterwards, Andrews — given his divided nature — both reviles and excuses himself.

Arthur Calder-Marshall defines Lucy as "a very improbable vamp ... introduced ... to seduce the hero into doing his duty and justify the philosophic pattern" of the novel. (Source: Calder-Marshall, 373)

LUCY (*This Gun for Hire*). She is a thin, blonde dancer for Collier, who is directing *Aladdin*. Davis thinks he might like to take her to lunch but invites Ruby instead.

LUIGI (*The Comedians*). He is an Italian electrical engineer Brown knows slightly and sees when both are gambling at the casino.

LUIS (*The Power and the Glory*). Luis, 14, is a pious woman's son. She reads the story of the young martyr called Juan to Luis and her two daughters. Luis isn't impressed, nor does his melancholy father encourage his faith. Luis admires the armed lieutenant but after he executes the whisky priest spits at the lieutenant's revolver. Luis becomes sad that the heroic priest, and three politico-military heroes — Francisco Madero (1873–1913), Pancho Villa (c. 1877–1923), and Emiliano Zapata (c. 1879–1919) — are now dead. But that night a priest, secretly replacing the executed one, raps quietly at Luis's bedroom door.

LUIS (*Rumour at Nightfall*). He and a fellow Spaniard are at an inn table when Chase and Crane join them. Fat Luis wanted to marry Señora Monti's daughter Eulelia, purchased a bed in anticipation of success, but wouldn't accept her without a dowry.

LUKITCH (*Orient Express*). He is a clerk at the Subotica railroad station. Lukitch and another clerk play cards with Ninitch, a stupid soldier they cheat.

LULU (*The Human Factor*). She and Mimi have their names beside their flat-bells, which Castle notes as indicative of Old Compton Street evening action. (Are the two prostitutes?)

LUNARDI (*The Captain and the Enemy*). Jim Baxter finds a photograph of a man named Lunardi in Jim's room in Liza's basement flat. Lunardi is seen rising in a balloon from Richmond Park, where Jim once lived.

LUXEMBURG CONSUL (*Our Man in Havana*). He is a guest at the European Traders' Association banquet.

MABEL (*England Made Me*). Kate Farrant in conversation with her twin brother Anthony remembers Mabel as one of his several girlfriends.

MACDONALD, JAMES RAMSAY (*Travels with My Aunt*). Aunt Augusta tells Henry she once attended an important literary figure's funeral, also attended by Edward Carpenter, Dr. Havelock Ellis, [James] Ramsay MacDonald ([1866–1937] British statesman), E[dith]. Nesbit, [George] Bernard Shaw and his wife, and H. G. Wells.

MACDOUGALL (*Our Man in Havana*). He is a guest from Scotland at the European Traders' Association banquet. MacDougall tells Wormold he has taken over from McIntyre. Though harmless, MacDougall scares Wormold by offering him a drink from his flask.

MACDOUGALL, HENRY ("The Case for the Defence"). He testifies that he nearly ran Adams down with his car shortly after Mrs. Parker's murder.

MCINTYRE (*Our Man in Havana*). He is evidently a Scottish businessman. MacDougall tells Wormold he is has replaced McIntyre and is attending the European Traders' Association banquet as McIntyre's substitute.

MACLEAN, (DONALD) (*The Human Factor*). In conversation with Hargreaves and Percival, Daintry mentions Maclean and Burgess as Secret Service men from years ago. Later Percival calls Maclean, as he does Burgess, "an advanced alcoholic."

Donald Duart (Duard) Maclean (1913–1983) was a diplomat in the British Foreign Service, served in France and Egypt, was assigned to sensitive positions in Washington, D.C., tried to undermine the joint efforts of American, Canadian, and British atomic researchers, and gave his Soviet contact agents details about American cooperation with European countries to establish America's Marshall Plan (proposed [1947] by George Catlett Marshall [1880–1959]) to help rebuild post-war Europe. Warned by Kim Philby* that he was under suspicion, Maclean defected to Russia (1951) and was temporarily joined by members of his family through Swiss connections (1953), by which time the degree of his work for the Soviets was known. Greene was very friendly with Maclean.

MACLEOD, JOSEPH (*The Ministry of Fear*). He presents the 6:00 p.m. news on the radio. Rowe and Mrs. Purvis, his landlady, listen to it.

Michael Shelden discusses a friend of Greene's named Joseph Macleod; they knew each other during their three years together in Oxford. Macleod became a successful radio announcer. (Source: Shelden, 117–18, 337)

MACPHERSON (*Brighton Rock*). He is a Brighton bookie.

MACPHERSON (*This Gun for Hire*). Calkin while chatting with the superintendent mentions MacPherson in connection with gambling activity of a man named Baines.

MAGIOT, DR. (*The Comedians*). He is a tall, elderly, dignified, well-established heart specialist in Haiti. From almost the moment the two met, he became Brown's father figure and wise companion. Dr. Magiot told Brown he admired Brown's peppy mother. Magiot is a non-practicing Catholic but doesn't believe in Voodooism either. He does favor Marxism and supports the rebellious insurgents. Magiot helps Brown dispose of the body of Dr. Philipot, with whom he recalls studying anatomy in Paris. Magiot behaves so as to establish Brown's cover-up story, unused, after the two get Jones out of Luis Pineda's embassy. Probably for doing so Magiot is murdered by the Tontons Macoute.

In a *Collected Edition* introduction, Greene says Magiot is based on a former Minister of Health he met in Port-au-Prince. He might have fashioned Magiot's name with some letters of the last name of Paul Eugène Magloire, president of Haiti (1950–1957), whose coup François Duvalier opposed (1950) and whom Duvalier replaced (1957). Norman Sherry contends that intellectual aspects of Magiot are partly based on a friend of Greene named Dr. Lherisson, while Magiot's fine appearance was suggested to Greene by the Catholic cardinal of Bombay, with whom Greene once had tea (December 1963). Bernard Diederich, whom Greene knew in Haiti and the Dominican Republic, and Al Burt write of a Major Lherrisson, the pro-Duvalier commander of a garrison at Ouanaminthe, Haiti, who held a voodoo ceremony, spilled bull blood, and let his soldiers smear it on their faces to ward off rebels' bullets. Michael Shelden praises Magiot for being "portrayed as articulate, independent," but adds "he is more of a disembodied voice than a flesh-and-blood human being," and "probably the most boring character in the book." In *Getting to Know the General*, Greene mentions Diederich as a personal friend. (Sources: Diederich and Burt, 259; Greene, *The Comedians, Collected Edition*, vii; Greene, *Getting to Know the General*, 20–33 passim, 44, 132, 162–65 passim, 209–10; Shelden, 441; Sherry III, 341, 440)

MAIS (*Brighton Rock*). He is a rich brewer, pointed out by Crab to Cubitt at the Cosmopolitan.

MAISIE (*Brighton Rock*). She is a bony little waitress at Snow's. Rose works briefly with her. It seems odd that Greene named two inactive characters Mais and Maisie in one novel.

MAKIN (*The Heart of the Matter*). Scobie remembers this man was a missionary in Africa, with its unforgiving climate, and had to be sent to an asylum in Cheslehunt, England.

Greene may have derived the name Makin from Makeni, a town in Sierra Leone that he probably visited.

MALCOTT, MISS (*The Heart of the Matter*). She survived the torpedo attack on the vessel carrying Helen Rolt, among others. On shore at Pende, Miss Malcott, gray but stalwart, wants to proceed to Lagos (Portugal), where she will work for the Education Department. Scobie lets her have his place in the van returning to Freetown.

MALING ("Alas, Poor Maling"). Maling is the secretary of the Simcox Newsprint Company. His stomach rumbling ruins a tax-saving merger of the company and the Hythe Newsprint Company. You see, his tummy sounded an air-raid alarm but couldn't manage an all-clear follow-up.

MALLEA, EDUARTO (1923–). Argentinian novelist. *See* Montez.

MALLOCK, SIR WILLIAM (*The End of the Affair*). He is an old, respected insurance expert who advised [David] Lloyd George (1863–1945) in matters of National Insurance. Bendrix meets him at a dinner party at Henry and Sarah Miles's home. At Sarah's cremation, he glances disapprovingly at Bendrix.

MALLOWS (*This Gun for Hire*). He is a hard-working medical student, criticized by Fergusson for not joining in the school rag.

MANAGER, THE (*England Made Me*). In one of his reminiscences, Farrant recalls that the Manager wanted to see him, probably to fire him from some job.

MANAGER OF OTRACO, THE (*A Burnt-Out Case*). At Governor Guelle's party, this official and the Director of Public Works worry about Querry, who has just arrived. O.T.R.A.C.O. stands for Office de l'Exploitation de Transports Coloniaux (the Congolese transportation administration).

MANAGING EDITOR, THE (*The Quiet American*). He is Fowler's London editor. Fowler writes him from Saigon asking not to be transferred to London.

MANDER (*This Gun for Hire*). He is the treasurer at St. Luke's, hence is involved in the jumble sale.

MANDERS (*Brighton Rock*). He was evidently the headmaster at Lancaster College, from which Drewitt graduated.

MAN FRIDAY (*The Comedians*). In conversation with Brown, the British chargé calls the government driver assigned to Jones "his Man Friday."

MANGEOT, MADAME (*The Tenth Man*). She is Michel Mangeot's and Thérèse Mangeot's mother. The sick old woman is mountainous, sloppy, and wise; her wisdom, however, is to be doubted because of a concomitant "vacancy of ignorance." Her shopkeeping background renders her unable to accept the implications of the fact that through Michel's death she and Thérèse have inherited Chavel's fortune. She dislikes Chavel when he appears, as Charlot. Shortly after Carosse's arrival, she dies, attended by the village priest.

MANGEOT, MICHEL (*The Tenth Man*). He is a thin young prisoner, among the 30 prisoners held by the Germans as hostages. His nickname is Janvier. When the prisoners draw to see which three are to be executed, he is the 10th man to draw. His slip is fortunately unmarked. Chavel draws a marked one, which he exchanges with Janvier, who wants to die rich. In return Chavel bequeaths his fortune to Janvier's mother Madame Mangeot and his sister Thérèse Mangeot.

MANGEOT, THÉRÈSE (*The Tenth Man*). She is Madame Mangeot's daughter and Michel Mangeot's sister. Thérèse is young, slender, with a pleasantly shaped mouth but an enigmatic personality. She so dislikes inheriting Chavel's house and money at the cost of Michel's life that she tells Charlot (really Chavel) that she has thought of burning the house down, She focuses all of her thoughts on hating Chavel. Chavel delays proposing to her; Carosse does not. Chavel's unmasking both Carosse and himself, at a fatal cost, dissolves Thérèse's corrosive hate.

MANN (*The Name of Action*). He is the Cochem passport officer. He and Muller, the customs officer, board Weber's arms-laden barge. Mann accepts Chant's passport but wants to tarry and chat with him about Tottenham Court Road, in London, which Mann visited. His doing so delays but doesn't prevent Weber's bribing Muller.

MANN, RACHEL ("Murder for the Wrong Reason"). This white-faced brunette with impetuous lips was the ambitious actress in whom both Collinson and Mason were interested. She may have been the indirect cause of Collinson's murder.

MANNERS, MISS ("Men at Work" [1940]). She is Richard Skate's assistant. They work for the Book Committee in the Ministry of Information.

Doubtless by sheer coincidence, Judith Martin (b. 1938), the American writer of the popular *Washington Post* weekly column on etiquette, adopted the pen name Miss Manners.

"THE MAN WHO STOLE THE EIFFEL TOWER" (1956). Short story. (Characters: Chester, the Minister of Education.)

The narrator easily loaded the Eiffel Tower onto 102 trucks and reclined it in a field near Chantilly. Motorists courteously tolerated the traffic jam. A taxi driver took an American tourist named Chester and his girlfriend to the empty site. Chester called it a memorial. The driver complained he was disoriented by street-name changes. The narrator suggested he take his fares to the Tour d'Argent. Workers at the Eiffel Tower ignore its absence; they're paid anyway and simply frequented nearby happily busier cafés. The Tour d'Argent also enjoyed brisker trade. Returning the Tower required the narrator's staging diversions, including an oration delivered by a friend posing as the Minister of Education. The narrator was standing by the re-erected Tower when Chester and his girl were taxied there again, griping that, once more, they were shown the wrong attraction.

This ridiculous fantasy satirizes the ignorance of tourists, with a side swipe at taxi men and a blast at American speech patterns. Chester mangles English, when he is made to say "'Tsa," meaning "It is a" and "'Tsnot," meaning "It is not"; unaccountably, he speaks acceptable French. Chester's dippy girl is more interested in French food than in French landmarks.

MANUEL (*The Power and the Glory*). He is a youthful playmate of young Luis.

MANVILLE, LORD CHARLES ("When Greek Meets Greek"). When this aristocrat employed Lord Driver as a servant, Driver learned to raise his eyebrows like an aristocrat too.

THE MAN WITHIN (1929). (Characters: Andrews, Francis Andrews, Mrs. Andrews, Bill, Braddock, Mrs. Butler, Carlyon, Joe Collier, Druce, Farne, Garnet, Elizabeth Garnet, George, Hake, Cockney Harry, Thomas Hilliard, Jennings, Lucy, Sir Henry Merriman, Edward Parkin, Petty, Edward Rexall, Richard Tims.)

Part One. 1. Three years earlier, Francis Andrews, son of Andrews the late tough smuggler off the Sussex coast of England near Shoreham, with Carlyon and two other smugglers, evaded capture. In the process, they killed an officer and are being hunted. Andrews defines himself as self-divided — timorous bully outside, self-critic within. On a third dark February night Andrews, pursued by Carlyon for being an informer, finds refuge in a two-story cottage near Hassocks. Inside is a strange girl named Elizabeth, whose step-father Jennings has just died. His candle-lit body is there.

2. When Mrs. Butler, the servant woman, enters next morning, Elizabeth dishonestly introduces Andrews as her brother, home from sea.

3. The priest preaches over Jennings's corpse. The villagers follow the cart through mist to the cemetery. After the burial, Elizabeth, estranged from her thirsty neighbors, gets Andrews to disperse them. The two head toward her home. Angry at being unfed, he vacillates between needing comfort and fearing exposure. Andrews spies Carlyon, tall, low-browed like a monkey, in the foggy road, his back turned. A confederate whistles to Carlyon. Andrews retreats.

4. Andrews taps at Elizabeth's window. She thinks it's Jennings's spirit but admits Andrews. She serves him tea and bread. He jests at her religious feelings, says women can't understand men. She offers him Jennings's stocking, to replace his worn one. He feels half chivalrous, half lustful. Hearing Carlyon outside, Andrews scurries to the other room, spies through the keyhole, clutches his knife, and recalls the time Carlyon killed a crewmember for committing rape. Carlyon tells Elizabeth that he and his gang are cargo and whisky smugglers, killed a revenuer, escaped gaol, but that Andrews became a Judas to them, must be found, explain, and die. Elizabeth fences Carlyon's queries: Andrews rested here last night, went north, and her brother just left the house after tea, will be back. Carlyon warns her to avoid his rough world and remain in her peaceful one. She asks whether the two worlds are distinct. He leaves.

5. Andrews, emerging, decides not to be evasive, must gain comfort, will explain. His father was a cunning smuggler; abused Andrews and his mother; she died; his father put him in

a fine school in Devon, mainly to boast about him; his father died, was dumped at sea, left boat and savings to Carlyon; Carlyon took him into his smugglers' crew; but, distressed by his father's example, he turned cowardly, and finally betrayed the crew by an anonymous letter to the Customs. Elizabeth listens like a pale saint, invites him to stay and dispel her loneliness, and tells her story. When her father died, her mother obtained money from her family, kept the cottage, and admitted Jennings, a Customs-office employee, as a boarder. He bought the place for her mother to leave Elizabeth in financial comfort. After her mother died, when Elizabeth was about 11, he paid rent to her, stayed on, let her cook and clean for him, sent her to school in Shoreham, read his Bible sporadically, and took long walks. She chanced to read the parable of the unjust steward to him. Since he had skimmed smugglers' customs payments, its message relieved his conscience. When Elizabeth was about 18, she ran off, returned late, and he entered the unclothed girl's bedroom with a strap. She said she wouldn't be forced; she hinted for a year that his patience would be rewarded — until, self-disgust torturing him, he died. She half-regrets her innocence, suggests Andrews clear his conscience by informing at the Assizes in Lewes against the crew. Andrews says Carlyon alone would have such courage, feels the need of maternal-breast comfort, is goaded by Elizabeth, and says he'd prefer her loving arms to any court appearance. Still, he promises to go to Lewes and consider testifying. The two bed down, separately.

Part Two. 6. Andrews awakens, is reluctant to keep his promise, leaves his knife as a memento, feels briefly brave, and starts his 12-mile walk to Lewes by the downs rather than the risky road. Although he knows Elizabeth feels safe with her God, Andrews half-prefers a devil's protection. When he rationalizes that he can see Lewes and then depart, his "inner critic" calls him a coward. He enters Lewes in the cold evening. Proceeding to France would expose him to authorities and prevent his revisiting Elizabeth. At a raggedy inn a stranger orders him double brandies, lets him pay with his dwindling funds, and leaves. A stranger approaches; Andrews mentions the Assizes; they dispute about justice; and Andrews says the smugglers are murderers. The man calls himself Farne; Andrews introduces himself as Absalom. Getting drunk, he tries to sketch saintly Elizabeth. Farne invites him to the nearby White Hart hotel for food and rest.

7. Farne, a barrister, leads Andrews to a room, introduces him to Sir Henry Merriman, a superior barrister. Lucy, indifferent Sir Henry's lovely young mistress for three years, is there. Sir Henry asks if Andrews is Carlyon. Jolted, he identifies himself as Andrews. Sir Henry knows Andrews wrote the letter incriminating Carlyon. Lucy orders Andrews a steak. He feels relieved to be caught by others' initiative, dines, ogles Lucy. Henry tells her to retire, orders Andrews to testify against Carlyon tomorrow in court. When Farne opts for justice despite the danger of prejudiced juries, Henry says he prefers martial law for smugglers. Andrews balances dangerous honesty against returning to Elizabeth. Henry promises him a clerkship in London. Andrews swaggeringly follows luscious Lucy toward her room upstairs, desire's "prick" making him discount Elizabeth. After mutually encouraged tentative groping, Lucy promises to sleep with Andrews next night if he'll help Henry win his case tomorrow.

8. Rainy dawn. With much pomp, Sir Edward Parkin, Assizes justice, arrives. Andrews is embarrassed when marched into the witness room. Sir Henry tells the jury to use reason, then summarizes the case against the smugglers: Thomas Hilliard commanded several revenuers (February 10), ordered 10 smugglers disembarking from their *Good Chance* to surrender, was fired upon, captured six while three escaped, and found his agent Edward Rexall shot dead. Braddock, for the defense, tries to get Hilliard to admit he needed to bolster his reputation by a beach coup. Hilliard counters he acted on information from a letter, now missing. Braddock queries Bill, an old gauger, and mentions Richard Tims, a half-witted young arrested smuggler. Andrews is called to witness. His inner critic reminds him of his pact with Lucy. Knowing Elizabeth would be proud of his thoughtless bravery, he answers Henry's questions, fingers the accused (Druce, Hake, Richard Tims, and three others), says he wrote the letter, knew of the trap, hid on the beach; names Carlyon, Joe Collier, and Cockney Harry, all of whom escaped. He doesn't point

to Cockney Harry, sitting boldly in the gallery. To Braddock's questions, Andrews says for three years he was disrespected by the *Good Chance* crew, except for Carlyon. Andrews rants about his brave but hateful father and his own cowardice, says he escaped to the Hassocks. Braddock promises to prove Andrews stayed many days with a woman named Elizabeth, who called him her brother. In rebuttal, Andrews extols Elizabeth ecstatically.

While Andrews sleeps in the corridor, the trial drones on. Four prisoners read perjured statements prepared by their solicitors. Hake, the toughest smuggler, warns the jury about Judgment Day, swears he wasn't on the beach, says loony Tims shot Rexall for teasing him, promises to deal with that Judas (Andrews) and his woman. Tims is pronounced unfit to defend himself. Braddock parades effectively perjurious witnesses for the accused. Farne tells Sir Henry that Andrews proved useless. Mrs. Butler, brought by Braddock, completes the rout.

Sir Henry persuades the jury to remain, dinnerless like himself, to hear his professional summation and render a verdict that night. The prisoners are acquitted. The crowd rejoices. Farne says duty charges must be removed from spirits for justice to prevail. Andrews awakens, feels betrayed, is told by Henry to trade Sussex for London, is promised money tomorrow, is escorted by reluctant guards to the White Hart.

9. A waiter hands Andrews an invitation from Lucy, which he ponders in his room. Since his court action should satisfy Elizabeth, whom his heart loves, he feels entitled to a toss with Lucy, for whom he rationally lusts. Cockney Harry enters Andrews's room, thankful for not being fingered. He warns Andrews that Carlyon, Joe, and Hake plan to terrorize Elizabeth, while Carlyon also plans to kill Andrews. Rationalizing that Elizabeth is safe from chivalric Carlyon, Andrews enters Lucy's room, hesitates, is taunted, seems to see Elizabeth's face, succumbs. By morning he regrets having "wallowed," feels "dirtier," mentions suicide. Lucy discusses the inefficacy of conscience.

Andrews strides into the downs, afraid only of death, sad at forgetting his oft-repeated sinfulness, praises the quality of his dreams, thinks of Carlyon, and would like to embarrass that ape-faced, romantic, danger-loving hero. Andrews remembers when Carlyon — tough, sure, with a musical voice — reported to his school, said his father was shot dead, bragged he owned the *Good Chance,* got Andrews to join the crew only to be demeaned for not resembling his father. Observing Elizabeth's cottage, does Andrews feel love or fear? Are Carlyon, Hake, and Joe there? Should he escape? He opens the door, finds all empty, would happily see Elizabeth but for Lucy's having sullied him, prays, prepares a breakfast for two. Elizabeth appears, suffused in golden light.

Part Three. 10. Elizabeth tells Andrews she expected him, regrets asking him to go riskily to Lewes, admires him for leaving his knife, is his friend. He says this: He betrayed her with a harlot; the court knows Elizabeth sheltered him; she is unique; lust isn't love; Carlyon and others are coming; she must gather funds, go to London; he lacks courage to defend her. He silently asks his inner critic to inspire him. Silence answers. He hopes fear will eject him. No. She wins. He stays, strengthens the door, loads her gun, learns neighbors are too distant to help, expresses fear of death extinguishing him, envies her faith in God. She calls their predicament "fun," praises the non-devilish part of him that left the knife, tells him to emphasizes his goodness, gets him to declare he loved and loves her.

They embrace sans consummation in darkness, discuss their future, eternity, her faith, their imminent danger, fear and death, peace overcoming hate, her unaging laughter and trust of him. He summarizes his actions in Lewes. She says they must separate and meet in London, orders him to tidy the place, hears his quarrelsome response, goes shopping before Carlyon's expected twilight attack. He fears Jennings's interloping spirit. Elizabeth returns with news: Tims escaped; Cockney Harry was seen near Chichester; authorities seized the *Good Chance*; Carlyon is loose but pursued; the other smugglers were rearrested on new evidence. Andrews ponders heroic Carlyon's loss of ship, anger, need to exact "punishment." He won't "soil" Elizabeth until marriage, vows selfless devotion. They express their love, forgive each other for "this mess," embrace. Dusk descends like a veil. When he reiterates his cowardice, she recalls his recent bravery, glances outside, fiercely orders him to fetch water from the well past the trees, promises a kiss "soon."

11. Returning, Andrews spies Collier's bulk in the open door, runs off, is critical of Elizabeth for neither shouting a warning nor shooting Collier, feels trapped, sees a house ahead, tells the farmer there that smugglers have Elizabeth and he should rush to Shoreham and earn a reward for reporting them, borrows a horse and rides back. Tim is posted on the road, but Andrews hits him and rides on. Elizabeth's trust erases fear. Entering the cottage, he finds Carlyon downcast, Elizabeth dead, drooping like a doll. He prays she lives yet. Carlyon says Collier tortured her for information about Andrews, she stabbed herself with Andrews's knife, and Collier left. Andrews and Carlyon reconcile. Andrews momentously concludes that his father caused his beloved's death, but that since he inherited his father's spirit, which imbued him with lust and cowardice, he himself killed her. Why live 50 years alone? Ah, he plans differently, persuades Carlyon to escape. Andrews figures hate for Carlyon was a game, physical love for Elizabeth, a dream. Both his heart and his mind deny notions of "an immortality and a resurrection."

Footsteps grate outside. Andrews embraces dead Elizabeth. The authorities burst in. Andrews tells them Carlyon is gone, he killed the girl with his own knife, points to his name on it, is led away by the gloomy men. Andrews, self-divided no longer, becomes his inner critic. Anticipating darkness, and with peaceful curiosity, seeing a pale face before him — neither pitying nor disapproving, but shining wisely, sanely — Andrew silently retrieves his knife from an officer's belt.

Titles considered for *The Man Within* were *Dear Sanity, The Divided Heart, Flight,* and *One Within*. The title used is based on the epigraph from Sir Thomas Browne: "There's another man within me that's angry with me." *The Man Within* was an immediate success. Two editions were sold pre-publication, followed by six reprintings in six months. Some 13,000 copies were soon in print. Translations in Danish, Dutch, German, Norwegian, and Swedish quickly appeared. Greene describes Andrews's handwriting as resembling his own, with drooping capital letters. The name Carlyon resembles the middle name of his younger brother, Hugh (Carleton) Greene.* Norman Sherry notes added autobiographical elements: Andrew's devotion to Elizabeth reflects Greene's worship of Vivienne Dayrell-Browning (*see* Greene, Vivien); Vivien's spirituality helped stabilize Greene, as Elizabeth does Andrews; Andrews's shoddy sexual escapism echoes Greene's own before he married Vivienne (and later). Anthony Mockler says the novel may be read as Greene's "confession to Vivienne, and as a plea for her understanding and forgiveness."

Ronald G. Walker explains that of 20 novels by Greene he studied, *The Man Within* has the fewest narrative divisions, only 14, averaging just over 5,000 words each. Daphna Erdinast-Vulcan notes that *The Man Within* is Greene's first novel among several in which the protagonist is "stamped by a lost childhood." The best parts of the novel are the inn and court scenes, although even there Greene doesn't evoke a sense of the early 1800's, the time of the action. Greene says "*The Man Within* is very young and very sentimental. It has no meaning for me today, and I can see no reason for its success."

Right. It is weak in characterization, motivation, and plot. Andrews is ludicrous when he imagines himself as Hansel seeking his lost Gretel; when he finds her, as Elizabeth, he doesn't help her to flesh-and-blood adulthood. Robert Pendleton says that *The Man Within* "teeters uneasily between interior revelation and boys' smuggling adventure." David Lodge suggests that Greene usually handles the conventions of melodrama ironically, but cites *The Man Within* to object that "[s]ometimes the irony is not sufficiently subtle and controlled to transform the melodramatic stereotypes." This novel is best approached as a confused allegory, in which a maturing male's split psyche (cowardly/brave, lecherous/loving) is agitated by contrasting feminine influences (harlot/madonna), and in which good wins — incompletely.

Gene D. Phillips and Quentin Falk discuss the movie based on *The Man Within* (1947; U.S. title, *The Smugglers*), starring Michael Redgrave (as Richard Carlyon) and Richard Attenborough (Francis Andrews). (Sources: Erdinast-Vulcan, 16; Falk, 48–51, 209; Greene, *A Sort of Life,* 196; Lodge, 11; Mockler, 55; Pendleton, 56; Phillips, 103–06; Shelden, 115, 139, 372–75; Sherry I, 361, 365, 366; Walker, 224–25, 231)

MARCEL (*The Comedians*). He was a black waiter in the Trianon and also Brown's mother's obedient lover. She willed Marcel 33 shares of her hotel. When she died and Brown bought his shares, Marcel deliberately gambled the money away at the casino and hanged himself in Brown's mother's former bedroom.

In one of several keys to the title of the novel, Brown says that Marcel's killing himself for love may indicate that "he was no *comédien* after all," adding that "Death is a proof of sincerity." Norman Sherry summarizes newspaper accounts concerning several members of *Jeune Haiti*, an anti–Duvalier group, who were caught, tortured, and executed (1964); one of them was Marcel Numa, a black Haitian. (Source: Sherry III, 357–58)

MARCUS, SIR (*This Gun for Hire*). He is the wealthy Midland Steel owner, with headquarters in Nottwich. He has connections with the rich and politically powerful in England, France, central Europe, and the Middle East. Sir Marcus is old, frail, wispily bearded, and sick. He ordered Davis to hire Raven to kill the Czech pacifist, in order for the ensuing war to increase demand for his products. He tries to order Calkin to have Raven shot on sight. Aware of death's proximity, Sir Marcus calmly faces the fatal appearance of Raven in his office.

Sir Marcus is too caricatured to be totally credible. Greene says that "Sir Marcus ... is, of course, not Sir Basil [Zaharoff], but the family resemblance is plain." Sir Basil Zaharoff (1850-1936), an international armament contractor, was born in Turkey, supposedly of a Russian father and a Greek mother, and was associated with international steel, aviation, and oil companies. Unlike Sir Marcus, Sir Basil endowed university chairs in several countries. Malcolm J. Turnbull sees Sir Marcus as an example of the popular "interwar ... stereotype of the ... Jewish mastermind bent on attaining or maintaining control over international affairs." (Sources: Greene, *Ways of Escape*, 73; Turnbull, 9)

MARGARET ("Cheap in August"). So that Charlie Watson won't think his wife Mary is vacationing alone in Jamaica while he is in London, Mary fibs she's traveling with a fictitious companion she calls Margaret when writing Charlie.

MARGESSON, MRS. ("The Lieutenant Died Last"). She keeps Potter's post office and its only cash store. When the German lieutenant enters her store to tell her Potter is occupied by his men, she bravely tries to telephone the authorities but finds the line dead.

MARÍA (*The Honorary Consul*). She was a prostitute, from Córdoba, in Señora Sanchez's brothel. Fortnum respected her. She was stabbed to death.

MARÍA (*The Honorary Consul*). She is the house servant working for Charley Fortnum, then for Clara Fortnum, in his camp.

MARIA (*Our Man in Havana*). She is a fat actress at the Shanghai Theatre. Doubling as a prostitute, she offers to help Wormold when he attends the theatre performance seeking Teresa.

MARIA (*The Power and the Glory*). She is the mother of the whisky priest's child Brigitta. After seven years, he visits them briefly. Although Maria helps him escape from the lieutenant, she cannot admire him and says his execution would constitute a mock martyrdom.

MARIA (*Travels with My Aunt*). She is the daughter of the fat, meat-devouring customs officer. They are at the dinner party Augusta and Visconti host at Asunción.

MARIA ("Under the Garden"). She is Javitt's haggard, old-looking female companion. She is slovenly and balding, has hands spotted and twisted like a bird's claw, and speaks in squawks through a roofless mouth. Javitt has found her to be an accomplished tunnel digger and praises her so-called ugliness by saying she could have posed for modern painters, for example, the artist who once depicted a three-eyed woman. She frightens Wilditch. Javitt says her real name isn't Maria.

MARIE (*Our Man in Havana*). She is a French schoolmate of Milly Wormold. She enlightens Milly by telling her that true love is always a *coup de foudre*.

MARINA (*England Made Me*). This is the name of a character in Professor Hammersten's play.

MARION, AUNT (*Loser Takes All*). She is Cary's aunt, with whom she has lived since Cary's parents were killed in a German air raid on London. Cary is sad to disappoint Aunt Marion by marrying in Monte Carlo rather than London, as originally planned.

MARK (*Our Man in Havana*). He is Wormold's sister Mary's son. Wormold sends Mark postage stamps for his collection, forgetting that Mark started collecting when he was six, is now older than 17, and probably has discontinued collecting.

MARK, SIR (*Brighton Rock*). He is someone Lady Angeline looks at fondly in a romance Pinkie says he read.

MARLENE (*It's a Battlefield*). She works in the Battersea match factory, as one of 150 girls there.

MARLOWE (*Our Man in Havana*). Wormold informs Hasselbacher that Marlowe is hospitalized and can't attend the birthday party Wormold plans for his daughter Milly.

MARQUEZ (*Monsignor Quixote*). He is or was a Salamanca stockbroker who, according to Diego, Zancas's friend from student days in Salamanca, was both rich and pious. After Marquez and his fertile wife had five children, he was given some advice by Diego, then practiced *coitus interruptus* without conscience qualms by a system of having his butler supervene by signaling a guest's arrival, but was distressed anew when Diego introduced the warning that preplanned interruption isn't "unforeseen necessity."

Greene spends three pages thus over-satirizing Catholic moral niceties for comic relief in a novel 50 percent comic relief anyway.

MARQUIS (*The Ministry of Fear*). He owns a fish saloon and bravely shows his sign after an air raid.

MARSDYKE, MRS. (*The Power and the Glory*). She is Tench's mother-in-law, in England. Tench writes his long-absent wife, Sylvia Tench, in care of Mrs. Marsdyke.

MARTA (*The Honorary Consul*). She is Rivas's admiring, intelligent wife and loyal servant. Originally from an Asunción *barrio,* she cleans the hut occupied by Rivas's gang, cooks stew for them after they kidnapped Fortnum, and persuades Rivas, whom she always calls "Father," to conduct Mass on their final Sunday. She and Pablo evidently survive the gory finale.

MARTHA ("The Blessing"). She is a pro-Nazi German correspondent's wife, pudgy and "prehensile." The anti–Nazi reporters feel duty-bound to cuckold the correspondent, and she is indiscriminately happy to comply — on the present occasion with Collins in his hotel room.

MARTIN (*The Honorary Consul*). He is Sir Henry Belfrage's Consul. Belfrage says that, unlike Fortnum, "Old Martin" can't buy cars officially and then sell them.

MARTIN, POPEY ("The Hint of an Explanation") *see* **DAVID**

MARTÍNEZ, COLONEL (*The Captain and the Enemy*). He is an officer in the National Guard of Panama. His General (Omar Torrijos Herrera) orders him to keep tabs on the Captain, Quigly, and Jim, to prevent any incident that might delay or halt the signing of the Canal Treaty by Panamian and American authorities. Though short, tubby, and unmilitarily mild in appearance and mien, Martínez is anything but unmilitary. He finds Jim's memoirs and mistakenly thinks references to King Kong are code messages to the Captain.

Norman Sherry equates Greene's Colonel Martínez with real-life Colonel Boris Martínez, whom Sherry calls Torrijos's "affable and gracious sidekick." Martínez may not understand the message of King Kong, but Greene surely did. Once again, he demonstrates uncanny cleverness, in light of the everlasting appeal of this Beauty-and-the-Beast story, by making use of it in *The Captain and the Enemy*. Greene would surely have relished seeing the most recent movie remake of *King Kong* (Universal Pictures, 2005), especially because of its computer-generated images. (Sources: Pryce-Jones; Sherry III, 567)

MARTINEZ, SEÑOR ("An Appointment with the General"). He is the General's adviser and arranges particulars for Marie-Claire Duval to interview the General. She complains that Martinez, who has been chauffeuring her around the country, speaks only Spanish. So the General orders English-speaking Sergeant Gurdián to take over. The real-life model of Martínez is José Martínez, according to Leopoldo Duran. Greene was driven about in Panama by Professor José Martínez, a security-guard sergeant under Herrera Omar Torrijos Herrera (1929–1981) and nicknamed Chuchu. (Sources: Duran, 64–68; Greene, *Getting to Know the General*, 25 and passim)

MARTINS, ROLLO (*The Third Man*). He is a British author of cheap Westerns — pen name Buck Dexter. Martins, 35, is a long-legged, womanizing, heavy drinker. Harry Lime, his idol since their schooldays, invites him to Vienna to write about international refugees. When Martins arrives, he is told Harry was killed in a car accident. Attending the funeral, Martins meets Colonel Calloway, who is investigating Harry's criminal past. Martins soon meets Anna Schmidt, Harry's girlfriend. Crabbin mistakes Martins for British novelist Benjamin Dexter and invites him to lecture — disastrously — on the contemporary novel to Crabbin's literary group. Martins later sees Harry, alive and cocky. Martins arranges to meet Harry at the Prater wheel, is disgusted at his callousness, and cooperates with Calloway. They lure Harry into the open and follow him through Vienna's sewer system, where Harry kills Bates, one of Calloway's soldiers, and where Martins kills Harry.

Peter Wolfe comments on the name Rollo Martins: "Calm and lucid [Martins], rash and extravagant [Rollo], Martins becomes the forked inconsistency God and the Devil both use in Greene to carry out their wills." Why does Wolfe also think Martins displays a "faintly homosexual hero-worship of Lime"? For the movie version, Greene made Martins an American with a new first name, "Holly." Greene explains it came to him after he "looked through an anthology of bad American verse in search of a prename, and found Holl[e]y — Thomas Holl[e]y Chivers [1809–1858] had some renown in the nineteenth century." (Sources: Greene, *Carving a Statue*, 8; Wolfe, 124).

MARY (*Our Man in Havana*). She is Wormold's married sister, in Nottingham, England. Wormold writes Mary once a year, while he is touring. This year Wormold reminds her of their going to a bull fight in Madrid one winter. Mary has a son named Mark.

MASON (*The Honorary Consul*) *see* **FORTNUM, CHARLEY**

MASON (*The Human Factor*) *see* **FORTNUM**

MASON, DETECTIVE-INSPECTOR ("Murder for the Wrong Reason"). He was in love years ago with the actress Rachel Mann, in whom Collinson was more successfully interested. This was when Mason, then called Arthur Callum, was a struggling young medical student. After Mason, later a policeman and now a Scotland Yard. detective-inspector, finds Collinson murdered, he lets an ambitious though bumbling constable take credit for solving the mystery by leading him to understand this: Arthur Callum, a suspect, is Mason; Collinson had been blackmailing Callum-turned-Mason.

MASON, MRS. (*This Gun for Hire*). Alice mentioned her as a gossipy Soho neighbor.

MATHER (*This Gun for Hire*). He was James Mather's brother. The brother sought identity through belonging to and being disciplined by an organization. Failing to do so, he committed suicide by drowning.

MATHER, JAMES (*This Gun for Hire*). He is a doggedly competent Scotland Yard detective sergeant. Mather has been engaged for six months to Anne Crowder, who calls him Jimmy and loves him less than he loves her. Mather and Saunders pursue Raven from London to Nottwich, at first only because of his supposed theft of bank notes. Mather works with Nottwich policemen and learns Raven is a suspected assassin. While Mather tries to capture Raven by dangling from a painter's platform outside Sir Marcus's offices, Saunders kills Raven. Mather and Anne may be able to marry more quickly than otherwise because she received reward money for informing on Raven.

Mather seems to be too smart a detective to

be so uncertain of himself in matters of love, marriage, and doubts. Peter Wolfe links Mather the pursuer and Raven the pursued by ingeniously comparing their names. The first name of each is James. The last name of each repeats, in order, the vowels in James. The name Mather "begins with a nasal and ends with the letter *r*," while the name Raven begins with that letter and ends with a nasal." Wolfe adds that "the medial constant of each bisyllabic surname ... is a fricative." (Source: Wolfe, 60)

MATTHEWS, FLOSSY (*It's a Battlefield*). She was a rape-and-murder victim on Stretham Common. The Assistant Commissioner ponders the case while walking to his flat.

Although Michael Shelden objects to the fact that Flossy's murder remains unsolved, it is obvious that Greene wishes to show criminal detection to be often unendingly ongoing. Shelden also stretches minuscule lines in the novel to hint that Conrad Drover may have had something to do with Flossy's death. (Source: Shelden, 177, 179)

MAUD (*The End of the Affair*). She is Sarah Miles's maid. Alfred Parkis makes underhanded use of Maud during his search, on Bendrix's orders, for information about Sarah's alleged lover. After Sarah dies, Maud is understandably curt to Bendrix.

MAUD (*England Made Me*). She is a former girlfriend of Anthony Farrant. When he and his twin sister Kate are discussing his girlfriends, he mentions that Maud was nearer 40 than 30, was blonde and "overblown about the blouse," and gave him presents that he "popped" (i.e., pawned).

MAUDE, MR. (*The Ministry of Fear*). He is a guest at Mrs. Bellairs's séance. He displays a fawning interest in Frederick Newey. Neither man figures in later action.

MAVERICK ("Special Duties"). He is an agent whom Ferraro employs to buy pictures for him, sometimes at Christie's auction establishment.

MAVIS ("The Bear Fell Free"). Baron sees Mavis's hat on the hat stand at Earl's Court.

MAX (*Our Man in Havana*). He is the dachshund owned by the head waiter at the Nacional Hotel. Wormold deliberately spills the poisoned drink Carter intended for him. Sadly, Max laps it up and dies in agony.

Wormold tells Beatrice that he survived the poison attempt and that "It was the dog that died." As Neil Sinyard observes, Wormold is quoting Oliver Goldsmith's humorous lines from "An Elegy on the Death of a Mad Dog": "The man recovered of the bite, / It was the dog that died." (Source: Sinyard, 67)

MAXIME (*A Burnt-Out Case*). Rycker egotistically tells Querry that his wife recorded in her childish diary that her mother wrote her that Maxime had five puppies but omitted mention of Rycker's having been decorated by Governor Guelle.

MAYOR OF BOURGE, THE (*The Tenth Man*). He is one of the 30 prisoners held by the Germans as hostages. He is unnaturally but understandably proud of his big silver watch and disputes about the exact time with Pierre, a fellow prisoner who owns an alarm clock. At war's end, the Mayor happens to tell Carosse about Chavel's exchanging his fortune, including a house, for Michel Mangeot's life.

"MAY WE BORROW YOUR HUSBAND?" (1962). Short story. (Characters: Alec, Mrs. Clarenty, Mrs. Harris, William Harris, Lou-Lou, Stephen, Tony, Travis, Peter Travis, Poopy Travis, Colin Winstanley.)

1. The novelist-narrator William Harris, twice married, about 50, is in an Antibes hotel in autumn. He watches vacationers from his balcony while writing a biography of the Earl of Rochester. He spots London interior decorators Stephen, almost 50, and his boyfriend Tony, over 30. Stephen sports a cheek bruise after a sailor rebuffed the duo in Corsica. In come honeymooners Peter Travis, over six feet and slim, and Poopy Travis, tall, slender, and attractive to Harris. He figures, however, that the ages of the couple total about 45. The homosexual pair spy them also. The narrator feels like warning them.

2. At breakfast, Stephen and Tony chat with Harris, see Poopy, and make snide remarks. Tony appears to hate her. Harris wonders why

the prowling homosexuals regard absent Peter as prey. Poopy smiles at Harris. Peter appears. Stephen sniffs Peter's lotion. Peter pauses. The homosexuals smile discourteously.

3. Poopy looks lovable and sad to Harris. Stephen and Tony try to enlist Harris by criticizing the dysfunctional honeymooners and suggesting Poopy for him. She catches Harris's full name, says she's heard of his books. Peter appears for breakfast. The homosexuals invite him, and Poopy, to the Saturday horse races at Cagnes. Stephen will bus with Peter, and Tony will drive Poopy in their tiny car. Their laughter upon returning indicates that the homosexuals are proceeding more cautiously than they did at Corsica.

4. One evening Harris sees Poopy crying outside the Musée Grimaldi. She tells him the three men are inspecting Picassos inside—Peter doing so to avoid her. She blames herself, says she went virgin into marriage and Peter is "sensitive." Harris blurts that she should take her husband home, to Rome, anywhere. Poopy is glad Peter has found new friends in Stephen and Tony. Harris simply can't say they're seducing Peter, silently wonders: Peter married as cover for his homosexuality? to seek "normality"? is confused by differences marriages make? Harris barges into Stephen's room. Tony lolls there. Harris says they should leave Peter alone. The homosexuals' response: Harris should seduce Poopy; Peter's father wants heirs; Poopy's mother has "lucre"; Poopy wouldn't believe Harris if he revealed what they've said; Colin Winstanley, whom they know and who is Peter's friend back home, may have seduced him; they're saving Peter from damp-salad Poopy and Poopy for Harris.

5. Three mornings later, Stephen in Tony's presence asks Poopy if they can borrow her husband to drive in their car to Peille. Peter is agreeable. Can Harris take Poopy to lunch? Fine.

6. At Lou-Lou's for fish soup and wine, Harris resists telling Poopy life after sex is companionable, mentions his work on quickly burned-out Rochester, suddenly asks what's wrong with her marriage. She wants to walk a bit with him. He tells her again to take Peter home, but she's too dumb for explanations. She says things are her fault, Peter can't achieve a climax, must hate her, dislikes her small breasts.

Harris resists trying to sleep with Poopy in time for her marriage to be annulled for non-consummation, hopes perhaps Peter slugged Tony, and gets Poopy to her room.

7. Tony phones Harris at 8:30 p.m. about a delay and asks him to take Poopy to dinner. The two drink too much before and after eating. She talks stupidly about her casual reading while he mentions Rochester again. The three young men return: Stephen, morose at the wheel, and later; Tony, singing; Peter, on Tony's lap. Poopy helps Peter to their room. Tony tells Harris they prompted "*petit Pierre*" to a realization—earlier actions at his school admittedly alerted him—that he wasn't "*impuissant,*" indeed is superbly virile. Alone with Harris, Tony adds that Stephen's rheumatism has recurred.

8. At breakfast alone, Harris wonders: Tony and Stephen feel ashamed? Peter in pain? Harris should have cautioned Poopy. But Poopy appears, is delighted, and says this: Peter has two new friends; she's grateful to Harris; Tony plans to redecorate Peter's and her home; it'll take six months; Stephen will be busy with a client elsewhere. Harris moves out. He wouldn't want to see Peter pretending further and can't help Poopy. Peter suffers from "the wrong hormones"; Harris, from "the wrong age."

A. A. DeVitis reports that "[a]lthough the situation in the ... story ['May We Borrow Your Husband?'] had actually occurred at St. Jean-Cap Ferrat, he [Greene] transferred it to nearby Antibes." Richard Kelly reminds readers that "[l]ike Greene, William Harris is a writer staying in Antibes while working on a biography of the earl of Rochester. Greene, in fact [Kelly adds], published a biography of the earl in 1974," all of which is important since Greene's Harris is therefore "predisposed to explore the wit and sexuality" abounding in Antibes. (The biography is *Lord Rochester's Monkey*.)

Neil Sinyard notes that "May We Borrow Your Husband?" provided the basis for a British television film (same title, 1986) starring Dirk Bogarde and Charlotte Attenborough. In his book about Catherine Walston,* Greene's favorite married mistress, William Cash entitles one pertinent chapter "May I Borrow Your Wife?" (Sources: Cash, 108–30; DeVitis, 177; Kelly, 54; O'Prey, 57; Sherry III, 408; Sinyard, 158)

MAY WE BORROW YOUR HUSBAND? AND OTHER COMEDIES OF THE SEXUAL LIFE (1967). A collection of 12 short stories. Greene says that it "was ... written ... in a single mood of sad hilarity, while I was establishing a home in a two-roomed apartment over the port at Antibes," and that "perhaps the stories ... are an escape in humor from the thought of death." He continues by wondering how anyone, without the therapy of writing, composing music, or painting, can, trapped "in the human condition," escape "madness, ... melancholia, ... panic fear." Norman Sherry says Greene told an interviewer soon after *May We Borrow Your Husband? and Other Comedies of the Sexual Life* was published that sales had already hit 25,000 copies. Sherry adds that French reviewers, smugly happy that Greene had chosen to live in Antibes, went overboard in praising the collection but "were right to recognize the beginnings of an amused tolerance towards human sexual behaviour in his latest work." (Oh, how bright those French reviewers were in 1967. Greene was tolerant about sex from his undergraduate days and soon indicated as much in his writings.) Paul O'Prey calls the entire 12-story collection "slick, cynical and ... slight." (Sources: Greene, *Ways of Escape*, 283, 285; O'Prey, 57; Sherry III, 408)

MAYDEW, MISS (*This Gun for Hire*). She is Lord Fordhaven's daughter and has the lead in *Aladdin*, being produced in Nottwich. To avoid aristocratic functions she was expected to attend, she went into acting and also writes essays for women readers. Her real name is Binns.

MEADMORE, MRS. (*The Name of Action*). She is a liberal society lady in whose house in Mayfair, London, Chant meets Kurtz, a romantic exile from Trier. Her doing so starts Chant, bored and feeling useless, on his adventures.

MEGRIM, GENERAL ("The Last Word"). More than 20 years earlier (but in the distant future), this impetuous military man tried unsuccessfully to assassinate Pope John. Soon thereafter, General Megrim died.

MEMBER OF PARLIAMENT, THE (*The Quiet American*). Fowler recalls how dull it is for him to explain the situation in Vietnam to visitors, including this one.

MEMENTO MORI (*Brighton Rock*). This is the prophetic name of the racehorse Spicer bets on. Ida Arnold's horse Black Boy wins, while Memento Mori places and Spicer is soon murdered.

"MEN AT WORK" (1940). Short story. (Characters: Bone, H. Graves, D. Hill, R. King, Lawrence, B. Lewis, F. Lewis, Lowndes, Miss Manners, Priestley, Savage, Richard Skate, Wilkinson.)

During World War II, would-be dramatist Richard Skate has a useless Ministry of Information job. His assistant, Miss Manners, handles the telephone. She and her colleagues refer to each other by their initials. R.S.'s message is that his house in the country survived an air raid. The regular weekly Book Committee meeting convenes. Skate consults his meaningless agenda. R. King, chairman of the Books Division, plans a pamphlet explaining the war effort. D. Hill says the Stationery Office will object. When Wilkinson suggests "a clarion-note to women," his writing ability gets debated. F. Lewis dozes. Bone's controversial pamphlet about the British Empire, though in print, was revised to delete passages offending India, Canada, Australia, New Zealand, and the United States, and is now "unrecognizable" by Bone, who plans a written objection. Lowndes enters late, tipsy, to report that in recent daylight air raids the R.A.F. downed 50 German airplanes at a cost of 15 of theirs. Hill suggests printing Bone's rebuttal. R.S. blurts, "That'll show them," then feels like a traitor. R.S. agrees to confer with Priestley on a leaflet concerning meat marketing. R.S. opens a window, looks up, and sees the phosphorescent trails of British aviators "going home after work."

Michael Shelden writes that when Greene quit working at the Ministry of Information, he criticized it in "Men at Work," every detail of which he insisted was accurate but with names changed. Its most bitter passage is Skate's remembering that while his memos were inefficiently circulating about a suggested publication on "the French war-effort," Germany smashed the Maginot Line, hopped the

Somme, took Paris, and accepted France's surrender at Compiègne. (Source: Shelden, 289)

MENDEZ, FATHER (*Our Man in Havana*). Wormold recalls Father Mendez's preaching against the hydrogen bomb when Wormold, though a non-believer, attended Mass at Havana's Cathedral last Sunday.

Greene says that Father Mendez's message is that scientists who fancy they can make the earth a heaven are in reality making it a hell.

MENDRILL, MRS. MARIE (*The Confidential Agent*). She is the manageress of the shabby Bloomsbury hotel to which D. is ordered to report. She hulks, has a square, mannish face, and domineers Else Crole, her servant, and also K., another of D.'s contacts. Mrs. Mendrill murders Else, is confronted by testimony from Muckerji, confesses, and is adjudged insane.

MERDY ("Jubilee"). One of Chalfont's now-vanished friends, along with the Boob. Merdy and Book were probably gigolos. Chalfont surely is.

Merdy's name echoes, so to say, *merde* (vulgar French, "shit"), while "Boob" sounds close to "Poop," and the two men are asinine old buddies.

MEREDITH (*The Human Factor*). He was Castle's predecessor and, as Castle is now, was in charge of MI6.

MERLAN, MÈRE (*The Comedians*). She is the owner of a Petit Guave public house.

MERRIMAN, SIR HENRY (*The Man Within*). He is a competent old barrister at Lewes. Tall, thin, cold-voiced, he neglects his juicy young mistress, Lucy, who seduces Andrews. Sir Henry is effective at the trial, conducted under Sir Edward Parkin, of the six indicted smugglers, including Druce, Hake, and Richard Tims. Nonetheless, the smugglers are acquitted. Henry then offers Andrews protection and promises him getaway money.

MERRY MONARCH (*Brighton Rock*). This is a horse that runs in the race in which Black Boy wins and Memento Mori places.

MERSHAM, LADY (*The Confidential Agent*). She is the radio announcer whose "Hints to the Young Housewife" program D. hears while hiding in Emily Glover's empty flat.

MESTIZO, THE (*The Power and the Glory*). This Judas figure who betrays the whisky priest is unnamed. According to Norman Sherry, he is modeled on a man named Don Pelito. Sherry says the unattractive fellow used to be a clerk in the Predencia. (Source: Sherry III, xviii-xix, 183)

MEYERSDORF, GRÄFIN VON (*The Third Man*). She is an old countess who attends Crabbin's literary group, assembled to hear Martins lecture on the contemporary novel. Crabbin hustles Martins away before she can complete a question aimed at him.

MICHAEL (*It's a Battlefield*). He is the subject of drifting talk at the Berkeley Restaurant, when the Assistant Commissioner and the Home Secretary's secretary are eating there.

MICHAEL (*The Name of Action*). In a half-dreaming state, Chant remembers that Remnant once asked if he ever heard the captivating story of Michael and Loulou.

MICHAEL ("The Trial of Pan"). He was the prosecuting attorney in Lady Hope-Smithies's trial. Michael demolished Gabriel's defense of the generous woman.

MICK (*The Quiet American*). When Granger brings a drunk Frenchman to a bar, he calls him Mick and abandons him. Joe takes him to his own residence to keep him from harm.

MIDGE (*The Comedians*) see **DON JUAN**

MIGUEL (*The Honorary Consul*). He is a member of Rivas's gang in the hut. Miguel is a trigger-happy Guaraní Indian, unable to speak Spanish or English. When it was discovered that Fortnum was kidnapped by mistake, Miguel suggested drowning him immediately. At about the time Plarr emerges to speak with Colonel Perez, Miguel gets shot dead.

MIGUEL (*Our Man in Havana*). He is a black

employee at the Shanghai Theatre. Wormold sees Miguel sweeping up and bribes him to lead Beatrice, the real Teresa, and himself out of the theatre at the onset of the police raid.

MIGUEL (*Our Man in Havana*). When Beatrice sees a blind beggar at the Cathedral steps, Wormold's "creative instinct" prompts him to confide that the beggar, whose name is Miguel, isn't blind but is another of his secret agents, working gratis because Wormold once saved him from drowning.

MIGUEL (*The Power and the Glory*). He is a hostage the lieutenant seized at Concepción, the whisky priest's village. The priest sees Miguel in the jail yard.

MIGUEL (*Rumour at Nightfall*). He is Caveda's fat-necked, surprisingly agile leader of brave fellow guerrillas in San Juan. Enrique brings Chase to Miguel at the inn, where Enrique, Miguel, lightly armed, and the others in his squad are killed before San Juan falls.

MIKE ("The Destructors"). He is a member, nine, of the Wormsley Common Gang of boys. He laughs but is scared for laughing. Mike warns Trevor, called T., that Thomas is returning early from his Bank Holiday.

MIKE ("A Drive in the Country"). Mike, a self-confessed "Bolshie," is a friend of Fred's. After Fred commits suicide in the country, his girlfriend leaves, finds Mike at the roadhouse, and accepts a ride from him back to her home.

MIKE (*This Gun for Hire*). He is a friend of Buddy Fergusson, suggests kidnapping the museum mummy during the rag, and is walking ahead of Buddy when Raven forces Buddy into a garage.

MILAN, THE REVEREND SIMON ("When Greek Meets Greek"). He is a nice-looking old ex-convict whom Nicholas Fennick knew while both were in prison. Fennick will ply him with drinks and get him to write examination papers for students in Fennick's bogus St. Ambrose's College.

MILBANKE, MRS. (*This Gun for Hire*). While Raven is standing outside a Charing Cross Road theatre hoping to see Davis, he hears someone say that the author of *Loyalties* gave Mrs. Milbanke a check to support the Antivivisection Society.

Loyalties was a 1922 drama by John Galsworthy. Peter Wolfe notes that, "[i]ronically, a book that mentions John Galsworthy's play, *Loyalties,* has a protagonist who feels betrayed on all counts," and ticks them off— parents, poverty, harelip, orphanage, paymasters, the poor, the lawless. (Source: Wolfe, 57)

MILES (*The End of the Affair*). He was Henry Miles's father, who worked in Treasury.

MILES, HENRY (*The End of the Affair*). By 1939 he has been Sarah Miles's sexless husband for a decade, and is now in his mid-40s. He worked for the Ministry of Pensions until the war began, then was transferred to the Ministry of Home Security. His work is officially admired. Bendrix cultivates his friendship to observe him and more accurately depict a civil servant in his current novel. Henry grows suspicious of his wife Sarah's promiscuity, tells Bendrix about a detective named Savage he thinks of consulting, and only mildly frets when Bendrix takes over the case. He learns of but doesn't mind Bendrix's affair with Sarah. After her death, Henry gets Bendrix to live with him. While there, Henry, Bendrix, and Father Crompton discuss Sarah's religious faith. Bendrix develops genuine affection for poor, benighted Henry.

Norman Sherry, in explaining that the love affair of Bendrix and Sarah Miles is based on Greene's affair with Catherine Walston,* details how Catherine's husband, Harry Walston, somewhat resembles Henry Miles, although Walston succeeded in curtailing Greene's obsession. Michael Shelden equates the principals: "Harry became 'Henry Miles,' Catherine became 'Sarah Miles,' and Greene became the popular novelist 'Maurice Bendrix,' who narrates the story." Shirley Hazzard adds this: "Henry, which was the given name of Catherine Walston's husband, was heartlessly bestowed by Graham [Greene] on the betrayed and ludicrous husband in *The End of the Affair,* intense as a love letter, which, originating in Graham's first years with Catherine, was published in

1951—when that affair was far from ending, had still a decade to run"; Hazzard then lists Henrys in Greene's later fiction who are also somewhat spineless. William Cash devotes an entire book to Greene, the Walstons, and the Mileses. (Sources: Cash; Hazzard, 41–42; Shelden, 374; Sherry II, 223–37, 322–36, 378–79)

MILES, SARAH (*The End of the Affair*). She is Henry Miles's promiscuous wife, about 38 in January 1946, according to Bendrix's estimate. Henry's decade-long passionlessness partly excuses her conduct. Bendrix caters to Henry, as he and Sarah begin their lusty, hardly clandestine affair. She experiences love for Bendrix deeper than his for her. Her emotions become spiritually colored. Moments after they complete vigorous lovemaking at his place in June 1944, a V1 explosion smashes debris over Bendrix in the basement. She thinks he is dead and promises God to give him up should He revivify him. Bendrix comes to. His being alive puts Sarah into religious confusion unresolved by consultation with earnest Father Crompton. In a detailed diary Sarah records her development into a self-hating, self-denying, self-sacrificial, loving devotee of God. Her helping Lance Parkis and Richard Smythe with cures may be interpreted as divine intervention. Reading the diary impels Bendrix into a kind of reluctant faith.

Norman Sherry reports that Greene and Catherine Walston,* Harry Walston's wife, first fell in love while eating onions (as Bendrix and Sarah do), then contends that Sarah is virtually Catherine, whom Greene obsessively loved (1947–1951). William Cash, however, says that Yvonne Cloetta* was so disgusted by Sherry's contention that she stopped cooperating with him. A. F. Cassis regards Sarah as Greene's "first full-length portrait of a woman." Thinking of Sarah, Peter Wolfe notes that by the time *The End of the Affair* ends, sin has become something grace is built on. K. C. Joseph Kurismmootil, who extols Sarah, feels that soon after writing her last diary entry, "she would be ... gathered forever in the divine embrace." A. A. DeVitis says that "[i]n *The End of the Affair* the conditions for sainthood are explored and the possibility ... of the heroine's salvation portrayed." Evelyn Waugh (1903–1966) notes that "Sarah, after her death, begins to work miracles." Mary Warner writes that Greene's "perspectives on religious faith in this novel cannot be separated from the mysteries of the crucifix, the resurrection of the body, and the communion of saints.... Sarah Miles demonstrates most powerfully that that faith is won only through anguished self-denial." (It should be added that Sarah's apparently not noticing that her diary is missing is a considerable plot flaw.) (Sources: Cash, 23; Cassis, 28; DeVitis, 93; Kurismmootil, 161; Sherry II, 21–22, 223–37, 322–36, 375–76; Warner, 312; Waugh, 458; Wolfe, 28)

MILLET ("The Other Side of the Border"). He is the thin, gray, courtly-looking photographer in Denton. Hands intrigues him with lies about his African exploits. Millet's niece Ethel, eavesdropping in Millet's shop, is also impressed and is swept into marriage to Hands.

MILLY (*This Gun for Hire*). She is a brunette nurse that Buddy Fergusson is to have tea with next Saturday. Buddy imagines a seduction scene to follow, but frustration, as usual, will be the result.

MIMI (*The Human Factor*). She and Lulu have their names beside their flat-bells, which Castle notes as indicative of Old Compton Street evening action. The two could be prostitutes.

MINISTER, THE (*The Power and the Glory*). He is an official to whom Trixy Fellows would report the lieutenant if he dared search her home for the whisky priest.

MINISTER, THE (*The Quiet American*). When Fowler first meets Pyle and a car exhaust makes a noise, Pyle wonders if a grenade caused the sound and says the Minister, presumably American, would find it "awkward" if a grenade killed any Americans. Fowler sarcastically replies that "Congress wouldn't like it."

MINISTER OF DEFENCE, THE ("An Old Man's Memory"). This British official is inexplicably with Mrs. Thatcher when she greets the arrival of the French train out of the Channel Tunnel. It emerges, but news soon comes that the British train has been destroyed in the tunnel.

MINISTER OF DEFENSE, THE (*Our Man in Havana*). Wormold identifies his imaginary Teresa as this official's mistress.

MINISTER OF EDUCATION, THE ("The Man Who Stole the Eiffel Tower"). The narrator gets a friend to pretend he's the Minister of Education and orate, thus diverting traffic while he returns the Eiffel Tower to its proper place.

MINISTER OF THE INTERIOR, THE (*The Confidential Agent*). He is an ambitious cabinet member in the home country of D., who fears the young fellow may have betrayed him.

MINISTER OF THE INTERIOR, THE (*The Honorary Consul*). He is an official at the British Embassy in Buenos Aires. Colonel Perez is ordered by the provincial Governor to fly down and confer with him about Fortnum.

MINISTER OF THE INTERIOR, THE (*Our Man in Havana*). Milly Wormold tells her father that Captain Segura told her that someone shot at the Minister of the Interior and that Engineer Cifuentes thought he was the target (and probably was).

THE MINISTRY OF FEAR (1943). Novel. (Characters: Barnes, Beale, Beavis, Mrs. Bellairs, Bridges, Brothers, Collier, Cost, Conway, Lady Cradbrooke, Crooks, Tom Curtis, David, Davis, Davis, Mrs. Dermody, Dunwoody, Lady Dunwoody, Lord Dunwoody, Ernest, Fishguard, Dr. Forester, Fullove, Graves, Griggs, Anna Hilfe, Willi Hilfe, Isaacs, Jack, Johns, Jones, F. G. J[ones]., N. L. J[ones]., Keyser, Joseph Macleod, Marquis, Mr. Maude, Minny, Frederick Newey, Mrs. Frederick Newey, Miss Pantil, Perry, Poole, Prentice, Mrs. Purvis, Rennit, Mrs. Rennit, Alice Rowe, Arthur Rowe, Mrs. Rowe, Miss Savage, Sinclair, Mrs. J. A. Smythe-Phillips, Spot, Still, Major Stone, Mrs. Stone, Tatham, Canon Topling, Trench, Mrs. Troup, Vane, Doris Wilcox, Henry Wilcox, Mrs. Wilcox, Wilson.)

Book One: *The Unhappy Man*. Chapter 1: "The Free Mothers." 1. London, summer Sunday afternoon. Arthur Rowe attends a fête to raise money to comfort mothers of the free nations. He buys Charlotte M. Yonge's *The Little Duke* (1854, by Charlotte M. Yonge [1823–1901]) and has his palm read by Mrs. Bellairs. She tells him to bet 4 lbs. 8½ oz. as the weight of the tasty cake, being raffled. He does and wins. Clergyman Sinclair asks Rowe to auction the cake to raise additional funds. No. A stranger (Cost) rushes in, reports to Mrs. Bellairs, and professes to bid correctly. Rowe keeps his cake.

2. Rowe, for two years an ex-journalist, rents quarters from Mrs. Purvis, who owns her Guildford Street house, near bombed and boarded places. He displays his cake and enjoys a slice. Pitying sweets-addicted Mrs. Purvis, he gives her some. They tin the remainder.

3. Next day Poole, crippled but strong, rents from Mrs. Purvis. He, Mrs. Purvis, and Rowe have tea and cake, which Roe slices with his schoolboy's knife. An air raid sends Mrs. Purvis for the shelter. Poole says he's investigated Rowe, calls him too intelligent, like himself, to support war efforts. Rowe attempts a patriotic rebuttal. Poole crumbles more cake. Rowe thinks his tastes funny. Poole says Rowe wasn't supposed to win the cake. Suddenly the place is bombed. Poole collapses. Rowe is rescued.

Chapter 2: "Private Inquiries." 1. Rowe learns Poole was hospitalized with concussion but disappeared with friends. Rowe consults Rennit, of the Orthotex detective agency. Rennit offers reasons for Poole's wanting the cake. Rowe explains that the tea tasted of the poison hyoscine and confesses to Rennit, as follows.

2. Rowe poisoned his wife, was jailed (one year), tried for murder, but acquitted on the grounds that it was a mercy killing — but mercy for whom? — and offers Rennit money to investigate.

Chapter 3: "Frontal Assault." 1. Rennit assigns the case to agent Jones, who combines seediness, cunning, and fear. They pooh-pooh Rowe's theory that if killed by hyoscine-laced liquid (as Rowe's wife was), Rowe's death would be ruled suicide. They prefer to consult Mrs. Bellairs and identify Poole alone. Walking through Holburn's stony rubble, Rowe remembers killing for pity but can't feel self-pity.

2. Rowe goes the Free Mothers' office, meets Anna Hilfe and her brother Willi Hilfe, explains about the cake, his suspicions about it, and hiring Jones. Rolfe obtains Mrs. Bellairs's

address. Willi says he and Anna are Austrian refugees from Hitler. Lady Dunwoody phones Willi. Timid Anna reminds Rowe of his wife. Anna is distressed when Willi taxis with Rowe to Mrs. Bellairs — avoiding Jones on the street, since Willi wants him uninvolved.

Chapter 4: "An Evening with Mrs. Bellairs." Mrs. Bellairs introduce Rowe and Willi to her guests: Dr. Forester; Cost, businessman; Miss Pantil, painter; Frederick Newey and his friend Mr. Maude; Collier, former waiter and stoker, now a poet. A phone call for Rowe disconcerts everyone; Anna whispers to him to leave without telling Willi.

When Willi approaches, Rowe fibs that he left word for Jones at the Free Mothers and Jones just phoned. Willi gets Rowe to remain, sit holding hands with Cost and Miss Pantil in a darkened, locked room, for a séance. He feels fear and pity. A strange voice says only "Arthur, why did you kill ... [?]" Rowe yells. Cost drops Rowe's hand. Dazzling lights. Cost is seen to be stabbed to death, by Rowe's schoolboy's knife — gone from his pocket. Forester and Willi promise to protect Mrs. Bellairs. Rowe asks to go to the lavatory. Willi escorts him there. Rowe admits Anna phoned him. Willi tells him to knock him out, go "underground" to avoid inevitable rearrest, and in a week seek Hilfe.

Chapter 5: "Between Sleeping and Waking." Rowe stays overnight in a crowded air-raid shelter. Hearing sirens and bombs, he dreams and half-dreams — childhood garden, not convincing his simpering mother he committed murder, dog-bitten rat he killed in pity, lovely girl he daren't kiss, homey asylum.

Chapter 6: "Out of Touch." 1. Over breakfast in Chapham, Rowe reads newspaper accounts of raids but nothing about the séance murder, summarizes his action for police in writing but doesn't mail it, phones Rennit about last night, and learns Jones is missing. Rowe wanders, sad he can't day-dream, and feels despair.

2. Rowe watches Rennit's office from a book auction across the street, suspects a loiterer of being a detective also watching, and muses about his trial, friends loyal and otherwise, the probably innocent cake, being unwanted now even as an air-raid warden. He phones Anna. Scared for him, she tells him to keep distant.

After a corner-house lunch, he goes by bus to Henry Wilcox, a Battersea friend, to request cash for a check. He finds Wilcox, a bumbling warden cared for by his suspicious mother and awaiting a funeral procession: Doris, his wife, also a warden, was just killed when a bombed wall collapsed on her.

Chapter 7: "A Load of Books." 1. Rowe counts his remaining 35 shillings, approaches the Embankment, contemplates suicide. The idea of justice intrudes, despite his awareness that childhood innocence is betrayed in the adult world. The dead hero of *The Little Duke* is forgotten. He poisoned his wife to end his pain, not hers; she knowingly accepted his intent — in fear of him? Rowe longs for surcease of anguish.

2. An ugly man calling himself Fullove approaches Rowe, feeds birds some bread, and says his heavy suitcase contains landscape-gardening books he must deliver. Rowe remembers seeing Fullove at the auction, pities him, offers to lug the case. Fullove takes Rowe by taxi to the Regal Court hotel and asks him to leave the case for Mr. Travers. A stolid page shows him Room 6. There is Anna.

Anna says she came here to warn him. The room is a spacious, unoccupied flat. To his questions about Willi, Mrs. Bellairs, cake, etc., Anna, in a familiar-sounding voice, responds thus: "They are bad," can stand others' pains; newspaper accounts of Rowe's mercy killing prove his harmlessness; she'll leave with him now; ring for the page to escort them. Phone, lights, heater all fail; door is bolted. Hearing an intruder, Rowe seeks a weapon. The suitcase may contains heavy bricks, not books. He opens it.

Book Two: *The Happy Man*. Chapter 1: "Conversations in Arcady." 1. Early spring (four months later). Rowe, called Richard Digby, with scarred forehead and bearded, has amnesia, remembers nothing past age 18, and is in a private sanatorium (self-sustaining by farm- and hunting-lands) run by Dr. Forester for the shell-shocked, self-admitted and without rights. Attending him is Johns, who worships Forester for his beneficent, advanced psychoanalytical expertise. Johns briefs Rowe about the war.

2. Johns takes Digby to Forester, who says he's looking better and leaves him with a woman who knows him.

3. Anna enters, unrecognized. She says he fell over her during a bombing and saved her. Since she must let him recover the past himself, she parries comments concerning his recent reading about Hitler, also when asked names herself, says she's Austrian, he shouldn't wish to leave these lovely surroundings, but she's supposed to help him regain his memories gently. He wonders what he was, could still be. She calls him Arthur and leaves for now.

4. Digby reads war news over breakfast. Johns idealistically talks about international economics, Napoleon's defeat, German materialism; says Forester has written about psychoanalyzing "Nazidom"; says there's a German Ministry of Fear designed to blackmail "so-called leaders." Digby summarizes his newspaper reading about Ministry of Home Security plans not needed for a certain meeting, then mysteriously missing, then available, with everything queried by an M.P. Digby theorizes the papers could have been photographed in that interval they were missing. Johns says that notion hit the papers after Digby's arrival here but suffered governmental quashing. Digby wonders if another person held such photos and would be pursued by other ministers of fear.

5. Digby happily wanders past a garden, seemingly designed for children, to a stream and a pool, with a small island in it. Major Stone regards it as something to be militarily occupied and gets muddy trying. Still and Fishguard play tennis and chess argumentatively but reconcile to avoid being committed, like overly tearful Davis, to the sick bay — really an off-limits, solitary-confinement cell. Johns summons Poole to help him find Stone. Poole, crippled but massive, asks Digby if they're acquainted. Digby says no, but memory stirs.

6. Anna revisits Digby, urges him to remain, be happy, avoid remembering. She mentions her brother. Memories agitate Digby. They kiss like adolescents.

7. Next day. No paper, no visit from Johns. Recollection of Poole's leaving sick bay scares Digby. Reading Tolstoy's comments — signaled by pencil marks, incompletely erased — on antipatriotic non-resistance tempt Digby to believe military killings release enemies from pain. The thought dizzies him. Should one kill a beloved?

Forester enters, trailed by disconsolate Johns. Forester tells Digby this: I am disappointed, have ordered your newspapers stopped; Johns mustn't discuss the war with you; you can't be released yet; Poole criticized your detective-like behavior; Stone is in sick bay; Miss Hilfe cannot revisit you.

Chapter Two: "The Sick Bay." 1. Digby feels that Forester is dishonorable. When he sees Poole drive Forester elsewhere, Digby plans to consult with demented Stone in sick bay.

2. First Digby examines Poole's room, full of hero-worship books, dirty clothes, tobacco stink, and other masculine untidiness. Tinges of memory return. Digby locates Stone, who screams deliriously, demonstrates he's not entirely demented by hinting that Barnes, an inmate, may have been killed and buried in the pond island, and promising to remain firm until Digby can help. Hearing Forester's car, Digby camps in Johns's room.

3. Digby reads Johns's marked newspapers, about some politician wrongly accused of handling a document carelessly, then about Arthur Rowe. His record of crime and accompanying photograph don't interest Digby.

4. Johns enters. Digby terrifies him by criticizing sanatorium protocol, asserting his intent to escape, and praising Stone, whom he says he just visited. Johns calls Forester brainy, sensitive, and caring. Suddenly Forester enters. Digby challenges him about Stone's spotting Forester and Poole. Forester says one patient's asking about his illness led to his suicide, shows Digby the newspaper photograph of a murderer named Rowe, and threatens Digby with Rowe's data. Digby retreats to his room, stares into his mirror, and remembers more — Poole eating cake, Forester, bloody body, sad woman, life returning to him.

Book Three: *Bits and Pieces.* Chapter 1: "The Roman Death." Rowe escapes by train to London, surrenders himself at Scotland Yard, and is interviewed by Beale, a policeman who partially believes him as fragments of his past resurface. Rowe is surprised to learn he's not wanted for murder. His identifying a living man (Cost) by a photograph startles Beale.

2. Rowe, taken to Prentice, a detective, mentions his cake and Mrs. Bellairs's séance. Prentice grills him about Forester's private sanatorium of voluntary patients, Cost's so-called murder, and a missing man's picture (Jones's). When Rowe calls him a detective, of the Orthotex, Prentice

adds details — Free Mothers, cake, Rowe's phoning Rennit about being a murderer. Bewildered, challenged by life, Rowe offers assistance, names Anna Hilfe, says they were lovers perhaps. Prentice mentions the Regal Court.

3. Prentice leaves, returns with the hotel clerk (Davis), who identifies Rowe as the man with the heavy suitcase. Prentice takes both men by taxi to a tailor shop. Prentice explains much — fête; cake, containing top-secret microfilm, smashed during air raid; Rowe surviving hotel bomb, disappearing with amnesia, being blamed. By design, Prentice enters the shop first and asks for a fitting. When Rowe follows, he recognizes as Cost the tailor, called Ford — not dead after all. Keeping steady, Cost makes a phone call and starts it by labeling himself now hopeless — this, even after Davis, following on cue, calls him Travers. Cost-Travers-Ford pierces his own throat with cutting shears.

Chapter Two: "Mopping Up." 1. Prentice and Rowe race to Mrs. Bellairs's home, filled with policemen. When confronted with Prentice's summary and Rowe's appearance, Mrs. Bellairs wilts. When Forester phones her, he is identified. Prentice orders a Scotland Yard speedster, viciously tears apart Mrs. Bellairs's place for clues, tells her she may hang, and off he and Rowe drive.

2. While proceeding to Forester's sanatorium, Prentice tells Rowe that Forester could be blackmailed in inefficiently policed counties' crime havens, and accidentally names Dunwoody as an enemy courier of documents. Police let them into the sanatorium, where they find Johns has shot Forester.

3. This because Forester euthanized Stone, Nazi style. Sinclair, the vicar summoned by Forester, is there, sees Rowe, who doesn't recognize him. Prentice orders Sinclair home. Johns confesses he heard Forester and Poole talking about tumor-afflicted Stone, rushed for the patient Davis's hidden gun, was too late to save Stone, but shot theoretical-purist, practical-villain Forester and malignant Poole too. Prentice ransacks Poole's photo laboratory in the sanatorium but finds no film negative. In the pond island, Prentice's men unearth detective Jones's remnants.

Chapter 3: "Wrong Numbers." Prentice deposits Rowe, his memory returning, in a hotel near Hyde Park, with £5. Having concealed from Prentice his having observed Cost, fatally resigned, dial BAT 271 but missing the final number, Rowe tries that sequence plus last numbers, unsuccessfully, until ...

Book Four: *The Whole Man*. Chapter 1: "Journey's End." 1. Rowe hears Anna's voice, hangs up puzzled, locates her Battersea address by scanning numbers in the phone directory, and on the way there chances to meet Henry Wilcox. This triggers recollection of man with suitcase.

2. Rowe finds Anna's flat, is admitted. He tells her about Cost's phoning, about Forester's death, and Poole's, and is pleased when she says she's relieved they're gone. But she adds he and she probably won't untangle everything, and in fact hopes not, for his sake. Queried, Anna answers thus: Willi has the film; Willi faked Cost's murder to make Rowe hide; Willi tried to kill Rowe and Anna with the suitcase bomb; Rowe's loss of memory enabled him to be let live. She agrees Willi must be stopped, says he's asleep here, will be smuggled tonight to Ireland by Lady Dunwoody. Anna resolves to brain Willi with a brass candlestick. They awaken him. He has a gun, reviews much with Rowe, offers to swap restoring Rowe's total memory for his own escape, but adds Anna wants Rowe as is, not as was. Anna breaks Willi's wrist, disarms him, orders Rowe to wait outside, and promises to retain Willi. When Anne emerges, she gives him the rolled film, and says she let Willi escape. Rowe checks the film; it is not the one.

3. Rowe requires Anna to say where Willi has gone. Surrendering happiness, she says Willi, with a one-bullet gun, was to escape on Paddington's 7.20 train. Confused, Rowe taxis through jittery night scenes, boards the train, and finds bandaged Willi with a stone-deaf lady winding wool with him, extracts his pocketed gun, and demands the negative. Recognizing defeat, Willi leaves the train alongside Rowe, and in a lavatory gives him his suit coat and Rowe's own knife. He cuts Willi's second copy of the film out from where Cost tailored it in. Willi wants his gun, to avoid torture-interrogation. No. Willi vengefully reveals Rowe's unwanted past — married, he poisoned his wife — and gloats Anna hoped he'd never remember that. Memories flood. Rowe surrenders the gun and exits as Willi shoots himself.

4. Rowe walks to Battersea, finds Anna, realizes she loved and will love only Digby, and therefore says Willi killed himself without revealing Rowe's past. He must atone for everything by lovingly living a lie with ignorant, loving Anna.

Greene wrote *The Ministry of Fear,* according to Norman Sherry, during the last months of his duty with the British Colonial Office in Freetown, Sierra Leone (March-August 1942). Discarded titles were *The Worst Passion of All* (obviously Rowe's obsessive pity) and *The Man Who Forgot.* In a *Collected Edition* introduction, Green snidely suggests that he wrote downward in this, his favorite "entertainment," to an immature audience of the sort attracted to Michael Innes (pen name of John Innes Mackintosh Stewart — JIM Stewart [1906–1994] — he ultimately wrote 131 mystery novels.) Greene adds that Innes's audience includes the occasional university professor. Michael Shelden reports that *The Ministry of Fear* sold 18,000 copies in its first period of publication.

A clever feature of *The Ministry of Fear* is Greene's use of quotations from Yonge's *The Little Duke* as epigraphs to foreshadow emotions stirred in successive chapters. In Greene's novel are at least 160 similes and metaphors, many concerning childhood and others of startling charm. The word "pity" is used 29 times. Peter Wolfe puts it simply: "Pity frets Rowe's nerves and addles his mind." A. A. DeVitis contends that "[p]ity is ... the dominant theme of the book," and that it "creates in its advocate [Rowe] a sense of responsibility" which "sets him apart from his fellow beings" while also "paradoxically" requiring him "to love them the more for being apart." Cates Baldridge says that, although we can understand how Rowe's personal misery causes him "to demonize pity in ... categorical terms," we should be puzzled when Prentice "reacts strongly" to Rowe's "reluctant admiration" after Willi shot himself to avoid capture. Prentice adverts to one of Greene's frequently quoted lines, to the effect that the passion of pity, necessarily mature, is worse than the outlived passion of sex itself. Remembering *The Ministry of Fear* and later Greene novels, W. H. Auden says that "[j]ust as Balzac comes back again to avarice and Stendahl to ambition, so, in book after book, Graham Greene analyzes the vice of pity, that corrupt parody of love and compassion which is so invidious and deadly for sensitive natures." The fact that Book Four of *The Ministry of Fear,* which is entitled "Journey's End," has a first chapter but no second chapter implies that Rowe's psychological journey hasn't ended and his wretched future is indescribable. *The Ministry of Fear* borders on the fantastic. For example, the hero observes, thinks, and talks far more than is credible before, during, and after German air-raids — which Greene survived personally and describes movingly, especially for readers still alive and also remembering. David Lodge complains that "*The Ministry of Fear* applies the devices of the prewar thrillers to the circumstances of the London Blitz and the activities of fascist spies, with an effect that sometimes comes near self-parody."

Movie rights to the novel were sold prepublication for £3,250. In the movie (1943), Rowe becomes Stephen Neale (played by Ray Milland); Neale's wife takes the poison all by herself; Neale doesn't go to any clinic for amnesia; the cake is temporarily lost near a bomb crater; Anna (called Carla) Hilfe shoots her brother to death, etc. Greene disliked the movie, in which potentially thrilling pieces are inadequately integrated. The book's 33 numbered sub-chapters signal cinema-like quick-changing locales and times. (Sources: Auden, 94; Baldridge, 92; DeVitis, 39, 40; Greene, *The Ministry of Fear, Collected Edition,* vii, xiii; Phillips, 29–31; Shelden, 356; Sherry II, 146–48; Wolfe, 103)

MINNY (*The Ministry of Fear*). She is a pet cat. When Rowe phones a wrong number, someone screams that David must have told him Minny was killed in last night's air raid.

MINTY, FERDINAND (*England Made Me*). Bent, weak, and yellow, and a graduate from Harrow, this Britisher has been a hand-to-mouth reporter in Stockholm 20 years. He also works in Professor Hammarsten's language school and is partly supported by monthly allowances from family solicitors Scott and James back home. Minty becomes friendly with Farrant, who can sell him insider secrets of the company built and controlled by Krogh, whose secretary and mistress is Farrant's twin sister Kate. Minty knows Captain Gullie, a Harrow man and Sir Ronald's British legation military attaché. Minty sadistically keeps an injured spider under a tooth glass. Minty, a misogynist, lends Farrant his bedroom for a tryst with Lucia Davidge.

In a *Collected Edition* introduction, Greene says he planned for Minty to be a minor character but he kept intruding. (Source: *England Made Me, Collected Edition,* x)

MINTY, MRS. (*England Made Me*). She is Minty's mother. His Aunt Ella writes him about his mother's failing memory.

MIRIAM (*The Captain and the Enemy*) see **MURIEL**

MOLLINSON, MISS (*England Made Me*). She was an early employer of Kate Farrant. Kate's father disapproves of her going to a play with her employer.

MOLLISON (*This Gun for Hire*). He has been Sir Marcus's valet for years, hates him, warns Raven that Marcus has rung the alarm bell. After Raven shoots Marcus, Mollison tells Raven that Anne Crowder was his betrayer.

"THE MOMENT OF TRUTH" (1988). Short story. (Characters: Arthur Burton, Hogminster, Dolly Hogminster.)

Arthur Burton, a waiter for 20 years at a Kensington restaurant renamed from The Queen's to Chez Auguste, may have cancer. Death approaches like a crime one can confess to strangers but not to friends. Maybe to Mrs. Hogminster? She and her husband, both Americans, having booked Arthur's window table twice, seem amiable. Burton helps them choose from the menu, in which the English dishes are in both English and French. When they mention shopping, Arthur recommends eating nearer Jermyn Street stores. But they want one of Arthur's tables next night. They arrive late — barely in time to be given it by Arthur's impatient manager.

Arthur tells the Hogminsters he'll miss tomorrow (Wednesday) because of a hospital appointment. They express sympathy, discuss Hogminster's own medical check-ups, and promise to dine Thursday at what Mrs. Hogminster calls Chez Augustine, before flying Friday to New York. Arthur's sugar-coated ominous news from the physician is bad. Surgery required. Arthur, though unafraid of death, hopes to share some words about it with Mrs. Hogminster. On Thursday the manager assigns the Hogminsters a more secluded table. After dinner Mrs. Hogminster has a grateful word with Arthur — about bargains purchased St. Jermyn shops, owing to his recommendation. Arthur, deflated, proceeds to the kitchen.

The manager gives Arthur an envelope from Mrs. Hogminster. Wondrously relieved, Arthur waits to open it until he is abed in the hospital that night. Out come three one-pound notes and a letter thanking "Dear Arthur" for enjoyable visits to Chez Augustine and for the Jermyn Street sales tip.

Perhaps the extra-alone, extra-ill can best appreciate Arthur's quandary. Revealing his very human condition to intimates, if he had any, would somehow be a betrayal; and so when his desire to tell a seemingly sympathetic stranger is frustrated, the result is an ironically typical blow life often delivers to the elderly. Most readers surely know, and some surely are, Golden Oldies like Arthur.

MONEGASQUE CONSUL, THE (*Our Man in Havana*). He is one of the guests at the European Traders' Association banquet. He exports Havana cigars.

MONSIGNOR QUIXOTE (1982). Novel. (Characters: the Archbishop, the Bishop of El Toboso, the Bishop of Motopo, Diego, Señor Diego, Father Enrique, Father Felipe, Father Francesco, Doctor Galván, Father Gonzales, Father Herrera, Father José, Father Leopoldo, Marquez, Professor Pilbeam, Monsignor Quixote, Rocinante, Ronald, Teresa, Enrique Zancas.)

Part One. I: "How Father Quixote Became a Monsignor." Father Quixote's parish is El Toboso, province of La Mancha. He drives his red-colored old Seat 600, dubbed Rocinante in honor of his supposed ancestor Don Quixote's old horse, to buy wine. He encounters the Bishop of Motopo, a friendly Italian, whose Mercedes has stalled on the way to Madrid. Quixote drives him to his home for lunch until his car can be repaired. He tells his housekeeper Teresa to prepare his steak for two. She tells him it's horse meat. He plies the Bishop with wine, and he commends the meat. The Bishop rests. Quixote checks the Mercedes. No petrol. He inserts enough, greases his hands, and tells the Bishop he adjusted things and all's well. Weeks pass. A letter comes from Quixote's unfriendly Bishop of El Toboso: The Pope, at the grateful Bishop of Motopo's request, has elevated Quixote to monsignor.

II: "How Monsignor Set Off on His Travels." 1. Quixote's wise Communist friend, Enrique Zancas, was mayor of El Toboso, but has been ousted by presumably dishonest reactionaries. Sancho, as Quixote calls Zancas, offers him vodka — new to Quixote — and the two amiably but intelligently dispute, as usual. Sancho proposes a holiday drive to Moscow. Quixote suggests Rome, pleading Rocinante's frailty. Resting, Quixote dreams he climbed a tree and dislodged an empty nest.

2. The Bishop grants Quixote vacation time, after which he may be transferred, and sends as his El Toboso replacement the shrewd Father Herrera. Teresa dislikes Herrera. He and Quixote disagree about justice vs. love and about weighing moral theology against instinct in advising repentant sinners.

3. Sancho and Quixote pack Rocinante. Sancho prefers heading for Cuenca so Quixote can buy monsignor-style purple socks. Quixote rules for Madrid. Rocinante's boot has cases of Manchegan wine and some books, including Heribert Jone's *Moral Theology* (and items by Lenin and Marx).

III: "How a Certain Light Was Shed upon the Holy Trinity." Sunset finds Quixote and Sancho short of Madrid. By an abandoned outhouse they open Teresa's emergency parcel — cheese and sausage — dispute Cross vs. Hammer and Sickle (both symbols protesting injustice) and the Inquisition (Torquemada then Franco) vs. USSR (Stalin then Brezhnev), "monsignor" vs. "comrade." They drink two sunlit bottles of wine, then a small bottle. When Sancho expresses puzzlement about the Trinity, Quixote explains by analogy with the two bottles — God the Father, God the Son — and the half bottle — God the Holy Spirit. All different, all same substance; partake of one, partake of three, with the small bottle providing "the extra spark of life," and perhaps enabling their friendship to continue. Quixote suddenly feels he sinned by demeaning the Holy Ghost through comparing it to the small bottle. Sancho comforts him by opening another standard-size bottle.

IV: "How Sancho in His Turn Cast New Light on an Old Faith." Sheep interrupt their morning drive toward Madrid. Sancho wonders why Christ was called a shepherd, since sheep get slaughtered. They agree Generalissimo Francisco Franco was evil. Should he be damned? God, not Dante, should decide. Are Marx, Lenin, Matthew, Mark all infallible? The two men's doubts may make them more affectionate than shared faith could. Sancho retells the Prodigal Son story: Son felt stifled by bourgeois father's Job-like riches, took inheritance early, gave it away, worked on pig farm, returned home through temporary weakness, then was pig farmer again under bearded surrogate father, who taught him capitalism even when democracy subjugates workers. On to Madrid. Sancho, evidently well-heeled, treats Quixote to a sucking-pig and aristocratic-wine luncheon at Botin's, a former fascist hangout.

2. Sancho would spring for rooms in the glittering Palace Hotel, but Quixote demurs, Rocinante stops in front of a hostelry, and the two crash there. Quixote dreams that their friendship and understanding reconciled their "disparate faiths." At twilight Sancho rouses him to shop for purple socks, which should impress possible Guardia Civil. Sancho insists on shimmering nylons and matching "bib" (*pechera*) from a supercilious salesman, whom Sancho's needling makes suspicious. Quixote and Sancho discuss whether Franco is in Hell, then Pontius Pilate, Fidel Castro, the evolutionary Roman Empire. They bypass restaurants with saints' names, have a poor secular meal washed down with wine. Quixote, declining a third bottle and fearing to relate his conciliatory dream to Sancho, recalls Herrera's insisting that a Gospel advocating discipline by fear is better than one recommending love. Quixote thought Herrera hoped to goad him into reportable heresy. The travelers return to the hostelry. Sancho agrees to read Jone's moral book, to put him to sleep. Quixote, briefly sleepless, recalls his siesta dream that Christ, appealing from the Cross when challenged to do so, was saved. Ah, no agony. No rolled-away stone, no empty tomb, Roman soldiers knelt.

Jerusalem citizens approach in adoration. Christ's mother and disciples are joyful. No ambiguity. No doubt. Therefore no need for faith. Awakening, Quixote prays to be saved from such absolute certainty.

3. In the morning, the scared-looking landlady tells Quixote to write their names and destination. Equivocating, he writes Barcelona. Maybe they'll go there.

V: "How Monsignor Quixote and Sancho Visit a Holy Site." Sancho directs Quixote to drive toward Salamanca. Sancho opines that with pure Communism the state will wither, just as with universal Catholicism the papacy would. Quixote counters: Pure Communism, no need to fight injustice; what to do? Sancho: Cure diseases, find new energy sources. Quixote: Death would be welcome. Sancho: Transplanting organs might end deaths. Quixote: I prefer happy death, then "something further." Sancho dilates on Jone's strict *coitus interruptus* theory and its misapplication for birth control by Marquez, who was the friend of a student friend of Sancho. He directs Quixote to Franco's gigantic cross in the Valley of the Fallen. They enter the enormous tomb, festooned with tapestries and saints' statues. Sancho: Everything was built by Franco's prisoners. Quixote: Siberian-camp workers similarly toil. After praying for everybody, Quixote drives Sancho on. A Guardia jeep passes. The travelers have a road-side lunch. Sancho says that while he was a student in Salamanca he slept with the daughter of a druggist who had contraceptives; afterwards, Sancho used to apologize to Saint Teresa, of nearby Avila. Quixote prefers Saint Francis of Sales to the author Jone, and thinks Calvin resembled Lenin and Stalin. At the moment Sancho humorously dons Quixote's collar, two policemen appear. They check the car, examine their papers, look at their books, dislike the Lenin essays, briefly think Sancho with the collar must be the monsignor. Queried, Sancho says they stayed last night at the Palace and aim for Avila tonight. The cops leave. Sancho says it's too bad the cops' parents didn't practice birth control. Quixote: God's law mustn't be broken. Sancho: Fathering an unwanted child might be worse than murdering someone for a good reason. Quixote: God is merciful. Sancho: In Africa, in India, with poverty, disease? Quixote: Sufferers go to Heaven. Sancho: Hell, perhaps. Silently, Quixote tells himself to believe. They discuss appetites — for cheese, for sex. Silently, Quixote remembers *The City of God* by the experienced Augustine. Sancho lewdly refers to Jone. The cops drive by. Sancho suggests Segovia instead of Avila for now. Sancho asks whether Quixote was ever in love with a woman. Yes, with Martin (of Lisieux, known as Saint Thérèse). Sancho says his beloved woman is dead. Quixote prays for her. They drive to a hotel, happily near the Church of Saint Martin. In his room, Quixote knows he hasn't traveled far, but his ancestor Don Quixote didn't either. He opens *The Love of God* by Saint Francis de Sales. Advised by a random passage to speak even to the inanimate, he apologizes to his Rocinante for hard driving.

VI: "How Monsignor Quixote and Sancho Visit Another Holy Site." In the morning, Quixote dons his *pechera*. They drive. Sancho compares his being imprisoned during the Civil War to a monastery regimen, although interrogators differ from abbots. At Arévalo they see tattered circus posters; Sancho wonders how Quixote would baptize a two-headed newborn. Afternoon finds them in Salamanca, where Sancho studied and where Quixote wished he had, instead of in Madrid. Sancho mentions a priest whose half-belief lectures inspired him; the man got exiled for his liberalism. Quixote identifies that lecturer as Unamuno. Sancho says many conservatives were happy when he (Miguel de Unamuno [1864–1936]) died. Quixote says now that Sancho fully believes "the prophet Marx," he needn't think for himself or know "the dignity of despair." They visit Unamuno's tomb, a box in a wall. Goaded, Quixote says he prayed for Unamuno and, yes, for Stalin and Hitler.

VII: "How in Salamanca Monsignor Continued His Studies." Sancho, remembering his student days, guides Quixote to a certain place for rest. In Sancho's first-floor room, Quixote mistakes a bidet for a foot bath, a handy condom for a balloon he even blows up, and — tardily — the girl with champagne for what she is. He goes to his third-floor room to read Marx but can't wish him a good night.

VIII: How Monsignor Quixote Had a Curious Encounter in Valladolid." Quixote suggests Valladolid, where Cervantes completed his book — that biography of Quixote's ancestor. On the way, Sancho is disappointed that Quixote doesn't query him about last night. After seeing Cervantes's home, they have lunch. Quixote says Marx had much in common with Don Quixote and reads, loudly, from Marx's *Communist Manifesto* about "chivalrous enthusiasms" being swept away. After Sancho points to an eavesdropper who resembles a secret policeman, Quixote continues in whispers. The two debate about increase of vacation time and decrease of pauperism, Communism vs. humanism, religion (as Marxism or Christianity), politics (nationalism, imperialism, economics, wars). The eavesdropper leaves. Quixote reads Marx's praise of historical bourgeoisie inventiveness, explicates it as Marx's unacknowledged love of the bourgeoisie, and says Marx as a colonial governor might have saved the Spanish empire. Once outside, Sancho spots the eavesdropper, steers Quixote to a bar, slips out back to reconnoiter. The eavesdropper enters, steers Quixote into a lavatory, and asks to be confessed. The man says he's an undertaker, just buried his own priest Father Gonzalez, shows the coffin's brass handles, confesses he stole them, says undertakers do that pretty regularly. Quixote chops theological niceties to himself, tells the man to say he's sorry for proudly thinking such a sin is important, mumbles absolution, and the fellow bows and leaves. Quixote tells Sancho he feels inadequate and has a fourth bottle of that nice new drink Sancho showed him — tonic water.

IX: "How Monsignor Quixote Saw a Strange Spectacle." Sancho takes Quixote to his first-ever movie, *A Maiden's Prayer,* a porno flick. Sancho finds it mild. Its exhausting exercise involving tangled limbs puzzled Quixote. Sancho says it was simulating love-making. Quixote replies that he thought such activity was simpler, more pleasant, that those grunts and squeals sounded like suffering, unlike expressions of love for God. That night he opens *The Love of God,* reads about magnetized iron leaping toward adamant hence loving it; the movie had leaping too but no "lively love." Driving next day, Quixote tells Sancho he's afraid since he's never felt jumpy sexual desire he can't pray to resist its temptation. He quietly prays to lose his indifference, to be forced to confront temptation, to feel human shame.

X: "How Monsignor Quixote Confronted Justice." While driving toward León, Quixote and Sancho stop to rest. While Sancho cools some wine in a river, Quixote returns to the car for some cheese. A few minutes later, Quixote and a Guardia walk down to Sancho. The cop asks if they saw a certain dangerous robber on the road. Quixote answers questions in Latin (to avoid lying). Warning them to be on the lookout, the Guardia leaves. Quixote reveals to Sancho that he hid the robber in Rocinante's trunk. When they let the ragged fellow out, he pulls a revolver, demands Quixote's shoes first and a ride to the León cathedral next. Once they get there, the robber disappears. Quixote tries to pray in the cathedral. Sancho gets him to buy new shoes. Worried about events back home, he telephones Teresa to reassure her he is in León. She tells him the police are checking into his whereabouts, since they tried unsuccessfully to find him in Avila. She adds that Herrera tattled to the bishop, who wants to have Quixote declared insane. Sancho cannot persuade Quixote to abandon faithful Rocinante.

2. Outside León, Sancho asks Quixote whether he prefers Burgos or Osera next. Quixote opts for the Trappists of Osera. Sancho is relieved: Franco's headquarters were at Burgos. They share three bottles of wine. Quixote, teased by Sancho about his ancestor Don Quixote, retorts that his own adventures are based on saints' books, on his dead ancestor's, on chivalry. They contrast Marx and God — each tangible to his followers. Quixote feels as out of control as those lovers in that flick, then sleeps and snores.

3. Sancho dreams he was carrying those purple socks and located Quixote, who was weeping. Sancho awakens, finds the socks but no Quixote. He sees an American couple with a Renault near Rocinante. They give him some rolls, and by using a dictionary and gestures they communicate: Quixote was carried away.

Part Two. I: "Monsignor Quixote Encounters the Bishop." 1. After feeling a sensation of motion and then dreaming of three funny balloons, Quixote awakens back home in El Toboso. Doctor Galván, his friend for almost 30 years, and Teresa are there. He learns that through Herrera, the Bishop, and a politician related to Galván, Quixote was located, given a soothing injection, and brought home. The Bishop wants to see him. "Bugger the bishop," he says, surprisingly, in Spanish.

2. For guidance Quixote is reading from *Spiritual Letters* by Jean Pierre de Caussade (1675–1751) when Herrera announces the Bishop. He disparages Quixote's recent actions and association with that Communist ex-mayor. Quoting the Gospels in justification, the two priests wrangle about Quixote's wine, clothing, attending *A Maiden's Prayer,* giving a robber his shoes, fibbing to the Guardia, vacationing with a Communist, etc. Quixote debates so challengingly — even praising parts of Marx's *Manifesto* — that the Bishop upbraids him for thinking dangerously, calls his responses "ravings of a sick mind," and will pray for him, consult Galván, and write the Archbishop.

II: "Monsignor Quixote's Second Journey." 1. Sancho toots the horn of Rocinante, ready outside, painted blue, with a new number. While Herrera is at confessions, Sancho enters Quixote's residence, picks some locks, and equips Quixote for travel. He has his collar, purple socks, and new shoes, gives faithful Teresa a kiss on the forehead, and takes from her a letter from the Bishop.

2. The garage assistant who delayed Herrera by lying at confession rushes up. Quixote absolves him. Since Sancho and Quixote broke the law helping a robber, where can they drive now? Not to Alicante. To Mora and the Toledo mountains. They stop for wine from Rocinante's back seat, and sausages and cheese from Teresa. They compare and contrast themselves — two friendly survivors, with off-beat beliefs, torn between faith and doubt, hardly helped by books. Quixote concludes that absolute knowledge would be terrible. He reads the Bishop's letter: Quixote is under suspension. Good. He's justified in running. Sancho confesses he was tempted to drive alone and escape via Orense into Portugal. They decide to stay temporarily with the Osera Trappists.

III: "How Monsignor Quixote Had His Last Adventure Among the Mexicans." They can't cross to Bragança, Portugal, because Quixote lacks a passport. Sancho prefers Portuguese Communists to Euro-Communists, says Stalinists unlike Jesuits don't "turn with the wind," says Trappists are Catholic Stalinists. They seek to replenish their wine supply from Señor Diego, recommended by a villager, encounter a so-called Mexican who was refused wine with which to bribe his priests, but are admitted by José, Diego's priest-grandson, when they explain the wine is for Trappists. Diego serves the adventurers excellent wine, ham, and much talk: José, driven from his parish by dishonest priests and rich Mexicans buying land here, should have married and managed Diego's vineyards; Communists, when controlling production centers, install managers but could never manage a living vineyard. Quixote calls Diego's wine honest and beautiful. Since Stalin's intentions wouldn't be toasted, Sancho won't toast the Pope's, adding that no one knows chivalric Don Quixote's intentions, and that today Quixote and Sancho parody their models' intentions. Sensing Sancho's unaccustomed sadness, regret, even despair, Quixote wonders where their "voyage" will end. Diego explains: Mexicans, born here, left, made money, and returned, and fancy they can buy their way to Heaven by bribing regional priests. When Diego warns about an imminent money-laced procession to Our Lady in the village, Quixote must go see; Sancho will accompany him. Giving them two cases of wine, Diego thanks them for visiting.

2. They drive past several banks in Learig catering to Mexican money and then past villagers approaching the feast. Quixote arms himself, with collar and *pechera,* as Don Quixote did, with Mambrino's helmet. Worshippers explain that a rich man won the auction, has earned salvation, and heads Our Lady's procession, while others paying less march nearby. The Virgin's clothing is plastered with peseta notes, franc notes, and even a $100 bill. Despite Sancho's warning, Quixote calls the event blasphemous. He is rebuked and threatened. Though bloodied over an eye by the priest's swinging censer, he tears money down, is commended by one dissident, and the procession turns riotous. Sancho rushes Quixote, giddy now, into the car and off. Quixote costs valuable time by stopping to urinate.

IV: "How Monsignor Quixote Rejoined His Ancestor." 1. Behold the 12th-century monastery at Osera. In the dusk, statues of old popes and old knights seem alive. Visitors who speak seem like tourists landing on a silent island.

2. Father Leopoldo, the Trappist superior and an expert on (René) Descartes (1596–1650), has just cooked a wretched lunch for his visitor, Professor Pilbeam, who teaches at Notre Dame, in the United States, and is an expert on (Saint) Ignatius (of) Loyola (1491–1556). Leopoldo and Pilbeam are debating in the library — Descartes's practicality — fact — vs. Saint Ignatius's idealism — fiction — when gunshots ring out. The Guardia pursued Quixote's car and shot the tires. It crashed into the church wall, and Quixote bashed his head. Sancho says he is the ex-mayor named Zancas but nicknamed Sancho, his friend is Monsignor Quixote of El Toboso, the car is Rocinante; Pilbeam calls it all Cervantes's fiction. Leopoldo quips about fiction or fact, tells some monks to get Quixote and Sancho inside, orders the Guardia to back off, threatens to telephone the Orense bishop to rebuke them, and has Pilbeam phone for a doctor. On their way to a guest room, Quixote mutters about church and Mass, and Leopoldo graciously says "monsignor" and "tomorrow." The doctor stitches Quixote's cut forehead, suggests rest, maybe an x-ray later. The Guardia, having checked, phone Leopoldo that Quixote is deranged and Zancas is a Communist. So what?

3. Sedated, Quixote sleeps, stirs, imagines he's home, calls Leopoldo "Galván," hopes the Bishop won't burn his books, asks about Rocinante, and learns from Sancho she's safely garaged. Quixote babbles about lambs, elephants, books, a musical fart, Mambrino's helmet, sinfully discussing the half bottle, and items out of Cervantes which Pilbeam can interpret. Quixote offers Sancho a kingdom, which he agrees to journey for. Quixote mentions love hopping, then sitting erect in bed repeats "Bugger the bishop." Saying "no balloons," he stumbles out, leads the others into the church, starts a speedy Mass in Latin. Certain phrases resemble night lights in a child's dark room. He swallows invisible paten from unseen chalice. He calls Sancho "compañero," has him kneel, and falls dead. He is caught by Sancho, who says, "Compañero, I'm Sancho."

4. Quixote's Bishop will come soon, and Quixote's body will be returned to El Toboso. Ex-mayor Zancas and Pilbeam, both preferring fact, discount Leopoldo's belief that Descartes would say only that no one *saw* wafer and chalice last night. Leopoldo adds that Quixote *knew* the 30-year Communist Sancho received communion. Leopoldo says that if wine can turn to blood, air can turn to wine. As Pilbeam considerately drives him to Orense, Zancas feels less free, compares Rocinante, a smashed metal animal, and Monsignor Quixote, his "brain in fragments," strangely cannot feel hatred for dead Franco and yet fearfully feels continued love for Quixote despite his being dead and separated from him. For how long? Why?

Greene and his priest-friend Leopoldo Duran drove around Spain (July 1976, July 1977). They visited many of the places described in *Monsignor Quixote,* and drank, ate, and talked much as Quixote and Zancas do in the novel. Greene often played devil's advocate (Sancho) to Duran (Quixote). Duran later wrote that Greene told him their journey would form a basis for *Monsignor Quixote.* Greene wrote Duran and conferred with him while composing the novel, which he began late in 1977 and completed early in 1982. Yvonne Cloetta* says that Greene liked *Monsignor Quixote* best among his novels

According to Norman Sherry, Greene wrote *Monsignor Quixote* mostly in Antibes, France, during which time he resembled Cervantes's Quixote by chivalrously making windmills of the Mafia, to help Antibes regain chivalric repute. It seems that Greene had been studying the French Mafia on the Côte d'Azure, and its influence on politicians, the police, attorneys, and judges. He felt a special animus against Daniel Guy, who was an often-convicted criminal (1960–1970) and, worse, was also the despised, sadistic husband of Martine Cloetta Guy, the daughter of Yvonne Cloetta,* Greene's ultimate mistress. Sherry and Duran say Guy was protected by corrupt authorities in Nice. Greene published articles in French newspapers and assembled his courageous diatribe against French criminal activity in *J'Accuse: The Dark Side of Nice* (1982), published in English and French, and soon banned in France. Greene's movie-director friend Bryan Forbes (b. 1926) recalls in his autobiography meeting with Greene in Antibes and hearing him casually discuss the possibility of his being the victim of drive-by assassins because of his outspoken criticism of crime in the region. In *Getting to Know the General: The Story of an Involvement,* Greene explains that when he told General Torrijos about Yvonne's dangerous son-in-law, Torrijos offered to "send a man to France to teach a lesson" to him. Greene couldn't condone this "violent solution."

Valerie Sedlak says that "In *Monsignor Quixote,* Graham Greene not only completes a circle begun with *Brighton Rock,* but also marks the conclusion of a spiritual search begun forty-four years earlier." Jae-Suck Choi says that "Greene's *Monsignor Quixote* is to Cervantes' *Don Quixote* as Unamuno's *The Life of Don Quixote and Sancho* [1927] is to *Don Quixote,*" then details similarities in Unamuno's and Greene's respective handling of Quixote. Peter Green suggests that a source of *Monsignor Quixote* could be *Mondo Piccolo: Don Camillo* (1948; trans., *The Little World of Don Camillo* (1950) by Giovanni Guareschi (1908–1968); it concerns simple priest, Communist villagers, Communist mayor. Wolfgang G. Müller relates Greene's "conception of *Monsignor Quixote*" to two postmodern theories, which are that "individual texts constantly refer to other texts" and also that "fiction and reality are indistinguishable." The "other texts" are Cervantes's *Don Quixote,* Miguel de Unamuno's classic, and the Bible. Duran writes that Greene was incredibly moved when he visited Unamuno's simple grave in Salamanca. Mark Bosco links *Monsignor Quixote* and *Doctor Fischer of Geneva or The Bomb Party,* since both "showed Greene's surprising stylistic turn to fablelike compositions: the stark realism of his narrative style was fused with romantic idioms that heightened the symbolic weight of his characters." Refuting critics who categorize *Monsignor Quixote* as Catholic or anything else viz-a-viz religion and politics, Bosco concludes that it "is overwhelmingly more Catholic than Communist, more Christian than humanist, and more a new development — stylistically and thematically — than a mere coda to Greene's celebrated Catholic cycle." Bosco discusses the novel as it relates to Catholic liturgy, Christology, and Marxism. It may be added that it is unified by several devices. Picaresque narratives are always sewed together by journey motifs. Dramatic diversities of Greene's two principals squeeze their story together. Providing unifying musical background noise are Quixote's and Zancas's references and allusions, eventually predictable and sometimes tiresome, to their respective ancestors in Cervantes's masterpiece.

Quentin Falk, David Parkinson, Neil Sinyard, and Cedric Watts mention the television adaptation of *Monsignor Quixote* (1985, with Alex Guinness playing Quixote). It is interesting that *Beloved Quixote: The Unknown Life of John Middleton Murry* (1986) is the title of the biography of John Middleton Murry (1889–1957) by his daughter Katherine Middleton Murry (b. 1925). Greene knew about both Murrys. (Sources: Bosco, 130, 139; Choi, 188; Duran, 126–27, 212–21 passim, 253–59; Falk, 198; Forbes, 125–27; Green, 35; Greene, *Getting to Know the General,* 185, 186; Müller, 161; Parkinson, 698; Sedlak, 577; Sherry III, 637–55 passim; Sinyard, 158; Watts, 81; West, 247–48)

MONSTER OF THE CHEMINS DE FER (*Travels with My Aunt*). While on the Orient Express, Augusta tells Henry about this killer. The Monster traveled on French railroads, offered brassieres to various girls, and killed those who chose improperly. He was caught, made a good confession, was given absolution, and was guillotined.

MONTAGU, SIR JOSEPH (*Brighton Rock*). This gentleman is paged at the Cosmopolitan while Pinkie is talking with Colleoni.

MONTEZ (*The Honorary Consul*). He is a young novelist in Buenos Aires, whom Saavedra complains to Plarr he encouraged, only to find that Montez had just published a well-written essay praising novels by Mallea and Sabato while contending that Saavedra's epic poem *Martín Fierro* was adversely affecting Argentine novels.

Mentioning fictional Saavedra's fictional rival Montez in this way gives Greene an opportunity to link the two to real-life Argentine novelists Eduarto Mallea (b. 1923) and Ernesto Sabato (b. 1911), both deservedly popular during the time of the action of *The Honorary Consul.*

MONTEZ (*The Power and the Glory*). He is the father of a hostage murdered in Concepción, the whisky priest's village.

MONTEZ, PEDRO (*The Power and the Glory*). He was a hostage, shot in Concepción, the village of the whisky priest, who dreams about Pedro being shot in the forehead.

MONTGOMERY (*Doctor Fischer of Geneva*). He was the husband, deceased, of Mrs. Montgomery, one of Fischer's party guests. Fischer criticizes her for remaining married to her husband 20 years because of his wealth.

MONTGOMERY, LADY ISOBEL ("Under the Garden"). She was a society woman who opened a charitable fête, according to the 1885 newspaper Wilditch reads aloud to Javitt. Hearing the word "fête" prompts Javitt to lecture on "fate."

MONTGOMERY, MRS. (*Doctor Fischer of Geneva*). She is a blue-haired widow and the only woman guest at Fischer's parties, for which she occasionally shops, selects gifts, and serves as a toadying hostess. She likes Jones but calls him Smith.

MONTI, EULELIA (*Rumour at Nightfall*). She is a proud San Juan woman, 26, the conflicted daughter of radically distinct parents. Beautiful, with bronze-shadowed black hair, green eyes, and ivory skin, Eulelia gives herself, one night only, to Ramon Caveda to spite her dowry-seeking mother. This interests Chase pronto and Crane soon. Eulelia appeals differently to both men, which results in her forsaking Caveda for Crane and Chase's betraying Crane and surviving sadly with her.

Two unacceptable aspects of *Rumour at Nightfall* are Eulelia's self-confessed poor English turning fluent and her marrying Crane hours after meeting him.

MONTI, SEÑOR (*Rumour at Nightfall*). He is Eulelia's religious, gentle, inept father. Scholarly Monti studies the lives of saints. Eulelia says she inherited her best qualities from him.

Greene oddly also reports that Monti read works by the British poets Edmund Campion (1540–1581) and Robert Southwell (c. 1561–1595). Both were Jesuit priests accused of treason and hanged. Monti may have studied saints' lives in the 1870s, but Campion was not beatified until 1886, Southwell not until 1929.

Greene, however, long retained his interest in Catholic martyrs. Anthony Mockler suggests that Greene's trip to Mexico (1938) was partly inspired by *Edmund Campion* (New York: Sheed & Ward, 1935), the martyr's biography by Greene's Catholic friend Evelyn Waugh. Greene favorably reviewed Waugh's book (*Spectator,* November 1, 1935), saw obvious parallels between violently anti–Catholic Elizabeth England and anti–Catholic Mexico (in the 1920s and 1930s), and unsuccessfully sought travel funds from Catholic-publisher Frank Sheed. Greene went to Mexico anyway to observe conditions (1938), and wrote *The Lawless Roads* (1939; American title, *Another Mexico*) and *The Power and the Glory* (1940). Decades later, Greene lectured on "The Virtue of Disloyalty" in Hamburg, Germany (1969), and took the occasion to call Southwell, contemporary to Shakespeare and bravely disloyal to murderously anti–Catholic Britain, "a greater hero" than Shakespeare, who remained politically expedient. Norman Sherry discusses Greene's admiration of Southwell but doesn't mention Monti or *Rumour at Nightfall* while doing so. (Sources: Mockler, 132–33; Sherry III, 486, 487)

MONTI, SEÑORA (*Rumour at Nightfall*). She is Eulelia's mother. Her half-crazy venality and materialism cause her to put Eulelia, beautiful and innocent, on the auction block. Caveda, Eulelia's one-night lover, fears her mother would betray him for the reward money. Señora Monti is skinny, with dyed hair, glittering left eye, thin and hungry lips, and metallic voice. Her having the last word in the novel bodes ill for Eulela's and Chase's future.

MOON ("A Discovery in the Woods"). This tallest man ever known in the village of Bottom was reputedly almost five feet high.

MOREL, ANNE (*A Burnt-Out Case*) see **MOREL, MARIE**

MOREL, MARIE (*A Burnt-Out Case*). She was a girlfriend of Querry, probably in Belgium. He lured her away from Hoghe, her boyfriend. When Rycker repeats to Querry the gossip concerning his love affairs, Querry corrects him: Marie was the girl's name, not Anne;

she was 25, not 18; she killed herself not for love of him but to escape him; her city was not Bruges. When Querry is telling Marie Rycker his fairy tale about the King and the jeweler, he says the jeweler had a mistress named Marie, who lived at 49 rue des Remparts.

MORENO, JULIO (*The Honorary Consul*). He is the main character in Saavedra's novel *The Taciturn Heart,* which Plarr reads unenthusiastically. Moreno's wife leaves him for a young, unemployed, alcoholic laborer, then returns. Plarr guesses the ending will involve Moreno's having a knife fight with the youth, predestined to killed Moreno.

MORENO, SEÑORA (*The Honorary Consul*). She is the wayward wife of Julio Moreno in Saavedra's novel *The Taciturn Heart.* She deserts Julio, goes to a seaside city, consorts with an unemployed drunk, and returns to Julio, who finds the drunk and dies in a fight with him.

Could Greene's depiction of this woman be interpreted as Greene's warning to husbands of his mistresses to avoid him?

MORGAN, HARRY (*Our Man in Havana*). He is a real-estate man in from Miami and drinking at the Seville-Biltmore bar. He overhears Hasselbacher pretending to Wormold he's won $140,000 in the lottery. Morgan expresses wonder. So Hasselbacher offers this confusing solipsism: Morgan and the lottery winnings exist if Hasselbacher perceives them and don't if he doesn't. Hasselbacher adds that if Wormold invented Morgan he would call him Pennyfeather and claim he was Oxford-educated.

Perhaps Greene gave this evidently successful land-dealing American the name he did to suggest a relationship with Henry Morgan (1635?–1688), the successful buccaneer who also knew something about Caribbean coastal real estate.

MORIN, PIERRE ("A Visit to Morin"). He is a French novelist, a member of the Academy, now nearly 80, and a non-practicing Catholic retired in a village near Colmar, Germany. The narrator Dunlop sees him avoid communion at Christmas Eve Mass. The two converse at Morin's home. Morin fiercely denies he has only his belief, not his faith. For 20 years he avoided confession, partly because he had a mistress he wouldn't pretend he'd ever leave. Her death five years ago killed "my sex," he says. Now he fears participating in the sacraments could deprive him of his faith.

Philip Stratford opens his comparison of Greene and François Mauriac (1885–1970) by quoting "A Visit to Morin" and suggesting the relationship of Greene, Mauriac, and Morin. (Greene told Leopoldo Duran that Stratford's book, which was published in 1964, was "the best on my work.") Norman Sherry follows with parallels between Morin and Greene, concerning Catholicism and also their responses to misguided critics of their writing. Significant is Morin's telling Dunlop he couldn't confess illicit sexual relations with his mistress without having any "firm purpose of amendment." So for 20 years Morin absented himself from grace. Likewise Greene, who, says Sherry, refused communion, not for 20 but for 30 years. Jae-Suck Choi observes that "Monsignor Quixote [in Greene's *Monsignor Quixote*], like Morin ..., distinguishes between belief and faith and makes more of faith than of belief." Thomas A. Wendorf comments that "Morin ... believes his writing of fiction has somehow emptied him of belief.... The implication is that writing narrative can deplete the writer's sense of mystery." (Thus with Greene too?) (Sources: Choi, 195; Duran, 305; Sherry III, 250, 688–89; Stratford, ix; Wendorf, 646)

MORROW ("The Other Side of the Border"). He was Morrow's father, deceased. He was a parson, in or near Liverpool. Danvers reminds Morrow that he knew his father.

MORROW ("The Other Side of the Border"). He becomes a victim when he is persuaded by Danvers, general manager of the New Syndicate in Liverpool, to join Hands in a West African gold-seeking expedition. Morrow returns and reports disasters occurring in their 1936–1938 venture and involving Colley, Billings, and deaths, including those of a hundred blacks.

Greene doesn't specify the nature of the disasters.

MORROW, MRS. ("The Other Side of the Border"). She is Morrow's mother. When Colley joins Hands and Billings in the latter's photograph shop in West Africa (1936), he calls Morrow an uppity prig and says he's writing his Sunday letter to "Mamma."

"MORTMAIN" (1963). Short story. (Characters: Julia Carter, Philip Carter, Josephine Heckstall-Jones.)

Philip Carter, 42, a fiction writer, lived 10 stormy years with Josephine Heckstall-Jones, a successful fashion designer whose jealous, hysterical temperament made his brand-new marriage to Julia seem to augur serenity. Julia, however, alarms Carter by hoping for Josephine's continued friendship. The Carters honeymoon in Athens. Josephine, who cried at the wedding, writes him there. Julia gets upset when Philip attempts to conceal the letter, which mentions Josephine's using her kept key to retrieve things from Philip's home. Julia admires "wonderful" Josephine's letter. The Carters return to London and find that Josephine has prepared electric fires against the autumn chill and left Julia a letter. It says she and Philip had to fight London's chill when they returned from southern France, and she's leaving the key under the doormat.

Their marriage is nice until, in November, Josephine's "time-bombs" start exploding. In his desk Philip finds a note saying goodnight to him and much love. Julia won't let him destroy the note and voices sympathy for Josephine, who, poor thing, lost him. They decide to flip the mattress, only to find a letter underneath from Josephine to Julia, about how Greece, which she and Philip never visited, is probably nice. Julia rebukes Philip for sarcastically suggesting an edition of Josephine's letters. In his telephone directory he finds a list of necessary numbers, done on Josephine's recognizable typewriter. Josephine calls Julia an angel for such consideration. The mailman delivers a copy of the Paris *Vogue,* which features sketches by Josephine and includes a card saying she took out the subscription for them. That evening Philip reads from Robert Browning to Julia in a homey way. His selection starts well until, first, he comes to the part about two close people shadowed by a third, and, second, a note inserted after that page — Josephine wishes Philip good night between the pages of his — and her — favorite book. He throws everything down and says "bitch." Finding the note, Julia appreciates Josephine's having good memories, and wonders about hers to come, with wrongheaded Philip. That night things are cool. In the morning, sure enough, there's a letter in his writing pad, beginning "Darling."

Richard Kelly explains that "mortmain," a legal term, "refers to the transfer of property ... for perpetual ownership," and explicates thus: "Josephine has not transferred her emotional property ... for perpetual ownership by her rival." It may be added that when Greene describes Josephine's handwriting, now "abhorrent" to Philip, as precise, tiny, and in black ink, he may intend to suggest that her "main" has an intention as black as "mort." Greene's handwriting was tiny and often black but almost never precise. "Mortmain" was the subject of a 1976 television production. *See Shades of Greene.* (Sources: Falk, 215; Kelly, 58)

MORTON ("The End of the Party"). He is Francis Morton's and Peter Morton's father. When Francis sees preparations for his parents' evening meal, he senses their indifference to his anxiety attack.

MORTON, FRANCIS ("The End of the Party"). He is Peter Morton's very slightly younger and far more timid twin brother. They are nine. Francis dreams of death, fears life in general and darkness in particular, fights against attending Colin Henne-Falcon's 10th birthday party, plays hide-and-seek in the dark there, and is literally scared to death.

Part of the name Morton suggests death. Norman Sherry details ways in which Francis is similar to Greene himself as a child. (Source: Sherry I, 15, 71–72, 277)

MORTON, MRS. ("The End of the Party"). She and her husband are the parents of nine-year-old twins, Peter Morton and Francis Morton. When timorous Francis begs to stay home, Mrs. Morton insists that his real fears of darkness and death are nothing, and requires both twins to attend Colin Henne-Falcon's 10th birthday party. While playing hide-and-seek, as the children did at last year's party, Francis dies in darkness.

MORTON, PETER ("The End of the Party"). He is Francis Morton's minutes-older twin brother. More self-reliant, he tries to comfort Francis when the two are playing hide-and-seek at Colin Henne-Falcon's 10th birthday party, touches him in the darkness, whispers to comfort the silent lad, only to find him dead when the lights come on again. Eerily, Peter fears Francis's fright is now transfused into his own blood stream.

MOSES ("The Trial of Pan"). God has a brief vision of this sternly somber "minister."

MOSS, B. ("The Other Side of the Border"). He is the religious man who answers Billings's cable applying to replace Baines, who has died in their West African town. B. Moss says he himself is arriving on the 16th.

Oddly, an American clothing store established in 1989 is named B. Moss.

MOULT (*Orient Express*). He is a commercial rival of Myatt's currant business in Constantinople. Eckman says Moult tried to buy the stock of Leo Stein, Myatt's associate there.

MOYNE, CHARLIE (*Brighton Rock*). He is a raffish-looking panhandler near Carter & Galloway. Ida Arnold gives him a pound, even though she has walked to Carter's to save bus fare.

MSLOZ (*The Comedians*) see **BROWN**

MUCKERJI, MR. (*The Confidential Agent*). He is a respectful, courteous Hindu living in the hotel managed by Mrs. Mendrill. Muckerji takes notes on public actions and thoughts for an organization that samples public opinions. His making his observations available to the police results in Mrs. Mendrill's confession that she murdered Else Crole.

MULLER (*The Name of Action*). He is the customs officer at Cochem. He is a towering man, with supercilious eyebrows and a heavy moustache. Weber is usually able to bribe Muller to let contraband items through to Trier. But the presence of Mann, the loquacious passport officer, threatens Weber's success in doing so and in his and Chant's getting their arms shipment by.

MULLER, CORNELIUS (*The Human Factor*). He is a special BOSS agent, of Dutch Reformed Church persuasion and with gold-rimmed glasses. Castle despises Muller. In South Africa, Muller wanted Castle to work under him and tried to blackmail him by threatening to have him discharged for violating apartheid laws by marrying Sarah MaNkosi (*see* Castle, Sarah). Muller comes to London to confer with Castle about the Uncle Remus project. The Castles have him to dinner. Replacing Davis when he is murdered, Muller feeds Castle false information to transmit to the Soviets, which obliges Castle to defect.

MULLER, FRAU ("The Root of All Evil"). She is the sturdy wife of Muller, who is one of the wine-drinking clubmen.

MULLER, HERR ("The Root of All Evil"). He is one of the wine-drinking clubmen.

"MURDER FOR THE WRONG REASON" (1929). Short story. (Characters: Collins, Nellie Collins, Hubert Collinson, Groves, Rachel Mann, Detective-Inspector Mason, Saunders.)

1. Stabbed in the heart, Hubert Collinson screams, may have seen the wall mirror used by his girlfriends, and dies. Someone hears the cry, breaks the locked door, sees the corpse.

Detective-Inspector Mason, who entered, is middle aged, gray, and tidy. He blows his whistle out the window for police reinforcements, phones his office, reports Collinson's death, orders expert Groves to come. Smirking, Mason admits a neighbor-beat constable, tells him Collinson was a blackmailing womanizer deserving death. The ambitious constable impresses him by saying evil people sometimes aren't killed for good reasons. Mason agrees the killer might have escaped by the window and wonders who locked Collinson's door.

Mason orders the constable to break open Collinson's locked box and seek paper evidence. Only bills and receipts, sir. Mason says this may be a difficult case, after which, having done private-inquiry work, he'll retire.

Mason, melancholy, sees his face reflected in that of Collinson, a fellow trusted to do wrong. Mason knew nothing virtuous about him, figured the cunning fellow would have rationalized his misuse of power. Mason muses on his own private inquiries. The constable finds an undated letter. Swaying, Mason reads its familiar writing: Arthur Callum vows that if Collinson won't admit him, he'll thrash him in the street.

Mason can imagine where this cheap notepaper was purchased. The constable, eager for promotion, theorizes: Callum had a grudge. Mason reminds him he said bad people are rarely killed for good reasons, adding Callum sounds like someone with a good reason but the faded ink suggests a 10-year-old letter. When Mason says he knew Callum years ago, the constable suggests nabbing Callum ahead of Scotland Yard reinforcements.

2. Mason enters Callum's unlocked, unforgotten room, sees the familiar mantelpiece engraving of Lazarus rising, books, bed, tobacco pouch, other litter. Shouting "Callum," he sees Callum's face; the years that have lined Mason's face with surly melancholy spared Callum, young, with sick-looking eyes.

Mason apologizes for lateness. Callum agrees it's late. Years separate them. Mason says Collinson was murdered tonight. Callum rejoices. Mason mentions bad men aren't always killed for good reasons, says Callum had reason, flourishes Callum's letter, adds he alone knows the knife was Callum's, silently recalls when 15-year-old Callum bought it in Camden Town, engraved it, hid it, adds he knows why the letter was written, before he and Callum separated.

Mason's knowledgeable memory of cynical young Rachel Mann, whom both men knew, derives more from Callum's mind, stained as in an old mirror. Callum vowed patience to gain Rachel, who at 25 wanted him but desired a publicized acting career more, gained access to theatrical-entrepreneur Collinson, whom Callum wrote threateningly but too late. Mason knew Rachel was professional toward Collinson while remaining amiably fond of Callum. Mason rages, thinking dead Collinson not only learned intimate secrets about Rachel through their commercial relationship but was until an hour ago indifferent concerning those secrets, which Callum would have prized indefinitely. Mason upbraids himself for seeming jealous, whereas Callum, if knowing Rachel was Collinson's mistress, would still marry her. But she wouldn't.

Rachel offered Mason 45 minutes of sex before dinner with Collinson. Mason tells Callum he should have accepted, should then merely have compared notes with Collinson instead of killing him. Mason knows Callum didn't kill him, which he had good reason to do 20 years ago. Mason forgets the constable, forgets Groves, driving close. Mason, briefly angry, wishes too-chivalrous Callum, with an unselfish reason, had acceptably committed the murder. Oddly addressing a potential arrestee, smiling Mason says no court would have hanged you.

Mason tells Callum a Piccadilly streetwalker would have sufficed, biologically; additionally, he, not Mason, caused the present "mess." Yet Callum and this room have left an impress on Mason, now truly tortured.

Staying inside, Mason knows Collinson wasn't killed for blackmailing, tells Callum he couldn't bring him back, suddenly encounters dark-dressed, red-lipped Rachel still young. Mason tells ever-silent, unfeeling Rachel this: Collinson is dead, better earlier, never so now; she wasn't the reason for his murder; she was the right reason earlier, should have married misunderstood Callum, who wanted to be a doctor and serve, wrongly desired serving her but ended serving self; you and I know that dull deadliness; you wrecked Callum; Collinson's death was required but not for any wrong reason; I killed him; you caused Callum to meet him.

Mason tells Rachel: He won't arrest now-safe Callum; let's suppose you married him. Swaying, Mason forgets his corrupt, deceitful climb to Scotland Yard eminence but instead remembers tenderly, passionately proposing marriage to her. In Callum's littered room he recalls her "infamous proposal" in negative reply, winces, then thinks about biology and laughs.

3. Two minutes have passed. Laughing, lowering the letter, Mason tells the constable this: Callum isn't the wanted one; I've held private inquiries; you'll surpass Groves triumphantly; this letter is 15 years old; I knew Callum, the long-dead quarrel, the woman concerned. Mason leads the constable to agree that Callum, once an impoverished medical student, wasn't worth blackmailing; also that,

since the knife was bent, it had to be leaned on, ergo, elderly killer.

Mason gets the constable to agree no old killer could escape out window, down 30-foot drain-pipe. Mason quietly sees no evidence of Rachel in Collinson's room. Mason queries the fuddled constable about the locked-door key, then produces it.

Mason says killer killed, exited, locked door, smashed it open, observed corpse, then — tired of his prospects — persuades the constable to handcuff him, and explains everything: Mason was Callum, and killer wasn't jealous young lover but corrupt old policeman and blackmail victim. Yes, bad men aren't always killed for good reasons. Groves enters. Mason praises the constable for solving the crime.

Banishing vision of a relenting Rachel, Mason orders astonished Groves to take his statement. Listeners here and later in court were troubled, but not so Rachel, dead 10 years.

"Murder for the Wrong Reason," though early, is Greene's most complex short story. Greene confesses — believe it or not — that when he reread it "more than sixty years later" he couldn't "detect the murderer before he was disclosed." Most critics ignore the story, which requires rereading for fuller alleged comprehension. After analyzing it in detail, Richard Kelly complains that Greene doesn't clarify either what Collinson blackmailed Mason for or how Rachel died. Is Kelly's addendum helpful — that "the blackmail may have been about women, or a woman, or the death of a woman"?

Though evidently never the basis of a film, "Murder for the Wrong Reason" has one uniquely beautiful cinematic touch. When Mason is in Collinson's flat and imagining he is revisiting Callum's flat, the chiaroscuro lighting effects are identical in both places. (Sources: Greene, *The Last Word*, viii; Kelly, 72)

MURIEL (*The Captain and the Enemy*). She is Jim Baxter's maternal aunt. Jim's selfish father dislikes her. Jim, who doesn't like her either, resents her unloving visits to him at school. When the Captain rescues Jim from school, Muriel engages a detective to locate him. By a slip of the tongue at one point, Jim's father misnames her Miriam.

MURPHY (*England Made Me*). When Krogh reminisces about doing construction work on a bridge in Chicago, he recalls his friends Murphy, O'Connor, and Williamson there. Krogh's memory of the three men is triggered when Farrant uses the verb "neck" (i.e., kiss and caress) in conversation with him.

MUSKER, CORAL (*Orient Express*). She is a young dancer in London. Coral is on her way by train from Ostend to London to be a chorus-line girl in Dunn's Babies, a show in Constantinople. She is befriended and willingly seduced by Myatt, who encourages her to believe she will be his Constantinople mistress. She is arrested by the police at Subotica for aiding Czinner; escapes with Czinner and Grünlich, hides in a shed with Czinner after he has been mortally wounded by a soldier under Hartep's command, and is recaptured. Mabel Warren, a reporter, gains Coral's release, after which she will interview Coral and probably make some lesbian moves toward her.

It is thought that Coral was partly modeled on Anna Sten (1908–1993), the leading actress in the movie entitled *Die Mörder Dimitri Karamazov* (1931, directed by Fedor Ozep [1895–1949]), which Greene saw in Oxford (1932). Sten, born Anjuschka Stenski Sudakewitsch in Kiev, went to Hollywood (1933) and starred in several movies, among them *Nana* (1934) and *The Nun and the Sergeant* (1962). (Sources: Sherry I, 410–11; Watts, 25)

MYATT, CARLETON (*Orient Express*). He is a commercially sharp Jewish merchant, and a member of Myatt, Myatt and Page, London importers of currants. He is chronically suspicious of associates and rivals alike, whereas his father Jacob is more trusting. On the train from Ostend to Constantinople, Carleton Myatt makes nice to and seduces Coral Musker, a dancer from London, and promises she'll become his Constantinople mistress. After Myatt learns she has been detained by authorities in Subotica for helping Czinner, another passenger, he tries unavailingly to rescue her, and proceeds to Constantinople. Once there, Myatt straightens out business difficulties involving his agent Eckman and his rival Leo Stein, forgets Coral and goes after Stein's half-Jewish niece Janet Pardoe, whom he also met on the train.

Greene gave Myatt the first name he did because of the middle name of Hugh Carleton Greene,* Greene's younger brother. It seems likely that "Mr. Eugenides, the Smyrna merchant / Unshaven, with a pocketful of currants" (T. S. Eliot, *The Waste Land*) was in Greene's mind when he has Myatt offer Coral some currants from a supply in his pockets. Izmir (Smyrna) is only 160 miles south-southwest of Istanbul (Constantinople). Michael Shelden surprisingly states that many readers may view Myatt as "a good character," but then concludes, not surprisingly, that Myatt is "coarse and selfish." Malcolm J. Turnbull generously praises Greene for characterizing "not altogether unsympathetic" Myatt in such a way as to "express ... alarm at increasing levels of antisemitic activity in Europe [in 1932]." (Sources: Shelden, 166, 167; Turnbull, 61)

MYATT, JACOB (*Orient Express*). He is Carleton Myatt's father, head of the currant-importing firm of Myatt, Myatt and Page. Carleton regards his father as too trustful.

"MY GIRL IN GAITERS" *see* **"WORK NOT IN PROGRESS"**

NAISMITH (*Loser Takes All*). He is evidently a business associate of Sir Walter Blixon. The others are in Dreuther's office with Dreuther and Bertram. At one point, Blixon gets Naismith to have lunch with him.

THE NAME OF ACTION (1930). Novel. (Characters: Adolph, Oliver Chant, Crane, Anne-Marie Demassener, Paul Demassener, Frau Ertzüger, Fritz, Fritz, Frau Gruner, Bertha Kapper, Joseph Kapper, Karl, Captain Kraft, Kurtz, Sebastian Lintz, Loulou, Michael, Mann, Mrs. Meadmore, Muller, Peter Remnant, Frau Schultz, Struber, Frau Struber, Peter Torner, Weber, Frau Weber.)

Part I: Chapter I. Oliver Chant meets Kurtz, exiled by Paul Demassener, Dictator of Trier in the Rhenish Palatinate, east of Luxemburg, at liberal Mrs. Meadmore's London home. Chant agrees to take £3,000 to Trier, and meet and finance Kurtz's revolutionary friends Joseph Kapper and Peter Torner. Seven days later, Chant arrives by train and is thrilled by being body-searched.

Chapter II. Trier, Eastertime. Life deadened by the Dictator. From his gasthaus room, Chant takes an introductory letter from Kurtz to shoemaker Sebastian Lintz. Kapper and Torner are there. They speak English and German. Promising money, Chant sees their secret printing press, which will spread propaganda to make the people disrespect and distrust Demassener. Anne-Marie Demassener, his wife, drives up, having cut her wrist when her windshield broke in an accident. She sees Chant, identifies the conspirators, says Demassener knows where they meet but doesn't fear their propaganda, and chortles when Kapper shows his revolver. Chant is solicitous about her wrist. She invites him to dinner tomorrow at the palace.

Chapter III. Chant, their only guest, observes, first, Demassener, tall, stooped, proud of shuttering the too-sexy cabarets for seducing his people from work, and, second, gorgeous, half-French wife Anne-Marie. She calls Demassener puritanical. They speak English. Captain Kraft, reporting, says the mother of a prisoner just executed asks to see the Dictator. When she wants her son's body and to have a Mass performed, Demassener says the burial of this atheist will be inside prison grounds but a priest may attend. She asks if Frau Schultz, whose son was also shot, may attend his burial. No. Kraft ejects her. Anne-Marie rebukes her husband and exits. Demassener, lonely and happy for Chant's audience, explains: He isn't greedy for power as visiting journalists think, but is saving his province for Germany, though not Republican Germany. He closed Frau Schultz's brothel. He hates freedom, which bestializes people. He reviles the trivial poetry by a certain Jew (Kapper), whom Chant says Londoners praise. Demassener says after the French abandoned Trier and the Rhineland, republicans took over. His friend Struber was murdered by three republicans. Demassener organized a funeral procession with a thousand armed men, struck back, seized city control, and exiled Kurtz. Chant, though wavering, still savors adventuresome rebellion. And he wants Anne-Marie. The two men see her playing the piano. Her eyes and Chant's meet. After goodnights, Chant smells enchanting magnolias, asks a servant how to leave through the garden, then eavesdrops as Demassener tells his wife that "this boy" (Chant) is in love with her. Demassener tries to embrace her. She says she's tired of waiting, sees peeping Chant, who walks away. Anne-Marie enters the garden, seemingly bored. Chant tells her he saw her photograph, is infatuated, came to Trier to see her and for another, secret, reason. They embrace and kiss.

Chapter IV. Chant climbs the garden wall, gets lost, is afraid of being arrested after curfew, is followed by a policeman, whom Kapper, also following Chant, shoots and kills. They swing the corpse into the nearby Moselle River and hide in Kapper's house, also nearby. Kapper orders his slovenly wife Bertha to go cover the policeman's blood in the road with strips of dripping liver to deceive the street cleaners. Kapper boasts that this unplanned violence is weaker than his propagandistic poetry and Torner's pictures, and shows Torner's cartoon of Anne-Marie consorting lasciviously with a French soldier — already posted everywhere. Outraged, Chant says he won't finance Kapper's plans and storms out.

Chapter V. Chant goes to the palace next morning, tells Anne-Marie he's leaving, but hears she'd like the boyish fellow to attend her birthday celebration. A servant admits the keeper of the *Rhine Maiden,* a barge from Coblenz. Afraid of Kraft, he informs Anne-Marie that his dog Fritz dragged a policeman's body from the river. She tells him to wait in the kitchen, to report to the Dictator. Anne-Marie wonders if she'll be murdered also. Chant says her husband can't love her if he lets Torner's cartoons be shown. Anne-Marie and Chant come close to confidences, but turn sarcastic. He says he loves her and leaves, his thoughts of last night's murder obscuring thoughts of last night's kiss.

Part II: Chapter VI. Aware of Anne-Marie's loyalty and wanting the coming struggle to be honorable, Chant finds a dozen would-be revolutionaries at Kapper's place. Chant countermands any assassination attempt on the Dictator but will finance smuggling arms via the Moselle for a thousand loyal townsmen. They decide to buy arms at Coblenz, bribe a customs official, off-load near Pallien, and attack on the Dictator's wife's birthday, six days hence.

Chapter VII. While Weber, a barge owner, goes to Coblenz to dicker for arms, Chant supervises mailing printed instructions to key rabble-rousers, ordering action when the first shots are fired. Kapper, Lintz, and Torner, though pessimistic, obey. Kapper translates Chant's faulty German. They plan to isolate the palace and hope for popular support, even from the police. Days pass. Afraid no message from Weber will come, Chant climbs the palace wall, spies on a party of elderly guests dancing, sees Anne-Marie rebuking Demassener, sending him away, smiling into the garden darkness.

Chapter VIII. One morning a coded telegram from Weber signals Chant to take the train to Coblenz. Shadowed by a tall man with a newspaper, Chant books a hotel room, walks out the kitchen, escapes to a rendezvous spot — a fake to mislead more of the Dictator's men — as Weber, arriving, says. The two proceed instead to Crane, a fat American arms dealer, in a building where the Moselle joins the Rhine. Long dickering, plus Crane's phoning Chant's bank, yields only 500 revolvers, five machine guns, and ammunition, soon hidden on the barge under barrels of Rhine wine. Weber and Chant take their barge and tug through afternoon sunshine into river darkness at Cochem. Mann, the passport officer, samples Weber's wine and dilly-dallies with Chant to talk about London, which Mann once visited. Muller, the customs officer, is suspicious; but Weber's hints about a coming popular uprising, his and Chant's menacing postures, and 500 marks from Chant get him off again.

Chapter IX. A couple of hours after midnight Weber and Chant dock near the Pallien bridge, across which is Trier. Weber points to his house, where, he says, his trustworthy wife awaits them. Kapper boards, reveals plans for cohorts to carry the arms into Weber's house circuitously avoiding police patrols, posts Chant on a road as a lookout, and disappears. Time drags. Chant sees a speedy car's headlights, steps in its path to be killed and end it all, but it swerves into a tree. Anne-Marie, the driver, is unhurt. They resist asking each other what's happening. Kapper emerges from the darkness, recognizes Chant, says the guns are safe, thinks shadowy Anne-Marie is Chant's evening trollop, and leaves. Walking with Chant, Anne-Marie names and praises Kapper. Bickering, the pair find a gasthaus and tell the blowsy manageress they want hot drinks. She brings brandy to a private room. After awkward verbal feints, Anne-Marie hints at Demassener's impotence and says she was another man's mistress before her five-year marriage. Passion trumps Chant's now-ended bewilderment by her disrobing.

Part III: Chapter X. The morning finds Chant satisfied. Anne-Marie, now gone, promised to meet him in Trier's Church of Our Lady, 8:00 p.m. He makes his way to Weber's home. Frau Weber, good wife, good Catholic, offers him soup, knows about the attack, says Weber is returning to Coblenz, and trusts in God's will. Chant wants to marry Anne-Marie and settle for a dull, certain married life. In the church, he sees old women at the Stations of the Cross and a sexton with a safely coffined priest, ponders the act of prayer, and hears Anne-Marie. The double upshot: Chant offers to rescue her from an unconsummated marriage; Anne-Marie regards him as nothing but a harmless man satisfying her "lust" briefly and believes life with the Dictator, who will probably defeat the rebels, is satisfactory. She leaves Chant in the church.

Chapter XI. Today is Anne-Marie's much-touted birthday. Streets are decorated. Thoroughly drunk, Chant babbles to Kapper that he slept with an impotent man's wife. Kapper soon guesses their identities and leads Chant to his home. While Chant sleeps, Kapper writes, prints, and distributes broadsides about impotent, cuckolded Demassener. Learning this, Chant hastens to Demassener. Disconsolate, he wants Chant to disavow the lying broadside and then duel him. Equivocating, Chant reassuringly says Anne-Marie never loved Chant. Demassener produces loaded pistols, one for each, and says when the clock strikes, in a minute, they may fire. Anne-Marie, who heard everything and approaches, retorts that the broadside is truthful, says she gave Demassener five years of loyalty, hints she has given nobody love, which she'll bestow when she pleases. Kraft enters, impolitely reports a crowd has filled the square. Demassener orders him to go fire on the crowd. Refusing, Kraft says a people's deputation wants in. No, says Demassener. But Kapper, Torner, and a gunman with a syphilitic scar enter. Demassener reviles Kapper's poetry. When Kapper says the revolt owes everything to Frau Demassener and Chant, Demassener tries to shoot Kapper but is gravely wounded by the scarred gunman. The people, with vicious effigies of horned Dictator and loose wife, joyfully reestablish the Republic. Kapper gets Demassener to a train, deliberately delayed and bound for Luxemburg. Anne-Marie won't leave but asks Chant, who will accompany Demassener, if her husband asked for her. He did, but Chant lies that he didn't. On the train, a Chicago reporter, concerned about the inexplicable delay, asks Chant what happened. Otherwise uncommunicative, Chant identifies his wounded "friend" as Demessaner. The reporter contemplates a scoop.

W. J. West says that a literary influence on *The Name of Action* is "Defeat" (1924), a short story by Geoffrey McNeill-Moss (1886–1954; pseudonym, Geoffrey Moss), which concerns unsupported French-separatist efforts in the Trier area and which Greene read, resulting in his vacationing in the Palatinate (1924). Michael Shelden puts it thus: Greene's visit as "a secret German propagandist" to the Trier region (1924) provided local-color details first used in Greene's essay "The French Peace" (*Oxford Outlook,* June 1924) and used again in *The Name of Action*. Before completing the novel, Greene wanted to revisit Trier (August 1929), the lovely beauty of which he adored, but a Greek cruise intervened. He did go again to Trier, according to Norman Sherry so briefly (one night, 1930) that his "failure to renew his impressions of the town earlier was to be fatal for the novel." Sherry reports that two suggested titles, soon discarded, were *Falls the Shadow* and *Heretics in Love,* and that Greene's friend Winifred Ashton (1888–1965; pen name Clemence Dane), prolific novelist and playwright, suggested the title. It comes from Hamlet's "To be, or not to be" soliloquy, ending with the notion that a conscience makes one a coward,

> And enterprises of great pitch and moment
> With this regard their currents turn awry
> And lose the name of action.

Greene quickly disliked *The Name of Action* and once wrote that "the only good thing about the book was its title," that the work was "false and ... derivative." Few critics bother with it. While discussing it as a politico-espionage adventure story and Bildungsroman, Robert

Pendleton touches on its similarities to Joseph Conrad's *Under Western Skies,* "The Secret Sharer," *The Arrow of Gold,* and *Lord Jim.* Philip Stratford praises Greene mainly for three scenes in it — Chant's running from the policeman through dark streets, Chant's avoiding the plainclothesman in busy Coblenz, and Chant's bribing Muller — "with as much ingenuity and suspense as similar scenes in any of Greene's later thrillers." Shelden also finds two "masterly" episodes — Chant's helping to dispose of the policeman Kapper murdered, and Chant's meeting with Anne-Marie in the Catholic church. W. J. West overemphasizes Greene's presentation of Catholicism, which, given the speed of Chant's vacillating actions, seems unimportant.

Greene rightly decided to suppress both *The Name of Action* and *Rumour at Nightfall* as inferior and unrepresentative novels. *The Name of Action* is overwritten, grossly if sometimes pleasantly. Much dialogue seems tailor-made for a class-B movie. Given the action Chant finds himself in, it is grotesque that he pauses and psychoanalyzes himself, mixing wandering memories and thoughts the while. The novel tries to cohere by fugue-like sets of numerous contrasts — idealism/realism, light/dark, talk/action, head/heart, wake/sleep, faith/doubt, danger/safety, worry/indifference, plus a coda escape from violence. (Sources: Greene, *A Sort of Life,* 197, 204; Pendleton, 60–62; Shelden, 141–42, 144, 504; Sherry I, 381, 382; Stratford, 100; West, 24–29 passim, 50)

NANCY (*Travels with My Aunt*). She and Miss Truman run the Abbey Restaurant in London. Henry has a lonely Christmas dinner there.

NAOMI (*The Human Factor*). She is a popular film star's first wife. In a gossip magazine, Castle reads the actor's comments about their unsatisfactory sex life.

NELL (*The Confidential Agent*). Someone in Benditch shouts to Nell that Lord Benditch's agent is stopping at the Red Lion.

NELSON, CHICK (*The Comedians*). This young patron of the Trianon praises his girlfriend's backstroke in the hotel swimming pool.

NESBIT, E[DITH] (*Travels with My Aunt*). Aunt Augusta tells Henry she once attended an important literary figure's funeral, also attended by Edward Carpenter, Dr. Havelock Ellis, [James] Ramsay MacDonald, E[dith]. Nesbit ([1858–1924] English woman of letters), [George] Bernard Shaw and his wife, and H. G. Wells.

NEWALL (*The Heart of the Matter*). He and Forbes, both old, survived the torpedo attack on the ship carrying Helen Rolt, among others. (Newall is spelled Newhall in British editions.)

NEWEY, FREDERICK (*The Ministry of Fear*). He is a sandaled guest at Mrs. Bellairs's séance. Mr. Maude treats him attentively. Neither man appears later.

NEWEY, MRS. FREDERICK (*The Ministry of Fear*). She is Newey's wife and, according to him, wants him home from Mrs. Bellairs's séance early, before anticipated air raids.

NEWHALL (*The Heart of the Matter*) see **NEWALL**

"THE NEW HOUSE" (1923). Short story. (Characters: Handry, Mrs. Handry, Samuel Josephs.)

Handry, an architect, has spent 20 years in a nearby village perfecting dream plans for a fine house to fit modestly onto rich Samuel Josephs's thousand acres, which include hills, woods, and park-like space. This while he also erected modest cottages for other clients. Josephs rejects Handry's drawings, demands instead a landmark visible for miles, says Handry should accept his tentative offer of £5,000 and whip up something astonishing. Handry refuses grandly, storms out, but is aware he'll soon knuckle under apologetically because he has a wife and family.

A cyclist deplores to his companion the ruination of the noble philanthropist Josephs's lovely view by the local materialistic architect's insistence upon this "monstrosity," especially since Josephs is never here. A little fellow is standing near, hears them, calls the house "fine" and "imposing," says he once had different ideas but now appreciates its inspiration, introduces himself as Handry the architect, and slopes into the darkness.

This early short story is a Chinese box with ironies within ironies. Handry not only loses his aesthetic idealism but also comes to accept, with a light now in his eyes, the crass materialism of Josephs, who not only hypocritically tells Handry to be guided by poetic light — the way he allegedly conducted his business — but also so deplores the building he demanded that he won't come within eyeshot of it. Moreover, cycling visitors misunderstand, praise money-grubbing Josephs, hate the loss of a nice view, and criticize the local architect, who at first tried to preserve it.

Greene may also be implying that Handry, like other artists, should have preferred celebate professional dedication to marrying and siring costly children. Is Greene including an undercurrent of regret that he not only married and had children but also created less than artistically pure work because of all those energy-sapping mistresses?

NEWMAN (*Travels with My Aunt*). He is the late Sir Oswald Newman's son and is the secretary of the International Federation of Thermofactors.

NEWMAN, ROSE URQUHART (*Travels with My Aunt*). She is Sir Oswald Newman's widow. They had three sons.

NEWMAN, SIR OSWALD (*Travels with My Aunt*). On the boring Dover-to-London train ride, Henry reads Newman's obituary. He married Rose Urquhart (1928), had three sons with her, was Permanent Secretary in the Ministry of Works, retired, arbitrated a 1950 building dispute, and died, age 72. Henry muses that his father died before meeting Sir Oswald, then wonders if Rose loved Oswald and her labor-secretary son as Miss Paterson loved Henry's father.

"THE NEWS IN ENGLISH" (1940). Short story. (Characters: David Bishop, Mary Bishop, Mrs. Bishop, the Colonel.)

Mary Bishop lives in Crowborough with Mrs. Bishop, her mother-in-law. Lord Haw Haw of Zeesen isn't broadcasting. The women listen to his replacement, nicknamed Doctor Funkhole by the outraged British, and recognize Mary's absent husband David Bishop's voice over the radio, spouting anti–British, pro–German lies. David was a mathematics teacher at Oxford, went to Germany to lecture, is still there. Mrs. Bishop, patriotically despising her son, says the authorities must be informed. Mary hesitates, thinking he could be tried for treason eventually.

Gossipers says David left England to avoid military service. Mary hears David appeal directly to his wife to believe his truths and adds "The fact of the matter is." These words were their secret telephonic clue. She scribbles something down.

Next day Mary rushes to the War Office, tells a tweedy Colonel about their code: David would phone and say "The fact of the matter is," and initial letters of words following would spell a message. Last night's signal? "SOSPIC." The Colonel consults the Admiralty, returns, and tells Mary that the neutral ship *Pic* was sunk this morning and that her SOS if more timely would have saved 200 lives. He orders Mary to continue this secret work, tell absolutely nobody, and expect the newspapers to continue reviling Doctor Funkhole.

Four weeks pass. David sends more messages, concerning Berlin regiments and personnel on leave. The Colonel praises David to Mary for brave duty but cautions that it would be difficult for David, now endangered but watched by enemy agents, to be rescued from Germany, where he and Mary often vacationed. Nonetheless, the Colonel decides to signal in England's counter-news broadcasts in German, using the David-Mary code, that David should visit a station on the Cologne-Wesel railroad line, where an agent might help him escape. The broadcast includes a false report of a sabotage event there.

One night, to David's mother's disgust but Mary's delight, David, who obviously got the message, gloats that the sabotage story was untrue and that he's going there to investigate for his truth-telling colleagues.

Next day Mary prays, imagines David's step-by-step approach to safety, and feels reassured when Funkhole doesn't broadcast that evening. Next night Mrs. Bishop taunts Mary to listen. Mary figures David is free but tunes in Zeesen anyway. Horrifyingly, David broadcasts in their code about news from Wesel concerning certain U-boats refueling and adds a calm farewell to his dear wife. Mrs. Bishop, never understanding, wishes her unwanted, cowardly son had never been born, while Mary, weeping, hopes that one day her "damned hero" of a husband is recognized as such.

Lord Haw Haw, really William Joyce (1906–1946), was born in Brooklyn, New York, grew up in England, was a member of the British Union of Fascists founded (1932) by Sir Oswald Ernald Mosley (1896–1980), migrated to Germany (1939), broadcast taunting Nazi propaganda in English to Britain throughout World War II, and was captured (1945), tried and found guilty of treason, and hanged in Wandsworth Prison, outside London (1946). One illustration by Paul Hogarth for Greene's *It's a Battlefield* is of grim Wandsworth.

"The News in English," though gut-wrenching, is technically inferior. Greene never clarifies David Bishop's behavior. Why leave England? He was never an officially sanctioned double agent. What motivated his broadcasting Haw-Hawkish messages? How could he imagine that Mary, if she made sense of his attempts to communicate in code, could persuade officials to take note? It is unbelievable that Mary could scribble first letters of a sufficient number of words delivered at unsuspiciously normal speed to intercept a valuable message. If the two Mrs. Bishops got along so badly, why didn't the younger one live in Oxford and support her childless self? The younger could surely have broken silence with the older, revealed the code in solemnly sworn confidence, and made her likewise tragically proud of their David. David Parkinson mentions a film treatment of "The News in English," written in 1940 but evidently now lost. (Sources: Hogarth, 31; Parkinson, 702)

NGAMBO, MARK (*The Human Factor*). He is a South African black nationalist. Castle gives Muller information about him, probably knowing Muller already has it — which Muller says he does.

NICARAGUAN AMBASSADOR, THE (*Travels with My Aunt*). He, the British Ambassador, and the Dutch Ambassador attend Visconti's party in Asunción.

NIKOLA (*Orient Express*). He owned a Belgrade restaurant. According to the driver Myatt hired to drive him to Subotica, journalists commandeered the restaurant during the sensational trial of General Kamnetz.

NILS (*England Made Me*). He is a smart young journalist on the staff of a Stockholm newspaper. Minty regards him as a kind of assistant.

NINITCH (*Orient Express*). He is a big, mentally limited frontier guard in Subotica. He stolidly endures a life of poverty, with a wife and child. He is cheated at cards by clerks in the railroad station and is ordered about by Major Petkovitch. Ninitch fails to guard Czinner, Coral Musker, and Grünlich properly. When he helps locate Czinner, dead in the shed with Coral, Petkovitch orders him to shoot Czinner in the mouth. First forcing Coral to look away, he does so.

Greene gives Ninitch a name resembling the word "ninny"; however, his wordless behavior, in front of Coral, before he is ordered to shoot Dr Richard Czinner's corpse, is an epiphanic moment in the novel.

NINITCH, MRS. (*Orient Express*). She is the soldier Ninitch's loving wife and the mother of his child. While he is on duty at the railroad station, she brings him a neatly wrapped sandwich.

NOBODY TO BLAME. An unfulfilled film project by Greene during his brief sojourn in Hollywood (mid-1940s). (Source: Parkinson, 700, 704–05)

NORA (*The Power and the Glory*). She is Trixy Fellows's sister, in England. Nora writes Trixy that she and her husband Captain Fellows will be welcome to stay with her a while when they return home.

NORMA (*It's a Battlefield*). She is one of the 150 girls working at the Battersea match factory.

NUMBER ONE ("A Discovery in the Woods"). He is one of the three boys Pete persuades to join him and Liz in exploring the woods beyond Bottom. Number One has sunken eyes, refuses to take the vow of silence, and is dragged along griping all the way.

NUMBER THREE ("A Discovery in the Woods"). He is another of the three boys who explore the woods with Pete and Liz. Number Three says he is indifferent to laws. He likes to kick stones.

NUMBER TWO ("A Discovery in the Woods"). He is another of the three. He is reliable and stable, but timid.

OBREGÓN, ÁLVARO (1880–1928). Mexican soldier and politician. After a varied army career, he was president of Mexico (1920–1924), suppressed the revolt of Adolfo de la Huerta (1923-1924), was reelected president (1928), but was assassinated days later.

Greene christens as the *General Obregon* the vessel using the port near where Tench and others live in *The Power and the Glory*.

O'BRIEN (*The Honorary Consul*). Sir Henry Belfrage praises Plarr for being really British, unlike the O'Briens and the Higginses around here.

Is Greene thus indicating an anti–Irish bias in some British functionaries?

O'BRIEN, PAT (*The Third Man*). He is an American military police soldier. He is part of the international patrol led by a Russian soldier when Anna Schmidt is arrested. He protests against the Russian's conduct and insists on being present when the uncouth fellow orders Anna to get dressed.

Greene reviewed *The Irish in Us* (1935) and *Page Miss Glory* (also 1935), two American movies starring Pat O'Brien (1899–1983), whom, Greene complains, he doesn't like and who even "makes my [Greene's] flesh creep." (Source: Parkinson, 51, 54)

OCHS, HENRY S. (*The Comedians*). He and his wife are described by Smith, in his dispatch back home, as Philadelphia residents and as having entertained Smith and his wife before the Smiths boarded the *Medea*.

O'CONNELL (*The Human Factor*) see **CONNOLLY**

O'CONNOR (*England Made Me*). When Krogh reminisces about doing construction work on a bridge in Chicago, he recalls his friends O'Connor, Murphy, and Williamson there, and says Aronstein was a friend at another time.

O'CONNOR, FATHER ("Dear Dr. Falkenheim"). He was a priest waiting with members of his congregation to see the helicopter flying Father Christmas over a crowd of children in Browne's department store parking lot.

OKAPA, HENRY (*A Burnt-Out Case*). He is a native living near the leproserie. His having his bicycle deliberately damaged by a Christian is one subject of the superior's sermon on Klistian's Christians' sins.

OLD CROWE (*Brighton Rock*). He is a white-haired, short-sighted codger living in the Russell Square apartment building where Ida Arnold lives. The two play his ouija board seriously.

"AN OLD MAN'S MEMORY" (1989). Short story. (Characters: the French Ambassador, the Minister of Defense, the President of France, Mrs. [Margaret] Thatcher.)

The narrator, writing in 1995, complains that old people have short memories, Still, he recalls seeing television coverage of the 1994 celebration of the opening of the Channel Tunnel. At Dover, Mrs. Thatcher, the Minister of Defense, the French Ambassador, and others watched the French train emerge. At Calais, the President of France headed a group awaiting the British train. News of its having been blown up while under the Channel interrupts Mrs. Thatcher's speech. Who were the terrorists? The IRA, with connections in Germany and Gadaffi? The Iranians, because the British supported Rushdie and because the United States shot down a non-military Iranian airliner? Those Channel Tunnel bombs killed more American than English passengers. Security measures during the construction of the Channel Tunnel were thorough and publicized. But only a little Semtex sufficed to destroy that airplane over a village in Scotland, and the Channel Tunnel took four years to construct — ample time to bribe workers to sketch plans and for others to plant Semtex in a cassette. Two years later. No arrests. But plans to rebuild and reopen the

Tunnel, at great expense, by 1997. Yes, old men's memories are short. But will passengers forget 1994, board the Channel Tunnel trains in 1997, and travel underwater but above rotting corpses in still-lower depths?

The following historical events are relevant: The Channel Tunnel, a joint English-French engineering marvel, was begun 1987, completed 1991, and formally opened May 1994. It connected Folkestone, England, and Sangatte, near Calais, France. The English Channel had separated the two countries by 21 miles of water. The railroad trip now takes 35 minutes. Margaret Thatcher (b. 1925) was the Prime Minister of United Kingdom (1979–1990). Muammar al-Qaddafi (Moammar El-Gadhafi; b. 1942), Libya's dictator, was suspected of complicity in the terrorist bombing of a Berlin discotheque (April 5, 1986); Qaddafi was also thought to have connections with the Irish Republican Army. United States bombed Tripoli and Benghazi, Libya, in retaliation (April 25, 1986). The Iranian government under Ayatollah Khomeini (1900–1989) held 52 American hostages (November 4, 1979–January 21, 1881). Pan American flight 103 exploded over Lockerbie, Scotland (December 21, 1988), killing all 259 passengers aboard, including 189 Americans, and 11 persons on the ground. The United States shot down an Iranian airline over Iranian waters, killing all 286 people aboard (July 3, 1988). The United States announced (November 14, 1991) that two Libyan nationals were to be charged for the Lockerbie bombing. Qaddafi surrendered two Libyans to Holland (April 5, 1999) for trial under Scottish law for the bombing; one suspect was found guilty, the other, acquitted (January 31, 2001). *The Satanic Verses* (1988) by Salman Rushdie (b. 1947), a Bombay-born British writer, so offended the Islamic world that Iran's Ayatollah offered a reward to assassinate him (1989). Rushdie apologized, declared his continuing Islamic faith, hid (to 1991), made limited appearances (to 1995), and then began going out freely again. Qaddafi announced that he was giving up his nuclear-arms program (2003).

Richard Kelly correctly noted (in 1992) that "An Old Man's Memory," a futuristic piece, is better read not as a "new short story by Graham Greene," as it was announced, but as "a dire warning to the English government about the potential for sabotage of the Channel Tunnel between Dover and Calais, scheduled for completion in 1994." The civilized fraction of the 21st-century world surely hopes and prays that Greene's 1989 scenario never becomes an actuality. (Source: Kelly, 85–86)

OLO, THOMAS (*A Burnt-Out Case*). He is a native living near the leproserie. The Superior when preaching says that if Olo's radio were stolen, it would be an example of Klistians' (Christians') sinfulness.

ONE WITHIN see *THE MAN WITHIN*

ONOKO, MRS. (*The Heart of the Matter*). She is involved in a larceny case. Scobie attends the hearing while his mind is occupied with thoughts of suicide.

ON THE WAY BACK: A WORK NOT IN PROGRESS (1982). See "An Appointment with the General." (Source: Greene, *Getting to Know the General*, 53, 55–57, 72, 87–88, 175, 182, 186)

OPIE (*Orient Express*). He is a pretentious Anglican minister. Opie busies himself on the train preparing an anthology to show more profundity than mere Catholic selections could provide. Opie's comments on religion, and occasionally cricket, confuse and put off, in turn, Grünlich, Czinner, and Savory.

ORIENT EXPRESS (*Stamboul Train*, 1932; American title, *Orient Express*, 1933). Novel. (Characters: Captain Alexitch, Anna, Ruby M. Ayers, Campbell, Carl, Con, Dr. Czinner, the Hon. Carol Delaine, Dick, James Douglas, Sidney Dunn, Eckman, Emma Eckman, Edwards, Elsie, Flo, Lord Gathaway, Josef Grünich, Colonel Hartep, Hobbs, Isaacs, Ivy, Jervis, Jim, John, Joyce, Kalebdjian, General Kamnetz, Kolber, Kruger, Lukitch, Moult, Coral Musker, Carleton Myatt, Jacob Myatt, Nikola, Ninitch, Mrs. Ninitch, Opie, Page, Janet Pardoe, Amy Peters, Herbert Peters, Major Petkovitch, Phil, Quin C. Savory, Spot, Stavrog, Leo Stein, Mrs. Stein, Sutliffe, Emmy Tod, Mabel Warren.)

Part One: "Ostend." I. It is April. The purser helps passengers leaving a British ship to board the Ostend-to-Istanbul train. A Jewish currant importer (Carleton Myatt), of Myatt, Myatt and Page, tips with reluctant generosity for a private compartment. A thin, pretty dancer (Carol Musker) talks with Peters and his wife Amy. A clergyman (Opie) reads. A man calling himself Richard John, schoolmaster, longs for sleep. Quin C. Savory, popular novelist, and some Cook's tourists are also aboard. Leaving at sunset, the train passes through Bruges in darkness.

II. Myatt dines in the restaurant car, observes others, worries about his Jewishness and about a business deal he and his father Jacob are planning with Leo Stein and Eckman in Constantinople. Myatt converses with Coral, learns she has a gig with Dunn's Babies in Constantinople, helps her when she faints. John ministers to her, says she has a weakened heart and needs rest. Putting her in his sleeper, Myatt dozes in the corridor and dreams of prostitutes, Coral's legs, business.

Part Two: "Cologne." I. Mabel Warren, an unattractive London *Clarion* gossip columnist in Cologne, says goodbye to pretty Janet Pardoe, her paid-for lesbian lover (for two years) now going on holiday. Mabel was to interview Savory before the train left. She sees a passenger she can get a scoop by interviewing. She pays a porter 80 marks to take a message to her boss about her delay with Savory, flashes her reporter's pass, boards the train, and finds the passenger she saw. Calling himself Richard John, he is Dr. Richard Czinner, a Communist. Mabel saw him testify five years ago (August 1927) in Belgrade against child-raper General Kamnetz. Kamnetz got off with Colonel Hartep's connivance, and Czinner has been on the run since.

Coral sees Myatt dozing, lets him into his compartment, which he boasts cost him £10. Although they squabble, she is grateful, especially when he compliments her and persuades her to have breakfast with him in the diner. Pointing out the Rhine, he mentions the Jewish poet Heine. Coral thinks of bothersome theatrical Jews.

Also breakfasting, Mabel tells Janet that Czinner must be planning to return to Belgrade. Scrutinizing Myatt and Coral, Mabel figures on exploiting Coral in her scoop regarding Czinner and perhaps sexually. Coral exits.

Mabel follows, pretends weakness, asks Coral to fetch a physician to her compartment. Mabel locates Czinner's compartment, rifles his bag, seizes a Baedeker with markings indicating a Communist uprising in Belgrade slums, finds Savory, a pompous fake Cockney hack, interviews him. Returning to Czinner's compartment, she orders brandy and waits. Czinner returns, comments on her theft, and replies to her information about the uprising by pointing out a report in a newspaper he just bought when the train stopped at Würzburg. An unsuccessful uprising started three days too early, before his planned heroic arrival. So he'll deboard at Vienna. Saying she'll interview him there, she leaves the disheartened man, who thinks about his past glories and present uselessness.

II. Mabel sees Janet talking with Savory. Mabel writes her cousin Con a letter about redecorating her flat, and about Janet, Savory, Coral, and Czinner.

Coral watches Myatt fussing over account books. They chat. She silently wonders if he wants intimacy. He says he dreamed about her last night. She agrees to visit his compartment tonight. The train gets to the Austrian customs at snowy Passau.

Part Three: "Vienna." I. Josef Grünlich is a clever, petty, fat, Catholic criminal, known to the police. Tonight, armed, Grünlich sneaks through Anna's window, purportedly to make love with her. Anna is a maid working for Kolber, assistant manager of the Vienna railroad station. Grünlich traps her in her bedroom, goes to Kolber's safe, starts to melt its door to get money inside, plans to dump Anna and escape by train to Passau. Kolber, however, returns early and holds a revolver on him. Anna emerges, starts to make excuses, but falters. Grünlich distracts Kolber and shoots him dead. Anna faints. Grünlich, proud of gaining greater stature as a criminal though without getting Kolber's funds, exits, hears Anna's screams and two responding policemen, and gets to the railroad station. Needing money to escape by the Istanbul express, he snatches an attractive handbag from a woman who just put it down to telephone.

Mabel has left the train here at Vienna, believing Czinner was doing so, as he said. She is arranging coins at a booth to phone London with her stories — about important Czinner and trivial Savory — when she discovers her handbag gone. Czinner doesn't appear. She figures he's still aboard. She pleads with railway agents to reboard but, with neither ticket nor money, is refused. She coolly phones her stories.

II. The diner is crowded. Coral talks with Myatt over resistance-dissolving wine. She suggests that rather than quicky love tonight they might start living together in Constantinople. Other people's chatter swirls about: Peters and Amy, whose stomach is upset, discuss Myatt and Coral; Peters envies Myatt; Grünlich, safely aboard but worried he didn't ditch his gun, discusses cricket and religion with Opie; others discuss beer. Myatt gets Coral to compare his juicy currants and Stein's dry ones, wonders about shaking up the Constantinople office. Savory observes the moonlight and the Danube, ponders describing them cinematically, is glad he invited Janet Pardoe to talk later. Coral is apprehensive about Myatt; after all, though, he was kind when she fainted. Czinner remembers the oppressed, the old trial, his impudent British students; anticipates mobs of journalists he must soon face; must arrange his answers, remember he struggled not for Belgrade's poor but the world's, must insist he protested against the militant, nationalistic part of the Social-Democratic party.

III. Coral gets her bag in the section where the Peterses are. Amy calls her a tart for going after Myatt. Coral rebukes her, then cries. Seeing her embarrassment, Czinner explains he is a doctor and last night ordered a sleeper for her, and calls the Peterses bourgeois.

Alone, Czinner remembers his parents' sacrifice to get him through medical school, after which he concluded he could never prescribe necessary medicines for the impoverished masses and lost his faith in God. He finds Grünlich in his compartment, having rifled his bag. Grünlich explains he is a Socialist, has just escaped the police, needs money. Czinner, knowing he won't need funds in Belgrade, sends him off with £5, feels guilty traveling first class. A guard reports snow ahead. Czinner wishes he could confess to a priest, spots Opie writing, learns he is preparing an Anglican, non-Catholic anthology. Asked about confession, Opie says that psychiatrists give better advice than priests, through according the penitent power as well as intention to make a new start. Savory drops by, says writers are penitents. Opie counters that novels are certainly confessions if dreams told to psychiatrists are. Czinner leaves, confused.

Coral reports to Myatt's sleeper, says she loves him, thus interrupting his work on figures and Eckman correspondence. He warms to her. She inspires generosity in him. He fondles her. She disrobes. Their jerky encounter reveals her virginity to him. She says a girl "has to learn some time." She wants a second session in Constantinople. He promises a London flat. He suggests an in-train dinner party (£2 "a head") to toast his "mistress."

Part Four: "Subotica." I. In the Subotica station-master's office, Lukitch the clerk, and a parcels clerk are cheating Ninitch, a stupid soldier, at cards, and are discussing the Red revolt in Belgrade. A local telephone call summons Major Petkovitch from the barracks. Colonel Hartep in Belgrade orders him to get a certain passenger off the Stamboul train and hold him.

II. On the train, Coral awakens joyfully, hardly remembering last-night's pain. She rouses Myatt. At breakfast they discuss sharing a Constantinople hotel room. The train stops at Budapest, then Subotica, to shunt some cars.

Czinner escorts Coral outside, gives her a letter to mail from Istanbul. A soldier, however, arrests both. Grünlich decides to travel all the way to Constantinople but gets held, searched, and his "cannon" confiscated. Czinner tells Coral he is a Communist and will probably be shot in Belgrade. Hartep and his assistant, Captain Alexitch, arrive to take charge of Czinner, Coral, and Grünlich, but lunch first with Petkovitch.

Coral prays for Myatt to rescue her. She and Czinner know he won't. A guard leads them away through the snow, along with Grünlich.

III. On the train, stalled beyond Subotica and requiring a new engine, Myatt dreams of sharp business dealings, awakens, misses Coral, and haggles with a fiddler to play at his planned diner dinner.

In the station Hartep says martial law has been declared since the Belgrade uprising and, despite Petkovitch's legal objections, convenes a court martial: Czinner is a perjured criminal, Coral helped him, Grünlich concealed a weapon.

When Myatt learns from flirty Janet that Coral is back in Subotica, he hires a man to drive him back to help her.

While Coral naps and dreams, and Alexitch turns yes-man, Hartep overrides Petkovitch, convicts Czinner of treason, gives Grünlich a month in jail, and orders Coral deported. Czinner starts a political rejoinder, loses his rhetoric, is sentenced to death in three hours. He reminisces about the improverished. He and Coral sing briefly. Her future will resemble her past, after all.

Myatt's driver tells him about the Belgrade uprising, gets to Subotica. Myatt tries but can't warn his Constantinople associate about his delay, conscientiously seeks Coral, is met by anti–Semitic rebuffs and honest ignorance, thinks again of Janet, and returns to the car. Its engine is frozen.

IV. Ninitch is posted in the dusk outside the station. Grünlich boasts he murdered his daughter's violator, then unscrews the door lock with Czinner's paper cutter while Czinner at the window distracts Ninitch, who tells him a foreigner came and was asking questions. He was Myatt, Coral figures. Czinner tells Ninitch he treated Ninitch's sick father and gets Ninitch to go for wine for the three prisoners, who then rush out. Grünlich disappears in the snowy darkness. Coral runs more slowly. Czinner makes little distance, is shot at from afar and wounded. Coral pulls him into an abandoned shed.

Myatt's driver finally starts his engine. They hear gunfire. Myatt thinks of old pogroms but still wants to help Coral. Grünlich suddenly jumps into the car, is shot at. Off they speed. Myatt recognizes Grünlich, queries him, but is answered with experienced cunning. No, no girl was back there.

Coral tends to delirious Czinner reluctantly but gently, through the long cold night.

The daring driver speeds off with Myatt and Grünich. They are stopped by police seeking someone else, are let go.

During the night, Czinner dies. Coral regards his coarse, humorless old face quizzically. Petkovitch and his officers drive up, find Coral and Czinner. One soldier turns Coral away as another shoots Czinner's head. She retches. Suddenly Mabel Warren rushes in, rescues Coral, outtalks the officers, and gets her into a car — for Vienna, an exclusive interview, and perhaps something more intimate.

Part Five: "Constantinople." Kalebdjian, an Armenian clerk at the Blue Mosque hotel, helps two gushy American girls to a tour, then greets Myatt, sweeping in with Janet Pardoe and Savory in tow. In Myatt's room Leo Stein is waiting, tells him Eckman has disappeared, shows him Eckman's signed agreement with Stein, says Moult has dropped negotiations, wants and will fight to be a director of Myatt's firm. Stein arms Myatt by revealing this: Janet's parents are dead, her mother was Stein's sister, he and his wife want to employ Janet here, he'd like to sell out soon and play golf. Myatt thinks Janet, being half-Jewish, would make an acceptable wife. Myatt and Stein taxi to Eckman's place, learn from his wife Emma that Eckman may remain away. The two proceed to a dingy office Myatt owns, learn from faithful Joyce working there that Eckman is still absent, and return to the hotel for late lunch with Janet and Savory. Janet gossips to Uncle Leo about Myatt's affair with Coral on the train and his mad drive to and from Subotica, but declines to discuss Mabel Warren or Czinner. Savory butts in but gets squelched by Stein. Queried by smut-loving Stein, Myatt merely says he bought Coral a ticket and she loved him.

Myatt raps at Janet's room door, watches her finish dressing, persuades her to ignore Savory, dine with him in nearby Pera, and have drinks at a garden place. He spots Grünlich — twice seen and soon forgotten — then sees Dunn's Babies — is Coral dancing there? He boasts to Janet about a non-affair in a Pera hotel. She says she's tired of living with Mabel. Stein hovers near. Myatt can easily seal the deal, forgets Coral, and asks Janet to dump Mabel for him.

Greene's popularity and bank account swelled when the Book Society selected *Stamboul Train* for its December 1932 choice, guaranteeing a distribution of 10,000 copies to its members. Soon at least 26,000 copies were sold in England and the United States. Greene sold movie rights to *Stamboul Train* for £1,738 to Twentieth Century-Fox in 1932, although he regarded the result, entitled *Orient Express,* a technically incompetent transformation of his plot into something cheap and sentimental. In a *Collected Edition* introduction, Greene says that the movie was worse than three earlier films featuring express trains and that the British Broadcasting Company television adaptation of his novel (1962) was still worse. Quentin Falk is pleased that the movie "pared away the book's ultimately rather tiresome preoccupation with anti–Semitism." Michael Tracey discusses the BBC adaptation, in which "sex in the raw" scenes displeased Greene and his brother Hugh Greene,* the BBC General Director at the time.

Orient Express gains unity via varied incidents on, off, and near the train, and has cinema-like effects involving chiaroscuro movements. A. F. Cassis admires Greene's "good use of the closed setting of the speeding train." Robert Pendleton contends that Greene adapted the narrative device of action on a moving train from *The Thirty-Nine Steps* (1915) by John Buchan (1875–1940), whom Michael Shelden calls Greene's "boyhood hero." In an essay on Buchan in *The Lost Childhood and Other Essays,* Greene says *The Thirty-Nine Steps* established "a pattern for adventure-writers." The ambivalent messages in Greene's novel concerning religion and politics reflect his recent conversion to Roman Catholicism, his dabbling in and reading about Communism, and his dismay at European social misery. Descriptive details derive from his seeing Constantinople during a quick Greek-island cruise (1930), his third-class trip from Ostend as far as Cologne (April 1931), and his reading in books by more affluent authors, including *Constantinople, Old and New* (1915) by Harrison Griswold Wright (b. 1875) and *Orient Express* (1927) by John Dos Passos (1896–1970). Greene subtitled his novel *An Entertainment,* which it often is, especially in Part Five. For example, in nearby paragraphs Emma Eckman peers from under her fancy hat "like a mouse lost in a wardrobe" and Leo Stein blows his nose "in an honest emotional way." Better, Grünlich's brief time in poor Anna's bedroom is, as Grahame Smith notes, "macabre comedy." Greene wastes wordage on Myatt's and Coral's dreams, and on Greene's own now-dated political lamentations. (Sources: Cassis, 19; Falk, 20, 206; Greene, *Stamboul Train, Collected Edition,* ix; Greene, *The Lost Childhood,* 104; Pendleton, 69; Phillips, 14, 20; Shelden, 91, 170; Sherry I, 409, 422, 475; G. Smith, 24; Tracey, 225–26; Watts, 25–27)

THE OTHER SIDE OF THE BORDER (1936). Novel fragment. (Characters: Anderson, Baines, Bates, Billings, Colley, Cudlow, Jimmy Danvers, Sir Frederick, Hands, Hands, Ethel Hands, Mrs. Hands, Millet, Morrow, Morrow, Mrs. Morrow, B. Moss, Ted, Vandi.)

Part One: "The Map." After two years, Morrow, young but ill, returns to England in weather cold off the Mersey. Reporting to Danvers, general manager of the New Syndicate, Morrow resigns and warns him not to trust Hands's judgment, because of difficulties with the gold, with deaths, and with Colley and Billings. Morrow will put everything in writing. The waiting-room map shows coast, rivers, and mountains, where the explorers had been, near Zigita.

2. Hands takes a train from Metroland to Denton, his hometown. His head is full of future action — though not yet connected to anyone named Morrow, Danvers, or Billings, or to the hundred blacks dead (1936–1938). Hands visits his widowered father. Being pro–Fascist, Hands ridicules his father's liberalism and says he's applied by mail for jobs. Exiting the smelly house, Hands visits Millet, Denton's photographer who took many passport photos for him. Hands lies about his dangerous African adventures. Millet's niece (Ethel) eavesdrops.

3. Though hoping for non-success, Hands receives a letter from Danvers of Liverpool's New Syndicate requesting an interview on Wednesday, March 5, gets there, and sees a four-year-old magazine (February 1932) featuring Jimmy Danvers. Danvers surprisingly employs Hands to go with Colley and a trustworthy "boy" named Morrow to seek gold. Danvers produces some gray stratified rock, meaning nothing to Hands.

4. Outside London's Victoria railway station Colley, 33, remembers clerking in Brazil at 17 and drinking excessively in Africa, feels sad and lonely, has three brandies, and boards a Liverpool-bound bus to seek some employment outside hopeless England that Hands said might suit him.

5. Danvers impresses a reporter. Danvers praises Hands's pioneering if not actual mining experience, hints at dangers in transporting anticipated gold from a practically medieval, black-infested section of West Africa across the border into respectable British Territory, and

plans to place a newspaper item announcing issuance of 200,000 ordinary-stock shares. His imagination envisions a shiny new office building, premium shares, but no gold.

6. Hands shows his father a map of West Africa where the tiny six-town country is, inland from the French colony. Old Hands thinks both about the impoverished natives and about pride he'll feel when his son is famous. Hands saunters off to impress Millet and Ethel.

Part Two: "The Expedition." Billings, a failure in an African town, has found God but barely survives as a photographer. When Baines, the local priest, dies, Billings cables England applying to replace him. No luck. Suddenly Hands, married to Ethel, appears, saying he landed today. He and Billings recall failing five years earlier. Now flush with money and plans, Hands heads a gold-seeking expedition, has already hired Colley and a prig named Morrow, but also wants Billings. The two share Billings's treasured brandy. Billings dreams of bringing God to the natives. Colley enters, is sad brandy's gone, and criticizes uppity Morrow. Hands, Billings, and Colley resemble lying criminals.

In a "Note" preceding T*he Other Side of the Border*, Greene explains he abandoned it for two reasons: *Brighton Rock* demanded his immediate time to complete it; Hands was insufficiently different from Anthony Farrant in *England Made Me*. Greene adds that he inaccurately described the West African port town where Hands finds Billings but was pleased at his handling of Denton, based on the town where he was born (i.e., Berkhamsted). Richard Kelly complains that in this novel fragment "too many failed characters [are] competing for attention," Colley gets too much wordage, and Billings's religiosity further distorts the focus.

It is difficult, though not important, to date events in the story. Moreover, one date is incorrect. When Hands reports to Danvers's office on Wednesday, March 5, he sees a 1932 magazine. Wednesday fell on March 5 in 1931 and not again until 1942. (Source: Kelly, 92)

O'TOOLE, JAMES (*Travels with My Aunt*). He is Lucinda O'Toole's tall, thin, gray, divorced father. An American, O'Toole is a CIA agent, long seeking Visconti for allegedly stealing a Leonardo da Vinci drawing. O'Toole meets Henry on the river boat to Asunción; pretends he's investigating the cost of living, malnutrition, and illiteracy in the region, talks with Henry about Lucinda, springs Henry from jail in Asunción, attends the dinner party given by Augusta and Visconti there, and pays Visconti $10,000 for the drawing (a forgery).

Greene makes O'Toole a CIA buffoon by having him record how long it takes him to urinate daily and having him conclude he thus piddles away 36 hours annually. Norman Sherry compounds matters by quoting Greene's O'Toole's recording eight urinal stops on July 28 totaling 4 minutes, 31 seconds, and then by indiscreetly reporting that Greene's own diary records "columns of [such] numbers ... in his own hand." Sherry adds that Trevor Williams, an academic statistician, wrote Sherry after Greene's death that Greene met Williams and modeled O'Toole after him. Sherry's proffered proof is that Williams was an American, knew statistics, and had trouble with one of his children. (Source: Sherry III, 497)

O'TOOLE, LUCINDA (*Travels with My Aunt*). This vivacious American hippie, 18, nicknamed Tooley, is the product of divorced parents. Tooley leaves her boyfriend Julian in Paris, takes the Orient Express to Istanbul, tells Henry she thinks she's pregnant (not so), and jaunts with other young Americans to Katmandu, Vientiane, and Goa. She worries her father James O'Toole, a CIA agent. Henry regards her as gentle, sweet, and uncorrupted by her mother.

O'TOOLE, MRS. (*Travels with My Aunt*). She is James O'Toole's divorced wife and Lucinda O'Toole's mother. When James tells Henry his wife was corrupting their daughter by bringing boyfriends home, Henry sticks up for the uncorrupted girl. Mrs. O'Toole was last heard of in Bonn with friends.

OUR MAN IN HAVANA (1958). Novel. (Characters: Sister Agnes, Aunt Alice, the Ambassador, the Ambassadress, the American Consul-General, Angelica, Mrs. Ashworth, Baronin, the Bishop, Dr. Braun, Brewer, William Carter, the Chief, the Chief Engineer, the Chief of Police, the Director of Posts and Telegraphs, Engineer Cifuentes, Cooper, Davis, the Director of Posts and Telegraphs, Raul Dominguez, Raul Dominguez, Edith, Uncle Edward, Ethel, Ferdinand of Castile, Granny Brown, Hans, Dr. Hasselbacher, Dr. Emma Hasselbacher, Mr. Hilton, Henry Hawthorne, Henry, Humpelnicker, Miss Jenkinson, Joe, Great-aunt Kate, Little Dwarf Doodoo, Lopez, the Luxemburg Consul, MacDougall, McIntyre, Maria, Marie, Mark, Marlowe, Mary, Max, Father Mendez, Miguel, Miguel, the Minister of Defense, the Minister of the Interior, the Monegasque Consul, Harry Morgan, Thomas Earl Parkman Jr., Vincent C. Parkman, Pedro, Señor Perez, Señora Perez, the Permanent Under-Secretary, Miss Pfunk, the President, the Reverend Mother, Rodriguez, Rudy, Luis Sanchez, Maria Sanchez, Santa Teresa, Savage, Segura, Captain Segura, Seraphina, Sergeant, Mrs. Beatrice Severn, Peter Severn, Mrs. Slater, Svenson, Teresa, Teresa, Miss "Pony" Traggers, Hiram C. Truman, White, James Wormold, Mary Wormold, Milly Wormold.)

Part One: Chapter 1: 1. Havana, January. Dr. Hasselbacher, carefree, and James Wormold, vacuum-cleaner salesman, enjoy drinks at the Wonder Bar. Wormold, soon to celebrate his daughter Milly's 17th birthday, worries about his latest model, because its name, the Atomic Pile Cleaner, is offputting nowadays.

2. An inquisitive, English-speaking man (Henry R. Hawthorne) enters Wormold's store, where his assistant Lopez is reading dirty magazines, and discusses vacuum cleaners. Mention is made that Wormold's daughter is in the American convent school.

Chapter 2. Pretty Milly comes home, with harmless youths emitting wolf-whistles in her wake. She puts some cumbersome shopping in her room and wheedles her father into promising to buy Seraphina, an expensive horse, from Captain Segura, the Vedado police chief. Milly's shopping includes saddle, bridle, bit, whip.

Chapter 3: 1. A bank teller cashes Wormold's withdrawal of $250 and courteously says his account is $50 overdrawn.

2. Wormold avoids Hasselbacher and drinks at Sloppy Joe's, less frequented since a stray bullet recently killed a tourist there. Entering, Hawthorne identifies himself as a British Secret Service agent here recruiting Caribbean-area spies, warns Wormold about Hasselbacher, and insists on meeting Wormold tonight — room 501, Seville-Biltmore.

3. Wormold chats with Milly at bedtime. He feels one doesn't gain from experience. She says she prays that her long-absent mother, whom he says he still loves sometimes, will become a good Catholic again but never return to them, and adds she's happy her prayers for a horse are coming true.

Chapter 4: 1. En route to Hawthorne, Wormold ignores pimps and smut peddlers, encounters Hasselbacher, is diverted first to have a drink and then to seek a lottery ticket for Hasselbacher, and arrives late. Hawthorne bewilders Wormold by assuming he'll patriotically serve England at $150 a month plus expenses, and by chattering about opening Hasselbacher's mail, citing page and line from Charles Lamb's *Tales from Shakespeare* (Everyman edition) for coded messages written in invisible ink or "bird shit."

2. Milly tells Wormold she'll eat cheaper food so they can afford to join the Country Club — to stable her horse there.

"Interlude in London." Hawthorne informs the Chief about his new Havana Agent 59200/5 (i.e., Wormold), who wants to join the Country Club for contacts with the wealthy. The Chief envisions Wormold as an admirably traditional British merchant, belonging in Kipling times, but for added security tells Hawthorne to order the Secret Service secretaries' pool boss Miss Jenkinson to dispatch a Spanish-speaking secretary for Wormhold. Miss Jenkinson will send Beatrice, whose qualifications cause Hawthorne qualms.

Part Two: Chapter 1: 1. Ash Wednesday, February. Wormold receives a dispatch from London at Havana's British consulate and laboriously deciphers the Lamb message. Reckoning he must send pithy messages in return for Country Club membership (as well as Milly's horse), he decides to recruit Lopez. Lopez foolishly thinks Wormold wants him as his pimp.

Over drinks at the Wonder Bar, Wormold tells Hasselbacher he has been recruited to provide secret information, is promptly advised to invent reports and agents, but is warned Hasselbacher won't be his agent. Wormold warns they are trying to "trace" Hasselbacher.

3. Wormold obtains professional names

from the Country Club membership list, orders Lopez to gather sugar- and tobacco-industry statistics and other data, and fakes an economics report. Summoned to the consulate, Wormold accepts three-months' pay, secretly wrapped.

Chapter 2: 1. Wormold sends word to Hawthorne concerning a recruiting trip he'll take by car, for $50 daily.

2. After driving to Cienfuegos, Wormold writes his sister Mary, in Northampton, England, describing the region, the Chief Engineer off the *Juan Belmonte,* and old memories, and enclosing stamps for his nephew's collection. Wormold will call that engineer another agent.

3. Car trouble in Santa Clara forces Wormold to continue by bus to Santiago, swarming with troops and rebels. After talking with his vacuum retailer there, Wormold is stopped after curfew and roughed up by the police until he mentions he knows Captain Segura. Wormold retrieves his repaired car and returns to Havana.

Chapter 3. March dispatches await Wormold, telling whom to hire, whom not. Hasselbacher phones in anguish. Wormold rushes over, finds Wormold's apartment ransacked, and some 30-year-old, possibly incriminating documents gone. Wormold feels guilty, grows angry at Hawthorne and his ilk. If innocent ones like Milly can believe in miracles, the Secret Service will swallow his grotesqueries. So he writes that Raul Dominquez, a drunken Cuban airline pilot, revealed he saw military constructions in the Oriente mountains outside Santiago. Using his Atomic Pile Cleaner as a pattern, he creates a drawing of military constructions, professedly from Engineer Cifuentes (a Club member).

"Interlude in London." Hawthorne flies to London. He and the Chief examine Cifuentes's drawing, of machines transported by lorries and mules to a forest edge. Hawthorne wonders what the drawing reminds him of. An aide has foolishly likened the drawing to vacuum-cleaner parts; a weapon worse than the H-bomb may be in the offing; Agent 59200/5 must hire aerial photos the Chief can show his atomic-research people; Beatrice Severn, Miss Jenkinson's Spanish-speaking recommendation sent Hawthorne, needs a radio-operating helper.

Part Three: Chapter 1. Celebrating Milly's 17th birthday at the Tropicana, Wormold, Hasselbacher, and champagne-guzzling Milly discuss Shakespeare and the Lamb book that Hasselbacher borrowed from Wormold. Segura invades their table, meets Hasselbacher, gets rebuked by Milly, reminds her he chauffeurs her from her convent, wants to dance. A woman sitting with two K.L.M. pilots halts Segura's plan by squirting him with a soda siphon. He gallantly but menacingly accepts her apology, bows to everybody, says all drinks are on him, leaves. Wormold orders champagne. The siphoneer introduces herself as Beatrice Severn, tells Wormold she's his assigned secretary and his work is great but so dangerous he needs an assistant. Milly dances with Hasselbacher.

Chapter 2: 1. Wormold develops files of imaginary informants. Milly asks him if he wants to marry Beatrice, who arrives, answers inquisitive Milly's questions about her ex-husband (Peter), a UNESCO intellectual, and promises Wormold a safe.

2. Workers, with a huge safe, and also Rudy, Wormold's ostensible accountant, arrive at Wormold's apartment, where Beatrice and Rudy are both bunking. Passersby gather, recognize Beatrice as the siphoneer, and applaud. Beatrice sets the safe's combination based on Wormold's birthdate ("19-6-14"), loads his files in it, expresses both espionage expertise and uneasiness. Rudy unpacks his smuggled-in radio.

Chapter 3: 1. Wormold feels he must invent colorful reports. Rudy needs military photographs for microfilming. Beatrice would relish some romancing with that pilot Raul Dominguez, whose alluring past Wormold spins. He has Beatrice report news that Raul may be deported to Spain for on-duty drunkenness, then gets her to authorize $1,700 for Raul to fly around Oriente first.

2. With an advance of $1,500, Wormold and Beatrice enjoy langouste at a harbor fishhouse. He worries about Raul's fancied flight plan, figures on having him crash and disappear. Beatrice hints at awareness of Wormold's fabrications. His reply is to hint he needs money for Milly. Hasselbacher happens by, and they go to his apartment for drinks. Beatrice wonders about his past. He says he was in the German army but left Germany (1934). He puts *Tristan*

on the gramophone; its plot causes Wormold to think Beatrice is as unreal as Tristan's beloved. Beatrice finds a photograph of Captain Hasselbacher. A man phones Hasselbacher that Raul is a car-crash victim.

Part Four: Chapter 1: 1. Home at 2:00 a.m., Wormold and Beatrice get news from Milly: Cifuentes was shot at; Segura is investigating. Wormold worries that Cifuentes, whom he hasn't met, and a real-life Raul are endangered. Beatrice, fearing for herself and Wormold, suggests their lying low and telling his agents to do likewise.

2. Wormold and Beatrice go to the Shanghai Theatre. His imagined agent, Teresa the fat nude dancer, is supposedly there. Outside, pimps and pornographic-card salesmen surround them. Inside, they see dancers and a porno film. Wormold tells Beatrice their edition of Lamb's *Shakespeare* differs from Hasselbacher's Everyman edition. A possible connection to Raul disturbs her. Wormold and Beatrice enter the nudes' dressing rooms. A police raid starts. Wormold bribes a skinny nude really named Teresa and a black stage hand named Miguel to help them escape.

3. Wormold and Beatrice, with Teresa aboard, drive to Professor Luis Sanchez's fancy residence. Sanchez and his mistress emerge. She thinks Wormold is spying on them, at the behest of Maria Sanchez, the professor's absent wife. When Wormold says Cifuentes was shot at, the present mistress, loud and lewd, says she knows Cifuentes and jealous Sanchez wanted him shot. Sanchez, unruffled, saunters inside.

4. Half-tempted to confess everything, Wormold returns to his car. Beatrice and Teresa are there, surrounded by police, who take them all to Captain Segura's office. Segura says Sanchez complained about Wormold, quizzes him about this ill-clad Shanghai dancer, warns him to avoid Sanchez's wife, asks if he plays draughts, says Hasselbacher is bad company, and plays a recording of the phone call. A stammerer is calling "H-Hasselbacher" about Raul's death. Wormold swears he knew no Raul. Segura lets everyone go. Beatrice extols Wormold's professional lying and returns alone to Milly.

Chapter 2. Wormold finds Hasselbacher dressed in his tight World War I uniform. They talk. Hasselbacher reveals this: Raul Dominguez was a real-life drunk pilot; Hasselbacher, after his residence was tossed and his research into blue coloring in cheese destroyed, informed against Raul and Raul was killed; Hasselbacher borrowed Wormold's Lamb from Milly and broke the code, worries about the Oriente photographs; he never got over fatally bayoneting a Russian, became a doctor to save lives. Wormold phones home, learns from Beatrice that she and Milly are safe.

"Interlude in London." The Chief personally prepares a splendid dinner for the Permanent Under-Secretary. They discuss spy news from the Caribbean, agree the Americans are stingy with information, are uneasy about the Russians, and grieve that their Havana man's best agent died just before his aerial-photography mission.

Part Five: Chapter 1. Over a game of draughts at a free-drink joint, Segura summarizes Wormold's drive to Cienfuegos, etc., doubts he's any secret agent, thinks Hasselbacher's associates are wrong, believes Hasselbacher plays a minor role but knows crypography, mentions Jamaica, feels spies surround Cuba, theorizes why Cifuentes was shot at, categorizes the "torturable" and others, says he admires Milly, expresses doubts as to Wormold's employees. Thus warned, Wormold leaves, drunk on daiquiris, encounters Beatrice, wonders if she suspects he's agentless, tells her Miguel, the beggar nearby and supposedly blind, works for him. Beatrice details her escape plans if Wormold is caught. He says Segura tells him about Communists among his policemen. Beatrice fears sweets-addicted Rudy lives a secret life.

Chapter 2: 1. Milly persuades Wormold to accept an invitation from Dr. Braun, president of the European Traders' Association, to address its annual meeting. Rudy brings a scary order from Hawthorne to report to Kingston.

2. Wormold finds Jamaica dirtier than ever. Hawthorne tells Wormold he harbored suspicions about him because those drawing resembled vacuum parts until reports have it that enemies plan to poison Wormold at the Traders' lunch. Wormold bravely says he'll go and try to avoid possibly poisoned Morro crabmeat.

3. On the airplane back, Wormold meets William Carter, a snobbish, vulgar rival vacuum salesman from Nottwich, who will be at

the Traders' lunch. Wormold tells Beatrice his life was threatened and notices she has removed her wedding ring.

Chapter 3: 1. Milly tells Wormold his speech will be sensational. Beatrice wants him not to go. He says he must earn his money. He also wants to impress her.

2. The Traders display their wares at the Nacional Hotel convention. Outside, Hasselbach solemnly warns Wormold to stay away, he'll be poisoned. Wormold sees Carter, introduces him to Hasselbacher, feels better entering the dining room with fellow-Britisher Carter.

3. The tables are organized by nationalities. Wormold sits with a Scotchman named MacDougall, refuses liquor and Morro crabs, refuses Highland malt from MacDougall's possibly poisoned flask, but feels better when Carter takes some. Amid idle talk, Wormold frowns as his plate of food is innocently passed along but then removed by the head-waiter. Wormold shares MacDougall's whisky with MacDougall and Carter. The American Consul-General intones about spiritual and commercial links among democratic countries. Called to speak next, Wormold needs another drink. Carter pours him some from his flask but says "h-hurry," stammering as Hasselbacher's phone caller did. The German head-waiter's dachshund Max enters, laps up nervous Wormold's deliberately overturned drink, and dies.

4. Wormold tells Beatrice he survived but the dog died.

Chapter 4: 1. Segura visits Wormold, asks for Milly's hand in marriage. Wormold waffles. Segura lists troubles Wormold may have caused — Raul's death, Cifuentes shot at, Max poisoned — threatens to revoke Wormold's residence permit, then escorts him to the Wonder Bar, where Hasselbacher has just been shot dead. Wormold blames Carter, a new name to Segura, tells him to torture the head-waiter for information, and silently longs to leave Havana with Milly.

2. While Wormold considers how to kill Carter, he hears Beatrice coaching Milly on flowers, perfumes, flirting. Milly asks if Beatrice loves daddy. Wormold enters, tells them about Hasselbacher, asks Milly — who doesn't want to marry "old" Segura — to invite him to play draughts tonight and bring his secret list, and adds they're returning to England. Alone, he confesses his bogus "spying" to Beatrice. She is delighted, says she loves him, praises his loyalty to Milly, prefers loyalty to love rather than to country.

Chapter 5: 1. Wormold welcomes Segura, says Milly won't marry him, explains that the draught pieces are miniature whisky bottles from his souvenir collection and that a player capturing his rival's piece drinks it, thus evening the odds. Long games end in Segura's victory and therefore drunken unconsciousness. Wormold takes Segura's gun.

2. Wormold phones Carter, says the headwaiter poisoned his aged dog, and invites Carter to visit brothels with him. They meet at Carter's Seville-Biltmore hotel, drive to a striptease, have drinks, drive on, step out before a brothel. To get both of them riled, Wormold hints at Carter's poisoned whisky. Wormold draws Segura's gun. Carter confesses he was ordered to kill Hasselbacher because of Wormold's convincing drawings, and reaches for something. Wormold fires, misses, is glad. Carter shoots.

Chapter 6: 1. Home again, Wormold tells Beatrice he fired and missed, Carter fired and missed, he fired and killed poor lamentable Carter, returned the wiped-clean gun to Segura, still asleep, microfilmed Segura's list of spies, put the tiny image on a stamp and mailed it with other stamps to headquarters.

2. Called before the Ambassador in his fancy residence, Wormold is informed thusly: Segura told the Ambassador that Wormold accepted pay to send home misleading information from non-existent sources, forged a document supposedly owned by Segura, knew Carter, now dead; the Ambassador has reported Wormold to the Foreign Office; Wormold should fly to England pronto.

3. Rudy burns codes, will fly to Kingston with Beatrice. She will proceed to London to learn her next assignment. Perhaps Basra, in the Persian Gulf? Milly sells her horse back to Segura, will fly on K.L.M. with Wormold via Montreal to London.

4. Before Wormold and Milly take off, Segura tells him Dr. Braun is leaving with those construction drawings for Switzerland. Thence to Moscow, Bonn, Washington, Bucharest?

"Epilogue in London." 1. Wormold reports to headquarters, waits outside, sees glum

Hawthorne enter and then leave with two military men. Beatrice, exiting, tells Wormold to enter. The Chief says Wormold will remain in London, teach new spies, be given a medal.

2. Beatrice explains events to Wormold: Chief said they'll use certain rumors extrapolated from Wormold's reports, rebuked Hawthorne for not seeing the construction drawings were based on vacuum parts, decided exposing their man in Havana would be embarrassing, will say those enemy constructions failed and were dismantled. Beatrice says she blasted one and all for their phony international patriotism. Wormold and Beatrice decide to wed. As they kiss, Milly enters. She says the two fortunately are "pagans" and goes shopping. Beatrice says Wormold's microfilm was over-exposed and hence useless, dances with him, and fears he won't "be quite mad enough" for her.

In *Ways of Escape,* Greene discusses the genesis of *Our Man in Havana.* Alberto Cavalcanti, the Brazilian movie director, asked Greene for a script (1946). Greene replied with a one-page outline of a spy story to be cast in 1938 in Tallinn, Estonia, and to involve a husband who fakes intelligence reports to pay for his wife's extravagant spending habits. Nothing came of the proposal because Greene's purpose was to ridicule agents in the British Secret Intelligence Service (SIS), and British film censors said they would never issue a certificate of approval for such a plot. Greene made revised use of the idea in *Our Man in Havana.* Michael Shelden offers proof that Greene first planned to set this novel in Lisbon.

Norman Sherry reports much about Greene and the SIS; Cuba; Fulgencio Batista y Zaldivar (1901-1973), Cuba's ruthless dictator (1940–1944, 1952–1959); Fidel Castro (b. 1927), Cuba's present tyrant; and early reviews of *Our Man in Havana.* The satire of SIS antics is based on Greene's wartime experiences and observations when he worked for SIS, in offices at St. Albans and Ryder Street, London (1943–1944). He wrote *Our Man in Havana* over the course of two years (October 1956-June 1958). He visited Cuba six times (1957–1966). During his first visit, he smuggled winter clothes to Castro's rebels in Oriente. Reviewers praised Greene for having more astute intelligence about Cuba than the SIS could provide. Columbia Pictures bought film rights for $100,000 (October 1958). Greene and movie-director Carol Reed* visited Havana together (October 1958); the novel was published simultaneously in England and America (October 1958). Greene and Reed went to Brighton to work on the film script (October-November 1958) and to Havana to film it (March 1959). Ronald Bryden asked Greene about the criticism by Castro-era Cubans of *Our Man in Havana* for its "lightness," for its not "exploring Cuba in depth"; Greene rationalized that his first visits to Cuba were brief, added that later a Russian ambassador told him he urged Castro to read the novel, and said that, yes, the Cubans had forgiven Greene.

When Greene published *The Tenth Man* (1985), he included *Nobody to Blame,* a plot outline for a movie, never made, which concerns a British sewing-machine salesman in Baltic Latesthia, who makes extra money by faking intelligence reports to London. He accidentally reports the German invasion of Poland (later occurring in 1939) and becomes a decorated hero. Details of the slapstick plot foreshadow elements in *Our Man in Havana.*

Our Man in Havana takes place January-March 1958. This is made clear when mention is made that the Cuban president's rule is "creaking dangerously towards its end." The president in the novel (*see* President) was Batista, president and dictator, who was overthrown by an armed revolt led by Castro and sent into exile (January 1, 1959). When Wormold, on his way to the Consulate to accept his pay, views "a February sky," he remembers today is Ash Wednesday. Ash Wednesday fell on February 19th in 1958. Wormold is fibbing, to someone, when he tells the Santiago police he is 45 and tells Beatrice he was born December 6, 1914; these statements, if true, would erroneously place the year of action a year later. Maybe Greene enjoyed imagining the action of his novel to be occurring even as he was completing his report of it, in 1958. Although Hasselbacher tells Beatrice he left Germany in 1934, Wormold, admittedly a skillful liar, tells Hawthorne that Hasselbacher has lived in Cuba 30 years, then tells Beatrice more than 20. Wormold may be excused if he tells the police he is a year older than he is, for a modicum of sympathy. Readers of Greene may be excused for ignoring these forgettable dates.

Grahame Smith calls *Our Man in Havana* "Greene's first novel in an extended comic vein"; says "it triumphantly demonstrates the critical truism that comedy is every bit as serious a form as tragedy"; praises that form for its use of "interlocking patterns" (for ex., the phrase "part of the drill," the refrain of the popular song about "madness," similes about undertakers, mausoleums, graves, tombs); and analyzes "the absurdity of the basic situation" with its "farcical framework." Comedy, yes. Farce, yes. But when sweetly bungling Wormold causes the deaths of Raul, innocent pilot, and Hasselbacher, innocent philosophical cheese student, and certainly when he decides to kill Carter, the story becomes dark comedy, no longer farce. Smith, recognizing as much, concludes that the novel is "deeply serious" even while it is "gloriously funny." Greene's having Wormold shoot Carter in self-defense is a copout. Georg M. A. Gaston regards *Our Man in Havana* as proof that at the time he was writing it "Greene was undergoing a significant development in his outlook," and that the beliefs and acts of Wormold, Beatrice, Hasselbacher, and Milly partly dramatize "the idea which becomes prominent in Greene's thoughts thereafter — that the existential absurdity of life is allied to the positive, necessary values of comedy and farce."

Sherry and Quentin Falk report that before *Our Man in Havana* was published, Greene's agent expressed the hope of selling film rights for $125,000, that Alfred Hitchcock offered £25,000 for movie rights but was quoted an asking price of £50,000. Greene disliked Hitchcock's melodramatic touches in his movies (beginning in the 1930s), would never sell to him, and finally accepted less money so as to script with and work again with Reed. The movie (1960) stars Alec Guinness (as Wormold), Maureen O'Hara (Beatrice), Noël Coward (Hawthorne), Ralph Richardson (the Chief, called "C"), Ernie Kovacs (Segura), Burl Ives (Dr. Hasselbacher). Gene D. Phillips explains how the movie follows the novel closely and has splendid comic touches in some scenes. The best is Wormold's chess game with Segura, the chess pieces being miniature liquor bottles. Michael Meyer describes visiting Greene's residences and seeing his "army of tiny whisky bottles which airlines give to their ... passengers and which multiplied over the years like a child's collection of toy soldiers." Christopher Hawtree reports that Greene and Coward criticized each other but Coward readily accepted £20,000 to play Hawthorne. Hawtree discusses an opera (1962) based on Greene's novel, composed by an Australian named Malcolm Williamson and using a libretto by Sidney Gilliat. (Source: Bryden, 88; Falk, 145, 212; Gaston, 74; Greene, *Ways of Escape,* 246–59; Hawtree, 16–17, 48; Shelden, 426, 516; Sherry III, xxix, 55, 102–04, 108, 123, 135–41; G. Smith, 138, 139, 147; Phillips, 86–89)

"THE OVER-NIGHT BAG" (1965). Short story. (Characters: Bertha, Cooper, Henry Cooper, Mrs. Cooper, Mrs. Cooper, Sir Bernard Spilsbury, Tiny.)

Henry Cooper is flying from Nice to London. At the airport, a telegram from his mother says he'll be welcome back home. He takes a window seat, places his over-night bag in the central seat, and is bothered when an obese woman takes the aisle seat and puts a handbag on his over-night bag. He straps the seat-belt over both bags. She re-reads her letter from "cuddly Bertha" to "darling Tiny." Tiny wonders what Cooper's over-night bag contains. A dead baby, he says. He adds that it's cheaper to carry it than pay to freight it, that his wife wouldn't trust a foreign coffin, that, yes, he'll have to declare the baby, "acquired abroad," at customs. She sees him go through customs while she's held for having undeclared gifts for Bertha. Cooper takes a hired car home. He asks the driver to turn down the heat because a dead baby is in his over-night bag. The driver assures him that "the little perisher" should "keep" longer than oldsters. They nearly have a fender bender. The driver says not to worry, he's read corpses don't bruise. Queried, Cooper says the baby is his wife's, not his. The driver is glad, asks about an undertaker, and learning Cooper will keep the baby overnight at home advises placing it precautionarily in the frig. Home at last. Cooper is hugged by his mother, notes she's displaced his favorite picture, a reproduction of a Hieronymus Bosch, and says during his "adventures" abroad he found a little toe in his marmalade. English? she wonders. No, foreign. She says she could understand a finger. He says he didn't complain but did display the toe plainly on his plate. His mother bakes a shepherd's pie while Cooper, tidy man, goes to unpack.

Richard Kelly offers two opposing interpretations. Cooper is "carrying his wife's dead baby home for burial." Or Cooper "makes up stories to shock those around him and to give meaning [h-mm?] to his own dreary reality." Adumbrating the first interpretation, Kelly asks questions about wife, son living with mother, infanticide. Bulwarking the second interpretation, Kelly suggests Cooper's "grotesque imagination" is understandable given his liking Bosch, then half-implies Bosch's delight at a severed toe on a dish. Kelly concludes that Greene teases the readers about what's in the bag to reinforce his central belief that "a fictional narrative is the most significant version of reality available to us." Greene later recalled that, when asked, he told George Price, the Prime Minister of Belize, that Cooper's over-bag contained nothing.

"The Over-night Bag" was the subject of a 1976 television production. *See Shades of Greene.* (Sources: Falk, 215; Greene, *Getting to Know the General,* 146; Kelly, 64)

OWTRAM, JACK (*The Confidential Agent*) *see* **K**

PABLO (*The Captain and the Enemy*). He is the reliable, stolid, armed bodyguard Colonel Martínez assigns to Jim Baxter. Jim sees the makings of a revolutionary in Pablo's humble nature.

PABLO (*The Honorary Consul*). He is a pockmarked Negro member of Rivas's gang. Pablo and Diego Corredo are Argentinians. Pablo's wife and child are dead. All he has is the hut where the gang hides after kidnapping Fortnum by mistake. Pablo, more temperate than his colleagues, evidently survives the gory finale, along with Marta.

PAGE (*Orient Express*). He is a partner in the London firm Myatt, Myatt and Page, which is controlled by Jacob Myatt and his son Carleton.

PAGE (*This Gun for Hire*). She was a girl on whom Dr. Yogel operated well, according to Raven. This suggests that she recommended the crooked physician.

It is likely, since Raven says Yogel performed Page's "trick fine," that she had an abortion. Norman Sherry quotes Greene to the effect that a partial model for Dr. Yogel was a Hindu physician whom Greene consulted in Battersea, London, when he had severe stomach pains (September 1926), and whose drab consulting room gave evidence of a diminished practice. (Sources: Greene, *A Sort of Life,* 134; Sherry I, 318)

PAINE (*The Third Man*). He is a big, powerful, courteous soldier under Colonel Calloway's command. When Martins tries to hit Calloway, Paine slugs Martins in the mouth, then drives him to his hotel. When Martins hides after attempting to lecture to Crabbin's literary group, Paine finds him and addresses him gently.

PAMELA ("The Bear Fell Free"). Pamela is someone Baron sees right after Tony Farrell takes off on his fatal flight.

PAN ("The Trial of Pan"). He is the lithe, curly-haired, fun-loving fellow who wins a kind of acquittal. God carelessly lets him plead his case in music so effectively that the 12 jurymen, the 45 innocents, and the three guilties all disappear from court.

PANTIL, MISS (*The Ministry of Fear*). She is a guest at Mrs. Bellairs's séance. Mrs. Bellairs tells Rowe that Miss Pantil paints inner-world objects in rhythmical shapes and colors.

PAPA DOC (*The Comedians*) *see* **DUVALIER, FRANÇOIS**

PAPAL NUNCIO, THE (*The Comedians*). He is mentioned as a Catholic official accredited to Haiti but now in Rome, obviously because of political and religious unrest.

PARDOE, JANET (*Orient Express*). She is the bisexual paid companion of Mabel Warren, a lesbian journalist in Cologne. Janet's parents are dead. Her mother was Leo Stein's sister. Janet boards the train for Constantinople, to visit Uncle Leo and his wife there. On the way, Janet meets Myatt, Savory, Coral Musker, and other passengers. In Constantinople, Janet dumps Savory in favor of Myatt, who, being Jewish, is glad she's half-Jewish.

Norman Sherry reports that Greene received a letter from a woman in Pennsylvania who said that her name was also Janet Pardoe, and who added that she was attractive like the Janet Pardoe in his novel but not stupidly and egotistically parasitic like her. (Source: Sherry I, 441)

PARKER, COLONEL ("Doctor Crombie"). He was an eccentric man and remained one of Doctor Crombie's few patients after Crombie resigned as the Bankstead school physician.

PARKER, MRS. ("The Case for the Defence"). She was the woman murdered by one of the Adams twins.

PARKES, D. C. (*The Heart of the Matter*). An Indian fortune teller tells Wilson that Parkes gave him a letter attesting to his good work.

With this name, is Graham Greene punning on parks in the District of Columbia?

PARKIN, SIR EDWARD (*The Man Within*). Short, plump, and white-handed, Sir Edward is the pompous, snuff-sniffing judge at the Assizes in Lewes. The six captured smugglers are tried before him. All are acquitted.

PARKINSON (*A Burnt-Out Case*). He was the father of Montagu Parkinson. Montagu, worrying that his mild malaria has been misdiagnosed, tells Querry that old Parkinson was diagnosed with a duodenal ulcer but died evidently of something worse.

PARKINSON, MONTAGU (*A Burnt-Out Case*). He is a successful London *Post* journalist. Gross at 18 stone (252 lbs.), he specializes in scandal and travels widely. Parkinson tracks down Querry, gains inaccurate information about Querry from Rycker, and interviews Querry. Though aware of his distortions of the truth, Querry foolishly talks at length with him. Parkinson's first piece on Querry, calling him the saintly escapist architect and comparing him to Albert Schweitzer (1875–1965), is so sensational — even being translated into French and republished — that more coverage is to follow. Parkinson quotes and misquotes famous writers, and in the process assigns and misassigns their names to what he quotes.

For comic relief, Greene overdoes the matter of Parkinson's incomplete knowledge of Browning, Conrad, Herodotus, Hood, Horace, Keats, Landor, Poe, Shakespeare, Shelley, Suetonius, Swinbourne, and Virgil. Greene felt that many journalists who interviewed him were as cavalier with the truth as Parkinson. Heinz Antor criticizes Parkinson's sensationalizing his obituary on Querry by headlining it "Death of a Hermit. The Saint Who Failed," but says that Querry "has indeed attained a kind of humane sainthood through his charitable work in the lepers' colony."

Michael Shelden stretches in saying that, "[a]s his name suggests, Parkinson is suffering from a degenerative disease that is as bad as leprosy: with every story he writes, he moves further and further from the truth." Norman Sherry notes that journalists pestered Greene when he landed at Leopoldville to start his foray into the leprosy-infested Congo and then lied in print about him. Sherry then asks: "Could Parkinson be a manifestation of generalized anger ... who has no particular source?" Sherry nominates as Parkinson's partial model Ronald Matthews (1903–1966), a respected but opportunistic journalist whom Greene pub-crawled with and whose subsequent unauthorized book *Mon Ami Graham Greene* (1957) Greene not only felt betrayed by but also despised for its errors. (Sources: Antor, 104; Shelden, 434; Sherry III, 198, 200–04)

PARKIS, ALFRED (*The End of the Affair*). He is a simple, relentless detective working under Savage and hired by Bendrix to discover the identity of Sarah Miles's supposed lover. Parkis, a widower, has a droopy moustache and a hang-dog expression. He discovers that the alleged lover is Richard Smythe, an atheistic tutor that Sarah consults. Parkis obtains Sarah's diary and gives it to Bendrix, who reads it to his betterment.

PARKIS, LANCE (*The End of the Affair*). He is Parkis's son, 12. He helps his father at stakeouts. Bendrix takes Lance along to the home of Richard Smythe and his sister Miss Smythe. Bendrix introduces himself as Bridges and Lance as Arthur James Bridges, his son. Sarah Miles speaks to Lance once. Later, dangerously ill and feverish, Lance mumbles as though talking to Sarah, dreams she promised him a gift, and his father brings him one of Sarah's book of fairy tales. As a seemingly miraculous consequence, Lance recovers. Parkis tells Bendrix that Lance was named after Lancelot, who — he wrongly says — found the Holy Grail. Bendrix's mean-spiritedly corrects Parkis. Bendrix thinks he might have been motivated by jealousy of Parkis's innocence.

PARKIS, MRS. (*The End of the Affair*). Deceased, she was Alfred's wife and Lance's mother. Alfred refrained from discussing sordid details of his detective work with her. He says if there's a heaven she's there. Since she died after surgery, Alfred resists having Lance operated on for what is probably appendicitis.

PARKMAN, THOMAS EARL, JR. (*Our Man in Havana*). When he and Milly Wormold, then 13, were students in the convent school, young Thomas pulled her hair. She got even by pouring petrol on his shirt tail and lighting it.

PARKMAN, VINCENT C. (*Our Man in Havana*). When Wormold finds Parkman's name on the Country Club membership list, he plans to make Parkman a fictional secret agent with political savvy. But by London cable, Wormold learns Parkman is probably an American spy.

PARTRIDGE (*England Made Me*). He was senior chaplain at Harrow when Minty was there. When Minty mentions him, Farrant starts to discuss him but can't because, though pretending to be a Harrow man, Farrant isn't.

PARTRIDGE (*The Human Factor*) *see* **CASTLE, MAURICE**

PASSERATI (*Travels with My Aunt*). When Detective-Sergeant Sparrow asks Henry if Augusta ever mentioned Passerati, and also Cossa, Stradano, and Tiberio Titi, the answer is no.

PATERSON, MISS DOROTHY (*Travels with My Aunt*). She was one of Richard Pulling's mistresses. They met on a London bus, began an affair, and while vacationing in Boulogne he died in his Dolly's devoted arms (1923). During the war, she taught English at the Lycée in Boulogne, her wartime alias being Poupée. When Henry and Augusta are seeking his father's grave in the Boulogne cemetery on the anniversary of his death (October 2), they encounter Miss Paterson decorating it, invite her for tea, and learn details of her relationship with Richard.

In his book illustrating Greene's novels, Paul Hogarth's "The Cemetery, Boulogne-sur-Mer" is especially fine. (Source: Hogarth, 133)

PATMORE (*It's a Battlefield*). He is crime reporter Conder's contact in Scotland Yard.

PATRICIA (*The Human Factor*). She is Brigadier Tomlinson's niece and works in his secretarial pool. To annoy her, Castle addresses her as Pat, which she doesn't like.

PATSY ONE-EYE ("Church Militant"). Father Donnell mentions her as someone at his residence whom the Archbishop may encounter to his discomfiture.

PATTERSON (*England Made Me*). He was a person at Harrow, as was Henriques, before Farrant's time there, according to Minty when he and Farrant are discussing the school. Minty knows Farrant never attended Harrow.

PAUL, FATHER (*A Burnt-Out Case*). He is one of the priests at the leproserie. He and Brother Philippe handle its electrical problems.

PAULINE ("Chagrin in Three Parts"). She was widowed Madame Emmy Dejoie's lesbian partner, whose dexterity enabled Emmy to discover her own "capacity for love."

PAYNE (*Travels with My Aunt*). In one of Augusta's yarns, Miss Comfort loved a coward named Courage, married Payne, and killed herself in a comfort station.

PEACOCK (*Rumour at Nightfall*). He is a London newspaperman. Chase remembers Peacock and Verity as companionable fellow drinkers with him, as well as happy sharers of dirty stories.

PEDRO (*The Honorary Consul*). Rivas remembers a Pedro as his well-to-do family's gardener.

PEDRO (*The Honorary Consul*). He is Sir Henry Belfrage's cook. Belfrage petulantly complains to Lady Belfrage that Pedro, in that dreadful "Yankee custom," thrice has wrongly fried his egg on both sides.

PEDRO (*Our Man in Havana*). He is thin Teresa's sick boyfriend.

PEDRO (*The Power and the Glory*). He is a Catholic living near the Lehrs. He attends the whisky priest's Mass.

PEDRO (*The Power and the Glory*). He is Luis's playmate.

PEDRO (*The Power and the Glory*). He is Brigitta's 10-year-old playmate.

PEDRO (*The Power and the Glory*) see **BRIGITTA**

PEDRO, FATHER (*The Honorary Consul*). According to Marta, Father Pedro in Asunción said Mass effectively even though he slept with women. So why can't her husband, Father Léon Rivas, do so?

PEDRO, FATHER (*Rumour at Nightfall*). He is mentioned by women praying in a church near San Juan that Chase enters to escape from rain. The priest doesn't appear.

PEMBERTON (*The Heart of the Matter*). He is a widowed, retired bank manager in England. His son Dicky wrote him, then committed suicide.

PEMBERTON, DICKY (*The Heart of the Matter*). He was the assistant district commissioner, 25. When Butterworth, his superior, fell ill, Pemberton was ill-advisedly promoted. Immaturity and loneliness, plus too much liquor and mounting gambling debts, forced him to write his father apologetically and then hang himself. Scobie determines Pemberton owed money to a store manager employed by Yusef. Did Yusef therefore indirectly cause Pemberton's death?

PENELOPE (*The Human Factor*). She is a member of the Secret Intelligence Service's secretarial pool. When Cynthia grieves after Davis's death, Penelope substitutes for her.

PENKOVSKY (*The Human Factor*). In conversation with Daintry about eliminating Davis, Percival remarks that after the Soviets tried Penkovsky for treason they happily didn't kill him. Davis mentions Penkovsky to Castle.

Without the slightest elaboration, W. J. West mentions "the famous Russian MI6 agent Penkovsky" and indexes him as "Penkovsky, Oleg Vladimirovich." (Source: West, 241, 282)

PENNY, LUKE (*Our Man in Havana*) see **WORMOLD, JAMES**

PENNY, MRS. (*This Gun for Hire*). She works at the jumble at St. Luke's, puts a low price on a nice hat Lady Cundife donated, and buys it herself.

PENNYFEATHER (*Our Man in Havana*) see **MORGAN, HARRY**

PENRITH (*This Gun for Hire*). He is a thug who Raven tells Anne Crowder was hurt when he went soft on a girl.

PERAUD, LIEUTENANT (*The Quiet American*). Fowler meets this serious Frenchman on the river near Phat Diem. Peraud, a Freemason, regards the successful bombing of buildings in Phat Diem as a judgment leveled at his fellow soldiers' "[Catholic] superstitions."

Norman Sherry hints that Lieutenant Peraud is based on a friend of Greene's (incompletely) named Captain Mathei. (Source: Sherry II, 394)

PERCIVAL, DR. EMMANUEL (*The Human Factor*). He is a merciless physician now not practicing but established as a liaison official between Hargreaves's MI6 workers and biological-warfare agents. Percival is a stout, rubicund lover of choice wines, special foods and fish, and fishing rather than hunting. He regards espionage as a game. When he and Daintry seek to plug security leaks caused by Castle, they follow flimsy evidence against Davis, and Percival murders him by dropping aflatoxin in his whisky. After Castle defects to Moscow, Percival invites Castle's wife Sarah to a gourmet lunch and scares her heartlessly.

Michael Shelden reports that Greene wrote to his brother Raymond Greene,* a physician, to ask how to make death by murder seem to be the result of natural causes, and that "[a]fter doing a little research, Raymond found the perfect solution and conveyed the details in a letter to his brother, who put them into the novel almost verbatim." Norman Sherry adds details by quoting Greene's letters to Raymond (May 15, 1967; June 2, 1967) and one of Raymond's replies (October 15, 1972). Paul O'Prey sees Percival as "a vivid, frightening portrait of a ruthless institutional mind," as "a man not only without ideals, but without morals or conscience," hence a dazzling Greene rendition of pure evil. Thomas Michael Stein says that when Percival advises Daintry to be as indifferent to others as a square of one color is to adjacent squares of other colors in "that Nicholson" painting, he is referring to "Painting 1937" by Ben Nicholson (1894–1962); Stein shows how, in life and in many of Greene's characters, the human factor tries to counter amoral, pragmatic indifference. (Sources: O'Prey, 139; Shelden, 481; Sherry III, 606–08, 861; Stein)

PEREZ, COLONEL (*The Honorary Consul*). He is the intelligent, efficient, cool provincial Chief of Police where Plarr lives. Both men know they were both Margarita Escobar's lovers. When Fortnum was kidnapped, Perez guessed Fortnum wasn't their intended target. Perez suspects Plarr of complicity, knows he sleeps with Clara Fortnum, and urges him to avoid trouble with the kidnappers. Perez and his men surround the hut of the kidnappers, Fortnum, and Plarr at the end.

PEREZ, SEÑOR (*Our Man in Havana*). He is a man for whose children Milly Wormold tells her father she could be a governess. Wormold objects to the idea, because Perez is currently living with his fourth wife.

PEREZ, SEÑORA (*Our Man in Havana*). She is Señor Perez's fourth wife.

PERMANENT UNDER-SECRETARY, THE (*Our Man in Havana*). He is an official who, when he is a guest of the Chief, is served a really nice dinner — biscuits, cheese, garlic, gravy, roast, and wine.

PERRIN (*A Burnt-Out Case*). He operates a plantation located near the road between the leproserie and Luc. Marie Rycker knows the Perrins.

PERRIN, LIEUTENANT (*The Quiet American*). Captain Trouin tells Fowler that both he and Perrin have slept with a half-breed he and Fowler see at the opium house.

PERRIN, MRS. (*A Burnt-Out Case*). She is probably the wife of Perrin, a plantation operator. They are mentioned a few times.

PERROT (*The Heart of the Matter*). He is the officious district commissioner at Pende. Scobie and others go there to assist survivors of the torpedoed ship. Perrot informs Scobie that he has been on duty there since 1939.

Does Greene unnecessarily cloud the religious atmosphere of *The Heart of the Matter* by having Perrot descend from Huguenots?

PERROT, MRS. (*The Heart of the Matter*). She is the Pende official's wife and is helpful when Scobie visits. Her listening to music on the radio from England indicates her homesickness.

PERRY (*The Ministry of Fear*). Arthur remembers him as one of several friends who deserted him once they heard he was on trial for murder.

PETE ("A Discovery in the Woods"). He is the only child of dwarfish, twisted parents. His fisherman father says Pete is nine. His stuttering mother says he's seven. Pete leads three other boys and Liz in an exploration of the woods beyond Bottom. They find luscious blackberries and then the wreck of a sea-going vessel, containing among other mysteries scattered bones, dangerous-looking yellow rust, and a beautiful, straight-boned, six-foot skeleton.

A. A. DeVitis says that Pete, through his urge to explore, "represents the future," while Liz, whom Pete suddenly finds pretty, represents "intuition and the promise of beauty." (Source: DeVitis, 177)

PETER (*Travels with My Aunt*). When first

leaving Augusta's flat over the Crown and Anchor, Henry hears an obscene girl rebuking a bloke named Peter.

PETERS (*The Confidential Agent*). He is a detective. Pete and his sergeant go to the embassy representing D.'s country to arrest D. on suspicion of his murdering Else Crole.

PETERS, AMY (*Orient Express*). She and her husband Herbert are passengers on the train to Constantinople. She complains of a weak stomach. When she calls Coral Musker a tart for liking Carleton Myatt, both her husband and Czinner object.

PETERS, HERBERT (*Orient Express*). He is Amy Peters's husband. They are traveling on the train to Constantinople.

PETIT PIERRE (The Comedians). He is a courageous little Haitian journalist who dresses flamboyantly, writes dangerous columns often exaggerating the truth or falsifying, cadges drinks in establishments by publicizing events therein, and is watched by the Tontons Macoute. Petit Pierre helps Brown.

Petit Pierre is patterned after Aubelin Jolicoeur, the Haitian journalist. Greene mentions him both in a *Collected Edition* introduction and in *Ways of Escape*. Flamboyant in his trademark white suit and sporting a gold-tipped cane, Jolicoeur published gossip about Haitian high society for 50 years. He died peacefully at his home in Jacmel, Haiti (2005). Ian Thomson, who met Jolicoeur, reports the following: "He was a Mister Facing-Both-Ways, a man who had clung mollusc-like to the centers of corruption and power, and never allowed himself to be on the side of the losers. For two years Jolicœur was Secretary of State at the Ministry of Education." When Greene died, Jolicoeur wrote an appreciation of him for the London *Guardian,* in which he expressed gratitude for Greene's converting him, as Petit Pierre, into a living legend and untouchable. Michael Shelden adds that Truman Capote introduced Greene to Jolicoeur, discusses Jolicoeur briefly, then gratuitously asserts that Greene's presentation of Jolicoeur as Petit Pierre was racially motivated. (Sources: Greene, *The Comedians, Collected Edition,* x; Greene, *Ways of Escape,* 276; Shelden, 438–49, 441; Thomson, 44, 45)

PETKOVITCH, MAJOR (*Orient Express*). He is the commanding officer of the Subotica frontier guards. Captain Alexitch is his assistant. Short, thin, and sporting gold pince-nez, Petkovitch caters to Colonel Hartep when he arrives from Belgrade. Petkovitch does object, though ineffectually, when Hartep conducts a quick court martial resulting in Czinner's death sentence. Petkovitch humiliates Ninitch, a frontier guard, by ordering him to shoot Czinner's corpse in the head.

PETTY (*The Man Within*). He is a little old solicitor. He generously offers to defend Richard Tims at the smugglers' trial at the Assizes in Lewes, does so, then naps in court. Tims, however, is declared mentally incompetent.

PFUNK, MISS (*Our Man in Havana*). She is the K.L.M. stewardess. Hans, a K.L.M. pilot, tells Wormold at the Tropicana bar he wants to marry her but is refused.

When it is said that Wormold thinks Hans pronounced her name thus, it seems likely Greene wants the reader to think slightly otherwise.

PHAM-VAN-TU (*The Quiet American*). He is an accountant at the Banque de l'Indo-Chine in Saigon. When Fowler, who knows him, sees him dancing with his wife in a civilized manner, he recalls that Pham-Van-Tu studies William Wordsworth's poetry and write nature poems himself.

PHAM-VAN-TU, MRS. (*The Quiet American*). She is the wife of a Saigon bank accountant. Fowler sees the two dancing decorously.

PHAN-VAN-MUOI (*The Quiet American*). He is the husband of a woman related to General Thé. Heng tells Fowler that when Phan-Van-Muoi found discarded plastic moulds and traces of Diolacton powder in his garage, he sought to report the matter to Pyle. This information convinces Fowler that Pyle is providing explosives to Thé.

PHAN-VAN-MUOI, MRS. (*The Quiet American*). She is related to General Thé.

PHELPS, MONTAGUE (*This Gun for Hire*). He is a well-dressed, hair-oiled lecturer, about 42, and with an M.A. He discourses, somewhat superciliously, on how to cure stammerers. After shooting Raven, Saunders, who stammers, attends Phelps's free class for diversion.

PHIL (*Orient Express*). Coral Musker remembers him as one of her slightly successful theatrical friends. Others are Dick, Flo, and Ivy.

PHILBY, (KIM) (*The Human Factor*). When Daintry, Hargreaves, and Percival discuss slack security at MI6, Philby is mentioned along with Blake, Burgess, Maclean, Vassall, and the Portland affair.

Harold Adrian Russell Philby (1912–1988) was a notorious, brilliantly clever British double-agent during and after World War II. Philby, called Kim, was born in Amballa, India, the son of Harry St. John Bridger Philby, a British member of the Indian Civil Service, and Dora Johnston Philby. Philby entered Trinity College, Cambridge, joined the Cambridge University Socialist Society (1929–1933), began associating with pro–Communist students Anthony Blunt, Guy Francis de Moncey Burgess,* and Donald Duart Maclean* (1932), joined the Soviet Counter-Intelligence Service (1933), was active in pro–German and pro–Hitler work (1934), and was a correspondent for the London *Times* in Spain ostensibly to report favorably on Francisco Franco's activities during the Spanish Civil War but really to arrange (unsuccessfully) for Franco's assassination (1937). Philby was a *Times* war correspondent in Arras, France (1939), worked with the British Secret Intelligence Service (SIS, MI6) in London (1940–1945) as head of the section monitoring anti–Communist, anti–Soviet counter-intelligence work (1945). Knighted (1946), Philby was appointed secretary of the British Embassy in Istanbul, Turkey (1947, actually heading SIS there). He was SIS representative in Washington, D.C., working with Burgess, Maclean, the FBI, and the newly formed CIA (1949–1951). Warned by Philby (1950), Burgess and Maclean defected to the Soviet Union. Philby was asked to resign (1951). Harold Macmillan (1894–1986), when Foreign Minister, asserted in parliamentary debate that there was no incriminating evidence against Philby (1955). Philby was assigned to Beirut, Lebanon, as a stringer for the *Observer* and the *Economist,* while working for the SIS (1956). Interrogated at last by British agents, Philby confessed, disappeared, and resurfaced in Moscow, where he was granted political asylum and awarded a lifetime pension (1963). Philby published *My Silent War* (1968), was temporarily neglected by the KGB (1969–1972), visited Cuba (1978), and died in Moscow.

Philby, who had homosexual experiences, was married four times. His first marriage (1934–1946) was to Alice Kohlman; his second (1946–1957), to Aileen Furse, producing five children; his third (1959–1968), to Eleanor Pope Brewer; and his fourth (1971) to Rufina Ivanovna. Eleanor Philby wrote *Kim Philby: The Spy I Loved* (1968). Rufina Philby wrote *The Private Life of Kim Philby: The Moscow Years* (2000).

Greene knew Philby well; was one of Philby's deputies (1941–1944); probably knew about his Communist past and anti–British actions, and resigned from under him (June 2, 1944); suspended writing (1963) *The Human Factor* because its protagonist Maurice Castle's actions too closely resemble Philby's; resumed friendship with Philby and published *The Human Factor* (1978); and visited Philby, by invitation from Mikhail Gorbachev, in Moscow (September 1986), and again (September 1987, February 1988), last seeing Philby three months before his death. Greene reviewed (1968) both *Kim Philby: The Spy I Loved* and *My Silent War,* having also written the introduction of the latter. Greene records two dreams he had about Philby: Philby recruited Ernest Hemingway to write about Hong Kong refugees; Philby visited Greene in London in 1980.

Anthony Cave Brown quotes a London *Sunday Telegraph* interview in which Greene, if asked what he would do if he discovered during the war that Philby was a Soviet agent, said he'd give Philby 24 hours to escape and then report him. Philby retained great fondness for Greene, and Greene was cavalier in his friendship with this notorious "Master Spy" operating to the disadvantage of England, the United

States, and other Allies during and long after World War II. Greene's good friend Michael Meyer turns critical when, as he puts it, "Greene retained his affection for Kim Philby." Most veterans of Allied armies and navies from World War II would agree with Meyer, not Greene. Philby, who caused many Allied casualties, should have been arrested and tried for treason. (Sources: Brown, 583, 601; Greene, *A World of My Own*, 17, 23; Meyer, 225; Rufina Philby, 401–28)

PHILIPOT (*The Comedians*). He is the son, six, of Dr. Philipot and his wife. The boy asks for ice cream while he and his mother are following the funeral cortège of his father as far as the Trianon.

PHILIPOT, DR. (*The Comedians*). He is the Secretary for Social Welfare. Dr. Magiot tells Brown he and Philipot studied anatomy together in Paris. Brown met Philipot only once. Smith has a letter of introduction to present to Philipot. But he has displeased Duvalier's administration and, hoping to spare his family grief, commits suicide in Brown's Trianon swimming pool. Brown and Magiot hide his body, but it is soon found, abused, taken from its coffin, and ultimately may be placed in the palace of François Duvalier as a zombie to scare off would-be assailants.

Robert Heinl and Nancy Heinl, Bernard Diederich and Al Burt, and Robert I. Rotberg present evidence concerning the abuse of a Haitian politician's corpse which parallels Philipot's post-mortem fate. Clément Jumelle was the Finance Minister under Paul Eugène Magloire, president of Haiti (1950–1957), but angered Duvalier by having the timerity to want to run for president. When Duvalier's reign of terror began, Jumelle hid for 21 months with peasants and in holes in the ground, then stumbled disheveled into the Cuban embassy (April 1959), and died of uremia, age 42. When his body was being taken by hearse to the Church of the Sacred Heart in Port-au-Prince, Duvalier's police stopped the procession, battered some of the mourners, and buried the body in a voodoo ceremony. According to rumors, the police disinterred it so that the heart and other organs could be made into a voodoo charm and placed in Duvalier's palace to ward off enemies. Rotberg says that "[t]his incident obviously provided the basis for the interrupted funeral [of Philipot] in Graham Greene, *The Comedians*." (Sources: Heinl and Heinl, 597; Diederich and Burt, 139; Rotberg, 218)

PHILIPOT, HENRI (*The Comedians*). He is Dr. Philipot's nephew. This Philipot limps, because as a child he had polio. He studied at the Sorbonne, admires Charles Baudelaire's works, and is a would-be poet himself. Disgusted by the Haitian government, Philipot becomes a revolutionary, attends a voodoo ceremony to become bellicose, and asks Brown to encourage Jones to obtain weapons and join the insurgents. Jones, among others, is killed during a border skirmish. Philipot survives and is driven to safety by Brown. Ironically, the voodoo priest scorches Philopot's arm to purify and strengthen it, but he breaks it after the clash with Haitian soldiers.

Bernard Diederich and Al Burt describe how a sugar-cane planter named Riobé was wrongly suspected of planning to kidnap François Duvalier's children, was seized by the Tontons Macoute and murdered, and his family property confiscated. Riobé's son Hector went underground (May 1963). Hector and his men attacked a police station, gathered weapons, killed many opponents, but were driven into the mountains and destroyed by field weapons and mortars. With his last bullet, Hector killed himself (July 1963). Greene, in Haiti at the time, heard about these events. Norman Sherry finds a parallel between Henri Philipot's intention to avenge his uncle's death and events in the Riobé family, especially with respect to Hector. (Sources: Diederich and Burt, 244–46; Sherry III, 331–32, 354)

PHILIPOT, MME. (*The Comedians*). She is Dr. Philipot's beautiful wife, then widow, somewhat under 40. Brown helplessly watches her being humiliated by Captain Concasseur and his men during her husband's funeral procession. His coffin is taken by them and delivered to Haitian headquarters, and Clement Dupont and Hercule Dupont, the funeral directors, are arrested.

PHILIPPE, BROTHER (*A Burnt-Out Case*). He is a member of the religious order managing the leproserie. Older than the priests there and speaking only Flemish, Philippe and Father Paul manage the electrical work.

PHILIPS (*The Human Factor*). When Hargreaves and Percival are discussing the possibility that Castle is the security leak, Percival asks if Hargreaves has consulted "5." Saying yes, Hargreaves adds that Philips is going to monitor Castle's phone again.

PHUONG (*The Quiet American*). She is Fowler's mistress. Fowler met Phuong, then 18, two years earlier, when he saw her dancing at the Grand Monde in Cholon, a Chinese suburb in Saigon. Phuong's parents are dead. Her sister is Miss Hei. Their father was a Hué mandarin. Phuong, whose name means "Phoenix," is little more than Fowler's obedient but inscrutable sex toy. She knows Fowler is married. Phuong and Fowler have a room on the rue Catinat. She prepares bamboo pipes for his opium smoking, pops into bed when he beckons, but takes up with Pyle when his proposal of marriage would seem to provide security and a chance to see America, and when she hears Fowler is being recalled to London. Fowler's recall is cancelled. Pyle is murdered. Phuong returns to Fowler. When Fowler's wife Helen agrees to a divorce, Phuong naively dreams of accompanying him to London.

Several years after *The Quiet American* was published, U.S. and South Vietnamese military forces launched a pacification operation to capture or kill Viet Cong agents operating in South Vietnamese villages (1968). Although the effort was successful in "neutralizing" more than 81,000 Viet Cong suspects (by 1972), it was criticized for confirmed or alleged stories of revenge, torture, bribery, and murder tactics employed to succeed. By coincidence, the operation was called Phung Hoang, "The Phoenix Program."

Greene took the name Phuong from that of his editor friend René Berval's Vietnamese girlfriend. The two lived, according to Norman Sherry, at 104 rue Catinat, Saigon. Sherry adds that René's Phuong was not beautiful like Greene's Fowler's Phuong, whose beauty reflects that of the real-life sister of the mistress of Mathieu Franchini, the real-life manager of Saigon's Majestic hotel. (Source: Sherry II, 409–11)

PIDOT (*The Tenth Man*). He is a friend of Carosse. When Corosse sees Chavel at a urinal in Paris, Corosse mistakes him for Pidot, then pays Chavel to deliver a message to Pidot.

PIERPOINT (*It's a Battlefield*). He is the Leeds prison executioner, as the chief warder explains to the Assistant Commissioner.

PIERRE (*The Tenth Man*). He is one of the 30 prisoners the Germans hold as hostages. He is an engine driver, owns an alarm clock, and argues with the Mayor of Bourge, a fellow prisoner, about the precise time.

PIERRE ("Two Gentle People"). He is evidently Marie-Claire Duval's husband's latest homosexual partner. Or so she judges when she hears "little yelps and giggles" through her bedroom wall.

PIETRI (*The Quiet American*). He is a Sûreté officer, married to the Tonkinese owner of the Pax Bar in Hanoi. Pietri, a Corsican, prefers Marseilles to Corsica but quietly prefers Hanoi to either. Fowler plays dice with him when Fowler is in Hanoi.

PIG ("A Shocking Accident") *see* **JEROME**

PIG (*The Confidential Agent*). He is one of several fun-loving young people at the Lido. He may be voyeuring when he looks into D.'s room there. When D. asks what he wants, Pig says he thought the room was Chubby's.

PIHLSTRÖM (*England Made Me*). Minty mentions Pihlström as a rival journalist.

PIKER (*Brighton Rock*). He is a waiter at the Peacehaven hotel where Pinkie and Rose stop. Pinkie knew him at school and tries to lord it over him.

PIKER, ALFRED (*This Gun for Hire*). He is Nottwich's mayor. He was a good sport when he was dunked by medical students at an earlier rag. During the mock air-raid drill, Calkin suggests that it's an opportune time, what with gas masks and all, for Piker to hop into a strange woman's bed.

PIKER, MRS. (*This Gun for Hire*). She is the

vapid wife of Alfred Piker, Nottwich's mayor. She worries Mrs. Calkin by bringing her Pekinese dog, Chinky, to the Calkinses' party. Sir Marcus, the featured guest, dislikes dogs.

PILBEAM, PROFESSOR (*Monsignor Quixote*). He is an American teacher-scholar from the University of Notre Dame. A lapsed Catholic, Pilbeam is perhaps the greatest living authority on Ignatius Loyola. He is visiting the Trappist monastery at Osera when Father Quixote crashes his car there. Father Leopoldo, the head priest at the monastery, prefers Descartes to Loyola, verbally jousts with Pilbeam, and is therefore philosophically more sympathetic toward Quixote than Pilbeam is.

PIM ("The Bear Fell Free"). Baron sees Pim's hat on the hat stand at Earl's Court.

PINECOFFIN (*Brighton Rock*). This name is shouted by a page at the Cosmopolitan when Pinkie is unsuccessfully seeking a room for Rose and himself after their marriage.

Perhaps Greene is using this idiotic name to foreshadow the fact that Pinkie's matrimonial bed will be a coffin — if his body is ever found.

PINEDA, ANGEL (*The Comedians*). He is Martha and Luis Pineda's only child, five. Brown regards the fat, dark-eyed, sweets-sucking little cheater as a demon (despite his name) interfering with his affair with Martha. Jones likes the kid and plays games with him. Martha's maternal attachment to Angel keeps Brown worried about the viability of their affair.

PINEDA, LUIS (*The Comedians*). He is the fat, supercilious ambassador, nearly 50, representing a small, unnamed South American country and assigned to Haiti. He told Brown he studied at the College of Saint Ignatius, somewhere in South America. Lonely and evidently possessing little sexual energy, Pineda is the husband of Martha Pineda, Brown's mistress. If Pineda suspects the two, he remains remarkably tolerant. His dog is named Don Juan.

Norman Sherry suggests that this cuckolded husband is patterned on Henry Walston, the husband of Catherine Walston,* one of Greene's lovers. (Source: Sherry III, 379, 385–88)

PINEDA, MARTHA (*The Comedians*). She is Luis Pineda's young, dissatisfied wife, Angel Pineda's loving mother, and Brown's mistress. Brown met Martha at the casino and immediately started a torrid but basically miserable affair with her. Her German father, a Lutheran and a Nazi, was hanged in the American zone for war crimes during World War II. Martha's pretending to like Jones while he resides in sanctuary at the Pineda embassy apartment annoys Brown and may contribute to his not following her when Luis is transferred.

Norman Sherry theorizes that Brown's affair with Martha reflects "the secret concerns of Greene's life, not Brown's; Catherine's distress [*see* Walston, Catherine], not Martha's; Lord [Henry] Walston's vexations, not Ambassador [Luis] Pineda's." Father Thomas Gilby (d. 1975) was a Dominican priest and professor whom Greene, Catherine, and others knew and whose alleged sexual misconduct Shelden, Sherry, and William Cash mention. Yvonne Cloetta* says she felt that Martha Pineda came closest of any of Greene's female characters to be patterned after her. (Sources: Cash, 233–34; Cloetta, 83; Shelden, 360–61; Sherry II, 304; Sherry, III, 379, 392–400, 613–14; Sinyard, 66)

PINK, MOLLY (*Brighton Rock*). She is a London secretary, 18 and fat. Hale tries to invite for lunch both Molly, who is in Brighton for holiday, and her friend Delia to insulate him from Pinkie. Pinkie enters and spoils Hale's plan. Ida Arnold finds Molly in London and queries her about Hale.

It seems strange that Greene would give Molly the last name Pink when his arch-villain is Pinkie.

PIPER (*The Human Factor*). Piper and Taylor are MI6 agents who search dead Davis's flat for clues. When Piper finds some Robert Browning poems marginally marked with "c" (meaning Cynthia, whom Davis loved from afar), he is foolishly suspicious.

Percival reads some marked lines aloud and Piper responds by saying they sound like poetry; thus Greene pokes too blatant fun at the stupidity of British intelligence agents in general.

PIPPITT, MARY (*The End of the Affair*). According to a program Bendrix finds in one of

Sarah's books, Mary Pippitt played the violin during a July 23, 1926 recital, in their school.

PLARR, DR. EDUARDO (*The Honorary Consul*). He is the son of Henry Plarr, missing in Paraguay, and his wife, now living in Buenos Aires. Dr. Plarr, thin-faced and in his early 30s, never married, and after studying in Buenos Aires began practice in a small city 600 kilometers north. His friends include Humphries, Saavedra, Bergman, Gruber, Señora Sanchez and several of her prostitutes, Perez, three mistresses — Margarita Escobar, Señora Lopez, and Señora Vallejo — and most recently Fortnum (who calls him Ted) and his wife Clara, also Plarr's lover. Reared Catholic, Plarr now believes in just about nothing, partly because his father deserted the family when Eduardo was 14, and partly because he hates his self-centered mother. Plarr is drawn into the kidnapping of Fortnum by Plarr's childhood friend Léon Rivas. Plarr dangerously tends to Fortnum, first ill, then wounded. Perez's warnings to Plarr are unavailing. At the end, Plarr demonstrates loyalty, courage, and perhaps something like "love," a word he dislikes.

Michael Shelden says this: Plarr's "portrait ... is powerfully rendered"; unlike most adulterers in Greene's fiction, Plarr is completely isolated; his sexual actions are rendered in graphic detail unusual in Greene; the reader is concerned about Plarr's fate because Greene blends "comedy and tragedy" in presenting him. Incidentally, the sex-prompted images Greene puts in Plarr's head are disgusting.

Norman Sherry demonstrates that at different times Greene planned for Fortnum to die, Plarr to survive and consort with Clara briefly, Plarr to die saving Fortnum as his surrogate father. Sherry theorizes that Greene, because of a conscience troubled by exposure of his adultery with Yvonne Cloetta,* made Plarr's end somewhat honorable. But why must Sherry contend that by killing Plarr off Greene was committing a kind of mock suicide? Greene, after all, put down pencil not pistol, and lived. Mark Bosco remarks that "Plarr resembles a type of character that ubiquitously populates Greene's later novels — a jaded rationalist who casts an ironic glance at the wasteland of modern life," but that he spiritually profits once he understands "lack of love ... [to be] ... a sickness ... he has failed to diagnose correctly" and "faith ... not [to] be ... an absurdity." (Sources: Bosco, 108; Shelden, 477, 478; Sherry III, 552, 556)

PLARR, HENRY (*The Honorary Consul*). He was Dr. Eduardo's idealistic British father. He remained in Paraguay to oppose General Stroessner, was captured, was ignominiously held in a police station 15 years, and when 71 was shot to death trying to escape with Aquino Ribera, a tortured fellow prisoner.

PLARR, SEÑORA (*The Honorary Consul*). She is Henry Plarr's once-beautiful Spanish-Paraguayan wife and Dr. Eduardo Plarr's mother. She was in her early 30s when her husband sent her and Eduardo to safety in Argentina, remained in Paraguay, and was captured and shot 15 years later. Now in her early 50s, Señora Plarr lives in Buenos Aires on money provided by Eduardo, who visits her every three months or so. She is incredibly self-absorbed, is triple-chinned with dewlaps, uses cosmetics, and is addicted to sweets, has tea occasionally with Lady Belfrage, and lets Father Galvão help her rationalize her useless life. She attends Eduardo's funeral with Father Galvão.

THE POINT OF DEPARTURE. The working title for *The End of the Affair* (*which see*). Greene liked *Point Depart,* the French translation of "point of departure." (Source: Cash, 203)

POMPILIA ("A Little Place off the Edgeware Road"). She is a character in the silent movie Craven sees. Betrayed by Augustus, Pompilia evidently stabs herself.

POOLE (*The Ministry of Fear*). He is a crippled, strong-shouldered photographer for the spy ring. He rents rooms from Mrs. Purvis in an effort to swipe Rowe's hidden film. His attempt to poison Rowe fails. During an air raid, Poole is rendered unconscious with a concussion but is whisked away from the hospital. When Rowe is put in Dr. Forester's sanatorium, Poole aids Forester, manages sick bay, helps him murder Major Stone, and is shot by Johns, Rowe's disaffected attendant. Prentice tells Rowe that Poole specialized in photographing bees.

POPEY MARTIN ("The Hint of an Explanation") *see* **DAVID**

PORTLAND (*The Human Factor*). Percival mentions "the Portland affair" when he, Daintry, and Hargreaves are discussing possible sources of security leaks.

A celebated espionage trial (1961) followed investigative work by MI5 agents, Special Branch officers, and the wives of several agents. Ethel Gee, Harry Houghton, Helen and Peter Kroger, and Gordon Arnold Lonsdale were convicted. Gee was a middle-aged, security-cleared, sex-hungry spinster filing clerk at the Detection Establishment. Houghton served at the British Embassy in Warsaw (1950) and at the secret naval Underwater Detection Establishment, Portland (beginning 1950). Houghton and Gee lived together. The Krogers were KGB moles who escaped an FBI dragnet in the United States and became booksellers in Ruislip, London. Lonsdale was really Konon Trofimovich Molody, a top Soviet spy in England using the name of a deceased Canadian businessman and functioning as Houghton's controller (1952). Houghton transmitted documents from Gee to Lonsdale in men's lavatories. British agents' wives followed Houghton to the Krogers. Gee and Houghton received 15-year sentences, were released (1971), and married each other; the Krogers were exchanged (1969) for a British lecturer imprisoned in Russia for subversive conduct; Lonsdale received a 25-year sentence but was exchanged for a British spy (1964). Anthony Cave Brown reports that the Krogers knew Julius Rosenberg (1918–1953) and his wife Ethel Rosenberg (1915–1953), that Kim Philby* vouched for their innocence (both, convicted of spying for the Soviet Union, were executed), and that Lonsdale was caught because he was circumcised but pretended to be a man who hadn't been.

Greene undoubtedly knew about and relished these juicy stories. The Ruislip booksellers remind one of Halliday and his son (*The Human Factor*). Nefarious exchanges in lavatories in Greene's fiction are too numerous to mention. (Source: Brown, 530, 575)

PORTON (*The Human Factor*). When Castle tells Davis that Percival is a liaison officer from a bacteriological-warfare establishment, Davis says that the Porton place scares him, because if the atomic bomb is abolished there is still weaponry from "deadly test-tube[s]."

Davis's shivers are prophetic, because Percival kills him with aflatoxin obtained from a Porton colleague.

At Porton Down, Wiltshire, 20,000 volunteers were experimented on (beginning in 1916) by scientists using nerve gas, mustard gas, and other poisons. Many victims complained of cancer and other diseases. Operation Antler was one experiment (1939–1989). The Gulf War syndrome appeared in returning military personnel (early 1990s). Complaints were stonewalled. A criminal inquiry was held (1999) after it was learned that some volunteers were told the experiments were conducted to find a cure for the common cold. RAF serviceman Ronald Maddison, 20, was, in great secrecy, given a dab on sarin on one shoulder; he quickly died (1953). The verdict (1953) that his death had been caused by "misadventure" was quashed (2002), and a new inquest was ordered. Greene undoubtedly knew about Operation Antler in general and Airman Maddison in particular and would have mordantly delighted in knowledge of later events, had he lived to learn of them.

POST WARDEN X (*The Comedians*) *see* **BAXTER, J.**

POTTIFER, CHARLES (*Travels with My Aunt*). Augusta tells Henry about Charles Pottifer. He was a tax-hating tax collector who started a fake money-losing company, paid fees to directors including Augusta, and to circumvent death engaged a post-mortem answering service for his phone.

THE POWER AND THE GLORY (1940). Novel. (Characters: Anita, Henry Beckley, Brigitta, Brigitta, James Calver, Catarina, Father Miguel Cerra, the Chief of Police, the Chief of Police, the Chief of Police, Captain Charles Fellows, Coral Fellows, Trixy Fellows, the Governor, Señora Jiminez, Padre José, Juan, Lehr, Miss Lehr, Mrs. Lehr, the Lieutenant, Lopez, Luis, Manuel, Maria, Mrs. Marsdyke, the mestizo, Miguel, the Minister, Montez, Pedro Montez, Nora, Pedro, Pedro, Father Quintana, Henry Tench, Sylvia Tench, the Whisky Priest.)

Part One. Chapter 1. "The Port." Henry Tench, British dentist, for 15 or more years in a godforsaken Mexican village circled by vultures, waits for the *General Obregon* to deliver an ether cylinder before it proceeds to Vera Cruz. He sees an ugly little stranger approach. In English, he says he's a doctor seeking Lopez. Tench tells him Lopez has been shot. Learning he has brandy, Tench warns that only beer, controlled by government monopoly, is legal. In Tench's miserable house the two share drinks from the stranger's bottle. A child comes and asks for a doctor to cure his ill mother. Saying he was "meant to miss" the *Obregon,* the stranger accompanies the child by mule into darkness.

Chapter 2. "The Capital." Raggedy policemen return to barracks. At 9:30 p.m., lights out. The prisoners get fined for infractions. The lieutenant, dapper and aggressive, and consumed with hatred for the Catholic Church, talks with the jefe (Chief of Police), who has a toothache. The Governor wants a certain clever fugitive priest caught and shot within a month. He avoided the Red Shirts by not taking a boat to Vera Cruz. The lieutenant looks at the poster of James Calver, wanted for robbery and murder in Houston. The lieutenant says he could lure the priest by executing hostages.

The lieutenant walks home, gets into bed, hears beetles explode against his wall, relishes thoughts of shooting priests.

In the Academia Commercial, a woman reads from something by Father Miguel Cerra to her rapt young daughters. It concerns Juan, a pious lad deserving of martyrdom. Luis, her son, is indifferent. She tells her husband she worries about Luis, who asks about that traitor Padre José and about "that whisky priest" they briefly housed.

Padre José, 62, and 40 years a priest, sits in cold darkness, reviling himself. Married for two years, the fat, pig-eyed man is unhappy until his bony wife calls him to bed. Amid hiccups, he acquiesces. Children outside scoff at him.

Chapter 3. "The River." Captain Charles Fellows, an American Banana Company worker, chugs home in his motorized canoe, and greets Trixy, his fever-stricken, life-and-death-fearing wife. Their skinny daughter Coral, about 13, takes Fellows to the lieutenant. He warns Fellows, a foreigner, to turn in the whisky priest, if seen nearby again, declines a drink of gaseosa, strides off. Coral whispers that the priest is in their banana barn and takes her reluctant father to him. Fellows tells him to leave when darkness falls.

Coral takes the priest food and beer. She tells him it is March 7, He says that in six weeks the rains will turn the roads too muddy for pursuers for six months and it's his duty to God not to be caught. She says she lost faith in God at age 10. Saying he'll pray for her, he leaves hugging his attaché case.

The priest sees some mud-and-wattle huts, talks to an oldster, is warned about the soldiers and told there's coffee but no food, is aroused from sleep to hear confessions from sinners awaiting any priest for five years now. A boy stands guard. The villagers believe the priest weeps for their sins.

Chapter 4. "The Bystanders." Tench surprisingly starts a letter to his long-gone wife Sylvia in England but is interrupted when a patient arrives.

Padre José wanders into a cemetery, encounters a tomb marked Lopez, then a family burying their daughter, dead at age five. Asked poignantly for a prayer, Padre José feels momentarily proud but expresses fear and exits, seized by "the unforgivable sin, despair."

As soldiers march out of step to their barracks, the mother reads to her three children. The forbidden story concerns Juan's becoming a priest. When Luis doubts the whole story, she sends him to his father, who says not to worry, since they're all deserted.

Coral Fellows is tutored by her mother, using lessons from a London correspondence school. When Coral queries her mother about the existence of God, the answer is dismissively positive. Coral conscientiously orders Indian peons to get the banana shipment to the port. In the fierce sunlight, she feels unique pains.

The jefe, still suffering from toothache, plays billiards and reports to the inquiring lieutenant: Governor will hold him responsible to catch priest before rains; use any means to succeed. The lieutenant says he'll take hostages, first in the priest's parish of Concepción, then in his home town. The lieutenant walks off, gets a beer bottle thrown near him by Luis, shows him his Colt .38, and inspires the kid to want also to rid the region of Church, foreigners, and even politicians.

Part Two. Chapter 1. Feeling alternately exhilarated, despairing, unwelcome, the ragged priest enters his old village of huts, is greeted patiently by Maria, and asks about Brigitta. Some villagers reverently kiss his hand. He learns a hostage was shot in Concepción. Maria presents brandy saved for him, then brings in Brigitta, their malicious-eyed, sniggering daughter, seven. Brigitta wonders if he's that Yankee murderer sought by police, mocks him, leaves. He ponders theological matters, in immense confusion, then rests. He holds a predawn Mass, preaches intelligently that painful suffering precedes heavenly peace, hastily delivers the Host to unwashed, anxious, famished, sighing villagers. Suddenly the police enter. The lieutenant, on horseback, questions everyone. Maria tells him that the disguised priest, unrecognized from an old photograph the lieutenant has, is her husband and Brigitta is their daughter. The lieutenant seizes a hostage named Miguel. The priest, though aware his duty is to avoid capture, offers himself, instead, as a useless laborer, whom the lieutenant rejects. The intruders leave. The villagers, full of personal hate but devotional loyalty, tell him to head north. The priest and Maria speak, then part in anger and sorrow. Seeking his ruined case in wet rubbish, he retrieves some religious papers and encounters graceless, charmless Brigitta. She rebukes him, giggling, screeching. To God, he barters his soul for her salvation, and kisses her awkwardly.

On his banana-laden mule the priest follows the lieutenant's tracks, encounters a dozing, malarial-eyed mestizo (half-caste) with two yellow teeth, discusses the American murderer, and gets across water toward his birth-town Carmen. He's followed, then accompanied, by the offensively ingratiating mestizo, who calls himself a Christian and in darkness guides him to rest in an abandoned hut. Cannily queried by the mestizo, who calls him father, the fear-beset priest knows the man "was ... Judas."

The priest dreamily recalls his 10th-anniversary ordination ceremony in Concepción: He drank much wine, collected Altar Society funds, discouraged ideas of a charity society, recommended starting a parish school, mentioned violence up north. Stirring, he thinks he might have imitated humble Padre José's defection but for ambition, pride, and awareness of God's presence. He laments he can't be his people's martyr. Suddenly, like an oil gusher, the mestizo calls him father again, confesses sins of "treachery, violence, and lust," and asks for God. In the morning, the priest tries to escape; but the mestizo awakens, clings to him, and they take turns riding the mule, with the feverish mestizo speaking of the 700-peso reward for the priest. Admitting he's a priest, he lets the mocking man ride off toward Carmen and heads west alone.

Chapter 2. In the capital city, the priest, now in a drill suit (bought at a river store), gets a beggar to take him to a beetle-infested hotel to find some wine for 15 pesos, for Masses. In one room they await the Governor's cousin, who finds a bottle of brandy and another of wine in a mattress. They all drink copiously. The jefe enters, accepts the illegal wine himself by calling it beer, reports some hostages shot, and says an informant will soon finger the one uncaught priest, probably here in the capital. The wine bottle is empty. Clutching the nearly empty bottle of brandy, the priest departs in nocturnal rain.

Ducking into a cantina, he accidentally jostles a Red Shirt playing billiards. When the fellow notices the priest's brandy bottle, the priest exits, is chased by merry amateur and professional man-hunters alike, is refused admittance by Padre José, is arrested for smuggling brandy. He discards his religious papers, silently reviews his life, pleads guilty, says he lacks pesos for a fine, is barely noticed by the dapper lieutenant, gives the name Montez to the sergeant, who pushes him into a jail room full of stinking, hairy men and a few women.

Chapter 3. Amid swirling talk by prisoners, the priest hears the word "bastard," thinks of his daughter, and says good priests should teach others to love those innocent borne in sin. When someone says he speaks like a priest, he reveals he is one, calms their fears for him, says he'll be soon identified and shot, admits he's afraid. One says that Christianity creates cowards, that toothaches are worse than quick death. Denying he's a martyr, the priest preaches to some inmates, admits to a pious woman prisoner that he has a child. He can't regret the sin that caused such beloved fruit. He mentions the reward on his head. No prisoner wants blood money. The pious woman, jailed for owning holy books, wants to be confessed. He resists. Noisy lovemaking in a corner infuriates her. His excusing sins, even in fallen angels, makes the woman wish him dead. He tries but can't express comforting words for her. He briefly dreams of a bleeding child he can't help. He tells God he must escape, for Him.

Sudden daylight. Faces all about. The sergeant orders him to empty the pails from all six cells into a cesspool past the water tap. In the last cell is the mestizo, held on guest status, given beer, and ordered to be on the lookout for the priest. He is aware that if he informs against the priest already jailed he'll get no reward. The priest feels God saved him. Soon the unobservant lieutenant questions him, gives him five pesos, and orders him out.

Chapter 4. A week later finds the famished priest at the deserted banana station and entering the Fellows's abandoned house. An Indian stares and him, then departs. The priest sees a partly gnawed bone on the kitchen floor, fights a crippled dog for it, and eats the raw meat left on it. On the veranda, he reads some puzzling English poems in one of Coral's correspondence-school books. Rain suddenly attacks. He finds a leaky hut. An Indian woman peers in. Resembling something from the Stone Age, she weeps. In the hut, he finds a boy, about three, shot three times. She returns. He calls himself a priest. She kisses his hand. He washes the boy, who dies. They must bury him. Speaking mostly Camacho, she repeats *Americano* and *iglesia* (church). For burial?

With the corpse strapped on her back, the Indian feeds the priest sugar lumps and leads him up and down muddy slopes for two days and nights to a deserted plateau with Christian crosses. She sets the baby down, crosses herself, and remains. Since this is faith, will the child miraculously live? But why should God further punish the innocent?

The priest leaves her, suffers aches and trembles, climbs into a forest with monkeys and hissing snakes, crosses the border, encounters an armed man, identifies himself, and, called "Father," is taken to the devout region's barracks-like "church."

Part Three. Chapter 1. The priest, unconscious, is taken to the neat farm bungalow of Lehr, a German who escaped military service by coming here via the United States. A widowered Lutheran, Lehr lives with his unmarried sister, from Pittsburgh. Lehr clothes and feeds the priest, lets him bathe in the river, and criticizes inessentially luxurious Catholicism.

The priest goes to the village, demands pesos for Masses after baptisms, is treated by a commercial fellow to brandy, agrees to buy three bottles later, and distractedly hears hours of routine confessions in Lehr's barn. He returns to talk with Miss Lehr, rests, and in the morning holds Mass for innumerable Mexicans and Indians. As he is about to depart with a guide and two mules for Las Casas and safety, the mestizo appears, tells the doubting priest that the Yankee murderer was shot by the police, escaped, is dying near the border, is a good Catholic, and has begged in writing for the priest. Doubting most of this, the priest, regarding escape as a dream, feels curiously cheerful, accepts sandwiches from Miss Lehr, thanks the Lehrs, rides with the mestizo to the village, and gives the anti–Catholic schoolmaster 45 pesos for school supplies, says he won't need money, and heads south with his sin-burdened mestizo.

Chapter 2. Seven hours later the priest pays and dismisses the muleteer and his mules, and walks with the mestizo toward a rock-surrounded Indian village. They pause, bicker with each other, split a bottle of brandy, and ascend a slope. Inside a hut is the murderer, who whispers "Beat it" to the priest. Instead, the priest asks him to confess, since he is a Catholic. The dying man beseeches the priest to arm himself with his gun and knife. While the priest lectures him and, while being offered conditional absolution, he dies.

The lieutenant, with a dozen policemen, is outside; the mestizo, nowhere. The lieutenant and the priest sit on boxes in the hut. Rain begins. The priest produces a deck of cards, a gift from Lehr, and shows the lieutenant some tricks. They talk. The priest, reviling himself explicitly, defends the Church; the lieutenant, proud of listening to enemy ideas and praising his politics, berates the Church. He calls the priest a martyr; the priest denies the praise. Rain ends in the afternoon. They bury the murderer. The stealthy mestizo reappears, asks for the priest's blessing, is told to give away the blood-money reward and pray, is told the priest will pray for him, and "complacently" says he'll pray for the priest.

After a hard, rainy ride until midnight, the group rests. The priest and the lieutenant, who gripes he has shot three men because of the priest, dispute about the wealthy, the poor, the heart, the mind, God, love, violence, peace; to the lieutenant's sneer that the Church is hypocritical, the priest answers that "God *is* love."

In the hot afternoon they reach the capital. The lieutenant says the priest must be hoping for a miracle. No, God needn't keep him alive for any good to others; further, people call miracles something else. The lieutenant agrees to let Padre José hear the priest's confession. They pass the cemetery and the wall where prisoners are shot.

Chapter 4. The acidulous lieutenant asks Padre José, over his fat wife's protests and street urchins' guffaws, to hear that whisky priest's confession. José is willing only to pray for him.

The lieutenant reveals all this to the priest: José won't come, tomorrow the priest will be shot, here's some contraband brandy, everyone must die, being shot is painless after a second. Returning to his office, the lieutenant discards the two "wanted" posters, sleeps, dreams of laughter and an exitless corridor. The priest swigs his brandy ineffectively, confesses unsatisfactorily, remembers Brigitta, asks for his damnation and her salvation, prays for all those persons recently seen, names his sins, looks out at hammocked policemen, regards his last eight years as grotesque, imagines saints abandoning him, nods off, dreams of tasty dishes and communion he can't share and the banana-station girl. He awakens, feels he barely missed happiness, feels useless going to God with empty hands, will soon be forgotten. Only being a saint counts now.

Part Four. In the hot hotel, Fellows swabs Trixy's forehead with a perfumed handkerchief. He says a priest — maybe the one they sheltered — is getting shot today. Fellows has reluctantly agreed to return to England and Trixy's sister Nora. He remembers influential things the condemned priest told their daughter.

With his equipment moved into the jefe's office, Tench is drilling the man's most carious tooth and mentioning a letter from Mrs. Tench, suddenly religious and wanting a divorce, when through the window he sees the priest being dragged to his execution. Rifles crash. The lieutenant's final shot. The jefe moans in pain. Tench, lonely and determined to leave the country, remembers what is now a mere heap outside.

The pious mother reads once again the story of Juan, martyred for his religion, smiling at death, praying for his executioners, now in heaven. Luis wonders if, as with Juan, someone soaked the priest's blood in a handkerchief today, to cut it into relics. Luis sees the lieutenant purposefully striding home. He pats his revolver. The boy carefully spits on it. In bed that night, Luis dreams that the priest, dressed for burial, winked at him. A knock on the door awakens Luis. He admits a tall stranger. He has an introduction from a friend of the señora and says he is a priest. The boy quickly kisses the man's hand.

Greene was able to vivify both Mexican scenery and Mexican anti–Catholicism because of his trip (1938), partly by mule, through the states of Chiapas and Tabasco, and to the whisky priest's Ciudad del Carmen. Greene's impression-loaded travel book, *The Lawless Roads: A Mexican Journey* (1939), preceded publication of *The Power and the Glory*. His writing of the novel was threatened by a call-up for military service (December 1939), but he received a deferment (to June 1940). Published in wartime (March 1940), *The Power and the Glory* according to Norman Sherry sold slowly (perhaps 12,600 copies) until VE Day (8 May 1945), then did nicely into the 1950s (perhaps 42,000 more copies). Viking, Greene's American publishers then, changed the title (until 1946) to *The Labrynthine Ways* (1940), probably because the popular British author Phyllis Eleanor Bentley (1894–1977) had just published a novel entitled *The Power and the Glory* (1940). The controversial theology in Greene's novel stirred both Vatican criticism (1953) and brisk sales, notably in France, especially after Greene's admired friend François Mauriac (1885–1970) wrote a preface for a French translation (1948). Greene wrote that in a personal interview with him Pope Paul VI said he had read the novel and brushed off earlier Holy Office criticism of it. Leopoldo Duran adds that Greene told Pope Paul VI that the censoring critic was Cardinal Pizzardo.

Richard Hoggart contends that *The Power and the Glory* is forceful because of "three main structural features": simple "overall pattern," "visual quality of the scenes," and quick "transition[s] between those scenes." Greene told Marie-Françoise Allain that *The Power and the Glory* should be read as a 17th-century drama in which the leading characters symbolize "a virtue or a vice, pride, pity, et cetera." A. A. DeVitis elaborates by saying that "allegory lends the events ... an excitement ... beyond the melodramatic adventure of flight [by the priest] and pursuit [by the lieutenant]." The former exemplifies "an old, corrupt, and God-ridden world of religion," the latter, "a new political order," i.e., an "enlightened and philanthropic world of a power cult." DeVitis adds that the two main characters "are satirically antithetical," each being made to suggest "what the other should be" and each emphasizing "the pity that is in the other while denying the evil." In the allegory, the mestizo is the Judas figure, whose betrayal of the priest, as DeVitis notes, triggers the priest's sudden avoidance of grace and his reversing the role of the lieutenant from pursuer to pursued.

Grahame Smith avows that "the best extended piece of writing in his [Greene's] whole career" may well be his dramatic presentation of the priest's dismal night in the inferno-like jail cell. Smith reviews the elements of this inferno: grated door, foul smells, sound of weeping, blackness, mosquitoes, sex sounds, piety, companionship. At the Dantean opposite, "the laughter in *The Power and the Glory* celebrates, perhaps, the entrance of a soul into paradise," says R. W. B. Lewis. More metronomic rhythms are established by Greene's skillful pattern of true then false then true foreshadowings, as the priest expects freedom then expects nothing, then expects, then ... Arthur Calder-Marshall, constantly negative, says that *The Power and the Glory* fails because "there is too much action — the game of hide-and-seek — and too little development."

Gene D. Phillips discusses the movie made of *The Power and the Glory*. It was entitled *The Fugitive* (1947), starring Henry Fonda (priest), Pedro Armendariz (lieutenant), J. Carroll Naish (informer). The priest is not an alcoholic; the lieutenant, not the priest, is the father of the illegitimate child; only the replacement priest's shadow is seen. Greene disliked the script and never saw the movie. A dramatization of the novel debuted in London (1956), then was revised partly by Greene and staged in London (1959), with Paul Scofield (priest). A CBS television production of the novel (1961) starred Laurence Olivier (priest) and George Scott (lieutenant) and omitted the replacement priest entirely. (Sources: Allain, 129; Calder-Marshall, 374; DeVitis, 74, 75, 78; Duran, 38–39; Greene, *Ways of Escape*, 89–90; Hoggart, 87; Lewis, 12; Phillips, 108–12; Sherry II, 41–43; Sherry III, 7–8; G. Smith, 79)

PRENTICE (*The End of the Affair*). He works for Savage in his detective agency. Prentice inconsiderately criticizes Alfred Parkis, who also works there, in Alfred's son Lance's presence.

PRENTICE (*The Ministry of Fear*). He is a Scotland Yard detective, experienced, astute, thin, and long of limb. Prentice grills Rowe, believes much of his story, confides in him, and takes him along when he invades the shop where Cost works as a tailor named Ford, and when he searches Mrs. Bellairs's house and Dr. Forester's sanatorium. Rowe's concealing the fact that he memorized most of the numbers Cost used when phoning Anna Hilfe enables Rowe to find Anna and pursue her brother Willi.

Brian Diemert discusses parallels between Prentice and Sherlock Holmes; both are affected, intellectual, dislike the seemingly innocent English countryside, expose similarly evil plotters, and "assume an air of authority that is at least bordering on arrogance and at most fascist." Michael Shelden suggests that when Prentice tears Mrs. Bellairs's residence apart looking for evidence, Greene makes the search "a kind of rape" to show his own belief in the immorality of his countrymen in wartime. (Sources: Diemert, 169; Shelden, 335)

PRESIDENT, THE (*The Honorary Consul*). He is the President of Argentina. He can't ask General Stroessner of Paraguay to do anything about the kidnapping of Fortnum. Stroesser won't since he's busy fishing in southern Argentina.

Later Greene wrote that Stroessner was indeed on a fishing holiday when a botched kidnapping — Paraguayan consul instead of Paraguayan ambassador — was reported to him, and that he was interested only in his fishing. Happily, the consul was released. (Source: Greene, *Ways of Escape,* 303)

PRESIDENT, THE (*Our Man in Havana*). He is the president of Cuba. His regime is close to ending. Since the latest assassination attempt, he no longer sleeps in his palace. Captain Segura tells Wormold he is preparing a report for the president on Wormold's list of spies.

In 1958 Cuba's endangered president was Fulgencio Batista y Zaldivar (1901–1973). He was a mixed-blood Cuban laborer, strong-arm leader during the successful Sergeants' Revolution (1933), commander of the army and then president (1940–1944). Batista headed a corrupt, oppressive regime, and amassed a fortune of $20 million. He retired in Miami, returned to Havana, seized power (1952–1958), and became a tyrannical dictator notorious for gangsterism, assassination of opponents, and ballooning corruption.

Overthrown by Fidel Castro and his rebels (December 31, 1958), Batista escaped with an estimated $300 million, and died in Spain. Enrique Oltuski provides details of horrors committed during Batista's reign of terror. Norman Sherry indicates Greene's partial awareness of their extent, beginning when Greene returned to Havana (October 13, l958), after *Our Man in Havana* was published, for the purpose of arranging its filming. Sherry adds that Greene was too much an early admirer of Castro to realize that both Castro and especially his brother Raul Castro were as brutal as Batista. (Sources: Oltuski; Sherry III, 136–39, 148–49)

PRESIDENT, THE (*The Quiet American*). He is the President of Vietnam. After Pyle's murder, Joe tells Fowler the High Commissioner is conferring with the President.

PRESIDENT OF FRANCE, THE ("An Old Man's Memory"). He is with Mrs. Thatcher greeting the arrival of the French train at Dover, after it passed through the Channel Tunnel. Word comes that explosions destroyed the British train still in the tunnel.

PREWITT (*Brighton Rock*) *see* **DREWITT**

PRIDE (*The Honorary Consul*). This is the name Fortnum calls his Land Rover, which he drives around as his "steed." His wife Clara damages it.

PRIESTLEY ("Men at Work"). He is mentioned by R. King, chairman of the Books Division in the Ministry of Information, as one of the "right authors" to be appealed to for help. King suggests that Skate might check with Priestley about leaflets concerning meat marketing.

Priestley may be fictitious here. More likely, however, Greene is jibing at J. B. Priestley,* whose review of Greene's *The Man Within* irritated Greene and who later caused Greene trouble in connection with his characterization of Quin C. Savory, the novelist in *Stamboul Train.* (Source: Sherry I, 435–37)

PRIESTLEY, J. B. (1894–1984). John Boynton Priestley, British man of letters, attended Cambridge, was a newspaper essayist and critic, wrote novels (*The Good Companions* [1929] and *Angel Pavement* [1930] being the most popular), and experimental plays (1932–1952). Among his later books are *The Edwardians* (1970) and *The English* (1973). Priestley was also director of *New Statesman and Nation.*

Priestley was a member of the committee of the Book Society (1932), founded (1928) and designed to select a book each month to distribute to its 10,000 members. However, Priestley resigned from the committee (1932) and could not therefore directly influence committee decisions. And yet, when *Stamboul Train* (1932) was being considered as the December selection by the Book Society, Priestley was asked to review it. He read an advance copy, alerted a Book Society director that he felt the popular hack novelist Quin C. Savory in *Stamboul Train* was a satirical partial portrait of himself, and threatened a libel suit should the novel be published without specific alterations he demanded. The director wired Greene, who revised parts and had to share expenses in reprinting and rebinding 1,300 pages. Greene called Priestley's novel *Faraway* (1932) flabby, verbose, and poorly structured, reviewed his *Albert Goes Through* (1933) and called it unoriginal, has Ida Arnold in *Brighton Rock* (l938) possess a copy of *The Good Companions* (obviously to show her poor taste in novels), adversely reviewed Priestley's *Let the People Sing* (1939), but praised Priestley in a *Spectator* essay (December 13, 1940) for his rousingly patriotic Sunday evening wartime broadcasts. He also has R. King, of the Books Division in the Ministry of Information, in "Men at Work," lump "Priestley" among "right authors." (Sources: Mockler, 71–72; Sherry I, 430–37, 439–41; Sherry III, 259n)

PRINCE (*The Quiet American*). Pyle tells Fowler his first dog was named Prince, after the Black Prince. Duke is Pyle's dog in Saigon.

PRINCE BISHOP, THE (*The Quiet American*) *see* **THE BISHOP OF PHAT DIEM**

PRINCESS, THE (*England Made Me*). She is the wife of the Crown Prince of Sweden. When Krogh and Farrant attend the opera, they see the Crown Prince and the Princess there too.

The Princess was Lady Louise Alexandrine Mountbatten (1889–1965), the second spouse of Prince Gustav. His first spouse was Margaret Victoria Wettin (1882–1920).

PRISKETT ("When Greek Meets Greek"). He is an Oxford chemist. Nicholas Fennick and Elisabeth Cross meet at Priskett's place to hatch plans to start St. Ambrose's College in Oxford. Priskett will teach science in the phony school.

PROLOGUE TO PILGRIMAGE. This is the title of a novel Greene wrote while he was a student at Oxford. Earlier, it was called *Anthony Sant*. It remains unpublished (Sources: Shelden, 132; Sherry I, 72).

PROFESSOR, HERR ("Dream of a Strange Land"). He is a retired medical doctor, 67 and living on a secluded estate 20 minutes from the capital. He reads only professional books, still treats a few patients, and won't illegally treat a former patient suffering from leprosy. Yielding to pressure, however, Herr Professor violates anti-gambling laws by letting Herr Colonel turns Herr Professor's estate into a casino to surprise Herr General, a gambling addict. Herr Professor and the leper ultimately resemble doppelgängers as they stare at each other through the windows of an estate now in an oneirically strange land.

"PROOF POSITIVE" (1930). Short story. (Characters: Dr. Brown, Colonel Crashaw, General Leadbitter, Major Philip Weaver.)

Colonel Crashaw, president of a local Psychical Society, agreed to let Major Philip Weaver lecture. The meeting takes place in a music room of The Spa, attended by bored old ladies and retired military officers struggling to seem attentive. Weaver about 60, is tall, thin, dark, with a stubborn nose, eyes expressing satire, and a handkerchief emitting the sickly smell of lilies. When General Leadbitter wants to smoke, Weaver says smoke bothers him and Crashaw says "influenza throats" are common in this bad weather. Weaver says his malady is cancer. He scratchily lectures about spirit's immortal power over matter, promises an anecdote about signs and wonders in proof, but delivers only snatches from Shakespeare and St. Paul and a touch about Simla. Crashaw finds everything digressive though subtly juxtaposed. Dr. Brown sends a note to Crashaw: Weaver is ill, should quit talking. When Weaver announces positive proof, Crashaw flourishes his watch — to no effect. From Weaver's dead-pan face comes a mewing sound, then gibberish resembling séance noises. He sits, his head falls back, and Brown rushes forward. Brown removes Weaver's scented hanky, smells something ugly, and pronounces Weaver dead — and, judging by his rotten-fruit face, for at least a week. Crashaw morosely concludes that the man's spirit, positively enough, outlasted his flesh, experienced eternity, and after seven days with no physical support collapsed into nonsensical verbosity.

"Proof Positive" won a 10-guinea prize when Greene submitted it to the *Manchester Guardian*. Richard Kelly contends that the stress in the story on the smell of putrefaction represents an "instance of Greene's puritanical castigation of the mortal flesh," and adds that "[h]is brahmin sense of cleanliness may in part be an explanation for his attitude." However, Greene unpuritanically, even uncleanly, revelled in fleshly delights now and again. Also, what can A. A. DeVitis mean when he finds it "difficult to read 'Proof Positive' ... as anything but a humorous vindication, perhaps unintentional, of Philip

Weaver's belief that the spirit can exist beyond the body"? (Sources: DeVitis, 169; Kelly, 32)

PUCKLER, FRAU ("The Root of All Evil"). She is the respected, unsuspecting wife of much-disliked Herr Puckler, whose death frees her to become affianced to the Superintendent of Police.

PUCKLER, HERR ("The Root of All Evil"). He is a vinegary little citizen of B—, disliked by the wine-drinking clubmen. Puckler has gimlet-like eyes that bore into his victims' foreheads while he numbs them with talk. His inability to locate the wine-drinking clubmen precipitates the action, which ends when a chamberpot is dropped over his head and he dies.

PULLEN (*The Human Factor*). He is an MI5 officer who attends the beginning of a conference convened by Hargreaves to improve communications between MI5 (counter-espionage) and MI6 (espionage).

PULLING, ANGELA (*Travels with My Aunt*). She was Augusta Bertram's sister and Richard Pulling's ever-virginal wife. After Augusta gives birth to Richard's son Henry, Richard and Angela raise him as theirs. When Angela dies, Henry first meets "Aunt Augusta," at Angela's funeral. Henry remembers Angela as kind but stern.

Augusta tells Henry that Angela faked her pregnancy by padding herself with progressively larger pillows. Norman Sherry says Catherine Walston* used the same subterfuge. She faked a pregnancy with pillows, went to Dublin, and was recorded as having given birth (July 18, 1949) to James Patrick Francis Walston, who more likely was Catherine's adulterous husband Harry Walston's baby by a girlfriend. William Cash, doubting all this pillow talk, theorizes that Harry's pregnant lover may have been "Twinkle," the long-serving nanny of the Walston children. Both Sherry and Cash mention *Travels with My Aunt* in connection with this Walston family secret. (Sources: Cash, 181–84; Sherry II, 320–22)

PULLING, HENRY (*Travels with My Aunt*). He is the narrator and reluctant hero. A bachelor retired Southwood bank manager, Henry meets Aunt Augusta Bertram at his mother Angela (Bertram) Pulling's funeral. Augusta changes his life by taking him on travels — to Brighton, Paris, Istanbul, and Asunción, Paraguay. She introduces him to some of her friends and associates, including Zachary Wordsworth, Colonel Hakim, and Visconti. Henry's encounter with Lucinda O'Toole on the Orient Express out of Paris gives him welcome contact with a sweet if dangerous youngster. His troubled but affectionate association with free-spirited Augusta makes Henry aware that his hobby of raising dahlias was escapism, and he moults into a new personality. He was born in 1913, calls himself a non-religious Anglican, and is in his 50s.

Walter O'Grady contends that Greene presents Henry Pulling as a twentieth-century parody of Dionysus, "the twice-born God." Far from being reborn through association with Augusta, he will "resume his abandoned occupation and become the trusted accountant" of Augusta's smuggler friend Visconti, and, unlike Dionysus, will never enjoy any "sexual frenzy" with "his prospective bride"; nor will depleted Augusta and over-the-hill Visconti frenzy much either. (Source: O'Grady, 505, 520)

PULLING, JO (*Travels with My Aunt*). He was Henry Pulling's uncle, 15 years older than Richard Pulling, Henry's father. Henry never knew he had an uncle until Aunt Augusta informed him. She adds Jo was a fat bookie, addicted to travel. Augusta bought Jo a run-down mansion outside Venice, where he suffered a stroke. Its 52 rooms enabled him, with his nurse's help, to "travel" to a new room every week. He died trying for #52.

PULLING, RICHARD (*Travels with My Aunt*). He was Angela Pulling's husband, Henry Pulling's father, and the lover of Rose, Augusta Bertram, and Dorothy Paterson. Richard was an easy-going building contractor, and lolled about a lot reading romantic fiction, including works by Sir Walter Scott and Francis Marion Crawford (1854–1909), and poetry in *The Golden Treasury of Songs and Lyrics* (1861, 2nd series, 1896) assembled by Francis Palgrave (1824–1897). His favorite book was Scott's *Rob Roy*, in the pages of which Henry happens upon a photograph of Augusta as a teenager. Richard died October 2, 1923, and would, says Augusta, be about 85 if still alive.

PURVES, BILL ("The Lieutenant Died Last"). He is a poacher on absent Lord Drew's grounds in Potter. While plying his trade, he sees some German soldiers who have parachuted into town, to disrupt its important communication system. Purves, a veteran of the Boer War and World War I, finds it exciting fun to use his trusty Mauser rifle to shoot and otherwise kill some of the Germans and capture the rest.

PURVIS, MRS. (*The Ministry of Fear*). She is Rowe's widowed landlady. Rowe takes pity on her addiction to sweets and lets her munch on his mysterious cake. Her renting rooms to Poole nearly costs Rowe his life.

PYLE, ALDEN (*The Quiet American*). He is "the quiet American," a young, idealistic American employed by the American Economic Mission in Saigon, Vietnam. Influenced by York Harding's economic and political theories, Pyle seeks to develop a Third Force, independent of Communists and French colonialists alike. Fowler meets Pyle, is amused by his political naiveté but annoyed when Pyle attracts Fowler's mistress Phuong. Pyle is open about his sudden love of and proposal of marriage to Phuong, remains overtly friendly with Fowler, and saves his life when both are in a combat zone outside Phat Diem. Pyle goes too far when he supplies explosives to General Thé, supposedly in favor of third-force activities but resulting in a deadly blast in Place Garnier, Saigon. Fowler is outraged when Pyle steps in civilians' blood on the street and says he must get his shoes polished. Fowler therefore engineers Pyle's murder.

Greene excessively demeans Pyle, who says he had the disadvantage of being an only child, is a poor dancer, speaks French badly, was called Bat by his schoolmates because — he tells Fowler — he's blind as a bat but sees well at night. When Pyle asks Fowler to call him Alden, Fowler says he prefers Pyle because "Pyle has ... associations"— obviously anatomical. Greene probably figured the name Alden would make some readers think of timid John Alden, who in Henry Wadsworth Longfellow's *The Courtship of Miles Standish* was an inept lover manqué from Pyle's puritan Boston area. Matt Steinglass says that "Pyle's courtship of Phuong is ... too rushed, too programmatic, to be credible."

Norman Sherry discusses two candidates as possible models for Pyle. One was a naive Britisher named Jollye whom Greene met in Malaya (December 10, 1950). Jollye saw a beautiful Chinese taxi dancer in the City Dance Park, met her, escorted her home, admired her, told her about his work, and was assassinated by terrorists. Another candidate, though denied by Greene according to evidence presented by Christopher Hawtree and regarded as unlikely by Sherry, was Colonel Edward Lansdale, an American CIA agent who tried to develop opposition to the Communists, who was the only American operative close to Trinh Minh Thé (the model for General Thé), and who had a dog always close to him. Skip Willman writes that Lansdale was the director of Operation Mongoose (beginning in 1961), the purpose of which was to disrupt Cuba under Fidel Castro and to encourage Cubans to overthrow Castro and establish a pro–U.S.A. government, and that Lansdale was the model for Colonel Edwin Hillendale, the ugly hero of *The Ugly American* (1958), by William Lederer and Eugene Burdick. Willman adds that "[a] less flattering portrait of Lansdale emerged in Graham Greene's *The Quiet American,* in which Lansdale was apparently the model for Alden Pyle, an idealistic menace of a CIA agent, although Greene publicly denied it."

Other models abound. Michael Shelden finds one for Pyle in Emmet John Hughes, Ivy League graduate, protégé of Henry Luce of *Time-Life,* and religious, anti–Communist journalist whose career beginning in the 1950s Pyle's might have echoed had he lived. When Hughes was an editor for *Life* in the 1940s, he commissioned Greene for several Southeast Asian assignments. The upshot was disaffection in Greene, who, Shelden says, soon thereafter ridiculed the naiveté of Hughes and Luce in *The Quiet American*. Shelden also names another American on whom Pyle is patterned: Leo Hochstetter, an American economic-aid official, perhaps really a CIA operative with a third-force agenda, in Saigon in the early 1950s. Sherry plays down the resemblances of

Hochstetter and Pyle. (Sources: Hawtree, 126–27; Shelden, 388, 391, 399; Sherry II, 414–19; Steinglass, 34; Willman, 195)

PYLE, MRS. (*The Quiet American*). She is Alden Pyle's son. She collects glass.

PYLE, PROFESSOR HAROLD C. (*The Quiet American*). He is Alden Pyle's father, 69. Professor Pyle is a world-renowned expert on underwater erosion, collects Darwin manuscripts, and is an isolationist. He and his wife have a house on Chestnut Street, Boston. Joe, the Economic Attaché, says he knew the Pyles and Professor Pyle's face was "on the cover of *Time* the other month."

This *Time* name-dropping is intended to remind readers that Greene's face also graced a *Time* cover. The issue appeared October 29, 1951, weeks after the action of *The Quiet American* begins. The name Harold Pyle is close to that of Howard Pyle (1853–1911), the American illustrator-author. Among other works, Pyle wrote and illustrated *The Merry Adventures of Robin Hood* (1883). When Vigot wonders if the movie Fowler saw on the night of Pyle's murder was *Robin Hood,* Fowler says no, it was *Scaramouche.* (Source: "Shocker")

QUERRY (*A Burnt-Out Case*). He is an internationally known architect. Querry specialized in church designing, is now in his late 50s, is a former womanizer disgusted by his selfish treatment of women attracted to him, a lapsed Catholic not attending Mass for 20 years and professing to belief in nothing, and an ex-professional tired of his work. He is a "burnt-out case," i.e., feeling and experience have eaten him hollow, much as a leper is burned out when leprosy has consumed all it can and leaves its victim free to wander. Querry seeks the relief of nothingness at Dr. Colin's Congo leproserie but develops a Christian love for his servant "boy" Deo Gratias, friendship with the priests and one brother, admiration of and intellectual challenges with Colin, energy for planning a new hospital, and selfless regard for Marie Rycker. Querry is undone by outside forces: Parkinson interviews and publicizes misinformation about him; Rycker misunderstands him; Marie spreads lies about him. Querry's mother was English. Querry, evidently from Belgium, speaks English, French, and Flemish.

When Greene fictionalizes about Querry as the subject of a cover essay in *Time,* 10 years earlier, he is obviously thinking of his own identical journalistic fame, having been the subject himself of a cover essay (*Time,* October 29, 1951—the year 1951 being equal to 1961, the publication date of *A Burnt-Out Case,* minus 10).

Querry's problems, though carried to extremes, parallel many of Greene's. Both felt burned out professionally, had been consumed by sex, and had religious doubts. Greene felt that writing *A Burnt-Out Case* had vaporized his creative energy; he unnecessarily feared he might write nothing more of consequence. Yvonne Cloetta* says that Querry was Greene's alter ego and that writing about him severely depressed him, once even causing him to vomit. Greene wrote at great length about Querry in *Ways of Escape.*

A. A. DeVitis believes that Querry's name may be "suggestive of his search and longing." Norman Sherry wonders whether the name conflates "query," suggesting that Querry questions God, and "quarry," suggesting God's hounding of Querry. K. C. Joseph Kurismmootil concludes that "Querry certainly is not offered to us as a hero. Had he challenged God like Faustus, or even like Job, or gone and damned himself with the boy hero of *Brighton Rock,* we might speak of some strain of heroism.... Querry ... is an anti-hero like most Greene characters.... He is done with life, the success, money, and women.... In Querry ... the seed of faith has taken deep roots but it must struggle hard ... if it is to yield fruit." (Sources: Cloetta, 14–15; DeVitis, 116; Greene, *Ways of Escape,* 259–67; Kurismmootil, 183–84; Sherry III, 179n)

THE QUIET AMERICAN (1955). Novel. (Characters: Anne, the Bishop, Mme Bompierre, the British Minister, Chou, Connolly, the Commander-in-Chief, Corinne, Madame Desprez, Dominguez, M. Dubois, Duke, Captain Duparc, the First Secretary, M. Flic, Gustave, Helen Fowler, Thomas Fowler, François, Granger, Bill Granger, Mrs. Granger, York Harding, Heng, the High Commissioner, Joe, Miss Hei, the Managing Editor, a Member of Parliament, Mick, the Minister, Lieutenant

Peraud, Lieutenant Perrin, Pham-Van-Tu, Mrs. Phan-Van-Tu, Phan-Van-Muoi, Mrs. Phan-Van-Muoi, Phuong, Pietri, the President, Prince, the Prince Bishop, Alden Pyle, Mrs. Pyle, Professor Harold C. Pyle, Simon, Captain Sorel, General Thé, Captain Trouin, Vigot, Madame Vigot, Warren, Wilkins.)

(Please note: Flash-forwards to the time after Pyle's death are presented in past tense; main, non-retrospective action, in historical present.)

Part One: 1. Thomas Fowler, the narrator, was a British reporter in Saigon (gone from England five years). He sent news about the Indo-China war to his London newspaper. He recalled that one February night he was waiting in his rue Catinat room for Alden Pyle, a quiet American, to return. Phuong (20, from Annam, Vietnam), Fowler's lovely girlfriend for two years, until Pyle took her from him and promised marriage, waited with Fowler, worried because Pyle was suddenly missing. She prepared some opium pipes for Fowler. Vigot, of the French Sûreté, summoned them, told only Fowler that Pyle had just been killed, and had Fowler identify the body. Fowler recalled meeting Pyle last September. After telling Vigot details to establish his alibi and filing a report concerning Pyle's death, Fowler accompanied Phuong to his room, told the stoical girl Pyle was *assassiné*, smoked more opium, and so to bed.

2: I. Last September. Fowler meets Pyle. This quiet representative of the Economic Aid Mission was earnest, book-learned about the complex war, naive. He thinks his mentor York Harding's idea of a Third Force, free of both Communism and colonialism, will bring peace to Indo-China. Fowler updates Pyle on conditions: Communist Vietminh, favored by China, battling French around Hanoi and north; French in daylight control south; General Thé, opposing both Communists and French around Tanyin. Pyle theorizes about Thé favorably. Fowler, tired of politico-military puzzles and neutral, returns to Phuong.

II. Back to February. Fowler went to dead Pyle's flat. Vigot was there. He and Fowler wondered who killed Pyle: Vietminh, Vietnamese police, Caodaists (Catholic-Buddhist-Confucian cultists) recently abandoned by Pyle's friend Thé, French police? Pyle's black dog (Duke) was missing. Vigot said Communists killed Pyle. Fowler talked critically to the American Economic Attaché (Joe) about Pyle's unacceptable "innocence" and American materialism.

3: I. In September Fowler and Phuong, drinking together, are invited by boyish-looking Pyle to meet Joe (the American Economic Attaché). Bill Granger, a loud American reporter, just back from Hanoi, enters, ogles Phuong, talks dirty, drinks, explains how the French fly him over battlefields and how he then fakes reports. He takes Pyle in a trishaw to a brothel entrance. Pyle's quiet courtesy endears him to Fowler, who decides to protect the dangerously innocent fellow. Fowler, with Phuong along, extricates Pyle, suddenly suspects he's virginal. Pyle expresses sympathy for those prostitutes.

II. At dinner, Phuong's sister, Miss Hei, approaches Fowler, has disapproved of his affair with Phuong, wants her to marry well (Fowler's wife is in England), and butters up Pyle when he's introduced to her. Hearing she was a secretary in Singapore, Pyle will try to hire her for an office job. He dances awkwardly with Phuong, and when a floor show seems obscene, says they should all leave. Touched by Pyle's inexperience, Fowler thinks this: Phuong may leave him, love is temporary, death a gift.

4: I. Fowler goes from Nam Dinh to Phat Diem, a city attacked by the Vietminh, to cover real war action. Fowler sees frightened citizens crowding into the Roman Catholic cathedral, with its European priest and nuns tending casualties. He debates the priest about God and the "unmanly" Catholic act of confessing. Fowler advances with a noonday French Foreign Legion patrol. They see corpses in a canal, advance, rest. The sentries go forward; two shots; woman and child dead. The radio orders them back. They rest in a cold, shattered building. Fowler offers the soldiers the whisky he brought. They play cards. French mortar fire at 3:30 a.m. will scatter the Vietminh. Suddenly Pyle appears, with thermos, food, toiletries, sleeping bag.

II. Pyle tells Fowler he bought a boat, drifted with the current, is ashamed of Granger's rudeness, is in love with Phuong, and wanted to clear that with him. Fowler replies that he's married. Mortar fire cancels sleep. Pyle calls Fowler's response to his revelation about loving Phuong "swell" and adds they both have her "interests" in mind. Fowler retorts he cares only about her body. Pyle says he understands Phuong, who should marry and have children, which her sister conned him into thinking she wants; he adds he'd transfer if she preferred Fowler (who months later wondered if dead Pyle understood Phuong would be sleeping with Fowler again).

5: I. Pyle leaves later that morning. Delayed three weeks by damaged roads and no room on military airplanes, Fowler back in Saigon has a letter from Pyle saying he's down south with an American trachoma team and plans to win Phuong fair and square. Fowler plans for no long future (but, surprisingly, outlived Pyle, he noted later). Fowler attends a press conference in Hanoi, with a handsome French colonel in charge. Granger bullies him about unmentioned French casualties in a just-announced battle involving heavy enemy losses. Fowler snidely hints at the current stalemate in Korea. Incensed at Granger, the colonel says Americans should send the French more helicopters to transport their wounded before they died in the field. Fowler files no report on Phat Diem. An honest account would get censored. He prefers to remain, thus keeping Phuong from Pyle. Fowler learns he's promoted to foreign editor, must return to London soon (in April). He chats with a French officer from Corsica about returning to England, which, he adds, isn't home, since Saigon now is.

Part Two: 1. Back in Saigon, Fowler doesn't spoil their remaining months by mentioning his transfer to Phuong, who is nonplussed that Pyle hadn't visited her in weeks. She tells Fowler that Pyle imports things secretly. Drugs for his medicine team? No, plastics. (Perhaps to make toys?) Fowler writes London asking not to be transferred. Pyle calls on him, brings his dog Duke, talks with stupifying candor, is happy when Phuong enters, and has Fowler translate his stolid proposal of marriage. Fowler tells her not he but Pyle can marry her, then lies that he's not leaving her. Pyle adds he's robust and will inherit $50,000 at his father's death. Things get dicey. Pyle asks Phuong to come with him now. No. He finishes a drink, bows at her, says he wishes Fowler could marry her, leaves. Fowler, checking his paunch, thinks he should have mentioned his departure orders, writes his wife Helen, reports his promotion and return to London, respectfully requests divorce and immediate answer. He tells Phuong about this letter and his transfer. She says she'd like to accompany him to England, divorce or no divorce, then prepares his opium.

2: [I]. A week or more later, Fowler attends the annual Caodaist festival in sultry Tanyin, 50 miles northwest of Saigon. He endures what he regards as its religious hypocrisy, and, after the speeches, sees Pyle there too, beside his stalled Buick and the polite Tanyin commandant. Fowler finds relief in the cool 20-year-old Cathedral, decorated with Christian, Buddhist, and Confucian artifacts. He reminisces about Helen, war casualties he has seen, Helen again. Fowler reluctantly offers Pyle a lift in his car. The Buick will be delivered once repaired.

II. Driving out of Tanyin into sniper territory, they run out of gas. Thieves in town probably siphoned most of it. They walk in sudden darkness to a French watch tower. Fowler climbs in.

III. Two timid young Vietnamese guards sit inside. Pyle enters. Cynical Fowler and naive Pyle discuss religion and politics. Pyle defends York's and Thế's third-force theory. Fowler praises hard-working peasants; criticizes present-day, harmful American and British liberals, former British policies in India and Burma, and American and British news accounts; and ridicules fighting for so-called liberty. With 10 cold hours to wait, Fowler descends to get a blanket from the car. An explosion and gunfire are followed by yells. Returning to the tower, he finds that Pyle has one guard's sten gun. Time drags. Pyle asks about Phuong, confesses his sexual innocence. Fowler mentions his varied experiences, his "need" of Phuong, her immature love modes, his fear of loneliness and a nursing-home finish, his preference for death now. A foreign voice from outside startles everyone. Silence. They leave the guards. Fowler jumps off the ladder, twists an ankle. Pyle follows. A Viet bazooka shatters the tower.

IV. Fowler's leg is hit (broken) by debris falling. One guard remains alive, weeping. Pyle returns from the nearby rice field, half-carries Fowler, resisting being saved, into deep water. A bren gun fires. Footsteps on the road. The Viets torch the car. Fowler says Pyle could have left him to be killed and had Phuong to himself. Pyle replies they both prefer playing the game fairly, neither could leave the other. Pyle lays Fowler flat, walks to the next tower for aid. Fowler hears the guard still crying, faints, and when Pyle returns is rescued. The guard died.

3: I. After treatment at the Legion Hospital, Fowler hobbles upstairs (with a stick), his leg splinted, to Phuong, who says Joe hired her sister and Fowler has a letter. From his wife, it is tender and tough, reminds him of his habitual infidelities, and refuses a divorce. Feeling rightly injured, sad at paining Helen, he lies to Phuong that Helen may release him soon, and smokes lots of opium. He writes Pyle to thank him for saving his life and to say his wife is divorcing him — thus assuring himself of continuation of short-term pleasure.

II. Fowler visits Dominguez, his loyal, intelligent assistant. They discuss Pyle's dangerous belief in the Third Force. Dominguez tells Fowler he should see Chou, a source of information, at the Quai Mytho. Fowler goes there, meets old opium-addicted Chou, is shunted to Heng, who in Phan-Van-Muoi's nearby junk-filled garage shows him a plastic mould, from an American shipment and discarded as defective. Heng says Phan-Van-Muoi, whose wife is related to General Thé, found suspicious Diolacon powder residue in a drum near the mould and discussed it with Pyle. Assured of Fowler's neutrality, pro–Communist Heng says if an incident occurs in Saigon his side will be wrongly blamed. Fowler promises not to betray Heng as his informant.

III. Fowler's rest is disturbed when Phuong brings Pyle in. Fowler learns Phuong's sister translated Helen's letter for her. While the two men argue, Phuong casually looks at a British picture book, upsidedown. Pyle says he can give Phuong "love" and security. Fowler cheerfully admits he lied to Pyle, who replies he won't now fight fair either. Fowler says "love" is a Western concept, he'll use Phuong while he can, she'll survive both of them, Pyle will get hurt but is free to play with his pro-democratic plastics.

Part Three: 1: I. Almost two weeks after Pyle died, Fowler saw Vigot again. Over dice and vermouth, Vigot reported that Pyle's dog was found, its throat slit. Fowler invited Vigot to come to his flat at 11:00 p.m. to converse further.

II. Fowler becomes jealous of Pyle, suspicious of Phuong. Heng invites Fowler to be outside a certain store at 10:30 a.m. There, he sees police rush up, seize three bicycles from many there and throw them into a fountain, where they explode at 11:00 a.m. Heng shows Fowler that his own bicycle has a fake tire-pump attached, shaped like that suspicious mould. Alerted by Heng, the police could prevent only part of the damage, since 10 bicycles also exploded elsewhere. Communists were blamed in all reports except Fowler's, which originally called the event General Thé's "demonstration" but got altered. Some days later, Fowler enters Muoi's deserted garage, its personnel off to Thé's sacred-mountain retreat. Fowler finds an old press, white powder, no drum, no mould. He goes home. Phuong has packed and vanished.

III. Lonely Fowler goes to Pyle's office. Pyle is absent. Joe greets him, while Miss Hei, Phuong's sister, watches furtively. Fowler interrupts loud-mouthed Joe, says Pyle has stolen his Phuong, sarcastically advises her sister to be sure Pyle's settlement papers are notarized, wants Pyle to phone, then weeps in the lavatory.

IV. Fowler proceeds to Haiphong, flies with French pilots at safe heights to watch bomb drops, then goes illegally with his friend, a B-26 French pilot named Captain Trouin of the Squadron Gascogne, on multiple vertical bombing runs near the Chinese border. Fowler gets air-sick. While returning, they sink a sampan on the Red River and view a lovely sunset.

V. That night Trouin and Fowler go to a parlor where Fowler smokes some opium. Trouin tells Fowler he was born in Vietnam, is a loyal pilot, has bombed his home town, predicts the war will be lost and politicians will accept peace terms available "at the beginning," and recommends a half-breed prostitute to Fowler, who lies down with her. Memory of Phuong makes him impotent.

2: I. Fowler returns to his Saigon flat and finds that Dominguez has admitted Pyle. Fowler checks mail from his editor: General De Lattre's death means Fowler must stay in Saigon another year. Pyle says he plans to marry Phuong in a family ceremony back home (Boston). Fowler feels his aged cynicism can't defeat Pyle's youthful innocence and mistaken idealism. He warns Pyle not to trust Thé, who is a bandit, not a national democrat, but instead to let Joe handle these American messes.

II. Weeks pass. Fowler seeks a new flat near the Place Garnier, hears two American girls say "Warren" said they should leave the Place by 11:25. A violent explosion rips the luxurious Pavilion hotel five minutes later. Fowler sees Pyle approaching, snarls at him that the bloody carnage was American-designed, blames Thé's supporters, figures Pyle warned Phuong to stay away, and heads for Heng.

Part Four: 1. Vigot arrived at 11:00 p.m. at Fowler's place, as requested, to discuss Pyle's death. By probing Fowler's alibi, Vigot ascertained that he had time and indeed saw Pyle the night he was killed, further, that Pyle's dog Duke had cement in his paws from some nearby construction.

2: I. Fowler leaves the corpse-strewn Place Garnier, locates circumspect Heng, says Pyle was to blame. Heng agrees but says Thé is unbalanced. Fowler says childish Pyle must be stopped but adds no journalist's report would carry sufficient weight. Heng suggests Fowler signal by reading a book at his sunset window if Pyle will accept Fowler's invitation to dinner about 9:00 p.m. at the Vieux Moulin.

II. Fowler asks Pyle by note to come see him yet hopes he won't. Dominguez visits Fowler, who says he won't file a report on the Garnier massacre, asks Dominguez to leave. Pyle and Duke drop by. Pyle tells Fowler this: Thé was in town, he cautioned Thé to control his demonstrations, but he still needs Thé. That does it: Fowler takes a book to his window, asks Pyle to dine with him at the Moulin about 9:00, sees a trishaw driver look up and leave. Pyle reminisces about his parents, has a drink, and leaves with Duke.

III. Fowler walks out, chats with a reporter named Wilkins, goes to a swashbuckler movie, takes a trishaw to the Moulin, where noisy Granger is. Soon Phuong will be free of Pyle, Fowler thinks. Granger, drunk, asks him to come outside, away from all those "Frogs," says he learned by cable today his young son has polio. Fowler goes home, waits until midnight, sees Phuong on the street.

3. Vigot quit questioning Fowler and left. Phuong returned after seeing a movie with her sister, and summarized its plot for Fowler. He told her that Granger, who she said was also at the movie, was relieved because he heard his son was better. Fowler and Phuong agreed they were happy, as of yore. He lay down with her, opened a just-arrived telegram. Helen was starting divorce proceedings. Ecstatic, Phuong said she'll become "the second Mrs. Fowlair." She kissed Fowler, who permitted her to rush off and tell her sister.

Greene worked on *The Quiet American* almost two and a half year (March 1952–June 1955). He parades his awareness of place by including more than a dozen geographical names, in addition to Saigon street names. The book was carried by many G.I.'s in Vietnam, not entirely for its political prescience. It was published in England (December 1955) and in America (March 1956). It is based mainly on Greene's first of four Saigon junkets, beginning January 1951 and including many trips throughout the war-torn country that year, and then again in 1952, 1953, and 1955 (interviewing Ho Chi Minh [1890–1969] in 1955). The anti–American currents caused animosity among some of Greene's Yankee fans and reviewers. Sherry opines that since Greene "was such an accurate chronicler of the period [Vietnam after the French withdrawal], anti–Americanism in some form had to appear in the novel because strong anti–Americanism was historically present, most of it emanating from the French." Sherry continues: "The Americans were pouring in arms and economic aid of all kinds, but it did not make them loved by the French — generosity often provokes envy.... American prodigality often aroused in the French an impotent malice." And, finally, "[i]n contrast to the French anti–Americanism, Greene's 'anti–Americanism' is tame." Still, Greene must have been in unique turmoil. His 22-page introduction to *The Quiet American* is longer than any other introduction in the *Collected Edition*. (With respect to Vietnam, Michael Shelden is as biased against Greene as Sherry is biased against America.)

A. A. DeVitis calls Fowler "an unreliable narrator whose motives must be fully appreciated if the novel's theme is to develop cogently through the action," the theme being that "human beings involved in a political and ethical dilemma" (or a dozen such) fail in their struggles toward solutions. While in their existential traps, some of these characters are presented in comic ways. Miriam Allott notes that "Pyle and Fowler at cross purposes are often ... entertaining...; and in association with the delightful and uncomprehending Phuong, whom they both love, they also demonstrate their author's skill in mingling the funny and the sad." Fowler images himself and Phuong at one point thus: "She lay at my feet like a dog on a crusader's tomb, preparing the opium." Similes like that one, of obedient bitch offering comfort to dead fighter in alien land — often are signposts directing readers to respond emotionally to a given situation. Peter Mudford, far from being troubled, even confused, by Greene's flashbacks and flash-forwards, which muddy the narrative flow in *The Quiet American,* expresses admiration. He says that "[i]n the end, Fowler will be compelled to become *engagé*.... Rather I should say at the beginning, for Greene with his skill at manipulating narrative and time begins with Pyle's disappearance." Doing so, however, makes any serious narrative climaxing impossible. Matt Steinglass judges that, of all Greene's novels, *The Quiet American* "most tightly wraps his trademark sexual and political concerns in a neat, explosive package." V. S. Pritchett, discontent with *The Quiet American,* feels that only "minor figures ... in the war scenes are individualized; ... Fowler is mere self-pity; Pyle is a flat profile."

The reference to General De Lattre is to General Jean Joseph Marie Gabriel de Lattre de Tassigny (1889–1952), the distinguished French military hero who was placed in command of French forces in Indo-China (1950) to oppose Vietnamese forces led by Vo Nguyen Giap. Greene later wrote about meeting De Lattre in Vietnam, being befriended by him, taking advantage of De Lattre's trust, lamenting the death of De Lattre's son in a Viet Minh ambush, and touching on De Lattre's military mistakes (1951). Yvonne Cloetta* notes that Greene liked De Lattre and was liked by De Lattre, who, however, was suspicious of Greene. Saigon's Place Garnier, full of bicyclists, is presented in a watercolor in Paul Hogarth's book illustrating Greene's novels.

The movie based on *The Quiet American* (1957) starred Michael Redgrave (as Fowler), miscast as Pyle the World War II hero Audie Murphy (1924–1971), had Phuong played by a minor Italian actress (Giorgia Molland), and violated Greene's purpose by making the American position intelligent and making Fowler the dupe of Communists and strongly motivated by desire to recoup Phuong, who rejects him. Quentin Falk is generous in his comments on the movie; Gene D. Phillips, less so. Christopher Hawtree demonstrates that Greene regarded the movie as a politically dishonest travesty. Falk reports two items of interest. First, Greene gave his daughter Caroline film rights to the novel so she could buy a ranch in Canada with the proceeds. Second, soon after the movie was released, a dramatic version of the novel was staged in Moscow, which understandably pleased audiences, but not Greene, who saw one performance (1960) and despised it. He showed Marie-Françoise Allain photographs of the actors in it; they were cardboard cutouts with stiff stereotypical expressions. (Sources: Allain, 168n; Allott, 67; Cloetta, 140; DeVitis, 109, 110; Falk, 134–40; Greene, *Ways of Escape,* 163–73 passim, 187; Hawtree, 56–58; Hogarth, 95; Mudford, 43; Phillips, 139–44; Pritchett, 81; Shelden, 382–401 passim; Sherry II, 409, 417, 475–76, 478; Steinglass, 34)

QUIGLY, CYRIL (*The Captain and the Enemy*). He is a tall, thin, mysterious man. He tells Jim Baxter his friends call him Fred. He was born in Brighton, has a British passport, left England at 16, has lived in America. He tells Jim he works as a financial consultant for American newspapers, and constantly wants information for possible use in his columns and elsewhere. Colonel Martínez believes that Quigly, being pro–American, told Somoza's men about the Captain's flight plan and therefore is partly responsible for the Captain's crash and death. Martínez's hint that Quigly should seek American Zone protection results in Quigly's decamping and possibly arranging Jim's fatal accident.

Although the CIA goes unmentioned in *The Captain and the Enemy,* Quigly's actions have inspired several critics to name him as a CIA operative. For example, Haim Gordon mentions Quigly five times, each time saying Quigly is a CIA agent while saying nothing else about the novel. Judith Adamson also calls Quigly a CIA agent but adds that Jim is so "politically naive" that he confides in Quigly, "who is responsible for Jim's and the Captain's deaths." (Sources: Adamson, 180; Gordon, 2, 12, 17, 30, 42)

QUINTANA, CAPTAIN (*Rumour at Nightfall*). He is an officer under Colonel Riego. Quintana is diminutive, dapper, supercilious. Disagreeing with Chase, Quintana believes that their quarry, the guerrilla Caveda, could be bribed. During the San Juan uprising, Quintana is last seen trying ineffectively to surrender.

QUINTANA, FATHER (*The Power and the Glory*). He is a Las Casas priest Miss Lehr says she and her brother know. Father Quintana said he would return but didn't.

QUIXOTE, FATHER (*Monsignor Quixote*). He has been a priest at El Toboso 30 years. Modest and sympathetic toward the lowly, he knows his mission and applies to it lessons gained from reading the more loving books of Catholic theology. He believes that the Don Quixote of Cervantes's epic novel is his ancestor. Father Quixote names his old car Rocinante and dubs as Sancho his closest friend, Enrique Zancas, a Communist. Quixote's faithful servant is Teresa. Trouble begins when the Bishop of Motopo causes Quixote to become a monsignor. Quixote and Sancho take a holiday together. Quixote rooms in a brothel, sees a porno film, hears a confession in a lavatory, helps a robber evade the Guardia—all in touching innocence. The Bishop of El Toboso and prim Father Herrera lack any understanding of Quixote and want him committed. Trouble ends for Quixote when, driving Rocinante with Sancho along, he crashes into the wall of the Trappist monastery at Osera.

Norman Sherry says Greene told Father Leopoldo Duran he would be the model for Monsignor Quixote; he partly is, although Sherry discounts it basically. Robert Hoskins starts analyzing "Father Quixote" thus: "Innocence itself, so often conceived in Greene's earlier novels as lost, or hopelessly inadequate to deal with the world, or positively dangerous ..., is restored here to its proper theological role as a saintly virtue." Anne T. Salvatore contends that "the portrayal of the monsignor is ... complicated, for ... Greene's ambiguous attack/defense method ... seems to confuse the reader's judgment of the priest's human worth." A. F. Cassis notes that Quixote exemplifies "the importance of doubt" and the error "of smugness and certainty." (Sources: Cassis, 29; Hoskins, 257; Salvatore, 98; Sherry III, 668)

RACHEL ("The Second Death"). She is a compliant farm girl with whom an unnamed dying fellow was intimate. He may have fibbed to encourage the narrator, also unnamed, to believe he too could have his way with her.

RAMAGE (*Loser Takes All*). Bertram says he and Cary could honeymoon at Le Touquet but prefer Bournemouth because the Ramages would be at Le Touquet. Cary adds that Le Touquet has a casino where Bertram would "lose all our money." A nice bit of foreshadowing.

RAMSGATE, MISS ("Under the Garden"). She is Maria's and Javitt's beautiful daughter. When Wilditch sees multi-angled, cheesecake photographs of her as a contestant in a Miss England contest, he falls in love—with beauty—and determines to seek her in continent after continent for immediate marriage. It is possible that a woman in Africa came close to being his ideal, since he mentions having a mixed-class daughter.

RANK, FATHER (*The Heart of the Matter*). He is the Catholic priest in Freetown, Sierra Leone. He was more at ease in Northampton, England, but went to Africa 22 years ago to try to serve God better. He has taken no leave for 12 years. Father Rank has tousled gray hair, drinks, laughs boisterously, is aware of his limited ability, and associates with Tallit the Christian Syrian. He and Scobie know each other well. Father Rank tries to help Scobie when he confesses having committed adultery with Helen Rolt, but he is stymied when Scobie says he'll keep on seeing Helen. Despite Scobie's death by suicide, Father Rank tells Helen Scobie he can't believe Scobie is damned to Hell.

Norman Sherry notes that during Greene's service in Sierra Leone as an Intelligence agent he met a priest named Father Mackie, many of whose traits are reflected in Greene's Father Rank. A. A. DeVitis contends that Father Rank is necessary in the novel, "for Greene's overall dramatic technique in the construction of plot demands ... that someone restore balance and order in the world after ... passions have spent themselves." Paul Hogarth includes a watercolor of the Catholic Church in Freetown, Sierra Leone. (Sources: DeVitis, 92; Hogarth, 75; Sherry II, 136)

RAVEN (*This Gun for Hire*). He was James Raven's criminal father, was in jail when James was born, and was hanged at Wandsworth six years after that.

RAVEN, JAMES (*This Gun for Hire*). He is the anti-hero of the novel. His father was hanged in prison. His mother committed suicide practically in front of him. Raven was reared in an orphanage, well-enough schooled but mistreated, partly by a dishonest chaplain. He respects Christ for his suffering but without respect for Christianity. Raven, a bitter, hardened man, 28, with a disfiguring harelip, is hired by Davis on steel-maker Sir Marcus's order to assassinate a Czech pacifist, thus generating a European war. When Raven learns Davis paid him in stolen bank notes with numbers known by the police, he determines on reckless, remorseless revenge. Raven follows Davis to Nottwich, where Sir Marcus lives, works, and rules; meets Anne Crowder by chance, saves her from Davis and confides in her; is shadowed by Anne's fiancé, the detective Mather, to whom Anne betrayed him; goes to Sir Marcus's building, with multiple fatal consequences.

In a *Collected Edition* introduction, Greene says Raven did not evolve from the melodramas of John Buchan (1875–1940), one of Greene's favorite authors, but wanted revenge after life played filthy tricks on him. Peter Wolfe explicates Raven's name as "Raven-raving," since at the outset the man commits "a sick crime rather than a rational one." Additionally, Wolfe notes that Raven, "like Iago, ... is twenty-eight years old" and extravagantly equates Raven to Christ and Judas.

It is worth noting that "corvo" is Latin for "raven," in light of the fact that Greene's characterization of Acky, also in *This Gun for Hire*, owes something to Greene's admiration of the eccentric author Baron Corvo (*see* Acky). Anthony Mockler first defines Raven as "the lumpenproletariat made flesh — undersized, brutal, self-centered, self-pitying, vicious," then adds that Greene "takes an almost perverse pleasure in loading the dice against his creature."

In discussing the movie based on *This Gun for Hire,* Carlos Clarens notes that, for Greene's Raven, Hollywood "substituted a monosyllabic gunsel in a raincoat — the first emblematic use of the garment — and removed the harelip." (Sources: Clarens, 178; Greene, *A Gun for Sale, Collected Edition,* v; Mockler, 118; Wolfe, 54, 54–55, 56, 69)

RAVEN, MRS. (*This Gun for Hire*). She was James Raven's mother. A few years after her husband was hanged, she committed suicide by inexpertly cutting her throat in the basement kitchen. The door being unlocked, Raven saw his bleeding, dying mother.

RAYMOND (*The Human Factor*). Castle, Davis, and even Percival go to Raymond's Revuebar, London hot spot, and enjoy drinks and Rita Rolls's striptease dance.

RECTOR, THE (*The Comedians*). He is an official at the Jesuit College of the Visitation, in Monte Carlo. When Brown is expelled, he promises the rector he will get in touch with Father Thomas Capriole in England — but doesn't.

REDAKTEUR, HERR (*England Made Me*). Minty addresses his newspaper superior thus. (In Swedish, "redakteur" means "director.") He criticizes Minty for his bad back, thin chest, and weak muscles, and recommends cold baths and no tea.

REED, CAROL (1906–1976). Carol Reed, the distinguished British movie director, was an actor, then producer, then director of dialogue (1932–1934), and finally director of several hits (1930s, early 1940s). During World War II he was commission captain in the British Army (1942–1945) and worked in the Kinematograph Service on patriotic, award-winning war-propaganda films. Reed was knighted (1952). His Hollywood movies, *The Agony and the Ecstasy* (1965) for one example, were box-office successes but weren't critically acclaimed.

However, *Oliver!* (1968), a musical movie based on Charles Dickens's *Oliver Twist,* won him an Oscar as best director.

Greene admired Reed's work early on. For example, in a review he enormously praised Reed's skill in directing *Laburnum Grove* (1936), based on a play by J. P. Priestley,* Greene's temperamental friend.

David Parkinson, Michael Shelden, and Norman Sherry detail Greene's friendship with Reed. Greene worked with Reed on *The Fallen Idol* (based on "The Basement Room"), which Greene scripted and Reed directed. Greene worked again with Reed when Alexander Korda* placed Reed under contract (1948) to direct *The Third Man,* which Greene scripted. Reed hired Orson Welles to play Harry Lime — for $100,000. Greene and Reed traveled together from England to New York to Santa Monica, California, to confer with the occasionally irascible David Selznick about *The Third Man* script (1948). Greene and Reed collaborated on *Our Man in Havana,* with Greene scripting, the two traveling to Cuba, and Reed directing (1959). *The Third Man* has been frequently regarded as the best British movie ever made. (Sources: Parkinson, 124–26 and passim; Shelden, 318–31 passim; Sherry II, 239–41. 253–55; Sherry III, 103, 135–42 passim)

REED, SIR HUBERT ("The Basement Room"). He must be a friend of Philip Lane's father. Philip remembers him not only as the withered Permanent Secretary who uses steel nibs and has a pen wiper in his pocket, but also as a possible figure in stories Philip dreams up.

This gentleman's name was surely suggested by that of Herbert Read (1893–1968). Read was a poet and critic, a University of Edinburgh professor of fine arts, and Greene's close friend. Read became Sir Herbert Read in 1953, 18 years after Greene created Sir Hubert Reed.

REES (*The Heart of the Matter*). He is a naval-intelligence man. Scobie temporizes to Helen Rolt, on the beach, by saying he was in a hurry trying to locate Rees.

REITH (*The Heart of the Matter*). He is the Chief Assistant Colonial Secretary, a willfully aloof snob. Scobie and the Commissioner joke about Reith's reputation.

REMNANT, PETER (*The Name of Action*). He is a casual friend with whom Chant has routine, uninspiring lunches in London.

RENNIT (*The Ministry of Fear*). He is the Orthotex detective agency director, with 30 years of experience mostly in divorce cases. Though reluctant to believe Rowe's claim that Poole tried to kill him, Rennit agrees for big money to check into it and assigns his man Jones to the job. Willi Hilfe or his henchmen kill Jones.

RENNIT, MRS. (*The Ministry of Fear*). She is Rennit's real or fictitious wife. He pretends to phone her while really phoning the police about Rowe.

REPRESENTATIVE OF THE BRITISH COUNCIL, THE (*The Honorary Consul*). He functions in the British Embassy in Buenos Aires. One of his jobs is to squire visiting poets around. During a cocktail party given by Sir Henry Belfrage, Plarr helps Sir Henry by untrapping Lady Belfrage from one such poet. Plarr can never remember the council representative's name, "for some Freudian reason."

REVEREND MOTHER, THE (*Our Man in Havana*). She was in charge of the convent school when Milly Wormold set fire to fellow student Thomas Earl Parkman Jr.'s shirt tail. Wormold, Milly's father, successfully appealed to the Reverend Mother for mercy by saying Parkman's pulling Milly's hair started the fracas.

REXALL, EDWARD (*The Man Within*). He was a revenuer serving under Hilliard during the attempt to trap the 10 smugglers off the *Good Chance*. Rexall was shot to death by a smuggler, later perhaps falsely identified as Richard Tims.

RIBERA, AQUINO (*The Honorary Consul*). He is a bearded, one-track Marxist. Ribera wanted to be a writer, smuggled American cigarettes from Panama, was imprisoned in Paraguay, was tortured into talking by having three fingers cut off, escaped in the caper during which Henry Plarr was killed. Belonging to Rivas's revolutionary gang, Aquino helped kidnap Fortnum, wields his gun in his one good hand, repeatedly suggests shooting Fortnum, and defeats Eduardo Plarr at chess when Plarr is held in the gang's hut. Colonel Perez's men storm the hut and kill Aquino.

Greene makes lugubrious points by tediously allowing Aquino to quote his poetic squibs satirizing social evolution and stressing death.

RICKARDS, JOCELYN (1924–2005). One of Greene's several lovers, Jocelyn Rickards was born in Melbourne, Australia, went to girls' grammar school, moved to Sydney with her family when her businessman father went bankrupt, studied in an art school (1938–1944), and exhibited successfully. She moved to London (1949) with Australian fashion-photographer Alec Murray, and was soon painting murals, designing interiors, designing costumes for stage shows and musical shows, and designing sets and costumes for movies. Her talent is revealed in the following movies, among others: *The Prince and the Showgirl* (1957), *Look Back in Anger* (1958), *The Entertainer* (1960), *From Russia with Love* (1963), *Blow-Up* (1966), *Alfred the Great* (1969), *Ryan's Daughter* (1970), and *Sunday, Bloody Sunday* (1971). Having developed friendships with men important in intellectual high-society, Jocelyn enjoyed an unrestrained sex life. She had affairs of varying intensities and lengths with countless men, including Murray, Leonard Rosoman (painter, whom she married, to her regret), Alfred J. Ayer (distinguished philosophy professor and multiple husband), John Osborne (distinguished playwright), and Greene.

Jocelyn met Greene at a National Book Show in London (1951), to which Ayer had taken her. At odds with Catherine Walston,* Greene was ready for substitute amours. When Ayer took a trip to Mexico, Jocelyn agreed to a tumultuous affair with Greene. Although Michael Shelden says she told him this relationship started in 1951, she herself and William Cash date it 1953. Shelden adds she told him that Greene, calling her Pixie, found her combination of girlish-boyish attributes stimulatingly androgynous. She affectionately recalls Greene's showing her London environs she never knew; taking her to dinners, the theater, the movies; visiting with her — and Ayer — the apartment shared by John Hayward, bibliophile and scholar, and T. S. Eliot, whom Greene esteemed. Jocelyn and Greene remained staunch friends. He owned and valued one of her paintings and also lent her his Capri villa (1958). Cash provides details of the Ayer-Greene-Rickards triangle. Norman Sherry says Greene told him his affair with Jocelyn lasted only weeks. Jocelyn wrote Greene (February 17, 1986) to congratulate him on being awarded the British Order of Merit. Earlier, stability entered Jocelyn's life when she permanently married movie director Clive Donner (1970). Later, she taught costume design at the University of Southern California. (Sources: Cash, 235–40; Rickards, 35–38, 46, 63; Shelden, 102, 409–12; Sherry II, 500; Sherry III, 237, 738, 865n26)

RIEGO, COLONEL (*Rumour at Nightfall*). Riego, a low-skulled, fair-haired Cantabrian, is a devout, tired veteran under General Diaz's command. Childless and widowered, Riego sadly remembers his deceased wife's adulteries, perhaps including an affair with the guerrilla Caveda, whom Riego is under orders to capture. Diaz rebukes Riego so severely that Riego urges Chase to help him get Caveda to regain military clout.

RIEGO, SEÑORA (*Rumour at Nightfall*). She was Colonel Riego's faithless wife, now deceased. One of her affairs may have been with Caveda — or so Caveda boasts in a letter retrieved by Riego's men and read to Riego.

RIMMER, KAY (*It's a Battlefield*). She is Milly Drover's sexy sister and the sister-in-law of Jim Drover, imprisoned for murder. Kay works in the Battersea match factory, attracts Philip Surrogate, and admires his flat, especially his big pink circular bed therein. She also goes for an overnight drive with Jules Briton, enjoys sexual relations with him at Berkhamsted, but doesn't greatly care when he doesn't propose marriage.

RITA (*Travels with My Aunt*). She is a prostitute in Paris. Wordsworth takes Henry to what he calls an A.1 "joint" and tries unsuccessfully to pimp for Henry and Rita, whom he calls a school teacher.

RIVAS (*The Honorary Consul*). He was Léon Rivas's father. A rich lawyer of the bourgeoisie of Paraguay, old Rivas avoided trouble by regularly contributing to the Partido Colorado before General Stroessner achieved power. Rivas fired Pedro, the family gardener, because he pocketed some pesos he found on a garden seat.

RIVAS, LÉON (*The Honorary Consul*). He is Plarr's friend from schooldays. Léon, who has big, jutting ears, studied in the seminary, became a priest, half-abandoned the priesthood, married Marta, became a Paraguayan revolutionary, and went into hiding for two years. His cohorts are Corredo, Marta, Miguel, Pablo, and Ribera. Rivas got information from Plarr about the American Ambassador, aimed to kidnap him for a prisoner exchange, but by mistake seized Fortnum. Dr. Plarr is summoned to treat Fortnum, tries to dissuade the gang, and talks tediously with Léon the while. Léon regards God as evil because He remains insufficiently involved in human problems, yet excuses God because, like everyone else, He has a "night side" and is evolving toward a "day side." Marta and some of the others call Léon "Father." He doesn't survive Colonel Perez's attempt to rescue Fortnum.

Leopoldo Duran states that Greene "immortalized Father Camilo Torres in the character of Father Rivas." Torres was chaplain of the University of Bogota, in Colombia, until his ouster for misbehavior. He became an armed member of the Communist party and a jungle guerrilla. To make a martyr of him, Communists betrayed him to the police, who killed him. Norman Sherry discusses resemblances between Rivas and guerrilla-priests Greene knew or heard about, including some he met while staying at the Grand Hotel in Asunción, Paraguay (July 1968). Among them was Father Oscar Marturet, whom Greene met in Corrientes province, Argentina (March 1970), and whom Sherry later also met and interviewed. Mark Bosco sees Rivas as "the postcolonial descendent of Greene's whiskey [sic] priest in *The Power and the Glory* ... transformed into the liberationist priest who preaches a gospel of freedom from the tyranny of the institutional Church, as well as from its alliances with capitalism and despotic regimes." Bosco regards Rivas's analysis of God as a "Manichean reduction" but also as containing "a deeper incarnational insight into God's immanent proximity," relating to "the French Catholic revival that Greene appropriated." A. F. Cassis says Father Rivas exemplifies "a blueprint of the role of the church in the face of social and political injustice." Greene and Sherry both strain credulity—Greene for having Rivas, while waiting for troopers to storm his hut, wonder whether to murder Fortnum or not, then read a detective novel to pass the time; Sherry, for seeing resemblances between Rivas and Christ. (Sources: Bosco, 110, 116; Cassis, 24; Duran, 74; Sherry III, 529–35, 687)

RIVAS, SEÑORA (*The Honorary Consul*). She was Léon Rivas's mother. She regularly ordered Pedro, the family gardener, to sweep up fallen flower petals, because they were "so untidy."

ROBINSON ("A Day Saved"). He is the narrator. He shadows a man whom he says he doesn't know but who is concealing something Robinson would kill him to get. Together they go by airplane instead of Dover-to-Ostend ship, drink excessively, then proceed by train to the strange man's destination, which is a home filled with hospitable people. Though invited in, Robinson remains outside, unhappy that the man saved a day by flying but wasted his own time. He hopes the man will similarly doubt himself and thus waste time. Finally Robinson, who has named the man Canby, Douglas, Fotheringay, Jones, and Wales, reveals that he too is Canby, Douglas, Fotheringay, Jones, Wales, and Robinson.

ROBINSON (*The Heart of the Matter*). He is a Freetown bank manager. Robinson is a hypochondriac, bitter for not being posted to Nigeria. He won't lend Scobie £250 to finance his wife Louise's South African vacation. The Commissioner tells Scobie that Robinson, treated by Dr. Travis and seemingly better, is ill, with two years to live.

ROBINSON, EDWARD RHODES (*Travels with My Aunt*). His is a name seen by Henry on a monument in the Boulogne cemetery. The inscription says he died in Bombay.

ROBINSON, MOLLY (*The Heart of the Matter*). She is the banker's wife, seemingly in fine health.

ROCA, LUIS (*Rumour at Nightfall*). He was a member of Colonel Riego's command. Roca, quiet and fair, was mortally wounded by guerrillas during an ambush suggested by Chase. Riego's wrenching prayers over the dying Roca should make Chase compassionate but don't.

ROCHE (*The Tenth Man*). He is a farmer in the Brinac region outside Paris. When he was a boy, he and Chavel were playmates. Roche had his right arm torn off by a tractor as a youth and grew sour. A local Resistance leader during the war, he doesn't recognize Chavel when Chavel returns to the neighborhood.

ROCINANTE (*Monsignor Quixote*). She is Father Quixote's faithful but aged Seat 600 car. Rocinante struggle up hills, rests under bridges, poops out occasionally, and when charging into a church wall becomes a metal carcass.

Mark Bosco says "Rocinante is given a place of honor throughout the novel, an inanimate creature worthy of Quixote's love and care." Peter Mudford even suggests that Rocinante's "performance shares with those who drive in her an idiosyncratic temperament, even a humanity to counterbalance their ideological disputes." (Sources: Bosco, 147; Mudford, 56)

RODRIGUEZ (*Our Man in Havana*). Wormold includes Rodriguez on his list of nonexistent agents, defining him as a night-club king.

RODRIGUEZ, DR. (*Travels with My Aunt*). He is an Asunción physician whom Visconti knows and who he says would be happy to prepare fake medical news to promote dishonest sales of the unnamed happy Czech's useless plastic drinking straws.

ROGER (*The Captain and the Enemy*) *see* **CAPTAIN, THE**

ROLLS, RITA (*The Human Factor*). She is a stripteaser at Raymond's Revuebar, where Castle, Davis, and Percival go one evening.

ROLT, HELEN (*The Heart of the Matter*). She is a girl, 19, from Bury St. Edmund, Suffolk, England. Her mother died 10 years ago. Her father is a clergyman. Married only three weeks, Helen was widowed when a German submarine torpedoed their passenger vessel and her husband John Rolt drowned. After 40 days in a lifeboat, Helen and a few others were rescued by a French ship and taken ashore at Pende. Scobie helps her recuperate in Freetown. They fall in love. When Scobie's wife Louise returns from South Africa, Scobie feels responsible for both women's well-being. In despair, he commits suicide to free them to regain happiness.

Gene D. Phillips argues that Scobie views Helen "as a surrogate for his own dead daughter and feels very protective toward her." Why then sleep with her? (Source: Phillips, 120)

ROLT, JOHN (*The Heart of the Matter*). He was Helen Rolt's husband but died at sea when their ship was torpedoed.

RONALD (*Monsignor Quixote*). He is an American who with his unnamed girlfriend stops their Renault outside León. Zancas questions them about Father Quixote, who has gone.

RONALD, SIR (*England Made Me*). He is the Minister of the British Legation in Stockholm. He recently published a book of poetry entitled *Viol and Vine*. Minty says Ronald is a fellow Harrow man. Krogh is a welcome legation visitor. Late in the action, Sir Ronald is off for a holiday in Scotland.

"THE ROOT OF ALL EVIL" (1964). Short story. (Characters: Anna, Herr Braun, Herr Dobel, the Grand Duke, Frau Hackenfurth, Mayor Kalnitz, Herr Kastner, Frau Muller, Herr Muller, Frau Puckler, Herr Puckler, Frau Schmidt, Herr Schmidt, the Superintendent of Police.)

The narrator's father, a German living in England, believed original sin triggered secrecy and practicing secrecy causes new sins.

Illustrating, the father tells the narrator about Schmidt's club, in 189-, in market-town B—. Schmidt bothered Frau Schmidt by domestic drinking. She wanted to visit other wives, knit, discuss their grandchildren's illnesses. He won't go to public houses and drink with cronies. She consults tough Frau Muller, who suggests wives meet weekly, sew, have coffee, share illness news. Frau Muller suggests Herr Muller invite the men in for drinks while wives are away. Fine. Until Frau Muller includes sweet Frau Puckler in the sewing circle. The men can't abide Puckler. He has gimlet eyes staring others into immobility, then talks them numb. Schmidt tells Muller all should meet secretly, drink in Braun's cellar. Six men do. Fine. Until Puckler, not locating them anywhere, gets Superintendent of police to send cops to find and foil their possible political plot. One of the six mislead cops each week. Fine. Until doing so leads to lying to wives. Also, decoy Schmidt one night becomes thirsty, seeks inn, but enters brothel. To escape, the madam dresses Schmidt as woman; he simpers past the cop. Fine? No; cops tell Superintendent the secret-society men meet in brothels; what's more, Puckler theorizes they disguise themselves as women to start anarchistic domestic infelicity. Worse, Puckler suspects big women of being transvestite men, pulls Frau Hackenfurth's wig off in failed effort at proof. Fine for two wine-bibbing weeks. Schmidt and Muller miss pasties wives baked for them, tell their associates. Braun suggests advertising for woman to prepare pasties for a men's club. Puckler sees Braun's ad, suspects the club, disguises himself as woman, gets hired by Braun, who never met Puckler, who bakes pasties in Braun's kitchen, hands them to Braun through cellar door, overhears converse within. Puckler takes notes of talk by Muller, Schmidt, Braun, Dobel, Kastner, and one anonymous man concerning weather, postman, vintages, cow, clock, dog, plum-duff, dead Mayor Kalnitz, 1886, 1887. Puckler tells doubtful Superintendent these words are codes, persuades him to assign bachelor cop, in female garb, to bake Braun's pasties while Puckler listens uninterruptedly. Fine. Until one wife spots Puckler buying the cop bloomers, gossips to other wives except Frau Puckler, who gets treated so solicitously that she pleads headache, leaves, accompanied by Frau Muller, who returns with this gossip: Puckler was unaccountably absent; Frau Puckler said Puckler said cop said Schmidt was wearing women's clothes. Fraus Schmidt, Muller, Dobel gossip foully, gossip being another sin, in narrator's father's view. Worse next. Frau Muller tells Muller everything; he remembers cook Anna's gimlet eyes, i.e., Puckler's. Clubmen surmise Puckler plans to poison their pasties for being excluded. Sinful revenge? When Puckler and disguised cop arrive, foul liquids, wood, etc. fall on them. Cop flees. Puckler is crowned with chamberpot, unremovable; he dies when it is hammered off. Inquiry follows, extended by Superintendent's pretending to believe Puckler's unaccepted theory and getting affianced to Puckler's comely widow.

The narrator's father lists the sins inevitably evolving from that secret club, ending with the sin committed by transvestite Sodomites. When the narrator asks for an explanation of Sodom, his father says he's too young to hear about such secrets.

Greene claims he dreamed the plot of "The Root of All Evil" and awakened in laughter. Thomas A. Wendorf says that the story "approaches farce and subverts its own original moral rigors." It is easily Greene's least worthwhile fictional effort. The only palatable ingredient in the slapsticky mix is the ironic conclusion. "The Root of All Evil" was the subject of a 1976 television production. The cast included Donald Pleasance. *See Shades of Greene.* (Sources: Falk, 215; Greene, *Collected Stories,* xi; Greene, *A World of My Own,* xxi; Wendorf, 650)

ROSE ("The Basement Room"). She is a sloppy policewoman who shambles into the station, is ridiculed by the sergeant, and doesn't help Philip Lane.

ROSE (*Travels with My Aunt*). Richard Pulling told Augusta that Rose, who worked in a flower shop, was his first sexual conquest.

ROSEN (*This Gun for Hire*). Sir Marcus remembers Rosen got seasick while cruising off Rhodes on Soppelsa's yacht and vomited on Mrs. Ziffo's dress.

ROUGEMONT (*The Human Factor*). He is a Free State farmer in South Africa. Of Huguenot ancestry, Rougemont speaks Afrikaans and English, has been assimilated into the Dutch life style, doesn't advocate apartheid, but is reconciled to being eliminated, as he told his friend Castle, when blacks take control of South Africa. Castle met Carson through Rougemont.

ROVER ("Across the Bridge"). He is the part-setter mongrel dog owned and routinely kicked by Calloway, a fugitive hiding in Mexico. When detectives take Rover over the bridge into the United States, Calloway follows. The detectives follow Rover to find Calloway. When one detective swerves his car to avoid Rover, he kills Calloway. Rover barks in "mongrel triumph" over his body.

ROW (*The Confidential Agent*). He is an Indian with a room in the hotel managed by Mrs. Mendrill. Her maid Else Crole tells D. that Mr. Muckerji is more respectable than Row.

ROWE, ALICE (*The Ministry of Fear*). She was Rowe's wife, whom he poisoned to end her painful terminal illness. Aware, however, that she could bear pain better than he could, he knows he acted more from self-pity than pity for her. This gnawing awareness contributes to his childishness and also his partial amnesia.

ROWE, ARTHUR (*The Ministry of Fear*). He was a journalist until he poisoned his terminally ill and suffering wife Alice, partly through pitying her but more through self-pity. Rowe was tried for murder but after much suffering was acquitted. He regressed to partial childishness. His winning a cake with dangerous film in it leads to his meeting siblings Anna and Willi Hilfe, attending Mrs. Bellairs's séance, believing he murdered Cost, being menaced by Poole, being injured in an air raid and thereafter suffering partial amnesia, living as Richard Digby in Dr. Forester's sanatorium, and helping Scotland Yard detective Prentice expose Willi's spy ring. By not telling Prentice everything, Rowe, who gradually regains more memories, is able to find Anna, pursue Willi, secure the second copy of the film, but also learn from Willi about killing Alice. Rowe and Anna love each other, but they are condemned to live lies together — Rowe pretending not to remember everything, and Anna, who knows everything, pretending she doesn't. Rowe's nickname at school was Boojie.

Quentin Falk is glad that in the movie version of *The Ministry of Fear* the hero is named Stephen Neale, since Falk regards the name Arthur Rowe as "dour and uninspiring." Is it possible that Greene in naming his murderer Rowe was thinking of the Yankees' "Murderers' Row," known to baseball lovers beginning in 1927? Probably not. (Source: Falk, 37)

ROWE, MRS. (*The Ministry of Fear*). She was Rowe's complacent mother. When Rowe tries in a dream to tell her that he is a murderer, she simperingly disbelieves him.

Norman Sherry suggests that Rowe's memory of his mother owes something to Greene's memory of Marion Greene,* his own mother. (Source: Sherry I, 35–36)

ROWLETT (*It's a Battlefield*). This rowdy person is drinking where Conder and Patmore have met to talk. Miss Chick, the bar maid, tells Rowlett to speak more "Quaietly [*sic*]."

ROY, HARRY ("A Drive in the Country"). While driving Fred's girlfriend to her home, Mike recognizes Harry Roy's dance music on his car radio.

RS (*England Made Me*). These are reference initials in the letter Scott and James, solicitors in England, used when they sent Minty his September [1930] monthly allowance. Since Minty recognizes these initials, RS may be Scott (*which see*).

RUBY (*This Gun for Hire*). She is the easy-come chorus girl who flirts with Davis, has a luncheon date with him at the Metropole, expects steak and onions and whatever later. When Davis doesn't show up, the porter Hallows treats Ruby to lunch.

RUDY (*Our Man in Havana*). He is a secret-service agent Beatrice Severn brings from London to Wormold's office to pretend to be his assistant accountant but really to handle radio communications. Ultimately, Rudy burns code materials and escapes by air via Jamaica.

RUMOUR AT NIGHTFALL (1931). Novel. (Characters: Ramon Caveda, Francis Chase, Michael Crane, Mrs. Crane, General Diaz, Emilio, Enrique, Jaime, Juan, Luis, Miguel, Eulelia Monti, Señor Monti, Señora Monti, Peacock, Father Pedro, Captain Quintana, Colonel Riego, Señora Riego, Luis Roca, Stephens, Verity.)

Part I. (1) For two years Francis Chase, London correspondent, has been in northern Spain, imbedded for six months with Colonel Riego, Captain Quintana, and other soldiers pursuing never-seen Ramon Caveda, a guerrilla still loyal to Don Carlos de Borbón the Pretender (1848–1909), who actually has fled (to France, 1872). In a failed ambush suggested by Chase, he and Quintana merely retrieve enemy materials — a letter, nun-like woman's photograph, broad gloves — which they take to Riego. The letter from Caveda to Miguel boasts of Caveda's elusiveness, Riego's ineptness, and Caveda's having slept with Riego's wife, deceased. Chase believes the photograph may lead to Caveda. Regarded by many Spaniards as a foreign heretic, Chase thinks Spain is "rotten."

(2) Next day Chase rides toward provincial San Juan, with the photograph, hoping to find the original and thus Caveda, whose name he hears women say in a church he enters during a rainstorm. He silently scoffs at their praying. They tell him nothing about the woman in the photograph. He enters an inn. Two conservative oldsters and a liberal youngster named Emilio greet him. Accepting wine, Chase hears talk about Caveda, whom one calls a robber of priests while Emilio praises his liberalism. They can't describe Caveda or identify the photographed woman. Michael Crane, a journalist-friend of Chase's, enters. Chase rides on to San Juan, stables his horse, goes to the inn, asks for his old room, but entering it finds Crane before the mirror.

(3) Crane explains he's quit journalism, was in Madrid a week, and advanced to San Juan to see Crane. They have wine in the courtyard. Crane says he heard in Madrid that Riego is disliked and Caveda may be bribed with a commission. Chase shows Crane the photograph. Crane seems attracted, borrows it, and says he'll help Chase find Caveda through her.

(4) After preparing a dispatch for his home office, Chase has dinner downstairs. Two courteous Spaniards tell Chase they identified the photographed woman for Crane, described her residence, and he left. She is Señorita Monti, 24. Luis, one of the two men dining, says he refused her when her mother demanded a dowry. Crane returns, says he saw the girl, her house, and a man with her, but was afraid of intruding. Chase, not believing in fate, not superstitious, and loving risks, seems Crane's mirrored opposite.

(5) That night Chase knocks on the Montis's door. Crane waits in shadows. Thin, metallic Señora Monti admits Chase, and thinks he wants to marry Señorita Monti, who appears. Chase says that he wishes to warn Caveda, lies that Caveda's gloves, which he brought, are his, and when frightening military shots begin sees tall, timid Señor Monti near his scholarly library. Señorita Monti blurts that Caveda was here tonight.

Part II. (l) To protect Señorita Monti, who speaks some English, from Chase's pressure, Crane, emerging, tells Chase he saw Caveda near the market. Chase waits outside, impatiently. Crane, sad to betray Chase, tells Señorita Monti he and Chase are Caveda's enemies. To Chase he describes Caveda, face hidden, leaving Señorita Monti's steps and entering a side-street inn. Crane accompanies brave Chase forward, through soldiers, into darkness and a bullet-riddled house. They see soldiers in the square shoot to death a man shouting on the balcony that Caveda's men destroyed the bridge. Chase tells Crane this: San Juan, pro-Caveda, is isolated from the south; Caveda is safe with peasants in mountains north; Riego will be summoned. Crane timidly tells Chase, who regards Señorita Monti as rotten, that he told her, perhaps because she is beautiful, that Crane is Caveda's enemy. Feeling endangered, Chase gives Crane the photograph, wants to telegraph his dispatch to London, but both see Señorita Monti under a streetlight. Chase reluctantly says Caveda is probably safe; she says the murdered shouter was her barber. Crane asks to escort her to "su casa." No. Chase gets sarcastic toward Crane, who watches her leave.

(2) Next noon Crane visits Señorita Monti. Her mother is asleep; her father, studying and praying. By gestures and trying out words, Michael Crane and Eulelia Monti name themselves. He understands that Caveda. though charming and handsome, isn't her lover — yet — yet he cost her the world. The words "peace" and "breasts" would draw Crane and Eulelia closer, but Chase, announced, enters. Sarcastic and embarrassed, he says Caveda is too fine and brave for soldiers to hunt. Eulelia so grudgingly agrees that Chase praises Caveda's non-religiosity, which bothers Eulelia, who denies

Caveda is her lover — but perhaps tomorrow — and would never be her friend. Chase regards her conduct as sinful for a Catholic. When she calls herself "low" like the two of them, Crane disagrees; Chase agrees. Pressed by Chase, she says she won't marry Caveda because he's not Catholic, might accord peace to Crane, also temporary security — as she did with Caveda — then openly offers her Ramon's useful letters to incredulous Chase, whom she calls a liar. Crane takes Caveda's letters, for their bitter truth. Chase doesn't want them read; Crane tosses them to Chase, who promises reportorial objectivity toward both Caveda and those murderous soldiers. Chase translates the letters aloud: Carlos abandoned Caveda and his fighters; Caveda wants money for his men to purchase farms, businesses, amnesty, and an army commission for himself; thanks Eulelia for sheltering him; asks for a photograph of her; fears Señora Monti would betray him for the reward. Eulelia says this: Caveda made her lie to her mother he was rich and sought marriage; she wouldn't wed him. A letter mentions an inn, where Eulelia equivocatingly admits she and Caveda made love — pleasant for him, disgustingly painful for her. Hearing enough, Chase gets Crane out, just as Eulelia says Caveda loves her, therefore needs forgiveness.

(3) Riding away with Chase, brothel-experienced Crane lusts to do with Eulelia's body what Caveda did. Chase fears she'll inform against them. Two troopers demand their papers, are impressed by Crane's photograph of Eulelia, leave. Crane discards the picture, knowing the original, therefore knowing truth and becoming fearless. Autumnal noon. San Juan lethargy. Crane calls Eulalia a whore; Chase says they shouldn't judge her, says he likes Crane, asks if Crane loves her. Afternoon rain. Emilio, having heard the word ("whore?" or "Caveda"?) enters, offers unsuccessfully to pimp for Crane, hints at news of Caveda, demands wine in their upstairs room, talks, but exits when treated curtly. In the corridor, Emilio whispers to the stone-faced female innkeeper, whose skinny husband Juan hears "Mañana" and walks down with him. Chase tells Crane to leave if he fears mañana. The two wonder if Caveda plans a town revolt tomorrow, during the barber's funeral. After talk about Spanish superstitions, Crane decides to remain. It pleases Chase not to lose him. Through their window they see drunk Emilio staggering beside Juan. Chase begs Crane to take Chase's first-rate horse, get past Aljerema to Madrid, wire Chase's dispatch to London. Crane agrees, sorrowfully, rides to the gate, is warned by a soldier about Caveda and danger, then sees Eulelia, who says she often rides hereabouts. She calls herself a moral sinner for sleeping with Caveda, once. They race to the tree line, lit by sunset. Will Crane forsake peace with her, take the dark road to an Aljerema inn? Eulelia return to her San Juan home? Asked why she succumbed to Caveda, Eulelia says her pleasant father's virtue and her materialistic mother's sin-urging combine within her. She wants Crane's friendship, not love, carelessly says Caveda was handsome, charming, once. She and Crane declare their love, but she won't let him stay, since she has long known Caveda's plans: He'll capture San Juan tomorrow. But Crane will stay, warn Chase, alert the Commandant (General Diaz). They discuss cowardice, love, the uncertain future. They see a Caveda recruit in the road ahead. Eulelia gets Crane to tell him she's Crane's wife, names herself. The recruit is astonished; Crane, distressed. She defines her eternity as "conscious peace"; he'd prefer peace right here. They return to San Juan. Where to stay? Not his inn, because of Chase. A church? He's a heretic. Her home? Her home is with him now. They enter a church. He fears Catholic implications and a possible God's nearness. Should Crane pity a suffering God? Pay God something to buy asked-for peace? He half-parodies a confession to her. She seriously confesses her love to him, saying such isn't blasphemy, whereas hatred, inflicting pain, ugliness are. A blundering, worn priest, approaching, regards them as affianced. Eulelia accepts the lacklogic of Crane's suggestion they have him marry them. He won't. Crane fulminates. Eulelia hesitates. Crane dislikes God's inflexibility here. Bullets fly, some inside the church. Crane figures he's the target, bravely pushes Eulelia toward the priest. Emilio has been killed outside. Crane has a vision of rings of light in the church, fears pain will follow, then feels peace broken, and half-envies the self-sacrificial old priest, now comforting a woman whose hand was pierced by a bullet. Eulelia, having stepped outside, returns with

her father to be witness, as the wounded woman will be, to Eulelia's and Crane's marriage. Done. Eulelie goes with her father to lie to her undeserving mother; Crane goes to tell Chase everything; they will gallop out of unsafe San Juan tomorrow. Ah, tomorrow. Crane rides in darkness toward the inn. Señora Monti stops him, names him as Señor Crane, Señor's Chase's friend, and says Eulelia wants Chase, a successful newspaperman. Crane scoffs and leaves, but hears her cackling victoriously.

Part III. (1) Chase is watching from the inn room, happy that Crane sent his dispatch, when Crane enters, says he's back to warn Chase of San Juan's doom tomorrow, told of it by Eulelia Monti, whom Chase reviles as Caveda's rotten Catholic mistress whose photograph Crane foolishly admired. Told Crane has married her, Chase deplores Crane's likely surrender to God, and his losing Chase's friendship. Crane says they have different beliefs now. Chase reckons Eulelia could be desirable but hates both Crane and Eulelia. Captain Quintana knocks and enters, says he conferred with General Diaz because of trifling troubles. When Crane suggests Caveda might be at the inn he entered yesterday, Chase feels superstition-loving Crane could betray him too. Quintana escorts Chase to Diaz's office. Diaz is criticizing Riego for being hospitable to a newspaperman. Chase boldly says he supposes Diaz is referring to him and adds he tried to help find Caveda. Diaz orders Chase out of the region tomorrow. Following Chase, Riego asks him to say where Caveda is, so he can capture him and blunt Diaz's rebuke. Silently admiring Caveda's unseen omnipresence, Chase tells Riego, not seriously, to ask Crane to betray Caveda. Riego leaves. Rationalizing vacillatingly, Chase neither follows to dissuade Riego nor warns Crane. Emilio's replacement offers Chase women but not Caveda's whereabouts. Chase, pistol in pocket, seeks the inn which Crane saw Caveda approach yesterday. The pimp follows but, hearing pursuers, clatters off. Chase is surrounded by several men. When he offers to tell Caveda something valuable, their leader (Enrique) takes him to the side-street inn and puts him in a room. Rationalizing in darkness, Chase concludes he's useless to Crane and Eulelia, both bathed in her light now; he saw her before Crane did; he can do nothing but save Caveda. A crone cackles about being Caveda's wet nurse. Chase finds two men—Miguel, Caveda's fat-necked "chief helper," and another—playing checkers. Chase, feeling mercilessly just, says an Englishman (Crane) followed Caveda to this inn last night and can identify Caveda, and Riego's men are coming soon. Miguel orders Enrique to post men strategically. Chase is assigned a room upstairs. He believes, muddled, that he not Eulelia will possess the mortally dead but spiritually suffering Crane, that his own spirit will die when his body does. He sleeps, dreams vividly about Eulelia, and returns to Miguel and Enrique at 4:00 a.m. Though Miguel orders patience, Enrique rushes to the window and is shot dead from outside. Soldiers fire ineffectively through the heavy door. Miguel whistles for his posted men to fire. Chase blames Crane for the ensuing melee. Miguel readies two pistols at the door, being splintered by a ramrod, tells Chase to alert men upstairs to pour boiling water on the intruders. A figure, with wounded and bleeding hands, who Chase hysterically mistakes for Chase, falls dying down the stairs. Men upstairs fire, curse, are fired at from opposite windows. When they don't help with the boiling water, Chase grabs the wet nurse. She asks about her precious Ramon and spills the pail. No help for Miguel now. Chase escapes to the roof. The door breaks. Miguel shoots twice, is killed. His men attack downstairs. Chase sees Quintana in the street waving a white handkerchief. Sunrise. San Juan flames under a bombardment. Does Chase again see Crane, with bleeding hands? Is Crane's skull cracking? Feeling sympathy toward Crane, Chase gets down to the street and safety.

(2) A woman says Señor Crane left maybe an hour ago. A bomb explodes near Chase. He approaches the Montis's house. A woman warns him soldiers were seeking a man there, saw him run toward them, shot him. Approaching the corpse, Chase calls "Michael," extends his hands, drops a gold coin. The touched dead flesh is neither friend nor foe. Chase speaks not to it nor its spirit but to his image of Crane: I killed you, unknowingly but not because you married; I hate it here; I would but can't share your pain, ended; I suffer, thus exist. Crane seems to reply that his spirit suffers. Tears

would bring Chase peace but don't come. Eulelia Crane arrives, says her mother locked Crane out; thus Eulelia, having her mother's instincts, killed him. Chase carries Crane to her room. She says Crane is happy; so will she be, through suffering. Chase, lonely, senses Crane possesses her still. She implores Chase to find peace through recognizing Crane's peace. Chase says this: Crane, betraying Caveda, her lover, deserved to be betrayed; Chase, mistaken for Caveda once, is her lover now. Producing a photograph of sensual Caveda, she says Crane, wanting Caveda, caused his own death. She invites Chase to go find his world. Afraid forgetting Crane's pain will end his, thus condemning him, Chase asks Eulelia to stay with him. Surprisingly, she agrees. Light floods him. Her mother approaches, eyes bright, hands forward, blessing their sorrowful union.

Michael Shelden, calling *Rumour at Nightfall* "plodding," says it is based on a novel to be called *The Episode* that Greene started but rejected. Shelden adds that it sold badly — about 3,000 in England and 1,018 in the United States — was unfavorably reviewed, and cost the publishers money.

Greene laments ever having written *Rumour at Nightfall*, saying "What did I know of Carlist Spain or Spain at all except from the pages of Conrad [specifically *The Arrow of Gold* by Joseph Conrad]?" Robert Pendleton expatiates on Conrad's influence. First, "sub-genres ... eclipse [many] a potentially strong plot" both in Conrad's fiction and in *Rumour at Nightfall*. Next, both it and Conrad's *The Arrow of Gold* are set in "exactly the same period of the Carlist wars." Finally, Conrad's frequent "themes of personal, romantic, and political betrayal" are present in *Rumour at Nightfall*.

Peter Wolfe finds both *Rumour at Nightfall* and *The Name of Action* to be "[w]eighted by psychological analysis, elaborate symbolism, and inflated language," with the result that they "exude a lulling atmosphere rather than tell a story." Robert Hoskins says that *Rumour at Nightfall* contains "some of the worst writing in all of Greene's novels."

All true. *Rumour at Nightfall* is unbalanced. Part I has five unnumbered but spaced sections. Part II has three, the third being 83 pages long. Part III has two, the first thrice the second's length. Greene's prose is rendered dull by hair-splitting psychoanalyzing, unparagraphed speech changes, overuse of the words "dark(ness)," "light," "peace," "shadow," "silence," "spirit," and "time," and overblown images, (which Norman Sherry calls "absurd"). Two examples of verbal attenuation among dozens: Crane's thinking that the priest's seeing him with Eulelia in the dark church would make the priest eager to indulge in "Rabelaisian raillery" about their future sexual pleasures and her future childbirth pains; also, sudden silence in a dark street is likened to ripples of tide water, circling a child's beach moat, receding, dissolving letters carved in the sand, avoiding previously spoken obscene words, and instead creating perfect "anonymity." Mark Bosco avoids this unsatisfactory novel, even though its three central characters say much about religion in general and Catholicism in particular. (Sources: Greene, *A Sort of Life*, 155; Hoskins, 14; Pendleton, 62, 63; Shelden, 141, 159; Sherry I, 395; Wolfe, 29)

RUSSE, FATHER (*The Tenth Man*). He was a priest at St. Jean de Brinac, who died (1943) after 40 years of service to the community. Chavel knew him and asks the new priest about him.

RUSSELL (*The End of the Affair*). Alfred Parkis tells Bendrix, while both are in the British Museum Reading Room, that he's working on the Russell case.

RUSSELL, (KEN) (*The Honorary Consul*). During the time of the Fortnum crisis, the British Embassy in Buenos Aires, peopled by Sir Henry Belfrage and Crichton among others, is agitated by more important demands for action telegraphed to it. One subject concerns the propriety of the British entry in the Mar del Plata film festival. It is "by some man called Russell" and is allegedly pornographic.

Greene thus gives a plug to his friend Ken Russell (b. 1927), a British film director who, according to Gene D. Phillips, would have faithfully adapted *A Burnt-Out Case* by using much of its original dialogue. The porno movie alluded to could be Russell's *The Music Lovers* (1971), a wild biography of Peter Tchaikovsky, but much more likely is *The Devils* (also 1971), a sensational depiction of atrocities in a 17th-century French convent. (Source: Phillips, 145, 146)

RUTTLEDGE (*It's a Battlefield*). He was a suspect in the Streatham Common murder. However, when fingerprinted, he was found innocent and released.

Michael Shelden points out that Raymond Greene,* Greene's brother, and Raymond's friend Hugh Ruttledge climbed one of the slopes of Mount Everest (1933). Shelden purports that Greene was jealous of their physical prowess and therefore named the murder suspect as he did. (Source: Shelden, 181)

RYCKER, ANDRÉ (*A Burnt-Out Case*). He is a middle-aged manager of a palm-oil factory near Luc. After six years of seminary study with Jesuits, he is wise in theological theory but hypocritically sanctimonious about sex. He has been married for two years to young Marie Rycker, whom he demeans and dominates. Rycker puts an erroneous religious spin on Querry's burned-out escapism and tells Parkinson that Querry is a saintly, selfless, heroic builder in remote Africa. When Marie lies to her husband that Querry as the father of her unborn child, Rycker arms himself and hunts for Querry.

Rycker's last name resembles that of Charles Ryder, the painter-narrator of *Brideshead Revisited* (1945) by Evelyn Waugh, Greene's close friend. In a *Collected Edition* introduction, Greene says Waugh feared he was being depicted in the character of Rycker. Norman Sherry posits that Querry's feeling compelled to listen to Rycker's complaints echoes "Greene['s] listening ... to hundreds of letters from troubled souls yearning to be heard." A. A. DeVitis observes that "for the dilettante theologian Greene has little more than contempt, and Rycker is the best example of this attitude." Paul O'Prey diagnoses Rycker as suffering "from what can only be called a spiritual inferiority complex." (Sources: DeVitis, 116; Greene, *A Burnt-Out Case, Collected Edition,* xi-xiv passim; O'Prey, 97; Sherry III, 195)

RYCKER, MARIE (*A Burnt-Out Case*). She is a naive, convent-bred young lady, whose favorite reading is romantic fiction. Marie's father worked in the Upper Congo for the same company dealing in palm oil that André Rycker, her future husband, does. Her father sent her delicate mother home, evidently to Belgium, to have her baby. Marie, married two years, dislikes life near Luc, even though she was "bred a *colon.*" When she meets Querry, who regards her as a child who can be trusted if he pities and befriends her, she lies that he is responsible for her pregnancy.

Norman Sherry contends that Marie Rycker and André Rycker are based on Yvonne Cloette* and her husband Jacques Cloette. Jacques, perhaps. Yvonne, never. (Source: Sherry III, 195, 252)

SAABATO, ERNESTO (1911–). Argentine novelist. *See* Montez.

SAAVEDRA, DOCTOR JORGE JULIO (*The Honorary Consul*). He is an aging, conservative novelist. Saavedra is proud of his Argentine family background. His great-grandfather was the provincial governor; his grandfather was killed in a duel with a gaucho. Also proud of alleged literary ability, Saavedra feels he has a demon whereas other writers merely have talent. Plarr, Saavedra's physician and indulgent friend, regards his novels as having "heavy music," showing awareness of "destiny," but naively regarding life as "noble or dignified." Humphries dismisses Saavedra as a "pompous ass." Saavedra, though aware of his limitations, is good at rationalizing. For example, he visits Señora Sanchez's brothel weekly for balance and for research into the poor among us. Plarr is impressed when Saavedra, for romance and adventure, volunteers to replace Fortnum as a hostage during the revolutionaries' botched kidnapping caper. Saavedra offers a fulsome eulogy at Plarr's funeral.

Greene's literary theories are totally opposite those he puts into Saavedra's head and writings.

SAGRIN ("A Visit to Morin"). He is a character in Pierre Morin's novel *Le Bien Pensant.* Sagrin's naturalistic rejection of orthodox Catholic dogma is thought, wrongly at it turns out, to reflect Morin's own beliefs.

SALLY (*The Confidential Agent*). She is Forbes's mistress, with lodgings in Shepherd's

Market. Forbes finds time for a quickie with Sally before whisking D. from London to Southcrawl. Forbes tells D. that Sally is a physical-fitness advocate.

Sally's address may contain a submerged pun. With his rod and his staff, Forbes, like a good shepherd, will look out for her, even mark her. Pun-seekers abound: Peter Wolfe suggests that "D. comes to see life through Rose Cullen glasses." (Source: Wolfe, 88)

SALLY ("A Shocking Accident"). She is Jerome's fiancée, 25. Jerome is happy when she responds to the report that his father was killed when a pig fell on him by asking, as Jerome did years earlier, what happened to the pig.

SALMON, MRS. ("The Case for the Defence"). She is the careful, honest witness, 56, in the Adams trial for Mrs. Parker's murder. Mrs. Salmon has a Scotch accent.

SAM (*Brighton Rock*). He is the owner of a place where some of Pinkie's gang drink. (He may be the Samuel mentioned later as a bookie.)

SAMPSON, LADY ("Under the Garden"). She is Sir Nigel Sampson's wife. Sir Nigel rushes his consultation with Wilditch because he must meet his lady at Liverpool Street.

SAMPSON, SIR NIGEL ("Under the Garden"). He is an eminent London surgeon, with tousled white hair and dressed in tweeds. Called by Dr. Cave into Wilditch's case, Sir Nigel performs a bronchoscopic examination, finds lung cancer, and advises surgery. Wilditch images Sir Nigel as a fisherman regarding patients dispassionately as objects to be reeled in.

SAMUEL (*Brighton Rock*). He is the bookie who works under Tate and pays Spicer when his horse Memento Mori places. He is also called Sammy. (He may be the Sam mentioned earlier as the owner of the place where Pinkie's friends sometimes drink.)

SAMUEL ("The Trial of Pan"). God has a brief vision of this intriguing, crafty "minister."

SANCHEZ, LUIS (*Our Man in Havana*). He is a fancy, white-haired professor of Comparative Education. Wormold finds his name on the Country Club membership list and puts him on his fake spy list as a source of information about economics. Wormold visits Sanchez's home and finds him dancing with his mistress, his wife Maria being absent. Sanchez points a revolver at Wormold, whom he thinks Maria has hired to investigate his love life. Wormold says he wishes only to warn him of possible danger, since Engineer Cifuentes has been shot at.

SANCHEZ, MARIA (*Our Man in Havana*). She is Professor Luis Sanchez's wife. While Maria is away from home, Sanchez welcomes his mistress there. The lovers are afraid of Maria, because she is the cardinal's cousin and got him to investigate them. Sanchez's mistress understandably suspects Wormold has been hired by Maria to spy on them.

SANCHEZ, SEÑORA (*The Honorary Consul*). She is the stout, dimpled, coldly smiling madam of the brothel frequented by Escobar, Fortnum, Plarr, and Saavedra, among others. María worked there but was murdered. Teresa also works there. Fortnum met Clara there. Señora Sanchez not only employed Clara but also taught her to read and write a little.

SANCHO (*Monsignor Quixote*) *see* **ZANCAS, ENRIQUE**

SANDALE, LORD ("The Basement Room"). He is a man whom Philip Lane and Baines see stepping out of the Army and Navy building. Baines is so happy that his mean wife is out of town that he doesn't envy Lord Sandale — at least, Philip thinks so.

SANGER, LORD GEORGE ("When Greek Meets Greek"). He is a person whose name Lord Driver tells his suspicious landlady is a "good Christian" name like his own. Evidently Sanger's title was as bogus as Driver's.

SANTA TERESA (*Our Man in Havana*). She is Milly Wormold's horse Seraphina's mother.

SATAN ("The Improbable Tale of the Archbishop of Canterbury"). This evil lunatic brings such warfare to Britain that the Archbishop of Canterbury shoots him. Dying, Satan tells the archbishop not to worry, because he is God and rashly made himself in man's image. Satan dies laughing.

SAUNDERS ("Murder for the Wrong Reason"). He is a Scotland Yard driver who is bringing Groves, an able detective, to Collinson's murder scene. While they are en route, Detective-Inspector Mason solves the mystery.

SAUNDERS (*This Gun for Hire*). He is a policeman doggedly loyal and grateful to Mather. Saunders's stammer doesn't diminish his effectiveness. He shoots Raven to death, after which he chances to see and attend a meeting held by Phelps to help stammerers.

SAUNDERS, MISS ("Special Duties"). She was hired by Ferraro, a Catholic businessman in London, as his assistant confidential secretary. She is to accumulate indulgences by praying for him. She came to him recommended as a convent prize-winner for piety. When one day Ferraro chances to check on her, he finds not only that she isn't praying at St. Praxted's, as she asserted, but also that the church doesn't exist and that she is with a boyfriend.

SAUNDERS, MRS. ("Special Duties"). She is the invalid mother with whom Miss Saunders is said to be living. At least this is what Hopkinson, Ferraro's secretary, tells Ferraro.

SAVAGE (*The End of the Affair*). His detective agency employs Prentice and Alfred Parkis. When Bendrix wants someone to investigate Sarah Miles, Savage assigns the job to Parkis.

SAVAGE ("Men at Work"). Miss Manners tells Skate, her supervisor in the Book Committee in the Ministry of Information, that Savage just telephoned to say he had joined the Air Force and wished to come over and show Skate his uniform. Skate answers that Savage was always a little "wild."

SAVAGE (*Our Man in Havana*). He is a secret-service agent in London. When the Chief and Hawthorne confab in London about Wormold's drawings of the non-existent military construction, the Chief says Savage said one sketch reminded him of vacuum-cleaner parts.

SAVAGE, MISS (*The Ministry of Fear*). She was a Cambridgeshire teacher who, Rowe tells his mother in a dream, used to read him stories about violence he and his mother thought didn't exist in the real world. He now knows it does.

SAVORY, QUIN C. (*Orient Express*). He is a popular novelist, whose *The Great Gay Round* has sold 100,000 copies. Boarding the train at Ostend, Savory intends to travel to Constantinople and beyond, to the Far East, to seek new material. Mabel Warren interviews him, finds his Cockney accent phony, and repeats in her column his dislike of D. H. Lawrence, James Joyce, and Bohemianism, and his preference for William Shakespeare, Geoffrey Chaucer, and Charles Reade. Janet Pardoe flirts with Savory on the train but dumps him in Constantinople to favor Myatt instead.

Quin Savory's *The Great Gay Round* title may owe something to that of F. Scott Fitzgerald's *The Great Gatsby* (1925), in which the name Quinn appears on the narrator Nick Carraway's list of Gatsby's summer guests. Greene's initials are "G.G.," like that of Fitzgerald's great novel. J. B. Priestley,* the British novelist, thought he was the model for the satirically depicted Savory and threatened to sue for libel unless parts of the book were altered to his specifications. Greene reluctantly complied. (Sources: Greene, *A Sort of Life*, 217–18; Greene, *Ways of Escape*, 30–31; Sherry I, 435–37)

SCHMIDT (*The Third Man*). He is the porter at Sacher's Hotel, where Martins stays. Crabbin tells Martins that Schmidt will give him daily meal tickets.

SCHMIDT, ANNA (*The Third Man*). She is a Hungarian actress in Vienna, living in the British zone and carrying fake Austrian documentation obtained for her by Harry Lime, whose mistress she was until he faked his death. Martins learns about her through Kurtz, meets her to learn more about his friend Harry, falls in love with her. Even after she learns Harry, alive and in hiding, illegally sold diluted penicillin that damaged and killed children, she still loves him. Harry curries favor with the Russians by informing them about Anna, who gets illegally seized by the Russians but is rescued by Colonel Calloway. Anna and Martins attend Harry's real burial and walk together into the sunset.

SCHMIDT, FATHER ("Church Militant"). He is a practical, old, white-haired priest. He lives with settled nuns at a well-managed, well-guarded mission in Niguru, Kenya. He is alarmed when the Archbishop announces plans to place French nuns in this Mau Mau region.

SCHMIDT, FRAU ("The Root of All Evil"). She is Herr Schmidt's wife, a little over 60.

SCHMIDT, HERR ("The Root of All Evil"). He is a leading member, over 70, of the wine-drinking club.

SCHULTZ, FRAU (*The Name of Action*). When Frau Gruner gets Demassener's permission to have a priest attend her executed son's burial, she asks for a similar favor for Frau Schultz, whose son has also been executed. Demassener refuses to listen to Frau Gruner and orders her removed.

SCOBIE, CATHERINE (*The Heart of the Matter*). She was Louise and Henry Scobie's daughter. Catherine died, age nine, in England, while Louise was with her, three years earlier. Henry was then on duty in Sierra Leone.

SCOBIE, HENRY (*The Heart of the Matter*). He is the assistant commissioner of police, in Freetown, Sierra Leone, having served there 15 years. A Downham school graduate and a veteran of World War I, Henry married Louise 14 years ago in Ealing, England. Both devout Catholics, they had a daughter, Catherine, who died at age nine. Louise calls Henry "Ticki," which he dislikes. Henry is good at his job until Louise, toward whom he feels more pity and responsibility than love, wants to vacation in South Africa. He borrows money for the trip from Yusef, a corrupt Syrian merchant; falls in love with Helen Rolt, a torpedoed-ship survivor; participates in diamond smuggling at the demand of Yusef, who blackmails him with an indiscreet letter Henry wrote Helen and Yusef obtained; feels guilty when he is suspicious of his servant Ali and Yusef has Ali murdered; and receives communion from Father Rank while not having repented committing adultery and after having been given absolution. To rid God of his vile presence and to provide peace for Helen and Louise, Henry Scobie commits suicide.

Cedric Watts notes that Greene's wife Vivien Greene* called him Ticki. William Cash confirms her use of this nickname and Greene's disliking it. A. A. DeVitis contends that "[p]ride is ... Scobie's great flaw of character, but ... commingled with a compassionate awareness of misery and unhappiness" in others. It may be added that the word "pity," in connection with Scobie's concern for others, is used often, though less than it is in either *The Ministry of Fear* or *The Heart of the Matter,* and also less here than the word "responsibility," again with reference to Scobie's constantly felt need to attend to others. K. C. Joseph Kurismmootil concludes that Scobie "was a sinner, and he was sinned against, but he was no worse than most of us; what evil he caused he did not himself will, but it was the fruit of his confusion; he was truly a better man than most." In discussing Louise's gripe to Father Rank about her husband's sinful life, Heinz Antor say that Greene, as well as Father Rank, regards the likelihood "of divine forgiveness" overriding "the worst of sins." George Orwell, in a review blasting *The Heart of the Matter*, says of Scobie this: "White through it all, with a stiff upper lip, he had gone to what he believed was certain damnation out of pure gentlemanliness." Orwell adds this: "If he believed in Hell, he would not risk going there merely to spare the feelings of a couple of neurotic women." Greene himself criticized his depiction of Scobie, saying that "the religious scruples of Scobie [are] too extreme," and further that his character "was intended to show [but did not?] that pity can be the expression of an almost monstrous pride." (Sources: Antor, 101; Cash, 62; DeVitis, 86; Greene, *Ways of Escape*, 125; Kurismmootil, 134; Orwell, IV 440, 442; Watts, 57)

SCOBIE, LOUISE (*The Heart of the Matter*). She is Henry Scobie's unbalanced, thin, awkward wife, 38. Both are Catholics. Since their young daughter Catherine's death, they have devolved into a marginalized couple. Louise dislikes colonial life in Sierra Leone, alienates fellow Britishers by professing excessive love of literature, and is led to believe she could write professionally. She fends off Wilson's immature advances. She indirectly causes Henry's downfall by insisting on a vacation in South Africa that he must borrow money to finance. Learning of her Henry's affair with Helen Rolt, Louise returns home, reminds him of his obligation to attend Mass, and is partly the cause of his suicide.

SCOTT (*England Made Me*). Scott and James are British solicitors. For 20 years they have sent Minty his £15 monthly family allowance. Minty is pleased when the September 20 [1930] one arrives. Since he recognizes RS as reference initials, Scott's first name may begin with the letter R. (*See* RS.)

"THE SECOND DEATH" (1929). Short story. (Character: Rachel.) The domineering, querulous, husbandless mother of an ugly, womanizing man, something over 30, finds the his friend, the narrator, staring at a caterpillar on a swaying leaf, crawling toward a twig, over a pool. He doesn't know whether it got to safety or dropped, because the woman rushes him to her son, who she says is dying in their house. The narrator, who first arrived in the village 10 years earlier and soon met the young fellow, enters the bedroom but doubts the fellow is dying. After all, the mother a while back thought her son was dead and "premature[ly]" hastened a funeral for him; a strange roadside doctor noticed the "corpse" was alive. Moreover, a week ago the narrator helped the fellow sneak out of the house to rendezvous with Rachel, a bosomy farm girl down the road. The village doctor, now in attendance, assures the narrator the fellow is dying and desires to unburden himself to his friend immediately. They talk. First, the fellow recalls that long-ago time when he was supposed to have died but how on the way to his burial he was saved by a doctor. Next, he confesses that among his sexual conquests was an innocent, ignorant girl. Finally, he says he dreamed of being dead, standing in the road, and a crowd around someone — that miraculous physician. He vowed to turn sinless following this "second chance," was decent a few years, but relapsed. Feeling that in death there is eternal consciousness, he beseeches the narrator to assure him that his encounter with death, together with the implications of his dream thereafter, represents the impossible. The narrator, jocose all along, glibly says such miracles are outmoded, otherwise they would have heard of similar ones. The dying fellow replies that there are such stories about miraculous cures managed in the village by that roadside healer, even one about a blind man cured by his touch. The narrator starts his negative talk again but then notices his clammy friend is dead. Shocked, he recalls that once, long ago, he himself felt a touch as of spittle on his eyelids and that, upon opening his eyes, saw a treelike man walking away accompanied by other trees.

Greene characterizes his narrator strangely. He is a pub-crawler, would have had his way with Rachel too except that she evaded him, hopes his friend will hurry up and die, delays revealing the truth about his encounter with a savior figure, and callously defines the dying man's mother as wretch, vixen, hypocrite. Which of course she may have been. Greene teases astute readers to remember the Bible while reading "The Second Death." The story combines echoes of Lazarus (John 11:1–45); a girl named Rachel, whose Biblical antecedent, though Jacob's beautiful wife, was also a duplicitous thief (Gen. 31:19, 34–35); Christ's curing the blind man by anointing his eyes with spittle-moistened clay and telling him to go wash at the pool of Siloam (John 9:6–7); and an hallucinated crucifixion scene. When the mother looks for the narrator, she finds him beside a pool and under trees. An archaic meaning of "tree" is the cross on which Christ was crucified.

Gangeshwar Rai explicates the endangered caterpillar as existential symbol, "suggestive of man's life in this world. The possibility of death [Rai continues] is always present, yawning like a chasm, before man. But most men remain lost in the illusions of life in this world." Richard Kelly regards the frantic mother as a widow, while A. A. DeVitis says that the narrator is also "dying." But, literally, is she, and is he? (Sources: DeVitis, 155; Kelly, 18; Rai, 107)

SECOND SECRETARY, THE (*The Confidential Agent*). He was an official at the embassy in London representing D.'s country. D. feels the secretary may be the only person he can trust there. When D. arrives, he learns secretary is no longer stationed there.

SECRETARY FOR PUBLIC WORKS, THE (*The Comedians*). He is one official partly responsible for the tourist site in the proposed city of Duvalierville, according to what the new Secretary for Social Welfare tells Smith.

SECRETARY FOR SOCIAL WELFARE, THE (*The Comedians*). He replaces the deceased Dr. Philipot, and is Colonel Gracia's fat, toothy aide. He shows Smith around the site of Duvalierville and tries to get him to participate in governmental fraud to their mutual advantage. Smith moves to Santo Domingo instead.

SECRETARY FOR THE INTERIOR, THE (*The Comedians*). He is an official Petit Pierre says Smith might ask to help Jones.

In *A House of Reputation* (c. 1957), Greene's disowned play, the inexperienced son of the powerful Minister of the Interior visits a pleasantly run brothel; meets Marta, a prostitute with no belief in love; falls in love with her; proposes marriage to her, is refused; ruins her in the belief that, by having his father close the place, she will come to him; she will move to the streets. (Source: Sherry III, 30l-l0 passim)

SECRETARY FOR TOURISM (*The Comedians*). The new Secretary for Social Welfare tells Smith at the Duvalierville site that this official is partly responsible for Duvalierville's eventual tourist site.

SECRETARY OF EDUCATION, THE (*The Comedians*). He is the official who, according to a Petit Pierre newspaper column, is announcing a six-year plan to eliminate illiteracy in north Haiti. Brown the narrator sarcastically adds that Hurricane Hazel (1954) permanently eliminated much illiteracy in the interior.

During the terrorist regime of François Duvalier* (1907–1971), president of Haiti (1957-1971), illiteracy remained at 90 percent.

SECRETARY OF EMBASSY (*Doctor Fischer of Geneva*). Jones won't drown himself, because he has had a phobia of death by drowning ever since a Secretary of Embassy pushed him into the deep part of a *piscine*.

The official must have served in France.

SECRETARY OF STATE, THE (*The Comedians*). He is a Haitian official about to leave for New York to report to the United Nations. Brown takes Smith to see him just in time to bribe him to effect Jones's release from prison.

SEGURA (*Our Man in Havana*). He was Captain Segura's father, deceased. Rumor has it that Captain Segura has a cigarette case made of human skin. Wormold asks him about it. He says the skin was taken from a police officer who tortured his father to death.

SEGURA, CAPTAIN (*Our Man in Havana*). He is a tough-tender police officer in Vedado, an Havana suburb. Known as the Red Vulture because he resorts to torture and mutilation, Secura gently courts Milly Wormold, to whom he sells a horse named Seraphina. The captain warns Wormold of various dangers, and plays draughts with him so drunkenly that Wormold borrows his revolver before going after Carter.

In *Ways of Escape*, Greene identifies the model for Segura. He was Captain Ventura, the "notorious police chief" of Fulgencio Batista y Zaldivar (1901–1973), dictator of Cuban (1940–1944, 1952–1959). Agreeing, Claudia Lightfoot says that "the infamous Captain Segura, chief of the Vedado police ... [,] is based on the equally infamous real person of police chief Ventura," during part of Batista's time. Enrique Oltuski provides chilling details concerning Estaban Ventura, Havana's chief of police. Ventura murdered students and revolutionaries. He was indicted by a courageous magistrate (1958) shortly before the fall of Batista, after which he escaped to exile in the United States (January 1959). Greene's fictional Segura is a bit too gentle toward Wormold, and far too gentle toward Milly, if one is to believe she is the object of his supposedly old-fashioned attentions. Greene is only half-right when he admits that he turned "savage" Ventura into "cynical" Segura. (Sources: Greene, *Ways of Escape*, 251–52, 257; Lightfoot, 91; Oltuski, 107, 294)

A SENSE OF SECURITY. Greene mentions *A Sense of Security* as the title of "a spy story" he started. (*See The Human Factor.*) (Source: Greene, *A Sort of Life*, 184)

SERAPHINA (*Our Man in Havana*) *see* **WORMOLD, MILLY**

SERAPHINA (*Our Man in Havana*). She is the chestnut horse Milly Wormold buys from Segura and later sells back to him. She gives her father breeding details: Seraphina is out of Santa Teresa by Ferdinand of Castile, and is registered in the stud book.

SERGEANT (*Our Man in Havana*). He is a policeman in Santiago from whom Wormold tries to gain sympathy by discussing his imaginary girlfriend Dr. Emma Hasselbacher.

SEVERN, MRS. BEATRICE (*Our Man in Havana*). She is Peter Severn's ex-wife, 31. Beatrice is the agent sent by the Chief in London, at Miss Jenkinson's recommendation, to assist Wormold in Havana, despite the fact that Beatrice, who is half-French, speaks French but not Spanish. She pleases Wormold by squirting Segura with a siphon at the Tropicana. She brings Rudy to help Wormold. She accompanies Wormold when he searches for his fake agents and discovers he fibs. The two fall in love and are together at the end in London.

Beatrice praises Wormold for being more loyal to love than to his country. This isn't surprising, given the gist of Greene's lecture, "The Virtue of Disloyalty," delivered in Hamburg, Germany (1969) and criticizing Shakespeare for never joining political rebels. Norman Sherry discusses the lecture and quotes extensively from it. Michael Meyer paraphrases Greene's expressed dislike of Shakespeare's *King Lear*. Leopoldo Duran presents Greene on Shakespeare more thoroughly, saying he disliked *Hamlet* and *The Tempest*, and preferred *Antony and Cleopatra*, *Othello*, and *Troilus and Cressida*. (Sources: Duran, 44–45; Meyer, 59; Sherry III, 484–88)

SEVERN, PETER (*Our Man in Havana*). He is evidently Beatrice Severn's handsome, immature ex-husband, 40. He rose from writing for popular magazines to covering UNESCO conferences.

SHADES OF GREENE. This is the clever title of a 1976 Thames Television series adapting 18 short stories by Greene. The series was produced by Alan Cooke, who advised with several story consultants, including Greene's brother Hugh Greene* and Greene himself. The following stories were adapted: "Alas, Poor Maling," "The Blue Film," "The Case for the Defence," "Chagrin in Three Parts," "A Chance for Mr. Lever," "Cheap in August," "The Destructors," "A Drive in the Country," "Dream of a Strange Land," "The Invisible Japanese Gentlemen," "A Little Place off the Edgeware Road," "Mortmain," "The Over-Night Bag," "The Root of All Evil," "Special Duties," "Two Gentle People," "Under the Garden," and "When Greek Meets Greek." (Sources: Falk, 215; Parkinson, 698–99)

SHAW, [GEORGE] BERNARD *(Travels with My Aunt)*. Aunt Augusta tells Henry she once attended an important literary figure's funeral, also attended by Edward Carpenter, Dr. Havelock Ellis, [James] Ramsay MacDonald, E[dith]. Nesbit, [George] Bernard Shaw (1856–1950], Irish-born man of letters) and his wife, and H. G. Wells.

THE SHIPWRECKED *see* ***ENGLAND MADE ME***

"A SHOCKING ACCIDENT" (1957). Short story. (Characters: Jerome, Sally, Wordsworth.)

1. Jerome, nine, is told to report to Mr. Wordsworth, housemaster of his school. It seems that Jerome's father, a widowed traveling writer, who Jerome has imagined was a gun runner of a Secret Service agent, has been in an accident. Jerome wonders in what romantic way. Was he shot? No. Wordsworth says a pig, kept and fed on a balcony in Naples, grew too heavy, broke the balcony, and fell on him and killed him. Wordsworth suppresses his laughter. Jerome asks what happened to the pig.

2. When Jerome tells about the event, he gets nicknamed Pig. Jerome often hears his paternal aunt ramblingly tell the story. When Jerome, now a chartered accountant, wonders whether anyone might wish to write the biography of his father, though undistinguished,

and seek details from him, he considers two responses — tell it so circuitously that no laughter ensues, or tell it with utter brevity. Jerome becomes engaged to Sally, still sweet at 25. Stalling, he tells her his father died in a street accident. Sally's only response is to warn him not to drive fast. He must introduce Sally to his aunt. She rambles about her brother's writings and concludes that he got letters from his readers after the pig fell on him. Sally merely exclaims about things happening out of a clear sky. Taxiing off with her and relieved she didn't laugh at how his father died, Jerome kisses her with unique passion and offers a penny for her thoughts. Sally wonders what happened to the pig. He says "they" probably ate it for dinner.

Richard Kelly observes that "A Shocking Event" represents "a comic genius [in Greene] that has never been fully realized or appreciated," showing, as it and certain other works do, "his sense of the absurd and the comic twists of life." A. A. DeVitis notes that the story delicately balances "farce and pathos." Quentin Falk reports that "A Shocking Accident" was made into a 25-minute movie (1982). (Sources: DeVitis, 179; Falk, 216–17; Kelly, 53)

SIMCOX, JOSHUA ("Alas, Poor Maling"). He founded the Simcox Newsprint Company, in the nineteenth century. His descendent, Sir Joshua Simcox, now heads the company.

SIMCOX, SIR JOSHUA ("Alas, Poor Maling"). He directs the Simcox Newsprint Company and wants to merge it with Wesby Hythe's Hythe Newsprint Company. But the stomach of Maling, his secretary, rumbles inopportunely and spoils the deal. Sir Joshua has a Yorkshire accent.

SIMMONS (*This Gun for Hire*). He is a serious medical student. Therefore Fergusson and his light-hearted fellow students criticize him.

SIMON (*A Burnt-Out Case*). He was a native who died in prison almost 20 years earlier. Colin tells Querry that the partially Christianized Africans in the region pray to Yezu Klisto and also to Simon, believing he will rise from the dead.

SIMON (*The Quiet American*). The Simon Frères shop is near Phan-Van-Muoi's garage.

SIMPSON, MRS. AMY (*It's a Battlefield*). She has been a servant for 60 years. She now cooks for the Assistant Commissioner at his flat, complains about his behavior, but is concerned for his well-being.

SINCLAIR (*The Ministry of Fear*). This clergyman, garbed in cylindrical black, is a member of the spy ring. He fails to persuade Rowe to put up for auction the cake he won at the fête. Sinclair reappears as a neighborly vicar at Dr. Forester's sanatorium when Prentice, Rowe, and others investigate activities there. Prentice orders Sinclair to return to his vicarage and remain there.

SKATE, RICHARD ("Men at Work"). He is a would-be playwright employed by the Book Committee of the Ministry of Information. His wife and daughter, who dislike him, live outside much-bombed London. Skate hates but endures his paper-pushing job. He brings a useless agenda to weekly committee meetings. After one verbose, procrastinating session, he looks out a window and sees R.A.F. pilots returning "home after work."

Anthony Mockler calls Skate "Skate/Greene." Greene worked in the Ministry of Information (1940), saw himself as a perfunctory functionary, left quickly, joined the Secret Intelligence Service (1941), and went to Sierra Leone. In "Men at Work," the Ministry building is described as tall, heartless, stuffy, smelly, and with its staff spreading like a fungus within. (Source: Mockler, 171)

SLATER, MRS. (*Our Man in Havana*). The teller at the bank where Wormold is withdrawing some money delays helping him when a man named Henry phones and the two chat about various matters, including their friend Mrs. Slater.

SMILEY ("The Blessing"). He is reporter Weld's chief. Smiley sent Weld to cover the Archbishop's tank-blessing ceremony perhaps knowing Weld's pacifism and hoping he would write unobjectively and thus damage his professional reputation.

SMITH (*The Captain and the Enemy*) see **BAXTER, JIM**

SMITH (*The Captain and the Enemy*) see **CAPTAIN, THE**

SMITH, MRS. (*The Comedians*). She is William Abel Smith's old-fashioned, contented, naively liberal wife. They have been happily married 35 years. The two are from Wisconsin, made trouble opposing racism in Nashville, Tennessee, and have come to Haiti to encourage vegetarianism. From a balcony of Brown's Trianon hotel, Mrs. Smith, in funny haircurlers, rebukes Concasseur and his men so bravely in her fractured French that she saves Brown from being beaten, perhaps even killed.

SMITH, WILLIAM ABEL (*The Comedians*). He is an old, strong, sincere, courageous idealist. He has pale blue eyes and white hair. He and his affectionate wife, both from Wisconsin, were roughed up in Nashville, Tennessee, for participating in freedom-bus rides. Smith ran on the vegetarian ticket and lost to President Harry S. Truman (1948). The Smiths voyage on the *Medea* to Port-au-Prince to start a vegetarian center but have too much sense to fall for fraudulent governmental officials requiring bribes. Smith attempts to help Brown and Jones. The Smiths take their vegetarian campaign to Santo Domingo. Smith tries to avoid observing pain because doing so implies criticism.

Greene by giving Smith the initials W.A.S. may be suggesting that his idealism, though laudatory, is passé. Also, when providing him two-syllable first and middle names, Greene may have thought of Gerard Corley Smith (1909–1997). This Cambridge-educated Smith was the British ambassador to Haiti (1960–1962), until he was expelled for officially complaining about President François Duvalier's terrorist tactics against Haitians and foreign residents alike. Cedric Watts suggests that the "anti–American theme [in *The Comedians*] is to some extent counter-balanced by the sympathetic portrayal of Mr. Smith, a liberal former presidential candidate, and his intrepid wife." But Greene unbalances his light, left-handed praise of the naive American Smiths by dropping hint after hint concerning American racism, intermittent support of Duvalier, arms aid to the Dominican Republic, the Pentagon, the CIA, and fat, silly, fun-loving American tourists. V. S. Pritchett calls the Smiths "slow-motion slapstick, but [he adds] they have their courage and dignity."

Norman Sherry finds parallels between the well-intentioned but naive Smiths and American artists Harry Gottlieb and his wife Eugenie Gershoy, both friends of Greene. They went to Haiti so that Gottlieb could teach native artists the technique of silk screening, the products of which they could sell to tourists. Haitian officials promised to help with materials but wanted kickbacks; nothing came of the venture. (Sources: Sherry III, 351–53, opp. 478; Pritchett, 84; Watts, 76)

SMUDGE (*Travels with My Aunt*). This was a dog Lucinda O'Toole once owned and liked to talk to. Therefore she tells Henry she'd like to call him Smudge, and does.

SMYTHE, MISS (*The End of the Affair*). She is Richard Smythe's live-in, invalid sister. She admits Bendrix, who poses as Bridges, and Lance Parkis, whom "Bridges" introduces as his son Arthur James Bridges. She gives Lance so much orangeade that he vomits when he gets outside.

SMYTHE, RICHARD (*The End of the Affair*). He is an atheistic, Rationalist preacher-tutor living with his sister Miss Smythe near Bendrix and Henry and Sarah Miles. Smythe has graceful hands and also handsome features, marred, however, by a strawberry birthmark on his left cheek. Sarah consults him in an effort to disbelieve in God, but his angry words backfire. Bendrix goes to Smythe wrongly thinking he is Sarah's lover. (*See* X.) Shortly before her death, Sarah kissed Smythe's repulsive birthmark. Smythe obtains a lock of her hair, which, along with the healing of his birthmark, shakes his own antireligious beliefs.

SMYTHE-PHILLIPS, MRS. A. J. (*The Ministry of Fear*). She is thanked by letter for donating flour and tea to the Free Mothers.

SNAKEY (*The Heart of the Matter*). She is a woman from Downham in a photograph owned by Harris. He and Wilson both recognize her partly because of her squint.

SNOW (*Brighton Rock*). His is the popular restaurant that figures in much action. One of Hale's Kolly Kibber tickets is placed there not by Hale but by Spicer, on Pinkie's order; Rose works there; Pinkie hides there; Rose is discharged from there.

SOREL, CAPTAIN (*The Quiet American*). He is a French officer at Phat Diem with whom Fowler plays a dice game. At the time, Fowler also passes his whisky around in the officers' quarters.

SOPPELSA (*This Gun for Hire*). He is a wealthy, influential friend of Sir Marcus. Soppelsa entertains Sir Marcus, Mrs. Cranbeim, Rosen, and Mrs. Ziffo, on his yacht when they are cruising near Rhodes.

SPARROW (*England Made Me*). While at Farrant's cremation, Minty is reminded he attended the funeral of Sparrow, his school chum.

SPARROW, DETECTIVE-SERGEANT JOHN (*Travels with My Aunt*). He is a short, middle-aged London policeman. His broken nose makes his face notable. Sparrow courteously questions Henry about Wordworth and his marijuana. Later, he and his superior, Detective-Inspector Woodrow, grill Henry about Augusta's involvement with Visconti and A.D.

Greene says that as a private joke he "christened" John Sparrow "after that elegant scholar the ex–Warder of All Souls." Echoing this, Norman Sherry asserts that "Sergeant Sparrow ... [is] not based on but nevertheless named after that generous Oxford scholar and poet, John Sparrow." This unexpanded reference is to John Hanbury Angus Sparrow (1906–1992). (Sources: Greene, *Ways of Escape*, 297; Sherry II, 494–95)

"SPECIAL DUTIES" (1954). Short story. (Characters: Father Dewes, Mrs. Ferraro, William Ferraro, Hopkinson, Maverick, Miss Saunders, Mrs. Saunders.)

William Ferraro, of the London firm Ferraro & Smith, is a wealthy Catholic businessman. For 10 years his imaginary-invalid wife has lived in a separate wing of their Montagu Square mansion. Fearing each day might bring death, she has installed Father Dewes, a wine- and whisky-bibber, in a room nearby. Ferraro, distressed after a bout with pneumonia three years ago but remaining busy, engaged a secretary named Miss Saunders, recommended as supremely devout, to go about London gathering Catholic indulgences for him. To date, she has accumulated 36,892.

On May 1, a springy Monday, Ferraro summons Miss Saunders to his office, reviews her typed lists of his indulgences for recent months, and learns she is going to St. Praxted's in Canon Wood to pray for him today. After a chophouse lunch, Ferraro is chauffeured about, sees ugly May-Day banners around Trafalgar Square, forgoes an impulse for some quality time in Richmond Park but instead proceeds to meet Miss Saunders at St. Praxted's. Ah, there is no such church. Another secretary provides him Miss Saunders's address. Going there, he spies on her. She is "inefficiently clothed" at an upstairs window, at least until a male arm gently "circled her waist." Back in Montagu Square, Ferraro, looking older, walks past his wall of French Impressionist paintings to his library, full of leather-bound volumes by dead authors. Chest pains. Decision time. He must find a more reliable personal secretary.

"Special Duties" satirizes the practice of Catholic doctrine of dispensing indulgences. The story has literary echoes, beginning with Geoffrey Chaucer's "Pardoner's Tale," the pardoner being a peddler of indulgences. Ferraro sounds like Ferrera, the Italian city which is the locale of "My Last Duchess" by Robert Browning, who also wrote "The Bishop Orders His Tomb at Saint Prexed's Church," that church, spelled without a "t," being in Rome. Greene's having Miss Saunders coin the name St. Prexted is delightful, the original Saint Prexedes being a second-century martyred virgin. Greene has Miss Saunders, surely a latitudinarian, hail from a convent he names Saint Latitudinaria. Why did Greene precisely date the action of "Special Duties"? May-Day fell on Monday in 1950. Any May-Day would have sufficed.

"Special Duties" was the subject of a 1976 television production. The cast included John Gielgud. *See Shades of Greene.* (Sources: Falk, 215; Kelly, 40)

SPICER (*Brighton Rock*). He is Pinkie's most troublesome gang member. Spicer and other thugs live in Billy Frank's rooming house. Older, pale, with bad bowels and a painful corn, Spicer has a girlfriend named Sylvie. He leaves a Kolley Kibber ticket at Snow's on Pinkie's order, to suggest that Hale was alive after really being murdered. When Spicer isn't standing firm and desires to buy into a pub with a friend in Nottingham, Pinkie tries to have Colleoni's men kill him. But they nonfatally attack both Spicer and Pinkie. So Pinkie pushes him over a rotten banister to his death. Spicer is called Spicey by friends.

SPILSBURY, SIR BERNARD ("The Overnight Bag"). Cooper's hired-car driver says he read in *The Cases of Sir Bernard Spilsbury* that corpses don't bruise.

SPOT (*The Confidential Agent*). He is a bald-headed guest at the Lido. A girl in pajamas asks him if a basketball game is starting.

SPOT (*The Ministry of Fear*). Rowe has a recurring childhood memory of a dog named Spot which so badly bit a rat that Rowe took pity on it and killed it.

SPOT (*Orient Express*). Coral Musker remembers that there was a dog named Spot when she went ratting in Nottingham with some miners.

STAMBOUL TRAIN (1932). Novel. See *Orient Express*

STARLING, CORPORAL (*The Third Man*). He is part of the Russian-controlled international patrol that seizes Anna Schmidt. Starling phones Colonel Calloway about the illegal action, and Calloway rescues her. When O'Brien, the American military police soldier, wrongly says the British don't know when they should make a proper stand, Starling doesn't bother to reply that he was at Dunkirk.

STAVROG (*Orient Express*). He figures inexplicably in Myatt's business-based dream, in which Eckman is criticized.

STEFENSON (*England Made Me*). He is an official in Krogh's company. Krogh feels no need to consult Asplund, Bergsten, and Stefenson about minor matters such as signing checks, since he has a rubber stamp with their signatures.

STEIN, LEO (*Orient Express*). His company boxes currants in Constantinople. When Myatt arrives, he associates with Stein, who is also Jewish, and learns he wants to buy into Myatt's London-based company, become a director, and soon retire to play golf. Myatt also learns that Janet Pardoe, whom Myatt met on the train, is Stein's niece, hence half Jewish, and has traveled to Constantinople to vacation briefly with Stein and his wife. Myatt figures he can negotiate profitably with Stein and perhaps also marry Janet.

It is probably only a coincidence that Gertrude Stein (1874–1946), the expatriate American woman of letters, had a brilliant brother named Leo Stein (1872–1947). Greene modestly opines that Leo Stein and Kalebdjian are "presented with excellent brevity." (Source: Greene, *Ways of Escape*, 33)

STEIN, MRS. (*Orient Express*). As Leo Stein's wife, she likes the idea of having his niece, Janet Pardoe, come from Cologne to visit them in Constantinople. The Steins may be able to help Janet.

STEINER (*Doctor Fischer of Geneva*). He was a clerk working for Kips. When Fischer discovered his wife Anna and Steiner innocently enjoyed listening to musical records together, he paid Kips to fire Steiner. Steiner became a music-shop clerk. When he sees Anna-Luise Jones, her face reminds him of Anna, and he collapses, is hospitalized, and is comforted there by Jones. Steiner visits Fischer during the bomb party, intending to spit in his "God Almighty" face. Instead, Steiner winds up pitying him.

Haim Gordon judges that Steiner for years "suffered from his own cowardice, from his acceptance of the wickedness of Dr. Fischer, from his viewing of Dr. Fischer as if he were as omnipotent as God Almighty." Gordon adds: "Need I add that neither Henry Pulling [in *Travels with My Aunt*] nor Mr. Steiner is a person who has attained integrity?" Additionally, one may add that the price of integrity is often a little more than little people can afford to pony up, and that some readers may regard Steiner as frightened, then hopeless, then ill, and at last commendably forgiving. (Source: Gordon, 87)

STEPHEN ("May We Borrow Your Husband?"). He is a homosexual interior decorator, pushing 50, and Tony's lover. While vacationing in Antibes, Stephen and Tony seduce Peter Travis, who is starting a honeymoon with Poopy Travis. Observing some of this action, Harris regards Stephen as stupid and Tony as intelligent and cruel. Tony drops Stephen in the end and leaves him the chore of mollifying their client Mrs. Clarenty.

STEPHENS (*Rumour at Nightfall*). Chase remembers drinking with Stephens in London. He also recalls that Stephens was too quickly agreeable and amiable.

STILL (*The Ministry of Fear*). Still and Fishguard, patients in Dr. Forester's sanatorium, are disputatious at tennis and chess, but always quickly reconcile through fear Forester will send them to his sick bay.

STODGER (*England Made Me*). While lying to Minty, a Harrow man, that he is also a Harrow man, Farrant says that he was a member of Stodger's house at Harrow.

STONE, MAJOR (*The Ministry of Fear*). He is a trim, slightly demented patient in Dr. Forester's sanatorium. Stone tells Rowe, confined there as Richard Digby, that he saw some suspicious digging in the island pond and wants to "enfilade" it. Rowe tries to rescue Stone from Forester's sick bay but is too late to prevent Forester from killing him.

W. J. West hints that Major Stone may be based partly on Greene's cousin Benjamin Greene, whose pacifist tendencies during the war got him detained when the government enforced Emergency Powers regulations and whose mistreatment Greene feared might include his being straitjacketed in a cell. Michael Shelden identifies Benjamin Greene as the Nazi-sympathizing, anti-Jewish, anti-American son, 6 feet 8 inches, of Edward Greene, the wealthy brother of Greene's father Charles Greene.* (Sources: Shelden, 20, 23; West, 100)

STONE, MRS. (*The Ministry of Fear*). She is or was Major Stone's wife. Stone tells Rowe that she rightly deserted him, presumably when he showed signs of mental derangement.

STOWE ("I Spy"). He is a tobacconist whose living quarters are above his shop. His wife is more loving than he. Their son Charlie prefers her to his father, whose notice of the boy seems only spasmodic. The man is arrested for an alleged unspecified crime.

STOWE, CHARLIE (*The Confidential Agent*). He is a Benditch coal miner who dislikes authorities. The anarchistic boy-gang spreads the falsehood that D. is hiding at Stowe's house, knowing he won't let the police in without a warrant and this distraction may help D.

STOWE, CHARLIE ("I Spy"). This boy, 12, sneaks one night into his father's tobacco shop for a smoke, to prove his manliness to his buddies. From concealment, he sees two policemen enter with his father, then take him away. This saddens and scares Charlie, who senses he resembles his father, since both do things in darkness.

Richard Kelly thinks Charlie's last name suggests he's a stowaway. (Source: Kelly, 19)

STOWE, MRS. ("I Spy"). She is the boisterous, kind wife of a passive husband. She is well liked by everyone, including their son Charlie.

STRADANO (*Travels with My Aunt*). When Detective-Sergeant John Sparrow asks Henry if Augusta ever mentioned Stradano, and also Cossa, Passerati, and Tiberio Titi, Henry answers no.

STRANGEWAYS ("A Visit to Morin"). He was Dunlop's French teacher at Collingworth school, when Dunlop was 16. Strangeways, from Chile, was swarthy; his father was a Wolverhampton engineer; his mother came from Louisiana. In class, Strangeways neglected French syntax, read aloud and was read to aloud, and launched with youthful abandon into literary criticism of the text.

STROESSNER, ALFRED (1912–2006). He was the long-time president of Paraguay (1954–

1989). Born in Encarnación, Stroessner had a German immigrant father and a Paraguayan mother. He attended military school (1928), fought in the Chaco War (Paraguay vs. Bolivia, 1932–1935), studied at the Brazilian Army College (1940–1941), supported the Partido Colorado (1947), and was a colonel when he participated in the failed military uprising against President Natalicio Gonzáles. Stroessner obtained sanctuary in the Brazilian Embassy and fled in exile to Argentina (1948). He succeeded in the coup deposing President Raimondo Rolón, helped install President Felipe Molas López, led the Partido Colorado, and became brigadier general (1949) and Commander-in-Chief of the armed forces (1951). Maneuvering to gain U.S. anti–Communist support, Stroessner ran as the sole candidate for the presidency, was elected president (1954), and re-elected nine times (to 1988). He rarely traveled overseas but did visit the United States (1968, 1977), Japan (1972), Spain (1973), and South Africa (1974). His totalitarian rule was marked by ruthless oppression of the opposition. He was overthrown by the Movimiento Del 2 Febrero led by General Andrés Rodriguez, who became president and restored constitutional democracy. Stroessner was placed under house arrest, was allowed to fly to Brazil, and gained political asylum there (1989). Stroessner has two sons — one was an air force officer; the other abused alcohol and other drugs. (Alfredo Stroessner is the General in *The Honorary Consul* and *Travels with My Aunt*.)

W. J. West summarizes Greene's interest in Paraguay, including his being understandably snubbed by Stroessner and his staff when they all attended a reception in Washington D.C. The occasion was the signing of the Panama Canal Treaty (September 7, 1977) by General Omar Torrijos Herrera (1929–1981), ruler of Panama, and President Jimmy Carter. Haim Gordon, who adds that Carter invited Stroessner to be a guest of honor while Greene accompanied Torrijos, puts the standard anti–American, pro–Communist spin on the event. Greene reports that Torrijos told him exactly how the Panama Canal could be sabotaged and rendered useless for three years. One wonders if, at the time, anti–Americans generally felt that what has amounted to the American surrender of the Panama Canal to agents of the People's Republic of China was yet another CIA plot. One also wonders whether Stroessner ever read Greene's "The Worm Inside the Lotus Blossom" (*Daily Telegraph Magazine*, January 3, 1969), which details Stroessner's incredible cruelty. David Pryce-Jones says that Stroessner was one of Greene's "favourite hate-figures." Norman Sherry, while busy praising Torrijos's actions with regard to the Panama Canal, presents its early history in a distorted anti–American fashion. Though without discussing Panama, Matt Steinglass generalizes that "Sherry['s] ... understanding of international affairs is not terribly sophisticated." Anti–American also is Greene's *Getting to Know the General* (1984), the general being Torrijos. In that book and also in *Ways of Escape*, Greene boasts of being snubbed in Washington, D.C., by Stroessner during the Treaty-signing ceremony. A healthy corrective to Greene's position is contained in David Pryce-Jones. (Sources: Falcoff, 36; Gordon, 27–28; Greene, *Getting to Know the General*, 9–16, 61–62, 118–19; Greene, *Ways of Escape*, 300; Pryce-Jones; Sherry III, 562, 859–60; Steinglass, 34; West, 211–13, 225)

STRUBER (*The Name of Action*). He was a friend of Demassener. Struber's being murdered by three gunman in a Trier café enabled Demassener to overthrow the republican government in the ensuing confusion and then create his dictatorship.

STRUBER, FRAU (*The Name of Action*). When her husband was murdered in Trier, she was left a widow with three children. Their marching in the funeral procession Demassener arranged helped him wrest political power from the republicans.

SUE ("Work Not in Progress"). The Bishop of Melbourne says that as an archdeacon he wondered if his dream was literally Sue.

SUMMERS ("The Destructors"). This thin, yellow boy is a member of the Wormsley Common Gang. He cooperates with Trevor, the new leader.

SUPERINTENDENT OF POLICE, THE ("The Root of All Evil"). He is alerted by Herr Puckler to the possibility that since the wine-drinking clubmen can't be located, they may be conspiring anarchists. After Puckler's death, the Superintendent becomes engaged to Frau Puckler.

SUPERIOR, THE (*A Burnt-Out Case*). He is the head of the mission and supervises work at the leproserie. He has arrived at a tolerant theological position concerning the African natives and their brand of Christianity. He smokes smelly cheroots and carries a supply in his World War I knapsack. When summoned to Luc by the Bishop, he looks upon his "bleak refectory" as the place where he spent his best years. He appoints Father Thomas to take charge.

According to Norman Sherry, this cheroot-addicted priest is partly based on a more quiet Father Superior at the leprosarium Greene visited at Yonda, Belgian Congo. (Source: Sherry III, 171–72)

SUPERMAN (*Travels with My Aunt*). He is or was a robust performer in Havana sex dives. Augusta tells Henry she saw Superman.

SURROGATE, MARGARET (*It's a Battlefield*). Margaret married Philip Surrogate when she was 20. She was a talented painter, first sponsored by Lady Caroline Bury. Ever since Margaret's death, Surrogate has kept her portrait and often talks to it.

According to Norman Sherry, Margaret Surrogate is partly modeled on Katherine Middleton Murry (1888–1923), the writer (pen name, Katherine Mansfield) best known for her short stories. She was married to man-of-letters John Middleton Murry (1889–1957), who survived and insincerely extolled her, in the process converting (says Sherry) "that tough, outspoken, sexually promiscuous woman into a different character." (Source: Sherry I, 467).

SURROGATE, PHILIP (*It's a Battlefield*). Surrogate is a writer of left-wing books and is a conceited, conflicted Communist dilettante. Kay Rimmer, a match-factory worker, encounters him at a Communist meeting and eagerly accompanies him to his flat. He impresses her with his library and especially his big pink circular bed. They are intimate the second time around, after which he apologizes to his deceased wife Margaret's portrait and breaks his promise to meet Kay again. When Lady Caroline Bury is interested in helping Jim Drover, convicted of murder, and invites Surrogate to dine at her mansion, he doesn't plead Drover's case well.

Norman Sherry details resemblances between Surrogate and author John Middleton Murry (1889–1957, especially concerning certain "intimacies of Murry's married life." His wife was author Katherine Middleton Murry (1888–1923, pen name Katherine Mansfield). Sherry says that when Katherine died, her widower praised her dishonestly in print. (Source: Sherry I, 467)

SUTLIFFE (*Orient Express*). Opie mentions Sutliffe and Hobbs as cricket players.

SVENSON (*Our Man in Havana*). He is a Swede in the glass business and attends the European Traders' Association banquet. The gloomy man speaks phrase-book English.

SYKES, DR. JESSIE (*The Heart of the Matter*). Dr. Sykes is a physician in the British colony at Freetown, Sierra Leone. She has thick glasses casting beams like a lighthouse. At the club, Scobie hears her say a good way of committing undetected suicide would be to fake an angina attack and ingest a hoarded bunch of pills prescribed for it.

SYLVIE (*Brighton Rock*). She is Spicer's girlfriend until Pinkie kills him. At a roadhouse, Sylvie, briefly tearful and drinking, leads Pinkie to a handy Lancia; but before any action on his part, he manifests non-compliance and drives with Cubitt and Dallow back to Brighton.

SYMOND (*It's a Battlefield*). He is a judge mentioned in court by a young barrister.

TALLIT (*The Heart of the Matter*). He is a young Syrian merchant. Tallit, who has a glass eye, and Yusef are business and smuggling rivals. Their animosity is worsened by religion: Tallit is Christian; Yusef, Muslem. Scobie, Father Rank, and Wilson are guests for dinner at Tallit's home. Yusef tries to frame Tallit by telling Scobie that Tallit is smuggling diamonds in the crop of his cousin's parrot. Tallit isn't arrested because no one will testify that the parrot belongs to Tallit's cousin.

TATE, JIM (*Brighton Rock*). Tate, a Brighton bookie 20 years, is hoarse and with bloodshot eyes. Calling her Ida "Turner," he accepts Ida Arnold's bet on Black Boy.

TATHAM (*The Ministry of Fear*). A Free Mothers' lady explains at the Sunday fête that Tatham furnished currants for the cake, which, made with real eggs, will therefore keep a while.

TAVELL, BOB (*Brighton Rock*). He is a Brighton bookie, from Clapton.

TAVERIL, LORD (*It's a Battlefield*). According to the shopman in the store where Conrad Drover goes to buy a weapon, Lord Taveril and Fred Jones are shooting together.

TAYLOR (*The Human Factor*). Taylor and Piper are MI6 agents who search dead Davis's flat for clues. When Taylor finds the names of three horses—Bonne chance, Kalamazoo, and Widow Twanky—on which Davis bet, he is foolishly suspicious they may be codes for something.

Greene's having Taylor tell Piper that Kalamazoo sounds like an African town is a blatant crack at British intelligence agents' stupidity.

TEARLE, CONWAY (*The Confidential Agent*). Conway, the seven-year-old boy whose sticky hand D. holds at the Russell Square underground station, was named Conway, according to his mother, because she and her husband saw a movie featuring Conway Tearle shortly before their baby was born.

Conway Tearle (1878–1938), a member of an American family of actors, appeared in at least 92 movies. Just before Conway, now seven, was born, his parents saw a musical film starring Tearle. The movie must have been *Gold Diggers of Broadway* (1929), in which Tearle was cast as Stephen Lee. *The Confidential Agent* was published the year following the actor's death.

TED ("The Other Side of the Border"). While Colley is on the London-to-Denton bus, he overhears an older woman caution a younger woman to expect trouble when Ted learns something.

TEMPLE, SHIRLEY (b. 1928). Child actress. Shirley Temple was born in Santa Monica, California, took dance lessons and appeared in a short film (1931), was featured in one scene in another movie (1934), and received a Special Academy Award and was named box-office number one (1935)—a success often repeated. By the end of 1938 Shirley had appeared in 40 movies, including *The Littlest Rebel* 1935), *Captain January* (1936), *Wee Willie Winkie* (1937), *Heidi* (1937), and *Rebecca of Sunnybrook Farm* (1938).

During the time Greene was an assiduous film reviewer (1935–1940), he and Shirley fell afoul of one another. At first, all had been well. He commended Shirley's energy in *The Littlest Rebel* (*Spectator*, May 24, 1936). But then he called *Captain January* "depraved" and "decadent," and Shirley therein a "mature," "voluptuous, "precocious" coquette (*Spectator*, August 7, 1936). Worse, in his *Wee Willie Winkie* review (*Night and Day*, October 21, 1937) he avowed that "totsy" Shirley was deliberately making herself sexually appealing, mainly to middle aged men and clergymen. Her Twentieth Century-Fox producers sued Greene and his publishers for libel (March 1938) and were awarded £3,500 in damages, with Greene ordered to pay £500 personally. Greene, Patsy Guy Hammontree, Anthony Mockler, David Parkinson, and Norman Sherry provide details.

Shirley Temple's later movie appearances were mostly undistinguished. She married John Agar (1945), had a daughter by him (1948), divorced him (1949), married Charles Alden Black (1950), and had a son (1952) and a daughter (1954) by him. As Shirley Temple Black, she was a delegate to the United Nations (1969–1970), U.S. ambassador to Ghana (1974–1976), U.S. Chief of Protocol (1976–1977), and U.S. ambassador to Czechoslovakia (1989–1992). Greene's opinions concerning Ms. Black's diplomatic career are unrecorded, but anti–American chortles would inevitably have accompanied them. (Sources: Greene, *The Graham Greene Film Reader*, 449–52; Greene, *Ways of Escape*, 62–67; Hammontree, 70–72, 231, and passim; Mockler, 136–38; Parkinson, xxvi-xxvii; Sherry I, 619–22)

TENCH (*The Power and the Glory*). Tench mentions this man, his father, from Southend, England, as a dentist, deceased.

TENCH, HENRY (*The Power and the Glory*). He is a dentist, stuck in Mexico 20 years. He planned to practice here five years and return to England with savings. The devaluation of the peso made this impossible. He notices that the whisky priest has a bottle and innocently invites him to his rickety home to share it, not knowing the priest's identity. Tench receives a letter from his wife, in England; she got religion, forgives his absence, wants a divorce. During the exact time of the priest's execution, Tench is treating the Chief of Police for a bad toothache and casually looks out the window at the firing squad in action.

Michael Shelden says Hilary Trench was the name Greene assigned at times to his alter ego, and a name he used as a pseudonym. Norman Sherry adds this: Greene called himself Hilary Trench as author of a prize-winning imitation of a letter by Henry James (1925) and a prize-winning poem about Finland (1940). The name Henry Tench is close to Hilary Trench, and the name Henry is identical to James's first name. An item of incidental interest here but of paramount importance generally: Michael Meyer reports that when Greene was once asked to name the three greatest novels his answer was *War and Peace*, *Tom Jones*, and one of the following — he couldn't say which — James's *The Ambassadors*, *The Wings of the Dove*, and *The Golden Bowl*. (Greene named a minor character Trench in *The Ministry of Fear*). (Sources: Meyer, 125; Shelden, 113, 119, 195; Sherry I, 158, 211, 276–77; Sherry II, 31–32, 40, 67)

TENCH, SYLVIA (*The Power and the Glory*). She is the deserted wife of Tench, the dentist stuck in Mexico. After a 20-year separation, she writes him she has joined the Oxford Group, forgives him, and asks for a divorce.

THE TENTH MAN (1985). Novel. (Characters: Carosse, Madame Carosse, Chavel, Chavel, Jean-Louis Chavel, Madame Chavel, Madame Chavel, Jules, Krogh, Lenôtre, Pierre Louchard, Mangeot, Madame Mangeot, Michel Mangeot, Thérèse Mangeot, the Mayor of Bourge, Pidot, Pierre, Roche, Father Russo, Toupard, Voisin, Madame Warnier.)

Part One: 1. Thirty men in prison obsess about time. They remember two others with wrist watches who were led off by guards, never returned, but afterwards the guards wore their watches. The Mayor of Bourge, one prisoner, has a silver watch, and disputes the time with a engine driver named Pierre, another prisoner, who has an alarm clock. Another prisoner is Jean-Louis Chavel, a Paris lawyer — unpopular and lonely.

2. Chavel can't understand why the Mayor hates him. They're all hostages. Chavel figures on victory soon for one side or the other, then freedom. Chavel tries to discuss travel with a thin young clerk called Janvier. Chavel tries to tell him about his inherited house in St. Jean de Brinac, a village outside Paris. Chavel tries to talk with Pierre about Brinac. Neither listens. All lapse into sleeplessness, confined in one 35' × 17' concrete shed, with outside buckets as their lavatory.

3. Next afternoon a stiff German officer says that since a military governor, a sergeant, and an unimportant French girl were murdered last night, three of their 30 will be executed tomorrow morning. The prisoners can determine which. Lenôtre, an elderly clerk, tears a letter into 30 pieces, marks crosses on three, and puts everything in the big shoe of Krogh, an Alsatian. They draw in reverse alphabetical order. Voisin draws a cross. Eight draw blanks. Janvier, the tenth man, draws a blank. When Lenôtre draws a cross, he starts writing a letter to his daughter. Three slips left. Chavel draws a cross.

4. Chavel rants hysterically that he's a man of property, should be spared, offers 100,000 francs to anyone who will replace him. The others try to calm him, pity him as the only rich prisoner, wonder how any recipient of his largesse could live to enjoy it. When Chavel offers his entire fortune — 300,000 francs, house, land, and possessions — Janvier wants to hear more.

5. To gripes from doomed Voisin and Lenôtre, Janvier replies he always wanted to die rich, gets Chavel to use pages from Lenôtre's pad to write "a deed of gift" to Janvier and then write Janvier's will bequeathing all to his mother and sister. Witnesses sign the documents.

Darkness falls. Janvier makes Chavel describe "my house." Oh, it's commodious. The 30 men rest. Chavel silently regards the path to the execution wall as likely more "desirable" than his "obscure" future.

Part Two: 6. Chavel, bearded and calling himself Jean-Louis Charlot, returns to the house he shut up four years earlier. The Germans shot Voisin, Lenôtre, and Janvier. The survivors reviled Chavel. He felt shame. Now he might drown himself in a river beyond his house, which looks run down. He needs work. He rings the bell.

7. In 1944 Chavel was released from prison with 300 francs, without papers, but with an prison slip mistakenly calling him Charlot. He wandered around liberated Paris, sought work as a teacher, as a salesman. At a urinal Chavel was accosted by an actor calling himself Carosse, who mistook him for someone he called Pidot. Carosse excused himself for collaborating when Germans occupied Paris, and bribed "Pidot" with a couple hundred francs to go tell his wife Carosse was escaping temporarily to Switzerland. Carosse left a puzzled Chavel, who mused again about drowning himself but first had an apéritif at his favorite café. He reminded Jules, the headwaiter, who he was. Jules rationalized about his serving Germans during the occupation, offered to put up Chavel for the night, inquired about his Brinac house. Sold, replied Chavel.

8. Chavel, calling himself Jean-Louis Charlot, rings the bell of his house. Janvier's reckless-looking sister, Thérèse, easily recognized, brusquely invites unkempt "Charlot" in for food. Everything is changed. He tells her he knew her brother, called Janvier, in prison. She says he was Michel (Mangiot), is dead, but their feeble-minded old mother thinks he bought this house for them and also thinks he is alive, successful, far away. The big-bosomed mother appears. Thérèse plies "Charlot" with bread, cheese, and wine, and asks about, not her brother, but Chavel, whose name she saw on documents from her brother. She would prefer her brother alive rather than this mansion, which she's tempted to burn down. She gets "Charlot" to describe Chavel — to spit in his face. Thérèse theorizes Chavel will worm his way to Heaven but she'll die damned. "Charlot" agrees to be her handyman a while.

9. Soon "Charlot" regards the Mangiots as squatters. Thérèse takes her mother to Mass, shops weekly. "Charlot" shops also, half afraid he'll be recognized. Riding on a cart, a crippled farmer named Roche, whom "Charlot" played with when they were boys, passes him, unnoticed. Thérèse fancies that "Charlot's" handwriting on a shopping list seems familiar.

10. Madame Mangiot is strange. Her late husband had a general store in Paris. He sent Thérèse to secretarial school and Michel to trade school. Both quit. Madame Mangiot kept the store, regarding its income as more real than absent Michel's "fairy gold." One night "Charlot" leaves his top-floor servant's bedroom to check his old bedroom. Thérèse finds him. She sits on the bed in her night gown half provocatively. She says Michel's death and her consuming hate for Chavel destroyed her faith, says one cowardly act by Chavel surely revealed himself to himself forever, says she'd relish shooting him. Judging Thérèse ruined, like Michel, "Charlot" feels despair.

11. Next morning "Charlot," telling himself he loves Thérèse, argues legalisms casuistically: Janvier caused his own death; giving Thérèse love would end her hate; hope can rejuvenate him. "Charlot" persuades Thérèse to walk to Brinac's market with him. Roche overtakes them, says he was a war-time partisan, demands to see "Charlot's" papers, says as a boy he knew "soft" Chavel, whom "Charlot" resembles, warns Thérèse about beggars everywhere. Thérèse tells Roche the villagers dislike her because of her inheritance.

12. Thérèse suggests she and "Charlot" eat in the unused dining room. He nearly betrays himself by approaching it. They see portraits of ancient Chavel ancestors. She jeers at their long noses. The door bell rings. A visitor (really Carosse) calls himself Jean-Louis Chavel.

Part Three: 13. When he histrionically names himself "Chavel," Thérèse spits in his face. Wiping dramatically, he says her brother before dying said willing her his house was his best gesture. "Charlot" orders him out. Phony "Chavel" says he's wanted as a supposed collaborator but was planted as an informer in the prison, and seems to recognize "Charlot" as (the real) Chavel. She says he should, since both were imprisoned together. When "Chavel" says "Charlot" wasn't in prison, is an impostor preying on Thérèse,

"Chavel" calls him Carosse, says Carosse called him "Pidot" once. Thérèse goes upstairs. Carosse pseudo-sacrificially prepares to leave in the rain. "Charlot" shouts to her that Carosse has left but secretly takes him to his own top-floor room to confab. Carosse explains that on the run as a collaborator he chanced to meet the mayor of a town beginning with "B," who told him about a man named Chavel who gave a house here for that tenth man's life. Carosse decided to seek the house, figuring the real Chavel wouldn't dare. Denying he is Chavel, "Charlot" says he knew Chavel in prison, and called Carosse "Chavel" before Thérèse, who obsessively figures Chavel would reappear.

"Charlot" finds Thérèse in the dining room. She says he looks more like those ancestral portraits than "Chavel" did. She confesses her own cowardice for not shooting him. Madame Mangiot enters, complains about noisy talk, listens as "Charlot" says he gave "Chavel" bread and let him out the back, then leaves. Thérèse seems sad that "Chavel," gone in the rain, is a broken link to her brother. "Charlot" says he knew him. When, of a sudden, he asks what she'll do when her mother dies, she counters that perhaps she'll marry — not Roche, maybe you. He turns tongue-tied. Her mother calls her — it's rosary time. Upstairs, Carosse boasts of his acting prowess, twits "Charlot" for not proposing to Thérèse, aroused by him. Carosse belches, yawns, sleeps. Searching Carosse's jacket, "Charlot" finds a revolver and papers concerning a man named Toupard dated March 30, 1939.

14. Next morning "Charlot," scraping his muddy shoes, lies to Thérèse he thought he heard someone in the shed. Her mother is gravely ill. "Charlot" fetches the young priest from St. Jean. He gives her the sacraments and blesses Thérèse, at her request.

Part Four: 15. Early that morning Carosse saw his wanted picture on the St. Jean police station wall, and also notice of a village murder (Toupard's). He returns to the shed, sees "Charlot" bring the priest and both leave again. Carosse rings the door. Thérèse answers. He says he heard about her mother's illness in the village, spins lies about Michel's execution at night, not in the morning as "Charlot" said, and is admitted. More lies blacken "Charlot" further. Carosse has a message from Michel. Though catching him in a lie that her brother had her photograph, she longs for that message.

16. Having smooth-talked Thérèse more, Carosse waits outside. "Charlot" approaches. Their heated talk reveals this: Wartime land transfers have been nullified by a timely decree; Carosse might marry Thérèse, since "Charlot" muffed his chance last night; Roche, farming nearby, could find Carosse the collaborator; Carosse murdered Toupard. Carosse stops fingering his pocketed revolver. They decide to victimize Thérèse together.

17. While Thérèse's mother was dying that night, Carosse and "Charlot" listened like conspirators. "Charlot" speaks outside with the young priest, who attended and who warns him thus: Thérèse is vulnerable; "Charlot," an educated man, must leave or else a female companion should reside with her; her sorrow could lead to lust. Before dawn, "Charlot" tells the departing priest he wants only "good" for Thérèse "Charlot" spies as Carosse embraces Thérèse and calls "Charlot" a liar, offers her his repentant self, and winks at "Charlot," who feels only "tenderness" toward her now. Although Carosse wiggles his hidden revolver, "Charlot" solemnly tells Thérèse he is Jean-Louis Chavel.

18. Thérèse doubts. Carosse mocks. Chavel labels Carosse charlatan and Toupard's wanted murderer, but fears she prefers a cheat to a coward. He explains he'll signal Roche, his boyhood playmate, there in the fields, by using his flashlight in their Redskin code. Carosse pulls his revolver. Chavel signals anyway. Carosse shoots him and escapes. Shot in the stomach but pretending he was missed, Chavel convinces her he's Chavel, tells her to report fast-fleeing Carosse as murderer-actor to the authorities, to get the priest to help her, but first to give him writing material for his full disclosure. He asks if her hate is gone. Yes. She exits. He writes non-bindingly about leaving his possessions, is happy about dying alone in his own home, but can sign only "Jean-Louis Ch." Meaning? "A crowning justice" releases him to peace.

In an "Introduction" to *The Tenth Man*, Greene includes distorted, partly disingenuous memories: MGM signed him (1944) to a multi-year contract, which gave MGM possession of everything he would be writing for some time. He wrote *The Tenth Man* (1944?), based partly on a diary entry (December 27, 1937) that he says dropped from all conscious memory but concerned political prisoners drawing decimation lots, an exchange of one fatal slip for property, and the survivor's visiting his relinquished house. A stranger suddenly wrote Greene (1983) that a story entitled *The Tenth Man* was being offered by MGM for sale. It evolved from a two-page plot outline of his. He thought little more about it. Then he heard MGM had sold serial rights to the book for big money, with royalties going to MGM. Finally he received a typescript copy, read it with pleasant surprise, and was happy to see it published by Bodley Head, his London publishers (1985, copyright MGM).

After his "Introduction," Greene includes unused plot sketches for two movies: "Jim Braddon and the War Criminal," about an innocent man who looks like a Nazi inspector of concentration camps; and "Nobody to Blame," prefiguring the plot of *Our Man in Havana* (which see).

Michael Shelden reports that numerous presses (1984) ballyhooed the "discovery" of a lost novel by Greene, who promoted the story in interviews by saying he'd forgotten all about the manuscript, etc. Shelden adds this: Greene did not forget; a 1979 bibliography of Greene lists *The Tenth Man* as an unpublished manuscript by Greene; when Greene sold the manuscript, along with other items, to the University of Texas, the batch included not only a letter from Greene's agent (March 30, 1967) indicating he had written to Greene about a collector interested in acquiring the work, but also Greene's reply that MGM owned the copyright. Shelden correctly concludes that the "discovery" of this new novel permitted Greene to have fun hoodwinking journalists, and in addition to create publicity and hence increase sales — in the process, however, displaying a combination of cleverness, wisdom, and cruelty. W. J. West naively believes that the events surrounding the surfacing of *The Tenth Man* represents "[a]n astonishing example of Greene's very weak memory of his own work," and adds that "[w]hen he was approached for comment by the press with news of the discovery he was completely mystified." Anthony Mockler calls the whole history of *The Tenth Man* "almost gothic in its complications." Indubitably through deference to Greene, Norman Sherry avoids all discussion of *The Tenth Man*. Greene had fun with the title: Carosse first tells the real Chavel that the Mayor of B called poor Janvier "the tenth man" and then adds, "quite a good title, that."

Paul O'Prey notes that "many of Greene's major themes are incorporated into the story [*The Tenth Man*] in miniature ... : betrayal, forgiveness, the moment of weakness or cowardice 'which happens to everyone once' and 'when it happens, you know what you've been all your life [Thérèse tells the real Chavel].'" O'Prey adds that *The Tenth Man* "is also, like *The Ministry of Fear*, the story of a man changing his identity ... Chavel ... becomes Charlot and he too [like Rowe] has the chance to start again through humiliation, destitution, and ... his love for Thérèse." Robert Pendleton feels that in writing *The Tenth Man* Greene was influenced by Joseph Conrad's *Under Western Skies*. Like Conrad's Razumov, Chavel tries to project guilt onto another, feels homeless, has a *Doppelgänger*. Where in the text is evidence supporting Rowland Smith's assertion that "*The Tenth Man* lovingly recreates the French scene, French architecture and French customs from the perspective of the island fortress, cut off from the possibility of travel to occupied France"?

Cedric Watts opines that "[i]t is hard to imagine that this overly ingenious novella [*The Tenth Man*] of double imposture could have become an effective film"; Watts is implying that MGM was wise not to try, once the novel was discovered. Still, Neil Sinyard reports it inspired an American television film starring Anthony Hopkins and Derek Jacobi (1988). *The Tenth Man* (1909) was the title of a mediocre play by W. Somerset Maugham (1874–1965) and inspired a British black-and-white movie (1936). Greene was an unqualified admirer of Maugham's voluminous and varied writings. Michael Meyer reports Greene told him that he spent an evening with Maugham, who "reminisced fascinatingly," but that Greene drank too much to be able to remember next morning anything Maugham said. (Sources: Meyer, 136; Mockler, 204; O'Prey, 54; Parkinson, 700; Pendleton, 87–88; Shelden, 10–11, 455; Sinyard, 158; R. Smith, 129–30; Watts, 81; West, 246)

TERESA (*The Honorary Consul*). She works in Señora Sanchez's brothel. Having engaged her, Saavedra is able to tell Plarr that she comes from Salta and that he is thinking of having Salta the setting of his next novel, in which Teresa might figure, transformed, as a one-legged girl.

TERESA (*Monsignor Quixote*). She has been Father Quixote's servant for more than 20 years. Ill-humored but loyal, she aids Quixote when Father Herrera and the Bishop of El Toboso make trouble. She has a square shape, buck teeth, and an "embryo moustache."

TERESA (*Our Man in Havana*). Wormold wants to include a woman, a veritable Mata Hari, in his fake-spy list. So he creates Teresa, and fictionalizes her as a fat dancer at the Shanghai Theatre, and as the mistress of the Director of Posts and Telegraphs and of the Minister of Defence, both.

TERESA (*Our Man in Havana*). Wormold and Beatrice go to the Shanghai Theatre, and he pretends to be looking for his fictionalized fat Teresa. A real dancer named Teresa answers when he timidly calls "Teresa." She is skinny but says in Spanish she is Teresa; he translates for Beatrice that she said she's Teresa's sister. Even though a stage worker says Teresa belongs to Pedro, she leaves with Wormold and Beatrice, is eventually arrested, but isn't harmed.

TERRY, MRS. (*The Confidential Agent*). She was Mrs. Bennett's poverty-stricken neighbor. When a royal family member visited Benditch and asked to look in at Mrs. Terry's house, he was told she was sick and Mrs. Bennett's could be seen instead. Mrs. Terry had sold most of her possessions and her house was bare, while Mrs. Bennett, rewarded for having been Lord Benditch's daughter Rose Cullen's nurse, lived more comfortably. The royal family could wrongly assume average miners lived well.

TESTER (*England Made Me*). In talking with Farrant, who pretends he's a Harrow man, Minty, who is one, says Tester was sentenced to six months for indecent assault at Harrow.

THATCHER, MRS. ("An Old Man's Memory"). Having recently won her fourth term (as Prime Minister of the United Kingdom), she has just seen the train from France exit the Channel Tunnel, and is orating when news arrives that underwater bombs have destroyed the British train with great loss of life.

Margaret Thatcher (b. 1925), distinguished British political leader, was elected a Parliamentarian (1959), Conservative Party leader (1974), and Prime Minister (1979–1990). Greene reviled Augusto Pinochet Ugarte (b. 1915), tyrant of Chile (1974–1998), who went to England (1998) but was later returned to Chile to face charges of horrible violations of civil rights and financial misconduct, along with many of his military and political associates, and members of his family. According to Marie-Françoise Allain, when Greene learned that Margaret Thatcher was selling arms to Pinochet (1980), he nicknamed her Thatcher-Zaharoff, after Sir Basil Zaharoff (1849–1936), the notorious arms dealer. At least twice, Greene told Leopoldo Duran that Pinochet was a "villain." (Sources: Allain, 104; Duran, 61, 294)

THÉ, GENERAL (*The Quiet American*). He is a former chief of staff of the Caodaists near Tanyin. Becoming a dissident, he plans to fight both the Vietminh and the French. Fancying that Thé can lead a third-force movement, Pyle supplies him with explosives. Thé uses them, however, to create carnage on the streets of Saigon. This leads Fowler to betray Pyle and cause his death.

General Thé is Colonel Trinh Minh Thé, the Caodaist chief of staff. Later Greene wrote briefly about him. Norman Sherry reports that the colonel's mutiny (June 7, 1951) from the Caodaists in Tay Ninh (Tanyin in the novel) made him troublesome to the Vietnamese in the south and to the French alike. (Sources: Greene, *Ways of Escape*, 170–72; Sherry II, 402–33 passim).

THÉRÈSE, SISTER (*A Burnt-Out Case*). She was a nun at the convent school attended by Marie Rycker, who recalls that Sister Thérèse broke her ankle. Marie reminisces about events such as this one in her restricted past to avoid listening to her drunk husband's complaints as they are driving home from Governor Guelle's party.

THIMBLERIGG (*The Heart of the Matter*). He is a junior officer Scobie sees at the club bar. He recently arrived at Freetown from Palestine.

THE THIRD MAN (1949). Novel. (Characters: Mrs. Bannock, Bates, Bracer, Colonel Calloway, J. G. Carey, Carter, Colonel Cooler, Crabbin, Benjamin Dexter, Wolfgang Gottmann, Hansel, Harbin, Koch, Ilse Koch, Kurtz, Harry Lime, Rollo Martins, Gräfin von Meyersdorf, Pat O'Brien, Paine, Schmidt, Anna Schmidt, Corporal Starling, Miss Wilbraham, Dr. Winkler.)

1. February in Vienna. British Colonel Calloway, the narrator, met Rollo Martins (British author, pen name Buck Dexter, author of cheap Westerns) at Harry Lime's funeral in the Central Cemetery. Divided into American, British, French, and Russian zones, Vienna is dreary, with rubble, partly repaired buildings, and the Innere Stadt controlled by all four powers.

2. February 7. Martins goes to the address of Harry Lime, his hero from school days 20 years earlier, now working in the International Refugee Office. Harry invited Martins to come write about refugees. Harry's neighbor (Koch) tells him Harry was killed by a car and is being buried at the Central Cemetery. Martins taxis there, sees the burial, is approached by Calloway, who feeds him several drinks, which he says he needs. Calloway, whom Martins misnames Callaghan, learns Martins knew Harry, tells Martins that Harry was a racketeer, identifies himself as from Scotland Yard, ducks to avoid getting slugged by Martins. Paine, Calloway's assistant, decks Martins and drives him to his hotel.

3. Crabbin, a British Council literary fellow, has been waiting for the esteemed novelist Benjamin Dexter, and asks if Martins is Dexter. Yes. Crabbin promises to finance him for a week if he'll lecture at his literary Institute tomorrow. Martins mentions Harry. Crabbin says Harry knew Anna Schmidt, a Josefstadt Theatre actress. Martins rests in his room, dreams of a frustrated appointment with Harry, is phoned by someone calling himself Kurtz (from the Russian zone), Harry's friend who was with him when he died. They'll meet tomorrow at a certain street in Old Vienna.

4. Martins meets Kurtz, with a toupée and signaling with a Buck Dexter novelette. He says he and a man named Cooler were near Harry's street before the accident; expresses fear Martins, seeking justice for Harry, will find something disreputable; but gives Martins Cooler's address, in the American zone.

5. After the Josefstadt matinée, Martins meets Anna, shares tea in her dressing room, learns this: Harry's dead; Anna wishes she were; Cooler gave her money from Harry; Cooler's testimony exonerated the driver of the car that killed Harry; he didn't die instantly on the street; his doctor was nearby; Harry was a racketeer; she knows Kurtz; maybe "poor Harry" was murdered. Anna gives Martins the doctor's address.

6. Martins visits Dr. Winkler, surrounded by crucifixes, including one he calls Jansenist. He reveals only that when he arrived Harry was dead, had been carried inside, and others said he was briefly conscious. Winkler saw a man with a toupée there.

7. Martins returns to Harry's rooms and visits his neighbor, Koch, now cordial. He says when Harry was killed, the driver stayed in the car and three men carried the body into the house. Martins wonders about the time of death, and about that third man. Having keys, Koch shows Martins Harry's flat, totally cleaned by Koch's wife Ilse. Koch says Kurtz took Harry's briefcase. Martins says he thinks Harry was murdered. Koch rebukes him and hustles him out. At his hotel is a message from Crabbin about the upcoming lecture.

8. Martins reads Harry's inquest reports, visits Cooler's flat about 5:00 p.m. After Cooler, an American colonel, plies him with three whiskies, Martins says Winkler said there was another man in the car that killed Harry, and he was dead not dying when being carried to the house. Martins asks about Harry's girl Anna. Cooler says he helped Harry fix her papers saying she was Austrian, because her father was a Hungarian Nazi and the Russians might grab her if they knew. Cooler gets a phone call. Martins asks if Harry were involved in any racket. Never.

9. Martins finds Anna at the address she gave him at the theatre. Both are lonely. The sky darkens. They hold hands. She would like him to talk about Harry. His whistling Harry's

favorite tune unnerves her. He says he doesn't trust Winkler, likes Harry's friend Cooler, wonders about Koch's mentioning a third man. Anna wants to meet Koch. Walking toward his place, they see a crowd. Koch is being carried out dead, of a cut throat. Suicide or murder? Hansel, a neighbor boy, says he heard someone ask Frau Koch earlier about the foreigner and glares at Martins. He retreats with Anna, who says Koch was murdered because there was a third man.

Leaving Anna about 9:00 p.m., Martins heads for his hotel but is swept, scared, into a British car and taken to Crabbin's literary session. Confused, drunk, and worried, Martins names Zane Grey as his favorite author, doesn't know James Joyce, is regarded as properly professionally stiff when he ignores queries from the audience about unknown names such as Stein, Virginia Woolf, Daphne du Maurier, John Galsworthy, [J. B.] Priestley,* and Layman. Martins signs guests' copies of Benjamin Dexter's novel *The Curved Prow* with his honest "B. Dexter." Calloway's man Paine enters looking for one Rollo Martins, who hides but is gently caught.

10. Calloway, whose men have followed Martins, interviews him. Sullen but honest, Martins says Harry was murdered, and an unnamed informant saw a third man and was murdered. Calloway names Koch as the dead informant. Martins says he also mentioned the third man to Cooler. Calloway says Cooler telephoned him. Now believing Martins, Calloway says Cooler profits in illegal tires but Harry was into something deeper. For that, Martins wonders, was he killed? Calloway describes the racket — penicillin stolen from military hospitals, diluted with sand, sold to civilian hospitals, resulting in children's insanity and sometimes death. Authorities got a criminal named Harbin to double-cross Kurtz, who gave them notes written by Harry. Harbin wrote Kurtz fingering Harry as ring leader. Calloway wants Martins to remain in Vienna until the third man is found.

11. Martins, now glad Harry, his fallen hero, is dead, gets liquored up and at 3:00 a.m. staggers to Anna, tells her about Harry's penicillin scheme, confesses his love for her, says he doesn't care whether Kurtz or the third man killed Harry. She too is glad he's dead, not rotting in prison, but cherishes her love of good-or-bad Harry. Martins leaves but in the moonlit street sees Harry Lime, who quickly vanishes past a kiosk.

12. Martins returns to tell Anna, but at 4:00 a.m. she was seized, the porter said, by an international patrol (one Russian, in charge this month; Corporal Starling, a British soldier; Pat O'Brien, an American soldier; and a useless French soldier) as a Russian national without proper documentation. Starling phones details to Calloway, who establishes a road block stopping the vehicle in the British zone, rescues Anna, and mollifies the Russian with a pack of good cigarettes.

13. Martins visits Calloway, whose junior officer, Carter, says Harbin left town. Carter suggests opening Harry Lime's grave. Learning Anna is safe in her room, Martins agrees to show Calloway the kiosk where he last saw that Harry impersonator. Ah, it has a stairway down to Vienna's sewer system. Calloway concludes Harry is alive — probably in the Russian zone — and may have wanted to get Anna there also. Only Martins can go there safely and talk with Harry.

14. Sunday afternoon. With *laissez-passer* papers, Martins enters the Russian zone and visits Kurtz, now without his toupée. Martins orders him to tell Harry to meet him immediately at the Big Wheel in the Prater park. Harry, whistling, appears, and the two ride the enormous Ferris wheel. Harry blithely reveals this: Anna was nice, briefly; he'll cut Martins in on penicillin profits; victims are unimportant little creatures; he betrayed Anna to the Russians to curry favor; he roams safely at night; Harbin is in that coffin; Martins is welcome to Anna; Martins surely wouldn't kill him and he won't kill Martins; he makes £30,000 a year; still Catholic, he believes the dead are happiest. Martins and Harry part.

15. After revisiting Anna, Martins tells Calloway she doesn't want Harry further but won't help anyone hurt him. Calloway tells Martins this: Harbin was in the coffin; they'll nab Winkler and let Cooler escape; Martins must entice Harry out.

16. Martins gets Cooler to warn Harry, who, cocky and fun-loving, will take the bait and rendezvous with Martins at a restaurant near a kiosk near a sewer. Calloway will post

forces nearby. At 1:15 a.m. Harry shows, sees two policemen changing posts, darts into the sewer, is pursued. A British soldier named Bates, bodyguarding Martins, chats with Martins about Tottenham Court Road. When Bates rushes in front of Martins, Harry shoots out Bates's flashlight. Appealing to Harry to surrender, Martins shines another torch. Harry emerges, fires and kills Bates, plunges into raging sewage, and sweeps past. Asked by Calloway to shoot, Martins, separated from the rest, wounds Harry, who climbs in pain toward a manhole, sees Harry, says in agony, "Bloody fool"—but of whom?—and Martins shoots him dead.

17. Calloway, Martins, and Anna attend Harry Lime's "second" burial. Afterwards, Calloway sees Anna walk off, Martins follow, and her hand hold his arm.

The three words "the third man" chime at least a dozen times in the novel, including six in the pivotal ninth chapter. Those words should call to mind the risen Christ walking beside two unseeing apostles on the road to Emmaus (Luke 24:l3–16). Perhaps Greene also wants readers to recall these lines from T. S. Eliot's *The Waste Land*: "Who is the third who walks always beside you? / When I count, there are only you and I together."

Norman Sherry discusses Greene's activities after the 1948 success of the movie *The Fallen Idol* (called *The Lost Illusion* in the United States), based on "The Basement Room." Greene was encouraged to write a film script for Alexander Korda* and Carol Reed* about the four-power occupation of Vienna (1947). Greene initially planned Harry Lime's rise from the dead to transpire in London. Greene flew to Vienna (February 1948), scouted the city thoroughly, proceeded to Rome and Capri, and wrote up his film plot first in story form. In his preface to the novel *The Third Man*, Greene contends that it was written to be seen not read. (Still, he happily revised it and received royalties when it was published, first in *American Magazine*, March 1949; then by Viking, 1950, then by William Heinemann, 1950 [with *The Fallen Idol*].)

Back in Vienna in June, Greene rendezvoused with Reed, explored the city's sewer system, visited the Russian zone, met the gorgeous young actress Alida Valli, and brain-stormed over the movie script with Reed. In August Greene and Reed together voyaged to New York, flew to California, met with David O. Selznick, and with minor setbacks touched up the script. Greene later described difficulties with Selznick.

Gene D. Phillips discusses the movie. Regarded as a classic, it stars Orson Welles (Harry Lime, now an American), Joseph Cotten (Holly Martins, also American), Trevor Howard (Calloway), and Alida Valli (Anna); the American Cooler becomes a Rumanian criminal named Popescu; Crabbin, becoming Crabbit, has a mistress; excised are Greene's cracks unflattering to British novelist E. M. Forster (1879–1970), partial model for Benjamin Dexter (*see* Dexter, Benjamin, and Wilbraham, Miss). Quentin Falk notes that Anna's being kidnapped by the Russians is gone. Anne Piroëlle contends that *The Third Man* illustrates "the possibilities of union that exist between fiction and film." Orson Welles created the often-quoted lines in the movie contrasting the accomplishments of the terrible Italian Renaissance and Switzerland, the centuries-old democracy that produced the cuckoo clock. Neil Sinyard raises this point concerning the movie (and the novel, by the way): "For all it is a great cinematic moment, it is never clear to me why Harry Lime reappears when he does. Where is he going? To see Anna? But by this time he is not interested in her: indeed he is safer if she continues to think he is dead. Why does he walk so unsuspectingly into that final trap?"

W. J. West reports that Greene helped René Raymond (1906–1985), eventually the author of more than 80 novels, to get his novel *More Deadly Than the Male* (1946) published. Raymond used the pen name Ambrose Grant for it. (The novel was later republished as by James Hadley Chase, another of Raymond's four pen names, the others being James L. Docherty and Raymond Marshall.) West adds that Greene and Raymond both were drinking companions of a man named H. E. Bates on Tottenham Court Road. West adds that "Chase," like Rollo Martins, wrote thrillers cast in America even though, like Martins, he "never set foot in America." (West is incorrect here: Raymond visited the United States twice, once going to Miami, once to New Orleans.) West adds that *More Deadly Than the Male* has a character named Callaghan. Finally West stretches to compare Lime and Greene, both of whom are "morally corrupt," then to compare Martins and "Chase," both of whom are basically "innocent." (At least West didn't accuse Greene of choosing the name Lime because limes are green. Nor does pun-loving Peter Wolfe mention Lima Greenes.)

Greene's mode of narrating *The Third Man* has challenged at least two critics. Phillips, after contrasting Maurice Bendrix, the unbalanced narrator of *The End of the Affair*, and Colonel Calloway, contends that Calloway "is a professionally detached observer who relays to the reader the events of the story as they happened." Not so. Calloway, though efficiently professional, is directly involved in much action, as when he rescues Anna, wades in sewage, tells Martins he won't report his killing Lime. Also, Calloway doesn't observe all of Martins's actions but relays them second-hand from Martins to the reader. In fact, Peter Wolfe feels that "Calloway's narration does not help the book, and, other than giving Greene practice for *The End of the Affair* (1951), serves no purpose in his 1950 [sic] entertainment." Wolfe adds that "it is unlikely that Martins should talk as much as Greene and Calloway say…. His [Calloway's] report contains extended speeches and psychological nuances which nobody but a first-hand observer could have noted." It seems likely that a fast reader of this novel might often believe Martins was the first-person narrator. (Sources: Falk, 82–83; Greene, *Ways of Escape*, 68–71; Phillips, 62–64, 123; Piroëlle, 85; Sherry II, 239–54 passim; Sinyard, 38; West, 113, 126–27; Wolfe, 126, 127)

THIS GUN FOR HIRE (1936). Novel. (Characters: Acky, Aitkin, Alice, Bacon, Baines, Ballard, Colonel Banks, Barker, Binns, the Bishop, Alfred Bleek, Mrs. Brewster, Major Joseph Calkin, Mrs. Calkin, Callitrope, Carter, Charlie, Chinky, Cohen, Collier, Constance, Coral, Mrs. Cranbeim, Crosthwaite, Anne Crowder, Lady Cundifer, Davenant, Davis, Dora, Dreid, Colonel Mark Egerton, Mrs. Egerton, Emma, Buddy Fergusson, Lord Fordhaven, Frost, Graves, the Great Dane, Green, Groener, Frau Groener, Hallows, Henry Harris, Mrs. Harris, Higginbotham, Rose Higginbotham, Mrs. 'Opkinson, Juicy Juliet, J.K., Jim, Joe, Jossy, Battling Kite, Kusack, Lance, Lucy, Macpherson, Mallowes, Mander, Sir Marcus, Mrs. Mason, Mather, James Mather, Miss Maydew, Mike, Mrs. Milbanke, Milly, Mollison, Mrs. Penny, Page, Penrith, Montague Phelps, Alfred Piker, Mrs. Piker, Raven, James Raven, Mrs. Raven, Rosen, Ruby, Saunders, Simmons, Soppelsa, Tiny, Watt, Druce Winton, Dr. Alfred Yogel, Mrs. Ziffo.)

One: 1. Christmas time. James Raven, a bitter gunman with an ugly harelip, regards murders as simply jobs. He goes to a certain (Jewish) minister's residence, cuts the phone wire, and rings the bell. His secretary Emma, who should have been gone, admits him. Raven gives the minister a letter of introduction, shoots him to death, kills Emma, leaves a certain paper and a suitcase for misleading clues, and departs.

2. Anne Crowder, actress, and James Mather, detective sergeant, are on a London bus. He loves her. She likes him but has an assignment out of town. They mention a week-old murder that might cause a war. As she walks toward her rooms, she clutches a musical record about Kew, Paradise, and Greenland, and sees a man with a harelip.

3. At a London Corner House, Raven, back from Calais, meets "Cholmondeley" (Davis), who is fat, flashes his emerald ring, orders a huge sweet dessert, and tersely pays Raven £200 in £5 notes for the job. On his way to his (Soho) room, Raven reserves a dress with a £5 note in a store for Alice as a joke. Alice is a hunchback servant who cleans for him and other roomers. He gives her the dress receipt, knowing she can't wear the dress. Approaching the attached café, he hears his name spoken. Two men (Mather and fellow-policeman Saunders) have found where he rooms. He listens in a telephone box by the stairs as they interview his inimical neighbors in the building, get his description, learn about the joke dress, and say they'll post a man across the street for someone to finger Raven. Alice starts to phone a friend to watch Raven's capture, but he flourishes his automatic and orders her to repeat what the detectives revealed: Raven's payment was in stolen, traced money. Now knowing "Cholmondeley" set him up, he escapes.

4. Anne got that temporary job and must tell Mather. He phones to break their date by

explaining he's on Raven's case, having traced his money. She says they'll see each other again in a few weeks. Understanding, he will see her off at Euston station.

5. A crime reporter says he has information about the robbery of that safe and a suspect evading capture. The reporter's cohorts ridicule him.

6. Anne boards her train. A fat man with an emerald ring sits nearby. Mather runs alongside, but she can't attract his attention. She and the fat man are both bound for Nottwich.

Two: 1. Raven goes to Dr. Yogel's office seeking harelip surgery. But when the crooked physician tries to put him under with gas while his hard-eyed nurse phones the police, Raven escapes. He stakes out a smut shop where Cholmondeley receives mail, sees him, follows his taxi to Euston railroad station, and boards the train after him.

2. Mather, Saunders, and their driver check dives in a futile search for Raven. Dawn. Mather reports to Kusack, his chief, at Scotland Yard. By now, news of the murder of a Czech politician allegedly by a Serb foments widespread war scares.

3. The train stops at Nottwich. Cholmondeley pushes past Anne to exit. Anne gets off, followed by Raven, who asks her to exchange her ticket for his, shows his automatic, invites her to breakfast, but she hurls hot coffee in his face. He forces her, baggage and all, to a cheap suburban development, and into an almost finished house. She mentions her theater job. He mentions his useless pound notes, his betrayer Cholmondeley, and the man's emerald ring. Anne remembers him. Raven's plan to kill her upstairs is interrupted by a salesman (Green) showing the house. Anne obtains two £5 notes from Raven, goes downstairs, and options the house.

4. Anne, Ruby, and other girls are rehearsing an *Aladdin* pantomime at the Royal Theatre for Collier, the director, when Davis (a.k.a. Cholmondeley), the show's (40 percent) backer, enters. He selects Anne to take to dinner — and for afterwards. They go to the Metropole, where he concentrates on lobster and sweets. From the porter (Hallows), she learns that Davis works at Nottwich's Midland Steel, fallen on hard times. Davis taxis Anne to 61 Khyber Avenue where a woman (Tiny) runs a bawdy house. Davis prepares for action but is reduced briefly to tears when Anne mentions the news account of the minister's secretary and also seeing a harelipped man. Davis rationalizes his minor role in the murder, says £500,000 are involved, and begins to smother her with a pillow.

5. Night hail. Raven wonders how to find Cholmondeley, recalls Anne's saying she didn't mind his harelip, suppresses unaccustomed tenderness, must remain killer-quick, figures she'll turn him in, and hides in a house garage. He hears jumbles of radio programs.

Three: 1. Late evening. Mather and Saunders arrive by train at Nottwich, confer with the capable police superintendent, already briefed by a Scotland Yard message, and with the blustery constable (Major Joseph Calkin). Mather checks city locations on a map, walks outside, and spots the Royal Theatre. Anne phoned him her local address, and he goes near it, hoping she's comfortable, then retires at the Crown hotel.

2. Next morning. A police sergeant phones Mather: Raven was seen sleeping in St. Mark's cathedral; Green, a housing-estate agent, brought in two of those widely reported stolen £5 notes, given him by a girl. Figuring she was Raven's accomplice on the train, Mather interviews Green, learning little. When the train ticket agent reports the girl had two suitcases and was the only woman deboarding, Mather figures she's Anne. He goes to the house that was being sold, speculates about Anne's and Raven's movements, learns nothing by phoning the theatre, and is told Miss Maydew will be at St. Luke's at two.

3. Mather watches church people at St. Luke's preparing for a jumble sale. It starts. He interviews Miss Maydew. She says the new girl dined with fat Davenant, who bought out Davis, and Collier should return from York tonight. Mather sees Anne's bag, a gift from him. She must be dead. He relishes the armed hunt. He sees a harelipped man nearby.

Four: 1. Hungry, stubbled Raven melts into a crowd, buys a paper, reads front-page war news and a meagre account of his theft of money, grows bitter at sight of a store-window Nativity scene, remembers his pseudo–Christian orphanage, mingles with women at a church sale, sees Anne's bag, and follows the old woman who bought it — not seeing a man (Mather) trailing him. As she enters 6l Khyber Avenue, Raven forces himself in also. Threatened, the crone (Tiny) calls Acky (her husband), who spouts theology dementedly. When questioned about the bag, the pair rouse Raven's suspicions. Knowing they won't call the police into what Raven recognizes as a bawdy house, he checks around. Behind a covered fireplace he finds Anne gagged and bound. He inordinately praises her, especially when Acky fells him with a poker and she grabs his dropped automatic and threatens Acky. Raven and Anne escape to a shed past the railroad. She thinks she recognizes a policeman (Mather) down the twilit street but stumbles along with Raven regardless.

2. Mather sees Raven and Anne, feels she's favoring the robber, and with Saunders follows both to a shed along the railroad. Unable to risk shooting, Mather posts men to surround the shed, returns to the police station until dawn.

3. The inspector phones Major Joseph Calkin, Nottwich's constable: Raven is surrounded, has a girl with him, will be captured at dawn. Calkin and his domineering wife invite Mrs. Alfred Piker, the wife of Nottwich's mayor, and Sir Marcus to dinner. Mrs. Piker brings her Pekinese dog. Calkin caters to aged, frail, super-rich Marcus, the mysterious power with an obscure international background in control of Midland Steel. Marcus confidentially tells Calkin that Davis saw Raven, and Marcus wants him killed pronto. Calkin says waiting until morning will keep policemen from possible death, and they will be needed soon in the inevitable war. Marcus is pleased, demands that Calkin phone headquarters and order that Raven be shot on sight, promising Calkin promotion to colonel if he obeys and trouble if he doesn't. While Calkin is hesitating beside his phone, his wife bellows at him.

4. Marcus is taken by chauffeur and then by Mollinson, his valet, to a building in the Tanneries, where he lives. Recalling his international influence, he expects war and big profits by exporting metals.

Five: 1. In the shed, Raven makes Anne comfortable with old sacks, admires her cooperation, and is furious when she says Davis (his "Cholmondeley") almost suffocated her. Raven feels briefly gentle in loyal Anne's presence. She talks about the old Czech man assassinated by Davis's gunman, says the Czech merely tried to improve conditions by clearing slums and building better homes. Raven defines his so-called home as a brutal orphanage, mentions his mother's sloppy suicide. He naps briefly. He hears Anne praying, scoffs, recalls how dream interpreters rid one of burdens, feels it's wrong to be soft toward her. She promises never to tell the police about him. So to test his hope he can trust her, he confesses killing a racing-gang rival named Battling Kite. She seems calm. So he tells her he dreamed about shooting an old woman through a door, shooting an old man, and leaving a paper. She retorts that was no dream. Agreeing, he feels uniquely happy. He can trust someone.

2. Anne, however, feels revulsion. She recalls accounts of the brutal political shootings — the Socialist's head, his secretary's eyes. Anne figures Raven must locate Cholmondeley and his boss. Then what? He tells her he read about Mather's being here. She must prevent war, but save Mather first. Raven sleeps, dreams of a Guy Fawkes fire with the murdered minister burning happily. A yellow fog rolls in. Raven says he'll sneak out to Midland Steel. Anne dons his coat and hat, will run to the right, be captured, and he can dart left — to kill someone. She doesn't know his target's name (Sir Marcus). Raven shivers in ragged clothes.

Six: 1. Saunders and other policemen surround the shed. Anne runs. Saunders mistakes her for Raven, whistles, warns, fires but misses. Other whistles indicate the real fugitive is elsewhere, also caught. Anne identifies herself, jocosely. Raven wounded a policeman and is gone.

2. Mather doesn't believe everything in Anne's puzzling story to him — about other people trying to kill her, Raven's needing to kill someone at Midlands to stop the impending war, his being framed by the pound notes, his killing Kite. Mather, all business, seeks Raven.

Seven: 1. The medical students stage a "rag" during Nottwich's mock air-raid drill. Led by Buddy Fergusson, they collar anyone not wearing the required gas mask. They trash the room of a conscientious student. Buddy and his pal Mike decide to arrest the mummy in the nearby museum for being maskless. Mike runs ahead.

Suddenly Raven appears and pulls his gun on Buddy, who recognizes the harelipped fugitive. Raven forces the terrified lad into a garage, strips, ties, and gags him, and walks out in Buddy's safe clothes and a gas mask toward Midland Steel.

2. Christmas morning. Davis attends an *Aladdin* rehearsal, confident Anne will be caught as doomed Raven's accomplice. Eyeing two chorus girls and sucking toffees, Davis domineers Collier and Miss Maydew. Davis ordered a Christmas tree for the rehearsal, and as it comes in he cuddles with peppy Ruby. They'll meet for lunch — 1 p.m., Metropole. Exiting, Davis is stopped by a gas-masked "doctor" in hospital garb. Thinking he is to be "arrested" in the mock drill for having no gas mask, Davis offers to pay a fine if they can go to his office. In mask-muffled tones, Raven agrees. A masked boy jeers Davis. Policemen bow. The two walk to Midland Steel, where Davis works. When a detective is posted there because Raven is loose, Davis hurries the "doctor" into the elevator and sends his secretary out to check train schedules for him. For safety Davis locks his doors and, relaxing, says Sir Marcus is his boss, offers Raven sweet wine, and on demand presents two £5 notes as his fine. Raven's asking if they are also phony identifies Raven, still masked. They go to Marcus, whom a valet tends and who, Raven ascertains by Marcus's beard-covered scar, had been in school with and knew the murdered Czech. Davis admits that Marcus, agedly calm, ordered Raven to do the killing for a £500,000 steel profit. Marcus rings an alarm. The police approach the locked door. Marcus, unworried by death, and Davis, having retched, argue. The valet derides both. Raven shoots Marcus dead. To Davis's excuse of only following orders, Raven says Davis tried to kill Anne, who, Davis counters, told the police Raven would be here. Raven shoots him, thus despairingly killing the remnants of his world — abandoned by mother, priest, doctor, woman. The valet suggests his escaping by the window. But Mather is there, on a painter's platform. Saunders shoots the door lock open and kills Raven.

Eight: 1. When Davis doesn't appear at the Metropole, the porter Hallows treats Ruby to lunch. Reading the midday paper about three dead makes them feel closer. Hallows praises Sir Marcus for giving Christmas turkeys.

2. Political experts check Sir Marcus's papers to verify Raven's comments about him to Anne, whom Mather orders taken to London for questioning. Saunders cleans up, has lunch, and attends a free class in the Masonic Hall to cure stammering, conducted by a man reminding him of dead Davis. Marcus's portrait is on the wall.

3. Calkin and the police superintendent meet, complain about Mrs. Piker's dog, and praise Marcus, whose order about shooting Raven on sight Calkin refused to transmit.

The superintendent says a bank cashier's daughter found in their garage Buddy without sufficient clothes, which Raven used.

4. Tiny listens, lovingly awed, as Acky intones what he is writing to the Bishop pleading to be reinstated in the church after what he calls bribed, perjured allegations of his sexual misconduct. Acky hints that the Bishop also visited the occasional haycock and fleshpot.

5. In the train's locked compartment, Anne broods: Raven, who trusted her, dead, alongside two others; no job now; Mather disaffected. He enters, says legations of countries needlessly mobilizing have been informed, Anne's story is a sensation; she prevented war, will receive a reward for her success. Anne suggests their immediate marriage, momentarily feels she must celibately atone for failing Raven, but then in unfettered joy sees London and home ahead.

Norman Sherry reports that Greene started writing *A Gun for Sale* early in 1935, worked on it while also writing *Journey Without Maps: A Travel Book* (1936), and soon completed the novel (January 1936). It was published first in the United States (June, as *This Gun for Hire*), then England (July, *A Gun for Sale*). Before publication, film rights were sold to Paramount Pictures for $12,000 (May). Nottwich is Greene's remake of Nottingham, where he was a journalist trainee for a few months (1926). But did Greene remain there long enough to see the city blessed, as Nottwich is, with a church bazaar, a student frolic, and an air-raid drill — all on Christmas Day?

Peter Wolfe, discussing both structure and theme in *This Gun for Sale*, comments that Greene "work[s] ... fuguelike variations of the underlying theme of the pursuit." Wolfe adds that "Greene shifts between the point of view of the hunter and that of the hunted; he devises chases within chases; he has chases reverse themselves; combining pursuit with self-discovery and expanding moral vision, he lays trails of red herrings, or sets false clues." Wolfe concludes that "[t]he crabwise rhythm of thin victories and losses describes the foggy, dual nature of things," because "Western Europe has no engine other than material self-interest." (Is Wolfe commenting only on Europe in the 1930s?) Wolfe faults *This Gun for Hire* for having "a coincidence-ridden plot," glaringly when the mock air-raid drill and the students' rag occur on the same day (and Christmas day at that). Greene's having Anne and Raven talk almost interminably while half-freezing overnight seems another flaw. David Lodge calls *This Gun for Hire* "a kind of secular rehearsal for *Brighton Rock* (1938), his first overtly Catholic novel."

Gene D. Phillips and Quentin Falk discuss the movie *This Gun for Hire* (1942). It has an altered plot: California becomes the locale, time is the 1940s, and armament conspirators become American traitors. Raven, played by Alan Ladd (sans harelip), obtains military secrets from American scientist, shoots him, delivers secrets to Raven's boss. Raven is betrayed by William Gates (Davis renamed, played by Laird Cregar) and pursued by Michael Crane (Mather renamed, played by Robert Preston), with help of girlfriend, dancer and F.B.I. mole Ellen Graham (Anne redone, played by Veronica Lake). The war-time ending makes Raven a patriot. Carlos Clarens discusses the movie as "a modest B-plus Paramount thriller" that "added a wicked American twist by making the capitalist villain ([played by] Tulley Marshall) a decrepit double for Henry Ford." James Cagney directed *Short Cut to Hell*, another movie remake (1957) of *This Gun for Hire*. (Sources: Clarens, 178; Lodge, 14; Phillips, 26–27; Falk, 27–33 passim. 212; Sherry I, 571–86 passim; Wolfe, 53, 72, 77)

THOMAS ("The Destructors"). He is a harmless old man, a retired builder and decorator. His house, built 200 years ago by Christopher Wren, is the only residence in Wormsley Common standing after bombings during World War II. Mr. Thomas, as the Wormsley Common Gang of kids courteously call him, is nicknamed Old Misery. Although Thomas minds his own business, Trevor, known as T., leads the gang in a careful plan to hollow and raze the once-stately mansion.

Yvonne Cloetta* tries to connect Thomas here and Greene's choosing the name Thomas at his Catholic baptismal ceremony. (Source: Cloetta, 53)

THOMAS, FATHER (*A Burnt-Out Case*). He is a priest, from Liège, who has served as the supervisor of the leproserie school two years and must remain four more before having a leave. His nervous callowness — he fears the dark — and inexperience make him judgmental and uneasy. He incorrectly sees saintliness in Querry, who calls him "a pious fool."

When Father Thomas confesses to Querry that if he remains at the leproserie much longer he may lose his faith, Greene makes it obvious that this Doubting Thomas is appropriately named.

THRIPLOW, HENRY ("The Lottery Ticket"). He is a well-to-do, pale-haired bachelor, about 40, living with his aunt in her flat in Kensington, London. His timidity causes him to vacation in places remote from tourists. This time he chooses an impoverished state in Mexico. When the lottery ticket he bought back in Vera Cruz wins, he offers to donate the money to a worthy cause. The bank manager advises with the corrupt Governor, and Thriplow's 50,000 pesos wind up enabling the Governor's corrupt Chief of Police to cause the death of the Governor's liberal rival.

Thriplow's unusual name comes from that of a Cambridgeshire village near a farmhouse owned by Greene's special mistress Catherine Walston* and her husband Harry Walston. Greene has little reason to have his character Thriplow tell the dead liberal's daughter, when he notices her sewing work, that he embroiders, unless Greene wishes to imply that some misguided anti–Fascists are gay. The Catholic woman's acceptance of affairs causes Thriplow at the end to recall some words remembered from his childhood concerning "one who had so loved the world" (*see* John 3:16). (Sources: Shelden, 358; Sherry II, 330)

"THE TICK OF THE CLOCK: A LEGEND" (1921). Short story. (Characters: None named.)

An old clock ticks in an old servant's attic-bedroom. She dusts, polishes, and winds it, even though it is always wrong by 10 to 90 minutes. Every night she hopes it will tell her something, but it only goes "tick-tock." Childless herself, she would lavish love on the children in the house; but they call her a witch, and so she can be affectionate only to the clock. (*See* Harris, H. R.)

Norman Sherry reprints this poignant piece, which appeared in Greene's school magazine *The Berkhamstedian* and in the London *Star* (January 18, 1921), and earned Greene three guineas. (Sources: Greene, *A Sort of Life*, 110–11; Sherry I, 103–04; Sherry II, 112)

TIERNEY (*The Heart of the Matter*). Tierney and Ducker are mentioned in Harris's copy of the *Downhamian* news bulletin as being capable soccer forwards.

TIGRE, EL (*The Honorary Consul*). He is the leader of the revolutionaries but never appears. Rivas follows his orders. Ribera complains that, unlike those he commands, El Tigre lives and dines well and safely.

TILLY (*Brighton Rock*). She evidently was a servant in Drewitt's house. When Pinkie goes to his house and asks where Tilly is, a strange girl says she has left.

TIMS, RICHARD (*The Man Within*). He is a wild, mentally challenged member of Carlyon's smuggling crew. He is captured along with five others. During their trial at the Assizes in Lewes, Tims is declared incompetent and released. Later it is claimed that Tims shot Rexall, the revenue agent. Still later Carlyon and his cronies post Tims outside Elizabeth Garnet's cottage to watch for Andrews.

TINKER BELL (*The Human Factor*). This is old Mrs. Castle's Burmese cat. Her son Maurice Castle's boxer Bullen would relish killing Tinker Bell.

Greene reminisced fondly about being taken as a child to London to see *Peter Pan* and being affected by Tinker Bell's death. (Source: Greene, *A Sort of Life*, 57)

TIN TIN (*The Comedians*). Tin Tin, almost 18, is one of Mère Catherine's brothel girls. Brown knew her two years earlier and remembers her fondly. When he visits the place again, Tin Tin is with Jones. (Tin Tin is "Tintin" in some editions.)

TINY ("The Over-night Bag"). This fat woman sits beside Cooper on the Nice-to-London airplane. Tiny questions him about what's in his over-night bag. She may be the lesbian lover of Bertha, who wrote to her "darling Tiny."

TINY (*This Gun for Hire*). She is defrocked, demented Acky's old, wrinkled, gray, dirty, evil wife. They run a Nottwich bawdy house. Davis takes Anne Crowder there and hides her in a fireplace. Tiny dotes on Acky's impressive but hypocritical verbosity. Raven sees Tiny with Anne's handbag, follows her, and rescues Anne.

TISSAND, M. (*Loser Takes All*). He works for Dreuther in Nice. Dreuther orders his secretary Miss Bullen to phone Tissand to make arrangements for Bertram's and Cary's arrival and wedding.

TITI, TIBERIO (*Travels with My Aunt*). When Detective-Sergeant Sparrow asks Henry if Augusta ever mentioned Titi Tiberio, and also Cossa, Passerati, and Stradano, he answers negatively.

TOADS (*Doctor Fischer of Geneva*). Anna-Luise Jones calls the toadying guests at her father Doctor Fischer's parties "Toads." The Toads are Henri Belmont, Richard Deane, Kips, General Krueger, and Mrs. Montgomery.

TOD (*The Heart of the Matter*). He is a junior officer seen drinking at the club bar with Thimblerigg.

TOD, EMMY (*Orient Express*). She is the chargirl in *The Great Gay Round*, Savory's popular novel. The Hon. Carol Delaine is to play Emmy Tod in the British movie production of the novel.

TOM (*Brighton Rock*). He is Ida Arnold's former husband. Her stolen handbag contains some of his love letters. She may let him return to her.

TOM ("Under the Garden"). He is the protagonist in Wilditch's story about his dream and fantasy under the garden.

Greene hinted in *A Sort of Life* that Tom here may "echo ... Tom Kitten" in Beatrix Potter's stories he enjoyed as a child. Beatrix Potter (1866–1943) wrote and illustrated some 23 children's books, including *The Tale of Tom Kitten* (1907), *Tom Kitten's Painting Book* (1917), and, in between, *The Roly Poly Pudding* (1908), in which larcenous rats almost cook Tom for dinner. Greene in *The Lost Childhood and Other Essays* mentions Tom Kitten and the rats. (Sources: Greene, *Lost Childhood*, 206; Greene, *A Sort of Life*, 52)

TOMLINSON, BRIGADIER (*The Human Factor*). He is a high-ranking MI6 officer who orders Castle and Davis to report to him to meet Daintry, Tomlinson's "new broom." Tomlinson has a white moustache (black when Castle saw him once, years back) and a pot belly.

TONI ("Two Gentle People"). He is a ballet dancer and is one of Marie-Claire Duval's husband's homosexual partners.

Addicted to sex as he was, Greene pornographically adds to his characterization of Toni by having him boast, mostly to strangers, that he modeled for the "stone phallus" prominent in Duval's living room.

TONY (*The Confidential Agent*). When D. tries to ask Captain Currie for information at the roadhouse north of Dover, Currie avoids him by saying he sees Tony and exits.

TONY ("May We Borrow Your Husband?"). Tony and Stephen, both interior decorators and homosexual lovers, are vacationing in Antibes. They spot Peter Travis, an inept bridegroom just starting his honeymoon with Poopy Travis, stalk him, borrow him from her, and seduce him. Tony leaves Stephen in anticipation of good times wrecking the Travis marriage back in England. Harris, who observes much of the action, regards Tony as bright and brutal, while Stephen is stupid.

"TOP HATS IN HELL" *see* **"WORK NOT IN PROGRESS"**

TOPLING, CANON (*The Ministry of Fear*). He is a religious figure working legitimately with the Free Mothers. Willi Hilfe thinks Topling, whom Anna Hilfe regards as honorable, might help Rowe locate Mrs. Bellairs.

TORNER, PETER (*The Name of Action*). He is a would-be revolutionary associated with Kapper in Trier. Shrill-voiced, mountainous Torner is called an artist but is mainly talented in drawing caricatures for posters satirizing both Demassener, the dictator, and his wife Anne-Marie. Demassener for too long tolerates the cartoons as harmless. Before meeting Torner, Chant foolishly romanticizes him as perhaps resembling Peter Paul Rubens.

TORT ("A Discovery in the Woods"). This is the name of one of the two sets of parents in Bottom who had more than one child. The other family is named Fox. The Tort couple produced triplets.

TOUPARD (*The Tenth Man*). He was a villager fifty miles from Paris. Carosse murdered, robbed, and stole papers from him. Chavel uses knowledge of Carosse's crime to help save Thérèse Mangeot.

TOUTE À TOI (*A Burnt-Out Case*). A former mistress of Querry signs a letter to him thus. He insincerely signed his letters to her that way too, but left her three months earlier. Her signing is probably sincere. Querry foolishly tells Marie Rycker about this "signature," and she uses the phrase to tell witnesses that she is all Querry's.

TRAGGERS, MISS "PONY" (*Our Man in Havana*). She is named as the author of *White Mare*, a novel Milly Wormold has in her room.

Most oddly, the publishers of the late Jules Watson (1917–2001) issued her novel *The White Mare* posthumously (2005).

TRAVELS WITH MY AUNT (1969). Novel. (Characters: Abdul, Abdullah, Ada, Amis, Augusta Beltram, Blennerhasset, Mrs. Blennerhasset, Mrs. Brewster, the British Ambassador, Annette-Marie Callot, Camilla, Edward Carpenter, Major Charge, the Chief of Police, the Chief of Police, Comfort, Cossa,

Courage, Harvey Crowder, Melany Curlew, William Curlew, Curran, Achille Dambreuse, Madame Dambreuse, Louise Dupont, the Dutch Ambassador, Edith, Dr. Havelock Ellis, Fernandez, Flageollet, the General, Frau General, Field-Marshal [Hermann Wilhelm] Goering, Colonel Hakim, Colonel Hakim, Hannibal, Hatty, Hughes, Miss Hughes, the Indian Queen, Julian, Sir Alfred Keene, Barbara Keene, Doris Keene, Knock-Me-Down, [James] Ramsay MacDonald, Maria, the Monster of the Chemins de Fer, Nancy, E[dith]. Nesbit, Newman, Sir Oswald Newman, the Nicaraguan Ambassador, James O'Toole, Lucinda O'Toole, Mrs. O'Toole, Passerati, Miss Paterson, Payne, Peter, Charles Pottifer, Angela Pulling, Henry Pulling, Jo Pulling, Richard Pulling, Peter, Rita, Edward Rhodes Robinson, Dr. Rodriguez, Rose, [George] Bernard Shaw, Smudge, Detective-Sergeant John Sparrow, Stradano, Superman, Tiberio Titi, Miss Truman, Councilor Trumbull, Visconti, Mario Visconti, Signora Visconti, Weissmann, H. G. Wells, Wolf, Detective-Inspector Woodrow, Zachary Wordsworth, Wilbur Wright.)

Part 1: Chapter 1. Henry (Pulling), the narrator (in his 50s), a never-married London bank manager, retired two years earlier. At the funeral and cremation of his mother (Angela Pulling, 85), he sees her sister Augusta (Beltram, 73) for the first time in more than 50 years. Aunt Augusta has high-piled red hair, prominent front teeth, and a direct manner. She implies that Henry's father (Richard Pulling, building contractor, dead over 40 years) was peppier than Angela and criticizes Henry's dahlia-cultivating hobby. He takes mamma's ashes in a steel urn.

Chapter 2. On the way to her flat by taxi, Augusta tells Henry that Angela remained virginal, and accepted as theirs Richard's Henry by another woman, who refused marriage.

Chapter 3. They approach Augusta's flat, above the Crown and Anchor pub. Zachary Wordsworth, a big, middle-aged black from Sierra Leone, opens Augusta's door. The flat has Venice-like decor, double bed, and Disney-appointed "snuggery" for Wordsworth. Over whisky, she tells Henry she once attended an important writer's funeral. She offers to take Henry traveling. He forgets his stepmother's paper-wrapped ash-urn, which Wordsworth hands him on the street. Henry has lunch at home, ponders Augusta's revelations, and plans a garden spot for the urn.

Chapter 4. Henry recalls that when Sir Alfred Keene, a bank client, died, his daughter Barbara, nearing 40, invited him to dinner. He almost proposed, but he gardened and she tatted. She reluctantly went to live with South African cousins. Augusta phones Henry to tell him the police raided her place, suspecting something because Wordsworth handed Henry a package. She told them about Henry's mother's ashes. Detective-Sergeant Sparrow and a policeman interview Henry, tell him Wordsworth's pockets revealed marijuana, and take the ash-urn for analysis. Henry phones Augusta, who says she gave Wordsworth £20 to skip to Paris. When she suggests some traveling, he replies she couldn't find Wordsworth in Paris. She suggests Istabul, where (General) Abdul is — a 1920s friend, heard from just today. Henry suggests Brighton instead.

Chapter 5. Brighton. Augusta recalls a man named Curran whose circus career 40 years ago ended when an elephant named Hannibal crushed his toe. Augusta finds Curran's friend Hatty, now a fortune-teller. The two women giggle while reminiscing. Over tea leaves, Hatty foretells aunt and nephew will travel adventurously. Henry doubts it.

Chapter 6. Augusta tells Henry about Curran. After his foot injury in Brighton, they started a church to marry dogs. Curran found suitable religious texts to sermonize about dogs' souls, but not those of cats or fish. Long disappeared, Curran would be 90 now.

Chapter 7. London. Henry phones Sparrow and learns his mother's ashes included cannabis. Sassing Sparrow, Henry feels rebellious like daddy. Augusta books passage for Henry and herself on the Orient Express, for Istanbul. Henry admires her eloquent anecdotes: Shakespeare play in Tunis; girl named Comfort who married coward named Courage; Henry's uncle Jo Pulling the bookie, who wanted to travel around the world, had stroke in Venice; she bought him run-down 52-room Milan *palazzo*; Jo traveled weekly therein, had stroke in room #51, died crawling toward room #52; Visconti helped her quit traveling with *la quindicina* (teen-aged prostitutes). Augusta tells Henry not to worry about money, also that, not knowing laws, she can't break any.

Chapter 8. After getting a neighbor to water his dahlias, Henry accompanies Augusta to Heathrow. Arranging for her red-ticketed suitcase to be shipped separately to La Bourget, she and Henry drink aloft and discuss smuggling and brothels, which Wordsworth, once a Heathrow loader, knew about.

Chapter 9. At La Bourget, Henry retrieves the uninspected suitcase, and Augusta engages a St. James and Albany Hotel suite. An elegant man calls on Augusta and manages her suitcased £10,000. Henry reassures himself of steadfast British morality by reading *Punch*. Outside, he encounters Wordsworth, who entices him to an A.1 joint, offers him a girl, is declined, and when queried about the marijuana says he meant no harm.

Chapter 10. The Albany. Henry asks Augusta if she ever wanted a baby. She names various lovers able to help but says she couldn't have traveled with a child. She reminisces about Achille Dambreuse, a metallurgist retired because of ill health. He and Augusta were orgiastic lovers six months in the Albany, until Achille, his wife, two of his four children, Augusta, and Louise Dupont, Achille's contemporaneous St. James mistress, all bumped into each other. Augusta lamented his embarrassed departure, because she wasn't the jealous type.

Chapter 11. After dinner at Maxim's, Henry and Augusta, in her couchette (#72), are ready for the Orient Express to leave the Gare de Lyon bound for Istanbul, when Henry sees Wordsworth. He laments the temporary loss of Augusta, his "bebi gel." Sitting on Henry's couchette (#71) is Tooley (Lucinda O'Toole), 18, heading beyond Istanbul, to Katmandu. She offers to share her cokes, chocolate, and ham.

Chapter 12. Past Lausanne, coffee and *brioches*. Past Bex, Henry loves the peaceful scenery, is tempted to disembark and leave Augusta. Tooley gives Henry a grubby cigarette, which turns out to be pot. She explains she's American, studying literature; her parents are divorced; her father is in the CIA; her boyfriend Julian argued with her because she forgot the pill and she's maybe pregnant; Wordsworth, in Paris, offered to help her; Julian is hitchhiking, to economize, to Istanbul.

Chapter 13. Milan. Augusta rushes to meet handsome Mario Visconti. Unseen for 30 years, he's her old friend Visconti's son, 45 or 46 now. The two, with Henry and Tooley, lunch. Mario, who writes verse drama and sponges, puzzles Henry, charms Tooley, orders food and drink knowledgeably, lets Augusta pay. On the train to Venice, Augusta tells Henry: Augusta dumped Curran in England; he took her savings; she got to Paris, met Mario's father, toured Italy with him; Jo Pulling willed everything to her; she gave Joe's *palazzo* to Mario; Visconti lost her money and his wife's trying to sell tomatoes to Saudi Arabians; when Visconti disappeared, she did business in Havana, then Rome; Visconti bumped into her there, amorously. When Henry criticizes Visconti, Augusta reviles Henry: Regret your mistakes, if you want to wallow; despise no one; learn, like your father, to cheat.

Chapter 14. The Belgrade station. Henry buys himself some food and cokes for Tooley. Through Venice in darkness. Tooley tells him this: Julian paints soup cans after Andy Warhol; her divorced mother married a foreign correspondent, lives in Bonn. Customs at Sezana. On to Ljubljana, Zagreb. Breakfast with Tooley at Belgrade's station hotel. Dreadful food at Sofia. Tooley maunders, then goes to her bunk. Henry finds Augusta checking an Istanbul map. She tells him she returned to England during the war, while Visconti supplied Germans with Italian art during the occupation in Rome, survived, wrote recently to Mario, who replied; hence their travels now. Augusta hints she has a tarred-over gold ingot, rambles that Mario told her his father dressed like a priest to evade arrest by Germans and had to hear one German officer's Italian girlfriend's confession, then that of Frau General, in whose staff car they escaped to Florence.

Chapter 15. As the train hits Istanbul, Tooley cheerfully tells Henry and Augusta "the curse" has obliterated pregnancy fears. She departs with several jolly Americans. The Pera Palace. Augusta, without an expected message from General Abdul, is upset. Henry taxis to the West Berlin Hotel, gets tearfully drunk, envies men dancing with each other, returns to Augusta. The phone announces Colonel Hakim's approach. Augusta orders Henry to unpack her heavy-based candle and light it. Hakim enters, questions her about Abdul, who has just been wounded trying to escape arrest on a 30-year-old Interpol warrant, searches her luggage and Henry's, and courteously departs. She tells Henry the gold-based candle was for Abdul to invest for old Visconti.

Chapter 16. London. Henry, happily home again, waters his dahlias, and reads a mistyped letter from Miss Keene, in Koffiefontein, South Africa. He picks up his father's copy of Sir Walter Scott's *Rob Roy*, finds a photograph of teenage Augusta therein, phones her to ask where his father Richard is buried. In Boulogne, she explains. He decides to take her there.

Chapter 17. London to autumnal Dover, Calais to Boulogne. In the evening, Boulogne reminds Henry of East Anglia. He and Augusta dine at the maritime rail station. She tells him about his father's friend William Curlew, whose wife Melany was so demanding in bed that the two men wrote her a lie about William's infidelity, hoping for his release; but Melany forgave and held on.

Chapter 18. By plan, Henry and Augusta visit Richard's grave on 2 October, the 40th or so anniversary of his death (1923). Present is a little woman with a wreath. She is Miss Paterson. Over afternoon tea she explains she met Richard on a London bus, they visited Boulogne on holiday, and he died in her arms. She now lives in Boulogne, where she taught English at the Lycée during the war. Augusta's asking shyly defiant Mrs. Paterson bitterly ironic questions bothers tender Henry, who turns critical.

Chapter 19. Miffed, Augusta goes to Paris on business; Henry, to rainy London and his now-dull routine. Six weeks pass. He phones the St. James and Albany, learns Augusta left for Cherbourg. He receives and answers a letter from Miss Keene. Lonely Christmas Eve finds Henry dining at a pseudo-festive little restaurant. At St. John's Church service Detective-Sergeant Sparrow awaits him, with Detective-Inspector Woodrow, his superior. Questioned, Henry says he last heard from his aunt in Boulogne, acknowledges knowing the names General Abdul and Visconti. He learns Abdul is dead and Visconti, a war criminal wanted by Interpol and mentioned by Abdul, is missing though long thought dead. Henry denies the men admittance to his aunt's flat.

Chapter 20. After Boxing Day, Henry goes to Augusta's flat. He finds a post card from A.D. (Achille Dambreuse) saying how *miraculeux* it was to bump, too briefly, into Augusta aboard ship after a years'-long *séparation*. Woodrow and Sparrow enter with a warrant, take A.D.'s card, search fruitlessly, admire Wordsworth's Freetown photo, and say Visconti may be dangerous for Augusta.

Part 2: Chapter 1. Six months pass. Henry gets a letter from Miss Keene so appealing he almost wires a marriage proposal. But a letter, with check enclosed, from Augusta orders him to sell her furniture, bring Wordsworth's sentimental Freetown photo, and come to Buenos Aires. Henry gets there, finds a message at her hotel to proceed not by air but by boat up La Plata and the Paraná and the Paraguay rivers to Asunción, Paraguay, where a distressed friend of hers is. On the Paraná, Henry has a pre-lunch gin, is accosted by a Spanish-speaking octogenarian for whom "a tall lean sad grey man" interprets. The oldster reads Henry's palm, accurately — come afar, journey nearly finished, reunion with someone, money once in your care. The other man, James O'Toole, says he's from Philadelphia, spouts guidebook-like information about the region, learns Henry is heading for Asunción. He queries Henry, who feels free to respond — until the man gives his nickname, "Tooley." At lunch, after O'-Toole questions two other men, Henry says O'Toole's daughter is in Katmandu. This worries O'Toole, who denies any connection with the CIA.

Chapter 2. Next morning, O'Toole doesn't appear. Henry reads his father's *Rob Roy* and chats with a Czech whose parents died, one during the war, one later. An unsuccessful plastic-straw manufacturer, the Czech now makes plastic material.

Chapter 3. On the Paraguay river, near Corrientes. Henry briefly goes ashore at Formosa, compares his past — so unlike Augusta's — to that "prison-house" image in William Wordsworth's Ode. Suddenly black Wordsworth appears, says Augusta told him to await Henry here, asks about his Freetown picture, and sneaks aboard. O'Toole spots him. After their final-night dinner O'Toole pours bourbon for Henry, who clams up when asked about Wordsworth. A cloudburst descends. O'Toole says Paraguayans smuggle scotch whisky and

American cigarettes, but at too great a risk for him to participate. Henry finds Wordsworth in his cabin, with his three-bladed boy's knife in hand. He says Augusta wants the photo, says she's with a pleading old timer now, not vigorous Wordsworth. Henry describes O'Toole. Wordsworth says O'Toole is dangerous and frightened Augusta's "fellah" in Asunción. Wordsworth takes the photo.

Chapter 4. Asunción. Everyone disembarks. Henry rejects O'Toole's offer to help at the embassy and dismisses his attention to Wordsworth, who gets Henry into a friend's taxi, which deposits them at an enormous old mansion. Augusta greets them, is happy Wordsworth has the photo, says Visconti hasn't returned yet. At dinner, served by Wordsworth, she isn't surprised O'Toole followed Henry, rationalizes Visconti's art-work crimes, says she brought Wordsworth from Paris for protection, has replenished sick Visconti's cash flow here, bought this mansion, and hints at smuggling via a Dakota (American C-47). Next day, no Visconti, now known as Izquierdo. Henry walks around corrupt, soldier-infested, sweet-smelling Asunción. Returning, he overhears both Augusta's rejecting Wordsworth's "jig-jig" abed and his spurning of her money. She wants only Visconti. Warned of danger, Wordsworth leaves. Augusta tells Henry she loves unarrestable Visconti, will help him make a fortune in Paraguay — he nearly did so in Saudi Arabia, then Italy — then maybe they'll go to Brazil. Henry says he might marry Miss Keene in England. Aunty derides the dullness of tatting and gardening, whereas smuggling here will thrillingly push back death's wall.

Chapter 5. Next morning, Henry attends the National Day parade, sees the General (President Alfredo Stroessmer), his colonels, and people waving red things indicating the Colorado political party. Augusta gave Henry a red scarf, which, after sneezing, he thoughtlessly uses to blow his nose. This offends the national color; so he gets knocked down, taken to the police station, punched until he mentions O'Toole and the American embassy, then is locked up. O'Toole appears, will help, admits he's "kind of" with the CIA, says the police got Wordsworth to talk jealously about smuggler Izquierdo, whom several — including noncommittal Henry — know as Visconti. Henry agrees to let O'Toole interview Augusta. O'Toole drives Henry to her mansion. She meets O'Toole, criticizes what he did to Izquierdo in Argentina, says Visconti is upstairs.

Chapter 6. Visconti, fat and missing some teeth, meets Henry, boasts to O'Toole he has money again, orders Augusta to bring champagne, tells O'Toole how he beat the Buenos Aires lie-detecting machine, listens to O'Toole's quid-pro-quo security offer, boasts of flying his loaded Dakota to Argentina with whisky and cigarettes from Panama and returning just now with furniture for the mansion. Visconti orders Augusta to produce the Freetown picture, peels off its backing, finds a Leonardo da Vinci drawing of a military dredge under it, and gives it to O'Toole for $10,000. O'Toole departs. Visconti confesses the picture is a copy, tears up Wordsworth's Freetown photo, and he and his Augusta retire.

Chapter 7. Next morning Henry gulps champagne while Visconti intones about rats' and his own rat-like survivability. Augusta voices plans for tomorrow's dinner and dance, tells Henry about a fellow named Charles Pottifer. He was a tax collector, hated taxes, faked a money-losing company, and hired a telephone answering-service to pretend after his death he was alive and busy. Henry reminisces about his dull English life, says he's happy here. Augusta pats her "darling boy."

Chapter 8. Visconti's "apotheosis" is a banquet with roast ox and many guests, including O'Toole. Henry polkas drunkenly with Camilla, the Chief of Police's lovely daughter, then talks outside with Maria, the customs officer's daughter, 14. Maria knows English and recites sad poetry. She and Henry like Tennyson. Visconti talks with the Czech about a scheme to sell his plastic straws. Guests leave. Henry naps, awakens before dawn, happily aware he won't return to England. Outside, he steps on Wordsworth's knife, then finds Wordsworth, killed by Visconti's mustachioed old bodyguard. Wordsworth romantically, fatally, tried once more to go woo his love. Henry addresses Aunt Augusta, dancing with Visconti, as "Mother." Henry orders Wordsworth's killer sacked. Henry, Augusta, and Visconti — the police have killed his unnamed partner — own their smuggling Dakota. Henry will wed Maria when she turns 16.

Greene's visit to Argentina and Paraguay (1968) is reflected in the last chapters of *Travels with My Aunt*, the action in which should be dated as close to 1968. (Some time references are confusing; if, however, Augusta was born around 1895 and is about 75, the action is roughly 1968. Also, Henry, born in 1913, is in his 50s.) Viking, Greene's American publishers, wanted the title changed because it sounded too much like *Travels with Charley* (1962) by their late best-selling author John Steinbeck (1902–1968). Greene refused, and London's Bodley Head published the novel (1969) with Greene's desired title, and so did Viking (1970). But Greene, miffed at Viking, contracted lucratively with Simon & Schuster for his next novel, *The Honorary Consul* (1974).

Both Michael Shelden and Norman Sherry discover incidents in Greene's life transmuted into *Travels with My Aunt*, and both downgrade the novel as a consequence. Shelden calls it "farcical," "full of obscure personal references" and "bad jokes." Sherry first calls it "a flawed gem," a "picaresque" work lacking "pace" and composed of "loosely connected" stories; then adds that Aunt Augusta is "not wickedly interesting, but merely a naughty old lady"; but finally commends Part Two for revealing Greene as "a novelist of merit." R. H. Miller calls *Travels with My Aunt* "a brilliant comic tour de force ... with a pace that dominates the novel and a concurrent emphasis on melodrama and on action over character." He especially likes its conclusion, which, he believes — since it means a new life for Henry in Paraguay and Argentina, with his birth mother, lucrative smuggling, and a teenage bride — "brings this wonderfully entertaining and skillfully developed story to a redemptive close for both mother and son." Volker Schulz discusses *Travels with My Aunt* not as a picaresque novel nor as *une education sentimentale*, but as a Bildungsroman, with Henry crossing from his dull world into that of his "aunt," which is a mobile, adventuresome, amoral, intense, pleasant, amorous region. Mark Bosco remarks that this novel "lacked the religious intensity of his [Greene's] earlier ones." Peter Mudford notes its "very distinctive theme: survival." Tell that to General Abdul, Zachary Wordsworth, and even James O'Toole. Leopoldo Duran says Greene wrote him that he thought highly of *Travels with My Aunt*, which was "serious," "sad," and happened "to be funny." Yvonne Cloetta* notes that Greene called *Travels with My Aunt* a sad farce with some humorous scenes. Is it too rigidly righteous to add that *Travels with My Aunt* is partly a rollicking would-be rationalization? Aunt Augusta is as fecklessly sexually abandoned as Greene himself.

Quentin Falk discusses the dreadful movie based on *Travels with My Aunt* (1972), starring Maggie Smith (as Aunt Augusta), Alec McCowen (Henry Pulling), Robert Stephens (Visconti), and Lou Gossett (Wordsworth). Falk reports that Katharine Hepburn (1907–2003), whom Greene wanted for Augusta, worked briefly with director George Cukor (1899–1983), but she was too old to do flashbacks presenting Augusta as a youth; so Hepburn quit even though Cukor let her do considerable script rewriting. The plot was changed: Dambreuse helps Augusta get hold of his wife's Amedeo Modigliani painting to ransom Visconti, who is Henry's father and who kidnaps himself and takes the cash. Greene despised the script writers' omission of the South American finale. Falk praises Smith's youthful flashbacks that Hepburn feared to try, but he deplores Henry's filmic loss of innocence with Tooley. (Sources: Bosco, 72; Cloetta, 27–28; Duran, 240; Falk, 165–68 passim, 213–14; Miller, 126, 130; Schulz; Shelden, 458, 462, 463; Sherry III, 490, 491)

TRAVERS (*The Ministry of Fear*) *see* **COST**

TRAVERS, PUFFIN (*England Made Me*). Gullie tells Farrant, while he and others are playing poker at Krogh's apartment, that Puffin Travers invited Gullie to shoot with him at a moor Travers has taken in Scotland.

TRAVIS ("May We Borrow Your Husband?"). He is Peter Travis's father, and has 3,000 acres in Hampshire, England, managed by Peter. The elder Travis breeds horses, wants his son to provide heirs, and knows Peter's bride Poopy Travis's mother has money.

TRAVIS, DR. (*The Heart of the Matter*). He is a recently arrived physician, serving at Argyll Hospital. Robinson, the terminally ill banker, recommends him to Scobie. Scobie consults him, feigns angina symptoms, and is given epi-van pills. He uses 12 of them to commit suicide.

TRAVIS, PETER ("May We Borrow Your Husband?"). He is tall, slim, in his early 20s, and is Poopy's bridegroom. They start a sexless honeymoon in Antibes. Harris stands by as Poopy, naively and wrongly blaming herself, loses Peter, probably forever, when Stephen and Tony, homosexual lovers, seduce him.

TRAVIS, POOPY ("May We Borrow Your Husband?"). She is Peter Travis's virginal bride at the start of their Antibes honeymoon — and later. Tall, slim, with big eyes, and in her early 20s, Poopy is appealing enough to Harris to make him want to warn her and sleep with her. He does neither, concluding she won't understand anything he says. When Stephen and Tony, amoral homosexuals, seduce Peter, Poopy hopes they'll all be friends back in England.

Could Greene have given Poopy her dumb name because he remembered reviewing *Poppy*, the 1936 movie in which W. C. Fields utters his famous line "Never give a sucker an even break"? Greene's Poopy is a sucker, to whom Stephen and Tony give no break.

Greene launches personal critical jibes by having Harris ridicule Poopy's taste in reading, which Harris labels almost unbearably innocent and which includes Dornford Yates (pen name, Cecil William Mercer [1885–1960]), Hugh Walpole (1884–1941), and Charles Snow (1905–1980). It seems obligatory to disagree when Michael Shelden not only accuses poor Poopy of trying "to seduce him [Harris] with candid talk about how neglected she feels" but also adds that "he braves this assault ... as the detached novelist whose interest in this sexual comedy is strictly professional." Harris regards Poopy as hopelessly trapped by inexperience and feels that, although he wishes he could help, no rational words could penetrate her naiveté. (Sources: Greene, *Graham The Greene Film Reader*, 121–22; Shelden, 75)

TRENCH (*The Ministry of Fear*). Willi Hilfe is eager to leave the Free Mothers' office and take Rowe to see Mrs. Bellairs. So, when Anna Hilfe reminds Willi he is to see Trench, he tells her to handle Trench herself.

Greene called his alter ego Hilary Trench and used that name as a pseudonym. (*See* Tench, Henry.)

TREVOR ("The Destructors"). Enraged unless he is called T., this adolescent, 14, is the son of an ex-architect. T. leads his Wormsley Common Gang of delinquent boys in a plan to destroy the home of Mr. Thomas, called Old Misery. Built 200 years ago by Christopher Wren, the fine mansion is the only one remaining in an region bombed during World War II. T.'s aesthetic theory is that destroying something beautiful can be a creative act. (Vandals and graffiti specialists, take note.)

Norman Sherry, finding Greene bits in T., reports that Greene had a "gloomy and morbid double personality" and that when "unpleasant" traits came to the surface he referred to himself as "Hilary Trench" and "H.T." The name Trench is close to Trevor, while H.T. is even closer to T. Daphna Erdinast-Vulcan thinks T. could be motivated in either of two contrary ways; his destroying Old Misery's house "may be either an act of defiance against the father who failed or an act of revenge against the social system which had failed the father." (Maybe T. is simply evil?)

Greene is partly T.'s obverse: T. allegedly practices creative destruction; Greene practices destructive creativity, since he often wrecked relationships and beliefs, then was inspired by losses to write. (Sources: Erdinast-Vulcan, 16; Sherry II, 67)

"THE TRIAL OF PAN" (1923). Short story. (Characters: Elijah, Gabriel, God, Lady Hope-Smithies, Lord Hope-Smithies, Isaiah, Michael, Moses, Pan, Samuel.)

The 12 jurymen are tired, having passed judgment on 48 persons, all dull cases. The 45 innocents included six prostitutes, 14 murderers, two robbers, a swindler. The three guilties were Anglican curate, bank director, Lady Hope-Smithies. The curate had thrown promiscuous tracts at people. The banker committed fraud. Lady Hope-Smithies, the worst, had given money to charity, punched the curate, had lost money playing bridge, had given a cousin a present. Gabriel, her counsel, put up a fight. Michael demolished his points: In return for charity, she received a winning lottery ticket good for a necklace; she slugged the curate because he objected to pugs; her husband paid her card losses; her cousin already had a legacy. Michael then worsened her case by noting she recited a lugubrious poem at concerts and kept six pet dogs, including two pugs and a Pekinese. God issued a summary condemnation, and the jury called her guilty

Now comes Pan's trial. The jury knows he's guilty but anticipates excitement. But it's dull. Charge after charge. Guilty. God looks up from his blotter, strokes his white beard; sees Pan's handsome face, lithe figure, curly hair; seems briefly to see stern Moses, repentance-crying Isaiah, crafty Samuel, cruel Elijah. Looking at God, Pan can't believe "this old, gloom-wrapped dotard could ... be ... [what] men [and women] ... deserted the old religion" for, and in so doing "turned from the old joys, and the old sweet terrors," accepted "bondage," "repression and gloom," surrendered passion for peace, pride for humility, desire for purity. From his position of "strength and eternal youth," Pan feels pity for judgmental God. God asks Pan if he can explain why judgment shouldn't be visited on him. Looking up at heaven's blue summer sky, God finds it uniquely difficult to concentrate. He seems to have been sitting in judgment a long time. He resists taking to the open air again, feels old. Pan smiles, feels pity again, decides to give God a chance, says he won't speak but will express himself in music. Accepting the challenge, God tells him to proceed. Thus begins the battle between the old, ever young, and newness already aging. Pan's creeping tune expresses forests, light and elves, desires and scariness. All in the court feel nice chills. God sits, smiles, thinks of former judgments. Pan's tune expresses joys, lusts, feasts, songs, dancing, shouts, flowers, fruits, wines, boys' and girls' limbs and kisses. Eyes sparkle in the rapt court. God laughs at having feared Pan's strength, closes his eyes, and jeers at the notion of such fun outmatching heaven's joys—the cross, sacred songs, purity, love, peace, incense, prayers, everlasting communion with the supreme maker. Pan continues: Come, embrace, kiss. God remembers age-old creation's work and half-forgotten elements therein. He feels his aching old head. He mustn't cry. The music fades. Asking for Michael, who doesn't answer, God opens his eyes. The room is empty. God, fatigued, scribbles on his blotter. No more trials, anyway. His beard seems longer. He doesn't feel terribly old. Look at him, aloft on his judgment seat, beneath the blue sky, playing solitary "noughts and crosses" on his blotter.

This early story, published in the *Oxford Outlook* (February 1923) and never reprinted, foreshadows Greene's lifelong debate with himself about the body vs. the soul, and hints at his more-than-timid discontent with God. In addition, "pity," one of the most loaded words in all of Greene's works, appears in this early story four times.

TRIFFEN, PETER (*The Confidential Agent*). While reminiscing about Rose Cullen, Mrs. Bennett recalls the time little Peter Triffen scared Rose with a windup toy mouse.

TROUIN, CAPTAIN (*The Quiet American*). Born in Vietnam, Trouin is a loyal but disillusioned French Air Force pilot stationed in Haiphong. He tells Fowler he may have bombed old friends of his father. He especially hates dropping napalm. He feels that the war is lost and that final eventual peace terms will resemble those proposed years earlier. Trouin takes Fowler on a vertical bombing run near the Chinese border, and, later, to an opium parlor in which there is a half-breed prostitute whom Trouin and his friend Lieutenant Perrin have hired and whom he recommends to Fowler.

Captain Trouin is patterned on Captain Pinquet of the Haiphong-based Squadron Gascogne. Pinquet took Greene on a dive-bombing mission near the Chinese border (November 15, 1951) (Source: Sherry II, 387–89)

TROUP, MRS. (*The Ministry of Fear*). Rowe remembers she kept a post office and a general store in Cambridgeshire when he was a child.

TRUEFITT (*Loser Takes All*). Bertram and Cary planned to honeymoon in Bournemouth rather than at Le Touquet, where the Truefitts would be and where, also, there is a casino that might tempt the honeymooners to gamble and lose.

Is Greene poking onomastic fun at all blissful Truefitts?

TRUMAN, HIRAM C. (*Our Man in Havana*). When Milly Wormold was 13 and was attending a convent school, she set afire the shirt tail of a bothersome boy and was threatened with expulsion. Her father successfully pleaded with the Reverend Mother, head of the school, by saying Milly's Catholic mother wouldn't want Milly to be sent to the Hiram C. Truman School.

The name Hiram C. Truman resembles that of Harry S. Truman.

TRUMAN, MISS (*Travels with My Aunt*). She is the big, noisy proprietress of the Abbey Restaurant in London, off Latimer Road. She was once an officer in the women's navy. Maybe that's why she likes to be called Peter. Her timid partner is Nancy. Henry has Christmas dinner at the Abbey.

TRUMBULL, COUNCILLOR (*Travels with My Aunt*). When Henry attends Christmas service at St. John's Church, he habitually sits in the pew under the stained-glass window dedicated (1887) to the memory of Councilor Trumbull, who saw to the building of a Cranmer Road orphanage, now a juvenile detention center.

TUMBRIL ("The Blessing"). He is a young Reuters correspondent covering the Archbishop's tank-blessing ceremony. At the local *taverna*, he badgers a native reporter by wondering how weapons can be blessed in an unjust war.

TURNER, HORACE ("Doctor Crombie"). He was an eccentric man who remained one of Doctor Crombie's few patients after his resignation as the Bankstead school physician was demanded. Turner devised a system to convert the national debt into a national credit.

TURNER, IDA (*Brighton Rock*) *see* **ARNOLD, IDA**

TWINING (*The Captain and the Enemy*). He is one of Jim Baxter's schoolmates. Since this bully is two years older than Jim and presumably stronger, Jim can't kick back at him.

"TWO GENTLE PEOPLE" (1967). Short story. (Characters: Yvonne De Gaulle, Duval, Marie-Claire Duval, François, Greaves, Greaves, Henry C. Greaves, Patience Greaves, Pierre, Toni.)

Two middle aged strangers, a man and a woman, happen to be sitting on a bench in the Parc Monceau at Antibes when two loutish teenagers walk by. One kicks a pigeon in their path, breaking one of its wings and one of its legs. The louts amble away. To put the bird out of its misery, the man deftly wrings its neck, then deposits it in a refuse can. The strangers begin to speak. The man, an American named Henry C. Greaves, says his grandfather was a British consul in Nice, and he, overage for the military during the war, did government work in India. The woman, Marie-Claire Duval, went to a finishing school in Margate, England. Both are married. Henry's wife, Patience, is dining elsewhere. Marie-Claire's husband won't return home until late evening. Henry and Marie-Claire timidly agree to have dinner together, at a modest *brasserie*. Henry says his father went to America for adventure; Henry, disliking modern American life, removed to France, which Patience dislikes. Henry and Marie-Claire enjoy fish, wine, and strawberries. Queried, Henry says he has no children. Nor has Marie-Claire, who adds that missing something is perhaps sad. They sit in comfortable silence. They seem in a tranquil married state. They delay their return to sadness with coffee, brandy. Once outside, they part. She calls him *vraiment gentil*. Their meeting came too late for any exchange of addresses.

Taxiing home, Marie-Claire steps softly toward her single bed. She wonders what man is in the next room with her husband. Toni, the ballet dancer? François, the painter? No. She hears the name Pierre; he must be new. Lying down with ear plugs, she thinks things might have been different if 15 years ago she had observed a gentle man out of pity kill a pigeon.

When Henry gets home, Patience is in red hair-curlers. She says she smells a Rue de Douai *fille* on him. No, he says, he had dinner at a *brasserie*. He prepares her sleeping drops in water. Asked what he's thinking, he says just that things might have turned out differently — a uniquely big protest, for him, against life.

Richard Kelly suggests that Henry and Marie-Claire are "on the brink of starting a love affair." (True?) Surely the theme of this poignant story is less about "lost opportunities" (in Kelly's words) than about how life passes one by and one cannot turn back. "Two Gentle People" was the subject of a 1976 television production. See *Shades of Greene*. (Sources: Falk, 215; Kelly, 68)

UNDERSECRETARY FOR OVERSEAS TRADE, THE (*The Confidential Agent*). Fortescue informs D. and Rose Cullen, while the three are in Emily Glover's flat, that this official was a guest of the Oxford Groupers that Emily and Fortescue belonged to.

"UNDER THE GARDEN" (1963). Short story. (Characters: Dr. Cave, Dean of Warbury, Sir Silas Dedham, Ernest, Howell, Javitt, Joe, Maria, Lady Isobel Montgomery, Miss Ramsgate, Lady Sampson, Mrs. Sampson, Sir Nigel Sampson, Tom, Wilditch, Wilditch, George Wilditch, Henry Wilditch, Mary Wilditch, Mrs. Wilditch, William Wilditch, Lady Caroline Winterbottom.)

Part One: 1. William Wilditch is a patient in London of Dr. Cave, whose x-rays of his lungs remind Wilditch of top-secret aerial photographs he scrutinized during the war. Dr. Cave wants Sir Nigel Sampson, eminent surgeon, to have a look.

2. A week later Sir Nigel conducts a bronchoscopic examination, causing "a nightmare memory" of pain for Wilditch, whom Sir Nigel then chats with. Wilditch has an elder brother (George), has a mixed-race daughter, and is unmarried. When Dr. Cave appears, Wilditch learns that to postpone death he requires surgery to remove an obstruction. Dr. Cave says there's always hope. Wilditch says he isn't curious about the future.

3. Wilditch, finished with wandering in Africa and the East and seeking reconnection with the past, takes a train to Winton, East Anglia, to revisit Winton Hall. When an unmarried uncle owned it, George, William, and their widowed mother, now deceased, summered there. George, widowed, inherited Winton Hall, remodeled it, sold part of the land. William and George, when boys, enjoyed the Dark Walk, the lake, and its island. Though occupying Winton Hall now, George is ignorant of what's under the garden.

4. George meets William at the station. They drive to Winton Hall. William mentions treasure they dug for in the chalk pit. George calls it "iron stuff," making William wonder if his dream was only something imagined. When William mentions the lake, George calls it a shallow pond, with its "island" within jumping distance from land. William wonders if he ever told George about "his dream, his game," with their dog Joe. George explains he now sleeps in Uncle Henry's former bedroom, he converted William's bedroom to a bathroom, William will use their mother's bedroom, George is a nonbeliever like their mother (and William too). George remembers the Dark Walk, its mystery, their mother's desire to clear it, William's secret actions. George remembers William wrote a story about the island, published in their *Warburian* school magazine. When William can't remember it, George says their mother wrote critical remarks in its margins. Once in the bedroom, William handles some of his mother's books that George couldn't sell, among them an old *Warburian* volume. Out pops a long-preserved letter from the Dean of Warbury to his mother, defending William's story for its imaginative quality, criticizing her for calling it "silly," and saying they obeyed her demand not to give William any religious instruction.

5. William begins reading his story, "The Treasure on the Island," written 40 years ago. Tom, the protagonist, built a raft, landed on the island, dug with a pick, found an iron ring, levered it up, found a downward passage, and entered hoping to find money to enable his widowed mother to send his elder brother to Oxford and retain their house, mortgaged to Sir Silas Dedham. From a cave he took pieces of eight and gold bars to surprise his mother with. A night storm caused a landslide that buried the cavern, but the treasure helped both home and brother. Before sleeping, William wonders why the story falsified the real adventure and omitted mention of the bearded man and the squawking woman. A storm breaks, as it did 50 years ago; William gets writing material from a desk and now writes what he really found, or dreamed he found.

Part Two: 1. William Wilditch probably got to the island by the Dark Walk, hid from his scared brother, and spent three or more days underground. William, seven, dreamed about getting to the island and its woods, feeling lost, seeing a one-legged man's footprint, digging under the exposed root of a tree, finding a cave.

2. He crawled into a declining passage, lit his way with matches, felt he was under the lake, heard a hiss and a quack, found and took some newspapers, one dated April 5, 1885 and smelling as though it had wrapped fish, went spiraling through corridors, heard a man ask Maria for his soup.

3. A dirty-looking old woman squawked. Wilditch identified himself as English. Around a corner he saw a big old one-legged man (later calling himself Javitt) with a white beard perched on a lavatory with a deep-dug drop. He asked Wilditch why he took their papers, then told him to read a passage for his supper here below. One news item concerned Lady Isobel Montgomery's garden fête, which caused Javitt to lecture about fate. News about the fête's treasure hunt distressed him. Wilditch asked about Maria. Javitt said since there are two sexes why distinguish whether she's mother, wife, sister, daughter, whatever? Wilditch said he must return home. Javitt replied he'll get used to this home in a year or so, must stay here where there's practically no death. Javitt, who resembled Wilditch's mother's gardener, whom she disliked, rambled but made profound sense. He advised Wilditch to be disloyal and become a double agent, and said life's "only important things" are laughter and fear. He said his excrement was alive and created life, including his own daughter. He hinted about treasure below his lavatory. They had lots of canned food. When Wilditch squirmed, Javitt gave him a gold chamberpot. Javitt showed him photographs of his daughter, Miss Ramsgate, in a semi-nude beauty contest. Wilditch fell totally in love with her, could face anything with her beside him, and remembers her to this day. Days and nights of talk followed.

4. Javitt lectured Wilditch. The upshot? Time for you people upstairs is different from time for Maria and me, and for you is also measurable differently, depending. You lost power when you were specifically named. Javitt is only a temporary name for you to hear, not repeat. Maria and I are ugly, like rogue plants (i.e., weeds), but when I midwifed at Ramsgate's birth, she became beauty out of ugliness. The ugliness of war leaves columnar ruins penetrating the sky to make it give birth to beauty. We rogues survive underground, with difficulty. To find Miss Ramsgate, you needn't preen to become attractive to her, because she has a taste for rogues and has a want seeking a want.

5. Wilditch learned more from non-existent Javitt than from anyone else. Javitt said monkeys behave better about death than humans with their preaching, funerals, monks' skulls. How to help the human race survive? Disloyalty, fake names, love of sex, indifference to time, riots. Wilditch walked and Javitt hopped under the lake, heard an automobile above. Wilditch wondered how any child could invent these accreting truths he's gaining. Occasionally, Javitt demanded obedience of him under threats and scared even Maria. To learn about the treasure, Wilditch wanted Javitt to discuss his daughter, which he calmly did, saying she had to leave but predicted her return to her roots here. Queried, he said he and Maria couldn't marry here, instead grew into each other, and out sprouted the daughter. Planning purposefully to find her, Wilditch was advised to formulate long expeditions, including to Africa and other continents save Australia but omitting the Poles because his daughter is warm. Silently recalling he has visited most continents, Wilditch told scoffing Javitt he (unlike George, he added silently) would work his passage before the mast with youthfulness on his side. This thought made him remember Dr. Cave's comment about hope — but time was short now. After broth next morning, Javitt said they're going to see his treasure.

6. Ah, momentous feeling, like the approach to sexual consummation or the fear of bombs. Maria, hatted, appeared. Javitt alone had tea, put a tea leaf on Wilditch's hand, and, reading it, prophesied Wilditch's search would take five decades. The three walked under the lake and, perhaps, under the inn, then a field and Howell's farm. Wilditch contemplated escaping. But they descended to a kitchen, like Wilditch's mother's. Maria unlocked a dresser, and Javitt unloaded a box of jewelry dazzlingly colorful, absolutely, undilutedly real, as in dreams, not life. Wilditch swarmed into piles of gems, unavariciously. He remembered he was to write mundanely of a family-saving treasure. Javitt displayed gorgeous treasures — necklaces, souvenirs, gold coins, engraved gems, more. Javitt

called a halt, had Maria leave everything dumped out, and they returned. Wilditch slept, exhausted, and dreamed of laughter and tears.

7. Wilditch thought of leaving, mostly to find Miss Ramsgate. He tied sleeping Javitt's hands. Javitt opened one eye, laughed, and praised his prodigal, his straying sheep, for learning fast, said nobody would believe what he might say about his under-garden adventure, advised him while seeking Miss Ramsgate to forget school learning and lie and be disloyal. Javitt gave Wilditch the golden po. Wilditch outdistanced Maria squawking in pursuit, exited above the tangled roots in a morning hour, must have dropped his po, greeted his dog Joe, and for many nights lay awake fearing Maria's advent through his bedroom door, but never fearing Javitt.

Part Three: 1. Wilditch finishes his long writing. The stormy night gives way to day. He leaves the house, sees the path to the Dark Way, and then Ernest, the gardener now old, looking a bit like Javitt, and saying that though Master George wanted him to retire there are things about the garden only he knows about. Ernest's talk resembles Javitt's. Queried, Wilditch says, yes, he was once enamored of black skin. Queried about Ramsgate, Ernest says a gardener travels enough doing a day's work; as for any under-lake tunnel, Ernest wonder why there'd be a need. Wilditch says maybe he dreamed about one. Queried, Ernest recalls Master William liked the lake, the island, running away from the missus, seeking something. Ernest recalls Wilditch missed his uncle's funeral, probably being off in Australia. Wilditch surprisingly expresses regret at not looking in Australia and now it's too late to go there. Ernest's comments upon time's present-day changed pace resemble Javitt's. .

2. Wilditch takes the Dark Walk to the pond, leaps, wets his shoes, gets to the island, penetrates the bushes to a tree. Everything seems mundane, like George's world, unlike the globe he wandered, determined perhaps by George's having read to him about Australian explorations. Perhaps it's his disease making him dreadfully tired. He finds a sawed-down oak, trips on its roots, squats, hopes to hear Maria or Javitt, but finds only a tin chamber-pot, its yellow paint flaking.

3. He sits there, small, unable to see the house. If this pot 50 years ago inspired his "afternoon-legend," why didn't he mention it in his school-story write-up? The idea that he must decide on something, yet again, makes curiosity gnaw like his cancer. The breakfast-bell rings. Mother had cause to worry.

Peter Mudford defines "Under the Garden" as "an allegorical account of the relation between the unconscious (what is underground), childhood experience, and journeys of exploration." This statement is a splendid beginning, but "childhood experience" must be expanded to specify Wilditch's trauma following his mother's suppression of spiritual enlightenment in the boy's education, and "journeys of exploration" must be explained to mean not only Wilditch's weary traveling in search of beauty and love but also his determination toward the likely end of his life to rewrite his schoolboy story more honestly. The psychological perceptions presented aslant in this curious story remain not totally discoverable. Norman Sherry avoids "Under the Garden" completely. It was the subject of a 1976 television production. *See Shades of Greene.* (Sources: Falk, 215; Mudford, 16)

URQUHART, ROSE (*Travels with My Aunt*) *see* **NEWMAN, ROSE URQUHART**

VALLEJO, GASPAR (*The Honorary Consul*). He is a finance-department official and, Plarr understands, the latest lover of Margarita Escobar, one of Plarr's ex-mistresses. Vallejo doesn't attend Plarr's funeral.

VALLEJO, SEÑORA (*The Honorary Consul*). She is Gaspar Vallejo's wife and one of Plarr's ex-mistresses. She attends Plarr's funeral, accompanied by Duran but not by her husband.

VANDE (*The Heart of the Matter*). He is a native black lad assigned to serve Helen Rolt, who curtly orders him to bring drinks. Scobie recognizes Vande as having served Pemberton, in bush country, until Pemberton's suicide.

VANDI ("The Other Side of the Border"). He is the West African native Billings recommends to Hands (1936) to be hired as the head man for black carriers he'll need for his expedition.

VAN DONCK, CAPTAIN (*The Human Factor*). He was a South African security official. This insolent, menacing-looking bully mainly watched while Muller, his supervisor, interrogated Castle in Pretoria in an unsuccessful effort to frighten him into cooperating after Castle's unlawful association with Sarah MaNkosi (*see* Castle, Sarah) had become known. After the Castles escape, Muller had Van Donck demoted.

VASSALL (*The Human Factor*). His name is mentioned by Percival in conversation with Daintry and Hargreaves after the latter's bird shoot. The security leak has Percival concerned, and he says various "old names [may be] thrown up," including Philby, Portland, and Vassall.

Anthony Cave Brown reports this: John Vassall, a homosexual Russian spy while serving as a British Admiralty clerk, was caught (1962). Harold Macmillan, by then Prime Minister (1957–1963) was so upset, feeling that a public trial would embarrass the Secret Intelligence Service, that he told a subordinate it would have been better to discover, control, and not detain Vassall. (Hargreaves often seems to feel that way about Davis.) Vassall was charged, tried, found guilty, and sentenced (1962) to 18 years in prison. (Source: Brown, 504, 530)

VEGA, SEÑORA (*The Honorary Consul*). When Escobar tries to needle Dr. Plarr by saying that Clara Fortnum might be his favorite patient because she's pregnant, Plarr retorts that Señora Vega is also pregnant but is Dr. Benevento's patient.

VELARDO, CAPTAIN RUBÉN (*The Honorary Consul*). He is a colleague of Colonel Perez. To Plarr, Perez scoffs at the idea that a bomb in a church remained unexploded because of divine intervention, which he says Velardo "half believes." Velardo says that Perez may laugh but the fact remains that there was no explosion.

VERITY (*Rumour at Nightfall*). Chase recalls drinking and sharing dirty stories with Verity and Peacock, all three of whom were newspapermen together in London.

VICAR ("The Lieutenant Died Last"). He is a religious figure in Potter. While the Germans are invading Potter, his wife is exchanging one detective novel for another in the local circulating library.

VICAR (*Loser Takes All*). He is the vicar at St. Luke's in Maida Hill, London. Cary, for perhaps one moment, feels that he will be sad if she and Bertram don't get married there.

VICTOR, CAPTAIN J. (*The Captain and the Enemy*) *see* **CAPTAIN, THE**

VIGOT (*The Quiet American*). He is an intelligent, painstaking French detective stationed at Saigon's Sûreté. Vigot has Fowler identify Pyle's body, interrogates Fowler on his whereabouts the night of the murder, and is aware that Fowler is lying. Fowler admires Vigot's reading of Blaise Pascal. When asked, Vigot tells Fowler he became a detective partly because of reading Émile Gaboriau (1835–1873), the French detective-fiction writer.

VIGOT, MADAME (*The Quiet American*). She is Vigot's blonde wife. Rumor has it that she betrays him with some of his junior officers.

VISCONTI (*Travels with My Aunt*). He is a clever, articulate Italian criminal long known and loved by Augusta. She defines him to Henry as a conscienceless "terrible twister" and says he must be 84 or 85 now. His actions include thievery, black-marketing, smuggling, impersonating a priest, handling "antiques," sponging on Augusta, and trading illegal whisky and cigarettes for furniture. He is pursued by James O'Toole of the CIA all the way to Paraguay but fools him with a forged drawing purportedly by Leonardo da Vinci. Visconti's bodyguard kills Zachary Wordsworth. Visconti's son is Mario Visconti.

Greene explains in *Ways of Escape* that the name Visconti comes from that of villainous Gian Galeazzo Visconti in *The Viper of Milan* (1906) by Marjorie Bowen (1886–1952), one of Greene's favorite novels when he was a youth (as he explains in *The Lost Childhood and Other Essays*). Greene adds that it was fun for him to have Detective-Sergeant Sparrow describe Visconti as a viper. Bowen's villain, the Duke of Milan, is also called "the Viper." (Sources: Greene, *Lost Childhood*, 15–17; Greene, *Ways of Escape*, 297)

VISCONTI, MARIO (*Travels with My Aunt*). He is old Visconti's handsome son. Mario was educated by Jesuits and fancies himself as a verse-drama writer. Augusta tells Henry that Visconti settled Swiss francs on Mario before the war, that Mario was lucky to have survived the war because he was "too sweet," and that he may get money from women — after all, he can make women laugh. After a 30-year separation, Augusta and Mario meet at the Milan railway station, with Henry and Lucinda O'-Toole. Lucinda immediately finds Mario attractive. Mario's calling Augusta "Madre mia" presumably suggests nothing but affection, because, according to Augusta, he regarded her as his "real mother." (Since Augusta tells Henry that she and Signora Visconti detested each other, could the cause have been that Augusta is Mario's mother?) Colonel Hakim calls Mario Augusta's stepson.

Greene said he named this character Mario "after my friend Mario Soldati, who once greeted me and gave me lunch in the Milan station with similar flamboyance." Quentin Falk and Norman Sherry amplify: Mario Soldati (1906–1999) was an Italian writer and filmmaker with whom Greene collaborated to produce an insignificant movie entitled *The Stranger's Hand* (1954), and with whom he visited brothels and enjoyed opium. (Sources: Falk, 165, 210; Greene, *Ways of Escape*, 297; Sherry III, 507, 508)

VISCONTI, SIGNORA (*Travels with My Aunt*). She is or was old Visconti's wife, of German extraction. She had money which her husband couldn't seize. Perhaps therefore he called her, according to Augusta, "the blonde cow." Augusta says she and Signora Visconti detested each other.

"A VISIT TO MORIN" (1957). Short story. (Characters: Dunlop, Durobier, Pierre Morin, Sagrin, Strangeways.)

1. The narrator, Dunlop, chances upon a novel by Pierre Morin in a Colmar bookstore. Some 20 years ago, in the 1930s, Dunlop studied Morin in his Protestant school in Collingworth in French classes conducted by Mr. Strangeways, a Catholic. Strangeways advised his students not to decide what Morin believed but to realize he wasn't his characters, and also to appreciate Morin's well-chosen words and his characters' vividness. Strangeways lent Dunlop some Catholic literary periodicals with a spectrum of criticism. Some critics found Morin a Jansenist; others, an Augustinian. Some approved of his character Durobier's orthodoxy; others, his character Sagrin's naturalism. Some paradoxically found heresy within Morin's orthodoxy. Dunlop is to find all this in Morin himself.

2. After combat service in France during the war, Dunlop, non-religious and single, is a talented catalogue writer for a London wine-importing company. He goes to Colmar at Christmas time for business and pleasure. The bookshop assistant tells him Morin, old and respected in Germany, lives in a village 15 miles away. At midnight Mass on Christmas Eve, Dunlop recognizes Morin, nearly 80, from old photographs. His eyes rove, near and far. Neither he nor Dunlop receives. Dunlop, his faith lost, wishes communicants could tell him why they believe. He speaks to Morin, tells him his novels have given him pleasure, and reveals, when courteously asked, he is a wine merchant. Morin offers Dunlop one chance to talk with him. Morin invites Dunlop to his home tonight to taste a special wine.

3. Morin drives Dunlop to his place, and treats him to what Dunlop calls excellent wine. After some harsh words, Morin launches into a discussion, soon fueled by brandy. The gist: Morin has lost his belief in God but not his faith; the reason he no longer believes is that the Church is true and so is what the Church taught him; he doesn't take communion because what if he did and his belief didn't return? Morin grimaces when Dunlop implicitly equates the ideas of Morin's extremist characters with Morin's own. Morin drives Dunlop to his hotel at last, and the two barely speak. Dunlop finds himself hoping that one of Morin's expressed certainties — that he no longer infects others with the disease of faith — is correct.

Greene says that his belief in God "never came by way of those unconvincing philosophical arguments which I derided in a short story I called 'A Visit to Morin.'" Greene wrote in a note for Leopoldo Duran (April 30, 1984) that he had "faith" but had "less belief" in God's existence. Richard Kelly explains that "[b]y belief Greene means an approach to God through formal theology and institutional ritual and dogma. Faith, on the other hand [Kelly continues], represents a personal acceptance of God's love." Elsewhere, Kelly adds, Greene asserted that faith is more than belief, is God's gift, whereas belief isn't. Cedric harshly labels "A Visit to Morin" "rather drily didactic." (Sources: Allain, 162–63; Duran, 289; Greene, *A Sort of Life*, 168; Kelly, 47, 48; Watts, 70)

VOISIN (*The Tenth Man*). He is one of the 30 hostages held by the Germans. A lorry driver, he draws the first slip, and it is one of three slips marked for death by execution.

VOLET, MADAME ("Chagrin in Three Parts"). She is Paul Volet's young, amazingly pretty wife. Paul has just left her. Madame Emmy Dejoie meets her at Félix's restaurant, gets her drunk, and persuades her to try lesbian love with her. Madame Volet is responsive to Emmy because Paul's lovemaking lacked variety.

VOLET, PAUL ("Chagrin in Three Parts"). He has left his pretty wife for another woman.

WAGNER (*The Quiet American*). He is an unidentified man, probably American, who warns two young American girls to get away from the Pavilion by 11:25 a.m.— obviously to avoid the explosion only minutes later. Fowler gets nowhere asking Pyle to identify Warren.

WALES ("A Day Saved"). This is one of the names by which Robinson refers to the man he is pursuing. Robinson also calls him Canby, Douglas, Fotheringay, and Jones.

WALSTON, CATHERINE (1916–1978). She was one of Greene's lovers. Born in Rye, New York, Catherine (Bobs) Macdonald Crompton, was the daughter of David Crompton, British-born New York stockbroker, and Lillian Macdonald Sheridan Crompton, amateur actress; and the sister of Bonté Walston Duran and Belinda Walston Straight. During a skiing vacation in New Hampshire, she met Henry ("Harry") David Walston (1912–1991). He was studying bacterial science at Harvard. Engaged three days later, she dropped out of Barnard College and married him (1935) in Wilton, New Hampshire, where her family had farm property. Harry was a non-practicing Jew (family name, Waldstein) and a luxury-loving, millionaire British Labor Party supporter. She told her sister Bonté she didn't love Harry. Both were habitually adulterous, but between times they had five children before Catherine encountered Greene. Their relationship began when Catherine wrote Greene, whose works she admired, that she intended to become a Catholic convert and wanted him to be her godfather (1946). Greene's wife Vivien Greene* substituted for Greene in the ceremony (September 12, 1946) at a Dorchester-on-Thames church, 15 miles south of Oxford. Catherine invited both Greenes to dinner at the Walstons' Thriplow farmhouse, on 2,500 acres near Cambridge (pre–Christmas, 1946) and at twilight flew them back to Oxford in a hired plane. When the beautiful, eccentric, alcoholic nymphomaniac's hair brushed Greene's face and she kissed him goodnight, he was smitten.

Aware that literature owes a "creative debt ... to adultery," William Cash relates elements in Greene's affair with Catherine to elements in his fiction, including "deep betrayal, sexual obsession, secret vows, jealousy, hatred, tortured religiosity, confessional walk-outs, guilt, despair, blasphemy and literary revenge." Catherine invited Greene to a cottage that she rented at Keel, Achill Island, on Ireland's west coast (April 1947). She also used the place with Ernest Bernard ("Ernie") O'Malley (1897–1957), another continuing lover. O'Malley had been an anti-treatyite Irish Republican Army general (1922–1923), and wrote *On Another Man's Wound* (1936) and *The Singing Flame: A Memoir of the Civil War, 1922–24* (1978) about his IRA experiences. He was also a poet, an editor, and an unhappy husband. He had married an American woman named Helen Huntington Hooker (1935); they had three children, two of whom she kidnapped and took to the United States (1950), after which they divorced (1952). O'Malley advised John Ford when he filmed *The Quiet Man* in Ireland (1952).

Greene's lovemaking with Catherine began at Achill. He also participated in the hospitality of both Walstons, and not only openly betrayed Harry by sleeping with Catherine here, there, and anywhere, but also tormented her by desiring to be exclusively possessive of her. Michael Shelden theorizes that one of Greene's motives in his affair with Catherine was to create a mutually hurtful emotional relationship with both Walstons. Cash adds to his portrayal of Catherine when he praises (and builds upon) Shelden's discovery of her "sexual appetite for Catholic priests that [Norman] Sherry missed or preferred to ignore." One was Father Thomas Gilby, a loose-living Dominican.

Catherine was repeatedly with Greene in Italy — Rome, Ravello, Siena, Venice, and especially Capri (1947–1955) — most romantically after he bought a villa called Rosaio in Anacapri (1948). She helped him redecorate the villa. James Patrick Francis Walston was born in Dublin (July 18, 1949). On record as Catherine's and Harry's son, James Walston was probably Harry's son by an unnamed woman; he was not likely Catherine's and Greene's son. Harry, aware that Catherine's affair with Greene was embarrassing their children, considered a separation from Catherine; so Greene suggested marrying her somehow (January 1950). Instead, Harry wept, but then walked and talked amiably with Greene. Between arguments, Greene and Catherine rendezvoused in Paris, Italy, and aboard the yacht of movie-mogul Alexander Korda* on the Mediterranean (1950). With a tour in Vietnam just completed, Greene met Catherine in Paris (January 1951) and also spent some days with her at the home of Evelyn Waugh, writer and friend (September 1951). They met in New York when he was there about filming *The End of the Affair* (February 1952).

Greene's affair with Anita Björk* (1956–1958) caused Catherine, to whom he indiscreetly wrote about Anita, to reconsider their love for each other, although she shared a bit more time with him on Capri (October 1958). After his stay in the Congo leper colony (1959), Catherine visited him in Jamaica (November 1959), where he was working on *A Burnt-Out Case*, and where they stayed in a place owned by Noël Coward. A trip by Greene to Moscow (1960) that she thought dangerous put more distance between them and increased her indifference.

Meanwhile, Greene had met Yvonne Cloetta* (1959). His and Catherine's love waned. Harry, for administrative services rendered to Britain, was made a Life Peer (1961), and Catherine became Lady Walston. She fell in Ireland, broke a hip and had surgery (1965), was hospitalized often thereafter, required a wheelchair, and abused alcohol worse. Greene and Catherine wrote each often, but while her letters to the end are generous Greene's are fuller of himself than of sympathy toward her. When she died of pancreatic cancer (September 2, 1978), Harry was at her side. She was buried at Thriplow. Greene avoided the funeral. Harry married Lady Elizabeth Stott (1979). Lady Elizabeth was the abandoned wife of Sir Nicholas Stott, MP, and she sold Catherine's collections of paintings for high prices. Harry refused — according to Cash — to sell Greene's letters to Catherine back to Greene for £10,000, selling them instead to Georgetown University, Washington, D.C., for $150,000. Catherine's husband Henry and her lover Graham died the same year.

The amorous Graham-Harry-Catherine triangle resembles the triangle that frames Maurice Bendix, Henry Miles, and Sarah Miles in *The End of the Affair*. Fowler's love for Phuong, and his consequent desire to divorce his wife Helen, in *The Quiet American*, parallel Greene's wish to shed his wife Vivien in order to pursue Catherine more effectively. Bob Cullen was allowed to peruse Greene's letters to Catherine, now in the Special Collections Library of Georgetown University. He was struck by "how much Greene lifted from his life and inserted more or less whole into his novels." In proof, Cullen relates aspects of Greene's affair with Catherine to major characters in *The Heart of the Matter* and especially *The End of the Affair*. (Sources: Cash, 14, 29, 30, 32, 77, 81–84, 109–10, 181, 283, 285; Cullen, 113; Shelden, 357–74 passim, 446, 484–85; Sherry II, 224–33, 316–36 passim, 375–76, 381–82, 405–09, 502; Sherry III, 61–62, 104–08, 223–24, 416–17, 620)

WARNIER, MADAME (*The Tenth Man*). She was a Chavel family servant. Jean-Luis Chavel, when he was a child, saw her take off her hair piece. This led the lad to conclude that hair was easily removable.

WARREN, MABEL ("The End of the Party"). She is a seemingly boyish girl, 13, who frightened little Francis Morton at Colin Henne-Falcon's ninth birthday party, when she touched him during a scary hide-and-seek game played in darkness. During Colin's 10th birthday party, Francis's twin brother Peter tries to comfort him by touching him during an identical party, and he dies in terror.

WARREN, MABEL (*Orient Express*). She is the Cologne-based columnist for the London *Clarion*. A square-faced, awkward lesbian, Mabel has paid for Janet Pardoe's companionship for two years. Mabel interviews Savory, the popular novelist, during the stop in Cologne of the train he is on. She spots Czinner, wanted by the anti-socialist government in Belgrade and also on the train. She rushes aboard, interviews him, and gets off at Vienna thinking he will also. When he doesn't, Mabel telephones her interviews to London, makes her way to Subotica, rescues Coral Musker, a passenger held there by the authorities, and hopes for another scoop with her story. Big Mabel also eyes little Coral for a possible new amour.

WARRENDER, MISS ("Doctor Crombie"). She was an eccentric woman and remained one of Doctor Crombie's few patients after his exceedingly embarrassing resignation as the Bankstead school physician. She kept 25 cats.

WATERBURY, PETER (*The End of the Affair*). He is a conceited literary critic to whom Bendrix reluctantly grants a dull interview. Bendrix is so attractive to Waterbury's compassionate girlfriend Sylvia Black, whom Waterbury demeans, that she accompanies him to Sarah Miles's cremation. Bendrix's plan to rob Waterbury of Sylvia ends when Sarah's mother interrupts by introducing herself to Bendrix.

WATSON (*The Human Factor*). He is Castle's chief. Watson, who tried unsuccessfully to be a barrister, is in charge of MI6, with Sections 6A, 6B, and 6C, and learns of the security leak. Castle suggests to Daintry that Davis, Castle himself, or even Watson could be the source.

WATSON, CHARLIE ("Cheap in August"). He is Mary Watson's husband. Charlie is a tall, thin, concave American, and is a Connecticut university professor of literature now doing research in London on *The Seasons* by James Thomson (1700–1748). Since Charlie is personally unexciting and chronically absorbed in his work, Mary, on vacation alone in Jamaica, finds Henry Hickslaughter a total opposite and hence, though repulsively fat, poignantly appealing.

Greene satirizes poor Charlie, and possibly American literary criticism to boot, by having him plan to write next about "the American image in European literature," featuring James Fenimore Cooper, Mrs. Frances Trollope, and so on, oddly, to Dylan Thomas.

WATSON, MARY ("Cheap in August"). She is dull Charlie Watson's wife. Mary, born in England, is now 39 and married for 10 uneventful years. The Watsons live in New England, where he teaches. While Charlie is doing research in London, Mary is vacationing alone in Jamaica. She strikes up a friendship with Henry Hickslaughter, and — long having yearned for some kind of adventure, even brief — comforts Hickslaughter, by talking, drinking, and sleeping with him.

WATT (*This Gun for Hire*). He is a medical student at Nottwich, too serious to participate in the student frolic. His long-range goal is a Harley Street practice in London. Fergusson and other frivolous students confront Watt in his room and trash it.

WEATHERALL, PETER ("A Drive in the Country"). While driving Fred's girlfriend back to her home, Mike asks her if she knows Peter Weatherall. She doesn't. Mike says he and his friends laughed when Peter, a chronic drunk, went missing once.

WEAVER, MAJOR PHILIP ("Proof Positive"). He is a retired army officer, about 60, dark, skinny, and with a satirical eye. Weaver obtains Colonel Crashaw's permission to lecture to the Psychical Society and does so, despite boring his audience of old ladies and retired officers. He casually reveals he has cancer, talks raspingly in an effort to alter everyone's notion "of the relative values of matter and spirit" by some positive proof, suddenly mews, whispers, collapses. Dr. Brown, a skeptical member of the audience, worried all along that Weaver looks mighty ill, rushes to offer aid. For good reason: Weaver, dead for at least a week, carried a handkerchief steeped in a heavy scent of lilies to disguise the fact.

WEBER (*The Name of Action*). He is a barge keeper who transports a cache of weapons and ammunition hidden under barrels of Rhine wine, from Coblenz to Trier, for possible use by the revolutionaries headed by Kapper and Chant. Weber and Chant bribe and then threaten Muller, the customs officer at Cochem, to pass the shipment through. Weber tells Chant he is happily married to a good Catholic wife.

WEBER, FRAU (*The Name of Action*). She is the admirable Catholic wife of Weber, the barge man. Plump, middle aged, and with steady eyes, she welcomes Chant to their home near the Moselle River, gives him soup, and tells him that the outcome of the revolution is in God's hands.

WEILL (*The Comedians*) *see* **BROWN**

WEISSMANN (*Travels with My Aunt*). He is a German who Colonel Hakim tells Augusta was approached by General Abdul for money to promote a scheme in Istanbul. Hakim adds that the CIA surveilled Weissmann and a Chicago meat packer named Crowder, whom Abdul also asked for money, and that all three have been arrested and are talking to him.

WELD ("The Blessing"). He is a tall reporter sent by his chief, Smiley, to cover the Archbishop's tank-blessing ceremony. He has pacifist sympathies and has already written his column on what will surely be an uneventful happening. But during the tedious blessing, he talks with an old man who says it's better to bless anything or anyone we can't love than to express hate, and, anyway, blessings don't save lives. Back at the *taverna* to resume drinking with fellow reporters, Weld talks about and demonstrates the old man's advice by gesturing a blessing over cigarettes — his enemy, his eventual killer — then lighting up and coughing.

WELLS, H. G. (*Travels with My Aunt*). Aunt Augusta tells Henry she once attended an important literary figure's funeral, also attended by Edward Carpenter, Dr. Havelock Ellis, [James] Ramsay MacDonald, E[dith]. Nesbit, [George] Bernard Shaw and his wife, and H. G. Wells ([1866–1946], English author).

WHEELER ("The Case for the Defence"). He was a neighbor of Mrs. Parker and testifies that he heard a thud on the evening of her murder. He testifies he saw Adams leave the scene.

"WHEN GREEK MEETS GREEK" (1941). Short story. (Characters: Lord Bellen, Elisabeth Cross, Frederick Driver, Lord Driver, Nicholas Fennick, Lord Charles Manville, the Reverend Simon Milan, Priskett, Lord George Sanger.)

1. Springtime. Nicholas Fennick and his niece Elisabeth are establishing a phony St. Ambrose's College, in Oxford, to take money from soldiers, teach by correspondence, and guarantee degree-diplomas in three terms. Fennick will teach history and classics; Elisabeth, economics; Priskett, who is a pharmacist, science. The three meet over Priskett's shop in Oxford to get started.

2. A disreputable man calling himself Lord Driver applies to St. Ambrose's for his son Frederick Driver, now at the Borstal reform school, and gets a letter admitting him. Lord Driver is proud that Frederick will be at Oxford and figures he can get credit as "a peer," pay the fees later, and have the Reverend Simon Milan, whom he met in prison himself, fake the written examinations for Frederick.

3. Oxford in autumn. Elisabeth is pleased when money pours in. Their students learn a little and get their diplomas. She wants this harmless racket to gain her a husband. Judging from Frederick's papers, mailed from London, he seems suitable. Fennick tells Elisabeth and Priskett that Lord Driver, who hasn't paid up yet, is coming to inspect his son's school. Elisabeth volunteers to taxi him from the station to Balliol College, pretend it's St. Ambrose's, show him around, and dump him back at the station.

4. Elisabeth escorts the somewhat preoccupied Lord all about and introduces him to "President" Fennick, handily near the Master's house. As the two men discuss Elisabeth, "the

two crooked minds ... move in harmony," and she seems suitable for Frederick. Fennick, believing the Drivers come from a military family, promises to award the young soldier his diploma in London, and to bring his niece along.

5. Elisabeth suspects Fennick has something better in mind than St. Ambrose's. At Paddington station, Lord Driver bustles up with his son. He says his house was damaged by a recent air raid; so the graduation ceremony is held in a Mount Royal hotel room. Fennick orates in Latin. The oldsters order whisky and shoo Elisabeth and Frederick out onto Oxford Street. Elisabeth says both her uncle and Fred's father hope for a wedding. Fred is agreeable. They alternately reveal truths: Lord Driver is his father; her uncle is no college president; Fred served at Borstal, not the military; the graduation ceremony was phony. When Fred supposes the wedding is off, she says she's free. They see a parade of fraudulent-looking politicians, advertisers, and soldiers in Hyde Park and along Park Lane. Talking things over, they reckon thusly: Fred's duped father will pay if he marries a college president's niece; Elisabeth's duped uncle will pay if she marries an aristocrat's son; they will commandeer the fake college and, with money, make money. They return to the hotel, announce wedding plans, and see the drinking duo's faces light up. The optimistic youngsters watch the oldsters haggle over their respective "settlements."

Readers of Greek ancestry, aware of the canard that Greeks are clever bargainers, probably didn't and don't appreciate the title of this yarn about manipulators manipulated. The Borstal system, first established at Borstal Prison, in Kent, England (1902), was designed to rehabilitate delinquent boys ages 16–21. It involved classes, vocational training, work, and counseling. The system was eventually abolished (1982). "When Greek Meets Greek" was the subject of a 1976 television production. It starred Greene's friend Paul Scofield, whose performance disappointed Greene. *See Shades of Greene.* (Source: Falk, 215, 216)

WHISKY PRIEST, THE (*The Power and the Glory*). This is the designation of the unnamed Catholic priest. He is the last priest not killed or otherwise immobilized by the anti–Catholic Mexican government. Small, homely, cagey, scared but devout, he regards himself as a failure because of sins of lust, pride, and incontinence; he and a woman named Maria carelessly had a daughter, Brigitta. His love of Brigitta he feels prevents thorough repentance. He conducts furtive Masses, longs to escape, but accepts God's requirement that he be a priest. He willingly enters a trap set for him by the lieutenant, his relentless pursuer, who supervises his execution.

The whisky priest was based on several real-life figures. Cedric Watts summarizes the clandestine life of Father Miguel Pro Juárez, a Jesuit priest who arrived at Vera Cruz (July 1926), violated Mexican law by administering Catholic sacraments, was captured, and was executed (November 23, 1927). Norman Sherry discusses Greene's meeting with a strange German named Kruger, who sailed with him from Mexico back to Europe (May 1938). Kruger told him that he had been jailed without reason in Mexico, had suffered in a filthy cell with assorted criminals, but retained a sweet, charitable spirit. Philip Stratford suggests that Father Damien (1840–1889), the saintly priest ministering to Hawaiian lepers but often criticized for alleged failings, intrigued Greene and helped him characterize the whisky priest.

Greene presents the whisky priest superbly. By turns, the man feels useful, useless, hypocritical, hopeful, hopeless; giggles, is grateful, brusque, demanding; strikes bargains more successfully with natives than (perhaps) with God; swigs brandy but not wine reserved for makeshift altars; worries, doesn't worry, about death; wants to be a saint, thinks at his execution he isn't, but surely qualifies. His heroism inspires young Luis, whose final action is a thrilling epiphany indicative of the priest's immortality. K. C. Joseph Kurismmootil says that the "priest's dignity is enhanced by the comparison drawn between him and Christ in His passion." Anthony Mockler feels that the one-paragraph description of the whisky priest's execution "is possibly Graham Greene's most affecting, and most restrained, description of death in any of his novels; ... a triumph of pity, terror — and imaginative empathy." (Sources: Kurismmootil, 87; Mockler, 155; Sherry II, 4; Stratford, 28–29; Watts, 178)

WHITAKER (*England Made Me*). As she falls asleep at one point, Kate Farrant says God made Whitaker and Loewenstein when He made the lamb. Is she thinking of the two as lamb-like victims or lamb-eating predators?

WHITE (*Our Man in Havana*). He is an agent under Hawthorne. The Chief in the Intelligence office in London commends Hawthorne when he says he authorized Wormold's extra expenses even though they are 10 times White's expenses.

WHITEHOUSE, MRS. (*The Human Factor*). When Castle listens to the radio for important news, he hears only an interview with Mrs. Whitehouse, who welcomes a report about a new campaign against pornography. The reporter announces Halliday's arrest of for selling a pornographic film to a 14-year-old.

WIDOW TWANKY (*The Human Factor*). The name of this horse, and those of Bonne chance and Kalamazoo, are found in Davis's flat by Taylor, an MI6 officer, who mistakenly assumes they may be connected with a code.

WILBER, MAJOR (*England Made Me*). Farrant remembers that when he was cadging drinks by fibbing at a military club about being near when a coolie threw a bomb, Major Wilber, who was at the scene of the explosion, exposed his dishonesty.

It is possible that the incident occurred in Bangkok, because Farrant recalls leaving Bangkok for Aden.

WILBERFORCE, MISS (*The Heart of the Matter*). She is an African who officially complains before Scobie about her landlady, whose brother is Corporal Laminah. Scobie has learned to remain neutral in such cases.

WILBRAHAM, MISS (*The Third Man*). She is a member of the audience assembled by Crabbin to hear Martins lecture on the contemporary novel. Thinking Martins, whose pen name is Buck Dexter, is the novelist Benjamin Dexter, she tells him she doesn't like his books because they don't tell good stories. (*See* Dexter, Benjamin.)

WILBUR (*The Honorary Consul*) *see* **THE AMERICAN AMBASSADOR**

WILCOX, DORIS (*The Ministry of Fear*). She was the wife of Rowe's loyal friend Henry Wilcox. She was a hockey-playing air-raid warden. When Rowe seeks money from Henry, he learns Doris was crushed to death by the collapse of a wall during a bombing. Her funeral procession is about to start.

WILCOX, HENRY (*The Ministry of Fear*). He is one of Rowe's friends. When Rowe was tried for murdering his wife, Wilcox was almost alone in sticking with him. When Rowe asks Henry to cash a check, Henry tells him his wife Doris was killed in an air raid. Henry was a neat chartered-accounting worker, but when Rowe sees him, he looks slovenly.

The name Henry Wilcox is close to that of Henry Wilcoxon, who starred in *The Crusades* (Paramount, 1935), a movie Greene raucously reviewed (*Spectator*, August 30, 1935). (Source: Greene, *The Graham Greene Film Reader*, 22–24)

WILCOX, MRS. (*The Ministry of Fear*). She is Henry Wilcox's fussy mother. She is caring for him now that his wife is dead.

WILDITCH ("Under the Garden"). He was William Wilditch's father, who died before the boy was seven. Mrs. Wilditch resented her husband's dying before he could provide the family with seaside vacations.

WILDITCH ("Under the Garden"). She is or was William Wilditch's mixed-race daughter, probably born in Africa.

WILDITCH, GEORGE ("Under the Garden"). He is William Wilditch's elder brother, more practical than William. George read stories of Australian explorers to William. George's wife Mary is deceased. George inherited Winton Hall from his and William's unmarried Uncle Henry Wilditch, improved the house, and sold off much of the land. George's children have no interest in the property. When the brothers meet again at the Hall after years apart, they are reservedly convivial. George recalls William as "a secretive little bastard." In his dream and fantasy, William, as Tom, fancies that he worked his passage before the mast, that his brother couldn't do so, that he preserved his brother for Oxford. Their mother, since George was her first child, called him "Wilditch One" when annotating their school magazine.

WILDITCH, HENRY ("Under the Garden"). He was George Wilditch's and William Wilditch's unmarried uncle. After the boys' father died, their mother summered with the family at Winton Hall, which Henry owned and later bequeathed to George.

Winton Hall is based on Harston House, the Cambridgeshire country home of Sir William Graham Greene,* Greene's uncle. In his discussion of "Under the Garden," Michael Shelden discusses Harston House and Ernest Northrop, Sir William's gardener. (Source: Shelden, 45–53 passim)

WILDITCH, MARY ("Under the Garden"). She was George Wilditch's wife, deceased.

WILDITCH, MRS. ("Under the Garden"). She was George Wilditch's and William Wilditch's mother, deceased. When she was widowed, she reluctantly took the boys to their Uncle Henry Wilditch's Winton Hall. She disliked the Dark Walk, which leads to the garden, the field, and the pond with its tiny island. She quarreled with Ernest, the gardener there. A Fabian socialist and therefore an avid reader of the reformer Beatrice Webb (1858–1943), Mrs. Wilditch ordered the teachers at Warbury school not to offer religious subjects to William and also opposed their trying to develop his imagination. His story about events under the garden therefore bothered her, and she annotated it negatively in the margins.

Paul O'Prey explicates the last words of the story, in which Wilditch, holding his tin chamberpot, says his mother had "reason to fear": "His mother had feared that his story of an underground search for hidden treasure was a symbolic expression of a religious 'curiosity.'" O'Prey suggests that Wilditch as a schoolboy disguised the story but that, since his mother is dead, he can now rewrite it more fully and more truthfully. (Source: O'Prey, 66)

WILDITCH, WILLIAM ("Under the Garden"). He is the hero-narrator. Perhaps dying of lung cancer, he goes from London to Winton Hall, in East Anglia, where as a child he summered with his widowed mother and elder brother George. He reads a story he wrote at school, at age 13, about a fantasy or dream he had at age seven, involving his going under the Winton estate garden, which has a small island in a small pond, and while underground meeting Javitt and Maria. Wilditch writes up his dream or fantasy in greater detail, in which he projects a future of seeking Miss Ramsgate, Javitt's and Maria's inspiringly beautiful daughter. The underground vision triggered his future wandering life. Wilditch tells one of his London physicians, Sir Nigel Sampson, he has a mixed-race daughter, perhaps the consequence of finding a woman close to his ideal Miss Ramsgate in Africa, one of the several continents he visited. An insight into Wilditch's mind is contained in a seminal statement Greene has him make upon seeing Javitt's display of jewels: "Absolute reality belongs to dreams and not to life."

Thomas A. Wendorf says that "Wilditch sees his life in terms of literal narratives that have competed in their influence." Therefore, it may be added, drawing an absolute time line in "Under the Garden" (1963) is properly impossible. Wilditch recalls distributing apples to soldiers at Winton Hall in August 1914 (was he therefore born about 1910? and is now about 53?). He compares his x-rays to World War II reconnaissance photographs he was assigned to study (hence an intelligence officer, about 30? in about 1940? — a date he mentions in connection with the war). He says his return to Winton Hall occurs 40 years after he, 13, wrote his story for the school magazine (hence he's now 53), and 50 years after his under-the-garden dream at age seven (hence 57 now). Useless here is Tom's declaration that Javitt's 1885 newspaper is almost 50 years old (hence, reading it at age seven, Tom would have been born in 1938 or a little later, hence now a teenager?). All this reckoning is unimportant, as is the conclusion that Wilditch is now probably in his mid-50s or so.

As for Wilditch's last name, does Greene mean it to mean he had a wild itch to travel in Greeneland, or that he had to tunnel a wild (underground) ditch to find Javitt? Greene must have felt as bold as James Joyce and D. H. Lawrence when he has little Wilditch relish hearing, for the first time in sustained conversation, Javitt's salty use of those two once-arresting four-letter words beginning, respectively, "s" and "f." Shocking when the boy heard them, whenever that was. Less so when Greene's readers encountered them in 1963. Nowadays not at all. Greene found it fortunate that he "happily" remembered his own "unpleasant ... bronchioscopy" (1960) when it came time to describe Wilditch's similar examination. (Sources: Greene, *Ways of Escape*, 296; Shelden, 52–53; Wendorf, 641)

WILKINS (*The Quiet American*). He is an Associate Press reporter Fowler sees near the Majestic on the night of Pyle's murder. They watch American bombers unloading. Wilkins deplores the absence of "fancy writing" in reports now. To establish his alibi, Fowler tells Vigot he saw Wilkins that night.

WILKINS (*The Human Factor*). He is a new employee at Section C of MI6, whom Watson tells Hargreaves he will investigate.

WILKINSON ("Men at Work"). He is a popular novelist now working for the Book Committee in the Ministry of Information. His request to energize women during wartime by writing a study was summarily refused.

WILKINSON, HENRY ("Cheap in August"). Charlie Watson, in London, mentions in a letter to his wife Mary in Jamaica, that Henry Wilkinson and his wife had been vacationing in Athens and had dinner in London with him evidently on their way home. Mary remembers them well and evidently has found them boring.

WILKINSON, MRS. ("Cheap in August"). She is Henry Wilkinson's wife. Mary Watson knows them both and evidently regards them as dull.

WILLIAMSON (*England Made Me*). When Krogh reminisces about doing construction work on a bridge in Chicago, he recalls his friends Williamson, Murphy, and O'Connor, and Williamson there.

WILLIE (*Brighton Rock*). This is the name of a person whom Pinkie overhears two old ladies discussing at the Cosmopolitan when Pinkie and Rose are there.

WILLIE (*The Human Factor*). He is a gloomy drinker at the club called White's. He talks about his crumbling marriage.

WILLIE (*This Gun for Hire*) see **DAVID**

WILSON (*Brighton Rock*). He is Rose's thin old father. He and his wife live in Nelson Place. Illiterate and moody, he pretends to be morally outraged at Pinkie's request for permission to marry underaged Rose. After haggling, Pinkie promises Wilson and his wife 15 guineas.

WILSON (*The End of the Affair*). When Bendrix goes to Smythe's house to confront him, his sister Miss Smythe opens the door. Bendrix asks if Wilson, non-existent, lives here.

WILSON (*The Ministry of Fear*). Rowe phones around to find to whom Cost phoned just before his suicide. At one point, he asks for Isaacs, only to be told he is speaking to Wilson.

WILSON, EDWARD (*The Heart of the Matter*). He is a British intelligence agent. He attended the Downham school (1923–1928), and is now a plump 32. He is sent to Freetown, Sierra Leone, supposedly an accountant for the United African Company but in reality to investigate diamond smuggling. First Wilson rooms with Harris in a Bedford Hotel flat. Then the two share a hut. Wilson discusses literature with Louise Scobie, Scobie's wife. He regards Louise as Scobie's superior and falls sentimentally in love. She briefly tolerates his immaturity but later fends him off, once by slapping at him and causing a nosebleed. His dislike of Scobie turns to hatred. Wilson learns about Scobie's affair with Helen Rolt, suspects him of smuggling, and after Scobie's death shows Louise that Scobie's diary entries about taking evipan were added and thus prove suicide.

Norman Sherry contends that Wilson is based on a friend of Greene's named Harwood, who was a Berkhamsted schoolmate and an R.A.F. intelligence officer at Freetown (1942), when Greene also served there. Anthony Mockler, reporting that Greene referred in his diary to a "secret work[er]" in Freetown as "LP," asserts that LP, still a "mystery" man, was "the prototype of the despicable Wilson." Greene complained that Wilson "obstinately refused to come alive." (Sources: Greene, *Ways of Escape*, 126; Mockler, 180; Sherry II, 112, 137)

WILSON, MRS. (*Brighton Rock*). She is Rose's mother, stupid and mean in appearance. She and her husband, both moody, agree to let Pinkie marry Rose after he bribes them.

WILSON, ROSE (*Brighton Rock*). She is a waitress at Snow's, calling herself 17 but only 16. She sees Spicer, one of Pinkie's mobsters, and not Hale, leave a Kolley Kibber under a tablecloth. Since this evidence could be used against Pinkie for Hale's murder, Pinkie contrives to meet and become attractive to her, even while treating her abominably. He marries her, illegally, to prevent her from testifying against him, and then persuades her to join him in a suicide pact, which he would never abide by. Rose is a uniquely confused, adoring Catholic, willing for love to be damned with Pinkie. Ida Arnold saves her life.

WILSON, SCHUYLER (*The Comedians*). He is an agent of a Santo Domingo bauxite mine. He is a big, fat American, with an "anonymous face." Having a letter of introduction, Brown applies to Wilson to be the company catering manager. The two disagree about Haitian politics, and Brown is rejected.

Greene goes out of his way to indicate the smug, surly ignorance of this American, who says he knows nothing about the Tontons Macoute — which is incredible.

WINCE-DUDLEY, MRS. ("The Basement Room"). She is a person about whom Philip Lane feels he can make up stories. He recalls her annual visit from Penstanley, Suffolk, with green umbrella and black handbag.

WINIFRED (*The Confidential Agent*). She is an English girl whom D. sees at Dr. Bellows's soirée with a German, who alleges he likes her because she typifies British female innocence.

Greene makes Winifred remarkably unpre- possessing. She is said to be bony, with bad teeth, and is probably a teacher.

WINKLER, DR. (*The Third Man*). He is a Viennese physician. Small, neat, and superclean, he collects religious relics which he doesn't value. Martins interviews him but learns only that Winkler, who was Harry Lime's doctor for a year or so, saw Harry only after the car accident and didn't attend the inquest.

WINSTANLEY, COLIN ("May We Borrow Your Husband?"). He is mentioned as Travis's friend. Colin, one of Stephen's clients, is perhaps also a homosexual. Poopy Travis naively anticipates fun back home, maybe before Christmas, with Peter, Colin, Stephen, and Tony.

WINSTON (*It's a Battlefield*). When Conder enters the newspaper office at one point, the Chief reporter is interrupted in his talk about Winston, whose head was bandaged.

WINTERBOTTOM, LADY CAROLINE ("Under the Garden"). Javitt and Maria laugh at the newspaper obituary concerning this woman. Javitt puns that he and Maria have "summerbottoms" by the stove under the garden. Hearing this, Maria "kwahked."

WINTON, DRUCE (*This Gun for Hire*). When Raven is hiding in the garage of a Nottwich house, he hears a cultivated voice, identified as Druce Winton's, reading lines from Alfred, Lord Tennyson's *Maud* on the BBC's evening National Programme. The verses cause Raven to conclude, rightly, that Anne Crowder, just another skirt, will betray him.

Peter Wolfe notes that both *Maud* and *This Gun for Hire* "use as settings the yards, squares, and streets of an industrial town," "[b]oth attack capitalism," "Raven and the narrator of *Maud* both have a parent who committed suicide," etc. Wolfe praises Greene for this proof of his "uncanny ability to turn his formal learning to the services of his art." (Source: Wolfe, 78)

WISECOCK, MRS. (*England Made Me*). Gullie names her as unsatisfactory for a part in an opera company he is planning.

WOLF (*Travels with My Aunt*). He was Frau General's husband's Irish wolfhound. Although Wolf preferred him to her, she took Wolf not her husband in his staff car with Visconti, impersonating a priest, to escape from Rome. A tank pursued them. Wolfe leapt out. Wolf was crushed by the tank into something, Visconti noted, resembling a biscuit "they make for children in the shape of animals."

WOODROW, DETECTIVE-INSPECTOR (*Travels with My Aunt*). He is a Scotland Yard special-branch officer. Austere Woodrow and courteous Detective-Sergeant Sparrow find Henry at Christmas church service and seek his cooperation in pursuing Wordsworth and in locating Visconti. They search Augusta's flat and find Achille Dambreuse's postcard sent from Panama to her.

WORDSWORTH ("A Shocking Accident"). He is the housemaster at Jerome's school. He calls the boy to his office, tells him his father has just been killed by a falling pig, and turns to suppress his show of amusement. Jerome asks what happened to the pig.

WORDSWORTH, ZACHARY (*Travels with My Aunt*). He is a big, gentle black man from Sierra Leone. He is called Zach and Zak. He was a loader at Heathrow, London, and a doorman at the Grenada Palace, London. When Augusta saw him, she liked him, and he became her devoted lover. Wordsworth deals in marijuana and implicates Henry by commingling pot ashes and Henry's deceased mother Angel Pulling's ashes. To avoid arrest, Wordsworth goes to Paris, then follows Augusta to Paraguay. While trying to see Augusta one more time, Wordsworth is killed by Visconti's bodyguard. His framed photograph of Freetown, Sierra Leone, conceals a picture Visconti sells to O'Toole.

Greene said he named "Augusta's black lover ... after a villainous district commissioner whom I had met more than thirty years before in Liberia." (Source: Greene, *Ways of Escape*, 297)

"WORK NOT IN PROGRESS" (1955). Short story. (Characters: the Archbishop of Canterbury, the Archbishop of Centerbury, the Bishop of Bath and Wells, the Bishop of Melbourne, Brown, Dick, Harry, Journalist, Sue.)

Greene precedes this piece, subtitled "My Girl in Gaiters," with a disclaimer, that its characters and events are fictitious. He explains he's often asked by friends to tell their children stories. Since plots of his future novels wouldn't be suitable, he'll sketch a long-planned musical comedy, entitled "My Girl in Gaiters," but adds that doing so may cost him a parent's trust.

Twelve Anglican bishops, in gaiters and black hats, sing a chorus, about authorizing prayers but avoiding Hail Marys. A Journalist cautions that since they have wrongly counted Bath and Wells as two, they are 12 not 13. One of their group has been kidnapped. Soon all will be, because 12 thugs, confusing "chasuble" and "chalice," snatched the real bishops, grabbed their chasubles for ransom, are holding the bishops in their underwear in a basement, and will imitate them at the upcoming Convocation at Canterbury. The thug leader is a woman, disguised as the Archbishop of Canterbury. The Bishop of Melbourne arrives, notes the fraud, and infiltrates the gang to do justice. He falls in love with the lady fake, who, requiting his love, confesses all. He decides to go home, but love prevents his blowing the whistle. The false archbishop telephones the Bishop, who is half-longing for his girl in gaiters. The phony expresses her love and encouragement. Calling her a liar, he hangs up.

Greene continues. He plans to write about the false bishops' approaching Canterbury but seeing they've been betrayed by their lady leader, who is being defended by her sudden lover. The true bishops, having escaped, arrive in their underpants and scatter the fakes. The staunch lovers sing an old-fashioned duet. His lines are about forgetting both Brown and Sue, and preferring to marry his love and settling in "a country curate." She doubts his willingness to sacrifice ecclesiastical ambition for a stranger in a pram; further, what about her whilom Dick and Harry? He'd be willing for his true love to expatriate with him.

Greene says his finale will feature the two boarding a ship for Australia, wafted by the thugs' song, entitled "Top Hats in Hell" and written by Greene's brother (Hugh Greene*) when he was BBC's Controller of Overseas Services.

The less added the better about this literary effort, which, according to Richard Kelly, "shows Greene shamelessly indulging in the pleasures of low comedy." (Source: Kelly, 79)

WORMOLD, JAMES (*Our Man in Havana*). Wormold, an Englishman, was born December 6, 1914, in Nice, married Mary, is divorced, has run a vacuum-cleaner distributorship in Havana 15 years, and lives with his daughter Milly, 17. Hawthorne, a secret-service agent from London, recruits Wormold as agent 59200/5 to spy on the enemy. Needing cash, Wormold concocts a list of fictitious sub-agents. London provides money, Mrs. Beatrice Severn as assistant, and Rudy as communications man. The names of some of his "agents" being identical to those of real persons causes embarrassments and even deaths. Although Wormold's fake military drawings are based partly on vacuum-cleaner parts, they disturb his superiors less than they should. These shenanigans alert Captain Segura, of the Havana suburb Vedado, and William Carter, an enemy agent. Wormold gets revenge on Carter, finds love with Beatrice, and is honored in London. When he picks up undeserved pay at the Consulate, it is in an envelope marked 59200/5, in an envelope marked Henry Leadbetter, in an envelope marked Mr. Luke Penny. Greene provides Wormold with a limp, for no reason. Wormold's ugly name is uglier when its two syllables are reversed, to "Old Worm." He is sad that almost no one calls him Jim.

Michael Shelden and William Cash, without relating him to James Wormold, identify an ex–Anglican priest named Brian Wormald as a lover among many lovers favored by Catherine Walston,* one of Greene's lovers. Cash adds that Wormald told him Catherine was a priest-seeking nymphomaniac. Norman Sherry reports that Greene used as models for Wormold's fake secret-service reports those of two real-life "spies" for Germany in World War II. One was a Czech businessman named Paul Fidrmuc (using the code name "Ostro"), who became a German citizen (1940), was a German intelligence agent in Denmark and Rome, settled in Lisbon, sent "reports" to Germany, and was known to British agents. The other was Juan Pujol García ("Garbo"), also known to British agents. Peter Wolfe notes the aptness of Wormold's selling vacuum cleaners: "It follows that a book centering on the idea that nature abhors a vacuum should also center on vacuum cleaners." Wolfe continues by blaming the electrical-power cut-off for creating Wormold's absence of business, by implying that political corruption siphons away the energy from the people, and by suggesting that an in-rush of insurrection results. In Robert Hoskins's view, Wormold relates to more grimly presented characters thus: "In a comic variation of Greene's serious themes, Wormold places loyalty to an individual [first Milly, then Beatrice also] over loyalty to the state [England] and its institutions [the Secret Intelligence Service]." (Sources: Cash, 75, 190, 243; Hoskins, 165; Shelden, 361–62; Sherry III, 131–32; Wolfe, 149)

WORMOLD, MARY (*Our Man in Havana*). Mary Wormold, a 36-year-old Catholic, is James Wormold's divorced wife and Milly Wormold's mother. Years ago Wormold came to Havana and met Mary and her family there, in the Floridita. She left him one October after six years of marriage and decamped with an American. He still loves her but only until Mrs. Beatrice Severn appears.

Claudia Lightfoot mentions El Floridita bar, on Calle Obispo, established in 1818 (as La Piña de Plata" [the Silver Pineapple]), as one of Ernest Hemingway's favorite watering holes. (Source: Lightfoot, 97, 124, 236)

WORMOLD, MILLY (*Our Man in Havana*). She is Mary and James Wormold's daughter. A devout Catholic, Milly attends a convent school, is 17 at her birthday party, and combines beauty, piety, and charming pep. Her buying a horse named Seraphina from Segura, her unsuccessful suitor, helps impel her father into the spy field. Milly accompanies her father and Beatrice to London. Milly's given name is Seraphina.

WRIGHT ("Doctor Crombie"). He was Fred's virile father, who, unknown to Fred, was suffering from cancer. Doctor Crombie's theory that repeated sexual activity causes cancer alarmed the ill fellow, perhaps.

WRIGHT, COLONEL (*The Heart of the

Matter). He is an intelligence officer sent from Cape Town, South Africa, to investigate Scobie's connections with Yusef and Tallit. Scobie equivocates in some answers to Wright's gruff questions.

WRIGHT, FRED ("Doctor Crombie"). He was a schoolmate of the narrator. Fred's visiting a prostitute led to his questioning Doctor Crombie, which led to his telling Fred that prolonged sexual actions caused cancer, which led to parental alarms.

WRIGHT, WILBUR (*Travels with My Aunt*). Augusta tells Henry she knew Wilbur Wright (1867-1912), flew with him on "several trips," but prefers quiet railroad stations to blaring airports.

Wilbur Wright flew exhibitions of a Wright brothers' airplane in France (1908) and Italy (1909), while Orville Wright (1871–1948) exhibited in Germany (1909). Therefore, if Augusta was born around 1895, as Henry reports, she must have been fetching indeed to catch old Wilber's fancy.

X (*The End of the Affair*). Bendrix thinks Sarah Miles has left him for a lover, whom he calls X. X turns out to be Richard Smythe, however. So Bendrix then looks for Y, who is non-existent.

Y (*The End of the Affair*). When Bendrix is proved wrong in thinking Richard Smythe is Sarah Miles's lover (whom he initially labels X), he imagines yet another non-existent lover and calls him Y.

YOGEL, DR. (*This Gun for Hire*). He is the crooked physician on Charlotte Street, London, visited by Raven. A girl named Page recommended Yogel to Raven, who wants his harelip operated on but escapes when Yogel wants to gas him unconscious so his evil-looking nurse can call the police.

When Greene had appendicitis in London, he consulted a Hindu doctor in Battersea. Greene says the fellow was shabby, inefficient, and "possibly ... illegal," and "left his trace, with another doctor, on some pages of *A Gun for Sale* [American title, *This Gun for Hire*]." Later, Greene says Yogel was partly based on "a certain police doctor near Blackfriars" whom Greene consulted in fear he had a venereal disease. Like Yogel, the fellow worked in "dingy rooms" and had an "abrupt furtive manner." (Sources: Greene, *A Sort of Life*, 187; Greene, *Ways of Escape*, 76)

YUSEF (*The Heart of the Matter*). He is a fat, hairy-chested Moslem Syrian merchant, and a rival of Tallit, who though also Syrian is a Christian. Yusef controls a black market in liquor, cotton, and much else, and is also a diamond smuggler. He has a curious relationship with Scobie, whom he admires for his honesty but whom he wants to corrupt and use. Feigning friendship, Yusef lends Scobie £250 to finance his wife Louise's vacation in South Africa. Yusef gives Scobie an unsuccessful tip to implicate Tallit in smuggling, gets hold of a revealing letter from Scobie to Scobie's mistress Helen Rolt, thus forces him to help a substantial diamond-smuggling venture, and even causes the murder of Scobie's loyal black servant Ali to silence him.

Greene later wrote that Yusef was the "one character [in *The Heart of the Matter*] ... for which I care." (Source: Greene, *Ways of Escape*, 126)

YVONNE, TANTE ("Two Gentle People"). Marie-Claire tells Greaves that when shopping once for cheese in Paris's Place de Madeleine she happened to rub elbows with Tante Yvonne, the wife of the General, there selecting some Brie.

Tante Yvonne was the nickname by which French sarcastically, or otherwise, addressed Yvonne Vendroux de Gaulle (1900–1979), wife of Charles de Gaulle (1890–1970), French military hero and long-time president of France (1958–1969). Aunt Yvonne was well known as a careful shopper for her family's dining. Greene happily made use of the name Yvonne, since his mistress when he wrote "Two Gentle People" was Yvonne Cloetta.*

Z. (*The Confidential Agent*). He is a citizen of the country D. and L. are both fighting for. L. reminds D. that D.'s fighters destroyed Z.'s pictures back home. This means that Z. is or was an artist or an art collector.

ZANCAS, ENRIQUE (*Monsignor Quixote*). He is El Toboso's ex-mayor, is a Communist, and is Monsignor Quixote's friend. Zancas once aspired to become a priest but is now devoted to Marx and Lenin. Without employment, the Mayor, as he is often called, suggests that he and Quixote travel together for a time. Quixote calls him his Sancho. While sharing adventures, they dispute amiably about their respective religions— Catholicism and Marxism. Zancas, more practical than quixotic Quixote, enables him to escape the clutches of the Bishop of El Toboso and Father Herrera, and helps him valiantly until Quixote's death, after which Zancas continues to be challenged by Quixote's spirit.

Jae-Suck Choi, pleased by the dying Monsignor Quixote's ultimate influence on Zancas, says that finally "[t]he 'Knight of Faith' has succeeded in implanting a new gospel in the mind of a materialist who was hostile to Christianity." Mark Bosco is more tentative: "In the end, Sancho's biological determinism and epistemological certainty are placed in doubt by his sharing in Quixote's mystical vision of the material world." (Sources: Bosco, 148; Choi, 199)

ZIFFO, MRS. (*This Gun for Hire*). She is someone Sir Marcus knows. She was one of several guests on Soppelsa's yacht cruising near Rhodes when seasickness caused Rosen to throw up on her black satin dress.

ZOE (*Brighton Rock*). She is a girlfriend mentioned by two sporty young drinkers at the lounge in Peacehaven where Pinkie and Rose stop before he plans to have Rose shoot herself to death.

When Greene has the sports discuss Zoe and her "hot" friend, he indubitably had his psychiatrist Kenneth Richmond's big-breasted wife Zoe in mind.

Bibliography

Adamson, Judith. *Graham Greene, The Dangerous Edge: Where Art and Politics Meet.* London: Macmillan, 1990.

Allain, Marie-Françoise. *The Other Man: Conversations with Graham Greene.* Trans. Guido Waldman. New York: Simon & Schuster, 1981.

Allott, Miriam. "The Moral Situation in *The Quiet American.*" *Graham Greene: Modern Critical Views.* Ed. Harold Bloom. NY: Chelsea House, 1987.

Antor, Heinz. "Graham Greene as a Catholic Novelist." *Graham Greene in Perspective: A Critical Symposium.* Ed. Peter Erlebach and Thomas Michael Stein. Frankfurt am Main: Peter Lang, 1991.

Armstrong, Tim. "The Seventies and the Cult of Culture." *The Cambridge History of Twentieth-Century English Literature.* Ed. Laura Marcus and Peter Nicolls. Cambridge: Cambridge University Press, 2004.

Atkins, John. "Sex in Greeneland." *Essays in Graham Greene: An Annual Review* 1 (1987): 47–60.

Auden, W. H. "The Heresy of Our Time." *Graham Greene: A Collection of Critical Essays.* Ed. Samuel Hynes. Englewood Cliffs, NJ: Prentice-Hall, 1973.

Baldridge, Cates. *Graham Greene's Fictions: The Virtues of Extremity.* Columbia: University of Missouri Press, 2000.

Barrett, Dorothea L. L. "Communism and Catholicism in *The Comedians.*" *Graham Greene in Perspective: A Critical Symposium.* Ed. Peter Erlebach and Thomas Michael Stein. Frankfurt am Main: Peter Lang, 1991.

Bear, John. *The #1 New York Times Bestseller...* Berkeley, CA: Ten Speed Press, 1992.

Boardman, Gwenn R. *Graham Greene: The Aesthetics of Exploration.* Gainesville: University of Florida Press, 1971.

Böker, Uwe. "'Mixed up and Caught up': Dimension of Political Experience in *The Quiet American* and *The Honorary Consul.*" *Graham Greene in Perspective: A Critical Symposium.* Ed. Peter Erlebach and Thomas Michael Stein. Frankfurt am Main: Peter Lang, 1991.

Bosco, Mark. *Graham Greene's Catholic Imagination.* NY: Oxford University Press, 2005.

Brown, Anthony Cave. *Treason in the Blood: H. St. John Philby, Kim Philby, and the Spy Case of the Century.* Boston and New York: Houghton Mifflin, 1994.

Bryden, Ronald. "Graham Greene Discusses Collected Edition of His Novels." *Conversations with Graham Greene.* Ed. Henry J. Donaghy. Jackson and London: University Press of Mississippi, 1992.

Calder-Marshall, Arthur. "The Works of Graham Greene." *Horizon* 1 (May 1940): 367–75.

Cash, William. *The Third Woman: The Secret Passion That Inspired the End of the Affair.* NY: Carroll & Graf, 2000.

Cassis, A. F. *Graham Greene: Life, Work, and Criticism.* Fredericton, N.B., Canada: York Press, 1994.

Cheney, Lynne. "Joseph Conrad's *The Secret Agent* and Graham Greene's *It's a Battlefield:* A Study in Structural Meanings." *Modern Fiction Studies* 16 (Spring 1970): 117–31.

Choi, Jae-Suck. *Greene and Unamuno: Two Pilgrims to La Mancha.* NY: Peter Lang, 1990.

Clarens, Carlos. *Crime Movies: From Griffith to the Godfather and Beyond.* New York and London: W. W. Norton, 1980.

Cloetta, Yvonne. *In Search of a Beginning: My Life with Graham Greene,* as told to Marie-Françoise Allain. Translated from the French by Euan Cameron. London: Bloomsbury, 2004.

Coulthard, A. R. "Graham Greene's 'The Hint of an Explanation': A Reinterpretation." Richard Kelly. *Graham Greene: A Study of the Short Fiction,* 120–24. New York: Twayne, 1992.

Cullen, Bob. "Matter of the Heart: Graham Greene's Letters to His Paramour, Catherine Walston, Trace the Hazy Line Between Life and Fiction." *Smithsonian* 33 (June 2002): 112–115.

DeVitis, A. A. *Graham Greene.* Rev. ed. Boston: Twayne, 1986.

Diederich, Bernard, and Al Burt. *Papa Doc: The Truth About Haiti Today.* New York: McGraw-Hill, 1969.

Diemert, Brian. *Graham Greene's Thrillers and the 1930s.* Montreal & Kingston: McGill-Queen's University Press, 1996.

Duran, Leopoldo. *Graham Greene: Friend and Brother.* Trans. Euan Cameron. London: HarperCollins, 1994.

Erdinast-Vulcan, Daphna. *Graham Greene's Childless Fathers*. NY: St. Martin's Press, 1988.

Erlebach, Peter. "Major Themes and Structural Ways of Arguing Meaning in Graham Greene's Novels of the 1940s and 1950s." *Graham Greene in Perspective: A Critical Symposium*. Frankfurt am Main: Peter Lang, 1991.

Falcoff, Mark. *Panama's Canal: What Happens When the United States Gives a Small Country What It Wants*. Washington, DC: AEI Press, 1998.

Falk, Quentin. *Travels in Greeneland: The Cinema of Graham Greene*. London: Quartet Books, 1984.

Forbes, Bryan. *A Divided Life: Memoirs*. London: Heinemann, 1992.

Gaston, Georg M. A. *The Pursuit of Salvation: A Critical Guide to the Novels of Graham Greene*. Troy, NY: Whitston Publishing Company, 1984.

Gordon, Haim. *Fighting Evil: Unsung Heroes in the Novels of Graham Greene*. Westport, CT: Greenwood Press, 1997.

Green, Peter. "The End of the Affair [review essay]." *New Republic*. January 24, 2005, 30–35.

Greene, Donald. "Graham Greene and Evelyn Waugh: 'Catholic Novelists.'" *Graham Greene: A Revaluation, New Essays*. Ed. Jeffrey Meyers. NY: St. Martin's Press, 1990.

Greene, Graham. *Carving a Statue, a Play*. London: Bodley Head, 1964.

_____. *Collected Stories*. New York: Viking, 1972.

_____. *Getting to Know the General: The Story of an Involvement*. London: Bodley Head, 1984.

_____. *The Graham Greene Film Reader: Mornings in the Dark*. Ed. David Parkinson. Manchester: Carcanet, 1993.

_____. Introductions in *Collected Edition*. 17 volumes, London: Heinemann, 1970–1976.

_____. *Journey without Maps: A Travel Book*. London: Heinemann, 1976.

_____. *The Last Word and Other Stories*. London: Reinhardt Books, 1990.

_____. *The Lawless Roads: A Mexican Journey* (1939). New York: Penguin Books, 1982.

_____. *The Lost Childhood and Other Essays*. London: Eyre & Spottiswoode, 1951.

_____. *A Sort of Life*. New York: Simon and Schuster, 1971.

_____. *Ways of Escape*. New York: Simon and Schuster, 1980.

_____. *A World of My Own: A Dream Diary*. Hammondsworth, England: Reinhardt Books, 1992.

Grobel, Lawrence. *Conversations with Capote*. New York: New American Library, 1985.

Hammontree, Patsy Guy. *Shirley Temple Black: A Bio-Bibliography*. Westport, CT: Greenwood Press, 1998.

Hawtree, Christopher, ed. *Graham Greene: Yours etc., Letters to the Press*. London: Reinhardt Books, 1989.

Hazzard, Shirley. *Greene on Capri: A Memoir*. New York: Farrar, Straus and Giroux, 2000.

Heinl, Robert, and Nancy Heinl. *Written in Blood: The Story of the Haitian People, 1492–1971*. Boston: Houghton Mifflin, 1964.

Higdon, David Leon. "'I Try to Be Accurate': The Text of Greene's *Brighton Rock*." *Essays in Graham Greene: An Annual Review* 1 (1987), 169–86.

Higgins, Michael W. "Greene's Priest: A Sort of Rebel." *Essays in Graham Greene: An Annual Review* 3 (1992), 9–23.

Hitchens, Christopher. Introduction to *Orient Express*. Graham Greene. New York: Penguin Books, 2004.

Hogarth, Paul. *Graham Greene Country*. Ed. Paul Hogarth. Foreword and Commentary by Graham Greene. London: Pavilion, 1986.

Hoggart, Richard. "The Force of Caricature." *Graham Greene: A Collection of Critical Essays*. Ed. Samuel Hynes. Englewood Cliffs, NJ: Prentice-Hall, 1973.

Hoskins, Robert. *Graham Greene: An Approach to the Novels*. New York and London: Garland, 1999.

Joannon, Pierre. "Graham Greene's Other Island." *Conversations with Graham Greene*. Ed. Henry J. Donaghy. Jackson and London: University Press of Mississippi, 1992.

Kelly, Richard. *Graham Greene: A Study of the Short Fiction*. New York: Twayne, 1992.

Kurismmootil, K. C. Joseph. *Heaven and Hell on Earth: An Appreciation of Five Novels of Graham Greene*. Chicago: Loyola University Press, 1982.

Lewis, R. W. B. "The 'Trilogy.'" *Graham Greene: Modern Critical Views*. Ed. Harold Bloom. NY: Chelsea House, 1987.

Lightfoot, Claudia. *Havana: A Cultural and Literary Companion*. Oxford: Signal Books, 2002.

Lodge, David. *Graham Greene*. New York: Columbia University Press, 1966.

Malamet, Elliott. *The World Remade: Graham Greene and the Art of Detection*. New York: Peter Lang, 1998.

McEwan, Neil. *Graham Greene*. London: Macmillan, 1988.

Meyer, Michael. *Not Prince Hamlet: Literary and Theatrical Memoirs*. London: Secker & Warburg, 1989.

Miller, R. H. *Understanding Graham Greene*. Columbia: University of South Carolina Press, 1990.

Mockler, Anthony. *Graham Greene: Three Lives*. Scotland: Hunter Mackay, 1994.

Monnier, Jean-Yves. "'Knowing' in *Brighton Rock*." *Graham Greene in Perspective: A Critical Symposium*. Ed. Peter Erlebach and Thomas Michael Stein. Frankfurt am Main: Peter Lang, 1991.

Mudford, Peter. *Graham Greene*. London: Northcote House, 1996.

Müller, Wolfgang G. "Graham Greene's *Monsignor Quixote*: An Intertextual Analysis." *Graham Greene in Perspective: A Critical Symposium*. Ed. Peter Erlebach and Thomas Michael Stein. Frankfurt am Main: Peter Lang, 1991.

O'Grady, Walter. "Parodies of Metanarratives in *Travels with My Aunt.*" *Perceptions of Religious Faith in the Works of Graham Greene.* Ed. William Thomas Hill. Bern: Peter Lang, 2002.

Oltuski, Enrique. *Vida Clandestina.* Trans. Thomas and Carol Christensen. New York: Wiley, 2002.

O'Prey, Paul. *A Reader's Guide to Graham Greene.* New York: Thames and Hudson, 1988.

Orwell, George. *The Collected Essays, Journalism and Letters of George Orwell.* Ed. Sonia Orwell and Ian Angus. 4 vols. NY: Harcourt, Brace, Jovanovich, 1968.

Ower, John. "Dark Parable: History and Theology in Graham Greene's 'The Destructors.'" Richard Kelly. *Graham Greene: A Study of the Short Fiction,* 125-34. New York: Twayne, 1992.

Parkinson, David. Introduction to *The Graham Greene Film Reader: Mornings in the Dark.* Ed. David Parkinson. Manchester: Carcanet, 1993.

Pendleton, Robert. *Graham Greene's Conradian Masterplot: The Arabesques of Influence.* NY: St. Martin's Press, 1996.

Philby, Rufina. *The Private Life of Kim Philby: The Moscow Years.* NY: Fromm International, 2000.

Phillips, Gene D. *Graham Greene: The Films of His Fiction.* NY and London: Teachers College Press, 1974.

Pierloot, Roland A. *Psychoanalytic Patterns in the Work of Graham Greene.* Amsterdam: Rodopi, 1994.

Piroëlle, Anne. "Graham Greene: Fiction and Film." *Graham Greene in Perspective: A Critical Symposium.* Ed Peter Erlebach and Thomas Michael Stein. Frankfurt am Main: Peter Lang, 1991.

Pritchett, V. S. *The Tale Bearers: Literary Essays.* NY: Random House, 1980.

Pryce-Jones, David. "Cracked by a Sound: Graham Greene in Panama." *Encounter* 64 (February 1985): 35-36, 38-39.

Rai, Gangeshwar. *Graham Greene: An Existential Approach.* New Delhi: Associated Publishing House, 1983.

Rickards, Jocelyn. *The Painted Banquet: My Life and Loves.* London: Weidenfeld and Nicolson, 1987.

Rotberg, Robert I. *Haiti: The Politics of Squalor.* Boston: Houghton Mifflin, 1971.

Salvatore, Anne T. *Greene and Kierkegaard: The Discourse of Belief.* Tuscaloosa and London: University of Alabama Press, 1988.

Scarpaci, Joseph, Robert Segre, and Mario Coyula. *Havana: Two Faces of the Antillean Metropolis.* 1997. Rev. ed. Chapel Hill and London: University of North Carolina Press, 2002.

Schulz, Volker. "'Passing the Border': The Two Worlds of *Travels with My Aunt.*" *Graham Greene in Perspective: A Critical Symposium.* Ed. Peter Erlebach and Thomas Michael Stein. Frankfurt am Main: Peter Lang, 1991.

Sedlak, Valerie. "Beyond Theology and Ideology: The Monsignor's Mystical Quest." *Perceptions of Religious Faith in the Works of Graham Greene.* Ed. William Thomas Hill. Bern: Peter Lang, 2002.

Sharrock, Roger. "Love and Pity: *The Honorary Consul* and *The Human Factor.*" *Graham Greene: Modern Critical Views.* Ed. Harold Bloom. New York: Chelsea House, 1987.

Sheldon, Michael. *Graham Greene: The Man Within.* London: Heinemann, 1994.

Sherry, Norman. *The Life of Graham Greene: Volume I: 1904-1939.* New York: Viking, 1989.

_____. *The Life of Graham Greene: Volume II: 1939-1955.* New York: Viking, 1994.

_____. *The Life of Graham Greene: Volume III: 1955-1991.* New York: Viking, 2004.

"Shocker." *Time.* October 29, 1951. 98-100, 102-04.

Silveira, Gerald E. "Greene's 'The Basement Room.'" *Explicator* 15 (December 1956): 13.

Sinyard, Neil. *Graham Greene: A Literary Life.* Houndsmills, Basingstoke, Hampshire: 2003.

Smith, Grahame. *The Achievement of Graham Greene.* Sussex: Harvester Press, 1986.

Smith, Rowland. "A People's War in Greeneland: Heroic Virtue and Communal Effort in the Wartime Tales." *Graham Greene: A Revaluation.* Ed. Jeffrey Meyers. NY: St. Martin's Press, 1990.

Stein, Thomas Michael. "'Watertight Boxes': Ben Nicholson's 'Painting 1937' and Graham Greene's Novel *The Human Factor.*" *Graham Greene in Perspective: A Critical Symposium.* Ed. Peter Erlebach and Thomas Michael Stein. Frankfurt am Main: Peter Lang 1991.

Steinglass, Matt. "The Heart of the Matter [review essay]." *Nation,* July 11, 2005, 30- 36.

Stratford, Philip. *Faith and Fiction: Creative Process in Greene and Mauriac.* Notre Dame: University of Notre Dame Press, 1964.

Thomas, Brian. *An Underground Fate: The Idiom of Romance in the Later Novels of Graham Greene.* Athens and London: University of Georgia Press, 1988.

Thomson, Ian. *"Bonjours Blanc": A Journey Through Haiti.* London: Hutchinson, 1992.

Tracey, Michael. *A Variety of Lives: A Biography of Sir Hugh Greene.* London: Bodley Head, 1983.

Turnbull, Malcolm J. *Victims or Villains: Jewish Images in Classic English Detective Fiction.* Bowling Green, Ohio: Bowling Green State University Popular Press, 1998.

VanDerBeets, Richard. *George Sanders: An Exhausted Life.* Lanham, MD: Madison Books, 1990.

Walker, Ronald G. "World without End: An Approach to Narrative Structure in Greene's *The End of the Affair.*" *Texas Studies in Literature and Language* 26 (Summer 1984): 218-41.

Warner, Mary. "Faith Born of Anguish: Sarah Miles as Profligate and Apostle." *Perceptions of Religious Faith in the Works of Graham Greene.* Ed. William Thomas Hill. Bern: Peter Lang, 2002.

Watts, Cedric. *A Preface to Greene.* London and New York: Longman, 1997.

Waugh, Evelyn. "The Heart's Own Reasons: Graham Greene's New Novel." *Commonweal* 54 (August 17, 1951): 458–59.

Wendorf, Thomas A. "Greene's Mystery Stories." *Perceptions of Religious Faith in the Works of Graham Greene*. Ed. William Thomas Hill. Bern: Peter Lang, 2002.

West, W. J. *The Quest for Graham Greene*. London: Weidenfeld & Nicolson, 1997.

Williams, Trevor L. "History over Theology: The Case for Pinkie in Greene's *Brighton Rock*." *Studies in the Novel* 24 (Spring 1992): 67–97.

Willman, Skip. "The Kennedys, Fleming, and Cuba." *Ian Fleming & The Cultural Politics of 007 James Bond*. Ed. Edward P. Comentale et al. Bloomington and Indianapolis: Indiana University Press, 2005.

Wolfe, Peter. *Graham Greene the Entertainer*. Carbondale and Edwardsville: Southern Illinois University Press, 1972.

Index

Page references to main or significant entries are in **boldface**. All titles are of works by Greene

Abdul (*Travels with My Aunt*) 9
Abdullah (*Travels with My Aunt*) 9
Acky (*This Gun for Hire*) 9
Across the Border 9
"Across the Bridge" 9–10
Ada (*Travels with My Aunt*) 10
Adams ("The Case for the Defence") 10
Adams (*It's a Battlefield*) 10
Adams, Mrs. ("The Case for the Defence") 10
Adams, Stanley 96
Adolph (*The Name of Action*) 10
After Two Years 10
Agbo (*The Human Factor*) 10
Agnes (*Our Man in Havana*) 10
Agnes, Mother (*A Burnt-Out Case*) 10
Aitkin (*This Gun for Hire*) 10
Akimbu, Marie (*A Burnt-Out Case*) 10–11
"Alas, Poor Maling" 11
Albert (*Doctor Fischer of Geneva*) 11
Alec ("May We Borrow Your Husband?") 11
Alexitch, Captain (*Orient Express*) 11
Alfred (*The End of the Affair*) 11
Ali (*The Heart of the Matter*) 11
Alice (*This Gun for Hire*) 11
Alice, Aunt ("The Basement Room") 11
Allen, Larry 127
The Ambassador (*The Confidential Agent*) 11
The Ambassador (*Our Man in Havana*) 11
The Ambassador of Panama (*The Honorary Consul*) 11
The Ambassadress (*Our Man in Havana*) 12
The American Ambassador (*The Honorary Consul*) 12
The American Consul-General (*Our Man in Havana*) 12
Amis (*Travels with My Aunt*) 12
Amy ("Jubilee") 12, 14
Ana (*The Honorary Consul*) 12
Anderson (*The Other Side of the Border*) 12
Andersson (*England Made Me*) 12
André (*The Comedians*) 12

Andrews (*The Man Within*) 12, 128
Andrews, Francis (*The Man Within*) 12
Andrews, Mrs. (*The Man Within*) 12
Angelica (*Our Man in Havana*) 13
Angeline, Lady (*Brighton Rock*) 13
Anita (*The Power and the Glory*) 13
Anna (*England Made Me*) 13
Anna (*The Human Factor*) 13
Anna (*Orient Express*) 13
Anne (*The Quiet American*) 13
Annette (*England Made Me*) 13
Anthony Sant 13
Antonio, Father (*The Honorary Consul*) 13
An Appointment with the General 13–14
Aranjuez, Senor (*The Heart of the Matter*) 14
The Archbishop ("The Blessing") 14
The Archbishop ("Church Militant") 14
The Archbishop (*The Comedians*) 14
The Archbishop (*The Honorary Consul*) 14
The Archbishop (*Monsignor Quixote*) 14
The Archbishop of Canterbury ("The Improbable Tale of the Archbishop of Canterbury") 46
Arden (*The Honorary Consul*) 14
Arias, Arnulfo 123
Arnold (*Loser Takes All*) 14
Arnold, Ida (*Brighton Rock*) 14, 25
Aronstein (*England Made Me*) 14–15
Ashton, Winifred 222
Ashworth, Mrs. (*Our Man in Havana*) 15
Asplund (*England Made Me*) 15
The Assistant Commissioner (*It's a Battlefield*) 15
Attention (*A Burnt-Out Case*) 15
Auguste, Philippe 134
Augustus ("A Little Place Off the Edgeware Road") 15
"Awful When You Think of It" 15
Ayers, Ruby M. (*Orient Express*) 15
Azikawe (*The Heart of the Matter*) 16

Bacon (*This Gun for Hire*) 16
Bagster, Flight-Lieutenant Freddie (*The Heart of the Matter*) 16
Bailey (*The Hesart of the Matter*) 16
Baines ("The Basement Room") 16
Baines (*The Other Side of the Border*) 16
Baines (*This Gun for Hire*) 16
Baines, Mrs. ("The Basement Room") 16
Baines, Mrs. (*The Human Factor*) 16
Baker (*The Heart of the Matter*) 16
Balfrage, Lady (*The Honorary Consul*) 22
Ballard (*This Gun for Hire*) 16
Banks, Colonel (*This Gun for Hire*) 16
Bannocks, Mrs. (*The Third Man*) 16
Barham (*It's a Battlefield*) 16
Barker (*Brighton Rock*) 16
Barker (*The Human Factor*) 16
Barker (*This Gun for Hire*) 16–17
Barker, Dr. (*The Human Factor*) 17
Barlow (*The Heart of the Matter*) 17
Barlow, Major ("The Lieutenant Died Last") 17
Barlow, Mrs. (*The Heart of the Matter*) 17
Barnes (*The Ministry of Fear*) 17
Baron ("The Bear Fell Free") 17
Baron, Peggy (*Brighton Rock*) 17
Baronin (*Our Man in Havana*) 17
"The Basement Room" (story) 17–19, 300
The Basement Room (collection of stories) 18
Basil (*Brighton Rock*) 19
Bates (*The Captain and the Enemy*) 19
Bates (*The Human Factor*) 19
Bates (*The Other Side of the Border*) 19
Bates (*The Third Man*) 19–20
Bates, H.E. 300
Bates, Joe (*The Confidential Agent*) 20
Bates, Mrs. Union-of-Writers (*The Human Factor*) 20
Batista y Zaldivar, Fulgencio 237, 256, 283
Batlow, Miss (*It's a Battlefield*) 20

Index

Batterson (*England Made Me*) 20
Baudelaire, Charles 99, 246
Baxter (*The Captain and the Enemy*) 20
Baxter (*England Made Me*) 20
Baxter, J. (*The Comedians*) 20
Baxter, Jim (*The Captain and the Enemy*) 20
Baxter, Mrs. (*The Captain and the Enemy*) 20
Beale (*It's a Battlefield*) 20
Beale (*The Ministry of Fear*) 20
Beale, George (*Brighton Rock*) 20
"The Bear Fell Free" 20–21
"Beauty" 21–22
Beavis (*The Ministry of Fear*) 22
Beckley, Henry (*The Power and the Glory*) 22
Belfrage, Sir Henry (*The Honorary Consul*) 22
Bellairs, Mrs. (*The Ministry of Fear*) 22
Bellamy (*The Human Factor*) 22
Bellen, Lord ("When Greek Meets Greek") 22
Bellows, Dr. (*The Confidential Agent*) 22
Belmont, Monsieur Henri (*Doctor Fischer of Geneva*) 22
Benditch, Lord (*The Confidential Agent*) 22–23
Bendrix (*The End of the Affair*) 23
Bendrix, Maurice (*The End of the Affair*) 23, 301
Benevento, Dr. (*The Honorary Consul*) 23
Benevento, Señora (*The Honorary Consul*) 23
Bennett (*It's a Battlefield*) 23
Bennett, Arthur (*The Confidential Agent*) 23
Bennett, Mrs. (*The Confidential Agent*) 23
Bentley, Phyllis Eleanor 254
Beresford, John Davys 23
Bergman (*The Honorary Consul*) 23
Bergson ("A Drive in the Country") 24
Bergsten (*England Made Me*) 24
Bernay (*It's a Battlefield*) 24
Bertha ("The Over-night Bag") 24
Bertram (*The End of the Affair*) 24
Bertram (*Loser Takes All*) 24
Bertram, Augusta (*Travels with My Aunt*) 24–25
Bertram, Mrs. (*The End of the Affair*) 25
Berval, René 247
Beyer (*England Made Me*) 25
Bill (*Brighton Rock*) 25
Bill (*The Man Within*) 25
Billings (*The Other Side of the Border*) 25
Bird's Nest (*Loser Takes All*) 25
The Bishop (*The Burnt-Out Case*) 25
The Bishop (*Our Man in Havana*) 26
The Bishop (*The Quiet American*) 26

The Bishop (*This Gun for Hire*) 25–26
Bishop, Arthur (*The Heart of the Matter*) 26
Bishop, David ("The News in English") 26
Bishop, Mary ("The News in English") 26
Bishop, Mrs. ("The News in English") 26
The Bishop of Bath and Wells ("Work Not in Progress") 26
The Bishop of Canterbury ("Work Not in Progress") 26
Bishop of El Toboso (*Monsignor Quixote*) 26
The Bishop of Melbourne (*Monsignor Quixote*) 26
The Bishop of Motopo (*Monsignor Quixote*) 26
Björk, Anita 27, 56, 131, 322
Black (*The End of the Affair*) 27
Black, Sylvia (*The End of the Affair*) 27
Black Boy (*Brighton Rock*) 27
Blackbeard (*The Heart of the Matter*) 27
Blacker ("The Hint of an Explanation") 27, 146–147
Blackie ("The Destructors") 27
Blake (George) (*The Human Factor*) 27–28, 245
Bleek, Alfred (*This Gun for Hire*) 28
Blendowe, Lord (*It's a Battlefield*) 28
Blennerhasset, Mrs. (*Travels with My Aunt*) 28
Blesserhasset, Mayor (*Travels with My Aunt*) 28
"The Blessing" 28
Blit (*The Human Factor*) 28
Blixon, Mrs. (*Loser Takes All*) 28
Blixon, Sir Walter (*Loser Takes All*) 28
Blue, Tony (*The Confidential Agent*) 29
"The Blue Film" 28–29
Boling (*The Heart of the Matter*) 29
Bolton, Lady (*The End of the Affair*) 29
Bompierre, Mme. (*The Quiet American*) 29
Bone ("Men at Work") 29
Bonne chance (*The Human Factor*) 29
The Boob ("Jubilee") 29
Boris (*The Human Factor*) 29
Bottomley, Ezra (*The Human Factor*) 29
Bourget, Andrew (grandson) 131
Bourget, Caroline (daughter) 131; *see also* Greene, Caroline
Bowen, Marjorie 319
Bowers (*The Heart of the Matter*) 29
Bowles (*The Heart of the Matter*) 30
Bowles, A.N. (*Loser Takes All*) 30
Bowles, Mrs. (*The Heart of the Matter*) 30

Boyston (*The Heart of the Matter*) 30
Bracer (*The Third Man*) 30
Braddock (*The Man Within*) 30
Bradshaw (*The Honorary Consul*) 30
"A Branch of the Service" 30–31
Brandon's Acre 31
Braun, Dr. (*Our Man in Havana*) 31
Braun, Herr ("The Root of All Evil") 31
Brewer (*Our Man in Havana*) 31
Brewer, Bill (*Brighton Rock*) 31
Brewer, Mrs. (*Brighton Rock*) 31
Brewett ("The Lieutenant Died Last") 31
Brewett, Mrs. ("The Lieutenant Died Last") 31
Brewster, Mrs. (*This Gun for Hire*) 31
Brewster, Mrs. (*Travels with My Aunt*) 31
Bridges (*The Ministry of Fear*) 31
Brighton Rock 31–36, 232, 305
Brigitta (*The Power and the Glory*) 36
Brigstock ("The Bear Fell Free") 36
Brigstock (*The Confidential Agent*) 36
Brigstock (*The Heart of the Matter*) 36
The British Ambassador (*The Honorary Consul*) 36
The British Ambassador (*Travels with My Aunt*) 36
The British Minister (*The Quiet American*) 36
Briton, Jules (*It's a Battlefield*) 36
Bromley, Mrs. (*The Heart of the Matter*) 36
Bromley, Teddy (*The Heart of the Matter*) 36
"Brother" 37
Brothers (*The Ministry of Fear*) 37
Brown (*The Comedians*) 37–38
Brown (*The Heart of the Matter*) 38
Brown ("Work Not in Progress") 38
Brown, Pinkie (*Brighton Rock*) 38
Browne (*The Captain and the Enemy*) 38
Browne (*The Human Factor*) 39
Browne, Sir Thomas 192
Browning, Robert 86, 216, 287
Brûle, Père (*The Heart of the Matter*) 39
Brutus (*The Comedians*) 39
Buchan, John 231, 267
Buffy (*The Human Factor*) 39
Bullen (*It's a Battlefield*) 39
Bullen, Miss (*Loser Takes All*) 39
Buller (*The Honorary Consul*) 39
Buller (*The Human Factor*) 39
Buller, Captain (*The Heart of the Matter*) 39
Burdick, Eugene 259
Burgess, Guy 22, 39, 161, 245
A Burnt-Out Case 39–45, 63, **160**, 322
Burton, Arthur ("The Moment of Truth") 45
Bury (*The Human Factor*) 45

Bury, Lady Caroline (*It's a Battlefield*) 45
Bury, Lord Justin (*It's a Battlefield*) 45
Butler, Inspector (*The Human Factor*) 45
Butler, Mrs. (*The Man Within*) 45
Butterworth (*The Heart of the Matter*) 45

C (*The Human Factor*) 45
Cagney, James 305
Calkin, Major Joseph (*This Gun for Hire*) 45
Calkin, Mrs. (*This Gun for Hire*) 45
Callitrope (*This Gun for Hire*) 45
Callot, Annette-Marie (*Travels with My Aunt*) 46
Callow (*The Honorary Consul*) 46
Calloway (*England Made Me*) 46
Calloway (*The Heart of the Matter*) 46
Calloway, Colonel (*The Third Man*) 46, 301
Calloway, Joseph ("Across the Bridge") 46
Calver, James (*The Power and the Glory*) 46
Camden, William 38
Camilla (*Travels with My Aunt*) 46
Campbell (*Orient Express*) 46
Campion, Edmund 214
Canby ("A Day Saved") 46
Caper ("The Blessing") 46
Capote, Truman 35, 244
Capriole, Father Thomas (*The Comedians*) 46
The Captain (*The Captain and the Enemy*) 46–47, 128
The Captain and the Enemy 47–52
The Cardinal of Bombay 187
Carey, Father ("The Hint of an Explanation") 52
Carey, J.G. (*The Third Man*) 52
Carl (*Orient Express*) 52
Carlota (*The Honorary Consul*) 52
Carlyon (*The Man Within*) 52
Carosse (*The Tenth Man*) 52
Carosse, Madame (*The Tenth Man*) 52
Carpenter, Edward (*Travels with My Aunt*) 52
Carpenter, Miss (*The Confidential Agent*) 52
Carson (*The Human Factor*) 52
Carter ("The Bear Fell Free") 52–53
Carter ("The Blue Film") 53
Carter (*The End of the Affair*) 53
Carter (*The Third Man*) 53
Carter (*This Gun for Hire*) 53
Carter, President Jimmy 51, 124, 290
Carter, John 125
Carter, Julia ("Mortmain") 53
Carter, Lionel A. 52–53, 53, 54
Carter, Mr. ("The Bue Film") 53
Carter, Mrs. (*The Heart of the Matter*) 53
Carter, Philip ("Mortmain") 53
Carter, William (*Our Man in Havana*) 53–54

Carthew, Molly (*Brighton Rock*) 54
Cary (*Loser Takes All*) 54
"The Case for the Defence" 54
Casement, Roger 25
Cassidy (*It's a Battlefield*) 54
Cassin (*Burnt-Out Case*) 54
Cassin, Mme. (*A Burnt-Out Case*) 54
Castillo (*The Honorary Consul*) 54
Castle (*The Heart of the Matter*) 54
Castle (*The Human Factor*) 54–55
Castle, Mary (*The Human Factor*) 55
Castle, Maurice (*The Human Factor*) 55, 245
Castle, Mrs. (*The Heart of the Matter*) 55
Castle, Mrs. (*The Human Factor*) 55–56
Castle, Roger (*The Human Factor*) 56
Castle, Sam (*The Human Factor*) 56
Castle, Sarah (*The Human Factor*) 56
Castro, Fidel 51, 123, 146, 208, 237, 256, 259
Castro, Raul 256
Catarina (*The Power and the Glory*) 56
Caterina (*The Honorary Consul*) 56
Catherine, Mère (*The Comedians*) 56
Cato (*The Comedians*) 56
Caussade, Jean Pierre de 211
Cavalcanti, Alberto 180, 237
Caveda, Ramon (*Rumour at Nightfall*) 56
Cerra, Father Miguel (*The Power and the Glory*) 56
Cervantes Saavedra, Miguel de 213
"Chagrin in Three Parts" 57
Chalfont ("Jubilee") 57
"A Chance for Mr. Lever" 18, 57
Chant, Oliver (*The Name of Action*) 58
Chantier, Philippe (*Loser Takes All*) 58
Chaplain (*It's a Battlefield*) 58
Chaplin, Charlie 59, 96
Charge, Major (*Travels with My Aunt*) 58
Charlie (*Brighton Rock*) 58
Charlie (*This Gun for Hire*) 58
Charteris, Celia (*Loser Takes All*) 58
Charters (*The Comedians*) 58
Chase, Francis (*Rumour at Nightfall*) 58–59
Chase, James Hadley 300, 301; see also Raymond, René
Chaucer, Geoffrey 287
Chavel (*The Tenth Man*) 59
Chavel, Jean-Louis (*The Tenth Man*) 59
Chavel, Madame (*The Tenth Man*) 59
"Cheap in August" 59–60
Chester ("The Man Who Stole the Eiffel Tower") 61
Chick, Miss (*It's a Battlefield*) 61
Chief (*It's a Battlefield*) 61

The Chief (*Our Man in Havana*) 61
The Chief Clerk (*The Honorary Consul*) 61
The Chief Engineer (*Our Man in Havana*) 61
The Chief of Police (*The Honorary Consul*) 61
The Chief of Police ("The Lottery Ticket") 61
The Chief of Police (*Our Man in Havana*) 61
The Chief of Police *The Power and the Glory*) 61
The Chief of Police (*Travels with My Aunt*) 61
The Chief Warden (*The End of the Affair*) 62
Chilton (*The Human Factor*) 62
Chine (*It's a Battlefield*) 62
Chinky (*This Gun for Hire*) 62
Chivers, Thomas Holley 195
Chou (*The Quiet American*) 62
Chubby (*The Confidential Agent*) 62
"Church Militant" 62
Cibber, Colley 174
Cifuentes, Engineer (*Our Man in Havana*) 63
Clara (*The Captain and the Enemy*) 63
Clara (*The Confidential Agent*) 63
Clara, Sister (*A Burnt-Out Case*) 63
Clarence (*Brighton Rock*) 63
Clarenty, Mrs. ("May We Borrow Your Husband?") 63
Clay, Father (*The Heart of the Matter*) 63
Clayton, Tubby ("The Bear Fell Free") 63
Cloette, Jacques 278
Cloette, Yvonne 63–64, 90, 131, 248, 249, 278, 322, 332
Clough, Colin (*The Human Factor*) 64
Cohen (*This Gun for Hire*) 64
Cohen, Alf ("A Drive in the Country") 64
Colin ("Dear Dr. Falkenheim") 64
Colin, Dr. (*A Burnt-Out Case*) 64–65
Colin, Mme. (*A Burnt-Out Case*) 65
Colleoni (*Brighton Rock*) 65
Colleoni, Mrs. (*Brighton Rock*) 65
Colley (*The Other Side of the Border*) 65
Collier (*The Ministry of Fear*) 65
Collier (*This Gun for Hire*) 65
Collier, Joe (*The Man Within*) 65
Collins ("The Blessing") 65
Collins (*England Made Me*) 65
Collins (*The Heart of the Matter*) 65
Collins (*It's a Battlefield*) 65
Collins ("Murder for the Wrong Reason") 65
Collins, Annie (*Brighton Rock*) 66
Collins, Beatrice (*The End of the Affair*) 66
Collins, Lady (*It's a Battlefield*) 66
Collins, Lord (*It's a Battlefield*) 66

Index

Collins, Mrs. (*The Heart of the Matter*) 66
Collins, Nellie ("Murder for the Wrong Reason") 66
Collins, T. (*Brighton Rock*) 66
Collinson, Hubert ("Murder for the Wrong Reason") 66
The Colonel ("The News in English") 66
Colonel, Herr ("Dream of a Strange Land") 66
The Colonial Secretary (*The Heart of the Matter*) 66
The Colonial Treasurer (*The Heart of the Matter*) 66
The Comedians 66–71
Comfort (*Travels with My Aunt*) 73
The Commander-in-Chief (*The Quiet American*) 73
The Commissioner (*A Burnt-Out Case*) 73
The Commissioner ("Dream of a Strange Land") 73
The Commissioner (*The Heart of the Matter*) 73
The Commissioner of Police (*A Burnt-Out Case*) 73
The Complaisant Lover 27
Con (*Orient Express*) 73
Concasseur, Captain (*Our Man in Havana*) 73
Conder (*It's a Battlefield*) 73
Coney (*It's a Battlefield*) 73–74
Coney, Rose (*It's a Battlefield*) 74
The Confidential Agent 74–77
"Congo Journal" 44
Connell (*England Made Me*) 77
Connett, Miss May (*This Gun for Hire*) 77
Connolly (*The Human Factor*) 77
Connolly (*The Quiet American*) 77
Conrad, Joseph 44, 51, 58, **100**, 160, 166, 223, 277, 296
Constance (*This Gun for Hire*) 77
The Consul (*The Honorary Consul*) 77
Conway ("The Bear Fell Free") 77
Conway (*The Confidential Agent*) 77
Conway (*The Ministry of Fear*) 77
Cooler, Colonel (*The Third Man*) 77
Cooper (*Our Man in Havana*) 77
Cooper ("The Over-night Bag") 77
Cooper, Henry ("The Over-night Bag") 77–78
Cooper, James Fenimore 323
Cooper, Major (*The Heart of the Matter*) 78
Cooper, Mrs. ("The Over-night Bag") 78
Coral (*This Gun for Hire*) 78
Corinne (*The Quiet American*) 78
Corkery, Phil (*Brighton Rock*) 78
Cornforth, William P. (*The Heart of the Matter*) 78
Corredo, Diego (*The Honorary Consul*) 78
Corvo, Baron 267
Cossa (*Travels with My Aunt*) 78
Cost (*The Ministry of Fear*) 78

Courage (*Travels with My Aunt*) 78
Coward, Noël 96, 322
Crab (*Brighton Rock*) 78–79
Crabbe (*It's a Battlefield*) 79
Crabbin (*The Third Man*) 79
Cradbrooke, Lady (*The Ministry of Fear*) 79
Craigie, David (pen name of Dorothy Glover) 125
Cranbeim, Mrs. (*This Gun for Hire*) 79
Crane (*The Name of Action*) 79
Crane, Michael (*Rumour at Nightfall*) 79
Crane, Mrs. (*Rumour at Nightfall*) 79
Crane, Stephen 79
Crashaw, Colonel ("Proof Positive") 79
Craven ("A Little Place off the Edgeware Road") 79–80
Crawford, Francis Marion 258
Crayshaw (*The Heart of the Matter*) 80
Crichton (*The Honorary Consul*) 80
Crikey (*The Confidential Agent*) 80
Crippen (*It's a Battlefield*) 80
Crole, Else (*The Confidential Agent*) 80
Crombie, Doctor ("Doctor Crombie") 80
Crompton, David 80, 321
Crompton, Father (*The End of the Affair*) 80
Crookham, Monty (*The Confidential Agent*) 80
Crooks (*The Ministry of Fear*) 80
Cross, Elisabeth ("When Greek Meets Greek") 81
Cross, Superintendent (*It's a Battlefield*) 81
Crosthwaite (*This Gun for Hire*) 81
Crowder (*Travels with My Aunt*) 81
Crowder, Anne (*This Gun for Hire*) 81
Crowe ("The Blessing") 81
Crowle, Mrs. Janet (*It's a Battlefield*) 81
The Crown Prince (*England Made Me*) 81
Cruickshank (*The Human Factor*) 81
Cubitt, John (*Brighton Rock*) 81
Cubitt, Mrs. (*Brighton Rock*) 81
Cudlow (*The Other Side of the Border*) 81
Cullen, Rose (*The Confidential Agent*) 81–82
Cundifer, Lady (*This Gun for Hire*) 82
Curlew, Melany (*Travels with My Aunt*) 82
Curlew, the Rev. (*Travels with My Aunt*) 82
Curlew, William Crowder (*Travels with My Aunt*) 82
Currie, Captain (*The Confidential Agent*) 82
Curtis, Tom (*The Ministry of Fear*) 82

Cynthia (*The Human Factor*) 82
Czinner, Dr. Richard (*Orient Express*) 82

D. (*The Confidential Agent*) 82–83
D., Mrs. (*The Confidential Agent*) 83
Daintry (*The Human Factor*) 83
Daintry, Elizabeth (*The Human Factor*) 83
Daintry, Colonel John (*The Human Factor*) 83
Daintry, Mrs. (*The Human Factor*) 83
Daintry, Sylvia (*The Human Factor*) 83
Dallow, Ted (*Brighton Rock*) 83–84
Dambreuse, Achille (*Travels with My Aunt*) 84
Dambreuse, Madame (*Travels with My Aunt*) 84
Damien, Father 325
Dansey, Colonel Claude 83
Danvers, Jimmy (*The Other Side of the Border*) 84
Davenant (*This Gun for Hire*) 84
David ("The Hint of an Explanation") 84
David (*The Ministry of Fear*) 84
Davidge (*England Made Me*) 84
Davidge, Lucia (*England Made Me*) 84
Davidge, Mrs. (*England Made Me*) 85
Davidge, Roderick (*England Made Me*) 85
Davidson ("A Chance for Mr. Lever") 85
Davis ("The Bear Fell Free") 85
Davis (*It's a Battlefield*) 85
Davis (*The Ministry of Fear*) 85
Davis (*Our Man in Havana*) 85
Davis (*This Gun for Hire*) 85
Davis, Arthur (*The Human Factor*) 85
Davis, Batty (*The Heart of the Matter*) 85
Davis, Father (*The Heart of the Matter*) 86
Davis, William (*The Human Factor*) 86
"A Day Saved" 86
Dayrell-Browning, Marion Greene-Armytage (mother-in-law) 130
The Dean of Students (*The Comedians*) 86
Dean of Warbury ("Under the Garden") 86
Deane, Richard (*Doctor Fischer of Geneva*) 86
"Dear Dr. Falkenheim" 86–87
Dechaux (*The Comedians*) 87
Dechaux, Mme. (*The Comedians*) 87
Dedham, Sir Silas ("Under the Garden") 87
Dedications (by Greene) 87
Defoe, Daniel 159
De Gaulle, Charles André Joseph Marie 87, 332

De Gaulle, Tante Yvonne ("Two Gentle People") 87
De Gaulle, Yvonne Vendroux 332
Deighton, Len 160
Dejoie, Jacques ("Chagrin in Three Parts") 87
Delaine, The Hon. Carol (*Orient Express*) 87
De Laszlo (*England Made Me*) 87
De Lattre de Tassigny, Jean Joseph-Marie (*The Quiet American*) 88, 263, 265
Delia (*Brighton Rock*) 88
Delia (*England Made Me*) 88
Demassener, Anne-Marie (*The Name of Action*) 88
Demassener, Paul (*The Name of Action*) 88
Dempster (*The Heart of the Matter*) 88
Dennys, Elisabeth Greene (sister) 88–89, 128
Dennys, Louise (niece) 88–89
Dennys, Nicholas (nephew) 88
Dennys, Rodney (breother-in-law) 88
Dentista ("The Lottery Ticket") 89
Deo Gratias (*A Burnt-Out Case*) 89
Dermody, Mrs. (*The Ministry of Fear*) 89
Derry (*The Heart of the Matter*) 89
Descartes, René 211
Desprez (*The Quiet American*) 89
"The Destructors" 89–90
Dewes, Father ("Special Duties") 90
Dexter, Benjamin (*The Third Man*) 90
Diaz, General (*Rumour at Nightfall*) 91
Dibba, Philip (*The Human Factor*) 91
Dick (*Orient Express*) 91
Dick ("Work Not in Progress") 91
Dickens, Charles 109
Dicky (*The Human Factor*) 91
Diederich, Bernard 187
Diego (*Monsignor Quixote*) 91
Diego, Señor (*Monsignor Quixote*) 91
Digby (*Brighton Rock*) 91
The Director of Agriculture (*The Heart of the Matter*) 91
The Director of Education (*The Heart of the Matter*) 91
The Director of Posts and Telegraphs (*Our Man in Havana*) 91
The Director of Public Works (*Burnt-Out Case*) 91
Dirty (*Loser Takes All*) 91
"A Discovery in the Woods" 91–92
Dobel, Herr ("The Root of All Evil") 92
"Doctor Crombie" 92–93
Doctor Fischer of Geneva or The Bomb Party 93 – 97
Dodo (*The Human Factor*) 97
Dolly ("The Bear Fell Free") 97
Dominguez (*The Quiet American*) 97

Dominguez, Raul (*Our Man in Havana*) 97
Don Juan (*The Comedians*) 97
Dongen (*England Made Me*) 97
Donnell, Father ("Church Militant") 97
Doppeldorf, Dr. ("Dear Dr. Falkenheim") 97
Dora (*This Gun for Hire*) 97
Doris (*Brighton Rock*) 97
Dos Passos, John 79
Douglas ("A Day Saved") 97
Douglas, James (*Orient Express*) 97
Down, Cora ("The Basement Room") 97
Dowson (*England Made Me*) 97
"Dream of a Strange Land" 97–98
Dreid (*This Gun for Hire*) 98
Dreuther, Herbert (*Loser Takes All*) 98–99
Drew, Lord Brewitt ("The Lieutenant Died Last") 99, 231
Drew, Jeff ("Dear Dr. Falkenheim") 99
Drewitt (*Brighton Rock*) 99
"A Drive in the Country" 99–100
Driver ("The Lieutenant Died Last") 100
Driver, Frederick ("When Greek Meets Greek") 100
Driver, Lord ("When Greek Meets Greek") 100
Drover, Conrad (*It's a Battlefield*) 100
Drover, Jim (*It's a Battlefield*) 100–101
Drover, Milly (*It's a Battlefield*) 101
Druce (*The Man Within*) 101
Druce, Captain (*The Heart of the Matter*) 101
Dubois, Alexandre (*The Comedians*) 101
Dubois, M. Desprez (*The Quiet American*) 101
Ducker (*The Heart of the Matter*) 101
Duke (*The Quiet American*) 101
du Maurier, Daphne 299
Duncan, Miss (*The End of the Affair*) 101
Dunlop ("A Visit to Morin") 101
Dunn, Sidney (*Orient Express*) 101
Dunne, J.W. 21
Dunstan (*The End of the Affair*) 101
Dunwoody (*The Ministry of Fear*) 101
Dunwoody, Lady (*The Ministry of Fear*) 101
Dunwoody, Lord (*The Ministry of Fear*) 101
Duparc, Captain (*The Quiet American*) 101
Dupont ("A Visit to Morin") 102
Dupont, Clement (*The Comedians*) 102
Dupont, Hercule (*The Comedians*) 102
Dupont, Louise (*Travels with My Aunt*) 102

Dupont, Madame (*Loser Takes All*) 102
Dupont, Mlle. (*The Heart of the Matter*) 102
Duran, Leopoldo 88, 131, 178, 212, 266
Duran, Miguel (*The Honorary Consul*) 102
Durand (*The Heart of the Matter*) 102
Durand, Jacques ("An Appointment with the General") 102
Durobier ("A Visit to Morin") 102
The Dutch Ambassador (*Travels with My Aunt*) 102
Duval ("Two Gentle People") 102
Duval, Jean ("An Appointment with the General") 102
Duval, Marie-Claire ("An Appointment with the General") 102
Duval, Marie-Claire ("Two Gentle People") 102
Duvalier, Dr. François (*The Comedians*) 102–103, 134, 187, 193, 246, 286
Duvalier, Jean-Claude 103
Duvalier, Simone Ovide 103

Eckman (*Orient Express*) 103
Eckman, Emma (*Orient Express*) 103
Edith (*Our Man in Havana*) 103
Edith (*Travels with My Aunt*) 103
Edward, Uncle (*Our Man in Havana*) 103
Edwards (*Orient Express*) 103
Egerton, Colonel Mark (*This Gun for Hire*) 103
Egerton, Mrs. (*This Gun for Hire*) 103–104
Ekman (*England Made Me*) 104
Ekman, Frau (*England Made Me*) 104
Elijah ("The Trial of Pan") 104
Eliot, T.S. 36, 109, 220, 269, 299
Ella, Aunt (*England Made Me*) 104
Ellis, Dr. Havelock (*Travels with My Aunt*) 104
Elsie (*England Made Me*) 104
Elsie (*Orient Express*) 104
Emanuel (*A Burnt-Out Case*) 104
Emil (*The Comedians*) 104
Emilio (*Rumour at Nightfall*) 104
Emma ("The Basement Room") 104
Emma (*The Gun for Hire*) 104
The End of the Affair 55, 64, 104–110, 125, 160, 301, 322
"The End of the Party" 110–111
England Made Me 111–114, 232
Enrique (*Rumour at Nightfall*) 114
Enrique, Father (*Monsignor Quixote*) 114
Entertainments (Greene's) 114
The Episode 114, 277
Ernest (*The Ministry of Fear*) 114–115
Ernest ("Under the Garden") 115
Ertzüger, Frau (*The Name of Action*) 115
Escobar, Gustavo (*The Honorary Consul*) 115

Index

Escobar, Margarita (*The Honorary Consul*) 115
Ethel (*Our Man in Havana*) 115
Evans (*The Heart of the Matter*) 115
Excoffier, Monsieur (*Doctor Fischer of Geneva*) 115

Falkenheim, Dr. ("Dear Dr. Falkenheim") 115
Fanatic Arabia 115
Fanshaw (*It's a Battlefield*) 115
Farne (*The Man Within*) 115
Farrant (*England Made Me*) 115
Farrant, Anthony (*England Made Me*) 115–116, 134
Farrant, Kate (*England Made Me*) 116
Farrell, Mrs. ("The Bear Fell Free") 116
Farrell, Tony ("The Bear Fell Free") 116
Faulkner, William 109
Faverjon, Madame (*Doctor Fischer of Geneva*) 116
Favorites (Greene's own) 116–117
Felipe, Father (*Monsignor Quixote*) 117
Félix ("Chagrin in Three Parts") 117
Fellowes (*The Heart of the Matter*) 117
Fellowes, Mrs. (*The Heart of the Matter*) 117
Fellows, Captain Charles (*The Power and the Glory*) 117
Fellows, Coral (*The Power and the Glory*) 117
Fellows, Trixy (*The Power and the Glory*) 117
Fennick (*The Confidential Agent*) 117
Fennick, Nicolas ("When Greek Mets Greek") 117
Ferdinand of Castile (*Our Man in Havana*) 117
Fergusson, Buddy (*This Gun for Hire*) 117–118
Fernandez (*The Comedians*) 118
Fernandez (*Travels with My Aunt*) 118
Ferraro, Mrs. ("Special Duties") 118
Ferraro, William ("Special Duties") 118
Ferreira, P. (*The Heart of the Matter*) 118
Ferry, Mme. (*The Comedians*) 118
Fetting, Lord (*The Confidential Agent*) 118
Feversham, Lord (*Brighton Road*) 118
Fidrmuc, Paul 331
Fielding, Henry 293
Fields, Gracie 25
Fields, W.C. 313
The First Secretary (*The Confidential Agent*) 118
The First Secretary (*The Honorary Consul*) 118
The First Secretary (*The Quiet American*) 118

Fischer, Anna (*Doctor Fischer of Geneva*) 118
Fischer, Doctor (*Doctor Fischer of Geneva*) 119–119
Fisher (*The Honorary Consul*) 119
Fisher, Jimmy (*The Heart of the Matter*) 119
Fishguard (*The Ministry of Fear*) 119
Fitzgerald, F. Scott 280
Flageollet (*Travels with My Aunt*) 119
Flic, M. (*The Quiet American*) 119
Flo (*Orient Express*) 119
Fonteyn, Margot 99
Forage (*The Honorary Consul*) 119
Forbes (*The Confidential Agent*) 119
Forbes (*The Heart of the Matter*) 119
Forbes, Brian 161–162, 212
Ford, Ford Madox 109
Fordhaven (*Thie Gun for Hire*) 119
The Foreign Minister (*The Honorary Consul*) 119–120
The Foreign Secretary (*England Made Me*) 120
Forester, Dr. (*The Ministry of Fear*) 120
Forster, E.M. 90, 300
Fortescue (*The Confidential Agent*) 120
Fortnum (*The Honorary Consul*) 120
Fortnum (*The Human Factor*) 120
Fortnum, Charley (*The Honorary Consul*) 120
Fortnum, Clara (*The Honorary Consul*) 120
Fortnum, Evelyn (*The Honorary Consul*) 120–121
Fotheringay ("A Day Saved") 121
Fowler, Helen (*The Quiet American*) 121
Fowler, Thomas (*The Quiet American*) 121
Fox ("A Discovery in the Woods") 121
Franchini, Mathieu 247
Francis de Sales 209, 210
Francisco, Father (*Monsignor Quixote*) 121
Franco, Francisco 129, 208, 209, 245
François (*The Quiet American*) 121
François ("Two Gentle People") 121
Frank, Billy (*Brighton Rock*) 121–122
Frank, Judy (*Brighton Rock*) 122
Frankie (*The Confidential Agent*) 122
Fraser (*The Heart of the Matter*) 122
Frau General (*Travels with My Aunt*) 122
Fred ("A Drive in the Country") 122
Frederick, Sir ("Thew Other Side of the Border") 122
The French Ambassador ("An Old Man's Memory") 122
"The French Peace" 222
Fritz (dog) (*The Name of Action*) 122
Fritz (man) (*The Name of Action*) 122
Frost (*This Gun for Hire*) 122
Fuerabbia (*The Honorary Consul*) 122

Fullove (*The Ministry of Fear*) 122
Fuzzy Wuzzy (*England Made Me*) 122

Gaboriau, Ëmile 319
Gabriel ("The Trsial of Pan") 122
Galloway (*Brighton Rock*) 122
Galsworthy, John 200, 299
Galvao (*The Honorary Consul*) 122–123
Garcïa, Juan Pujol 331
Garnet (*The Man Within*) 123
Garnet, Elizabeth (*The Man Within*) 123
Gathaway, Lord (*Orient Express*) 123
Galván, Doctor (*Monsignor Quixote*) 123
Gary Parrot (*Brighton Rock*) 123
General, Herr ("Dream of a Strange Land") 123
The General ("An Appointment with the General") 123
The General (*A Burnt-Out Case*) 123
The General (*The Captain and the Enemy*) 123–124
The General (*The Comedians*) 124
The General (*The Honorary Consul*) 124
The General ("The Last Word") 124
The General (*Travels with My Aunt*) 124
General Burgoyne (*Brighton Rock*) 124
The General Director of the National Bank ("Dream of a Strange Land") 124
General Manager (*England Made Me*) 124
Geoff (*The Comedians*) 124
George (*The Honorary Consul*) 124
George (*The Man Within*) 124
George, David Lloyd 188
Gershoy, Eugenie 286
Getting to Know the General 51, 63, 124, 153, 187, 213, 290
Gibbons, Stanley (*Brighton Rock*) 124
Giffey, Major 132
Gilby, Father Thomas 248, 322
GL (*England Made Me*) 124
Glover, Dorothy 14, 124–125, 130, 131
Glover, Emily (*The Confidential Agent*) 125
God ("The Trial of Pan") 125
Goering, Field-Marshal Herman Wilhelm 125
Golding, William 92
Goldsmith, Oliver 196
Goldstein (*The Confidential Agent*) 125
Goldthorb (*The Confidential Agent*) 126
Golz, M. ("A Chance for Mr. Lever") 126
Gonzalez, Father (*Monsignor Quixote*) 126
González, Natalicio 290

Gorbachev, Mikhail 245
Gottlieb, Harry 286
Gottmann, Wolfgang (*The Third Man*) 126
Gough, Henry (Greene's pseudonym) 76
Gouldsmith (*England Made Me*) 126
The Governor (*The Heart of the Matter*) 126
The Governor (*The Honorary Consul*) 126
The Governor (*The Human Factor*) 126
The Governor (*It's a Battlefield*) 126
The Governor ("The Lottery Ticket") 126
The Governor (*The Power and the Glory*) 126
The Governor of the Chaco (*The Honorary Consul*) 126
Gower (*England Made Me*) 126
Gracia, Colonel (*The Comedians*) 126
The Graham Greene Film Reader 292
The Grand Duke ("The Root of All Evil") 126
Granger (*The Quiet Man*) 126–127
Granger, Bill (*The Quiet American*) 127
Granger, Mrs. (*The Quiet American*) 127
Granny Brown (*Our Man in Havana*) 127
Graves (*The Ministry of Fear*) 127
Graves (*This Gun for Hire*) 127
Graves, H. ("Men at Work") 127
The Great Dane (*This Gun for Hire*) 127
Greaves ("Two Gentle People") 127
Greaves, Henry ("Two Gentle People") 127
Greaves, Patience ("Two Gentle People") 127
The Greek (*A Burnt-Out Case*) 127–128
Green (*This Gun for Hire*) 128
Greene, Barbara (cousin) 58, 145, 176
Greene, Benjamin (cousin) 289
Greene, Benjamin (great-grandfather) 128
Greene, Carleton (father-in-law) 130
Greene, Caroline (daughter) 90, 124, 265; *see also* Bourget, Caroline
Greene, Charles Henry (father) 12, 83, 88, 93, 118, **128**, 129, 130, 134, 289
Greene, Edward (uncle) 289
Greene, Elaine Gilbert Shaplen (sister-in-law) 129
Greene, Elisabeth (sister); *see* Dennys, Elisabeth Greene
Greene, Else Hofler Neumann (sister-in-law) 80, 129–130
Greene, Francis (son) 124, 131
Greene, Graham Carleton (nephew) 129, 131

Greene, Helga Mary Guinness (sister-in-law) 129
Greene, Herbert (brother) 100, 116, **128–129**, 130, 134
Greene, Sir Hugh (brother) 80, 84, 90, 114, 125, 128, **129–130**, 192, 231, 330
Greene, Marion Raymond (mother) 19, 56, 83, 88, 125, 128, **130**, 273
Greene, Molly (sister) 128, **130**
Greene, Raymond (brother) 128, **130**, 243, 278
Greene, Sarah Mary Manning Grahame (sister-in-law) 130
Greene, Vivien (wife) 12, 27, 45, 90, 114, 121, 123, 124, 125, **130–131**, 192, 281, 322
Greene, William (grandfather) 128
Greene, Sir William Graham (uncle) 115, **130**, 327
Greta (*It's a Battlefield*) 131
Grey, Zane 299
Grey Lady (*Brighton Rock*) 131
Griggs (*The Ministry of Fear*) 131
Grisson (*A Burnt-Out Case*) 131
Grisson, Mme. (*A Burnt-Out Case*) 131
Groener (*This Gun for Hire*) 131
Groener, Frau (*The Heart of the Matter*) 131
Groener, Frau (*This Gun for Hire*) 131–132
Groseli, Monsieur (*Doctor Fischer of Geneva*) 132
Groves ("Murder for the Wrong Reason") 132
Gruber (*The Honorary Consul*) 132
Gruelle, Governor (*A Burnt-Out Case*) 132
Gruelle, Mme. (*A Burnt-Out Case*) 132
Gruner, Frau (*The Name of Action*) 132
Grünlich, Josef (*Orient Express*) 132
Guareschi, Giovanni 213
Gullie, Captain (*England Made Me*) 132
A Gun for Sale see *This Gun for Hire*
Gurnián, Sergeant ("An Appointment with the General") 132
Gustav VI (Sweden) 81, 257
Gustave (*The Quiet American*) 132
Guy, Daniel 63, 64, 212
Guy, Martine Cloetta 212

H, Toc ("The Bear Fell Free") 132
Hackenfurth, Frau ("The Root of All Evil") 132
Hake (*The Man Within*) 133
Hakim, Colonel (*Travels with My Aunt*) 133
Hale, Charles (*Brighton Rock*) 133
Halifax (*The Heart of the Matter*) 133
Halifax, Mary (*The Heart of the Matter*) 133
Hall, Fred (*England Made Me*) 133
Halliday (*The Human Factor*) 133–134

Hallows (*This Gun for Hire*) 134
Hamit (*The Comedians*) 134
Hammarsten, Professor (*England Made Me*) 134
Hammond (*England Made Me*) 134
Hands (*The Other Side of the Border*) 134
Hands, Ethel (*The Other Side of the Border*) 134–135
Hands, Mrs. (*The Other Side of the Border*) 135
Hannibal (*Travels with My Aunt*) 135
Hans (*Our Man in Havana*) 135
Hansel (*The Third Man*) 135
Harbin (*The Third Man*) 135
Harding (*The Captain and the Enemy*) 135
Harding, York (*The Quiet American*) 135
Hargreaves, Sir John (*The Human Factor*) 135
Hargreaves, Lady Mary (*The Human Factor*) 135
Harris, H.R. (*The Heart of the Matter*) 135–136, 306
Harris, Henry (*This Gun for Hire*) 136
Harris, Mrs. ("May We Borrow Your Husband?) 136
Harris, Mrs. (*This Gun for Hire*) 136
Harris, William ("May We Borrow Your Husband?) 136
Harry (*Brighton Rock*) 136
Harry (*The Human Factor*) 136
Harry ("Work Not in Progress") 136
Harry, Cockney (*The Man Within*) 136
Hartep, Colonel (*Orient Express*) 136
Harwood 328
Hasselbacher, Dr. (*Out Man in Havana*) 136–137
Hasselbacher, Emma (*Out Man in Havana*) 137
Hatty (*Travels with My Aunt*) 137
Hawthorne, Henry R. (*Our Man in Havana*) 137
Hawthorne, Nathaniel 11
Haw Haw, Lord *see* Joyce, William
The Heart of the Matter 125, **137–143**, 322
Heckstall-Jones, Josephine ("Mortmain") 143
Hei, Miss (*The Quiet American*) 143
Heine, Heinrich 228
Helen (*The Heart of the Matter*) 143
Hemingway, Ernest 331
Heng (*The Quiet American*) 143–144
Henne-Falcon, Colin ("The End of the Party") 144
Henne-Falcon, Mrs. ("The End of the Party") 144
Henri (*A Burnt-Out Case*) 144
Henri, Father (*A Burnt-Out Case*) 144

Index

Henriques (*England Made Me*) 144
Henry (*Our Man in Havana*) 144
Herbert (*It's a Battlefield*) 144
Herrera, Father (*Monsignor Quixote*) 144
Heysan-Bretau (*It's a Battlefield*) 144
Hickslaughter, Henry ("Cheap in August") 144
Hickslaughter, Joe ("Cheap in August") 144
Higginbotham (*This Gun for Hire*) 145
Higginbotham, Rose (*This Gun for Hire*) 145
Higgins (*The Honorary Consul*) 145
The High Commissioner (*Ths Quiet American*) 145
Hilfe, Anna (*The Ministry of Fear*) 145
Hilfe, Willi (*The Ministry of Fear*) 145
Hill, D. ("Men at Work") 145
Hilliard, Thomas (*The Man Within*) 145
Hillman, Sir Terence (*The Confidential Agent*) 145
Hilton, Conrad 145–146
Hilton, Mr. (*Our Man in Havana*) 145
"The Hint of an Explanation") 146–147
Hitchcock, Alfred 238
Ho Chi Minh 264
Hobbs (*Orient Express*) 147
Hochstetter, Leo 259–260
Hochstrudel, Wilbur K. (*The Comedians*) 147
Hogarth, Paul 27, 39, 64–65, 132, 153, 170, 178, 180, 184, 225
Hoghe (*A Burnt-Out Case*) 147
Hogminster ("The Moment of Truth") 147
Hogminster, Dolly ("The Moment of Truth") 147
Hogpit (*The Confidential Agent*) 147
Holmes, Sherlock 255
The Home Secretary (*It's a Battlefield*) 147
The Honorary Consul 147–153, 160, 290, 312
Hoover, Herbert 178
A House of Reputation 56
Hope-Smithies Lady ("The Trial of Pan") 153
Hope-Smithies Lord ("The Trial of Pan") 153
Hopkinson ("Special Duties") 153
Hopkinson (*This Gun for Hire*) 154
Howell ("Under the Garden") 154
Hügel, Friedrich von 109
Hughes ("The Blessing") 154
Hughes, Emmet John 259
Hughes, John ("Mortmain") 154
Hughes, Miss (*Travels with My Aunt*) 154
The Human Factor 154–161, 162, 245
Humpelnicker (*Our Man in Havana*) 161

Humphries, Doctor (*The Honorary Consul*) 161
Hythe, Wesby ("Alas, Poor Maling") 161

"I Spy" 162–163
"The Improbable Tale of the Archbishop of Canterbury" 161
In Search of a Character 44
Indian Queen (*Travels with My Aunt*) 161
Innes (*Brighton Rock*) 161
Innes, Michael 206
"The Innocent" 160, 161–162
The Inspector (*It's a Battlefield*) 162
"The Invisible Japanese Gentlemen" 162
Isaacs (*The Ministry of Fear*) 162
Isaacs (*Orient Express*) 162
Isaiah ("The Trial of Pan") 162
It's a Battlefield 163–166
Ivan (*The Human Factor*) 166
Ivy (*Orient Express*) 166
Izquierdo, Captain (*The Honorary Consul*) 166

J., F.G. (*The Ministry of Fear*) 166–167
J., N.L. (*The Ministry of Fear*) 167
J'Accuse 88, 212
Jack (*England Made Me*) 167
Jack (*The Ministry of Fear*) 167
Jagger (*The Heart of the Matter*) 167
Jaime (*Rumour at Nightfall*) 167
James (*England Made Me*) 167
James, Father (*Brighton Rock*) 167
James, Henry 18, 45, 72, 90, 293
Jameson (*The Human Factor*) 167
Jane ("The Bear Fell Free") 167
Jarvis, George (*The Confidential Agent*) 167
Javitt ("Under the Gareden") 167
Jean, Father (*A Burnt-Out Case*) 167
Jefferson, Alfred (*Brighton Rock*) 167
Jenkinson, Miss (*Our Man in Havana*) 167–168
Jenks (*It's a Battlefield*) 168
Jennings (*The Man Within*) 168
Jerome ("A Shocking Accident") 168
Jervis (*Orient Express*) 168
Jim (*Orient Express*) 168
Jim (*This Gun for Hire*) 168
Jim Braddon and the War Criminal 168, 296
Jiminez, Señora (*The Power and the Gory*) 168
Joe (*Brighton Rock*) 168
Joe (*The Confidential Agent*) 168
Joe ("The Destructors") 168
Joe ("A Drive in the Country") 168
Joe (*The Human Factor*) 168
Joe (*Our Man in Havana*) 168
Joe (*The Quiet American*) 168
Joe (*This Gun for Hire*) 168
Joe ("Under the Garden") 168
Joey (*The Confidential Agent*) 169
John ("The Bear Fell Free") 169
John (*Brighton Rock*) 169
John (*Orient Exzpress*) 169
John, Pope ("The Last Word") 169

Johnnie (*Brighton Rock*) 169
Johns (*The Ministry of Fear*) 169
Joiner, Edward (*The Human Factor*) 169
Jolicoeur, Aubelin 244
Jollye 259
Jones ("A Day Saved") 169
Jones (*The End of the Affair*) 169
Jones (*The Ministry of Fear*) 169
Jones, Alfred (*Doctor Fischer of Geneva*) 169
Jones, Anna-Luise (*Doctor Fischer of Geneva*) 170
Jones, Fred (*It's a Battlefield*) 170
Jones, Sir Frederick (*Doctor Fischer of Geneva*) 170
Jones, "Gee-Gee" (*It's a Battlefield*) 170
Jones, H.J. (*The Comedians*) 170
Jones, Lady (*Doctor Fischer of Geneva*) 170
Jones, Mary (*Doctor Fischer of Geneva*) 170
Jordan, Neil 110
José (*The Honorary Consul*) 170
José, Father (*Monsignor Quixote*) 170–171
José, Padre (*The Power and the Glory*) 171
Joseph (*The Comedians*) 171
Joseph, Father (*A Burnt-Out Case*) 171
Jossy (*This Gun for Hire*) 171
Journalist ("Work Not in Progress") 171
Journey Without Maps 18, 58, 304
Joyce ("The End of the Party") 171
Joyce (*Orient Express*) 171
Joyce, William (Lord Haw Haw) 225
Juan (*The Honorary Consul*) 171
Juan (*The Power and the Glory*) 171
Juan (*Rumour at Nightfall*) 171
Juárez, Father Miguel Pro 325
"Jubilee" 171–172
Juicy Juliet (*This Gun for Hire*) 172
Jules (*The Tenth Man*) 172
Julian (*Travels with My Aunt*) 172
Jumelle, Clément 246
The Junior Minister (*The Honorary Consul*) 172

K. (*The Confidential Agent*) 172
K., F.J. (*The Heaart of the Matter*) 172
K., J. (*This Gun for Hire*) 172
Kalamazoo (*The Human Factor*) 172
Kalebdjian (*Orient Express*) 172
Kalnitz, Mayor ("The Root of All Evil") 172
Kamnetz, General (*Orient Express*) 172
Kapper, Bertha (*The Name of Action*) 172
Kapper, Joseph (*The Name of Action*) 173
Karl (*The Name of Action*) 173
Kastner, Herr ("The Root of All Evil") 173

Kate, Great-aunt (*Our Man in Havana*) 173
Keene, Sir Alfred (*Travels with My Aunt*) 173
Keene, Miss Barbara (*Travels with My Aunt*) 173
Keene, Doris (*Travels with My Aunt*) 173
Keyser (*The Ministry of Fear*) 173
Khomeini, Ayatollah 227
The King (*A Burnt-Out Case*) 173
King, R. ("Men at Work") 173
Kips (*Doctor Fischer of Geneva*) 173
Kite (*Brighton Rock*) 17, 173–174
Kite, Battling (*This Gun for Hire*) 17, 174
Kimathi, Dedan 62
Knock-Me-Down (*Travels with My Aunt*) 174
Koch (*The Third Man*) 174
Koch, Ilse (*The Third Man*) 174
Kolber (*Orient Express*) 174
Kolley Kibber (*Brighton Rock*) 174
Korda, Alexander 19, 65, 77, 99, 109, 143, 174, 268, 300, 322
Kraft, Captain (*The Name of Action*) 174–175
Kreuger, Ivar 96, 133, 175
Krogh (*The Tenth Man*) 175
Krogh, Erik (*England Made Me*) 96, 132, 175
Krueger, General (*Doctor Fischer of Geneva*) 175
Krueger, Madame (*Doctor Fischer of Geneva*) 175
Kruger 325
Kruger (*Orient Express*) 175
Kurtz (*The Name of Action*) 175
Kurtz (*The Third Man*) 175
Kusack (*This Gun for Hire*) 176

L. (*The Confidential Agent*) 176
The Labyrinthine Ways see *The Power and the Glory*
Lagerson (*England Made Me*) 176
Laker (*The Human Factor*) 176
Lamb, Charles 233
Laminah 176
Laminah, Corporal (*The Heart of the Matter*) 176
Lance (*This Gun for Hire*) 176
Lane ("The Basement Room") 176
Lane (*The Heart of the Matter*) 176
Lane, Mrs. ("The Basement Room") 176
Lane, Philip ("The Basement Room") 176
Lansdale, Colonel Edward 259
Lascot-Villiers, The Comte Yvette de (*The Comedians*) 176
Lascot-Villiers, The Comtesse Yvette de (*The Comedians*) 176–177
"The Last Word" 177
The Last Word and Other Stories 177, 180, 219
Laurie (*England Made Me*) 177
Laurin (*England Made Me*) 177
The Lawless Roads 185, 254
Lawrence ("Men at Work") 178

Lawrence, D.H. 169, 178
Leadbitter, General ("Proof Positive") 178
Le Carré, John 160
Lechat, Dr. Michel F. 44, 64, 131, 144
Lederer, William 259
Lehr (*The Power and the Glory*) 178
Lehr, Miss (*The Power and the Glory*) 178
Lehr, Mrs. (*The Power and the Glory*) 178
Leigh, Vivien 99
Lenôtre (*The Tenth Man*) 178
Leopoldo, Father (*Monsignor Quixote*) 178
Lever ("A Chance for Mr. Lever") 178
Lever, Emily ("A Chance for Mr. Lever") 178
Lewis, F. ("Men at Work") 179
Lherisson, Dr. 187
Li, Dr. (*The Confidential Agent*) 179
The Liberal (*The Confidential Agent*) 179
The Lieutenant (*The Power and the Glory*) 124, 179
"The Lieutenant Died Last" 179–180
Lime, Harry (*The Third Man*) 180
"Limited Edition" 180
Lintz, Sabastian (*The Name of Action*) 180
Little Dwarf Doodoo (*Our Man in Havana*) 180
"A Little Place off the Edgeware Road" 180–181
Liz ("A Discovery in the Woods") 181
Liza (*The Captain and the Enemy*) 181
Lockhart, John 84
Loder (*The Heart of the Matter*) 181
Loewenstein (*England Made Me*) 181
Lola ("The Innocent") 181
Long, Huey 178
Longfellow, Henry Wadsworth 60
Lopez (*The Honorary Consul*) 181
Lopez (*Our Man in Havana*) 181
Lopez (*The Power and the Glory*) 181
López, Felipe Molas 290
Lopez, Señora (*The Honorary Consul*) 181
Lord (*The Human Factor*) 181
"The Lord Knows" 181–182
Lord Rochester's Monkey 136, 197
Loser Takes All 19, 182–184
The Lost Childhood 307
"The Lottery Ticket" 184–185
Lou-Lou ("May We Borrow Your Husband?") 185
Louchard, Pierre (*The Tenth Man*) 185
Louise (*The Comedians*) 185
Loulou (*The Name of Action*) 185
Lowndes, B. ("Men at Work") 185
Lowndes, Mrs. (*The Captain and the Enemy*) 185

Loyola, Ignatius of 212
Lucas ("A Chance for Mr. Lever") 185
Lucia ("Across the Bridge") 185
Lucius ("A Little Place off the Edgeware Road") 185
Lucy ("The Hint of an Explanation") 185
Lucy (*The Man Within*) 185
Lucy (*This Gun for Hire*) 186
Luigi (*The Comedians*) 186
Luis (*The Power and the Glory*) 186
Luis (*Rumour at Nightfall*) 186
Lukitch (*Orient Express*) 186
Lulu (*The Human Factor*) 186
Lunardi (*The Captain and the Enemy*) 186
Luxemburg Consul (*Our Man in Havana*) 186

MacDonald, James Ramsay (*Travels with My Aunt*) 186
MacDougall ("The Case for the Defence") 186
MacDougall (*Our Man in Hanava*) 186
MacIntyre (*Our Man in Havana*) 186
Mackie, Father 266
Maclean, Donald 30, 39, 161, 186–187, 245
Macleod, Joseph (*The Ministry of Fear*) 187
Macmillan, Harold 245
Macpherson (*Brighton Rock*) 187
Macpherson (*This Gun for Hire*) 187
Madero, Francisco 186
Magiot, Dr. (*The Comedians*) 187
Magloire, Paul Eugène 103, 246
Mais (*Brighton Rock*) 187
Maisie (*Brighton Rock*) 187
Makin (*The Heart of the Matter*) 187
"Malaya, the Forgotten War" 129
Malcott, Miss (*The Heart of the Matter*) 187
Maling ("Alas, Poor Maling") 187
Mallock, Sir William (*The End of the Affair*) 188
Mallows (*This Gun for Hire*) 188
Man Friday (*The Comedians*) 188
"The Man Who Stole the Eiffel Tower" 189
The Man Within 189–192
The Manager (*England Made Me*) 188
The Manager of Otraco (*A Burnt-Out Case*) 188
The Managing Editor (*The Quiet American*) 188
Mancini, Tony 133, 187
Mander (*This Gun for Hire*) 188
Manders (*Brighton Rock*) 188
Mangiot, Madame (*The Tenth Man*) 188
Mangiot, Michel (*The Tenth Man*) 188
Mangiot, Thérèse (*The Tenth Man*) 188

Index

Mann (*The Name of Action*) 188
Mann, Rachel ("Murder for the Wrong Reason") 188
Manners, Miss 189
Manners, Miss ("Men at Work") 188–189
Mansfield, Katherine 45, 291; *see also* Murry, Katherine Middleton
Manuel (*The Power and the Glory*) 189
Manville, Lord Charles ("When Greek Meets Greek") 189
Marcel (*The Comedians*) 193
Marcus, Sir (*This Gun for Hire*) 193
Margaret ("Cheap in August") 193
Margesson, Mrs. ("The Lieutenant Died Last") 193
María (*The Honorary Consul*) 193
Maria (*Our Man in Havana*) 193
Maria (*The Power and the Glory*) 193
Maria (*Travels with My Aunt*) 193
Maria ("Under the Garden") 193
Marie (*Our Man in Havana*) 193
Marina (*England Made Me*) 193
Marion, Aunt (*Loser Takes All*) 194
Mark (*Our Man In Havana*) 194
Mark, Sir (*Brighton Rock*) 194
Marlene (*It's a Battlefield*) 194
Marlowe, Christopher 99
Marquez (*Monsignor Quixote*) 194
Marquis (*The Ministry of Fesar*) 194
Marsdyke, Mrs. (*The Power and the Glory*) 194
Marshall, George Catlett 186
Marta (*The Honorary Consul*) 194
Martha ("The Blessing") 194
Martin (*The Honorary Consul*) 194
Martin, Judith 189
Martínez, Colonel Boris (*The Captain and the Enemy*) 123, 194
Martínez, José 195
Martinez, Señor ("An Appointment with the General") 194–195
Martins, Rollo (*The Third Man*) 195, 300, 301
Marturet, Father Oscar 270
Marx, Karl 210, 211
Mary (*Our Man in Havana*) 195
Mason, Detective-Inspector ("Murder for the Wrong Reason") 195
Mason, James (*This Gun for Hire*) 195–196
Mason, Mrs. (*This Gun for Hire*) 195
Mather (*This Gun for Hire*) 195
Matthews, Flossy (*It's a Battlefield*) 196
Matthews, Ronald 240
Maud (*The End of the Affair*) 196
Maud (*England Made Me*) 196
Maude, Mr. (*The Ministry of Fear*) 196
Maugham, W. Somerset 296
Mauriac, François 59, 215, 254
Maverick ("Special Duties") 196
Mavis ("The Bear Fell Free") 196
Max (*Our Man in Havana*) 196
Maxime (*A Burnt-Out Case*) 196

"May We Borrow Your Husband" 196–197
May We Borrow Your Husband? and Other Comedies of the Sexual Life 22, 198
Maydew, Miss (*This Gun for Hire*) 198
The Mayor of Brouge (*The Tenth Man*) 196
McNeill-Moss, Geoffrey 222
Meadmore, Mrs. (*The Name of Action*) 198
Megrim, General ("The Last Word") 198
The Member of Parliament (*The Quiet American*) 198
Memento Mori (*Brighton Rock*) 198
"Men at Work" 198–199, 257
Mendez, Father (*Our Man in Havana*) 199
Mendrill, Mrs. Marie (*The Confidential Agent*) 199
Menzies, Stewart Graham 135
Merdy ("Jubilee") 199
Meredith (*The Human Factor*) 199
Merlan, Mère (*The Comedians*) 199
Merriman, Sir Henry (*The Man Within*) 199
Merry Monarch (*Brighton Rock*) 199
Mersham, Lady (*The Confidential Agent*) 199
The Mestizo (*The Power and the Glory*) 199
Meyersdorf, Gräfin von (*The Third Man*) 199
Michael (*It's a Battlefield*) 199
Michael (*The Name of Action*) 199
Michael ("The Trial of Pan") 199
Mick ("The Destructors") 200
Mick ("A Drive in the Country") 200
Mick (*The Quiet American*) 199
Mick (*This Gun for Hire*) 200
Miguel (*The Honorary Consul*) 199
Miguel (*Our Man in Havana*) 199–200
Miguel (*The Power and the Glory*) 200
Miguel (*Rumour at Nightfall*) 200
Milan, the Reverend Simon ("When Greek Meets Greek") 200
Milbanke, Mrs (*This Gun for Hire*) 200
Miles (*The End of the Affair*) 200
Miles, Henry (*The End of the Affair*) 200–201
Miles, Sarah (*The End of the Affair*) 116, 201
Millet (*The Other Side of the Border*) 201
Milly (*This Gun for Hire*) 201
Milton, John 38
Mimi (*The Human Factor*) 201
The Minister (*The Power and the Glory*) 201
The Minister (*The Quiet American*) 201
The Minister of Defence ("An Old Man's Memory") 201

The Minister of Defense (*Our Man in Havana*) 202
The Minister of Education ("The Man Who Stole the Eiffel Tower") 202
The Minister of the Interior (*The Confidential Agent*) 202
The Minister of the Interior (*The Honorary Consul*) 202
The Minister of the Interior (*Our Man in Havana*) 202
The Ministry of Fear 19, 202–206, 281, 296
Minny (*The Ministry of Fear*) 206
Minty, Ferdinand (*England Made Me*) 206–207
Minty, Mrs. (*England Made Me*) 207
Modin, Yuri 29, 30
Mollinson, Miss (*England Made Me*) 207
Mollison, *This Gn for Hire*) 207
"The Moment of Truth" 207
The Monegasque Consul (*Our Man in Havana*) 207
Monsignor Quixote 153, 207–213
Monster of the Chemins de Fe (*Travels with My Aunt*) 213
Montagu, Sir Joseph (*Brighton Rock*) 213
Montas, Lucien 103
Montez (*The Honorary Consul*) 213
Montez (*The Power and the Glory*) 213
Montez, Pedro (*The Power and the Glory*) 214
Montgomery (*Doctor Fischer of Geneva*) 214
Montgomery, Lady Isobel ("Under the Garden") 214
Montgomery, Mrs. (*Doctor Fischer of Geneva*) 214
Monti, Eulelia (*Rumour at Nightfall*) 214
Monti, Señor (*Rumour at Nightfall*) 214
Monti, Señora (*Rumour at Nightfall*) 214
Moon ("A Discovery in the Woods") 214
Moor, Dr. Elisabeth 24
Morel, Marie (*A Burnt-Out Case*) 214–215
Moreno, Julio (*The Honorary Consul*) 215
Moreno, Señora (*The Honorary Consul*) 215
Morgan, Harry (*Our Man in Havana*) 215
Morgan, Henry 215
Morin, Pierre ("A Visit to Morin") 215
Morrell, Lady Ottoline 45
Morrow (*The Other Side of the Border*) 215
Morrow, Mrs. (*The Other Side of the Border*) 215–216
"Mortmain" 216
Morton ("The End of the Party") 216

Morton, Francis ("The End of the Party") 110–111, **216**
Morton, Mrs. ("The End of the Party") **216**
Morton, Peter ("The End of the Party") **216–217**
Moses ("The Trial of Pan") **217**
Moss (*The Other Side of the Border*) **217**
Moult (*Orient Express*) **217**
Mountbatten, Lady Louise Alexandrine 81, 257
Moyne, Charlie (*Brighton Rock*) **217**
Muckerji, Mr. (*The Confidential Agent*) **217**
Muggeridge, Malcolm 85
Muller (*The Name of Action*) **217**
Muller, Cornelius (*The Human Factor*) **217**
Muller, Frau ("The Root of All Evil") **217**
Muller, Herr ("The Root of All Evil") **217**
"Murder for the Wrong Reason" **217–219**
Muriel (*The Captain and the Enemy*) **219**
Murphy (*England Made Me*) **219**
Murry, John Middleton 45, 291
Murry, Katherine Middleton 291
Musker, Coral (*Orient Express*) **219**
Myatt, Carleton (*Orient Express*) **219–220**
Myatt, Jacob (*Orient Express*) **220**

Naismith (*Loser Takes All*) **220**
The Name of Action **220–223**
Nancy (*Travels with My Aunt*) **223**
Naomi (*The Human Factor*) **223**
Nell (*The Confidential Agent*) **223**
Nelson, Chick (*The Comedians*) **223**
Nesbit, Edith (*Travels with My Aunt*) **223**
Neumann, Else 80
"The New House" **223–224**
Newall (*The Heart of the Matter*) **223**
Newey, Frederick (*The Ministry of Fear*) **223**
Newey, Mrs. (*The Ministry of Fear*) **223**
Newman (*Travels with My Aunt*) **224**
Newman, Sir Oswald (*Travels with My Aunt*) **224**
Newman, Rose Urquhart (*Travels with My Aunt*) **224**
"The News in English" **224–225**
Ngambo, Mark (*The Human Factor*) **225**
The Nicaraguan Ambassador (*Travels with My Aunt*) **225**
Nicholson, Ben 243
Nicola (*Orient Express*) **225**
Nils (*England Made Me*) **225**
Ninitch (*Orient Express*) **225**
Ninitch, Mrs. (*Orient Express*) **225**
Nobody to Blame 225, 237, 296

Nora (*The Power and the Glory*) **225**
Noriega, Manuel Antonio 51
Norma (*It's a Battlefield*) **225**
Northrop, Ernest 115, 327
Numa, Marcel 193
Number One ("A Discovery in the Woods") **225**
Number Three ("A Discovery in the Woods") **226**
Number Two ("A Discovery in the Woods") **226**

Obregón, Álvaro (*The Power and the Glory*) **226**
O'Brien (*The Honorary Consul*) **226**
O'Brien, Pat (*The Third Man*) **226**
Ochs, Henry S. (*The Comedians*) **226**
O'Connor (*England Made Me*) **226**
O'Connor, Father ("Dear Dr. Falkenheim") **226**
Okapa, Henry (*A Burnt-Out Case*) **226**
Old Crowe (*Brighton Rock*) **226**
"An Old Man's Memory" **226–227**
Oldfield, Maurice 55
Olivier, Laurence 99, 255
Olo, Thomas (*A Burnt-Out Case*) **227**
O'Malley, Ernest Bernard 321
On the Way Back 51, 227
Onoko, Mrs. (*Orient Express*) 117
Opie (*Orient Express*) **227**
Orient Express **227–231**
Orwell, George 281
The Other Side of the Border **231–232**
O'Toole, James (*Travels with My Aunt*) **232**
O'Toole, Lucinda (*Travels with My Aunt*) **232**
O'Toole, Mrs. (*Travels with My Aunt*) **232**
Our Man in Havana **232–238**, 268, 296
"The Over-night Bag" **238–239**

Pablo (*The Captain and the Enemy*) **239**
Pablo (*The Honorary Consul*) **239**
Page (*Orient Express*) **239**
Page (*This Gun for Hire*) **239**
Paine (*The Third Man*) **239**
Palgrave, Francis 258
Pamela ("The Bear Fell Free") **239**
Pan ("The Trial of Pan") **239**
Pantil (*The Ministrey of Fear*) **239**
The Papal Nuncio (*The Comedians*) **239**
Pardoe, Janet (*Orient Express*) **239–240**
Parker, Colonel ("Doctor Crombie") **240**
Parker, Mrs. ("The Case for the Defence") **240**
Parkes, D.C. (*The Heart of the Matter*) **240**
Parkin, Sir Edward (*The Man Within*) **240**

Parkinson (*A Burnt-Out Case*) **240**
Parkinson, Montagu 101, **240**
Parkis, Alfred (*The End of the Affair*) **240**
Parkis, Lance (*The End of the Affair*) **240–241**
Parkis, Mrs. (*The End of the Affair*) **241**
Parkman, Thomas Earl, Jr. (*Our Man in Havana*) **241**
Parkman, Vincent C. (*Our Man in Havana*) **241**
Partridge (*England Made Me*) **241**
Passerati (*Travels with My Aunt*) **241**
Paterson, Miss Dorothy (*Travels with My Aunt*) **241**
Patmore (*It's a Battlefield*) **241**
Patricia (*The Human Factor*) **241**
Patsy-One-Eye "Church Militant") **241**
Patterson (*English Made Me*) **241**
Paul, Father (*A Bunrt-Out Case*) **241**
Paul VI, Pope 254
Pauline ("Chagrin in Three Parts") **241**
Payne (*Travels with My Aunt*) **241**
Peacock (*Rumour at Nightfall*) **241**
Pedro (*The Honorary Consul*) **241, 242**
Pedro (*Our Man in Havana*) **242**
Pedro (*The Power and the Glory*) **242**
Pedro, Father (*The Honorary Consul*) **242**
Pedro, Father (*Rumour at Nightfall*) **242**
Pemberton (*The Heart of the Matter*) **242**
Pemberton, Dick (*The Heart of the Matter*) **242**
Penelope (*The Human Factor*) **242**
Penkovsky (*The Human Factor*) **242**
Penny, Mrs. (*This Gun for Hire*) **242**
Penrith (*This Gun for Hire*) **242**
Peraud, Lieutenant (*The Quiet American*) **242**
Percival, Dr. Emmanuel (*The Human Factor*) **242–243**
Perez, Colonel (*The Honorary Consul*) **243**
Perez, Señor (*Our Man in Havana*) **243**
Perez, Señora (*Our Man in Havana*) **243**
The Permanent Under-Secretary (*Our Man in Havana*) **243**
Perrin (*A Burnt-Out Case*) **243**
Perrin, Lieutenant (*The Quiet American*) **243**
Perrot (*The Heart of the Matter*) **243**
Perrot, Mrs. (*The Heart of the Matter*) **243**
Perry (*The Ministry of Fear*) **243**
Pete ("A Discovery in the Woods") **243**

Index

Peter (*Travels with My Aunt*) 243–244
Peters (*The Confidential Agent*) 244
Peters, Amy (*Orient Express*) 244
Peters, Herbert (*Orient Express*) 244
Petit Pierre (*The Comedians*) 244
Petkovitch, Major (*Orient Express*) 244
Petty (*The Man Within*) 244
Pfunk, Miss (*Our Man in Havana*) 244
Pham-Van-Tu (*The Quiet American*) 244
Pham-Van-Tu, Mrs. (*The Quiet American*) 244
Phan-Van-Muoi (*The Quiet American*) 244
Phelps, Montague (*This Gun for Hire*) 245
Phil (*Orient Express*) 245
Philby, Alice 245
Philby, Eleanor 245
Philby, Kim 29, 39, 55, 121, 161, 186, 245–246, 250
Philby Rufina 245
Philipot (*The Comedians*) 246
Philipot, Dr. (*The Comedians*) 246
Philipot, Henri (*The Comedians*) 246
Philipot, Mme. (*The Comedians*) 246
Philippe, Brother (*A Burnt-Out Case*) 246–247
Philips (*The Human Factor*) 247
Phuong (*The Quiet American*) 247
Picasso, Pablo 197
Pidot (*The Tenth Man*) 247
Pierpoint (*It's a Battlefield*) 247
Pierre (*The Tenth Man*) 247
Pierre ("Two Gentle People") 247
Pietri (*The Quiet American*) 247
Pig (*The Confidential Agent*) 247
Pihlström (*England Made Me*) 247
Piker (*Brighton Rock*) 247
Piker, Alfred (*This Gun for Hire*) 247
Piker, Mrs. (*This Gun for Hire*) 247–248
Pilbeam, Professor (*Monsignor Quixote*) 248
Pim ("The Bear Fell Free") 248
Pinecoffin (*Brighton Rock*) 248
Pineda, Angel (*The Comedians*) 248
Pineda, Luis (*The Comedians*) 248
Pineda, Martha (*The Comedians*) 248
Pink, Molly (*Brighton Rock*) 248
Pinochet Ugarte, Augusto 297
Pinquet, Captain 314
Piper (*The Human Factor*) 248
Pippitt, Mary (*The End of the Affair*) 248–249
Plarr, Dr. Eduardo (*The Honorary Consul*) 249
Plarr, Henry (*The Honorary Consul*) 249
Plarr, Señora (*The Honorary Consul*) 249
Pompilia ("The Little Place off the Edgeware Road") 249

Poole (*The Ministry of Fear*) 249
The Portland Affair (*The Human Factor*) 245, 250
Porton (*The Human Factor*) 250
Potter, Beatrix 307
Pottifer, Charles (*Travels with My Aunt*) 250
The Potting Shed 130
Pound, Ezra 96
The Power and the Glory 185, 250–255, 270
Preminger, Otto 161
Prentice (*The End of the Affair*) 255
The President (*Our Man in Havana*) 256
The President (*The Quiet American*) 256
The President of France ("An Old Man's Memory") 256
Prexedes, Saint 287
Price (*The Honorary Consul*) 256
Priestley, J.B. 256–257, 268, 280, 299
Prince (*The Quiet American*) 257
The Princess (*England Made Me*) 257
Priskett ("When Greek Meets Greek") 257
Professor, Herr ("Dream of a Strange Land") 257
Prologue to Pilgrimage 13, 257
"Proof Positive" 257–258
Puckler, Frau ("The Root of All Evil") 258
Puckler, Herr ("The Root of All Evil") 258
Pullen (*The Human Factor*) 258
Pulling, Angela (*Travels with My Aunt*) 258
Pulling, Henry (*Travels with My Aunt*) 258
Pulling, Jo (*Travels with My Aunt*) 258
Pulling, Richard (*Travels with My Aunt*) 258–259
Purves, Bill ("The Lieutenant Died Last") 259
Purvis, Mrs. (*The Ministry of Fear*) 259
Pyle, Alden (*The Quiet American*) 259
Pyle, Harold 259

al-Qaddafi, Muammar 227
Querry (*A Burnt-Out Case*) 260
The Quiet American 260–265, 322
Quigly, Cyril (*The Captain and the Enemy*) 265–266
Quintana, Captain (*Rumour at Nightfall*) 266
Quintana, Father (*The Power and the Glory*) 266
Quixote, Father (*Monsignore Quixote*) 266

Rachel ("The Second Death") 266
Racine, Jean 99
Ramage (*Loser Takes All*) 266
Ramsgate, Miss ("Under the Garden") 266

Rank, Father (*The Heart of the Matter*) 266–267
Raven (*This Gun for Hire*) 267
Raven, James (*This Gun for Hire*) 267
Raven, Mrs. (*This Gun for Hire*) 267
Raymond (*The Human Factor*) 267
Raymond, René 300
Read, Herbert 95, 96, 268
The Rector (*The Comedians*) 267
Redakteur, Herr (*England Made Me*) 267
Reed, Carol 19, 237, 267–268, 300
Rees (*The Heart of the Matter*) 268
Reith (*The Heart of the Matter*) 268
Remnant, Peter (*The Name of Action*) 268
Rennit (*The Ministry of Fear*) 268
Rennit, Mrs. (*The Ministry of Fear*) 268
The Representative of the British Council (*The Honorary Consul*) 268
The Reverend Mother (*Our Man in Havana*) 268
Rexall, Edward (*The Man Within In*) 268
Ribera, Aquino (*The Honorary Consul*) 268–269
Richmond, Kenneth 87, 128, 130, 333
Richmond, Zoe 87, 333
Rickards, Jocelyn 269
Riego, Colonel (*Rumour at Nightfall*) 269
Riego, Señora (*Rumour at Nightfall*) 269
Rilke, Rainer Maria 145
Rimmer, Kay (*It's a Battlefield*) 269
Riobé 246
Riobé, Hector 246
Rita (*Trsavels with My Aunt*) 269
Rivas (*The Honorary Consul*) 269–270
Rivas, Léon (*The Honorary Consul*) 270
Rivas, Señora (*The Honorary Consul*) 270
Robinson ("A Day Saved") 270
Robinson (*The Heart of the Matter*) 270
Robinson, Edward Rhodes (*Travels with My Aunt*) 270
Robinson, Molly (*The Heart of the Matter*) 270
Roca, Luis (*Rumour at Nightfall*) 271
Roche (*The Tenth Man*) 271
Rocinante (*Monsignor Quixote*) 271
Rodriguez (*Our Man in Havana*) 271
Rodriiguez, Andrés 290
Rodriguez, Dr. (*Travels with My Aunt*) 271
Roe, Thomas Chambers Windsor 22, 59, 96
Rolls, Rita (*The Human Factor*) 271
Rolón, Raimondo 290
Rolt, Helen (*The Heart of the Matter*) 271

Rolt, John (*The Heart of the Matter*) 271
Romain, Major Franck 73
Ronald (*Monsignor Quixote*) 271
Ronald, Sir (*England Made Me*) 271
"The Root of All Evil") 271–272
Rose ("The Basement Room") 272
Rose (*Travels with My Aunt*) 272
Rosen (*This Gun for Hire*) 272
Rougemont (*The Human Factor*) 272
Rover ("Across the Bridge") 273
Row (*The Confidential Agent*) 273
Rowe, Alice (*The Ministry of Fear*) 273
Rowe, Arthur (*The Ministry of Fear*) 273
Rowe, Mrs. (*The Ministry of Fear*) 273
Rowlett (*It's a Battlefield*) 273
Roy, Harry ("A Drive in the Country") 273
RS (*England Made Me*) 273
Rudy (*Our Man in Havana*) 273
Ruby (*This Gun for Hire*) 273
Rumour at Nightfall 223, 273–27
Rushdie, Salman 227
Russe, Father (*The Tenth Man*) 277
Russell (*The End of the Affair*) 277
Russell, Ken (*The Honorary Consul*) 277–278
Ruttledge (*It's a Battlefield*) 278
Ruttledge, Hugh 278
Rycker, André (*A Burnt-Out Case*) 278
Rycker, Marie (*A Burnt-Out Case*) 278

Saavedra, Doctor Jorge Julio (*The Honorary Consul*) 278
Sagrin ("A Visit to Morin") 278
Saïeth, Issa el 134
St. John of the Cross 109
Sais, Tatjana *see* Greene, Else Hofler Neumann
Sally (*The Confidential Agent*) 278–279
Sally ("A Shocking Accident") 279
Salmon, Mrs. ("The Case for the Defence") 279
Sam (*Brighton Rock*) 279
Sampson, Lady ("Under the Garden") 279
Sampson, Sir Nigel ("Under the Garden") 279
Samuel (*Brighton Rock*) 279
Samuel ("The Trial of Pan") 279
Sanchez, Luis (*Our Man in Havana*) 279
Sanchez, Maria (*Our Man in Havana*) 279
Sanchez, Señora (*The Honorary Consul*) 279
Sandale, Lord ("The Basement Room") 279
Sanders, George 96
Sanger, Lord George ("When Greek Meets Greek") 279
Santa Teresa (*Our Man in Havana*) 279

Satan ("The Trial of Pan") 279–280
Saunders ("Murder for the Wrong Reason") 280
Saunders (*This Gun for Hire*) 280
Saunders, Amanda Dennys (niece) 88
Saunders, Miss ("Special Duties") 280
Saunders, Mrs. ("Special Duties") 280
Savage (*The End of the Affair*) 280
Savage ("Men at Work") 280
Savage (*Our Man n Havana*) 280
Savage, Miss (*The Ministry of Fear*) 280
Savory, Quin C. (*Orient Express*) 280
Schack, Ekkehard von 137
Schmidt (*The Third Man*) 280
Schmidt, Anna (*The Third Man*) 280–281
Schmidt, Father ("Church Militant") 281
Schmidt, Frau ("The Root of All Evil") 281
Schmidt, Herr ("The Root of All Evil") 281
Schultz, Frau (*The Name of Action*) 281
Schweitzer, Albert 44, 240
Scobie, Catherine (*The End of the Affair*) 281
Scobie, Henry (*The End of the Affair*) 281
Scobie, Louise (*The End of the Affair*) 281–282
Scofield, Paul 325
Scott (*England Made Me*) 282
Scott, Sir Walter 258, 310
"A Second Death" 282
The Second Secretary (*The Confidential Agent*) 283
The Secretary for Public Works (*The Comedians*) 283
The Secretary for Social Welfare (*The Comedians*) 283
The Secretary for the Interior (*The Comedians*) 283
The Secretary for Tourism (*The Comedians*) 283
The Secretary of Education (*The Comedians*) 283
Secretary of Embassy (*Doctor Fischer of Geneva*) 283
The Secretary of State (*The Comedians*) 283
Segura (*Our Man in Havana*) 283
Segura, Captain (*Our Man in Havana*) 283
Seitz, Al 134
Selznick, David 268, 300
A Sense of Security 284
Seraphina (*Our Man in Havana*) 284
Sergeant (*Our Man in Havana*) 284
Severn, Mrs. Beatrice (*Our Man in Havana*) 284
Severn, Peter (*Our Man in Havana*) 284

Shades of Green 284
Shakespeare, William 38, 67, 112, 134, 214, 222, 233, 284
Shaw, George Bernard (*Travels with My Aunt*) 284
"A Shocking Accident" 284–285
Simcox, Sir Joshua ("Alas, Poor Maling") 285
Simmons (*This Gun for Hire*) 285
Simon (*A Burnt-Out Case*) 285
Simon (*The Quiet American*) 285
Simpson, Mrs. Amy (*It's a Battlefield*) 285
Sinclair (*The Ministry of Fear*) 285
Skate, Richard ("Men at Work") 285
Slater, Mrs. (*Our Man in Havana*) 285
Smiley ("The Blessing") 285
Smith, Ernest Friend 133
Smith, Gerard Corley 286
Smith, Mrs. (*The Comedians*) 286
Smith, William Abel (*The Comedians*) 286
Smudge (*Travels with My Aunt*) 286
Smythe, Miss (*The End of the Affair*) 286
Smythe, Richard (*The End of the Affair*) 286
Smythe-Phillips, Mrs. (*The Ministry of Fear*) 286
Snakey (*The Heart of the Matter*) 286
Snow (*Brighton Rock*) 287
Snow, Charles 313
Soldati, Mario 320
Somosa Debayle, Anastasio 51
Song of Roland 74
Soppelsa (*This Gun for Hire*) 287
Sorel, Captain (*The Quiet American*) 287
A Sort of Life 130, 192, 306, 307, 332
Southwell, Robert 214
Sparrow (*England Made Me*) 287
Sparrow, Detective-Sergeant John (*Travels with My Aunt*) 287
Sparrow, John Hanbury Angus 287
"Special Duties" 287
Spicer (*Brighton Rock*) 287–288
Spilsbury, Sir Bernard ("The Overnight Bag") 288
Spot (*The Confidential Agent*) 288
Spot (*The Ministry of Fear*) 288
Spot (*Orient Express*) 288
The Spy's Bedside Book 129
Stamboul Train see *Orient Express*
Starling, Corporal (*The Third Man*) 288
Stavrog (*Orient Express*) 288
Stefenson (*England Made Me*) 288
Stein, Gertrude 288
Stein, Leo (*Orient Express*) 288
Stein, Mrs. (*Orient Express*) 288
Steinbeck, John 312
Steiner (*Doctor Fischer of Geneva*) 288–289
Stephen ("May We Borrow Your Husband?") 289

Stephens (*Rumour at Nightfall*) 289
Stevenson, Robert Louis 130, 158
Still (*The Ministry of Fear*) 289
Stodger (*England Made Me*) 289
Stone, Major (*The Ministry of Fear*) 289
Stone, Mrs. (*The Ministry of Fear*) 289
Stowe ("I Spy") 289
Stowe, Charlie (*The Confidential Agent*) 289
Stowe, Charlie ("I Spy") 289
Stowe, Mrs. ("I Spy") 289
Strachwitz, Countess Barbara (cousin) *see* Greene, Barbara
Strachwitz, Count Rudolf 145
Stradano (*Travels with My Aunt*) 289
Strait, Belinda Crompton 80
The Stranger's Hand 320
Strangeways ("A Visit to Morin") 289
Stroessner, Alfred(o) 120, 124, 255–256, **289–290**
Struber (*The Name of Action*) 290
Struber, Frau (*The Name of Action*) 290
Sue ("Work Not in Progress") 290
Summers ("The Destructors") 290
The Superintendent of Police ("The Root of All Evil") 290–291
The Superior (*A Burnt-Out Case*) 291
Superman (*Travels with My Aunt*) 291
Surrogate, Margaret (*It's a Battlefield*) 291
Surrogate, Philip (*It's a Battlefield*) 291
Sutliffe (*Orient Express*) 291
Svanstrom, Ragnar 27
Svenson (*Our Man in Havana*) 291
Sykes, Dr. Jessie (*The Heart of the Matter*) 291
Sylvie (*Brighton Rock*) 291
Symond (*It's a Battlefield*) 291

T., H. (pseudonym) 313
Tallit (*The Heart of the Matter*) 291–292
Tate, Jim (*Brighton Rock*) 292
Tatham (*The Ministry of Fear*) 292
Tavell, Bob (*Brighton Rock*) 292
Taveril, Lord (*It's a Battlefield*) 292
Taylor (*The Human Factor*) 292
Tearle, Conway (*The Confidential Agent*) 292
Ted (*The Other Side of the Border*) 292
Temple, Doris 129
Temple, Shirley 292
Tench (*The Power and the Glory*) 293
Tench, Sylvia (*The Power and the Glory*) 293
Tennyson, Alfred, Lord 329
The Tenth Man 237, **293–296**
Teresa (*The Honorary Consul*) 297
Teresa (*Monsignor Quixote*) 297

Teresa (*Our Man in Havana*) 297
Terry, Mrs. (*The Confidential Agent*) 297
Tester (*England Made Me*) 297
Thatcher, Margaret ("An Old Man's Memory") 227, 297
Thé, General (*The Quiet American*) 259, 297
Thé, Trinh Minh 259, 297
Thérèse, Sister (*A Burnt-Out Case*) 297
Thimblerigg (*The Heart of the Matter*) 298
The Third Man 268, **298–301**
This Gun for Hire 301–305
Thomas ("The Destructors") 305
Thomas, Dylan 323
Thomas, Father (*Burnt-Out Case*) 305
Thomson, James 60
Thriplow, Henry ("The Lottery Ticket") 305
"The Tick of the Clock" 136, 305–306
Tierney (*The Heart of the Matter*) 306
Tigre, El (*The Honorary Consul*) 306
Tilly (*Brighton Rock*) 306
Tims, Richard (*The Man Within*) 306
Tin Tin (*The Comedians*) 306
Tinker Bell (*The Human Factor*) 306
Tiny ("The Over-night Bag") 306
Tiny (*This Gun for Hire*) 306
Tissand, M. (*Loser Takes All*) 306
Titi, Tiberio (*Travels with My Aunt*) 306
Toads (*Doctor Fischer of Geneva*) 306
Tod (*The Heart of the Matter*) 306
Tod, Emmy (*Orient Express*) 306
Toll, Paul 133, 175
Tolstoy, Leo 156, 157, 293
Tom (*Brighton Rock*) 306
Tom ("Under the Garden") 307
Tomlinson, Brigadier (*The Human Factor*) 307
Toni ("Two Gentle People") 307
Tony (*The Confidential Agent*) 307
Tony ("May We Borrow Your Husband?) 307
Topling, Canon (*The Ministry of Fear*) 307
Torner, Peter (*The Name of Action*) 307
Torres, Father Camillo 270
Torrijos Herrera, Omar 14, 51, 123–124, 194, 195, 213, 290
Tort ("A Discovery in the Woods") 307
Toupard (*The Tenth Man*) 307
Toute à Toi (*A Burnt-Out Case*) 307
Traggers, Miss "Pony" (*Our Man in Havana*) 307
Travels with My Aunt 152, 290, **307–312**
Travers, Puffin (*England Made Me*) 312

Travis ("May We Borrow Your Husband") 312
Travis, Dr. (*The Heart of the Matter*) 312–313
Travis, Peter ("May We Borrow Your Husband?") 313
Travis, Poopy ("May We Borrow Your Husband?") 313
Trench (*The Ministry of Fear*) 293
Trench, Hilary (pseudonym) 293, 313
Trevor ("The Destructors") 313
"The Trial of Pan" 313–314
Triffin, Peter (*The Confidential Agent*) 314
Trollope, Anthony 57
Trollope, Mrs. Frances 323
Trouin, Captain (*The Quiet American*) 314
Troup, Mrs. (*The Ministry of Fear*) 314
Truefitt (*Loser Takes All*) 314
Truman, President Harry S. 286, 315
Truman, Hiram C. (*Our Man in Havana*) 315
Truman, Miss (*Travels with My Aunt*) 315
Trumbull, Councillor (*Travels with My Aunt*) 315
Tumbril ("The Blessing") 315
Turner, Horace ("Doctor Crombie") 315
Twining (*The Captain and the Enemy*) 315
"Two Gentle People" 315–316

Unamuno, Miguel de 209, 213
"Under the Garden" 136, **316–318**
The Undersecretary for Overseas Trade (*The Confidential Agent*) 316

Vallejo, Gaspar (*The Honorary Consul*) 318
Vallejo, Señora (*The Honorary Consul*) 318
Vande (*The Heart of the Matter*) 318
Vandi (*The Other Side of the Border*) 318
Van Donck, Captain (*The Human Factor*) 318
Vassall (*The Human Factor*) 319
Vassall (*The Quiet American*) 245
Vassall, John 319
Vega, Señora (*The Honorary Consul*) 319
Velardo, Captain Rubén (*The Honorary Consul*) 319
Ventura, Captain Estaban 283
Verity (*Rumour at Nightfall*) 319
Vicar ("The Lieutenant Died Last") 319
Vicar (*Loser Takes All*) 319
Victorian Detective Fiction 125
Victorian Villainies 129
Vigot (*The Quiet American*) 319
Vigot, Madame (*The Quiet American*) 319

Villa, Pancho 186
"The Virtue of Disloyalty" 284
Visconti (*Travels with My Aunt*) 319
Visconti, Gian Galeazzo 319
Visconti, Mario (*Travels with My Aunt*) 320
Visconti, Signora (*Travels with My Aunt*) 320
"A Visit to Morin" 320–321
Voisin (*The Tenth Man*) 321
Volet, Madame ("Chagrin in Three Parts") 321
Volet, Paul ("Chagrin in Three Parts") 321

Wagner (*The Quiet American*) 321
Wagner, Richard 84, 112
Wales ("A Day Saved") 321
Walpole, Hugh 313
Walston, Catherine 19, 27, 56, 63, 64, 80, 109, 121, 125, 129, 131, 135, 200–201, 248, 305, **321–322**, 331
Walston, Harry 109, 135, 200–201, 248, 305, 317, 321–322
Warnier, Madame (*The Tenth Man*) 322
Warren, Mabel ("The End of the Party") 322–323
Warren, Mabel (*Orient Express*) 323
Warrender, Miss ("Doctor Crombie") 323
Waterbury, Peter (*The End ofd the Affair*) 323
Watson (*The Human Factor*) 323
Watson, Charlie ("Cheap in August") 323
Watson, Jules 307
Watson, Mary ("Cheap in August") 323
Watt (*This Gun for Hire*) 323
Waugh, Evelyn 109, 201, 214, 278, 322
Ways of Escape 62, 121, 152, 160, 172, 174, 180, 184, 193, 237, 244, 260, 265, 283, 288, 290, 292, 328, 329, 330, 332
Weatherall, Peter ("A Drive in the Country") 323
Weaver, Major Philip ("Proof Positive") 323–324
Webb, Beatrice 327
Weber (*The Name of Action*) 324
Weber, Frau (*The Name of Action*) 324
Weissmann (*Travels with My Aunt*) 324
Weld ("The Blessing") 324
Wells, H.G. (*Travels with My Aunt*) 324
West, Mae 14

Wettin, Margaret Victoria 257
Wheeler ("The Case for the Defence") 324
"When Greek Meets Greek" 324–325
The Whisky Priest (*The Power and the Glory*) 325
Whitaker (*England Made Me*) 326
White (*Our Man in Havana*) 326
Whitehouse, Mrs. (*The Human Factor*) 326
Widow Twanky (*The Hman Factor*) 326
Wilberforce, Miss (*The Heart of the Matter*) 326
Wilbraham, Miss (*The Third Man*) 326
Wilbur, Major (*England Made Me*) 326
Wilcox, Doris (*The Ministry of Fear*) 326
Wilcox, Henry (*The Ministry of Fear*) 326
Wilcox, Mrs. (*The Ministry of Fear*) 326
Wilcoxon, Henry 326
Wilditch ("Under the Garden") 326
Wilditch, George ("Under the Garden") 326–327
Wilditch, Henry ("Under the Garden") 327
Wilditch, Mary ("Under the Garden") 327
Wilditch, Mrs. ("Under the Garden") 327
Wilditch, William ("Under the Garden") 327–328
Wilkins (*The Quiet American*) 328
Wilkins (*The Human Factor*) 328
Wilkinson ("Men at Work") 328
Wilkinson, Henry ("Cheap in August") 328
Wilkinson, Mrs. ("Cheap in August") 328
Williams, Tennessee 60
Williamson (*England Made Me*) 328
Willie (*Brighton Rock*) 328
Willie (*The Human Factor*) 328
Wilson (*Brighton Rock*) 328
Wilson (*The End of the Affair*) 328
Wilson (*The Ministry of Fear*) 328
Wilson, Edmund 79
Wilson, Edward (*The Heart of the Matter*) 328–329
Wilson, Mrs. (*Brighton Rock*) 328
Wilson, Rose (*Brighton Rock*) 104, 328
Wilson, Schuyler (*The Comedians*) 329
Wince-Dudley, Mrs. ("The Basement Room") 329

Winifred (*The Confidential Agent*) 329
Winkler, Dr. (*The Third Man*) 329
Winstanley, Colin ("May We Borrow Your Husband?") 329
Winston (*It's a Battlefield*) 329
Winterbottom, Lady Caroline ("Under the Garden") 329
Winton, Druce (*This Gun for Hire*) 329
Wisecock, Mrs. (*England Made Me*) 329
Wolf (*Travels with My Aunt*) 330
Woodrow, Detective-Inspector (*Travels with My Aunt*) 330
Woolf, Virginia 299
Wordsworth ("A Shocking Accident") 330
Wordsworth, William 15
Wordsworth, Zachary (*Travels with My Aunt*) 330
"Work Not in Progress") 330–331
A World of My Own 21, 64, 98, 124, 130, 180
"The Worm Inside the Lotus Blossom" 290
Wormald, Brian 331
Wormhold, James (*Our Man in Havana*) 331
Wormhold, Mary (*Our Man in Havana*) 331
Wormhold, Milly (*Our Man in Havana*) 331
Wright ("Doctor Crombie") 331
Wright, Colonel (*The Heart of the Matter*) 331–332
Wright, Fred ("Doctor Crombie") 332
Wright, Wilbur (*Travels with My Aunt*) 332
Wright, Harrison Griswold 231

X (*The End of the Affair*) 332

Y (*The End of the Affair*) 332
Yates, Dornford 313
Yeats, William Butler 15
Yogel, Dr. (*This Gun for Hire*) 332
Yonge, Charlotte 202, 203, 206
Yusef (*The Heart of the Matter*) 332
Yvonne, Tante ("Two Gentle People") 332

Z (*The Confidential Agent*) 332
Zaharoff, Basil 193, 297
Zancas, Enrique (*Monsignor Quixote*) 124, **333**
Zapata, Emiliano 186
Ziffo, Mrs. (*Loser Takes All*) 333
Zoe (*Brighton Rock*) 333